Handbook of Communication Competence
HAL 1

Handbooks of Applied Linguistics
Communication Competence
Language and Communication Problems
Practical Solutions

Editors
Karlfried Knapp and Gerd Antos

Volume 1

De Gruyter Mouton

Handbook of Communication Competence

Edited by
Gert Rickheit and Hans Strohner

De Gruyter Mouton

ISBN 978-3-11-022603-4

Library of Congress Cataloging-in-Publication Data

Handbook of communication competence / edited by Gert Rickheit, Hans Strohner.
  p. cm. − (Handbooks of applied linguistics ; 1)
  Includes bibliographical references and index.
  ISBN 978-3-11-022603-4 (pbk. : alk. paper)
  1. Communicative competence.   2. Language and languages
  3. Communication.   I. Rickheit, Gert.   II. Strohner, Hans.
  P91.3.H34 2010
  418−dc22
                                                          2010010875

Bibliographic information published by the Deutsche Nationalbibliothek

The Deutsche Nationalbibliothek lists this publication in the Deutsche Nationalbibliografie; detailed bibliographic data are available in the Internet at http://dnb.d-nb.de.

© 2010 Walter de Gruyter GmbH & Co. KG, Berlin/New York

Cover design: Martin Zech, Bremen
Typesetting: Dörlemann Satz GmbH & Co. KG, Lemförde
Printing: AZ Druck und Datentechnik GmbH, Kempten (Allgäu)
∞ Printed on acid-free paper

Printed in Germany

www.degruyter.com

In memoriam

Hans Strohner
* 7. 6. 1945
† 19. 6. 2006

Introduction to the handbook series
Linguistics for problem solving

Karlfried Knapp and Gerd Antos

1. Science and application at the turn of the millennium

The distinction between "pure" and "applied" sciences is an old one. According to Meinel (2000), it was introduced by the Swedish chemist Wallerius in 1751, as part of the dispute of that time between the scholastic disciplines and the then emerging epistemic sciences. However, although the concept of "Applied Science" gained currency rapidly since that time, it has remained problematic.

Until recently, the distinction between "pure" and "applied" mirrored the distinction between "theory and "practice". The latter ran all the way through Western history of science since its beginnings in antique times. At first, it was only philosophy that was regarded as a scholarly and, hence, theoretical discipline. Later it was followed by other leading disciplines, as e.g., the sciences. However, as academic disciplines, all of them remained theoretical. In fact, the process of achieving independence of theory was essential for the academic disciplines to become independent from political, religious or other contingencies and to establish themselves at universities and academies. This also implied a process of emancipation from practical concerns – an at times painful development which manifested (and occasionally still manifests) itself in the discrediting of and disdain for practice and practitioners. To some, already the very meaning of the notion "applied" carries a negative connotation, as is suggested by the contrast between the widely used synonym for "theoretical", i.e. "pure" (as used, e.g. in the distinction between "Pure" and "Applied Mathematics") and its natural antonym "impure". On a different level, a lower academic status sometimes is attributed to applied disciplines because of their alleged lack of originality – they are perceived as simply and one-directionally applying insights gained in basic research and watering them down by neglecting the limiting conditions under which these insights were achieved.

Today, however, the academic system is confronted with a new understanding of science. In politics, in society and, above all, in economy a new concept of science has gained acceptance which questions traditional views. In recent philosophy of science, this is labelled as "science under the pressure to succeed" – i.e. as science whose theoretical structure and criteria of evaluation are increasingly conditioned by the pressure of application (Carrier, Stöltzner, and Wette 2004):

> Whenever the public is interested in a particular subject, e.g. when a new disease develops that cannot be cured by conventional medication, the public requests science to provide new insights in this area as quickly as possible. In doing so, the public is less interested in whether these new insights fit seamlessly into an existing theoretical framework, but rather whether they make new methods of treatment and curing possible. (Institut für Wirtschafts- und Technikforschung 2004, our translation).

With most of the practical problems like these, sciences cannot rely on knowledge that is already available, simply because such knowledge does not yet exist. Very often, the problems at hand do not fit neatly into the theoretical framework of one particular "pure science", and there is competition among disciplines with respect to which one provides the best theoretical and methodological resources for potential solutions. And more often than not the problems can be tackled only by adopting an interdisciplinary approach.

As a result, the traditional "Cascade Model", where insights were applied top-down from basic research to practice, no longer works in many cases. Instead, a kind of "application oriented basic research" is needed, where disciplines – conditioned by the pressure of application – take up a certain still diffuse practical issue, define it as a problem against the background of their respective theoretical and methodological paradigms, study this problem and finally develop various application oriented suggestions for solutions. In this sense, applied science, on the one hand, has to be conceived of as a scientific strategy for problem solving – a strategy that starts from mundane practical problems and ultimately aims at solving them. On the other hand, despite the dominance of application that applied sciences are subjected to, as sciences they can do nothing but develop such solutions in a theoretically reflected and methodologically well founded manner. The latter, of course, may lead to the well-known fact that even applied sciences often tend to concentrate on "application oriented basic research" only and thus appear to lose sight of the original practical problem. But despite such shifts in focus: Both the boundaries between disciplines and between pure and applied research are getting more and more blurred.

Today, after the turn of the millennium, it is obvious that sciences are requested to provide more and something different than just theory, basic research or pure knowledge. Rather, sciences are increasingly being regarded as partners in a more comprehensive social and economic context of problem solving and are evaluated against expectations to be practically relevant. This also implies that sciences are expected to be critical, reflecting their impact on society. This new "applied" type of science is confronted with the question: Which role can the sciences play in solving individual, interpersonal, social, intercultural, political or technical problems? This question is typical of a conception of science that was especially developed and propagated by the influential philosopher Sir Karl Popper – a conception that also this handbook series is based on.

2. "Applied Linguistics": Concepts and controversies

The concept of "Applied Linguistics" is not as old as the notion of "Applied Science", but it has also been problematical in its relation to theoretical linguistics since its beginning. There seems to be a widespread consensus that the notion "Applied Linguistics" emerged in 1948 with the first issue of the journal *Language Learning* which used this compound in its subtitle *A Quarterly Journal of Applied Linguistics*. This history of its origin certainly explains why even today "Applied Linguistics" still tends to be predominantly associated with foreign language teaching and learning in the Anglophone literature in particular, as can bee seen e.g. from Johnson and Johnson (1998), whose *Encyclopedic Dictionary of Applied Linguistics* is explicitly subtitled *A Handbook for Language Teaching*. However, this theory of origin is historically wrong. As is pointed out by Back (1970), the concept of applying linguistics can be traced back to the early 19th century in Europe, and the very notion "Applied Linguistics" was used in the early 20th already.

2.1. Theoretically Applied vs. Practically Applied Linguistics

As with the relation between "Pure" and "Applied" sciences pointed out above, also with "Applied Linguistics" the first question to be asked is what makes it different from "Pure" or "Theoretical Linguistics". It is not surprising, then, that the terminologist Back takes this difference as the point of departure for his discussion of what constitutes "Applied Linguistics". In the light of recent controversies about this concept it is no doubt useful to remind us of his terminological distinctions.

Back (1970) distinguishes between "Theoretical Linguistics" – which aims at achieving knowledge for its own sake, without considering any other value –, "Practice" – i.e. any kind of activity that serves to achieve any purpose in life in the widest sense, apart from the striving for knowledge for its own sake – and "Applied Linguistics", as a being based on "Theoretical Linguistics" on the one hand and as aiming at usability in "Practice" on the other. In addition, he makes a difference between "Theoretical Applied Linguistics" and "Practical Applied Linguistics", which is of particular interest here. The former is defined as the use of insights and methods of "Theoretical Linguistics" for gaining knowledge in another, non-linguistic discipline, such as ethnology, sociology, law or literary studies, the latter as the application of insights from linguistics in a practical field related to language, such as language teaching, translation, and the like. For Back, the contribution of applied linguistics is to be seen in the planning of practical action. Language teaching, for example, is practical action done by practitioners, and what applied linguistics can contribute to this is, e.g., to provide contrastive descriptions of the languages involved as a foundation for teaching methods. These contrastive descriptions in turn have to be based on the descriptive methods developed in theoretical linguistics.

However, in the light of the recent epistemological developments outlined above, it may be useful to reinterpret Back's notion of "Theoretically Applied Linguistics". As he himself points out, dealing with practical problems can have repercussions on the development of the theoretical field. Often new approaches, new theoretical concepts and new methods are a prerequisite for dealing with a particular type of practical problems, which may lead to an – at least in the beginning – "application oriented basic research" in applied linguistics itself, which with some justification could also be labelled "theoretically applied", as many such problems require the transgression of disciplinary boundaries. It is not rare that a domain of "Theoretically Applied Linguistics" or "application oriented basic research" takes on a life of its own, and that also something which is labelled as "Applied Linguistics" might in fact be rather remote from the mundane practical problems that originally initiated the respective subject area. But as long as a relation to the original practical problem can be established, it may be justified to count a particular field or discussion as belonging to applied linguistics, even if only "theoretically applied".

2.2. Applied linguistics as a response to structuralism and generativism

As mentioned before, in the Anglophone world in particular the view still appears to be widespread that the primary concerns of the subject area of applied linguistics should be restricted to second language acquisition and language instruction in the first place (see, e.g., Davies 1999 or Schmitt and Celce-Murcia 2002). However, in other parts of the world, and above all in Europe, there has been a development away from aspects of language learning to a wider focus on more general issues of language and communication.

This broadening of scope was in part a reaction to the narrowing down the focus in linguistics that resulted from self-imposed methodological constraints which, as Ehlich (1999) points out, began with Saussurean structuralism and culminated in generative linguistics. For almost three decades since the late 1950s, these developments made "language" in a comprehensive sense, as related to the everyday experience of its users, vanish in favour of an idealised and basically artificial entity. This led in "Core" or theoretical linguistics to a neglect of almost all everyday problems with language and communication encountered by individuals and societies and made it necessary for those interested in socially accountable research into language and communication to draw on a wider range of disciplines, thus giving rise to a flourishing of interdisciplinary areas that have come to be referred to as hyphenated variants of linguistics, such as sociolinguistics, ethnolinguistics, psycholinguistics, conversation analysis, pragmatics, and so on (Davies and Elder 2004).

That these hyphenated variants of linguistics can be said to have originated from dealing with problems may lead to the impression that they fall completely into the scope of applied linguistics. This the more so as their original thematic focus is in line with a frequently quoted definition of applied linguistics as "the theoretical and empirical investigation of real world problems in which language is a central issue" (Brumfit 1997: 93). However, in the recent past much of the work done in these fields has itself been rather "theoretically applied" in the sense introduced above and ultimately even become mainstream in linguistics. Also, in view of the current epistemological developments that see all sciences under the pressure of application, one might even wonder if there is anything distinctive about applied linguistics at all.

Indeed it would be difficult if not impossible to delimit applied linguistics with respect to the practical problems studied and the disciplinary approaches used: Real-world problems with language (to which, for greater clarity, should be added: "with communication") are unlimited in principle. Also, many problems of this kind are unique and require quite different approaches. Some might be tackled successfully by applying already available linguistic theories and methods. Others might require for their solution the development of new methods and even new theories. Following a frequently used distinction first proposed by Widdowson (1980), one might label these approaches as "Linguistics Applied" or "Applied Linguistics". In addition, language is a trans-disciplinary subject par excellence, with the result that problems do not come labelled and may require for their solution the cooperation of various disciplines.

2.3. Conceptualisations and communities

The questions of what should be its reference discipline and which themes, areas of research and sub-disciplines it should deal with, have been discussed constantly and were also the subject of an intensive debate (e.g. Seidlhofer 2003). In the recent past, a number of edited volumes on applied linguistics have appeared which in their respective introductory chapters attempt at giving a definition of "Applied Linguistics". As can be seen from the existence of the Association Internationale de Linguistique Appliquée (AILA) and its numerous national affiliates, from the number of congresses held or books and journals published with the label "Applied Linguistics", applied linguistics appears to be a well-established and flourishing enterprise. Therefore, the collective need felt by authors and editors to introduce their publication with a definition of the subject area it is supposed to be about is astonishing at first sight. Quite obviously, what Ehlich (2006) has termed "the struggle for the object of inquiry" appears to be characteristic of linguistics – both of linguistics at large and applied linguistics. Its seems then, that the meaning and scope of "Applied Linguistics" cannot be taken for granted, and this is why a wide variety of controversial conceptualisations exist.

For example, in addition to the dichotomy mentioned above with respect to whether approaches to applied linguistics should in their theoretical foundations and methods be autonomous from theoretical linguistics or not, and apart from other controversies, there are diverging views on whether applied linguistics is an independent academic discipline (e.g. Kaplan and Grabe 2000) or not (e.g. Davies and Elder 2004), whether its scope should be mainly restricted to language teaching related topics (e.g. Schmitt and Celce-Murcia 2002) or not (e.g. Knapp 2006), or whether applied linguistics is a field of interdisciplinary synthesis where theories with their own integrity develop in close interaction with language users and professionals (e.g. Rampton 1997/2003) or whether this view should be rejected, as a true interdisciplinary approach is ultimately impossible (e.g. Widdowson 2005).

In contrast to such controversies Candlin and Sarangi (2004) point out that applied linguistics should be defined in the first place by the actions of those who practically *do* applied linguistics:

> [...] we see no especial purpose in reopening what has become a somewhat sterile debate on what applied linguistics is, or whether it is a distinctive and coherent discipline. [...] we see applied linguistics as a many centered and interdisciplinary endeavour whose coherence is achieved in purposeful, mediated action by its practitioners. [...]
> What we want to ask of applied linguistics is less what it is and more what it does, or rather what its practitioners do. (Candlin/Sarangi 2004:1–2)

Against this background, they see applied linguistics as less characterised by its thematic scope – which indeed is hard to delimit – but rather by the two aspects of "relevance" and "reflexivity". Relevance refers to the purpose applied linguistic activities have for the targeted audience and to the degree that these activities in their collaborative practices meet the background and needs of those addressed – which, as matter of comprehensibility, also includes taking their conceptual and language level into account. Reflexivity means the contextualisation of the intellectual principles and practices, which is at the core of what characterises a professional community, and which is achieved by asking leading questions like "What kinds of purposes underlie what is done?", "Who is involved in their determination?", "By whom, and in what ways, is their achievement appraised?", "Who owns the outcomes?".

We agree with these authors that applied linguistics in dealing with real world problems is determined by disciplinary givens – such as e.g. theories, methods or standards of linguistics or any other discipline – but that it is determined at least as much by the social and situational givens of the practices of life. These do not only include the concrete practical problems themselves but also the theoretical and methodological standards of cooperating experts from other disciplines, as well as the conceptual and practical standards of the practitioners who are confronted with the practical problems in the first place. Thus, as Sarangi and van Leeuwen (2003) point out, applied linguists have to become part of the respective "community of practice".

If, however, applied linguists have to regard themselves as part of a community of practice, it is obvious that it is the entire community which determines what the respective subject matter is that the applied linguist deals with and how. In particular, it is the respective community of practice which determines which problems of the practitioners have to be considered. The consequence of this is that applied linguistics can be understood from very comprehensive to very specific, depending on what kind of problems are considered relevant by the respective community. Of course, following this participative understanding of applied linguistics also has consequences for the Handbooks of Applied Linguistics both with respect to the subjects covered and the way they are theoretically and practically treated.

3. Applied linguistics for problem solving

Against this background, it seems reasonable not to define applied linguistics as an autonomous discipline or even only to delimit it by specifying a set of subjects it is supposed to study and typical disciplinary approaches it should use. Rather, in line with the collaborative and participatory perspective of the communities of practice applied linguists are involved in, this handbook series is based on the assumption that applied linguistics is a specific, problem-oriented way of "doing linguistics" related to the real-life world. In other words: applied linguistics is conceived of here as "linguistics for problem solving".

To outline what we think is distinctive about this area of inquiry: Entirely in line with Popper's conception of science, we take it that applied linguistics starts from the assumption of an imperfect world in the areas of language and communication. This means, firstly, that linguistic and communicative competence in individuals, like other forms of human knowledge, is fragmentary and defective – if it exists at all. To express it more pointedly: Human linguistic and communicative behaviour is not "perfect". And on a different level, this imperfection also applies to the use and status of language and communication in and among groups or societies.

Secondly, we take it that applied linguists are convinced that the imperfection both of individual linguistic and communicative behaviour and language based relations between groups and societies can be clarified, understood and to some extent resolved by their intervention, e.g. by means of education, training or consultancy.

Thirdly, we take it that applied linguistics proceeds by a specific mode of inquiry in that it mediates between the way language and communication is expertly studied in the linguistic disciplines and the way it is directly experienced in different domains of use. This implies that applied linguists are able to demonstrate that their findings – be they of a "Linguistics Applied" or "Applied Linguistics" nature – are not just "application oriented basic research" but can be made relevant to the real-life world.

Fourthly, we take it that applied linguistics is socially accountable. To the extent that the imperfections initiating applied linguistic activity involve both social actors and social structures, we take it that applied linguistics has to be critical and reflexive with respect to the results of its suggestions and solutions.

These assumptions yield the following questions which at the same time define objectives for applied linguistics:
1. Which linguistic problems are typical of which areas of language competence and language use?
2. How can linguistics define and describe these problems?
3. How can linguistics suggest, develop, or achieve solutions of these problems?
4. Which solutions result in which improvements in speakers' linguistic and communicative abilities or in the use and status of languages in and between groups?
5. What are additional effects of the linguistic intervention?

4. Objectives of this handbook series

These questions also determine the objectives of this book series. However, in view of the present boom in handbooks of linguistics and applied linguistics, one should ask what is specific about this series of nine thematically different volumes.

To begin with, it is important to emphasise what it is not aiming at:
– The handbook series does not want to take a snapshot view or even a "hit list" of fashionable topics, theories, debates or fields of study.
– Nor does it aim at a comprehensive coverage of linguistics because some selectivity with regard to the subject areas is both inevitable in a book series of this kind and part of its specific profile.

Instead, the book series will try
– to show that applied linguistics can offer a comprehensive, trustworthy and scientifically well-founded understanding of a wide range of problems,
– to show that applied linguistics can provide or develop instruments for solving new, still unpredictable problems,

- to show that applied linguistics is not confined to a restricted number of topics such as, e.g. foreign language learning, but that it successfully deals with a wide range of both everyday problems and areas of linguistics,
- to provide a state-of-the-art description of applied linguistics against the background of the ability of this area of academic inquiry to provide descriptions, analyses, explanations and, if possible, solutions of everyday problems. On the one hand, this criterion is the link to trans-disciplinary cooperation. On the other, it is crucial in assessing to what extent linguistics can in fact be made relevant.

In short, it is by no means the intention of this series to duplicate the present state of knowledge about linguistics as represented in other publications with the supposed aim of providing a comprehensive survey. Rather, the intention is to present the knowledge available in applied linguistics today firstly from an explicitly problem solving perspective and secondly, in a non-technical, easily comprehensible way. Also it is intended with this publication to build bridges to neighbouring disciplines and to critically discuss which impact the solutions discussed do in fact have on practice. This is particularly necessary in areas like language teaching and learning – where for years there has been a tendency to fashionable solutions without sufficient consideration of their actual impact on the reality in schools.

5. Criteria for the selection of topics

Based on the arguments outlined above, the handbook series has the following structure: Findings and applications of linguistics will be presented in concentric circles, as it were, starting out from the communication competence of the individual, proceeding via aspects of interpersonal and inter-group communication to technical communication and, ultimately, to the more general level of society. Thus, the topics of the nine volumes are as follows:

1. Handbook of Individual Communication Competence
2. Handbook of Interpersonal Communication
3. Handbook of Communication in Organisations and Professions
4. Handbook of Communication in the Public Sphere
5. Handbook of Multilingualism and Multilingual Communication
6. Handbook of Foreign Language Communication and Learning
7. Handbook of Intercultural Communication
8. Handbook of Technical Communication
9. Handbook of Language and Communication: Diversity and Change

This thematic structure can be said to follow the sequence of experience with problems related to language and communication a human passes through in the course of his or her personal biographical development. This is why the topic areas of applied linguistics are structured here in ever-increasing concentric circles: in line with biographical development, the first circle starts with the communicative competence of the individual and also includes interpersonal communication as belonging to a person's private sphere. The second circle proceeds to the everyday environment and includes the professional and public sphere. The third circle extends to the experience of foreign languages and cultures, which at least in officially monolingual societies, is not made by everybody and if so, only later in life. Technical communication as the fourth circle is even more exclusive and restricted to a more special professional clientele. The final volume extends this process to focus on more general, supra-individual national and international issues.

For almost all of these topics, there already exist introductions, handbooks or other types of survey literature. However, what makes the present volumes unique is their explicit claim to focus on topics in language and communication as areas of everyday problems and their emphasis on pointing out the relevance of applied linguistics in dealing with them.

Bibliography

Back, Otto
    1970   Was bedeutet und was bezeichnet der Begriff 'angewandte Sprachwissenschaft'? *Die Sprache* 16: 21–53.

Brumfit, Christopher
    1997   How applied linguistics is the same as any other science. *International Journal of Applied Linguistics* 7(1): 86–94.

Candlin, Chris N. and Srikant Sarangi
    2004   Making applied linguistics matter. *Journal of Applied Linguistics* 1(1): 1–8.

Carrier, Michael, Martin Stöltzner, and Jeanette Wette
    2004   *Theorienstruktur und Beurteilungsmaßstäbe unter den Bedingungen der Anwendungsdominanz.* Universität Bielefeld: Institut für Wissenschafts- und Technikforschung [http://www.uni-bielefeld.de/iwt/projekte/wissen/anwendungsdominanz.html, accessed Jan 5, 2007].

Davies, Alan
    1999   *Introduction to Applied Linguistics. From Practice to Theory.* Edinburgh: Edinburgh University Press.

Davies, Alan and Catherine Elder
    2004   General introduction – Applied linguistics: Subject to discipline? In: Alan Davies and Catherine Elder (eds.), *The Handbook of Applied Linguistics*, 1–16. Malden etc.: Blackwell.

Ehlich, Konrad
    1999   Vom Nutzen der „Funktionalen Pragmatik" für die angewandte Linguistik. In: Michael Becker-Mrotzek und Christine Doppler (eds.), *Medium Sprache im Beruf. Eine Aufgabe für* die *Linguistik*, 23–36. Tübingen: Narr.

Ehlich, Konrad
  2006 Mehrsprachigkeit für Europa – öffentliches Schweigen, linguistische Distanzen. In: Sergio Cigada, Jean-Francois de Pietro, Daniel Elmiger, and Markus Nussbaumer (eds.), *Öffentliche Sprachdebatten – linguistische Positionen. Bulletin Suisse de Linguistique Appliquée/VALS-ASLA-Bulletin* 83/1: 11–28.
Grabe, William
  2002 Applied linguistics: An emerging discipline for the twenty-first century. In: Robert B. Kaplan (ed.), *The Oxford Handbook of Applied Linguistics*, 3–12. Oxford: Oxford University Press.
Johnson, Keith and Helen Johnson (eds.)
  1998 *Encyclopedic Dictionary of Applied Linguistics. A Handbook for Language Teaching.* Oxford: Blackwell.
Kaplan, Robert B. and William Grabe
  2000 Applied linguistics and the Annual Review of Applied Linguistics. In: W. Grabe (ed.), *Applied Linguistics as an Emerging Discipline. Annual Review of Applied Linguistics* 20: 3–17.
Knapp, Karlfried
  2006 Vorwort. In: Karlfried Knapp, Gerd Antos, Michael Becker-Mrotzek, Arnulf Deppermann, Susanne Göpferich, Joachim Gabowski, Michael Klemm und Claudia Villiger (eds.), *Angewandte Linguistik. Ein Lehrbuch.* 2nd ed., xix–xxiii. Tübingen: Francke – UTB.
Meinel, Christoph
  2000 Reine und angewandte Wissenschaft. In: *Das Magazin.* Ed. Wissenschaftszentrum Nordrhein-Westfalen 11(1): 10–11.
Rampton, Ben
  1997 [2003] Retuning in applied linguistics. *International Journal of Applied Linguistics* 7 (1): 3–25, quoted from Seidlhofer (2003), 273–295.
Sarangi, Srikant and Theo van Leeuwen
  2003 Applied linguistics and communities of practice: Gaining communality or losing disciplinary autonomy? In: Srikant Sarangi and Theo van Leeuwen (eds.), *Applied Linguistics and Communities of Practice*, 1–8. London: Continuum.
Schmitt, Norbert and Marianne Celce-Murcia
  2002 An overview of applied linguistics. In: Norbert Schmitt (ed.), *An Introduction to Applied Linguistics.* London: Arnold.
Seidlhofer, Barbara (ed.)
  2003 *Controversies in Applied Linguistics.* Oxford: Oxford University Press.
Widdowson, Henry
  1984 [1980] Model and fictions. In: Henry Widdowson (1984) *Explorations in Applied Linguistics 2*, 21–27. Oxford: Oxford University Press.
Widdowson, Henry
  2005 Applied linguistics, interdisciplinarity, and disparate realities. In: Paul Bruthiaux, Dwight Atkinson, William G. Egginton, William Grabe, and Vaidehi Ramanathan (eds.), *Directions in Applied Linguistics. Essays in Honor of Robert B. Kaplan*, 12–25. Clevedon: Multilingual Matters.

Contents

Introduction to the handbook series vii
Karlfried Knapp and *Gerd Antos*

Introduction 1

I. Foundations

1. The concept of communicative competence
   Gert Rickheit, Hans Strohner †, and *Constanze Vorwerg* 15

II. Acquisition

2. Language and neurophysiological development
   Ralph-Axel Müller and *Erica Palmer* 65

3. Cognitive foundations
   Katharina J. Rohlfing 103

4. First utterances
   Holly L. Storkel 125

5. Discourse acquisition
   Clair Pond and *Michael Siegal* 149

6. Literacy acquisition and its precursors
   Pekka Niemi 169

7. Sign language acquisition
   Vivian Gramley 187

III. Adult competence

8. Speaking and listening
   Thomas Holtgraves 207

9. Writing and reading
   Elke Prestin 225

10. Nonverbal communicative competence
    Nancy M. Puccinelli 257

11. Media competence
    Daniel Perrin and *Maureen Ehrensberger-Dow* 277

IV. Competence training

12. Communication training
    Annette Lepschy 315

13. Coping with the needs of presentation
    Mike Allen, Nancy Burrell, and *John Bourhis* 343

14. Training of writing and reading
    Eva-Maria Jakobs and *Daniel Perrin* 359

V. Language therapy

15. Developmental dyslexia: A developmental neurolinguistic approach
    Virgina W. Berninger, William Nagy, Todd Richards, and
    Wendy Raskind 397

16. Language disorders
    Martina Hielscher-Fastabend 441

17. The nature and treatment of stuttering
    Ashley Craig 499

Biographical notes 531
Keywords 537

Introduction

In our everyday life, communicative processes are relevant in almost all situations. It is important to know when you must say something which is adequate in the situation or when it is better to say nothing. Grice (1975) gave fundamental insights on the mechanisms of successful communication in his theory of conversational implicature. He presumes that conversation is a cooperative activity with at least minimal levels of coordination. According to his theory, interlocuters are expected to follow the *cooperative principle*: "Make your conversational contribution such as is required, at the stage at which occurs, by the accepted purpose or direction of the talk exchange in which you are engaged" (Grice 1975: 45).[1] Grice proposes four *maxims* which lead to behaviour consistent with the cooperative principle. The first one, the *quantity maxim*, which pertains to the expected amount of talk, is violated when speakers are over- or underinformative. The *quality maxim* involves the truthfulness of talk. The *maxim of relation* implies that speakers should make relevant contributions given the current topic and purpose of talk. The *manner maxim* concerns the clarity of talk, such as expectations that speaker will avoid obscurity or ambiguity. But Grice also suggests that competent communicators must be able to both follow and violate these maxims or communicative expectations. Grice calls such violations "flouting" the maxims. Speakers flout when they strategically violate a maxim to achieve some communicative purpose. Many nonliteral forms of speech, such as irony, sarcasm, or metaphoric expressions, could be seen as flouts. Such maxims are culture dependant and the children of each culture have to achieve the cultural forms of communication of the specific speech community if they want to achieve whole communication competence.

Communicative competence is fundamental for a successful life in our society as it is of great importance for all areas of life. Therefore, it is not surprising that communicative competence is the subject of many theoretical and empirical approaches and, in consequence, research on this topic is diverse. This observation is not new. Most of the editors of similar handbooks or authors of the same topic stated that there is a vast research literature on communicative competence. So, you may ask why are we creating a new handbook on this topic? The answer is simple: We focus our contributions on linguistic aspects of communication, whereas most of the current approaches are psychologically or sociologically motivated. In the centre of interest are linguistically oriented performances of different forms of communication and language acquisition. In recent years, important handbooks and overwiews were published, such as the *Handbook of interpersonal communication* by Knapp and Daly (2002), and the *Handbook of communication and social interaction skills* by Greene and Burleson (2003), or Berger's (2005) review on *Interpersonal communication: Theoretical perspectives, future prospects*.

2   Introduction

In the following, I will outline the content of the contributions to this handbook to inform the readers briefly, so that they can choose their chapters of interest.

In the first chapter "The concept of communication competence", Gert Rickheit, Hans Strohner, and Constanze Vorwerg discuss the theoretical, methodological, and practical relevance of the notion of communicative competence. They give a short historical overview of the discussion on the notion of communicative competence since the 1960s. In explaining the notion of communication, they focus on three aspects of communication: communication as information processing, as interaction, and as situational adaptation. In order to explicate the concept of communicative competence, they first look at its behavioural basis composed of many communicative skills, whereby the relation between competence and skill has to be clarified. The two most important criteria of communicative competence, i.e. effectiveness and appropriateness, are described, and the processes of communication are discussed. Communication is a social interaction and can, therefore, be described in terms of collective action and cooperation. The primary unit of analysis in this type of studies is the dyad or the social group – an approach allowing for analysing mutuality, group processes, and the dialectics involved. At the same time, communication takes place in terms of the cognitive processes involved, such as those underlying the production of messages to accomplish goals, the understanding of others' intentions, as well as the generation and interpretation of nonverbal behaviours. These cognitive processes have implications for the communicative competence of an individual; they largely determine the ability to communicate effectively and appropriately. Importantly, these cognitive processes are intertwined with emotional and motivational processing. Research fields devoted to the internal mental states and processes associated with communicative competence include the psycholinguistics of dialogue, psychological approaches to communication theory, social cognition, and cognitive pragmatics. Other topics of the first chapter are the discussion of theoretical approaches of communicative competence, and explanations of the development of communicative competence.

In the second chapter "Language and neurophysiological development", Ralph-Alex Müller and Erica Palmer review the literature of clinical, electrophysiological and imaging evidence. They describe methods for studying language in the brain which are suitable to reveal associations between language processing and particular brain regions. The development of tools for imaging the anatomy of the living brain has increased the opportunities for relating structure and function, which is one of the dominant questions of research on language in the brain. The authors report that stimulation and ablation studies provided evidence against the strictest forms of localisationism. The descriptions of specific tools for localising language processing in the brain (e.g., PET, fMRI) and tools for studying the temporal dynamic of language processing (e.g., ERP) are fundamental for a better understanding of the complex processes in the brain. In special sections, they describe links between brain development and language acquisition and links between genes and language acquisition. Concerning the plasticity of the human brain, they assume a limited plasticity in the mature brain and that the brain organisation for language is not fully determined at birth.

Katharina J. Rohlfing argues in the third chapter that "Cognitive foundations" are a phenomenon of the interaction between language and cognition. This interaction is present in infants' very early experiences, when perceptual information becomes transformed into conceptual thought as a basis for communicative competence. She suggests that prelinguistic sensitivity on an intersensory basis is the foundation for building up the sensitivity needed for receiving and interpreting communicative information and forming knowledge of objects and events. She assumes that some of this early prelinguistic sensitivity on an intersensory basis is still present in adults' linguistic competence. She also reports on neurobiological studies, which show a strong link between verbal action and action representation. So, she suggests that the mirror neuron system is not limited to hand movements, but can be extended to intentional communication. All the studies she reports on support the view according to which the speech process is closely related to the actoric system.

In her chapter "First utterances", Holly L. Storkel focusses on learning sounds and words in very young children. To begin to produce first words, the child must create three types of representation: phonological, lexical, and semantic representation. The phonological representation determines production accuracy and is partially developed through babble. The lexical representation corresponds to the sound sequence of a word as a whole unit and is accessed to produce or recognise a word. The semantic representation corresponds to the meaning of the word. Storkel points out that these three types of representation must be linked to one another so that language production and comprehension can occur. These findings describe the skills which allow a child to rapidly acquire these three types of representation. One basic cue to word segmentation and word recognition is word stress. The ability to use the predominant stress pattern as a cue for speech segmentation appears to emerge around 7.5 months of age. Direct evidence of infants' ability to use phonotactic or transitional probability to aid in segmentation is provided by several studies. It is clear that infants avail of useful cues to segment continuous speech. There are studies which investigated how infants integrate or weight these cues. This chapter shows in detail how infants learn the prosodic, phonemic, and phonetic cues needed to segment the speech stream into words. In doing this, infants are also gaining practice producing these same cues in their babble. This association between productive phonology and word learning has been observed in several studies. Storkel reports on studies which found that children may not store segmentally detailed information on the entire word form, but rather may store more holistic information about parts of the word form. According to these findings, lexical representations are initially holistic but develop into segmentally detailed ones, due to vocabulary growth.

Clair Pound and Michael Siegal examined children's conversational understanding and proficiency in discourse in terms of their responses to measures designed to determine their ability to detect ambiguous messages. According to Grice's (1975) theory, they describe "Discourse acquisition" by testing the extent to which children are capable of following the intended implications of speakers in conversation. They present empirical studies on the development of discourse processing. In these studies, children were tested as to their ability to follow the implications of questions on a range of tasks aimed at their distinguishing between reality and the phenomenal world of appearances. Some studies investigated the question of how children come to acquire non-literal interpretation. Other authors found that children below 6–8 years have difficulty in accepting true paraphrases of utterances of nursery rhymes. The research discussed by the authors shows that young children do possess an incipient grasp of the implications of conversation. In contexts where alternative interpretations of messages are made clear and they are prompted to attend to these, children show evidence of proficiency in conversation, such that they can respond well on a variety of tasks central to language and cognition. In sum, this chapter gives a differentiated overview of children's pragmatic development and discourse acquisition.

Pekka Niemi introduces into the problem of "Literacy acquisition and its precursors". He reviews components and processes of literacy acquisition, in which phonological awareness play a central role, but not the only one. Studies beginning from birth or during the first year of life show that there is a predictable path to phonological awareness and literacy acquisition beginning with phoneme discrimination and processing through acquisition of vocabulary and inflectional morphology. Other factors promoting literacy acquisition are also briefly reviewed, some of which are cognitive or linguistic in nature such as rapid automatic naming or metacognition, which is a child's ability to reflect upon his/her cognitive processes such as memory, learning, and comprehension. Others have social origins such as letter knowledge and task orientation. Finally, he discusses whether it is possible to delineate a predictable path from early language-related skills to beginning reading and spelling. Having reviewed a set of studies, he comes to the conclusion that literacy prognosis based on phonological awareness appears to be weaker than usually thought, but also states that there is no reason to jettison it. So, he considers that phonological awareness is a necessary, rather than sufficient, condition for literacy. In consequence, he discusses other probable factors needed in beginning literacy, such as letter knowledge, rapid automatic naming, motivation, and metacognition.

The use and acquisition of the sign language is a problem which has long been neglected in Germany. It is, therefore, commendable that Vivian Raithel deals with this problem in her contribution "Sign language acquisition", in which she shows how sign languages are acquired and how similar or even same types of mistakes are found in both the spoken and sign languages. It is assumed that the capacities that underlie language acquisition are not specific for the spoken or sign language. Hearing and deaf children both begin their language acquisition by babbling. But deaf children babble with their hands, whereas hearing children's babbling involves vocalisations. What they have in common is that they use babbling in order to discover the phonological structure of their language. A major difference between hearing and deaf children when acquiring a language is that hearing children spend a great deal of time looking at the objects referred to, pointed at, and named by their parents, whereas deaf children spend a great amount of time looking at their parents when spoken to, which leads to an asynchronicity between the linguistic input and the object of reference. But Raithel emphasises that the acquisition of sign and spoken language does not differ much aside from the modalities used. Children go through comparable stages in their language acquisition. In both, motherese is of great support because the rhythmical quality, the enlarged size of the signs, and the frequent repetitions assist the child greatly. Similarly, the process of simplification can be observed in both acquisition processes for the production of the first words.

The basics of communicative competence, i.e. "Speaking and listening", are discussed by Thomas Holtgraves. He emphasises that successful language use requires a variety of skills and knowledge above and beyond basic syntactic and semantic competencies. Language users must know what actions can be performed with words and how to go about constructing utterances to perform those actions. In face-to-face communication, the final form of an utterance plays a central role because it reflects the speaker's concern with controlling his facial expression and that of his or her interlocutors. Successful language use requires coordination, and greatly facilitating this requirement is the fact that people are both speakers and listeners. Speakers formulate their utterances with the goal of having their intentions recognised and recipients process a speaker's remarks with the goal of recognising those intentions. All interactants must be able to do this in such a way as to avoid offending each other. Holtgraves' basic assumption is that language is goal-directed behaviour with the goals existing at varying levels of abstraction. There are high-level goals such as face expression control, which are almost always operative, as well as lower-level goals, which are associated with a single turn or set of turns. He uses the concept of goals as a means of organising his chapter. In a first section, he discusses the linguistic mechanisms by which speakers can convey their intentions and perform speech acts. In a second section, he describes the cognitive processes involved in the recognition of the speaker's goals. In a final section, he considers some of the obstacles that speakers and listeners must overcome to use language successfully.

In her chapter "Writing and reading", Elke Prestin gives a review of studies from a psycholinguistic perspective. In a first section, she discusses the most influential models of writing processes. The overview shows that research on writing as a human competence is based on both process-oriented and product-oriented methods. She emphasises that, in spite of the diversity of methodological approaches, the development of models has been rather straightforward. The first models of the writing process were based on the notion of writing as a problem-solving task. It is obvious that the models are divided into different components such as planning, translating, and reviewing. There are models of competent writers as well as models which implement different levels of competence in writing. Recent models describe not only the writing process itself, but also include the social-cultural dimension of writing and individual factors such as motivation and memory. Common for all models is that writing in general is considered as (more or less) resource-demanding. In a second section, Prestin discusses psycholinguistic approaches to reading. According to the reported literature, she points out that a theory of reading must account for both the process which reading implies and the understanding of a given text that results from these processes. Recent empirical reading research is mainly based on on-line methods. Models of text comprehension tend to be quite detailed in their description of processes and the underlying components of text comprehension. The chapter ends with an integrated view on writing and reading as interdependent parts of human communication.

Nancy M. Puccinelli examines how nonverbal encoding and decoding work separately and in concert to aid individuals in successful communication in her chapter "Nonverbal communicative competence". Research suggests that nonverbal behaviour, such as facial expressions and body movement, communicates more information on what one is thinking or feeling than words. When nonverbal and verbal cues conflict, nonverbal cues are more likely to be believed. When verbal content is unclear, people seem to rely almost exclusively on nonverbal cues. Research on nonverbal behaviour focused on so called "molecular" cues such as number of smiles, frequency of eye contact, gestures, posture, touching behaviour, facial expressions, and vocal behaviour (e.g., tone of voice, pauses, and rhythm). More recently, there has been a shift toward a focus on more "molar", i.e. holistic, judgments of behaviour which examine a perceiver's overall impressions of an individual based on the individual's nonverbal behaviour. In the following sections, she emphasises that nonverbal behaviour plays a critical role in being a competent communicator. How effectively people encode their needs has a significant impact on their ability to achieve their goals. Similarly, the ability to accurately decode and appropriately respond to the cues of others is also a key to successful communication.

Introduction   7

The topic of Daniel Perrin's and Maureen Ehrensberger's chapter is research on "Media competence". In their opinion, journalistic media characterise an autonomous, socially relevant area of language use. Journalism forms an own area of communication. The concept of journalistic media is specified communicatively, socio-politically, and economically. The authors distinguish different types of media competence: media competence in everyday situations, in media situations, in media production. After a detailed discussion of these types of media competence, they give a definition of this term. "Media competence encompasses general, topic-specific, and event-specific abilities that together make it possible to solve tasks appropriately and effectively with medially-transmitted communication." In a special section, research on media competence is discussed. The authors present four areas of research in which the language products themselves as well as language use as a cognitive, social, and cognitive-social activity are investigated. One method from each of the four approaches is outlined and illustrated with an empirical research project that works primarily with this method. In another section, they give a detailed overview of specific research questions and findings in the area of appropriate and successful media-specific language competence in the context of journalist text production. The research is categorised in terms of variously complex settings for language use, then language functions, and finally linguistic structures. At the end of the chapter, the authors show some gaps in the research area of media competence.

Annette Lepschy proposes in her contribution "Communication training" a system of categories which helps to discern teaching and learning methods aimed at developing communicative competence. The learning target communicative competence has two dimensions: First, communicative competence aims at taking the participants from an intuitive problem awareness to an analytical one. Secondly, it endeavours to create a greater individual scope for interaction. These two dimensions include the capacity to interpret social norms and expectations in and for speech situations. The author distinguishes two different methods of teaching, i.e., representation methods and reviewing methods. Representation methods integrate a given communication reality into the teaching and learning process in order to work on them and translate the resulting alternatives into communicative action. These methods are simulation (role play), games, and exercises, whereas reviewing methods help perceive and apperceive the individual communication reality and produce action alternatives. These methods can be divided into reflective and analytical review methods. The author emphasises that methods of representation and review methods need to be viewed as integral parts of communication training. Both activating and receptive methods of representation and reflective and analytical review methods should be looked on not as competing but as complementary with regard to the learning target, i.e., the widening of the participants' scope for communicative actions.

"Coping with the needs of presentation" is discussed in the chapter by Mike Allen, Nancy Burrell, and John Bourhis. The chapter focuses on the presenter's level of anxiety as to how his/her communicative competence is perceived by others. The first part of the chapter outlines the impact such anxiety about communication by the communicator generates in the perceptions of message receivers. Communication situations are often important for the communicator. Therefore, the impact of importance is to provide the potential for the communicator to be nervous or apprehensive about the process or act of communicating. Apprehension reflects a situational basis related to the number of persons with whom the person is communicating. In the next section, the authors discuss treatments which minimise the impact of anxiety on presentation. There are principally three methods of reducing anxiety about communication events: Skill training, cognitive modification, and systematic desensitisation. The research demonstrates that all three methods of reducing communication apprehension are successful. The findings also suggest that the impact of the methods in combination are additive. The final section of the chapter considers the impact of anxiety about social interaction, as it may impact on the development of antisocial (criminal) sexual behaviours. The goal of this section is to provide an example of how low levels of competence in communication may play a role in behaviours not normally associated with lack of communication skill. The result of this discussion is that anxiety about communication and the corresponding impact on lack of competence may contribute to a variety of social problems.

Eva-Maria Jakobs and Daniel Perrin discuss approaches of "Training of writing and reading". They state that training tends to focus either on writing or reading competence; programmes that systematically relate writing and reading as a complex combination of skills are rare. The chapter focuses on the reading and writing processes of adults involved in text production, mostly professionally, in domains such as science, technology, administration, and public communication. Studies on text production show that reading processes systematically accompany the entire process of text development. Depending on the related text, two types of reading processes can be differentiated: production-oriented reading, to monitor the developing text product, and source-oriented reading, to understand texts being referred to that are written by other authors. Scientifically-based trainings require systematic knowledge at two levels: knowledge on conveying information and knowledge on the topic, in this case, text production. At the level of conveying information, trainers have to carry out and guide educational processes suitable to expand their trainees' repertoires of competences in a targeted way. At the level of subject matter, trainers have to provide theoretically and empirically sound knowledge. Special training fields are discussed in a separate section. The authors point out that text production training is directed to certain text production tasks which presuppose certain competences in written communication. Text production tasks and trainings can be differentiated according to their relationship to the text production setting, function, and structure. Since the observation of eye movements during reading has only been possible in special eye-tracking laboratory settings, there is a lack of empirically solid analyses of the interaction between reading and writing processes during text production.

In their review of "Developmental dyslexia: A developmental neurolinguistic approach", Virginia W. Berninger, William Nagy, Todd Richards, and Wendy Raskind discuss recent approaches to developmental dyslexia. In the first section, they give a short historical overview of the concept of developmental dyslexia, which is contrasted with other reading disorders. Genetic and neurological factors of dyslexia are presented in the following section. They state that dyslexia is a language disorder and the causal mechanisms are primarily phonological and not due to a general auditory deficit. An adequate analysis of dyslexia must consider the language basis of this disorder, which is best understood within a theoretical framework that distinguishes among different levels of language (i.e., the phonological, morphological, syntactical, semantical, and the discourse level) and that takes into account functional systems and models of language processing in relationship to working memory. The notion of levels of language is relevant to understanding the different kinds of reading and writing disabilities. The phenotype for dyslexia can be characterised in terms of the components of working memory all of which have a phonological component. The authors state that teachers are often not adequately prepared, conceptually or paedagogically, for the linguistic issues involved in reading and writing. This lack of teacher knowledge can contribute as much as biological factors to the observed reading and writing disabilities of dyslexics. The authors emphasise that recent research on brain imaging with instruction in written language points to nature-nurture interactions in learning written language. They also go into interesting detail on the interaction of brain and language learning. In their view, the brain is not an independent variable that causes language learning in and of itself, but, rather, also a dependent variable that changes in response to language input from the environment. They report numerous results of empirical dyslexia studies and, in the final section, they discuss theoretical issues in linguistics that are relevant to understanding developmental dyslexia in detail.

Ashley Craig describes "The nature and treatment of stuttering", especially treatment shown to be effective at reducing stuttering within children, adolescents, and adults. Stuttering can be seen as a communication disorder involving involuntary disruption to the fluency and flow of speech. It is prevalent throughout life with a predominance in males. It is believed to be a neurological disorder which affects the motor system of speech. Most children who stutter will begin to stutter before adolescence, most commonly between 2 and 5 years of age, with the highest peak at around four years. As verbal communication is known to be very important for successful social interaction, stuttering can create barriers to social and psychological development. The author discusses treatment rationale and regimens for stutterers, including treatment for young children, older children, adolescents and adults. He emphasises treatments that have been scientifically tested and shown to be effective in reducing stuttering to acceptable levels in both the short- and long-term, as well as in reducing levels of fears about communicating verbally. Regardless of the specialised treatment being applied, there are core components and principles that should always be employed by the clinician to ensure the effectiveness of stuttering treatment. Relapse (i.e., the return of stuttering following successful treatment) and maintaining treatment gains continue to be significant clinical problems in stuttering. From adult research, it is estimated that around a third of treated adults experience difficulties in maintaining fluency in the long term. Finally, the author states that cognitive-behavioural treatment that contains fluency enhancing strategies is effective in reducing stuttering in the majority of older children. The combination of Smooth Speech and EMG feedback presented within a cognitive behavioural regimen was shown to be effective in lowering relapse rates in children who had serious difficulties maintaining their fluency skills following their initial treatment.

In the last chapter, "Language disorders" are described by Martina Hielscher-Fastabend. She gives an overview of the basic brain mechanisms of language functions. She argues that the traditional localistic view of cortical representation of language functions postulates a central speech area, represented usually in the left hemisphere, which consists of a receptive and auditory word association region, connected to the adjacent areas in the parieto-occipital lobe as well as via the arcuate fasciculus to a speech production, word-sequencing region in the frontal lobe. But she discusses several examples which document that this picture of language centres and functions is too simple. Today's view of localisation, lesion, and function is not as strict as it has been formerly postulated. She describes the traditional classification of aphasia which is closely related to the neurobiological localisation. After this description, she discusses recent neurolinguistic approaches which have promoted more exact knowledge of the processes involved in the production, perception and storage of oral and written language. She emphasises that the planning of therapeutic and rehabilitative programmes have to consider the components of changed skills and language processing of aphasia patients and their individual, situational, and social coping potential. The specific problems of patients with language disorders demand the development of adequate diagnostic tools and therapeutic methods.

I dedicate this handbook to my friend and colleague Hans Strohner[†]. He was the initiator of this volume but died last year in the middle of work on this book so that he, unfortunately, could not experience its completion. I thank Constanze

Vorwerg for her many helpful comments and suggestions and Grainne Delany for her fruitful organisational and technical support of this volume.

All contributors to this handbook would be pleased if the book in hand were to stimulate further discussion in the complex domain of communication competence.

Bielefeld, February 2008																				Gert Rickheit

Note

1. The references in this introduction will be given in the first chapter of this volume.

I. Foundations

1. The concept of communicative competence

Gert Rickheit, Hans Strohner†, and Constanze Vorwerg

This chapter provides an overview of the concept of communicative competence from the perspective of the individual emphasizing empirical foundations. After stressing the notion's theoretical, methodological, and practical relevance and giving a short historical survey since the early 1960s, it relates communicative competence to the basic concept of communication and discusses criteria for communicative competence: efficiency and appropriateness. On the basis of these comments on relevance, history, and criteria, the chapter presents an overview of theoretical proposals and empirical research about the processes underlying communicative competence, specifically processes of message production, message reception, nonverbal behaviors and social problem solving, as well as underlying knowledge and representations. Finally, some relevant developmental aspects are addressed.

1. Introduction

The ability of people to reach their goals in social life depends to a large extent on their communicative competence. The notion of 'communicative competence' was introduced by Dell Hymes in the 1960s (1962, 1964, 1972) to emphasize that the knowledge of grammatical rules is not sufficient for speaking a language and for communicating. There is a shared belief in many societies that good communication has many constraints and that one of the most important constraints is the underlying ability of the interlocutors. As Steven Wilson and Christina Sabee (2003: 3–4) put it:

> Why have so many scholars, from so many fields, studied communicative competence within so many relational, institutional, and cultural contexts? Our hunch is that scholars, as well as the contemporary Western societies in which most live and work, widely accept the following tacit beliefs: (a) within any situation, not all things that can be said and done are equally competent; (b) success in personal and professional relationships depends, in no small part, on communicative competence; and (c) most people display incompetence in at least a few situations, and a smaller number are judged incompetent across many situations.

In this introductory part of the chapter, we approach the concept of communicative competence, first, from a discussion of its theoretical, methodological, and practical relevance, and second, from its historical development.

1.1. Relevance

Like most central concepts in empirical sciences, the notion of communicative competence comprises theoretical, methodological, and practical aspects. With respect to theory, the internal and external structure of the concept should be well defined and contribute to an embedding theory, together with other concepts. In methodological terms, the concept should be based on objective, reliable, and valid measurements, which are connected to successful intervention procedures. Finally, the concept should support the application of the theory to practice in real life.

Theoretical relevance. Communicative competence is a complex term with a rich internal and external structure. Regarding the internal structure, we have to relate it to subordinated terms such as effectiveness and appropriateness. Whereas *effectiveness* describes the outcome of communicative competence, *appropriateness* connects it with the situational conditions of the actual social interaction.

The external structure of a concept is given by its embedding theory and other related concepts of this theory. What is the relationship to similar concepts as performance or skill, and how can communicative competence be described in terms of knowledge, motivation, emotion, and behavior? And what processes and settings are important for a general and integrative theory of communicative competence? And finally, how is communicative competence developed, and how can this development be influenced?

Many of the discussions in this book will be devoted to these theoretically relevant questions.

Methodological relevance. Being closely connected to the theoretical relevance of a scientific concept, its methodological relevance must be clarified. Only on the basis of objective, reliable, and valid observation procedures is it possible to build up clear theoretical terms. In recent years, research has made remarkable progress with regard to good empirical studies.

Practical relevance. Theoretical and methodological quality provides a solid basis for the purposes of applied research. When looking into the by now about hundred-years-old history of linguistics, we will find many concepts whose relevance for practical application is anything but clear. The concept of communicative competence is a strong counter-example. From its first introduction into linguistics in the early 1960s, it was meant as a means to support practical procedures for assessment and intervention in real life settings. A large number of chapters in this book are devoted to giving an overview of the present state of art in these fields of application.

1.2. Historical overview

The scientific history of the concept of communicative competence began in the 1960s as a counter-movement against the so-called "linguistic competence" introduced by the structural linguist Noam Chomsky (1965), who based linguistic theory on an ideal speaker-listener with perfect linguistic knowledge, which is supposed to be unaffected by cognitive and situational factors during actual linguistic performance. Among others, the philosopher Jürgen Habermas (1970) and the sociolinguist Dell Hymes (1972) argued that Chomsky's concept could not serve as a relevant component in a theory of real-life communication. Habermas argued "that general semantics cannot be developed sufficiently on the narrow basis of the monological linguistic competence proposed by Chomsky" (1970: 137–138). But similar to Chomsky's idea of an idealized *speaker-hearer*, he idealized the *speech situation*: "Above all, communicative competence relates to an ideal speech situation in the same way that linguistic competence relates to the abstract system of linguistic rules. The dialogue constitutive universals at the same time generate and describe the form of intersubjectivity which makes mutuality of understanding possible. Communicative competence is defined by the ideal speaker's mastery of the dialogue constitutive universals irrespective of the actual restrictions under empirical conditions" (Habermas 1970: 140–141).

Habermas dissociates himself on the one hand from Chomsky criticizing his too narrow linguistic-competence idea, and on the other hand from Hymes' empirically founded communicative-competence idea. "I propose to use this term [communicative competence] in a similar way as Chomsky does with linguistic competence. Communicative competence should be related to a system of rules generating an ideal speech situation, not regarding linguistic codes that link language and universal pragmatics with actual role systems. Dell Hymes, among others, makes use of the term communicative competence in a sociolinguistically limited sense. I don't want to follow this convention" (p. 147). In contrast to Habermas, most of the authors of this handbook follow the empirically well-founded concept of communicative competence as it was developed by Hymes.

Contrary to Chomsky and Habermas, the sociolinguist Dell Hymes related his conception of communicative competence not only to theoretical, but also to practical needs. He argued that the theoretical and the practical problems converge. "It is not that there exists a body of linguistic theory that practical research can turn to and has only to apply. It is rather that work motivated by practical needs may help build the theory that we need" (Hymes 1972: 269).

Consequently, he rejected the dichotomy of competence and performance. Instead, he looked upon the two concepts as two sides of a coin: Performance is the observable part, and competence is the inferred ability to produce the observed performance in the future. Hymes suggested that both competence and performance may be influenced by special cognitive and social factors, and that their interrelationship should be investigated with empirical methods.

Instead of a dichotomy of competence/performance, Hymes (1972: 281) proposed that the following four questions should be asked for a comprehensive study of language and communication:

1. Whether (and to what degree) something is formally *possible*;
2. Whether (and to what degree) something is *feasible* in virtue of the means of implementation available;
3. Whether (and to what degree) something is *appropriate* (adequate, happy, successful) in relation to a context in which it is used and evaluated;
4. Whether (and to which degree) something is in fact done, actually *performed*, and what its doing entails.

The question of formal possibility refers to grammatical and cultural rules of an utterance or another communicative action. Both verbal and other communicative behavior can be judged according to its obeying to the rules within a formal system. The question of feasibility is based on psycholinguistic factors such as memory and other cognitive, emotional, and behavioral limitations caused by features of the human brain and body in relation to their physical environment. The question of appropriateness relates the communicative action to its social environment. The basic point is here what behavior can be expected in a specific communication situation. And the question of actual performance points to the necessity of empirical observation of a certain communicative event. In addition, its probability of occurrence should be registered because this probability contributes to the quality of the related competence.

Further important milestones in the development of a comprehensive notion of communicative competence were, among others, the contributions by John Wiemann (1977), and Spitzberg and Cupach (1984/1989). Research in interpersonal communication has been directed at understanding how communication is used in forming relationships and what factors play a role in social interactions. A central factor of John M. Wiemann's (1977) model of communicative competence is *interaction management*. His aim was to develop a theory of communication competence that was robust and that could be used to understand communication behavior in a particular situation. In this attempt, the importance of individual and relational goals, strategies and motivations for achieving these goals, planning routines, emotions, and cognitive abilities became evident. He developed a model composed of the following five dimensions: "(1) affiliation/support, (2) social relaxation, (3) empathy, (4) behavioral flexibility, and (5) interaction management skills" (Wiemann 1977: 197). His model is based on earlier approaches to the study of competence, such as Goffman's (1959) self-presentation approach, in which human is described as an actor who plays various roles to various audiences. According to Goffman, the competent communicator is one who is aware of the quality of encounters as demonstrated by her or his presentation of appropriate faces and lines and the support of the faces and lines presented by others. The second basis of Wiemann's model was the human-relation or T-group approach (Argyris 1962, 1965; Bochner and Kelly 1974). They mentioned five skills of communicative competence: (1) empathy, (2) descriptiveness, i.e., the manner in which feedback is given and received, (3) owning feelings and thoughts, (4) self-disclosure, and (5) behavioral flexibility. The social-skill approach by Argyle (1969) was the most important example for Wiemann's model. Argyle defined "skill" as an "organized, coordinated activity in relation to an object or a situation, which involves a whole chain of sensory, central and motor mechanisms" (p. 180). Argyle developed the following specific dimensions of communicative competence: (1) extroversion and affiliation, (2) dominance-submission, (3) poise-social anxiety, (4) rewardingness, (5) interaction skills, (6) perceptual sensitivity, and (7) role-taking ability. Because of their centrality to communicative competence, Argyle (1969) mentioned two general interaction management skills (1) "the ability to establish and sustain a smooth and easy pattern of interaction" and (2) the ability to maintain control of the interaction without dominating (pp. 327–328). Based on these three approaches to communicative competence, Wiemann (1977) developed his own model, which was tested in an experiment. Results indicated a strong, positive, linear relationship between interaction management and communicative competence. The conclusion from his study was that "the competent communicator is one who is other-oriented, while at the same time maintaining the ability to accomplish his own interpersonal goals. This other-orientation is demonstrated by the communicator being empathic, affiliative and supportive, and relaxed while interacting with others. [...] It is this communicative competence which enables a person, in a very real and practical way, to establish a social identity" (p. 211).

Similarly, Spitzberg and colleagues (Spitzberg and Cupach 1984; Spitzberg and Hurt 1987) identify four global constructs: interaction management, altercentrism, expressiveness, and composure, which are each represented by overt molecular behaviors. *Interaction management* is represented by such behaviors as questions, interruptions, and talk time, while *altercentrism* is indicated by head nods, body lean, and smiling. Vocal variety, appropriate use of humor, and appropriate facial expression are indicants of *expressiveness*, while vocal tension, object manipulation, and postural rigidity are associated with *composure*. Spitzberg and Cupach (1984) discuss the question whether competence should be defined as a trait or a state. Traits are viewed as dispositions while states are situational events or occurrences (Fridhandler 1986). They argue that: "competence *as a trait* ultimately must boil down to an individual effectively communicating across contexts – with different environments, with diverse goals and topics. This consistency of performance is really tantamount to general communicative adaptability and behavioral flexibility" (Spitzberg and Cupach 1984: 92).

In their "Handbook of Interpersonal Competence Research", Spitzberg and Cupach (1989) gave a well structured overview of the state of the art in this complex field. Their book "is a research book. As such, it is designed to present and assess approaches and techniques for studying and measuring interpersonal competence" (p. 4). They chose the term "interpersonal competence", because the term "refers to the process whereby people effectively deal with each other, as the most general term" whereas "the term *communicative competence* often implies a focus on appropriate symbolic behavior manifested in social and interpersonal contexts" (p. 6). The aim of their handbook was "to review existing measures of interpersonal communication and cognate constructs, in order to facilitate further research" (Spitzberg and Cupach 1989: 234).

The last milestone in the study of communication skills to mention here in our overview is the "Handbook of Communication and Social Interaction Skills", which was edited by John O. Greene and Brant R. Burleson (2003). Their book – with a focus on relationships instead of the individual – aimed at producing "the most comprehensive, authoritative source available on communication skills and skills enhancement – a volume with both practical and theoretical significance" (p. XIV). Bringing together a number of perspectives from different disciplines, such as social psychology, sociolinguistics, sociology, and communication, the book demonstrates the considerable progress that has been made in understanding skillful social interaction in different contexts and the significance of communicative skills for interpersonal relationships at various levels.

2. Communication

In most communication situations, we have two or more communication partners with some internal knowledge who are connected to each other by the following five links (see Fig. 1):

- Information transmission and feedback
- Informational medium
- Referential knowledge
- Partner knowledge and mindreading
- Physical and social situation.

Most researchers would certainly agree to this rough scheme of the underlying structure of communication. However, the concrete models of communication and communicative competence differ considerably (see, e.g., Wilson and

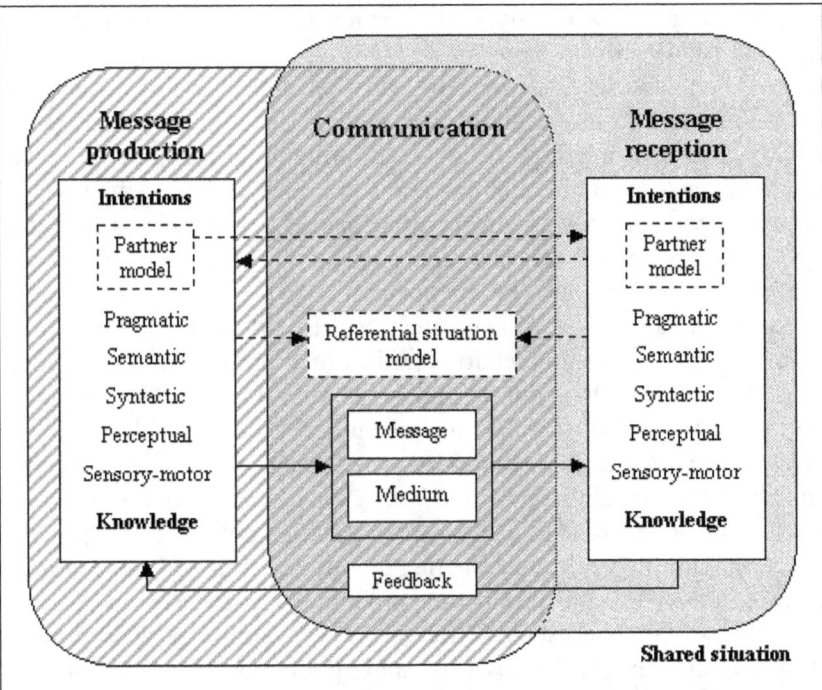

Figure 1. Structure of communication (based on Strohner 2001). Communication results from the overlapping of message production and reception processes, based on communicative intentions and different types of knowledge. The transmission of the message implies, among others, anticipatory processes on the side of the message producer, and inferential processes on the side of message recipient.

Sabee 2003; Berger 2005). In them, the integrated scheme is divided into many tiny parts, processes, and functions. Research projects are carried out, many of which yield empirically based, yet specific results. One question to ask is how to describe the overall structure of communication by integrating the obtained results of the different special projects. So, the problem is: How can a comprehensive and integrated theory of communicative competence be developed combining the various results in the broad area of communicative competence and how does this development relate to the basic notion of communication?

We suppose that in the field of communication the distinction of the following dimensions will be helpful:

– Communication as information exchange,
– Communication as mental-state reading and influencing,
– Communication as interaction,
– Communication as situation management.

In the following, we will only outline some theoretical approaches without going into a detailed discussion.

In every communicative event, information processing is a basic part. At least two independent information-processing systems are involved, which intentionally exchange messages using an informational medium. However, the wide-spread conception of communication as consisting of a sender encoding a message and sending it via an information channel to a receiver, who decodes it (based on Shannon and Weaver's information theory), grasps only part of the relevant processes in human communication.

In contrast to a code-based approach, there is wide agreement between cognitive approaches to communication that information processing includes very different activities such as knowledge and attitude activation, expectancies, evaluations, and goal-directed action planning. Theories within this *mental-states framework* (Bara, Cutica and Tirassa 2001) usually assume that communication is intentional and directed at affecting the other's mental states. Message production can be regarded as a goal-directed action including such processes as representing multiple goals, constructing hierarchical plans and executing behavioral programs. Message production processes are focused in *goals-plans-action theories* (e.g., Wilson 1990; Berger 1997; Waldron 1997) and *hierarchical theories* (e.g., Greene 1997). Relevant cognitive processes investigated are goal forming, planning, and anticipatory processes (see Section 4.1).

As far as message reception is concerned, the inferring of others' desires and intents is central. So, relevant cognitive processes include knowledge activation, the rational and emotional evaluation of the message contents, and the management of related attributions and expectations. Expectancies for other people's behavior and the recognition and interpretation of strategic violations are processes related to others' mental states in expectancy violations theories (e.g., Burgoon 1995). Causal judgments about the own communicative competence and about factors of communicative success are assumed to affect the setting of realistic goals and expectations in attribution theories (e.g., Weiner 1996). More generally, understanding a message may involve the recognition of others' feelings, intentions, and other mental states, based on inferential, empathetic, and executive abilities (see Section 4.2).

However, not even the understanding of the literal message can be explained solely in terms of information exchange. The cognitive basis of many mental activities involved in message understanding and production is the construction of *mental models* (Johnson-Laird 1983). A mental model is an internal representation with analogical relations to its referential object, so that local and temporal aspects of the object are preserved. It comes somewhat close to the mental images people report having in their minds whilst processing information. The great advantage of the notion of mental models, however, is its ability to include the notion of a *partner model* and the notion of a *situation model*. Thus, mental models can build a bridge to the other two dimensions of communication, namely interaction and situation.

Whereas theories in the mental-states framework look at the mental processes of the individual communication partners, interactional theories analyze dyads or groups investigating how the interlocutors react to each other and how well their actions fit together. According to Herbert Clark's theory, put forward in his book "Using Language" (1996), the basis of communication is the mutually shared knowledge of the interlocutors. The totality of the presuppositions individuals have concerning shared beliefs, knowledge, and assumptions constitutes their common ground. Common ground accretes with each succeeding conversational exchange, and each conversational exchange is interpreted with respect to the common ground that has accumulated to that point of individuals' joint activities (Clark 1994). There is a current controversy based on different empirical arguments about when common ground comes into play: right from the beginning of language planning vs. only either during monitoring or during communication problems (see Section 4.3).

Shared action and shared intentionality also form the basis for the development of language and communicative competence, according to Michael Tomasello's theory (2003). In his approach, the most basic skill underlying the ability to understand other people and to engage in shared activities is intention reading (Tomasello and Rakoczy 2003). This ability is related to the understanding of other people as intentional agents forming the groundwork for experiences in cultural activities using conventional symbols, which in turn results in more complex forms of understanding others' mental states (see also Sections 4.2 and 6).

An interaction theory focusing on mutual influence and relational processes is Giles' and colleagues' communication accommodation theory (Giles, Coupland and Coupland 1991). The authors emphasize that accommodation theory can describe processes both at the micro and the macro level within a single theoretical and interpretative frame. They argue that in conflict situations individuals tend to restore balance in altering such attributes of speech as dialect, accent, and other speech parameters in the direction of their interlocutors' speech style. Speakers may converge when they desire solidarity with their conversational partners, and they may emphasize differences, or diverge, when they wish to assert a unique individual or group identity.

Both phylogenetically and ontogenetically, communication in concrete situations is of fundamental importance (Cambell and Wales 1970). The evolution of language took place, for the most part, in the management of certain everyday tasks (Müller 1990). A prerequisite for the ontogenesis of language is a child's sensorimotor development, which also takes place within different situational contexts (Piaget 1975). More than seven decades ago, Bühler (1934: 23) spoke of a "situation theory of language" in contrast to "situation-distant speaking";

in doing so, he proceeded from a "concrete language experience", explained through his "Organon" model in which the referential field plays a prominent role. Therefore, language can be considered a versatile tool for situation management (Rickheit 2006).

Depending on their addressing specific components of communicative situations, media theories and social theories may be differentiated. Within the context of the new communication technologies, there are many approaches in studying mediated social interaction afforded by computers or Internet, video conferencing, and mobile telephone. Current communication research analyzes the specific conditions of computer-mediated communication and human-computer interaction (Berger 2005). Future research might benefit from interdisciplinary work in addressing the interaction of cognitive processing, social skills, and mediated communication.

3. Communicative competence

As already mentioned in the introduction to this chapter, communicative competence is of central importance not only for scientific purposes, but also for practical application. A certain amount and quality of communicative competence is needed not only in social interaction at the interpersonal level, but also at organizational and public levels, as well as for intercultural exchanges. Many individual and social problems in our societies arise, however, because people are not sufficiently competent with respect to certain aspects of communication. The consequences concern interpersonal relationships, academic and professional success, but also psychological and health problems. Higher levels of communicative proficiency facilitate a better social, psychological, and physical life.

In order to explicate the concept of communicative competence, we firstly look at its behavioral basis composed of many communicative skills. Therefore, the relation between competence and skill has to be clarified. Then the two most important criteria of communicative competence, i.e. effectiveness and appropriateness, are described.

3.1. Communication skills

Although there is great interest in the notion of communicative competence in science and real-life application, the concept is not easy to define in a general way. The reasons lie in the complexity of communication, the wide variety of related cognitive and social abilities, and also the huge situational variability. What we need in the field of communication, similar to the field of intelligence, is the specification of domain specific abilities. A recent handbook devoted to communication and social interaction skills edited by John Greene and Brant

Burlesen (2003) specifies a number of fundamental interaction skills, such as nonverbal communication skills, discourse and conversation skills, message production and reception skills, and impression management skills. The volume also discusses functional skills such as informing, explaining, arguing and persuasion, as well as specific skills in personal relationships and in public and professional contexts.

Specifying communication skills for a rather narrow range of particular behaviors and situations makes it easier to define them and to analyze methods for assessment and intervention. A certain skill is related to specific knowledge, emotion and, of course, sensory-motor behavior. In accordance with this conception, Brian Spitzberg (2003: 95) proposes the following definition of skills: "Skills, therefore, are generally thought to be manifestations of some underlying ability, which is a capacity for action. This capacity is typically conceptualized as a function of numerous motivation (e.g., confidence, goals, reinforcement potential, etc.) and knowledge (e.g., content and procedural knowledge, familiarity, etc.) components."

As any social behavior, communication skills are not independent of functional and situational influences. It often occurs that people manifest very different skill qualities in different situations, be it self-presentation, empathy or conflict management.

3.2. Effectiveness

Given that communication is enacted to reach a certain goal, a central criterion for communicative competence is effectiveness. This is a functional attribute, which may relate to the ability to achieve or to infer a speaker's meaning (e.g. that an utterance is meant ironic), or to the achievement of the goal behind this intent (e.g., that this irony is meant as a critique or as a joke; see 4.1). As Spitzberg and Cupach (1989) pointed out "effectiveness derives from control and is defined as successful goal achievement or task accomplishment" (p. 7). In cases where functions and goals of communicative actions are not clear, or if there are multiple functions, the analysis of effectiveness is problematic (see Chapter 2 in this volume).

In some situations, it is important to know not only that a certain action is accomplished, but also, how much time and energy consumption this has taken. The notion of efficiency refers to such a higher level of effectiveness.

3.3. Appropriateness

As already proposed by Dell Hymes (1972), a competent communication should be judged as appropriate according to the social factors in a given situation. Yet, here we should be very careful in not equating social factors with norms or rules, because in some situations it may be very appropriate to alter existing norms and rules or to establish new rules. Thus, the criterion of appropriateness is flexible enough to cover a vast variety of relations between communicative actions and their social environments. Following Spitzberg and Cupach (1989: 7), "appropriateness reflects tact or politeness and is defined as the avoidance of violating social or interpersonal norms, rules, or expectations".

After having reviewed several other criteria of communicative competence proposed in the scientific literature, Brian Spitzberg (2003: 98) concludes: "However, combining appropriateness and effectiveness provides a framework that most competence theorists accept as generally viable. Competence, according to the dual criteria of appropriateness and effectiveness, is the extent to which an interactant achieves preferred outcomes in a manner that upholds the emergent standards of legitimacy of those judging the interaction".

4. Processes implying communicative competence

Communication is social interaction and can therefore be described and studied in terms of collective action and cooperation. The primary unit of analysis in this type of studies is the dyad or the social group – an approach allowing for analyzing mutuality (e.g., Clark and Brennan 1993), group processes (e.g., Straus 1996) and the dialectics involved (e.g., Montgomery and Baxter 1998).

At the same time, communication is happening in terms of the cognitive processes involved, such as those underlying the production of messages to accomplish goals, the understanding of others' intentions, as well as the generation and interpretation of nonverbal behaviors. These cognitive processes have implications for the communicative competence of an individual; they determine largely the ability to communicate effectively and appropriately. Importantly, these cognitive processes are intertwined with emotional and motivational processing. Research fields devoted to the internal mental states and processes associated with communicative competence include the psycholinguistics of dialogue (e.g., Clark 1996; Pickering and Garrod 2004), psychological approaches to communication theory (e.g., Burgoon 1993; Schrader and Dillard 1999), social cognition (e.g., Tomasello (2003a) and cognitive pragmatics (e.g., Tirassa 1999; Sperber and Wilson 2002).

Some processes are specific for message production, others for message reception; while many underlying representations and knowledge structures are used for both conveying and reading intentions. In face-to-face communications, both are influenced by nonverbal behaviors. Additional processes are involved in situations where social problems arise, which require to be solved by communicative means and require particularly good communication skills. They will be addressed at the end of this section.

4.1. Message production: Conveying intentions and accomplishing goals

Speakers (as well as writers and signers) produce language in order to convey certain ideas to their interlocutors. They mean something by their utterance and want their communication partners to understand their intentions. A typical way to express this concern is the very frequent phrase "know what I mean" (with over one million occurrences on the internet). Accordingly, communicative meaning or speaker intention is conceptualized as the effect that the language producer intends to have on the addressee's mind. So for example, the sentence "I am trying to concentrate" may mean a desire for quietness and be intended to make someone stop talking or turn down the radio. The addressee's recognition of this speaker-meaning is the intended effect on the addressee's mind defining the basic criterion for a successful communication.

Ideas about communication as conveying and inferring communicative meaning have been strongly influenced by the "theorists of communication-intention" – Wittgenstein (1953), Austin (1962), Searle (1969) and the later Strawson (1971) and Grice (1975) – who regard intention or speaker-meaning as the central concept of communication. The proposed distinction between speaker-meaning (or communicative intent) and (literal) sentence meaning has been widely accepted in the field of communication and dialogue research, even though assumptions about the precise nature of the relation between them may differ. According to Sperber and Wilson (2002: 3), it is the objective of pragmatics to "explain how the gap between sentence meaning and speaker's meaning is bridged".

Intentionality lies at the heart of several cognitive approaches to human communication and language. Hörmann (1983: 233) emphasizes that "the listener does not understand the utterance; he understands the speaker. More precisely, he understands what the speaker, in this situation, wants the listener to think." Tomasello (2003b) argues that language is shared intentionality (see also Tomasello, Carpenter, Call, Behne and Moll 2005; Tomasello and Rakoczy 2003). According to Tirassa (1999: 419), "cognitive pragmatics is concerned with the mental processes involved in intentional communication". Canary and Cody (1993) emphasize the importance of interpersonal goals for communication, specifically self-representation goals, relational goals, and instrumental goals.

One task of cognitive models of message production is to describe how speakers (or writers etc.) manage to convey the communicative meaning intended. What cognitive processes are involved in producing literal or nonliteral language in a way that enables the auditory to understand what is meant – the basic criterion for a successful communication? And what means (such as nonverbal behaviors, intonation, explicit clarification, etc.) are used to signal the intended meaning? What processes are involved in judging its appropriateness in a situation? All those processes contribute to producing the message in a way that allows inferring whether it is meant as let's say a joke, or a reproach, or an offer to help.

As the intended meaning itself is determined in turn by the goals the language producer is pursuing, one might as well ask whether the communicative strategy chosen (e.g. irony, hyperbole, indirect request) is suitable to accomplish that goal. Even though the addressee might understand what was intended by an utterance, he or she doesn't necessarily act according to this intention. A request or an offer may be rejected; the child may be leaving the house without taking the jacket suggested by a caretaker, etc. Therefore, goal accomplishment (communicatively achieved) can be regarded as another possible criterion to judge how successful communication has been.

The relation between goal and intention has been discussed by Tomasello and colleagues, who propose following Bratman (1989, cited in Tomasello et al.) that "an intention is a plan of action the organism chooses and commits itself to in pursuit of a goal" (2005: 676). Concerning intentional communication, an utterance meant to be ironic may serve the goal to criticize the hearer (e.g., Haverkate 1990), or just to be humorous or to tease the addressee (e.g., Pexman, Glenwright, Krol and James 2005). The ironic intention has to be recognized on the one hand, the goal behind it is another aspect of intentional communication. To give another example, the remark "there's a draught" may be understood as an indirect request to close the window (successful communication in terms of conveying intentions); another question is whether the addressee will be fulfilling this request (successful communication in terms of goal accomplishment).

Cognitive models of message production describe several distinct stages of the process, such as (1) situation-dependent goal setting, (2) planning or "action assembly", and (3) enactment (Berger 2007; Burleson and Planalp 2000; Dillard and Solomon 2000; Wilson 2002). A number of cognitive processes associated with them have been proposed and partially supported by empirical evidence.

Speakers often pursue multiple goals simultaneously (see Wilson and Sabee 2003, for a review). On the one hand, goals are embedded in hierarchies: moving down the hierarchy, goals are subdivided into subgoals – moving up the hierarchy, higher-order goals and motives explain *why* somebody attempts to achieve a particular goal in a certain situation. On the other hand, the main goals underlying an utterance (e.g., eliminating annoying noise) are often accompanied by secondary goals (e.g., being polite, setting a good example, maintaining good relations with neighbors or colleagues). Some goals may be regarded as metagoals, such as social appropriateness or efficiency (Berger 1997).

According to Wilson's (1990) Cognitive-Rules (CR) model, associations (or "cognitive rules") between situational features and interaction goals are represented in long-term memory. Cognitive rules are assumed to have the form of implicit if-then rules. Spreading activation within this associative network may – after reaching a certain threshold level – trigger a cognitive rule, which in turn forms a goal. In that way, multiple goals can be formed simultaneously without substantial demands on processing capacity. Goal-forming processes may account for variations in communicative competence between speakers in a number of ways: Different speakers may vary with respect to their ability to form appropriate goals, which are accepted and recognized by other people (see Wilson and Sabee 2003, for a review), the level of specificity at which communication goals are represented in working memory (Meyer 2000), the accessibility of secondary goals (Meyer 2000, 2002), the sensitivity to a partner's goals (Berger 2000; Lakey and Canary 2002), and the flexibility to alter goals across situations (see Wilson and Sabee 2003). A review of the literature suggests that cognitive processes involved in goal-setting include the activation of goals depending on the representation of the current situation and by activating structures in long-term memory, a maintenance of goals in working memory, the representation of other people's goals based on theory of mind (see next section), the evaluation and coordination of divergent goals.

In the process stage of planning, the communicative goal is transformed into the plan of action chosen to achieve that goal. Plans for accomplishing communicative goals may vary widely in complexity. They may consist of a large number of hierarchically organized subgoals and steps involved in the preparation of a speech or in the arrangement of an appointment. They may also consist in the simple planning of a short sarcastic answer to a request. Planning complexity varies not only in dependence on situational demands, but also between speakers (Berger 1997). A higher level of plan complexity may be related to higher communicative competence if required by situational contingencies; however, it may also have debilitating effects on communication effectiveness, if plans for communication are so complex that they cannot be executed efficiently (see Berger 1997). The complexity of plans is also dependent on cognitive resource limitations and therefore affected by cognitive loads through too many goals or ambiguous situations (Waldron 1990).

Planning entails also the aspect of selecting parts of the activated pieces of knowledge for explicit verbalization. In Herrmann's (1983; see also Herrmann and Grabowski 1994) socially situated speech production model, selection, linearization and elaboration processes operate on the activated conceptual structures (for a distinction between speech production and message production, see Greene and Graves 2007). For example, to convey a request, the speaker might choose to express the own need, or the addressee's ability. An elaboration of activated knowledge structures might lead to a negation, or to a hyperbolic or an ironic expression. According to Action Assembly Theory (AAT), the conceptual structures underlying message planning consist of huge hierarchical networks in long-term memory, the "procedural records", which represent features of actions linked with situational conditions (Greene 1997). The subset of records that underlies the speaker's meaning to be conveyed (such as promising, or giving directions) is selected by receiving activation from already activated situational nodes and other feature-of-action nodes. A second process, "assembly" or "coalition formation" (see also Greene, Kirch and Grady 2000), integrates activated features of action into larger complexes of action specifications (a string of words, a syntactic frame linked with a particular noun and a particular verb, or specific activated words linked with the according motor programs). Greene (2006) assumes that the generation of utterance plans using the processes of activation and assembly can be based on either a complete retrieval from long-term memory (called "selection") or a novel construction (called "creation"), or a mixture of both. (Note that the term "selection" is used here for different processes than in Herrmann's account.)

Further cognitive processes involved in the planning of messages include anticipatory processes concerning the implications of actions and potential obstacles (Berger 1997; Waldron 1997; Wilson 1990) as well as executive control processes needed for planning, specifically those involved in monitoring, editing, and rehearsal (Jordan 1998). Therefore, problems with executive control hinder a speaker's ability to control planning processes in message production. In accordance with these considerations, research in neuropragmatics and neuropsychology has provided evidence for communicative consequences of executive dysfunction (such as impairments in goal setting, planning, inhibition of response and self-monitoring; Ylvisaker and Szekeres 1989). Similarly, executive function skills have proven important for the acquisition of alternative modes of communication in people with severe aphasia (Nicholas, Sinotte and Helm-Estabrooks 2005).

Action assembly theory also deals with the enactment of communicative plans. The hierarchical networks assumed in that theory extend to the very low-level nodes representing the configuration of concrete muscle movements (for facial expression, vocal articulation, or gestures). Sophisticated models of enactment based on a huge amount of empirical results concerning grammatical encoding, lexical access, phonological encoding, and phonetic encoding have been developed within speech production research (e.g., Bock 1982; Dell, Chang and Griffin 1999; Dell, Schwartz, Martin, Saffran and Gagnon 1997; Herrmann 1983; Levelt 1989; Levelt, Roelofs and Meyer 1999). Linguistic aspects of utterance production affecting intention understanding include pronunciation (e.g., Rosin and Swift 1999) and intonation (e.g., Chung 1988).

Several other – mainly motivational and emotional – factors have been shown to influence message production, including collaborative engagement (Tomasello et al. 2005), the ability to establish co-membership with the interlocutor by making the interaction more personalized (Kerekes 2006), stress-coping and self-esteem (Cegala and Waldron 1992), as well as transient mood (Forgas and Tehani 2005).

4.2. Message reception: Inferring intentions

Communicative competence comprises not only the ability to produce messages in a way that their intents can be inferred by others and that their interpersonal goals can be accomplished, but also the ability to receive messages conveyed by others. Therefore, an important part of cognitive processes involved in communicative competence deal with inferring the speaker's intentions.

Cognitive models of message reception usually assume two main stages in the processing of messages: (1) understanding literal meaning, and (2) understanding speaker's meaning (Airenti, Bara, and Colombetti 1993; Wyer and Adaval 2003). A third stage concerns the communicative effect on the addressee (such as forming a new belief), which is to a large degree dependent on evaluation processes. Additional phases of processing a communicative act, addressed by Airenti et al., include reaction (generating the intentions for a response) and overt response. These phases are not discussed here, as they overlap largely with processes of message production.

Understanding literal meaning or sentence meaning depends on a large number of cognitive processes, which are subject to theories of sentence processing (see for example, Gernsbacher 1990; MacWhinney and Bates 1989; Rohde and Plaut 2003) and which each constitute complex research areas in their own right. With respect to accounts of message reception, it is often emphasized that the literal meaning needs not be transmitted by linguistic means, but can also be conveyed in nonverbal communication (nodding or smiling or waving a hand) or in other ways (such as using pictures). These forms can be equivalent to linguistic means (for saying goodbye, or expressing joy or affirmation, or giving a route direction); their correct interpretation, i.e. inferring the intended meaning, depends on knowledge about the according cultural conventions (e.g., whether nodding is used for affirmation or for negation). In other instances, the intended literal meaning can only be conveyed by using language; deciphering it requires knowledge of the language rules and may depend on procedural knowledge providing a sufficiently fast activation of the intended knowledge structures. The linguistic representation of a sentence need not necessarily be complete, detailed and accurate (Ferreira, Bailey and Ferraro 2002).

The message is interpreted in terms of conceptual structures in long-term memory. As Wyer and Adaval (2003) point out, several alternative concepts may be assigned to a message, and which of them are activated may depend on their accessibility in long-term memory, which in turn may be influenced by factors such as recent activation, frequency of activation, and current goals. As people are often not aware of the factors that led them to apply one piece of knowledge rather than another one, biases can occur in interpreting messages. Another process contributing to literal message representation is the construction of current representations relating and instantiating generalized concepts based on imagination. It is now widely accepted that representing sentence meaning usually involves the construction of a representation of the situation described – besides wording-based and propositional representations. Such mental representations of what a discourse is about have become known as mental models (Johnson-Laird 1983) or situation models (van Dijk and Kintsch 1983) and consist of a mental simulation of the events described (see also Zwaan and Radvansky 1998; see Wyer and Radvansky 1999, for the comprehension of social information). Garrod and Pickering (2004) argue that the success of communication depends on the extent to which the interlocutors' situation models correspond in important aspects. The construction of situation models depends also on language skills (Zwaan and Brown 1996).

To infer the speaker's communicative intent, starting from the literal meaning, the addressee may take advantage of nonverbal clues, prosody, contextual information and information from long-term memory (such as knowledge about the partner or about cultural conventions). Using these types of information, the listener might interpret the sentence "It's raining," as advice to take an umbrella or as starting a small talk or as a response to an earlier argument. The representation of the message has been shown to depend on the listener's perception of speaker intention (specifically, attributed viewpoints), as evidenced by sentence recognition patterns (Wertsch 1975). An important indicator that the literal meaning deviates from the speaker's meaning and that a statement should not be taken literally at all would be a violation of communication expectancies. Communication expectancies are individual representations of norms for nonverbal behavior and language use. Both Griece's (1975) theory of conversational implicature and Burgoon's (1993, 1995) expectancy violations theory assume that competent communication involves following as well as strategically violating communication expectancies. In terms of Grice's theory, a speaker that violates one of the conversation maxims (quantity or informativeness, quality or truthfulness, relevance to topic and purpose of talk, and manner or clarity of talk) needed to converse in a cooperative way will be assumed by the addressee to adhere to the maxims at a deeper level. Therefore, the listener would reinterpret the message as being hyperbolic, ironic, sarcastic, humoristic, etc. According to expectancy violations theory, engagement in unexpected behavior of an interlocutor increases arousal, which leads to an orientation response, in which attention is shifted away from the topic of discourse to the interlocutor and the meaning of the violation itself. Studies based on expectancy violations theory have addressed mainly aspects of communicative effect and nonverbal communication (see below).

Understanding the speaker's meaning transmitted by an utterance can be regarded as an instance of *intention reading*, according to Tomasello et al. (2005) a most basic social-cognitive skill. The ability to form a fully developed theory of mind, to appreciate others' mental states and to form beliefs about what other people may think (called first order knowledge) or even about what other people belief other people to think (called second order knowledge) seems to be derivative of those more basic social-cognitive skills. Importantly, this basic mind-reading ability seems to be associated with a motivation to share psychological states with others, joint intentions and attention (shared intentionality) as well as well as emotions and experiences (see Tomasello et al.). Other authors propose that there is a specific, relevance-based sub-module, within the mind-reading module, dedicated to inferring the speaker's meaning (Sperber and Wilson 2002), or that there is an innate faculty to communicate (different from a language faculty; Tirassa 1999) – to explain the discrepancy between toddlers' lack of (first-order) theory of mind and ability to communicate (see Section 6). Generally, it can be assumed that understanding communicated messages often requires reasoning about the language producer's mental state (e.g., Bara, Tirassa and Zettin 1997).

The proposal that theory-of-mind abilities are necessary for understanding non-literal meaning has been put forward for understanding metaphor and irony (Happé 1993), deceit and sarcasms (Griffin, Friedman, Ween, Winner, Happé and Brownell 2006) and stories about double bluff, white lies and persuasion (Happé 1994). A number of studies have sought to validate or put to test hypotheses about the relationship between mind-reading or mentalizing abilities and understanding pragmatic, non-literal meaning – and also their possible relation with other cognitive functions, such as executive functions or semantic processing. The results are not clear-cut.

One type of evidence are findings about the neural bases of mind-reading and communicative abilities suggesting a relation; however, the specific contributions of different brain parts in these processes are not known in detail yet. Discourse deficits in understanding nonliteral meaning (but also in producing discourse) have been linked to right-hemisphere disorders (e.g., Bartels-Tobin and Hinckley 2005; Brady, Armstrong and Mackenzie 2006; van Lancker 1997; Winner, Brownell, Happe, Blum and Pincus 1998; Winner and Leekam 1991; for results concerning lateralization and interhemispheric integration, cf. also Cutica, Bucciarelli and Bara 2006; Huber-Okrainec, Blaser and Dennis 2005; Mitchell and Crow 2005; Paul, van Lancker-Sidtis, Schieffer, Dietrich and Brown 2003), and also to frontal lobe lesions and closed head injury[1] (e.g., Channon and Crawford 2000; Dennis and Barnes 2001; Pearce, McDonald and Coltheart 1998; Shamay, Tomer and Aharon-Peretz 2002), especially to prefrontal lesions. Mind reading (or mentalizing or theory of mind) has been associated in the neuroimaging and neuropsychological literature with the right hemisphere (Winner et al. 1998), and specifically with the medial frontal lobes (e.g., Fletcher, Happé, Frith, Baker, Dolan, Frackowiak and Frith 1995; Gallagher and Frith 2003; Stuss, Gallup and Alexander 2001; Shamay, Tomer, Berger, Goldsher and Aharon-Peretz 2005), and selective impairments have been found also for closed head injury (Channon, Pellijeff and Rule 2005). The assumption of a particular role of the medial frontal – as part of a brain system also including amygdala, temporo-parietal junction and orbital frontal cortex (Frith and Frith 2003; Siegal and Varley 2002) – has been challenged by both a reported case of intact theory-of-mind reasoning despite excessive damage to the medial frontal lobes (Bird, Castelli, Malik, Frith and Husain 2004) and findings highlighting the specific involvement of the right temporo-parietal junction (e.g., Saxe and Wexler 2005). Taken together, the neuropsychological and neuroimaging results suggest that a number of cognitive and affective processes work together in achieving theory of mind, such as making inference regarding beliefs and knowledge, perspective-taking, possibly imagination or mental simulation to represent the mental states of the self and the other or to anticipate behavior, using knowledge about the world and about the partner, affective mind-reading (probably related to empathy) and deriving emotional significance (Frith and Frith 2006; Shamay, Tomer and Aharon-Peretz 2005; Shamay-Tsoory, Tomer, Berger, Aharon-Peretz 2003; Siegal and Varley 2002) – and that these have also to be taken into account when discussing the role of mind-reading in interpreting communicative messages.

Other studies have tried to directly test whether there is a relationship between theory of mind and pragmatic abilities, such as understanding metaphor and sarcasm or distinguishing lies from jokes and irony from deception. Channon, Pellijeff and Rule (2005) found that study participants with closed head injury were impaired both in comprehending sarcastic remarks and in mentalizing about human actions described in stories and that mentalizing scores correlated with sarcasm comprehension. Other evidence linking sarcasm understanding to mentalizing ability was presented by Creusere (1999). In contrast, Martin and McDonald (2005) report a study in which theory of mind was not significantly associated with irony comprehension in individuals with traumatic brain injury; instead general inferential reasoning was a strong predictor (cf. also Bara, Tirassa and Zettin 1997; Frye, Zelazo, and Palfai 1995). In a study with children, semantic ability was a stronger predictor of performance on metaphor tasks rather than first-order mentalizing skills (Norbury 2005). On the other hand, a strong correlation between the ability to distinguish lies from jokes and the ability to attribute correctly second-order mental states was found by Winner and colleagues (1998), for both right-hemisphere brain damaged patients and a normal control group. Patients with ventromedial frontal lesions were significantly impaired in irony and faux pas, but not in second-order false beliefs in a study by Shamay-Tsoory and colleagues (2005b), considering social faux pas as a more advanced theory-of-mind test compared to first-order and second-order beliefs. They relate their results to a similar pattern described in Asperger syndrome (Baron-Cohen et al. 1999, cited in Shamay-Tsoory et al.). Altogether, these results fit well with the findings about neural bases, which suggested that several cognitive and processes contribute to theory of mind and that it may be partially impaired, and different theory-of-mind task may tap onto different aspects. Furthermore, the different processes involved in theory of mind may vary in their importance for different types of nonliteral meaning. One factor contributing to this may be the graded difficulty among speech acts found in studies with closed-head injured individuals for both linguistic communiation (Bara, Tirassa and Zettin 1997) and extralinguistic communication (Bara, Cutica and Tirassa 2001). In some instances, higher abilities in one contributing factor (such as superior semantic knowledge) might make up for deficits in another one (such as in theory-of-mind understanding) as proposed by Norbury (2005).

Several other processes contribute to message reception – some of them controversially discussed with respect to their relationship to theory of mind. These include more general and basic cognitive processes required for processing complex material, such as attention, working memory, and executive functions, but also processes more specific to social cognition and communication, such as interpreting facial expressions (e.g., Mah, Arnold and Grafman 2005; Shaw, Bramham, Lawrence, Morris, Baron-Cohen and David 2005) and emotional prosody (e.g., Paul et al. 2003; Trauner, Ballantyne, Friedland and Chase 1996), a special form of metacognition required for recognizing communicative intent directed at altering the mental state of the interlocutor (Amodio and Frith 2006), and restricting inference generation to the most likely outcomes (Lehman-Blake and Lesniewicz 2005).

Other authors reject the idea that understanding speaker's meaning follows understanding literal meaning. Glucksberg (1998) presents evidence supporting the conclusion that metaphor understanding is not necessarily optional: In a number of experiments did people comprehend metaphorical meanings as quickly and automatically as literal meanings. Moreover, understanding conventionalized metaphors may not so much be similar to a comparison process but more directly based on novel, extended senses of lexical entries. Similarly, indirect requests (such as "Close the window.") are not necessarily more difficult than direct requests (such "Can you close the window?"), as argued by Bara et al. (1997). While these cases clearly indicate that nonliteral meaning can be activated right from the beginning in communication understanding, it is not clearly whether these observations contradict the idea of two main phases in the processing of messages, or whether they are confined to cases were the meanings of words and phrases or gestures have been shifted or extended to include the originally nonliteral meaning.

A different question from understanding the message and inferring the speaker's intentions is the communicative effect the message has on the addressee. Listeners might well understand a speaker's intent to convince them of something, another question is whether they will believe it to be true and whether they believe the speaker to believe in it. To give another example, a listener's comprehension of an indirect request to open the window is different from their willingness to do so. It depends very much on private knowledge and motivations, but also on attributions of mental states to the language producers to what degree the interlocutor's mental states about the discourse topic are adjusted according to the message (Airenti, Bara and Colombetti 1993). Again, inferential processing plays an important part in this aspect of message reception. Emotional processes might be involved in appreciating humor, as understanding a humoristic story is not tantamount to appreciating its humor (cf. Barolo, Benuzzi, Nocetti, Baraldi and Nichelli 2006; Griffin et al. 2006). There is a huge amount of applied research available about what factors in the message and in the speaker's behavior contribute to reaching a communicative effect, such as persuasion (e.g., Sigall, Mucchi-Faina, and Mosso 2006), or compliance with safety recommendations (e.g., Laughery 2006) or medical treatment (e.g., Elliott and Jacobson 2006; Williams and Ogden 2004), and also how these interact with evaluation and attribution processes in the addressee (e.g., Briñol, Rucker, Tormala and Petty 2004; Campbell and Kirmani 2000; Wood 2000). These include the attribution of goals behind the communicative intentions perceived (e.g., why is somebody trying to convince me of something) and may also be related to secondary goals, such as maintaining good social relationships or being perceived as supportive. Altogether, communicative competence in understanding messages depends on all those processes involved in understanding literal meaning of utterances or nonverbal behavior, inferring intentions and goals, and relating them to the situation perceived, knowledge about the world and possibly metaknowledge about language use, as well as to the own motivations and intentions.

4.3. Underlying knowledge and representations

Communicative competence is based on a number of representations and knowledge structures underlying communication, which are used for both conveying and reading intentions. To understand and produce messages, we rely not only on our knowledge of the language at several levels (or nonverbal means to express ideas), general knowledge about the world, cultural schemata and represented constraints, specific situation models, and representations of our own mental and physical states, goals and intentions, but also assumptions about the other person(s) involved in the communication and about their goals, intentions, feelings, attitudes, opinions and knowledge. However, it is a matter of some controversy to what extent we need explicit representations of our interlocutors' mental states and fully fledged theories of mind in each and every case of communication.

According to Grice's theory, successful communication requires the speaker's intentions to be transparent (Grice 1975). That is, the listener must not only recognize the informative content of the utterance, but also the speaker's intention to inform, and the speaker's intention to have the listener recognize this intention to inform, etc. And the speaker would need to represent all these levels of intentions. So, this type of mutual knowledge (Searle 1969) would require an infinite sequence of metarepresentations that could hardly be mentally represented (Wilson 2000). The solution proposed by Grice himself to this dilemma is that communicators simply deem full transparency as achieved although it is not in effect achievable (Grice 1982). An alternative proposal stems from relevance theory, which distinguishes between informative and communicative intention and assumes a fully represented speaker's meaning to consist of a fourth-order metarepresentation involving the addressee's representation of the speaker's intention of the addressee's belief of the speaker's intention of the addressee's belief (see Wilson 2000).

Another type of mutual knowledge relevant to communication accounts is shared information or *common ground*, that is background knowledge and assumptions shared between speaker and addressee (e.g. Clark 1996; Clark and Brennan 1991). So, this is not mutual knowledge about communicative intentions, but rather shared knowledge about anything relevant to the contents of the conversation. For example, a definite reference such as "the movie" may be appropriate and understandable if both interlocutors know that the addressee watched a specific movie the night before and if each of them knows that the other one knows. Common ground may stem from community membership, physical co-presence, or linguistic co-presence (Clark and Marshall 1981), and is accumulated during conversation. This includes the process of grounding, in which both interlocutors assure themselves of the addressee's sufficient understanding of what has been said, as a basis for updating their common ground (Clark and Brennan 1991; Clark and Krych 2004). All these processes involve a mental representation of their interlocutor's mind – similar to the theory of mind discussed in the previous section. This modeling of the partner's mind is also assumed to provide the basis for partner-specific message production (see also Herrmann 1983; Herrmann and Grabowski 1994; the literature on situated speaking is reviewed in Rickheit and Vorwerg 2003).

There is debate about whether common ground is taken into account already during the initial processing (Metzing and Brennan 2003), or only later either during the monitoring of speech plans (Horton and Keysar 1996), or only in times of difficulty, when simple alignment mechanisms based on priming are ineffective (Pickering and Garrod 2004). Pickering and Garrod's interactive-alignment account of dialogue assumes that the interlocutors build similar linguistic representations and situation models based on largely automatic processes without need for a constant iterative formulation of mutual knowledge. At the time being, it is an empirical question how much knowledge about the partner's mind is necessary under what conditions and at which points in time during message generation and understanding. This dispute bears some interesting relations to the discussion presented in the previous subsection about basic mind-reading or intention-reading ability vs. a full-fledged theory of mind. Theory-of-mind skills and partner model seem to be phenomena that may be more or less developed in an individual and that consist of several aspects and facets more or less important to a communication dependent on task demands and situation.

4.4.   Generating and interpreting nonverbal behaviors

In face-to-face communication, nonverbal behaviors play an important role in communication and the ability to generate and to interpret appropriate and effective nonverbal behaviors contribute considerably to communicative competence. Gestures, facial expression and other body movements may be used by themselves to convey messages (e.g., Bara, Cutica and Tirassa 2001). They are also often interwoven with linguistic means to transmit the literal meaning, such as in communication about spatial information (Alibali 2005), or to clarify the communicative intent (or speaker-meaning). Frequently, they serve to pursue secondary goals (such as being perceived as polite or as communicatively competent, see Chapter 11, p. 275–310).

An important aspect of shared intentionality is the *coordination of attention* between interlocutors, which may be achieved by pointing, placing, and gesturing (Clark 2003; Clark and Krych 2004). An eye-tracking study showed that the more closely a speaker's eye movements were coupled with a listener's, the more successfully the listener comprehended the speech (Richardson and Dale 2005).

Gaze behavior is not only important in conveying the direction of attention, thereby providing a basis for joint attention, but also in direct eye contact – which may function to regulate interaction, express intimacy, exercise social control, or to provide information about liking and attraction, attentiveness, involvement, and the strength of feelings (Kleinke 1986). Gazing while speaking, or while listening depends very much on internal states, such as confidence or interest (see van Beek, van Dolderen and Demon Dubas 2006 for a review), but probably also on routinization. Complex neural networks are involved in gaze processing with specific regions of the temporal lobe and the prefrontal cortex being responsible for analyzing direction, social meaning, gaze monitoring and eye motion, partially depending on facially expressed emotion (Hooker, Paller, Gitelman, Parrish, Mesulam and Reber 2003).

Facial expressions are often indicative of emotions. Although they may also express other types of information, most research has focused on affective processing. Facial expressions may be produced intentionally to convey a message, they may mirror other people, or they may simply accompany emotions or mood without awareness. But even then they are important for conveying and inferring communicative intents – as communicative intents are frequently related to emotional states (such as in humor, teasing, threats, sarcasm or consolation). Some facial expressions, specifically smiling, are generally relevant for communicative competence and secondary goals, such as maintaining good relationships.

The ability to encode and express emotion facially and to decode facially expressed emotion is based on a number of internal processes and representations, such a as automatic activation processes and affect induction (Owren and Bachorowski 2003) possibly related to the mirror system (Iacobini, Woods, Brass, Bekkering, Mazziotta and Rizzolatti 1999), inhibition processes to mask negative emotions or inhibit culturally inappropriate expressions, and knowledge of culturally appropriate and possibly gender-dependent display rules. More controlled processes may dominate in situations when people try to modify their emotional expression (Feldman Barrett and Gross 2001). Nonverbal expressivity is related to the ability to identify and describe one's own feelings (Troisi, Chiaie, Russo, Russo, Mosco and Pasini 1996). As facial expressions are more likely to be displayed in social interaction (Chovil 1991), social perception seems to contribute as well. The accuracy of the recognition of emotion from facial expressions depends on shared cultural background and acquaintance, and the ability to perceive emotion differs between persons (see Elfenbein, Marsh and Ambady 2002 for a review).

Other channels of nonverbal communication are *body movements* and *manual gestures* – and besides them a number of other means, such as interpersonal space, touch, voice, head tilt, posture, or even pictures. Body movements and gestures can be used as cues to emotion (e.g., de Meijer 1989), but gestures do also aid both the production and the comprehension of speech (Driskell and Radtke 2003) and contribute to the conveying of the speaker's communicative intentions (Melinger and Levelt 2004). More gestures are produced at moments of relatively high conceptual load (Melinger and Kita in press).

Nonverbal expressivity is the ability to produce nonverbal behaviors for communication (see Burgoon and Bacue 2003). Relevant processes involved are the experience of identifiable emotion, presumably genetically rooted automatic motoric activations, inhibition processes, social cognition processes, and attentional and motivational processes, such as those leading to interest and arousal. Cultural influences are essential in modifying, inhibiting, or newly developing nonverbal expressions. Communicative goals and intentions play a central role in the functional model (Patterson 1982).

Nonverbal sensitivity is the ability to decode affect and emotion accurately (see Burgoon and Bacue 2003). Among the cognitive processes proposed in reactive, affect-based, equilibrium, and functional models are scripts, emotional labeling, expectancies and attributions (Patterson 1999). Expectancy theories put particular emphasis on nonverbal expectancy violations. People have expectancies about nonverbal behaviors, such as gaze, smile, or interpersonal distance. They anticipate their interlocutors' behavior based on internalized norms. Violations of those expectations, i.e. unexpected nonverbal behavior, triggers "a cognitive-affective appraisal of such behavior, leading to a valencing of the behavior(s) as positive or negative" (Burgoon, Newton, Walther and Baesler 1989: 97). In one experiment, Burgoon and colleagues found that high-involvement violations within a problem-solving discussion lead to greater attraction, credibility, and persuasiveness. Social judgment (e.g., Bargh 1989) and inferential processing (Cutica et al. 2006) are relevant processes with inferential load depending on conflicting mental representations.

4.5. Social problem-solving processes

In most cases, interpersonal communicative processes run fast and almost unconsciously. But when social problems arise, people tend to act more slowly and with more reflection concerning their actions and the related consequences. This is particularly true in the fields of organizational and public communication, where social problems may have a broader background and often result in career and financial difficulties. In the context of problem-solving processes, the basic concepts are problem, solution, problem-solving and solution implementation (D'Zurilla, Nezer and Mayden-Olivares 2004).

Problem-solving and solution implementation together result in the specific *problem-solving style* of a person. Problem-solving skills and solution-implementation skills often show only low correlations. Hence, some people might possess poor problem-solving skills but good solution-implementation skills, or vice versa. In addition to these skills, D'Zurilla et al. describe another central component of problem solving called *problem orientation*. Problem orientation is a meta-cognitive attitude comprising a person's general beliefs and feelings about problems as well as his or her own problem-solving ability.

The results of the empirical and theoretical analyses by D'Zurilla et al. suggest that a positive problem orientation and a rational problem solving style (as opposed to a impulsive or an avoidance style) contribute essentially to social-problem-solving competence. A positive problem orientation is a constructive attitude towards problem solving comprising optimism and a belief of self-efficacy. And a rational problem solving style is defined as a constructive problem-solving style applying effective problem-solving skills (problem definition, generation of alternative solutions, and decision making) and effective solution implementation, and evaluation skills.

When problems arise in communication, an especially high level of communicative competence is needed to analyze and solve the problems. Canary (2003) presents a review on some challenges for the use of effective and appropriate communication skills during interpersonal conflicts. He states that productive conflict behaviors are difficult to learn because the vast variation of conflict situations defies simple description and explanation of knowledge, emotion, and behavior components of the conflict. Moreover, a conflict often entails a broad spectrum of long-lasting influences including relational history, recurring differences, and ongoing tensions. Finally, an interpersonal conflict frequently occurs within stressful events, that challenge people's ability to use all their communicative competence.

One important factor is sensitivity to the goals of others (Lakey and Canary 2002). Therefore, inferential processes based on verbal and nonverbal cues, and mind-reading abilities seem to play a decisive role. Appreciation of both their own and their partner's goals may enable people to find ways how they can act both effectively and appropriately during conflict situations, as they come to understand the interdependence between their own and their partner's goals (Parks 1994). Appropriate communicative behavior also contributes to pursuing one's secondary goals (such as being perceived as communicatively competent, Lakey and Canary 2002). This is related to another factor of communicative competence related to conflict solving potential: the ability to keep in mind secondary goals at the same time while pursuing the main goals (see Section 4.1).

These representation of one's own and one's partner's goals provide the background for the choice of processes involved in the selection of communicative strategies. This strategic choice is influenced by emotional, cognitive and behavioral responses to a partner's opposition (Canary 2003). More specifically, Canary describes the following internal processes involved, based on the review of the literature. Initial reactions to situation with conflict potential (such as readiness to move toward, against or away) depend on personality factors that affect personal control and other response tendencies. Other processes concern assessments of the situation and attributions about an offender's or an interaction partner's intentions and about the cause of the problem. The ability to derive plausible and benevolent explanations underlies to an important degree a rational problem-solving style. The situation assessment is followed by decisions on the course of action, which depends on the goals an individual wants to achieve (including secondary goals). The message production is based on the conflict strategy chosen, i.e. the approach the person chooses to tackle the problem (such as to confront the other person in a cooperative manner). Different tactics can be deployed to pursue a problem-solving strategy, for example acceptance of responsibility, constructive metacommunication or solicitation of criticisms. Additionally, processes related to social interaction and possibly reconciliation following conflict termination may be important (Horowitz, Jansson, Ljungberg and Hedenbro 2006).

5. Settings of communicative competence

Message production and message comprehension may depend on the situation in which they are embedded. As emphasized in models of message production (see 4.1) and problem-solving behavior (see 4.5), the assessments of the situation form a basis for selecting appropriate and effective communicative means. In several models of message production, situation-action rules link situations with communicative means. However there are also interactions between situation perception, communicative competence, and messages. Situation features may affect the importance of secondary goals, in requests for example, and this effect of situation features on the importance of secondary goals depends on the request type (Meyer 2002). Other results show that the perception of the intimacy of a situation differs between competent and less competent communicators (Hazleton, Cupach and Canary 1987). These data suggest that communicative competence may also be a function of discriminative assessment of social situations.

In their book "An Atlas of Interpersonal Situations" Harold Kelley and colleagues (2003) present a systematic conceptual framework of social situations, which are also relevant for communication between the persons in these situations. This atlas provides a systematic theoretical approach for understanding the impact of situations on patterns of social interaction. The authors describe 21 of the most common situations that people encounter in everyday life. They explain the behavior of the interactants within the frame of interdependence theory, which stresses the manner in which people's outcomes are determined by the structure of their interaction with each other. "Our goal in writing this Atlas was to provide behavioral scientists with a tool for analyzing and understanding the influence of interpersonal situations on social interaction. We believe that there are important insights about human social behavior to be gained from systematic investigation of the properties of situations" (Kelley et al. 2003: 3). Their analysis considers a small set of key properties that define situations with interdependence between individuals. The analysis of the situations focuses on the following three aspects of interdependence: "the ways in which partners affect each others' outcomes, how they share information with each other, and the serial ordering of their responses" (Kelley et al. 2003: 7). The authors emphasize that their atlas is situation-centered, not theory-centered. Nevertheless, they use interdependence theory as their basic analytic tool.

Generally, situational factors may influence communicative processing in two respects: Firstly, they provide contextual information for judgments of emotion or intention; and secondly, long-term situational factors have an impact on the development of the ability to recognize emotions or intentions (see Elfenbein et al. 2002: 46f. for a review of research concerning attributions of facial expressions). On the other hand, our own feelings or bodily sensations may signal us whether a situation is problematic and requires detail-oriented, more systematic or elaborative processing, or whether a situation is benign and can be handled with our usual routines (see Schwarz 2002). So, in a sad mood – typically indicating a problematic situation – people are more likely to scrutinize and reject weak arguments in a persuasive message than they would be in a happy mood (e.g., Bless, Mackie and Schwarz 1992).

Different context categories may also play different roles in inferring communicative intent (Bosco, Bucciarelli and Bara 2004). Dillard and Solomon (2000) propose that context is conceptualized in terms of perceived regularities in social reality and that interpersonal goals follow from them. Context categories suggested by Bosco and colleagues are Access, Space, Time, Discourse, Move and Status. They provide data showing that the same utterance may adopt different communicative meanings according to the particular contexts in which it occurs. Moreover, different communicative skills may be relevant in different contexts, and communicative competence may vary between situations (see Rickheit and Vorwerg 2003 for a discussion of the relation between personal and situational factors in language production). The transferability of communicative skills acquired in certain settings to other situations (such as generalization from classroom to other contexts) is an often debated, empirical question.

The importance of specific communication skills may vary between different settings, for example between professional and personal contexts. And they may vary between different personal relationships, such as friendship, family, romantic relationship, or specifically long-distance relationship (e.g., Canary and Dainton 2003). And different facets of communicative competence may be particularly relevant in different professional roles and relationships, such as in supervisory relationships or as co-worker peers (e.g., Waldron 2003), for teachers or students, for health-care providers or patients, for buyers or sellers, and in international diplomacy. Negotiation skills are of especial importance for some them (e.g., Roloff, Putnam and Anastasiou 2003). Others require instructional skills (e.g., Daly and Vangelisti 2003), the competence of delivering bad news (e.g., Gillotti, Thompson and McNeilis 2002), or abilities that contribute to group decision making (Gouran 2003). Other aspects of communicative competence are essential in intercultural encounters (e.g., Wiseman and Koester 1993).

6. Development of communicative competence

Developmental issues bear on several aspects of the concept of communicative competence. The individual development of communicative competence is not only an important research area in its own right; it is also discussed to elucidate controversial or outstanding issues on the one hand and to provide a touchstone for theoretical assertions on the other hand. One such issue under discussion is the relation between intentionality, mentalizing and communicative abilities. As this aspect is very central for the concept of communicative competence, we will present the main lines of reasoning and related empirical findings in the following.

Given that communication involves the intention to convey a message on the part of the message producer (see 4.1), and the inferring of a speaker's message on the part of the message receiver (see 4.2), the question is how and when children develop communicative intentions and to what degree mind-reading abilities bear upon this development. Mind-reading abilities might be involved in understanding the other's intentions, but also in representing the other person as someone who is able to understand my intentions.

Children learn to mean long before they can use a lexical system to express their intentions; they may or they may not use imitations of adult phonology to express an intention during that early period (Halliday 1975). Infants typically come to employ gestures or sounds (or combinations of them) to make their intentions known around 9 or 10 months of age (Bates, Camaioni and Volterra 1975; Halliday 1975). However, there is a wide range of variability between children; some begin to produce words even earlier, some later, and most infants at 8 months of age use at least some gestures to signal their wishes (Fenson, Dale, Reznick, Bates, Thal and Pethick 1994). Examples include extending one's arms to be picked up, showing an object, or reaching to an object to get help in obtaining it. Generally, non-linguistic intentional communication appears prior to speech (e.g., Bruner 1975). Because communicative behavior does essentially not use conventional means of the target language during that phase, it has been termed the *illocutionary* phase (Bates et al. 1975). The emergence of intentional communication during that phase is preceded by a phase (called *perlocutionary* by Bates and colleagues) in which the mother is interpreting her child's behavior as if it was communicative and reacts accordingly. If the mother is consistent in her interpretations of the child's intents and reactions, the child may form a basis for a communicative use of such behaviors (e.g., Bruner 1975). During that phase – especially during about the first six months – infants either engage in purely *dyadic* interactions with the mother (or another key person) called *protoconversations* (Bateson 1975), or they focus on objects only.

In contrast, *coordinated person-object orientation* (Sugarman 1984) or *joint attention* (Scaife and Bruner 1975; Camaioni 1993) are regarded as essential in establishing communicative intentions. This type of *triadic* engagement involves both being responsive to the other person and participating in a shared activity; so, this activity means sharing intentions and perceptions with respect to something external to the mother-child dyad (Tomasello et al. 2005). This involves viewing the other person as pursuing goals and showing interest or attention. Whereas *proto-imperatives* (the infant's expressed wish to obtain something) could in principle be explained without assuming a representation of the other as having internal states, *proto-declaratives* (the infant's attempt to direct interest or attention) require an understanding of internal states, such as attention (Camaioni 1993). Accordingly, declarative pointing emerges later than imperative pointing, and it is linked to understanding others' intentions (Camaioni, Perucchini, Bellagamba and Colonnesi 2004). There is also a dissociation between the production of proto-imperatives and of proto-declaratives in autistic children (for a review, see Camaioni 1993). These deficits in triadic engagement and joint attention might be due to a difference between perceiving others as "agents of action" with desires and representing them as individual "agents of contemplation" (Camaioni 1993: 92) with interests and attentional states, or they might be explained by a lack of motivation to share psychological states with others (Tomasello et al. 2005), possibly related to problems in recognizing and sharing emotions with others (Hobson 2002).

According to Tomasello and colleagues, *intention reading* is one of the most basic social-cognitive skills and foundational for other mind-reading abilities. Experimental results suggest that 1-year-old infants are able to recognize others' intentions from gaze direction, emotional expression and reaching and grasping gestures (Phillips, Wellman and Spelke 2002; Sodian and Thoermer 2004). Other studies with children between 14 and 18 months found that the infants inferred the communicative intent of a gesture indicating a location in a hiding game (Behne, Carpenter and Tomasello 2005), that they imitatively learned actions even if the adult was not successful in performing them (Melzoff 1995) and that they learned only those that seemed intentional, not accidental (Carpenter, Akhtar and Tomasello 1998). Altogether, these results suggest that pre-speech infants are able to infer others' intentions including communicative intentions. The importance of joint attention for the development of communicative competence has been shown in another study, which provided evidence that early skills of gestural and linguistic communication are predicted by the quantity of time spent in joint engagement and the extent to which mothers used language that reflected their children's focus of attention (Carpenter, Nagell and Tomasello 1998).

All these results about the emergence of communicative skills suggest that early communicative acts depend on shared intentionality requiring intention-reading abilities; however, these mind-reading abilities seem to be very basic and do not imply that the infant's understanding of communicative intents is fully Gricean (see 4.3).

For 2-year-olds, the ability to share attention with an adult as well as the ability to talk about internal states is associated with the ability to cooperate with peers (Brownell, Ramani and Zerwas 2006). 2-year-olds may also use dynamic eye-gaze information to infer not only the focus of attention, but the desire of another person (Lee, Eskritt, Symons and Muir 1998). There are several proposals about how a fully developed theory of mind may build on these basic abilities (Baron-Cohen 2005; Wellman 1990). However, researchers from different approaches agree that there are different building blocks for a theory of mind and that inferring goals and intentions and joint attention are among the first to emerge, and that (first- and second-order) beliefs as well as metarepresentations develop only later (e.g., Stone 2006). The understanding of false beliefs is reported to emerge at approximately 4 to 5 years of age (Tomasello and Rakoczy 2003) – when communicative abilities are already clearly present. By the age of 3 to years, children have basically mastered most types of speech acts (McTear and Conti-Ramsden 1992); they start to interpret utterances non-literally between four and six years of age (Eson and Shapiro 1982).

Other developmental questions of relevance for the concept of communicative competence revolve around the development of conversational abilities (see Pond and Siegal in this volume) including the emergence of different speech acts (Bara, Bosco and Bucciarelli 1999) and the ability to distinguish between communicative intention and literal meaning (Beal and Flavell 1984), the intonation development (Wells, Peppé and Goulandris 2004), the development of nonverbal behavior (Guidetti 2002; Namy, Campbell and Tomasello 2004; van Beek, van Dolderen and Demon Dubas 2006) as well as the development of styles and appropriacy judgments (Leinonen and Smith 1994; Sachs and Devin 1976) and the mastering of specific communicative functions, such as promise, persuasion, irony and metaphor (Creusere 1999; Harris and Pexman 2003; Kline and Clinton 1998; Laval and Bernicot 1999; Norbury 2005). A concise summary of some research studies on the development of language pragmatics including approximate age of emergence is given by Adams (2002). Some aspects of communicative ability still develop up to the age of 17 years (Spector 1996) and during college time (Rubin, Graham and Mignerey 1990), and they may be further developed during adulthood, for example through communication courses (Greene, Sassi, Malek-Madani and Edward 1997).

7. Conclusion

The concept of communicative competence is of theoretical as well as methodological and also practical relevance. It has proven to be fruitful for theoretical developments, empirical research and a huge number of application areas. In fact, few concepts in language research have a comparable significance for applied research. Moreover, practical needs have always been a central motor of development for the concept.

To achieve communicative competence, a number of processes and factors work together, whose importance may vary dependent on the particular communicative situation involved. While there are several theoretical approaches possible, we have focused on empirically founded steps towards an integrative theory of communicative competence from the perspective of the individual. Although there are a large number of specific theories accounting for different aspects of communicative competence, many of them complement each other and converge in fundamental issues – even those from rather different approaches, such as the cognitive, mental-states framework and the social, interactive framework.

Acknowledgement. Preparation of this chapter was supported by the German Science Foundation (DFG) via the Collaborative Research Center "Alignment in Communication" (SFB 673).

Notes

1. According to Love and Webb (1992), the most predominant closed-head injury type is acceleration-deceleration trauma, which most often affects the prefrontal areas and the anterior portion of the temporal lobes.

References

Adams, C.
    2002   Practitioner review: The assessment of language pragmatics. *Journal of Child Psychology and Psychiatry* 43: 973–987.

Airenti, G., B. G. Bara, and M. Colombettik
    1993   Conversation and behavior games in the pragmatics of dialogue. *Cognitive Science* 17: 197–156.

Alibali, M. W.
    2005   Gesture in spatial cognition: Expressing, communicating, and thinking about spatial information. *Spatial Cognition and Computation* 5: 307–331.

Amodio, D. M. and C. D. Frith
    2006   Meeting of minds: The medial frontal cortex and social cognition. *Nature Reviews Neuroscience* 7: 268–277.

Areni, C. S. and J. R. Sparks
    2005   Language power and persuasion. *Psychology and Marketing* 22: 507–525.

Argyle, M.
    1969   *Social Interaction.* Chicago: Aldine Atherton.

Argyris, C.
    1962   *Interpersonal Competence and Organizational Effectiveness.* Homewood, Ill.: Irwin-Dorsey.

Argyris, C.
    1965   Explorations in interpersonal competence. *Journal of Applied Behavioral Science* 1: 58–83.

Austin, J. L.
　1962　*How to Do Things with Words.* Oxford, England: Oxford University Press.
Bara, B. G., F. M. Bosco, and M. Bucciarelli
　1999　Developmental pragmatics in normal and abnormal children. *Brain and Language* 68: 507–528.
Bara, B. G., I. Cutica, and M. Tirassa
　2001　Neuropragmatics: Extralinguistic communication after closed head injury. *Brain and Language* 77: 72–94.
Bara, B. G., M. Tirassa, and M. Zettin
　1997　Neuropragmatics: Neuropsychological constraints on formal theories of dialogue. *Brain and Language* 59: 7–49.
Bargh, J. A.
　1989　Conditional automaticity: Varieties of automatic influence in social perception and cognition. In: J. S. Uleman and J. A. Bargh (eds.), *Unintended Thought*, 3–51. New York: Guilford.
Barolo, A., F. Benuzzi, L. Nocetti, P. Baraldi, and P. Nichelli
　2006　Humor comprehension and appreciation: An fMRI study. *Journal of Cognitive Neuroscience* 18: 1789–1798.
Baron-Cohen, S.
　2005　The empathizing system: a revision of the 1994 model of the mindreading system. In: B. Ellis and D. Bjorklund (eds.), *Origins of the social mind. Evolutionary psychology and child development*, 468–492. New York: Guilford.
Bartels-Tobin, L. R. and Hinckley, J. J.
　2005　Cognition and discourse production in right hemisphere disorder. *Journal of Neurolinguistics* 18: 461–477.
Bates, E., Camaioni, L. and Volterra, V.
　1975　The acquisition of performatives prior to speech. *Merrill-Palmer Quarterly* 21: 205–226.
Bateson, M. C.
　1975　Mother-infant exchanges: the epigenesis of conversation interaction. *Annals of the New York Academy of Science* 263: 101–113.
Beal, C. R. and Flavell, J. H.
　1984　Development of the ability to distinguish between communicative intention and literal message meaning. *Child Development* 55: 920–928.
Behne, T., Carpenter, M. and Tomasello, M.
　2005　One-year-olds comprehend the communicative intentions behind gestures in a hiding game. *Developmental Science* 8: 492–499.
Bless, H., Mackie, D. M. and Schwarz, N.
　1992　Mood effects on encoding and judgmental processes in persuasion. *Journal of Personality and Social Psychology* 63: 585–595.
Berger, C. R.
　1997　*Planning Strategic Interaction: Attaining Goals Through Communicative Action.* Mahwah, NJ: Lawrence Erlbaum.
Berger, C. R.
　2000　Goal detection and efficiency: Neglected aspects of message production. *Communication Theory* 10: 156–166.

Berger, C. R.
2005 Interpersonal communication: Theoretical perspectives, future prospects. *Journal of Communication* 55: 415–447.

Berger C. R.
in press Communication: A goal-directed, plan-guided process. In: D. Roskos-Ewoldsen and J. Monahan (eds.), *Communication and Social Cognition: Theories and Methods*. Mahwah, NJ: Lawrence Erlbaum.

Bird, C. M., F. Castelli, O. Malik, U. Frith, and M. Husain
2004 The impact of extensive medial frontal lobe damage on 'Theory of Mind' and cognition. *Brain* 127: 914–928.

Bochner, A. P. and C. W. Kelly
1974 Interpersonal competence: Rationale, philosophy, and implementation of a conceptual framework. *Speech Teacher* 23: 278–301.

Bock, J. K.
1982 Toward a cognitive theory of syntax: Information processing contributions to sentence formation. *Psychological Review* 89: 1–47.

Bosco, F. M., M. Bucciarelli, and B. G. Bara
2004 The fundamental context categories in understanding communicative intention. *Journal of Pragmatics* 36: 467–488.

Brady, M., L. Armstrong, and C. Mackenzie
2006 An examination over time of language and discourse production abilities following right hemisphere brain damage. *Journal of Neurolinguistics* 19: 291–310.

Briñol, P., D. D. Rucker, Z. Tormala, and R. E. Petty
2004 Individual differences in resistance to persuasion: The role of beliefs and meta-beliefs. In: E. S. Knowles and J. A. Linn (eds.), *Resistance and Persuasion*, 83–104. Mahwah, NJ: Lawrence Erlbaum.

Brownell, C. A., G. B. Ramani, and S. Zerwas
2006 Becoming a social partner with peers: Cooperation and social understanding in one- and two-year-olds. *Child Development* 77: 803–821.

Bruner, J. S.
1975 From communication to language: A psychological perspective. *Cognition* 3: 255–287.

Bühler, K.
1934 *Sprachtheorie. Die Darstellungsfunktion der Sprache*. Jena: Fischer.

Burgoon, J. K.
1993 Interpersonal expectations, expectancy violations, and emotional communication. *Journal of Language and Social Psychology* 12: 30–48.

Burgoon, J. K. and A. E. Bacue
2003 Nonverbal communication skills. In: J. O. Greene and B. Burleson (eds.), *Handbook of Communication and Interaction Skills*, 3–50. Mahwah, NJ: Erlbaum.

Burgoon, J. K.
1995 Cross-cultural and intercultural applications of expectancy violations theory. In: R. Wiseman (ed.), *Intercultural Communication Theory*, 194–215. Thousand Oaks, CA: Sage.

Burgoon, J. K., D. A. Newton, J. B. Walther, and E. J. Baesler
   1989   Nonverbal expectancy violations and conversational involvement. *Journal of Nonverbal Behavior* 13: 97–120.

Burleson, B. R. and S. Planalp
   2000   Producing emotion(al) messages. *Communication Theory* 10: 221–250.

Camaioni, L.
   1993   The development of intentional communication. In: J. Nadel and L. Camaioni (eds.), *New Perspectives in Early Communicative Development*, 82–96. London: Routledge.

Camaioni, L., P. Perucchini, F. Bellagamba, and C. Colonnesi
   2004   The role of declarative pointing in developing a theory of mind. *Infancy* 5: 291–308.

Campbell, M. C. and A. Kirmani
   2000   Consumers' use of persuasion knowledge: The effects of accessibility and cognitive capacity on perceptions of an influence agent. *Journal of Consumer Research* 27: 69–83.

Campbell, R. and R. Wales
   1970   The study of language acquisition. In: J. Lyons (ed.), *New Horizons in Linguistics*, 242–260. Harmondsworth: Penguin.

Canary, D. J.
   2003   Managing interpersonal conflict: A model of events related to strategic choice. In: J. O. Greene and B. Burleson (eds.), *Handbook of Communication and Interaction Skills*, 3–50. Mahwah, NJ: Erlbaum.

Canary, D. J. and M. J. Cody
   1993   *Interpersonal Communication. A Goals-Based Approach.* New York: St. Martin's Press.

Canary, D. J. and M. Dainton (eds.)
   2003   *Maintaining Relationships Through Communication. Relational, Contextual, and Cultural Variation.* Mahwah, NJ: Lawrence Erlbaum.

Carpenter, M., N. Akhtar, and M. Tomasello
   1998   14- through 18-month-old infants differentially imitate intentional and accidental actions. *Infant Behavior and Development* 21: 315–330.

Carpenter, M., K. Nagell, K. and M. Tomasello
   1998   Social cognition, joint attention, and communicative competence from 9 to 15 months of age. *Monographs of the Society for Research in Child Development*, Vol. 63.

Cegala, D. J. and V. R. Waldron
   1992   A study of the relationship between communicative performance and conversation participants' thoughts. *Communication Studies* 43: 105–123.

Channon, S. and S. Crawford
   2000   The effects of anterior lesions on performance on a story comprehension test: Left anterior impairment on a theory-of-mind type task. *Neuropsychologia* 38: 1006–1017.

Channon, S., A. Pellijeff, and A. Rule
   2005   Social cognition after head injury: Sarcasm and theory of mind. *Brain and Language* 93: 123–134.

Chomsky, N.
1965 *Aspects of the Theory of Syntax.* Cambridge MA: MIT Press.
Chovil, N.
1991 Social determinants of facial displays. *Journal of Nonverbal Behavior* 15: 141–154.
Chung, D. M.
1988 The neglected role of intonation in communicative competence and proficiency. *The Modern Language Journal* 72: 295–303.
Clark, H. H.
1996 *Using Language.* Cambridge: Cambridge University Press.
Clark, H. H.
2003 Pointing and placing. In: S. Kita (ed.), *Pointing: Where Language, Culture, and Cognition Meet*, 243–268. Mahwah, NJ: Lawrence Erlbaum.
Clark, H. H. and M. A. Krych
2004 Speaking while monitoring addressees for understanding. *Journal of Memory and Language* 50: 62–81.
Clark, H. H. and S. Brennan
1991 Grounding in communication. In: L. B. Resnick, J. M. Levine, and S. D. Teasley (eds.), *Perspectives on Socially Shared Cognition*, 127–149. Washington: APA Books.
Creusere, A. C.
1999 Theories of adults' understanding and use of irony and sarcasm: Applications to and evidence from research with children. *Developmental Review* 19: 213–262.
Cutica, I., M. Bucciarelli, and B. G. Bara
2006 Neuropragmatics: Extralinguistic pragmatic ability is better preserved in left-hemisphere-damaged patients than in right-hemisphere-damaged patients. *Brain and Language* 98: 12–25.
Daly, J. A. and A. L. Vangelisti
2003 Skillfully instructing learners: How communicators effectively convey messages. In: J. O. Greene and B. Burleson (eds.), *Handbook of Communication and Interaction Skills*, 871–908. Mahwah, NJ: Erlbaum.
Dell, G. S., F. Chang, and Z. M. Griffin
1999 Connectionist models of language production: Lexical access and grammatical encoding. *Cognitive Science* 23: 517–542.
Dell, G. S., M. F. Schwartz, N. Martin, E. M. Saffran, and D. A. Gagnon
1997 Lexical access in aphasic and nonaphasic speakers. *Psychological Review* 104: 801–838.
Dennis, M. and M. A. Barnes
2001 Comparison of literal, inferential, and intentional text comprehension in children with mild or severe closed head injury. *Journal of Head Trauma Rehabilitation* 16: 456–468.
de Meijer, M.
1989 The contribution of general features of body movements to the attribution of emotions. *Journal of Nonverbal Behavior* 13: 247–268.
Dillard, J. P. and D. H. Solomon
2000 Conceptualizing context in message-production research. *Communication Theory* 10: 167–175.

Driskell, J. E. and P. H. Radtke
    2003   The effect of gesture on speech production and comprehension. *Human Factors* 45: 445–454.

D'Zurilla, T. J., A. M. Nezu, and A. Maydeu-Olivares
    2004   What is social problem solving?: Meaning, models, and measures. In: E. C. Chang, T. J. D'Zurilla and L. Sanna, (eds.), *Social Problem Solving: Theory, Research, and Training*, 11–27. Washington, DC: American Psychological Association.

Elfenbein, H. A., A. A. Marsh and N. Ambady
    2001   Emotional intelligence and the recognition of emotion in facial expression. In: L. Feldman Barrett and P. Salovey (eds.), *The Wisdom of Feeling. Psychological Processes of Emotional Intelligence*, 37–59. New York: Guilford.

Elliott, J. O. and M. P. Jacobson
    2006   Bone loss in epilepsy: Barriers to prevention, diagnosis, and treatment. *Epilepsy and Behavior* 8: 169–175.

Eson, M. and A. Shapiro
    1982   When 'don't' means 'do'. Pragmatics and cognitive development in understanding an indirect imperative. *First Language* 3: 83–91.

Ferreira, F., K. G. D. Bailey, and V. Ferraro
    2002   Good-enough representations in language comprehension. *Current Directions in Psychological Science* 11: 11–15.

Feldman Barrett, L. and J. Gross
    2001   Emotional intelligence: A process model of emotion representation and regulation. In: T. J. Mayne and G. A. Bonanno (eds.), *Emotions: Current Issues and Future Directions*, 286–310. New York: Guilford.

Fenson, L., P. S. Dale, J. S. Reznick, E. Bates, D. J. Thal, and S. J. Pethick
    1994   Early communicative ability: variability. *Monographs of the Society for Research in Child Development*, Vol. 59.

Fletcher, P. C., F. Happé, U. Frith, S. C. Baker, R. J. Dolan, R. S. J. Frackowiak, and C. D. Frith
    1995   Other minds in the brain: a functional imaging study of "theory of mind" in story comprehension. *Cognition* 57: 109–128.

Forgas, J. P. and G. Tehani
    2005   Affective influences on language use. Mood effects on performance feedback by experts and novices. *Journal of Language and Social Psychology* 24: 269–284.

Fridhandler, B. M.
    1986   Conceptual note on state, trait, and the state-trate distinction. *Journal of Personality and Social Psychology* 50: 169–174.

Frith, U. and C. D. Frith
    2003   Development and neurophysiology of mentalizing. *Philosophical Transactions of the Royal Society of London B: Biological Sciences* 358: 459–473.

Frith, C. D. and U. Frith
    2006   The neural basis of mentalizing. *Neuron* 50: 531–543.

Frye, D., P. D. Zelazo, and T. Palfai
    1995   Theory of mind and rule-based reasoning. *Cognitive Development* 10: 483–527.

Garrod, S. and M. J. Pickering
  2004   Why is conversation so easy? *Trends in Cognitive Science* 8: 8–11.
Gernsbacher, M. A.
  1990   *Language Comprehension as Structure Building.* Hillsdale, NJ: Lawrence Erlbaum.
Giles, H., N. Coupland, and J. Coupland
  1991   Accommodation theory: Communication, context and consequence. In: H. Giles, N. Coupland and Coupland (eds.), *Contexts of Accommodation,* 1–68. Cambridge: Cambridge University Press.
Gillotti, C., T. Thompson, and K. McNeilis
  2002   Communicative competence in the delivery of bad news. *Social Science and Medicine* 54: 1011–1023.
Glucksberg, S.
  1998   Understanding metaphors. *Current Directions in Psychological Science* 7: 39–43.
Goffman, E.
  1959   *The Representation of Self in Everyday Life.* Garden City, N.Y.: Doubleday Anchor.
Gouran, D. S.
  2003   Communication skills for group decision making. In: J. O. Greene and B. Burleson (eds.), *Handbook of Communication and Interaction Skills,* 835–870. Mahwah, NJ: Erlbaum.
Greene, J. O.
  1997   A second generation action assembly theory. In: J. O. Greene (ed.), *Message Production: Advances in Communication Theory,* 151–170. Mahwah, NJ: Erlbaum.
Greene, J. O.
  2006   Have I got something to tell you. Ideational dynamics and message production. *Journal of Language and Social Psychology* 25: 64–75.
Greene, J. O. and B. R. Burleson (eds.)
  2003   *Handbook of Communication and Social Interaction Skills.* Mahwah, NJ: Lawrence Erlbaum.
Greene, J. O. and A. R. Graves
  in press   Cognitive models of message production. In: D. Roskos-Ewoldsen and J. Monahan (eds.), *Communication and Social Cognition: Theories and Methods.* Mahwah, NJ: Lawrence Erlbaum.
Greene, J. O., M. W. Kirch, and C. S. Grady
  2000   Cognitive foundations of message encoding: An investigation of message production as coalition formation. *Communication Quarterly* 48: 256–271.
Greene, J. O., M. S. Sassi, T. Malek-Madani, and C. Edward
  1997   Adult acquisition of message-production skill. *Communication Monographs* 64: 181–200.
Grice, P.
  1975   Logic and conversation. In: P. Cole and J. Morgan (eds.), *Syntax and Semantics 3: Speech Acts,* 107–142. New York: Academic Press.
Grice, P.
  1982   Meaning revisited. In: N. Smith (ed.), *Mutual Knowledge,* 223–243. London: Academic Press.

Griffin, R., O. Friedman, J. Ween, E. Winner, F. G. E. Happé, and H. Brownell.
  2006   Theory of mind and the right cerebral hemisphere: Refining the scope of impairment. *Laterality* 11: 195–225.
Guidetti, M.
  2002   The emergence of pragmatics: forms and functions of conventional gestures in young French children. *First Language* 22: 265–286.
Habermas, J.
  1970   Toward a theory of communicative competence. In: H. P. Dreitzel (ed.), *Recent Sociology No. 2*, 115–148. New York: Macmillan.
Halliday, M.
  1975   *Learning How to Mean*. London: Edward Arnold.
Happé, F. G. E.
  1993   Communicative competence and theory of mind in autism: A test of relevance theory. *Cognition* 48: 101–119.
Happé, F. G. E.
  1994   An advanced test of theory of mind: Understanding of story characters' thoughts and feelings by able autistics, mentally handicapped and normal children and adults. *Journal of Autism and Developmental Disorders* 24: 129–154.
Harris, M. and P. M. Pexman
  2003   Children's perceptions of the social functions of verbal irony. *Discourse Processes* 36: 147–165.
Haverkate, H.
  1990   A speech act analysis of irony. *Journal of Pragmatics* 14: 77–109.
Hazleton, V., W. R. Cupach and D. J. Canary
  1987   Situation perception: Interactions between competence and messages. *Journal of Language and Social Psychology* 6: 57–63.
Herrmann, T.
  1983   *Speech and Situation: A Psychological Conception of Situated Speaking*. Berlin: Springer.
Herrmann, T. and J. Grabowski
  1994   *Sprechen. Psychologie der Sprachproduktion*. Heidelberg: Spektrum Akademischer Verlag.
Hobson, R. P.
  2002   *The Cradle of Thought. Exploring the Origins of Thinking*. London: Macmillan.
Hooker, C. I., K. A. Paller, D. R Gitelman, T. B. Parrish, M.-M. Mesulam and P. J. Reber
  2003   Brain networks for analyzing eye gaze. *Cognitive Brain Research* 17: 406–418.
Hörmann, H.
  1983   The calculating listener – or: How many are 'einige', 'mehrere', and 'ein paar' 'some', 'several', and 'a few'? In: R. Bäuerle, C. Schwarze and A. v. Stechow (eds.), *Meaning, Use, and Interpretation of Language*, 221–234. Berlin: de Gruyter.
Horowitz, L., L. Jansson, T. Ljungberg, T. and M. Hedenbro
  2006   Interaction before conflict and conflict resolution in pre-school boys with language impairment. *International Journal of Language and Communication Disorders* 41: 441–466.

Horton, W. S. and B. Keysar
  1996   When do speakers take into account common ground? *Cognition* 59: 91–117.
Huber-Okrainec, J., S. E. Blaser, and M. Dennis
  2005   Idiom comprehension deficits in relation to corpus callosum agenesis and hypoplasia in children with spina bifida meningomyelocele. *Brain and Language* 93: 349–368.
Hymes, D.
  1962   The ethnography of speaking. In: T. Gladwin and W. C. Sturtevant (eds.), *Anthropology and Human Behavior*, 13–53. Washington, DC: Anthropological Society of Washington. Reprinted in J. A. Fishman, 1968. *Readings in the Sociology of Language*, 99–138. The Hague: Mouton.
Hymes, D.
  1964   Introduction: Toward ethnographies of communication. In: J. J. Gumperz and D. Hymes (eds.), *The Ethnography of Communication,* 1–34. Washington, DC: American Anthropologist.
Hymes, D.
  1972   On communicative competence. In: J. B. Pride and J. Holmes (eds.), *Sociolinguistics*, 269–285. Harmondsworth: Penguin.
Ingerith, M. and S. McDonald
  2005   Evaluating the causes of impaired irony comprehension following traumatic brain injury. *Aphasiology* 19: 712–730.
Iacobini, M., R. P. Woods, M. Brass, H. Bekkering, J. C. Mazziotta, and G. Rizzolatti
  1999   Cortical mechanisms of human imitation. *Science* 286: 2526–2528.
Johnson-Laird, P. N.
  1983   *Mental Models: Towards a Cognitive Science of Language, Inference and Consciousness*. Cambridge, MA: Harvard University Press.
Jordan, J. M.
  1998   Executive cognitive control in communication: Extending plan-based theory. *Human Communication Research* 25: 3–38.
Kelley, H. H., J. G. Holmes, N. L. Kerr, H. T. Reis, C. E. Rusbult, and P. A. M. van Lange
  2003   *An Atlas of Interpersonal Situations*. Cambridge: Cambridge University Press.
Kerekes, J. A.
  2006   Winning an interviewer's trust in a gatekeeping encounter. *Language in Society* 35: 27–57.
Kleinke, C. L.
  1986   Gaze and eye contact: A research review. *Psychological Bulletin* 100: 78–100.
Kline, S. L. and B. L. Clinton
  1998   Developments in children's persuasive message practices. *Communication Education* 47: 120–136.
Lakey, S. G. and G. Canary
  2002   Actor goal achievement and sensitivity to partner as critical factors in understanding interpersonal communication competence and conflict strategies. *Communication Monographs* 69: 217–235.

Laughery, K. R.
  2006   Safety communications: Warnings. *Applied Ergonomics* 37: 467–478.
Laval, V. and J. Bernicot
  1999   How French speaking children understand promises: the role of future tense. *Journal of Psycholinguistic Research* 28: 179–195.
Lee, K., M. Eskritt, L. A. Symons, and D. Muir
  1998   Children's use of triadic eye gaze information for "mind reading". *Developmental Psychology* 34: 525–539.
Lehman-Blake, M. T. and K. S. Lesniewicz
  2005   Contextual bias and predictive inferencing in adults with and without right hemisphere brain damage. *Aphasiology* 19: 423–434.
Leinonen, E. and B. R. Smith
  1994   Appropriacy judgements and pragmatic performance. *European Journal of Disorders of Communication* 29: 77–84.
Levelt, W. J. M.
  1989   *Speaking: From Intention to Articulation*. Cambridge, MA: MIT Press.
Levelt, W. J. M., A. Roelofs, and A. S. Meyer
  1999   A theory of lexical access in speech production. *Behavioral and Brain Sciences* 22: 1–75.
Love, R. J. and W. G. Webb
  1992   *Neurology for the Speech-Language Pathologist*. Boston: Butterworth-Heinemann.
Mah, L. W. Y., M. C. Arnold, and J. Grafman
  2005   Knowledge following damage to ventromedial prefrontal cortex. *Journal of Neuropsychiatry and Clinical Neurosciences* 17: 66–74.
Melinger, A. and S. Kita
  in press   Conceptualisation load triggers gesture production. *Language and Cognitive Processes*.
Melinger, A. and W. J. M. Levelt
  2004   Gesture and the communicative intention of the speaker. *Gesture* 4: 119–141.
Melzoff, A.
  1995   Understanding the intentions of others: Re-enactment of intended acts by 18-month-old children. *Developmental Psychology* 31: 838–850.
Metzing, C. and S. E. Brennan
  2003   When conceptual pacts are broken: Partner-specific effects on the comprehension of referring expressions. *Journal of Memory and Language* 49: 477–496.
Meyer, J. R.
  2000   Cognitive models of message production: Unanswered questions. *Communication Theory* 10: 176–187.
Meyer, J. R.
  2002   Contextual influences on the pursuit of secondary goals in request messages. *Communication Monographs* 69: 189–203.
Mitchell, R. L. C. and T. J. Crow
  2005   Right hemisphere language functions and schizophrenia: the forgotten hemisphere? *Brain* 128: 963–978.

Montgomery, B. M. and L. A. Baxter
    1998   *Dialectical Approaches to Studying Personal Relationships.* Mahwah: Erlbaum.
Müller, H. M.
    1990   *Sprache und Evolution. Grundlagen der Evolution und Ansätze einer evolutionstheoretischen Sprachwissenschaft.* Berlin: de Gruyter.
Namy, L. L., A. L. Campbell, and M. Tomasello
    2004   The changing role of iconicity in non-verbal symbol learning: A U-shaped trajectory in the acquisition of arbitrary gestures. *Journal of Cognition and Development* 5: 37–57.
Nicholas, M., M. P. Sinotte and N. Helm-Estabrooks
    2005   Using a computer to communicate: Effect of executive function impairments in people with severe aphasia. *Aphasiology* 19: 1052–1065.
Norbury, C. F.
    2005   The relationship between theory of mind and metaphor: Evidence from children with language impairment and autistic spectrum disorder. *British Journal of Developmental Psychology* 23: 383–399.
Owren, M. J. and J.-A. Bachorowski
    2003   Reconsidering the evolution of nonlinguistic communication: The case of laughter. *Journal of Nonverbal Behavior* 27: 183–200.
Parks, M. R.
    1994   Communicative competence and interpersonal control. In: M. L. Knapp and G. R. Miller (eds.), *Handbook of Interpersonal Communication*, 589–618. Thousand Oaks, CA: Sage.
Patterson, M. L.
    1982   A sequential functional model of nonverbal exchange. *Psychological Review* 89: 231–249.
Patterson, M. L.
    1999   The evolution of a parallel process model of nonverbal communication. In: P. Philippot, R. S. Feldman and E. J. Coats (eds.), *The Social Context of Nonverbal Behavior*, 317–347. New York, Cambridge University Press.
Paul, L. K., D. van Lancker-Sidtis, B. Schieffer, R. Dietrich, and W. Brown
    2003   Communication deficits in agenesis of the corpus callosum: Nonliteral language and affective prosody. *Brain and Language* 85: 313–324.
Pearce, S., S. McDonald, and M. Coltheart
    1998   Interpreting ambiguous advertisements: The effect of frontal lobe damage. *Brain and Cognition* 38: 150–164.
Pexman, P. M., M. Glenwright, A. Krol, and T. James
    2005   An acquired taste: Children's perceptions of humor and teasing in verbal irony. *Discourse Processes* 40: 259–288.
Phillips, A. T., H. M. Wellman, and E. S. Spelke
    2002   Infants' ability to connect gaze and emotional expression to intentional action. *Cognition* 85: 53–78.
Piaget, J.
    1975   *Sprechen und Denken des Kindes.* Düsseldorf: Schwann.
Pickering, M. J. and S. Garrod
    2004   Toward a mechanistic psychology of dialogue. *Behavioral and Brain Sciences* 27: 169–226.

Richardson, D. C. and R. Dale
   2005   Looking to understand: The coupling between speakers' and listeners' eye movements and its relationship to discourse comprehension. *Cognitive Science* 29: 1045–1060.

Rickheit, G.
   2006   The constitution of meaning in situated communication. In: G. Rickheit and I. Wachsmuth (eds.), *Situated Communication*, 7–29. Berlin, New York: Mouton de Gruyter.

Rickheit, G. and C. Vorwerg
   2003   Situiertes Sprechen. In: G. Rickheit, T. Herrmann and W. Deutsch (eds.), *Psycholinguistics/Psycholinguistik. An international handbook/Ein internationales Handbuch*, 279–294. Berlin, New York: de Gruyter.

Rohde, D. L. T. and D. C. Plaut
   2003   Connectionist models of language processing. *Cognitive Studies* 10: 10–28.

Roloff, M. E., L. L. Putnam, and L. Anastasiou
   2003   Negotiation skills. In: J. O. Greene and B. Burleson (eds.), *Handbook of Communication and Interaction Skills*, 801–834. Mahwah, NJ: Erlbaum.

Rosin, P. and E. Swift
   1999   Communication intervention: Improving the speech intelligibility of children with Down syndrome. In: J. Miller, M. Leddy, and L. A. Leavitt (eds.), *Improving the Communication of People with Down Syndrome*, 133–160. Baltimore, MD: Paul Brookers.

Rubin, R. B., E. E. Graham, and J. T. Mignerey
   1990   A longitudinal study of college students' communication competence. *Communication Education* 39: 1–14.

Sachs, J. and J. Devin
   1976   Young children's use of age-appropriate speech styles in social interaction and role playing. *Journal of Child Language* 3: 81–98.

Saxe, R. and A. Wexler
   2005   Making sense of another mind: The role of the right temporo-parietal junction. *Neuropsychologia* 43: 1391–1399.

Scaife, M. and J. S. Bruner
   1975   The capacity for joint visual attention in the infant. *Nature* 253: 265–266.

Schrader, D. C. and J. P. Dillard
   1999   Goal structures and interpersonal influence. *Communication Studies* 49: 276–293.

Schwarz, N.
   2002   Situated cognition and the wisdom of feelings. Cognitive tuning. In: L. Feldman Barrett and P. Salovey (eds.), *The Wisdom of Feeling. Psychological Processes of Emotional Intelligence*, 37–59. New York: Guilford.

Searle, J.
   1969   *Speech Acts*. Cambridge: Cambridge University Press.

Shamay, S. G., R. Tomer, and J. Aharon-Peretz
   2002   Deficit in understanding sarcasm in patients with prefrontal lesion is related to impaired emphatic ability. *Brain and Cognition* 48: 558–563.

Shamay, S. G., R. Tomer, B. D. Berger, D. Goldsher, and J. Aharon-Peretz
 2005b Impaired 'affective theory of mind' is associated with right ventromedial prefrontal damage. *Cognitive and Behavioral Neurology* 18: 55–67.
Shamay-Tsoory, S. G., R. Tomer, and J. Aharon-Peretz
 2005 The neuroanatomical basis of understanding sarcasm and its relationship to social cognition. *Neuropsychology* 19: 288–300.
Shamay-Tsoory, S. G., R. Tomer, B. D. Berger, and J. Aharon-Peretz
 2003 Characterization of empathy deficits following prefrontal brain damage: The role of the right ventromedial prefrontal cortex. *Journal of Cognitive Neuroscience* 15: 324–37.
Shannon, C. E. and W. Weaver
 1949 *The Mathematical Theory of Communication.* Urbana: University of Illinois Press.
Shaw, P., J. Bramham, E. J. Lawrence, R. Morris, S. Baron-Cohen, and A. S. David
 2005 Differential effects of lesions of the amygdala and prefrontal cortex on recognizing facial expressions of complex emotions. *Journal of Cognitive Neuroscience* 17: 1410–1419.
Siegal, M. and R. Varley
 2002 Neural systems involved in 'theory of mind'. *Nature Reviews Neuroscience* 3: 463–471.
Sigall, H., A. Mucchi-Faina, and C. Mosso
 2006 Minority influence is facilitated when the communication employs linguistic abstractness. *Group Processes and Intergroup Relations* 9: 443–451.
Sodian, B. and C. Thoermer
 2004 Infants' understanding of looking, pointing, and reaching as cues to goal-directed action. *Journal of Cognition and Development* 5: 289–316.
Spector, C.
 1996 Children's comprehension of idioms in the context of humour. *Language, Speech and Hearing Services in Schools* 27: 307–313.
Sperber, D. and D. Wilson
 2002 Pragmatics, modularity and mindreading. *Mind and Language* 17: 3–23.
Spitzberg, B. H. and W. R. Cupach
 1984 *Interpersonal Communication Competence.* Beverly Hills, CA: Sage.
Spitzberg, B. H. and W. Cupach
 1989 *Handbook of Interpersonal Competence Research.* New York: Springer-Verlag.
Spitzberg, H. H. and H. T. Hurt
 1987 The measurement of interpersonal skills in instructional contexts. *Communication Education* 36: 28–45.
Stone, V. E.
 2006 Theory of mind and the evolution of social intelligence. In: J. T., P. S. and C. L. Pickett (eds.), *Social Neuroscience – People Thinking about People*, 103–129. Cambridge, MA: MIT Press.
Straus, S. G.
 1996 Getting a clue: The effects of communication media and information distribution on participation and performance in computer-mediated and face-to-face groups. *Small Group Research* 27: 115–142.

Strawson, P. F.
　1971　　Meaning and truth. In: P. F. Strawson, *Logico-Linguistic Papers*, 170–189. London: Methuen.
Strohner, H.
　2001　　*Kommunikation: Kognitive Grundlagen und praktische Anwendungen.* Wiesbaden: Westdeutscher Verlag.
Sugarman, S.
　1984　　The development of preverbal communication. In: R. L. Schiefelbusch and J. Pikar (eds.), *The Acquisition of Communicative Competence*, 23–67. Baltimore: University Park Press.
Tirassa, M.
　1999　　Communicative competence and the architecture of the mind/brain. *Brain and Language* 68: 419–441.
Tomasello, M.
　2003a　　The key is social cognition. In: D. Gentner and S. Goldin-Meadow (eds.), *Language in Mind: Advances in the Study of Language and Thought*, 47–57. Cambridge, MA: MIT Press.
Tomasello, M.
　2003b　　*Constructing a Language: A Usage-Based Theory of Language Acquisition.* Cambridge, MA: Harvard University Press.
Tomasello, M., M. Carpenter, J. Call, T. Behne, and H. Moll
　2005　　Understanding and sharing intentions: The origins of cultural cognition. *Behavioral and Brain Sciences* 28: 675–735.
Tomasello, M. and H. Rakoczy
　2003　　What makes human cognition unique? From individual to shared to collective intentionality. *Centennial Essay in Mind and Language* 18: 121–47.
Trauner, D. A., A. Ballantyne, S. Friedland, and C. Chase
　1996　　Disorders of affective and linguistic prosody in children after early unilateral brain damage. *Annals of Neurology* 39: 361–367.
Troisi, A., R. D. Chiaie, F. Russo, M. A. Russo, M. A., C. Mosco, and A. Pasini, A.
　1996　　Nonverbal behavior and alexithymic traits in normal subjects. *The Journal of Nervous and Mental Disease* 184: 561–566.
van Beek, Y., M. S. M. van Dolderen, and J. J. S. Demon Dubas.
　2006　　Gender-specific development of nonverbal behaviours and mild depression in adolescence. *Journal of Child Psychology and Psychiatry* 47: 1272–1283.
van Dijk, T. A. and W. Kintsch
　1983　　*Strategies in Discourse Comprehension.* New York: Academic Press.
van Lancker, D.
　1997　　Rag to riches: Our increasing appreciation of cognitive and communicative abilities of the human right cerebral hemisphere. *Brain and Language* 57: 1–11.
Waldron, V. R.
　1997　　Toward a theory of interactive conversational planning. In: J. O. Greene (ed.), *Message Production: Advances in Communication Theory,* 195–220. Mahwah, NJ: Erlbaum.

Waldron, V. R.
    2003   Relationship maintenance in organizational settings. In: D. J. Canary and M. Dainton (eds.), *Maintaining Relationships Through Communication. Relational, Contextual, and Cultural Variation*, 163–184. Mahwah, NJ: Lawrence Erlbaum.

Wellman, H. M.
    1990   *The Child's Theory of Mind*. Cambridge, MA: MIT Press.

Wells, B., S. Peppé, and N. Goulandris
    2004   Intonation development from five to thirteen. *Journal of Child Language* 31: 749–778.

Wiseman, R. L. and J. Koester (eds.)
    1993   *Intercultural communication competence*. Newbury Park, CA: Sage.

Wertsch, J. V.
    1975   The influence of listener perception of the speaker on recognition memory. *Journal of Psycholinguistic Research* 4: 89–98.

Wiemann, J. M.
    1977   Explication and test of a model of Communicative Competence. *Human Communication Research* 3: 195–213.

Williams, N. and J. Ogden
    2004   The impact of matching the patient's vocabulary: A randomized control trial. *Family Practice* 21: 630–635.

Wilson, S. R.
    1990   Development and test of a cognitive rules model of interaction goals. *Communication Monographs* 57: 81–103.

Wilson, S. R.
    2002   *Seeking and Resisting Compliance. Why People Say What They Do When Trying to Influence Others*. Thousand Oaks, CA: Sage.

Wilson, S. R. and C. M. Sabee
    2003   Explicating communicative competence as a theoretical term. In: J. O. Greene and B. Burleson (eds.), *Handbook of Communication and Interaction Skills*, 3–50. Mahwah, NJ: Erlbaum.

Winner, E., H. Brownell, F. G. E. Happé, A. Blum, and D. Pincus
    1998   Distinguishing lies from jokes: theory of mind deficits and discourse interpretation in right hemisphere brain-damaged patients. *Brain and Language* 62: 89–106.

Winner, E. and S. Leekam
    1991   Distinguishing irony from deception: Understanding the speaker's second-order intention. *British Journal of Developmental Psychology* 9: 257–70.

Wittgenstein, L.
    1953   *Philosophical Investigations*. Oxford: England: Basil Blackwell.

Wood, W.
    2000   Attitude change: Persuasion and social influence. *Annual Review of Psychology* 51: 539–570.

Wyer, R. S. and R. Adaval
    2003   Message reception skills in social communication. In: J. O. Greene and B. Burleson (eds.), *Handbook of Communication and Social Interaction Skills*, 291–356. Mahwah, NJ: Erlbaum.

Wyer, R. S. and G. A. Radvansky
　1999　　The comprehension and validation of social information. *Psychological Review* 106: 89–118.

Ylvisaker, M. and S. Szekeres
　1989　　F. Metacognitive and executive impairments in head-injured children and adults. *Topics in Language Disorders* 9: 34–49.

Zwaan, R. A. and C. M. Brown
　1996　　The influence of language proficiency and comprehension skill on situation model construction. *Discourse Processes* 21: 289–327.

Zwaan, R. A. and G. A. Radvansky
　1998　　Situation models in language comprehension and memory. *Psychological Bulletin* 123: 162–185.

II. Acquisition

2. Language and neurophysiological development

Ralph-Axel Müller and Erica Palmer

Traditional clinical approaches to the brain organization for language have in recent decades been complemented by neuroimaging techniques, most of which can be used with minimal risk in children. A growing literature mapping out developmental changes suggests that children activate grossly the same inferior frontal and temporo-parietal brain areas as adults during various types of language processing. However, there is some evidence indicating that typical left-lateralization becomes more robust with age and that frontal activity increases at the expense of posterior activation in visual cortices. While it is highly likely that genes play an important role in determining the brain organization for language, there is also ample evidence for high levels of plasticity. Early left hemisphere damage may result in reorganization of language in the right hemisphere, with often only subtle detrimental effects on language function. There is no consensus on why specific regions in perisylvian cortex are crucial for language processing, but evidence from animal and human studies suggests that Broca's area may become a 'language area' by virtue of its unique connectivity patterns, due to which several functional circuits crucial for language acquisition converge in inferior frontal cortex.

1. Introduction

Five millennia ago, the Egyptian author of the Edwin Smith papyrus (presumed to be the erudite Imhotep) noted loss of speech in a patient with a temporal wound (Critchley 1970). Although not all great minds have even considered the brain worthy of investigation – Aristotle regarded it merely as a cooling organ – the question of biological substrates for language has been with us for a very long time. Some answers to this question, as those advocated by craniologists and phrenologists around the turn of the 19th century (Gall and Spurzheim 1810), may sound rather silly to today's brain-savvy readers. How could anyone with respect for empirical evidence conclude from the observation of protruding eyes in a few eloquent subjects that language abilities were located right behind the eyes? Other answers, such as Marc Dax' observation in the early 19th century of speech loss after left hemisphere damage and Paul Broca's finding of inferior frontal damage in aphasic patient Leborgne (Broca 1861), were groundbreaking and painted the first strokes in today's rather complex picture of "language in the brain". In this chapter, we will first review some of this knowledge, which is based on a vast literature of clinical, electrophysiological and imaging evidence, and will then turn to the development of language in the brain, which is much less understood.

Since the mid-20th century, linguistics has been heavily influenced by the idea that language abilities and language processes are sharply distinct from other cognitive domains. In its strongest form, this view implies the autonomy (Chomsky 1965) and modularity (Fodor 1983) of at least some core linguistic components. This perspective on language has had important consequences for the interdisciplinary study of language. Noam Chomsky, whose groundbreaking work first formulated the idea of linguistic autonomy, considered the language ability (or 'universal grammar') as a biological object of study. Since the principles of universal grammar were innate, according to him, language development was to be ultimately explained by the genetic endowment of the human species (Chomsky 1976, 2002). This approach to language development had a fascinating and paradoxical effect on the field. On the one hand, it was probably mistaken in some of its basic assumptions pertaining to the autonomy of language development vis-à-vis other cognitive and sensorimotor domains (as we will discuss in Section 7). On the other hand, its nativism and biologism steered linguistics towards interdisciplinary research that has proven highly productive and thought-provoking. Ironically, many of the interdisciplinary studies examining language with the tools of behavioral genetics, developmental cognitive neuroscience, neurolinguistics, and related fields have yielded the very evidence that forces us to revise some notions of autonomy and innateness (Bates et al. 2003a; Karmiloff-Smith 1994; Müller 1996). This evidence will be reviewed in the following sections.

Chomsky's biological approach was paralleled and supported by Eric Lenneberg's "Biological Foundations of Language" (Lenneberg 1967), in which Lenneberg reviewed the neurophysiological, developmental, and evolutionary correlates of language. Although Lenneberg's review was admirably thorough and surprisingly modern for its time, the cognitive neuroscience of language acquisition has made considerable progress since then. Much of this progress derives from technological advances. For example, Lenneberg could have only dreamed of a non-invasive brain imaging technique that would map out language functions in children – a technique that is available to us today with functional MRI (see Section 3). Other advances have been conceptual, supported by a wealth of relevant data, but in some instances prompted by unreasonable theories and tales of caution, such as those of "language genes" (as discussed in Section 5 below).

2. Language in the brain

One approach to an understanding of language in the brain relies on associating components of language processing with particular brain regions. Such functional localization has been a challenge to scientists and philosophers for many centuries and continues to be so today. Part of the challenge lies in decomposing both language and the brain into meaningful units. Further, relating cognition and biology requires that the 'grain' (or resolution) of the units be comparable between the two fields of inquiry. In other words, an appropriate level of analysis must be determined.

The effort toward functional localization has benefited tremendously from advances in methods for studying the brain. Therefore, this section begins with a brief description of the methods that have made the greatest contributions to this effort. The remainder of the section discusses the progress that has been made in characterizing language in the brain.

2.1. Methods for studying language in the brain

The earliest links between brain structure and function were derived from post-mortem examinations of brain lesions. Some of the most influential reports concerned patients with aphasia who exhibited different types of language impairments that appeared to be associated with lesions to different portions of the brain. For example, Paul Broca (1861, 1866) identified a portion of the left inferior frontal gyrus as being involved in speech production. Some years later, reports of patients seen by Carl Wernicke (1874) suggested an association between deficits in language comprehension and lesions to the left temporoparietal junction (for anatomical terms, see Figure 1, p. 68).

These early reports led to the development of the first neurological models of language. Wernicke predicted that other types of aphasia could be expected based on disrupted connections between the posterior and anterior language centers. Ludwig Lichtheim (1885) fleshed out this model creating diagrams of the connections between language areas. Partly because of skepticism surrounding Broca's and Wernicke's reports, and partly because of a shift away from localizationist thinking, this model largely fell out of consideration until it was resurrected by Norman Geschwind (1970) almost a century later. Although many aspects of the so called "Wernicke-Geschwind" model have not withstood the test of time, it was important as a conceptual launching point for subsequent work on localization of language functions. The advent of tools for imaging the anatomy of the living brain has increased the utility of the lesion-behavior approach for relating structure and function, which remains one of the dominant approaches to research on language in the brain. Among the most advanced recent applications of this approach is 'voxel-based lesion-symptom mapping'

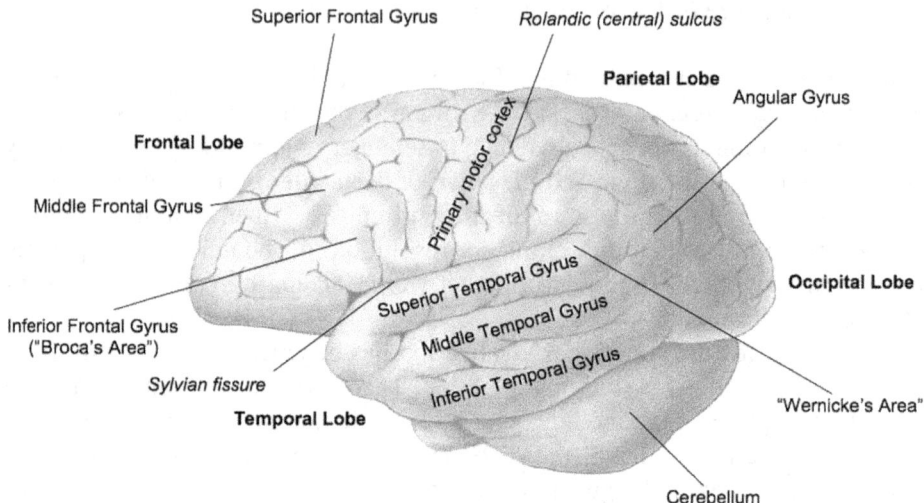

Figure 1. Main anatomical terms used in this chapter, indicated on the left hemisphere. Names of larger lobar subdivisions are shown in boldface, sulci are indicated in italics. Subcortical structures are not shown.

(Bates et al. 2003b), which determines for each brain location in 3-dimensional space whether damage is likely to result in behavioral impairment of a particular kind. Using this technique, Bates and colleagues found that impairments of verbal fluency were associated most consistently with lesions in insular cortex of the left hemisphere (rather than, as one might expect from the Wernicke-Geschwind model, with damage to Broca's area).

Progress in identifying brain regions important for language, particularly those related to speech, has also come from the study of patients undergoing brain surgery. In these patients, the effects of electrical stimulation of various brain regions can be observed during surgery. In addition, the consequences of removing portions of the brain can be tracked following surgery. Some of the earliest work of this type was performed by Wilder Penfield and Lamar Roberts in the 1950s (cf. Penfield and Roberts 1959). They determined that speech could be disrupted in various ways by stimulation of the language regions identified by Broca and Wernicke, and by stimulation of portions of left or right hemisphere sensorimotor and supplementary motor cortex. These findings were later supported and extended, notably by George Ojemann and colleagues (1991; see Figure 2).

Results of studies in surgical patients demonstrated that the relationships between language functions and brain regions were not as straightforward as the Wernicke-Geschwind model would suggest. For example, stimulation or removal of certain presumed language areas did not reliably produce language

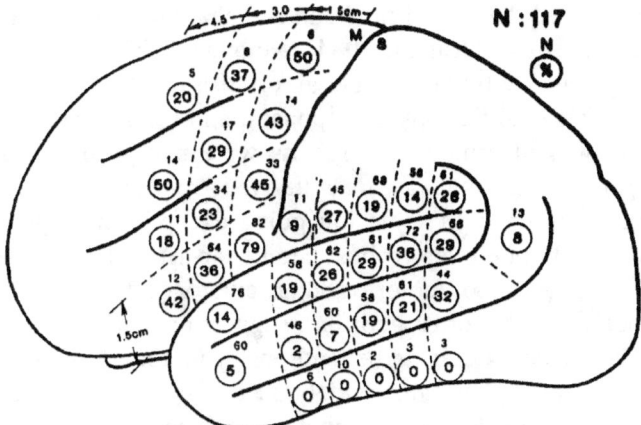

Figure 2. Results from electrical stimulation mapping by Ojemann and colleagues. The numbers in circles indicate the percentage of patients, in whom stimulation at the given site caused naming errors. The small numbers above each circle represent the total number of patients stimulated at the particular site. Results suggest that large regions of the left hemisphere are involved in processes that support naming. From Ojemann et al. (1991).

deficits of the type or severity that would have been predicted by the model. Furthermore, non-language functions such as short-term memory could be disrupted by stimulation of these areas, suggesting that they are not correctly classified as pure "language" areas. In short, stimulation and ablations studies provided evidence against the strictest forms of localizationism. In addition, this work lent support to an idea put forward by John Hughlings-Jackson one hundred years earlier that subcortical brain regions are important for language (cf. Kolb 1990). In particular, Penfield and Roberts, Ojemann and colleagues, and Irving Cooper and colleagues demonstrated that nuclei of the left thalamus participate in various speech and language processes (Ojemann and Mateer 1979).

Until the development of non-invasive methods for whole brain functional imaging in the late 1970s, studies of functional localization relied on examination of patients. Newer imaging methods, in addition to their important clinical applications, finally allowed for the study of healthy participants for research purposes. Among these is positron emission tomography (PET), which requires injection of radioactively labeled tracers into the blood stream. Due to increased blood flow, more active brain regions have a greater accumulation of the tracer, which is detected by the PET scanner. PET was first used in conjunction with cognitive tasks in the late 1980s, following methodological developments that allowed images to be averaged across subjects and functional activity to be related to brain anatomy (as reviewed by Raichle 2000). In addition, physiological studies have confirmed that blood flow and regional brain activity have a consistent relationship (Fox and Raichle 1984). Among the first PET studies of cognitive processing was one by Petersen et al. (1989), in which brain activity associated with input modality, spoken responses, and semantic demands during word processing was identified. The results were partly consistent with the model of left perisylvian language areas derived from clinical studies (as reviewed above), however, with some intriguing exceptions. In particular, Petersen and colleagues found very robust cerebellar activation for word generation even after subtraction of motoric and articulatory effects (i.e., subtraction of activity associated with word repetition), suggesting that the cerebellum may be involved in language processing beyond purely motoric functions.

Several years after PET became widely used in cognitive neuroscience research, developments in functional magnetic resonance imaging (fMRI) led to its use in cognitive experiments (e.g., McCarthy et al. 1993). FMRI measures the blood oxygenation level dependent (BOLD) response while subjects perform tasks in an MRI scanner. The BOLD response arises as neural activity results in local increases in blood flow and volume, and therefore increases in blood oxygenation. Oxygen metabolism also increases in these areas of the brain, but this increase is small in comparison to the increase in oxygenation (Buxton 2001). This net increase in oxygen changes the ratio of oxyhemoglobin to deoxyhemoglobin, resulting in increased BOLD contrast. While the specific neural underpinnings of the BOLD response are still under investigation (Logothetis and Pfeuffer 2004), repeated demonstrations of a reliable association between neural activity and the BOLD response have validated fMRI as a research tool. Its introduction for use in imaging cognitive tasks was facilitated by the fact that researchers using PET for similar purposes had already addressed many of the challenging analysis considerations. For example, in both PET and fMRI, functional images are registered to high-resolution images of brain anatomy acquired through structural MRI, to allow anatomical localization of functional effects. Unlike PET, however, fMRI does not require the injection of radioisotopes. Therefore, the availability of fMRI has reduced reliance on PET for many kinds of studies and has enabled researchers to study children and to perform very large numbers of scans on the same individuals in one session.

PET and fMRI are, however, not well suited for studying the temporal dynamic of language processing, since their temporal resolution is generally on the order of minutes (PET) or seconds (fMRI), whereas cognitive processes often occur within a few hundred milliseconds. Event-related potentials (ERPs) provide such temporal resolution. ERPs are recordings of the brain's electrical activity obtained via electrodes placed on the scalp. Electrical components specific to a cognitive event can be segregated from ongoing background activity by time-locking the recordings to an event of interest (e.g., presentation of a stimulus) and by averaging across a large number of trials. This results in a canonical waveform of the brain's electrical response to the stimulus. Precise localization of the neuronal sources of these responses is limited, but improving.

Various ERP components have been identified based on their latency and polarity, and related to specific aspects of cognitive processing. A number of these components are tied to language processing, some more specifically than others. For example, the mismatch negativity (MMN) is a negative waveform shift that occurs 100–250 msec following the presentation of a stimulus that differs in any of certain physical characteristics from a more frequently occurring standard stimulus (see Näätänen 1995 for review). While the MMN is not specific to language, it has found many uses in the study of language perception, such as determining whether infants detect a difference between two phonemes like "ba" and "ga" (Cheour et al. 2000). Two ERP components that are more specific to language are the N400 and the P600, both obtained from electrodes placed over centroparietal regions (Friederici 1997). The N400 is sensitive to semantic incongruities, as in the sentence "The box was too heavy to eat." The P600 is observed in response to syntactic anomalies, as in the sentence "He will walked." ERPs are valuable for characterizing the temporal dynamics of language processing in the brain, but localizing the neuronal generators underlying ERP components in the brain remains a challenge. Newer methods that combine high temporal and spatial resolution, such as magnetoencephalography (MEG), hold great promise for working toward this characterization in the future.

2.2. Functional localization of components of language processing

This section summarizes results of PET and fMRI studies identifying brain regions associated with early auditory and visual processing of words, lexicosemantic processing, language production, and postlexical processing.

Processing related specifically to spoken words primarily involves different portions of the temporal lobes, predominantly in the left hemisphere (Gernsbacher and Kaschak 2003; Hickok and Poeppel 2000). Certain posterior portions of the superior temporal gyri respond not only to auditorily presented language stimuli, but also more generally to auditory stimuli such as tones. Other bilateral posterior superior temporal regions and the right central middle temporal gyrus show greater responding to stimuli with complex acoustic properties, such as words and pseudowords (pronounceable, word-like letter strings), suggesting a possible role in linguistic processing. Portions of the left middle temporal gyrus show greater activity related to words than to pseudowords. A framework put forward by Hickok and Poeppel (2000) posits that in portions of the left middle and inferior temporal gyri, sound-based representations of words interface with their conceptual, more meaning-based representations. Another likely site important for linking sound and meaning is the inferior frontal cortex. For example, top-down information from inferior prefrontal cortex may facilitate the perception of spoken words (Marinkovic 2004).

Processing of written words, similar to other types of visual stimuli, originates from so-called early visual processing regions in the striate cortex of the occipital lobe. Processing then proceeds anteriorly to extrastriate cortex and higher-order visual association areas along the inferior surface of the occipital and temporal lobes, with representations of the written word form becoming increasingly abstract. For example, a region in the left fusiform gyrus is considered a "visual word form area". While processing in this region is not necessarily specific to words and word-like stimuli, evidence from literate adults suggests that it processes visual (but not auditory) words and word-like strings, and that this processing is insensitive to physical features of the stimulus such as case, size, and font, indicating a relatively abstract representation of the word form (McCandliss et al. 2003). Studies in patients with brain damage have implicated the left angular gyrus (near the junction of the temporal, parietal, and occipital lobes) in some stage of orthographic processing as well (Cohen et al. 2003).

Lexico-semantic processing, in which meaning-based representations of words are accessed from spoken or written stimuli, appears to involve a left-lateralized network of temporal, and frontal brain regions. Data from PET and fMRI studies are consistent with the literature on patients with semantic dementia (Mummery et al. 2000), suggesting a role of left anterior and inferolateral temporal regions, as well as the left temporoparietal junction (Wernicke's area) in semantic processing. MEG studies (Halgren et al. 2002) have used source modeling to identify the left superior temporal sulcus as the generator of the semantically-sensitive N400 component of the ERP waveform, described above. These results fit with fMRI and PET studies that report activity in similar regions during tasks with semantic demands (Pugh et al. 1996). In the frontal lobe, data from functional neuroimaging studies implicate left inferior frontal regions in semantic access and lexical retrieval (Petersen et al. 1989; Warburton et al. 1996).

Spoken language production involves access to phonological representations and their corresponding articulatory programs. The left posterior inferior frontal gyrus (Broca's area) and a central portion of the superior temporal gyrus appear to participate in generation or retrieval of phonological codes. The supplementary motor area (SMA), in frontal cortex near the midline, is known to be involved in motor planning, and there is evidence that it may also play a more specific role in preparation of articulatory programs. The cerebellum is involved in fine motor control, with medial portions linked specifically to language output (Fiez 1996). Less is known about the neural mechanisms of written language production, but there is some evidence that the angular gyrus, associated with orthographic processing in reading, is also important for orthographic processing related to spelling.

Processing at the sentence level requires a variety of syntactic operations. The complexity of these operations makes the identification of associated brain activity difficult to identify in any specific manner, particularly with the limited temporal resolution of hemodynamic methods such as PET and fMRI. However, studies of patients with deficits in various aspects of syntactic processing suggest that left anterior temporal cortex (Dronkers et al. 2004) and the left inferior frontal gyrus, including Broca's area (Fiebach et al. 2005; Indefrey et al. 2001), play important roles. MEG studies (Friederici et al. 2000) have used source modeling to identify similar left temporal and inferior frontal regions as the generators of the syntactically-sensitive P600 component of the ERP waveform, described above.

3. Developmental changes in brain activity associated with language processing

A large contribution to the study of developmental changes in the neural mechanisms of language processing comes from ERP research. This technique has allowed the inclusion of even very young children, who can be seated on a parent's lap during experiments and can be studied during passive listening. A first basic question concerns lateralization: Is the left hemisphere dominance for language, as it is typically found in right-handed (and most left-handed) adults, innate and potentially predetermined by genes; or is it an outcome of language development?

Neuroanatomically, leftward asymmetries of the planum temporale (a portion of Wernicke's area in the superior temporal lobe) have been observed in the fetus. This evidence is corroborated by auditory asymmetries detected in ERP and dichotic listening studies of neonates and infants (Werker and Vouloumanos 2001), consistent with limited recent evidence from fMRI studies in infants suggesting left-lateralizing temporal activation during speech stimulation (Dehaene-Lambertz et al. 2002; see Figure 3). However, there is also evidence pointing at greater right hemisphere language involvement during early stages of language acquisition. Mills et al. (1997) reported that ERPs distinguishing known from unknown words were bilateral in 13–17 month old infants, but left-lateralized in 20 month-olds. Furthermore, Neville & Mills (1997) found that a leftward asymmetry of ERPs to closed class (grammatical function) words, as observed in adults, was absent or even reversed in children under age 3 years. For children 5 years of age and older, Holcombe and colleagues (1992) reported that ERP asymmetries for semantic processing of sentence-final words were absent or inconsistent in children and became established only around age 13 years.

Figure 3. (A) Activation during sound stimulation (forward and backward speech) in 20 infants ages 2–3 months. Sites of significant activation in the left temporal lobe (indicated by the crosshairs) are overlaid in white onto structural MRI.
(B) Direct comparison between conditions shows greater activity for forward (compared to backward) speech in the left angular gyrus. From an fMRI study by Dehaene-Lambertz et al. (2002).

Figure 7. (A) PET activation studies in two subjects with progressive calcification of one hemisphere due to congenital Sturge-Weber syndrome. This disease is usually limited to a single hemisphere. During listening to sentences, the patient with right hemisphere damage shows a normal pattern of activation in left superior and middle temporal gyri, with slight additional activity in Broca's areas and in the temporal lobe of the affected right hemisphere. The patient with left hemisphere calcification shows almost a mirror image of activity in right temporal and inferior frontal regions. Activations are overlaid on resting blood flow images. Based on data from Müller et al. (1997; 1998b).
(B) Activations for sentence generation (compared to sentence repetition) in a patient with congenital onset left hemisphere damage, a patient with left hemisphere damage in the second decade of life, and in a group of healthy young adults. Early lesion is associated with extensive right frontal activation, whereas the late lesion patient shows left-lateralizing activity in inferior frontal and superior temporal lobes. Healthy adults show robust activity in left inferior frontal cortex. Note that images are shown in radiological convention, with sides inverted, as indicated in (A). Approximate slice locations are indicated on the small brain icons at the bottom. Based on data from Müller et al. (1999a; 1999b).

Figure 8. Examples of brain activation during covert word generation in three adult patients with a history of pre- and perinatal left hemisphere damage. All three subjects show activation in the right hemisphere that is not seen in control subjects. This activation, which is considered to reflect interhemispheric reorganization, varies strongly between individual patients, however. From an fMRI study by Staudt et al. (2002)

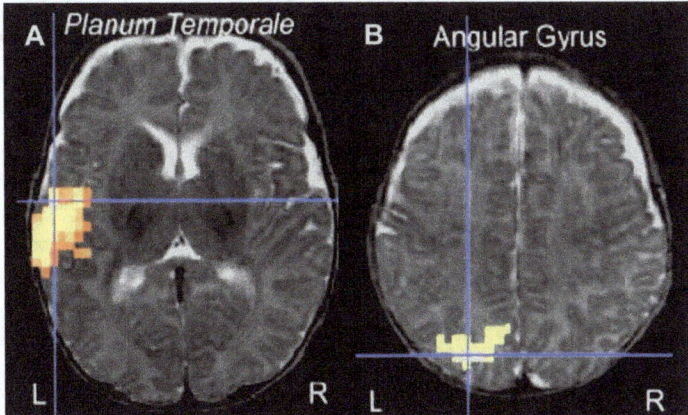

Figure 3

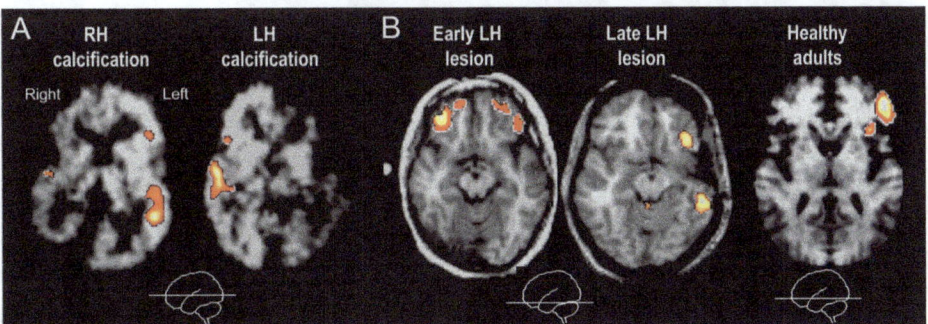

Figure 7

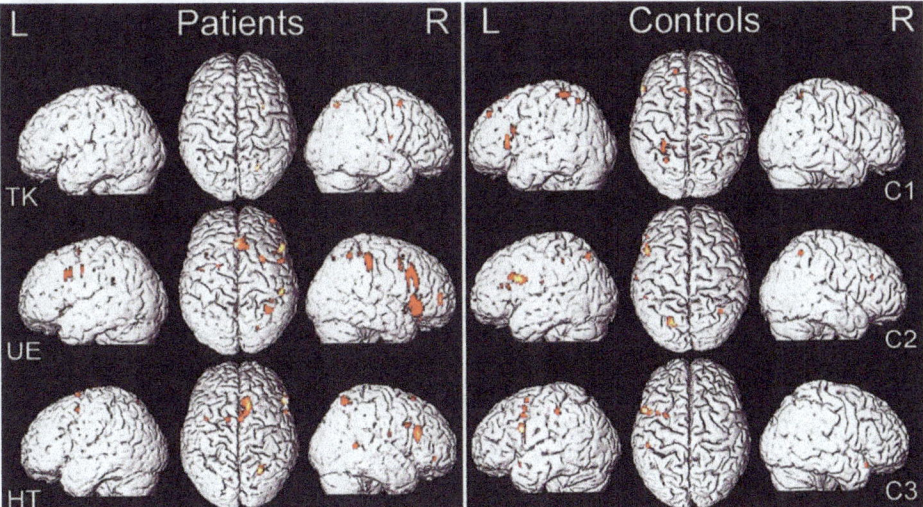

Figure 8

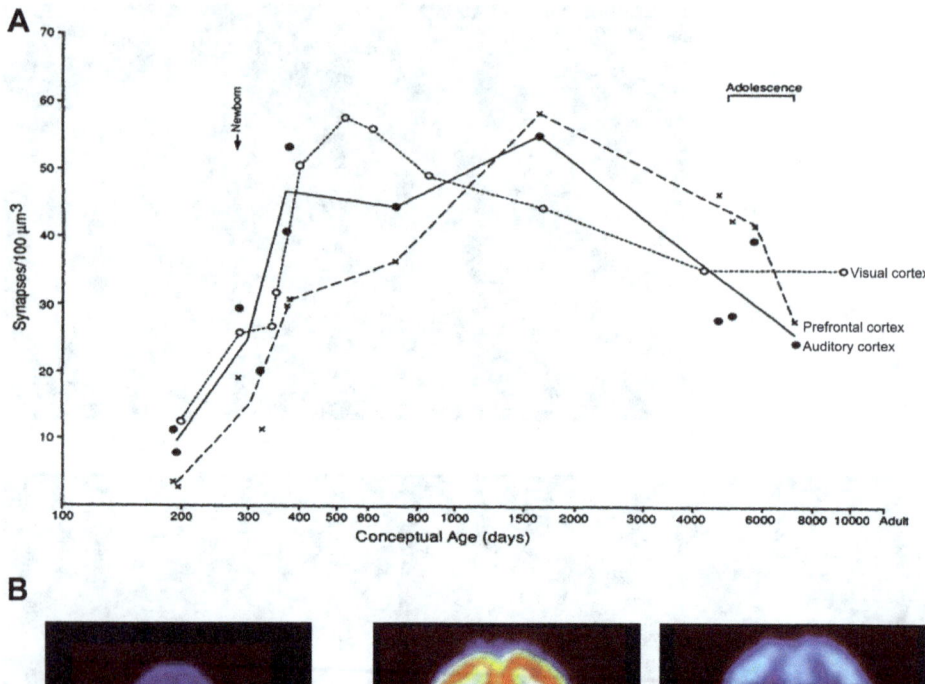

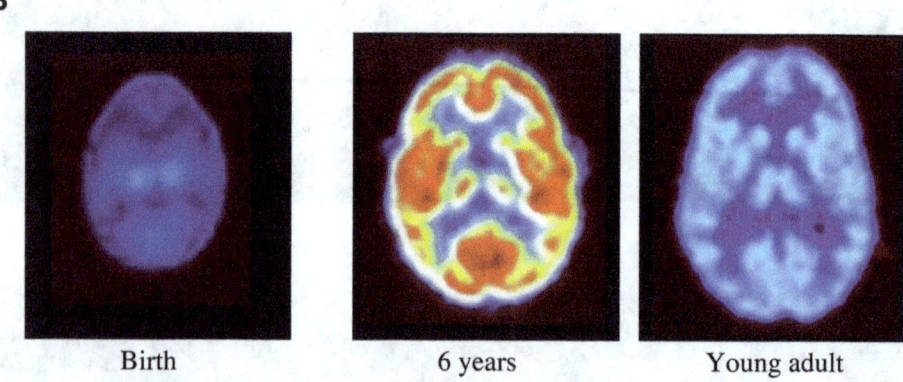

Figure 6. (A) Changes in synaptic density in primary auditory cortex (filled circles), primary visual cortex (open circles), and prefrontal cortex (middle frontal gyrus; x symbols) during development. The findings from Huttenlocher and Dabholkar (1997) show steep increases in synaptic density in the third gestational trimester and in the first postnatal year. High levels are maintained for several years, until synaptic density slowly declines to adult levels. Related age-dependent changes in glucose metabolism can be seen in (B). PET studies by Chugani et al. (1986) show much higher glucose metabolic rate in 6-year old children, compared to neonates and young adults. Adapted from Huttenlocher and Dabholkar (1997) and Chugani et al. (1991).

ERP studies have also addressed more general questions of developmental changes associated with language acquisition. For example, in a longitudinal study by Kuhl and colleagues (Rivera-Gaxiola et al. 2005), auditory ERPs were recorded from infants at 7 months and 11 months of age during passive listening to native and non-native phonetic contrasts. Data from this and other studies (Cheour et al. 1998; Kuhl 2000) comparing peak auditory ERP responses demonstrate that over this age range, discrimination sensitivity increases to native contrasts and decreases to non-native contrasts.

While Kuhl and colleagues focused on familiar vs. unfamiliar speech sounds, Mills and coworkers have applied auditory ERPs to study brain responses to familiar vs. novel words in slightly older infants (Conboy and Mills 2006; Mills et al. 1997). Mills et al. (1997) report that during passive listening to words, 13–17 month old children show broadly distributed ERP differences between comprehended and non-comprehended words. By about 20 months of age, however, differences between known and unknown words are limited to left temporal and parietal regions. These results may reflect an increasing brain regional specialization for lexical processing.

Moving from processing of individual words to sentence-level activation, Friederici and colleagues have used ERPs to examine syntactic processing in young children. In one study (Oberecker et al. 2005), children just under 3 years of age and a group of adults listened passively to sentences that were either correct or syntactically incorrect due to phrase-structure violations. In response to these violations, children demonstrated an early negative ERP component over left anterior electrode sites, followed by a P600 component. In adults, these components have been consistently associated with detection of phrase-structure violations. While the presence of these components in children suggests that at least some neural mechanisms of syntactic processing are in place at a young age, these components had a later onset and longer duration in the children than in the adults, indicating that development was ongoing. These findings are consistent with others in the literature that have revealed generally greater latencies for ERP components in children (Courchesne 1978; Holcomb et al. 1992).

Only in the past decade has fMRI come to be used for research in children. Despite the challenges associated with having young children perform a task while lying still in a noisy and confined space, fMRI results show promise for revealing changes in functional brain organization associated with language development. To date, fMRI studies of language development have focused on children ages 5 years and older. Because of the relatively small number of published studies and the differences among these studies in tasks, methods, and designs, conclusions about specific aspects of language processing have to be drawn with caution. While overall these studies suggest that grossly similar brain regions participate in language processing in children and adults, some intriguing age-dependent changes have been identified as well.

Gaillard et al. (2003), for example, reported that children ages 7–14 years showed activations in brain regions similar to those activated by adults during covert semantic fluency (generation of items appropriate to an aurally presented category, such as animals). This group also examined auditory story comprehension (Ahmad et al. 2003). The simple task and selection of age-appropriate stories allowed them to include children as young as age 5. They reported that even the youngest children showed activity similar to that previously observed in adults, most notably along the left superior temporal sulcus. Booth and colleagues (2003b; 2004) reported comparisons of 9–12 year old children and adults performing lexical processing tasks including spelling judgments, rhyme judgments, and semantic judgments to visually or aurally presented words. Under various task conditions, they observed greater activation in adults than in children in the inferior frontal and angular gyri.

Studies of language development using fMRI have also demonstrated that it is possible to observe differences in activation within groups of children. For example, Holland and colleagues (Szaflarski et al. 2006) conducted a longitudinal study of verb generation (hearing a noun and silently generating an appropriate verb; e.g., "ball" → throw), testing participants once a year for five years, starting at age 5, 6, or 7 years. Over these repeated observations, they saw increases in activity in left inferior and middle frontal gyri, left middle temporal and angular gyri, and right lingual and inferior temporal gyri. Other brain regions, including portions of left extrastriate and right anterior cingulate cortex, left superior frontal gyrus and left thalamus, showed decreased activity over the five-year period (cf. Figure 4). A recent study by Chou et al. (Chou et al. 2006) examined semantic judgments about written words in children ages 9–15 years. They reported that increasing age was associated with increased activity in the left middle temporal gyrus and inferior parietal cortex. Younger children, however, showed greater right superior temporal gyrus activation than older children.

One difficulty in interpreting data from developmental functional neuroimaging studies is that age and performance are often confounded. Thus, differences in brain activity across different age groups that are attributed to maturation may in fact be related to the ability to perform the tasks. Careful design of task paradigms that permit the distinction of developmental changes from effects related to performance and non-specific cognitive effort is therefore important. One possibility is manipulation of task difficulty for individual subjects or subject groups, so that performance is more comparable (Balsamo et al. 2006).

Another strategy for taking performance into account is illustrated in a study by Schlaggar and colleagues (2002), who used fMRI to examine brain activity during lexical generation tasks (verb, rhyme, and opposite generation to written words). Data were compared between groups of 7–10 year old children and adults whose performance on the tasks was statistically indistinguishable, and between groups of children and adults whose performance differed. In this

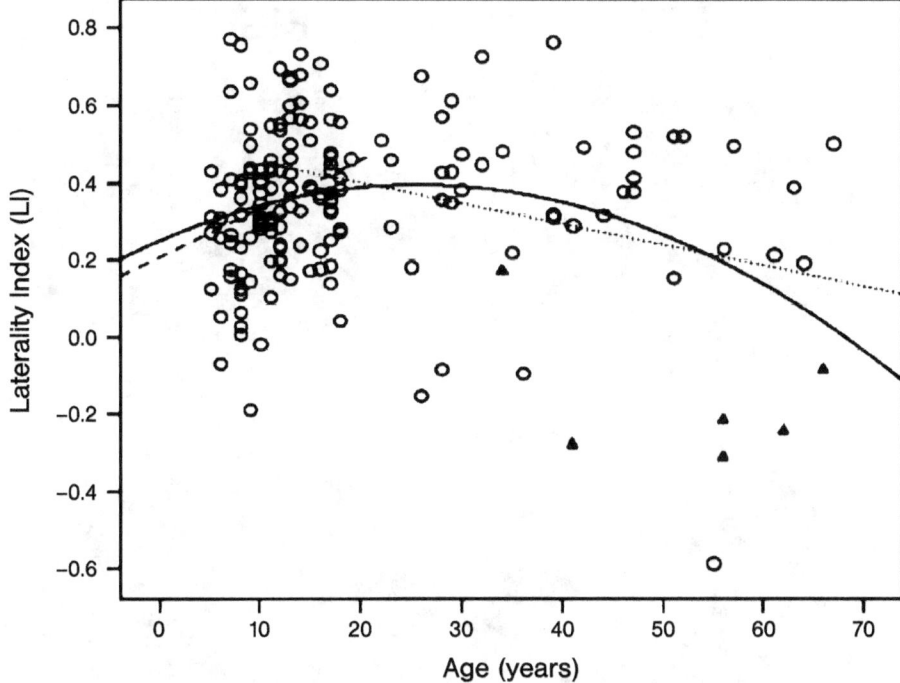

Figure 4. Hemispheric dominance for language as a function of age, based on fMRI activation findings in 170 healthy children and adults. Positive numbers in the upper half of the y-axis indicate leftward asymmetry of activation in Broca's and Wernicke's areas; negative numbers indicate rightward asymmetry. Circles and triangles indicate two different scanners used for data acquisition. Separate regressions were performed for children (A, dashed line), adults (B, dotted line), and all subjects together (C). The task was covert verb generation for aurally presented nouns. The results suggest that left lateralization increases throughout childhood and up to late adolescence, but slowly diminishes in adulthood. From Szaflarski et al. (2006).

way, it was possible to identify age-related regions (those in which activity differed between the age groups, independent of performance), performance-related regions (those in which activity differed based on performance, regardless of age), and age/performance-independent regions (those in which activity did not differ significantly among the groups). The trajectory of change in each of the age-related regions was then characterized by Brown and colleagues (Brown et al. 2005) by including lexical generation data from participants spanning the ages of 7 to 32 years. They demonstrated age-related increases in activity primarily in left frontal and parietal regions, and age-related decreases in activity in lower-level, more peripheral processing regions such as extrastriate cortex (Figure 5).

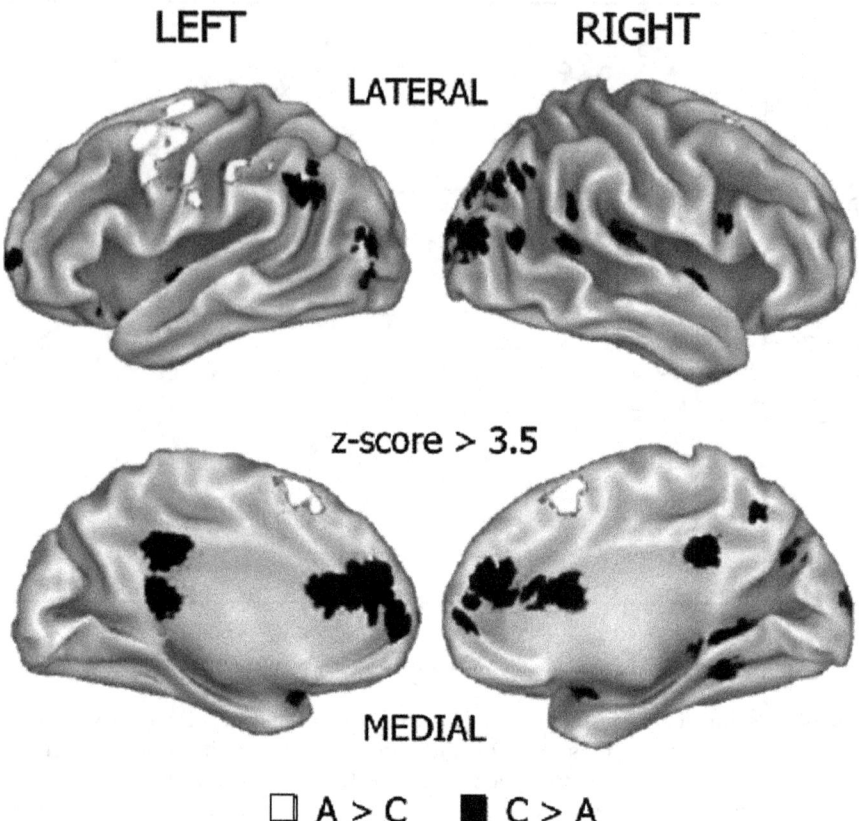

Figure 5. Age-dependent differences in activation for overt word production from an fMRI study in 95 children and adults, ages 7–32 years. White regions overlaid onto lateral and medial brain surfaces indicate greater activity in adults than in children (A>C), which is found mainly in frontal regions, such as premotor and supplementary motor cortex. Black overlays indicate regions with greater activity in children. These effects are extensive in posterior cortex, mostly in the occipital and parietal lobes, and in medial frontal and anterior cingulate regions. From Brown et al. (2005).

4. Links between brain development and language acquisition

Relating changes in brain development to the acquisition of language and other higher cognitive functions is one of the greatest challenges facing developmental cognitive neuroscientists. This section provides an overview of brain development, which encompasses both maturational and experience-dependent changes in neurobiology. The distinction between maturational (primarily genetic) and experience-dependent changes (i.e., those brought about by learning and environment) is conceptual, whereas in biological reality the two constantly interact. It is thus not possible, nor is it desirable, to characterize either one in isolation. The purpose of this section is to provide an overview of a typical series of changes that roughly characterize postnatal brain development.

4.1. Progressive and regressive principles of brain development

Human postnatal brain development has been studied in part through postmortem analyses, but primarily by neuroimaging methods such as MRI, by examination of glucose metabolism using PET, and by analogy with brain development in other primates. It appears that, by birth, the basic anatomical organization of the brain is in place; neurons have completed migration to their appropriate cortical locations, and major cortical gyri and sulci are identifiable. The volume of the brain at birth is roughly a quarter of its mature volume, and increases occur with different time courses for various cortical and subcortical structures (Toga et al. 2006). Many of these changes in volume are related to the substantial developmental changes in connectivity within and between regions.

A major component of these developmental changes is synaptogenesis, which is the formation of the junctions (synapses) through which neurons send and receive electrochemical signals. Following a general increase in synaptogenesis around the time of birth, synaptogenesis proceeds in a region-specific manner. Visual cortices, for example, are among the first to show increases in synaptogenesis, starting at approximately 3 months of age and reaching a peak around 6–8 months. While prefrontal cortex also shows an increase in synaptogenesis beginning at about 3 months of age, the time course is much more protracted than in visual cortex, with a peak in synaptic density well beyond the first year (Huttenlocher and Dabholkar 1997).

Synaptogenesis during the first two years of life is accompanied and followed by increasing myelination. Myelination is the process by which axons, the signal-transmitting projections from neuronal cell bodies, become insulated by a fatty sheath (myelin) that enhances conduction velocity. Increases in white matter (myelinated axons) contribute to the overall increase in brain volume that occurs through childhood. Myelination continues into the second decade of life, with prefrontal regions being among the last to attain mature levels (Giedd 2004). Myelination of fibers in lower cortical layers is also thought to underlie an apparent cortical thinning in children between the ages of 5 and 11 years (Sowell et al. 2004). Intriguingly, anterior and posterior language areas (Broca's and Wernicke's) show inverse age-dependent changes, suggesting very robust increases in cortical thickness that outweigh deep-layer myelination. Furthermore, age-dependent increases in the thickness of left inferior frontal cortex correlated with phonological abilities in the same sample of children. Improvements in motor skills, on the other hand, were associated with decreases in thickness of primary motor cortex (Lu et al. 2006).

These findings reflect that progressive events in brain development, such as synaptogenesis and myelination, are accompanied by regressive events. For example, there is extensive synaptic pruning, a process by which weaker or less active connections are eliminated (Kandel et al. 2000). Such pruning follows the extensive period of synaptogenesis described above, during which there is overgrowth, with synaptic density reaching approximately 150% of adult levels in 1 year old children (Huttenlocher 1994). The majority of synaptic pruning appears to occur in late childhood and early adolescence (cf. Figure 6, p. 76).

4.2. Relating functional and structural changes

The maturation of particular brain regions does not appear to be straightforwardly associated with the emergence of new skills or functions (cf. Bates et al. 2003a). Simply looking at changes in individual brain regions may only provide part of the picture. The relationship is likely more complex in that new functions are supported by changes in functional brain organization affecting both activity within a brain region and connections between brain regions, i.e., the emerging organization of distributed functional networks. An example of a framework for thinking about functional brain development in this manner is provided by the interactive specialization approach put forward by Johnson (2000; 2002; 2003), which takes into account both inter-regional and intra-regional changes.

In the interactive specialization framework, brain regions whose functional roles are initially not well defined compete with each other to perform certain kinds of processing, thereby altering connections among regions. At the same time, individual brain regions undergo functional fine-tuning, becoming most efficient at processing a particular class of stimuli or performing certain kinds of computations. These processes of inter-regional and intra-regional specialization influence each other to enhance tuning within selected brain regions and to shape a network of regions whose functional roles are more precisely defined. The process of interactive specialization may be related not only to maturational changes that support more efficient processing, but also to environmental factors. For example, there is evidence for changes in functional brain organization for word processing that are very closely tied to the size of a child's vocabulary, indicating the importance of language exposure in interactive specialization (Neville et al. 1992).

In considering how the interactive specialization framework might be applied more specifically to language development, some questions come immediately to mind: Which regions become specialized for language? Why these regions? How specialized are they? Is their specialization predetermined by genes or the outcome of experience and development? While these questions will remain under debate for years to come, some preliminary answers are provided by evidence from behavior genetics and the study of brain plasticity, which will be reviewed in the next two sections.

5. Language and genes

As already alluded to at the outset of this chapter, it was the groundbreaking work of Noam Chomsky that led linguists to consider their object of study as ultimately biological and determined by genes. Although psycholinguists may occasionally have been tempted by overly simple ideas of "language genes", the question is valid and important and a neurophysiological account of language development cannot ignore genetics. At the same time, the reader should be warned that the corpus of solid and relevant data remains extremely small and that no comprehensive and accepted theory of the link between genes and language acquisition is available today.

5.1. Genetic bases of language impairment

One approach to the genetic bases of language lies in the study of children with specific language impairment (SLI; i.e., language deficits in the context of otherwise normal development) that may be genetically based. For the population of children with specific language impairment at large, several quantitative trait loci (i.e., regions with genes suspected to contribute to SLI) have been identified on chromosomes 3p, 13q, 16q, and 19q (p and q indicating short and long arms, respectively; Newbury et al. 2005). An interesting familial aggregation of language impairment was described by Gopnik and colleagues (1990; 1991) in family KE. Initial studies in this family seemed to support a selective linguistic deficit relating to specific aspects of morphosyntax (such as past tense formation). This discovery was greeted with great enthusiasm in part of the linguistic community (e.g., Pinker 1991) because it appeared compatible with a gene-based modular architecture of linguistic subsystems, as proposed by Chomsky (1981). Even more intriguingly, the speech disorder in family KE was identified in subsequent studies as an autosomal-dominant trait involving a single gene on chromosome 7 (Fisher et al. 1998; Lai et al. 2001). These findings in family KE are consistent with independent evidence for strong genetic factors in the general SLI population (Bishop 2002; Tomblin and Buckwalter 1998). Indeed, recent studies indicate potentially distinct genetic factors underlying grammatical functions versus auditory working memory (Bishop et al. 2006).

Returning to family KE, it should be noted, however, that comprehensive examination of affected members does not support the initial impression of an exclusive or specific morphosyntactic deficit (Vargha-Khadem et al. 1995; Watkins et al. 2002a). Instead, affected (compared to unaffected family members) showed significantly lower nonverbal IQ scores as well as evidence of orofacial apraxia and impaired phonological working memory. Furthermore, anatomical MRI studies analyzed by means of voxel-based morphometry demonstrate gray matter reduction primarily in perirolandic sensorimotor cortex and the caudate nuclei in affected members compared to normal control participants (Watkins et al. 2002b), which appears to be more suggestive of neural defects in motor (rather than morphosyntactic) systems.

Nonetheless, family KE and the gene identified on chromosome 7 may serve as the best available example for a better understanding of potential links between genes, developing brains, and impairments of language acquisition. Before examining the role of this gene, it is important to review very briefly what is known more generally about the genetic impact on the regional functional differentiation of the developing brain. There is overwhelming consensus regarding regional functional specificity, both with regard to the mature and the developing brain. This implies that a neurobiological approach to developmental disorders of language should specifically target brain regions known for their role in language acquisition, despite the obvious added complexity of developmental links between lesion site and behavioral impairment (Thomas and Karmiloff-Smith 2002).

5.2. Genes and functional brain specialization

Some recent neuroanatomical studies have suggested very strong genetic factors affecting morphological variability (Bartley et al. 1997; Geschwind et al. 2002; Thompson et al. 2001). Following a review by Pallas (2001), one can distinguish between early regionalization, which is determined largely intrinsically and is thus under tight genetic control, and subsequent arealization, which is strongly affected by extrinsic and activity-driven factors. Knockout studies of regulatory genes, such as *Emx2* and *Pax6*, illustrate the impact of intrinsic factors on regionalization. In embryonic mice, these two genes are expressed in gradients along the antero-posterior and lateral-medial axes. In knockout models (i.e., in mice missing one of these genes), corresponding distortions of regionalization can be found. For example, *Pax6* knockout mice will have very small anterolateral cerebral regions, but disproportionately large posterior-medial regions (including very large visual cortex; O'Leary and Nakagawa 2002). Roughly the opposite pattern is found in *Emx2* knockout mice (Cecchi 2002).

Neocortical differentiation into fully specialized functional areas is, however, not strictly predetermined intrinsically (genetically), but instead largely driven by input information (i.e., afferent connections) and thus characterized by high levels of plasticity (O'Leary et al. 1994). Some compelling evidence for such epigenetic effects on arealization comes from transplantation and rewiring studies. Schlaggar and colleagues (1991) transplanted embryonic occipital cortex into the postcentral region in neonatal rats and found that "barrel fields" (separate representations for sensory hairs or whiskers normally found in primary somatosensory cortex) developed almost normally in this transplanted cortex. This implies that cortical tissue that would normally develop visual specialization in occipital cortex has the potential to develop somatosensory functions if transplanted into a brain region where it receives somatosensory information through fibers from the thalamus (Schlaggar et al. 1993). This type of functional malleability of developing cortex is called crossmodal plasticity and has also been documented in rewiring experiments by Sur and colleagues (1990), who experimentally connected retinal afferents in newborn ferrets to the medial geniculate nucleus (MGN) in the thalamus. MGN is normally an auditory structure connecting, in turn, to auditory cortex. Sur et al. (1988) found that following such rewiring both MGN and primary auditory cortex responded to visual stimulation. Indeed, such electrophysiological responses are functionally relevant and contribute to stimulus-appropriate behavior (von Melchner et al. 2000).

5.3. Language genes?

The evidence sketched above suggests that both intrinsic and extrinsic (or genetic and epigenetic) mechanisms are at work in determining a region's function in the mature brain. This implies that genes may play an important very basic role in creating brain substrates necessary for typical language acquisition, but that much of the regional functional fine-tuning is driven by connectivity and activity (i.e., ultimately by experience). Within this general framework, it is not surprising that the gene on chromosome 7, identified as the critical locus in language impaired members of family KE (as discussed above) is not a 'language gene' that would specifically code for grammatical abilities or narrowly specialized brain substrates. The gene involved – at first suggestively labeled *"SPCH1"* (Fisher et al. 1998) – was subsequently classified as a gene encoding forkhead transcription factors, therefore called *FOXP2* (Lai et al. 2001). Forkhead proteins are transcription factors that play important roles in various basic developmental processes, such as cell differentiation and proliferation (Marcus and Fisher 2003). Indeed, during embryonic development *FOXP2* is expressed far beyond the brain, for example, in the lungs and in the heart. From this perspective, the apparently more specific role of this gene in language impairment in family KE remains puzzling. More recent studies have shown a cosegregation of one coding change of *FOXP2* with verbal apraxia that could reflect a more specific link (MacDermot et al. 2005). Nonetheless, it must be noted that defects in this gene account for only a very small fraction of developmental language impairments. It is therefore likely that the *FOXP2* gene sheds light only on a small fraction of the links between genes and language development. These links are far from being completely understood, but the current evidence suggests that (a) the typically developing brain's capacity for language acquisition relies on the presence and interaction of a multitude of genes; and (b) these genes are shared, i.e., they also play other roles in the development of other brain systems and bodily systems outside the brain (for discussion, see Fisher 2005; Müller 2005).

The example of *FOXP2* may also be enlightening with regard to the phylogenetic emergence of language. While this gene is evolutionarily very old and highly conserved in vertebrate evolution, two amino-acid substitutions that distinguish humans from chimpanzees have been identified in the *FOXP2* sequence, suggesting the impact of selectional pressures within the last 200,000 years, which may be at least indirectly linked to language emergence (Fisher and Marcus 2006). The current knowledge of the role of *FOXP2* can thus help to modify the search for "language genes" that would correspond to the traditional Chomskian notion of evolutionarily discontinuous emergence of universal grammar due to specific mutations. In the last two sections, we will address the question of genetically anchored specific biological substrates for language, first reviewing evidence for plasticity in brain networks subserving language. Finally, we will reformulate the Chomskian quest, arguing that his overly exclusive view of language vis-à-vis other sensorimotor and cognitive domains needs to be broadened.

6. Damage and plasticity

In previous sections, we have discussed neurofunctional plasticity in the context of typical development (Section 3) and specifically with regard to the impact of afferent connectivity (Section 5.2). As described in Section 2.1, the study of adults with aphasia subsequent to localized brain damage served as the main knowledge source for neurolinguists until the emergence of functional neuroimaging techniques. Conclusions for healthy brain organization can be drawn from adult lesion studies on the assumption of limited plasticity in the mature brain. For example, the symptoms of non-fluent Broca's aphasia can be attributed to damage in the left inferior frontal lobe, assuming that there is only limited postlesional reorganization and that brain function in the patient can be equated to normal systems minus the function of a damaged anterior language area. While such assumptions are probably too simple even with regard to the mature brain, they are clearly wrong for the developing brain (Thomas and Karmiloff-Smith 2002).

Behavioral studies show that early-onset left hemisphere damage is often associated with delayed language milestones (Chilosi et al. 2005), but ultimately normal or near-normal language outcome, unless such damage is associated with seizure disorder (MacWhinney et al. 2000; Max 2004; Muter et al. 1997). In children with localized left hemisphere damage, it remains possible that intact parts of the left hemisphere may assume language functions. However, similarly good language outcomes are also seen in patients with left hemispherectomy (i.e., the removal or complete disconnection of an entire hemisphere), on condition that the right hemisphere remains intact (Boatman et al. 1999; Curtiss et al. 2001; Vargha-Khadem and Mishkin 1997; Vargha-Khadem et al. 1997). The behavioral literature would therefore suggest a potential for the right hemisphere to assume language functions in the face of massive left hemisphere damage early in life.

This indirect conclusion has been corroborated by functional neuroimaging studies. In a series of PET studies (Müller et al. 1997; 1998a; 1998b; 1998c), right hemisphere reorganization was observed in most children with early left hemisphere damage (Figure 7). In these subjects, right hemisphere activation was typically found in regions homotopic to left perisylvian language cortices. These studies also showed an enhanced potential for interhemispheric reorganization in the developing child brain, compared to the adult brain (Müller et al. 1999a; 1999b). A few functional MRI studies have more recently corroborated these findings. Staudt and colleagues (2002) found right-hemisphere activations in regions homotopic with left perisylvian language areas for silent word generation in adults with a history of congenital left periventricular lesions (Figure 8) – a finding corroborated more recently by Liegeois and coworkers (2004), who observed right-hemisphere dominance for language in five of ten adolescent patients with early onset damage due to diverse conditions. In a single-case study, language reorganization was examined in a child with Rasmussen's encephalitis before and after left hemispherotomy (extrathalamic white matter disconnection and callosotomy; Hertz-Pannier et al. 2002). Whereas word generation was associated with left frontal and inferior parietal activation before surgery, extensive right hemisphere activation was found after the resection.

The brief review in this section underlines that the brain organization for language is not fully determined at birth. While the ERP and imaging evidence on typically developing children suggest early biases of portions of the left hemisphere to assume a pivotal role in language acquisition (as reviewed in Section 3), the right hemisphere also has a similar potential early in life. Overall, the evidence is thus consistent neither with genetically driven predetermination nor with "equipotentiality" and exclusively epigenetic causes of functional specialization.

7. "Language areas": A developmental account

Current knowledge about the brain organization for language, as described in Section 2.2, is almost entirely based on evidence from healthy and brain damaged adults. This is related to scientific and conceptual pragmatism, since it is easier to acquire relevant data from adults and to draw conclusions about brain-behavior relationships at what is considered a 'steady-state' (compared to the dynamic changes of the maturing brain). However, this adultocentrist approach that considers children as not quite finished adults can be deeply misleading. The perspective taken in this section is informed by the constructivism of Swiss psychologist Jean Piaget (Piaget 1979), according to whom the cognitive system at any stage is erected on the building blocks of previous stages. With regard to brain-behavior links in the language system, this approach implies that it is preposterous (in the literal sense of putting the cart before the horse) to inspect the child brain in the search for language areas as defined by adult brain organization. Instead, we can study the maturing brain in search for explanations of why certain brain regions have come to assume language specialization in the adult brain.

7.1. Broca's area and the mirror neuron system

An exemplary case can be made with regard to Broca's area in left inferior frontal cortex. Despite some claims for highly specialized syntactic functions (Grodzinsky 2000), neuroimaging evidence shows overlapping cortex within this area involved in phonology and semantics as well (cf. Hagoort 2005). Indeed, a more comprehensive review of the literature suggests participation of the left inferior frontal gyrus in a large array of functions that are not even considered linguistic (Cabeza and Nyberg 2000). Among the examples are functions related to motor planning and action, such as imitation (Buccino et al. 2004; Iacoboni et al. 1999), motor preparation (Krams et al. 1998) and complex motor planning (Fincham et al. 2002), sequence learning (Haslinger et al. 2002), action imagery (Binkofski et al. 2000) and observation (Buccino et al. 2001), but also functions considered of executive nature, such as rule shifting (Konishi et al. 1998), response selection (Thompson-Schill et al. 1997), response inhibition (Kemmotsu et al. 2005; Rubia et al. 2001), perceptual fusion and resolution of audiovisual stimulus conflict (Dale and Buckner 1997; Miller and D'Esposito 2005), as well as working memory (Chen and Desmond 2005). Some of these findings can be considered reflections of inferior frontal participation in the mirror neuron system (Rizzolatti and Arbib 1998).

Mirror neurons were first observed in primate area F5, which is a likely homologue to human area 44 in inferior frontal cortex (Grèzes et al. 2003; Petrides and Pandya 1994) and thus to the core portion of Broca's area. Mirror neurons show increased firing rates for internally generated action as well as for corresponding externally observed actions (Fadiga et al. 2000), including actions performed with tools (Ferrari et al. 2005). While mirror neurons have been mostly studied using visuomotor conditions, the existence of multimodal auditory-visual-motor mirror neurons has also been demonstrated in monkey area

F5 (Kohler et al. 2002). The mirror neuron system, which additionally incorporates parietal cortex and the superior temporal sulcus, can thus be considered crucial to action understanding (Rizzolatti and Craighero 2004). More importantly, since this system affords a matching of self-generated actions to those observed in others, it is likely to provide a crucial component in the development of theory of mind, i.e., the ability to attribute intentions to other people's actions according to intentions underlying our own actions. The mirror neuron system is thus vital, not only for sensorimotor integration involved in language acquisition (e.g., the child's ability to imitate phonemes based on adult models), but in a deeper sense because it contributes to the understanding that verbal actions are meaningful, i.e., reflect the speaker's state of mind, intentions etc. (cf. Gallese 2003; Nishitani et al. 2005; Rizzolatti and Arbib 1998).

A large number of recent functional neuroimaging studies have documented that inferior frontal cortex participates in the described functions of the mirror neuron system in similar ways in adult humans as in monkeys. For example, activation in area 44 has been reported for action observation and imagery (Binkofski et al. 2000; Buccino et al. 2001), processing of action-related (compared to abstract) sentences (Tettamanti et al. 2005), as well as imitation (Grèzes et al. 2003; Heiser et al. 2003; Leslie et al. 2004), including imitation of lip forms (Nishitani and Hari 2002). Indeed, consistent with the idea that the mirror neuron system provides the basis of mentalizing abilities mentioned above, Iacoboni and colleagues (2005) showed inferior frontal activity related to the processing of intentions (as compared to simple action observation).

While the important role of Broca's area in the mirror neuron system is well documented, inferior frontal cortex also receives afferents from the ventral visual stream (Di Virgilio and Clarke 1997; Petrides and Pandya 2002) – a processing stream extending from visual cortex in the occipital lobe into inferior portion of the temporal lobe, which is crucial for the meaningful interpretation of perceived objects. Broca's area can thus be considered pivotal for language learning – not because it contains cortical tissue specifically predestined for morphosyntactic or other language functions (cf. Amunts et al. 2003) – but because a number of functional pathways providing crucial components for language learning converge in this brain area. The most important components are the mirror neuron system and dorsal stream (action understanding), the ventral stream (semantics), and executive components (working memory, response inhibition). The limited spatial resolution of functional neuroimaging techniques such as fMRI makes it hard to determine to what extent each of these components may be distinctly organized within inferior frontal cortex. In a recent review, Molnar-Szakacs and colleagues (2005) conclude that mirror neurons may themselves have working memory capacity, suggesting potential overlap of tissue involved in action understanding and executive components. Activity related to the mirror neuron system, such as action recognition, was also found to occur in close proximity to language-related activity (verb generation), with a distance of peaks below 10mm in many individuals (Hamzei et al. 2003).

Although the above example relates specifically to Broca's area, the approach to functional characterization will likely also apply to other presumed "language areas", such as Wernicke's area in posterior perisylvian cortex. The discussion of Broca's area suggests that its importance in language processing may be developmentally explained by this region's anatomical connectivity patterns and its participation in multiple functional networks that are important "ingredients" of language acquisition (see Müller in press for more extensive discussion).

8. Conclusion

The human ability to acquire languages ultimately rests on genetic endowment. Although there are a few intriguing genetic findings of changes in hominid evolution that may be related to language emergence, it is likely that many genes are involved in the phylogenetic emergence and ontogenetic acquisition of language. It remains open whether any genes may specifically code for language-related abilities. However, evidence for activity-driven (and thus not entirely intrinsic) specialization from developmental neuroscience suggests that the brain substrates for language functionally differentiate in part due to epigenetic processes. This is consistent with evidence for plasticity following damage to typical language regions in children. Further evidence was discussed regarding the precise functional characterization of Broca's area, the most universally accepted brain substrate for language processing, suggesting that this area's readiness for language acquisition relates to converging precursor functions (such as imitation, action understanding, attribution of intention, meaningful interpretation, working memory, and response inhibition). While a comprehensive explanatory model of the links between brain maturation and language remains unavailable, advances in functional imaging and neurophysiological techniques in the past decades promise to provide ever deeper insights into the nature and bases of language acquisition.

Acknowledgment. This review was supported by the National Institutes of Health, grants R01-NS43999 (RAM, EP) and R01-DC6155 (RAM). Thanks to Marisa Luna for technical assistance.

References

Ahmad, Z., L. M. Balsamo, B. C. Sachs, B. Xu, and W. D. Gaillard
2003 Auditory comprehension of language in young children: neural networks identified with fMRI. *Neurology* 60: 1598–605.
Amunts, K., A. Schleicher, A. Ditterich, and K. Zilles
2003 Broca's region: cytoarchitectonic asymmetry and developmental changes. *J Comp Neurol* 465: 72–89.
Balsamo, L. M., B. Xu, and W. D. Gaillard
2006 Language lateralization and the role of the fusiform gyrus in semantic processing in young children. *Neuroimage* 31:1306–14.
Bartley, A. J., D. W. Jones, and D. R. Weinberger
1997 Genetic variablility of human brain size and cortical gyral patterns. *Brain* 120: 257–269.
Bates, E., D. Thal, B. Finlay, and B. Clancy
2003a Early language development and its neural correlates. In: I. Rapin and S. Segalowitz (eds.), *Handbook of Neuropsychology: Child Neurology,* 525–592. Amsterdam: Elsevier.
Bates, E., S. M. Wilson, A. P. Saygin, F. Dick, M. I. Sereno, R. T. Knight, and N. F. Dronkers
2003b Voxel-based lesion-symptom mapping. *Nat Neurosci* 6: 448–50.
Binkofski, F., K. Amunts, K. M. Stephan, S. Posse, T. Schormann, H. J. Freund, K. Zilles, and R. J. Seitz
2000 Broca's region subserves imagery of motion: a combined cytoarchitectonic and fMRI study. *Human Brain Mapping* 11: 273–85.
Bishop, D. V.
2002 The role of genes in the etiology of specific language impairment. *J Commun Disord* 35: 311–28.
Bishop, D. V., C. V. Adams, and C. F. Norbury
2006 Distinct genetic influences on grammar and phonological short-term memory deficits: evidence from 6-year-old twins. *Genes Brain Behav* 5: 158–69.
Boatman, D., J. Freeman, E. Vining, M. Pulsifer, D. Miglioretti, R. Minahan, B. Carson, J. Brandt, and G. McKhann
1999 Language recovery after left hemispherectomy in children with late-onset seizures. *Ann Neurol* 46: 579–86.
Booth, J. R., D. D. Burman, J. R. Meyer, Dr. R. Gitelman, T. B. Parrish, M. M. and Mesulam
2004 Development of brain mechanisms for processing orthographic and phonologic representations. *J Cogn Neurosci* 16: 1234–49.
Broca, P.
1861 Remarques sur le siège de la faculté du langage articulé, suivies d'une observation d'aphémie (perte de la parole). *Bulletins et Mémoires de la Société Anatomique de Paris* 36: 330–57.
Broca, P.
1866 Discussion sur la Faculté du Langage und Aphasie traumatique. *Bulletins de la Société d'Anthropologie de Paris* 1: 377–85 & 396–9.

Brown, T. T., H. M. Lugar, R. S. Coalson, F. M. Miezin, S. E. Petersen, and B. L. Schlaggar
  2005   Developmental changes in human cerebral functional organization for word generation. *Cereb Cortex* 15: 275–90.
Buccino, G., F. Binkofski, G. R. Fink, L. Fadiga, L. Fogassi, V. Gallese, R. J. Seitz, K. Zilles, G. Rizzolatti, and H. J. Freund
  2001   Action observation activates premotor and parietal areas in a somatotopic manner: an fMRI study. *Eur J Neurosci* 13: 400–4.
Buccino, G., F. Binkofski, and L. Riggio
  2004   The mirror neuron system and action recognition. *Brain Lang* 89: 370–6.
Buxton, R. B.
  2001   *An Introduction to Functional Magnetic Resonance Imaging: Principles and Techniques.* Cambridge University Press.
Cabeza, R. and L. Nyberg
  2000   Imaging cognition II: an empirical review of 275 PET and fMRI studies. *Journal of Cognitive Neuroscience* 12: 1–47.
Cecchi, C.
  2002   *Emx2*: a gene responsible for cortical development, regionalization and area specification. *Gene* 291: 1–9.
Chen, S. H. and J. E. Desmond
  2005   Cerebrocerebellar networks during articulatory rehearsal and verbal working memory tasks. *Neuroimage* 24: 332–8.
Cheour, M., R. Ceponiene, A. Lehtokoski, A. Luuk, J. Allik, K. Alho, and R. Näätänen
  1998   Development of language-specific phoneme representations in the infant brain. *Nat Neurosci* 1: 351–3.
Cheour, M., P. H. Leppanen, and N. Kraus
  2000   Mismatch negativity (MMN) as a tool for investigating auditory discrimination and sensory memory in infants and children. *Clin Neurophysiol* 111: 4–16.
Chilosi, A. M., C. Pecini, P. Cipriani, P. Brovedani, D. Brizzolara, G. Ferretti, L. Pfanner, and G. Cioni
  2005   Atypical language lateralization and early linguistic development in children with focal brain lesions. *Dev Med Child Neurol* 47: 725–30.
Chomsky, N.
  1965   *Aspects of the Theory of Syntax.* Cambridge (Mass.): MIT Press.
Chomsky, N.
  1976   *Reflections on Language.* London: Temple Smith.
Chomsky, N.
  1981   *Lectures on Government and Binding.* Dordrecht: Foris.
Chomsky, N.
  2002   *On Nature and Language.* Cambridge: Cambridge University Press.
Chou, T. L., J. R. Booth, T. Bitan, D. D. Burman, J. D. Bigio, N. E. Cone, D. Lu, and F. Cao
  2006   Developmental and skill effects on the neural correlates of semantic processing to visually presented words. *Hum Brain Mapp* 27:915–24.
Chugani, H. T. and M. E. Phelps
  1991   Imaging human brain development with positron emission tomography. *J Nucl Med* 32: 23–6.

Chugani, H. T. and M. E. Phelps
  1986 Maturational changes in cerebral function in infants determined by 18-FDG positron emission tomography. *Science* 231: 840–843.
Cohen, L., O. Martinaud, C. Lemer, S. Lehericy, Y. Samson, M. Obadia, A. Slachevsky, and S. Dehaene
  2003 Visual word recognition in the left and right hemispheres: anatomical and functional correlates of peripheral alexias. *Cereb Cortex* 13: 1313–33.
Conboy, B. T. and D. L. Mills
  2006 Two languages, one developing brain: event-related potentials to words in bilingual toddlers. *Dev Sci* 9: F1–12.
Courchesne, E.
  1978 Neurophysiological correlates of cognitive development: changes in long-latency event-related potentials from childhood to adulthood. *Electroencephalography and Clinical Neurophysiology* 45: 468–82.
Critchley, M.
  1970 *Aphasiology*. London: Edwald Arnold.
Curtiss, S., S. de Bode, and G. W. Mathern
  2001 Spoken language outcomes after hemispherectomy: factoring in etiology. *Brain Lang* 79: 379–96.
Dale, A. M. and R. L. Buckner
  1997 Selective averaging of rapidly presented individual trials using fMRI. *Human Brain Mapping* 5: 329–340.
Dehaene-Lambertz, G., S. Dehaene, and L. Hertz-Pannier
  2002 Functional neuroimaging of speech perception in infants. *Science* 298: 2013–5.
Di Virgilio, G. and S. Clarke
  1997 Direct interhemispheric visuak input to human speech areas. *Hum Brain Mapp* 5: 347–354.
Dronkers, N. F., D. P. Wilkins, R. D. Van Valin, Jr., B. B. Redfern, and J. J. Jaeger
  2004 Lesion analysis of the brain areas involved in language comprehension. *Cognition* 92: 145–77.
Fadiga, L., L. Fogassi, V. Gallese, and G. Rizzolatti
  2000 Visuomotor neurons: ambiguity of the discharge or 'motor' perception? *International Journal of Psychophysiology* 35: 165–77.
Ferrari, P. F., S. Rozzi, and L. Fogassi
  2005 Mirror neurons responding to observation of actions made with tools in monkey ventral premotor cortex. *J Cogn Neurosci* 17: 212–26.
Fiebach, C. J., M. Schlesewsky, G. Lohmann, D. Y. Von Cramon, and A. D. Friederici
  2005 Revisiting the role of Broca's area in sentence processing: Syntactic integration versus syntactic working memory. *Hum Brain Mapp* 24: 79–91.
Fiez, J. A.
  1996 Cerebellar contributions to cognition. *Neuron* 16: 13–15.
Fincham, J. M., C. S. Carter, V. van Veen, V. A. Stenger, and J. R. Anderson
  2002 Neural mechanisms of planning: a computational analysis using event-related fMRI. *Proc Natl Acad Sci USA* 99: 3346–51.
Fisher, S. E.
  2005 Dissection of molecular mechanisms underlyiing speech and language disorders. *Applied Psycholinguistics* 26: 111–128.

Fisher, S. E. and G. F. Marcus
  2006   The eloquent ape: genes, brains and the evolution of language. *Nat Rev Genet* 7: 9–20.
Fisher, S. E., F. Vargha-Khadem, K. E. Watkins, A. P. Monaco, and M. E. Pembrey
  1998   Localisation of a gene implicated in a severe speech and language disorder. *Nat Genet* 18: 168–70.
Fodor, J. A.
  1983   *The Modularity of Mind.* Cambridge (Mass.): MIT Press.
Fox, P. T. and M. E. Raichle
  1984   Stimulus rate dependence of regional cerebral blood flow in human striate cortex, demonstrated by Positron Emission Tomography. *J. Neurophysiology* 51: 1109–1120.
Friederici, A. D.
  1997   Neurophysiological aspects of language processing. *Clin Neurosci* 4: 64–72.
Friederici, A. D., Y. Wang, C. S. Herrmann, B. Maess, and U. Oertel
  2000   Localization of early syntactic processes in frontal and temporal cortical areas: a magnetoencephalographic study. *Hum Brain Mapp* 11: 1–11.
Gaillard, W. D., B. C. Sachs, J. R. Whitnah, Z. Ahmad, L. M. Balsamo, J. R. Petrella, S. H. Braniecki, C. M. McKinney, K. Hunter, B. Xu, and C. B. Grandin.
  2003   Developmental aspects of language processing: fMRI of verbal fluency in children and adults. *Hum Brain Mapp* 18: 176–85.
Gall, F. J. and K. Spurzheim
  1810   *Anatomie und Physiologie des Nervensystems im allgemeinen, und des Gehirnes insbesondere.* Paris: Schoell.
Gallese, V.
  2003   The roots of empathy: the shared manifold hypothesis and the neural basis of intersubjectivity. *Psychopathology* 36: 171–80.
Gernsbacher, M. A. and M. P. Kaschak
  2003   Neuroimaging studies of language production and comprehension. *Annu Rev Psychol* 54: 91–114.
Geschwind, N.
  1970   The organization of language and the brain. *Science* 170: 940–4.
Geschwind, D. H., B. L. Miller, C. DeCarli, and D. Carmelli
  2002   Heritability of lobar brain volumes in twins supports genetic models of cerebral laterality and handedness. Proc *Natl Acad Sci USA* 99: 3176–81.
Giedd, J. N.
  2004   Structural magnetic resonance imaging of the adolescent brain. *Ann N Y Acad Sci* 1021: 77–85.
Gopnik, M.
  1990   Feature blindness: A case study. Language Acquisition: *A Journal of Developmental Linguistics* 1: 139–164.
Gopnik, M. and M. B. Crago
  1991   Familial aggregation of a developmental language disorder. *Cognition* 39: 1–50.
Grèzes, J., J. L. Armony, J. Rowe, and R. E. Passingham
  2003   Activations related to "mirror" and "canonical" neurones in the human brain: an fMRI study. *Neuroimage* 18: 928–37.

Grodzinsky, Y.
2000 The neurology of syntax: language use without Broca's area. *Behavioral and Brain Sciences* 23: 1–71.
Hagoort, P.
2005 On Broca, brain, and binding: a new framework. *Trends Cogn Sci* 9: 416–23.
Halgren, E., R. P. Dhond, N. Christensen, C. Van Petten, L. Marinkovic, J. D. Lewine, and A. M. Dale
2002 N400-like magnetoencephalography responses modulated by semantic context, word frequency, and lexical class in sentences. *Neuroimage* 17: 1101–16.
Hamzei, F., M. Rijntjes, C. Dettmers, V. Glauche, C. Weiller, and C. Buchel
2003 The human action recognition system and its relationship to Broca's area: an fMRI study. *Neuroimage* 19: 637–44.
Haslinger, B., P. Erhard, F. Weilke, A. O. Ceballos-Baumann, P. Bartenstein, H. Gräfin von Einsiedel, M. Schwaiger, B. Conrad, and H. Boecker
2002 The role of lateral premotor-cerebellar-parietal circuits in motor sequence control: a parametric fMRI study. *Cogn Brain Res* 13: 159–68.
Heiser, M., M. Iacoboni, F. Maeda, J. Marcus, and J. C. Mazziotta
2003 The essential role of Broca's area in imitation. *Eur J Neurosci* 17: 1123–8.
Hertz-Pannier, L., C. Chiron, I. Jambaque, V. Renaux-Kieffer, P. F. Van de Moortele, O. Delalande, M. Fohlen, F. Brunelle, and D. Le Bihan
2002 Late plasticity for language in a child's non-dominant hemisphere: a pre- and post-surgery fMRI study. *Brain* 125: 361–72.
Hickok, G. and D. Poeppel
2000 Towards a functional neuroanatomy of speech perception. *Trends in Cognitive Sciences* 4: 131–8.
Holcomb, P. J., S. A. Coffey, and H. J. Neville
1992 Visual and auditory sentence processing: A developmental analysis using event-related brain potentials. *Developmental Neuropsychology* 8: 203–241.
Huttenlocher, P. R. and A. S. Dabholkar
1997 Regional differences in synaptogenesis in human cerebral cortex. *Journal of Comparative Neurology* 387: 167–78.
Huttenlocher, P. R.
1994 Synaptogenesis in human cerebral cortex. In: Geraldine Dawson and Kurt W. Fischer (eds.), *Human Behavior and the Developing Brain*, 137–152. New York: Guilford.
Iacoboni, M., I. Molnar-Szakacs, V. Gallese, G. Buccino, J. C. Mazziotta, and G. Rizzolatti
2005 Grasping the intentions of others with one's own mirror neuron system. *PLoS Biol* 3: e79.
Iacoboni, M., R. P. Woods, M. Brass, H. Bekkering, J. C. Mazziotta, and G. Rizzolatti
1999 Cortical mechanisms of human imitation. *Science* 286: 2526–8.
Indefrey, P., P. Hagoort, H. Herzog, R. J. Seitz, and C. M. Brown
2001 Syntactic processing in left prefrontal cortex is independent of lexical meaning. *Neuroimage* 14: 546–55.

Johnson, M. H.
    2000   Functional brain development in infants: elements of an interactive specialization framework. *Child Dev* 71: 75–81.
Johnson, M. H.
    2003   Development of human brain functions. *Biol Psychiatry* 54: 1312–6.
Johnson, M. H., H. Halit, S. J. Grice, and A. Karmiloff-Smith
    2002   Neuroimaging of typical and atypical development: a perspective from multiple levels of analysis. *Dev Psychopathol* 14: 521–36.
Kandel, E. R., T. M. Jessell, and J. R. Sanes
    2000   Sensory experience and the fine tuning of synaptic connections. In: E. R. Kandel, J. H. Schwartz and T. M. Jessell (eds.), *Principles of Neural Science*, 1115–30. New York: Elsevier.
Karmiloff-Smith, A.
    1994   Précis of Beyond Modularity. *Behavioral and Brain Sciences* 17: 693–745.
Kemmotsu, N., M. E. Villalobos, M. S. Gaffrey, E. Courchesne, and R.-A. Müller
    2005   Activity and functional connectivity of inferior frontal cortex associated with response conflict. *Cogn Brain Res* 24: 335–342.
Kohler, E., C., C. Keysers, M. A. Umilta, L. Fogassi, V. Gallese, and G. Rizzolatti
    2002   Hearing sounds, understanding actions: action representation in mirror neurons. *Science* 297: 846–8.
Kolb, B.
    1990   Sparing and recovery of function. In: Bryan Kolb and Richard C. Tees (eds.), *The Cerebral Cortex of the Rat*, 537–61. Cambridge (Mass.): MIT Press.
Konishi, S., K. Nakajima, I. Uchida, M. Kameyama, K. Nakahara, K. Sekihara, and Y. Miyashita
    1998   Transient activation of inferior prefrontal cortex during cognitive set shifting. *Nat Neurosci* 1: 80–4.
Krams, M., M. F. Rushworth, M. P. Deiber, R. S. Frackowiak, and R. E. Passingham
    1998   The preparation, execution and suppression of copied movements in the human brain. *Experimental Brain Research* 120: 386–98.
Kuhl, P. K.
    2000   Language, mind, and brain: Experience alters perception. In: M. S. Gazzaniga (ed.), *The New Cognitive Neurosciences*, 99–115 (2nd Edition). Cambridge, MA: MIT Press.
Lai, C. S., S. E. Fisher, J. A. Hurst, F. Vargha-Khadem, and A. P. Monaco
    2001   A forkhead-domain gene is mutated in a severe speech and language disorder. *Nature* 413: 519–23.
Lenneberg, E. H.
    1967   *Biological Foundations of Language*. New York: Wiley.
Leslie, K. R., S. H. Johnson-Frey, and S. T. Grafton
    2004   Functional imaging of face and hand imitation: towards a motor theory of empathy. *Neuroimage* 21: 601–7.
Lichtheim, L.
    1885   On aphasia. *Brain* 7: 433–484.

Liegeois, F., A. Connelly, J. H. Cross, S. G. Boyd, D. G. Gadian, F. Vargha-Khadem, and T. Baldeweg
    2004   Language reorganization in children with early-onset lesions of the left hemisphere: an fMRI study. *Brain* 127: 1229–36.

Logothetis, N. K. and J. Pfeuffer
    2004   On the nature of the BOLD fMRI contrast mechanism. *Magn Reson Imaging* 22: 1517–31.

Lu, L. H., C. M. Leonard, P. M. Thompson, E. Kan, J. Jolley, S. E. Welcome, A. W. Toga, and E. R. Sowell
    2006   Normal Developmental Changes in Inferior Frontal Gray Matter Are Associated with Improvement in Phonological Processing: A Longitudinal MRI Analysis. *Cereb Cortex*

MacDermot, K. D., E. Bonora, N. Sykes, A. M. Coupe, C. S. Lai, S. C. Vernes, F. Vargha-Khadem, F. McKenzie, R. L. Smith, A. P. Monaco, and S. E. Fisher
    2005   Identification of *FOXP2* truncation as a novel cause of developmental speech and language deficits. *Am J Hum Genet* 76: 1074–80.

MacWhinney, B., H. Feldman, K. Sacco, and R. Valdes-Perez
    2000   Online measures of basic language skills in children with early focal brain lesions. *Brain and Language* 71: 400–31.

Marcus, G. F. and S. E. Fisher
    2003   *FOXP2* in focus: what can genes tell us about speech and language? *Trends Cogn Sci* 7: 257–262.

Marinkovic, K.
    2004   Spatiotemporal dynamics of word processing in the human cortex. *Neuroscientist* 10: 142–52.

Max, J. E.
    2004   Effect of side of lesion on neuropsychological performance in childhood stroke. *J Int Neuropsychol Soc* 10: 698–708.

McCandliss, B. D., L. Cohen, and S. Dehaene
    2003   The visual word form area: expertise for reading in the fusiform gyrus. *Trends Cogn Sci* 7: 293–299.

McCarthy, G., A. M. Blamire, D. L. Rothman, R. Gruetter, and R. G. Shulman
    1993   Echo-planar magnetic resonance imaging studies of frontal cortex activation during word generation in humans. *Proceedings of the National Academy of Sciences of the United States of America* 90: 4952–6.

Miller, L. M. and M. D'Esposito
    2005   Perceptual fusion and stimulus coincidence in the cross-modal integration of speech. *J Neurosci* 25: 5884–93.

Mills, D. L., S. A. Coffey-Corina, and H. J. Neville
    1997   Language comprehension and cerebral specialization from 13 to 20 months. *Developmental Neuropsychology* 13: 397–445.

Molnar-Szakacs, I., M. Iacoboni, L. Koski, and J. C. Mazziotta
    2005   Functional segregation within pars opercularis of the inferior frontal gyrus: evidence from fMRI studies of imitation and action observation. *Cereb Cortex* 15: 986–94.

Müller, R.-A.
  2005 Neurocognitive studies of language impairment: The 'bottom-up' approach. *Applied Psycholinguistics* 26: 65–78.
Müller, R.-A., R. D. Rothermel, M. E. Behen, O. Muzik, P. K. Chakraborty, and H. T. Chugani
  1999a Language organization in patients with early and late left hemisphere lesion: a PET study. *Neuropsychologia* 37: 545–57.
Müller, R.-A., R. D. Rothermel, O. Muzik, C. Becker, D. R. Fuerst, M. E. Behen, T. J. Mangner, and H. T. Chugani
  1998a Determination of language dominance by [15O]-water PET in in children and adolescents: a comparison with the Wada test. *Journal of Epilepsy* 11: 152–161.
Müller, R.-A.
  in press Language universals in the brain: How linguistic are they? In: M. H. Christiansen, C. Collins and S. Edelman (eds.), *Language Universals,* Oxford University Press.
Müller, R.-A.
  1996 Innateness, autonomy, universality? Neurobiological approaches to language. *Behavioral and Brain Sciences* 19: 611–631.
Müller, R.-A., M. E. Behen, R. D. Rothermel, O. Muzik, P. K. Chakraborty, and H. T. Chugani
  1999b Brain organization for language in children, adolescents, and adults with left hemisphere lesion: a PET study. *Progress in Neuropsychopharmacology and Biological Psychiatry* 23: 657–668.
Müller, R.-A., H. T. Chugani, O. Muzik, R. D. Rothermel, and P. K. Chakraborty
  1997 Language and motor functions activate calcified hemisphere in patients with Sturge-Weber syndrome: a positron emission tomography study. *Journal of Child Neurology* 12: 431–437.
Müller, R.-A., R. D. Rothermel, M. E. Behen, O. Muzik, T. J. Mangner, P. K. Chakraborty, and H. T. Chugani
  1998b Brain organization of language after early unilateral lesion: a PET study. *Brain and Language* 62: 422–451.
Müller, R.-A., R. D. Rothermel, M. E. Behen, O. Muzik, T. J. Mangner, and H. T. Chugani
  1998c Differential patterns of language and motor reorganization following early left hemisphere lesion: a PET study. *Archives of Neurology* 55: 1113–1119.
Mummery, C. J., K. Patterson, C. J. Price, J. Ashburner, R. S. Frackowiak, and J. R. Hodges
  2000 A voxel-based morphometry study of semantic dementia: relationship between temporal lobe atrophy and semantic memory. *Ann Neurol* 47: 36–45.
Muter, V., S. S. Taylor, and F. Vargha-Khadem
  1997 A longitudinal study of early intellectual development in hemiplegic children. *Neuropsychologia* 35: 289–298.
Näätänen, R.
  1995 The mismatch negativity: a powerful tool for cognitive neuroscience. *Ear Hear* 16: 6–18.
Neville, H. J., D. L. Mills, and D. S. Lawson
  1992 Fractionating language: different neural subsystems with different sensitive periods. *Cereb Cortex* 2: 244–58.

Neville, H. J. and D. L. Mills
  1997   Epigenesis of language. *Mental Retardation and Developmental Disabilities Research Reviews* 3: 282–92.
Newbury, D. F., D. V. Bishop, and A. P. Monaco
  2005   Genetic influences on language impairment and phonological short-term memory. *Trends Cogn Sci* 9: 528–34.
Nishitani, N. and R. Hari.
  2002   Viewing lip forms: cortical dynamics. *Neuron* 36: 1211–20.
Nishitani, N., M. Schurmann, K. Amunts, and R. Hari
  2005   Broca's region: from action to language. *Physiology* (Bethesda) 20: 60–9.
O'Leary, D. D. and Y. Nakagawa
  2002   Patterning centers, regulatory genes and extrinsic mechanisms controlling arealization of the neocortex. *Curr Opin Neurobiol* 12: 14–25.
O'Leary, D. D. M., B. L. Schlaggar, and R. Tuttle
  1994   Specification of neocortical areas and thalamocortical connections. *Annual Review of Neuroscience* 17: 419–439.
Oberecker, R., M. Friedrich, and A. D. Friederici
  2005   Neural correlates of syntactic processing in two-year-olds. *J Cogn Neurosci* 17: 1667–78.
Ojemann, G. A.
  1991   Cortical organization of language. *Journal of Neuroscience* 11: 2281–7.
Ojemann, G. A. and C. Mateer
  1979   Cortical and subcortical organization of human communication: Evidence from stimulation studies. In: H. D. Steklis and M. J. Raleigh (eds.), *Neurobiology of Social Communication in Primates: An Evolutionary Perspective*, New York: Academic Press.
Pallas, S. L.
  2001   Intrinsic and extrinsic factors that shape neocortical specification. *Trends Neurosci* 24: 417–23.
Penfield, W. and L. Roberts
  1959   *Speech and Brain – Mechanisms*. Princeton:
Petersen, S. E., P. T. Fox, M. I. Posner, M. Mintun, and M. E. Raichle
  1989   Positron emission tomographic studies of the processing of single words. *Journal of Cognitive Neuroscience* 1: 153–170.
Petrides, M. and D. N. Pandya
  1994   Comparative architectonic analysis of the human and macque frontal cortex. In: F. Boller and J. Grafman (eds.), *Handbook of Neuropsychology*, 17–58. Amsterdam: Elsevier Science Ltd.
Petrides, M. and D. N. Pandya
  2002   Comparative cytoarchitectonic analysis of the human and the macaque ventrolateral prefrontal cortex and corticocortical connection patterns in the monkey. *Eur J Neurosci* 16: 291–310.
Piaget, J.
  1979   *L'Épistémologie génétique*. Paris: Presses Universitaires de France.
Pinker, S.
  1991   Rules of language. *Science* 253: 530–535.

Pugh, K. R., B. A. Shaywitz, S. E. Shaywitz, R. T. Constable, P. Skudlarski, R. K. Fulbright, R. A. Bronen, D. P. Shankweiler, L. Katz, J. M. Fletcher, and J. C. Gore
    1996   Cerebral organization of component processes in reading. *Brain* 119 Pt 4: 1221–38.

Raichle, M. E.
    2000   A brief history of human functional brain mapping. In: A. W. Toga and J. C. Mazziotta (eds.), *Brain mapping: The Systems*, 33–75. San Diego: Academic Press.

Rivera-Gaxiola, M., J. Silva-Pereyra, and P. K. Kuhl
    2005   Brain potentials to native and non-native speech contrasts in 7- and 11-month-old American infants. *Dev Sci* 8: 162–72.

Rizzolatti, G. and M. A. Arbib
    1998   Language within our grasp [see comments]. *Trends in Neurosciences* 21: 188–94.

Rizzolatti, G. and L. Craighero
    2004   The mirror-neuron system. *Annu Rev Neurosci* 27: 169–92.

Rubia, K., T. Russell, S. Overmeyer, M. J. Brammer, E. T. Bullmore, T. Sharma, A. Simmons, S. C. Williams, V. Giampietro, C. M. Andrew, and E. Taylor
    2001   Mapping motor inhibition: conjunctive brain activations across different versions of go/no-go and stop tasks. *Neuroimage* 13: 250–61.

Schlaggar, B. L., T. T. Brown, H. M. Lugar, K. M. Visscher, F. M. Miezin, and S. E. Petersen
    2002   Functional neuroanatomical differences between adults and school-age children in the processing of single words. *Science* 296: 1476–9.

Schlaggar, B. L., K. Fox, and D. D. O'Leary
    1993   Postsynaptic control of plasticity in developing somatosensory cortex. *Nature* 364: 623–6.

Schlaggar, B. and D. O'Leary
    1991   Potential of visual cortex to develop an array of functional units unique to somatosensory cortex. *Science* 252: 1556–1560.

Sowell, E. R., P. M. Thompson, C. M. Leonard, S. E. Welcome, E. Kan, E., and A. W. Toga
    2004   Longitudinal mapping of cortical thickness and brain growth in normal children. *J Neurosci* 24: 8223–31.

Staudt, M., K. Lidzba, W. Grodd, D. Wildgruber, M. Erb, and I. Krageloh-Mann
    2002   Right-hemispheric organization of language following early left-sided brain lesions: functional MRI topography. *Neuroimage* 16: 954–67.

Sur, M., P. E. Garraghty, and A. W. Roe
    1988   Experimentally induced visual projections into auditory thalamus and cortex. *Science* 242: 1437–41.

Sur, M., S. L. Pallas, and A. W. Roe
    1990   Cross-modal plasticity in cortical development: differentiation and specification of sensory neocortex. *Trends in Neuroscience* 13: 227–233.

Szaflarski, J. P., S. K. Holland, V. J. Schmithorst, and A. W. Byars
    2006   fMRI study of language lateralization in children and adults. *Hum Brain Mapp* 27: 202–12.

Tettamanti, M., G. Buccino, M. C. Saccuman, V. Gallese, M. Danna, P. Scifo, F. Fazio, G. Rizzolatti, S. F. Cappa, and D. Perani
    2005   Listening to action-related sentences activates fronto-parietal motor circuits. *J Cogn Neurosci* 17: 273–81.

Thomas, M. and A. Karmiloff-Smith
    2002   Are developmental disorders like cases of adult brain damage? Implications from connectionist modeling. *Behavioral and Brain Sciences* 25: 727–50.

Thompson, P. M., T. D. Cannon, K. L. Narr, T. van Erp, V. P. Poutanen, M. Huttunen, M., J. Lonnqvist, C. G. Standertskjold-Nordenstam, J. Kaprio, M. Khaledy, R. Dail, C. I. Zoumalan, and A. W. Toga
    2001   Genetic influences on brain structure. *Nat Neurosci* 4: 1253–8.

Thompson-Schill, S. L., M. D'Esposito, G. K. Aguirre, and M. J. Farah
    1997   Role of left inferior prefrontal cortex in retrieval of semantic knowledge: a reevaluation. *Proceedings of the National Academy of Sciences of the United States of America* 94: 14792–7.

Toga, A. W., P. M. Thompson, and E. R. Sowell
    2006   Mapping brain maturation. *Trends Neurosci* 29: 148–59.

Tomblin, J. B. and P. R. Buckwalter
    1998   Heritability of poor language achievement among twins. *J Speech Lang Hear Res* 41: 188–99.

Vargha-Khadem, F. and M. Mishkin
    1997   Speech and language outcome after hemispherectomy in childhood. In: I. Tuxhorn, H. Holthausen and H. E. Boenigk (eds.), *Paediatric Epilepsy Syndromes and Their Surgical Treatment*, 774–84. John Libbey.

Vargha-Khadem, F., K, E. Watkins, K. Alcock, P. Fletcher, and R. E. Passingham
    1995   Praxic and nonverbal cognitive deficits in a large family with a genetically transmitted speech and language disorder. *Procedures of the National Academy of Science USA* 92: 930–3.

Vargha-Khadem, F., L. C. Carr, E. Isaacs, E. Brett, C. Adams, and M. Mishkin
    1997   Onset of speech after left hemispherectomy in a nine-year-old boy. *Brain* 120: 159–182.

von Melchner, L., S. L. Pallas, and M. Sur
    2000   Visual behaviour mediated by retinal projections directed to the auditory pathway. *Nature* 404: 871–6.

Warburton, E., R. J. S. Wise, C. J. Price, C. Weiller, U. Hadar, S. Ramsay, S., and R. S. J. Frackowiak
    1996   Noun and verb retrieval by normal subjects. Studies with PET. *Brain* 119: 159–179.

Watkins, K. E., N. F. Dronkers, and F. Vargha-Khadem
    2002a   Behavioural analysis of an inherited speech and language disorder: comparison with acquired aphasia. *Brain* 125: 452–64.

Watkins, K. E., F. Vargha-Khadem, J. Ashburner, R. E. Passingham, A. Connelly, K. J. Friston, R. S. Frackowiak, M. Mishkin, and D. G. Gadian
    2002b   MRI analysis of an inherited speech and language disorder: structural brain abnormalities. *Brain* 125: 465–78.

Werker, J. F. and A. Vouloumanos
    2001   Speech and language processing in infancy: a neurocognitive approach. In: C. A. Nelson and M. Luciana (eds.), *Handbook of Developmental Cognitive Neuroscience*, 269–280. Cambridge (MA): MIT Press.
Wernicke, C.
    1874   *Der aphasische Symptomenkomplex.* Berlin: Springer.

3. Cognitive foundations

Katharina J. Rohlfing

What are the cognitive foundations for our language competence? This question is related to mental prerequisites that make our linguistic knowledge possible. In the last two decades, new technologies for exploring what infants know within the first year of life raised fundamental questions about our cognition. Since then, research revealed infants' early abilities in the understanding of the physical world and development of abstract concepts about objects and events. New techniques enable us to examine linguistic knowledge before children actually start to speak. In addition, results from crosslinguistic studies challenged many earlier theories and presumptions about universal processes. Even though there are many attempts to bring the two strands of investigation together, the one focussed on language acquisition and the other on the conceptual development, it is still common research practice to consider nonlinguistic aspects of cognitive development and the development of linguistic abilities separately.

In this chapter, I will argue for cognitive foundations being a phenomenon of the interaction between language and cognition. This interaction is present in infants' very early experiences, when perceptual information becomes transformed into conceptual thought as basis for communicative competence. I will provide evidence suggesting that prelinguistic sensitivity on an intersensory basis leads to crucial knowledge building up sensitivity needed for receiving and interpreting communicative information and forming knowledge about objects and events. I will further argue that some of this early prelinguistic sensitivity on an intersensory basis is still present in adults' linguistic competence. In this approach, thus, language competence is viewed as a build-up rather than a process of maturation.

1. Introduction

What are the cognitive foundations for our language competence? This question is related to mental prerequisites that make our linguistic knowledge possible. In the last two decades, new technologies for exploring what infants know within the first year of life raised fundamental questions about our cognition. Since then, research revealed infants' early abilities in the understanding of the physical world and development of abstract concepts about objects and events. New techniques enable us to examine linguistic knowledge before children actually start to speak. In addition, results from cross-linguistic studies challenged many earlier theories and presumptions about universal processes. Even though there are many attempts to bring the two strands of investigation together, the one focussed on language acquisition and the other on conceptual development (e.g. Bowerman and Levinson 2001), it is still common research practice to consider nonlinguistic aspects of cognitive development and the development of linguistic abilities separately.

In this chapter, I will argue for cognitive foundations being a phenomenon of the interaction between language and cognition. This interaction is present in infants' very early experiences, when perceptual input becomes transformed into conceptual thought as a basis for communicative competence. I will provide evidence suggesting that prelinguistic sensitivity on an intersensory basis leads to crucial knowledge building up sensitivity needed for receiving and interpreting communicative information and forming knowledge about objects and events. I will further argue that some of this early prelinguistic sensitivity on an intersensory basis is still present in adults' linguistic competence. In this approach, thus, language competence is viewed as a build-up rather than a process of maturation

2. Early debates about language mirroring cognition

2.1. Universal concepts

In the last decade, many studies addressed the issue of whether and how language mirrors the nonlinguistic cognition, which discussions concern especially the domain of space and the precise nature of the relationship between spatial language and spatial cognition (e.g., Bowerman and Choi 2003). Space is an interesting domain because, in the literature, there are suggestions that we perceive spatial scenes in schematic forms (Barsalou 1999; Chatterjee 2001), which, in turn, correspond to linguistic counterparts in the form of meaning primitives. Recently, some important studies have been published shedding more light on infants' conceptual knowledge about space at the very early age of two to four months (e.g. Needham and Baillargeon 1993; Hespos and Spelke 2004; Baillargeon 2004). Their results suggest that children know a lot about space before they can talk about it and make use of this knowledge when starting to speak. Needham and Baillargeon's studies (1993; see also Baillargeon 2004) concern infants' understanding of spatial events. They tested whether four-and-a-half-month-old infants expect an object to fall when its support is removed. In the study, infants saw a possible and an impossible test event. In the possible event, a hand deposits a box on a platform and then withdraws, leaving the box supported by the platform. In the impossible event, the hand deposits the box beyond the platform and then withdraws, leaving the box suspended in mid-air with no apparent source of support. As an effect of this study infants looked reliably longer at the impossible event suggesting that they expected the box to fall and were surprised when it did not.

The infants' physical reasoning is changing in the course of development: Already 6-month-olds are more sensitive to the kind of support, which is needed so the objects do not fall. Needham and Baillargeon (1993) conclude that infants possess intuitions about objects' behavior, which changes with child's growing experience reflecting advances in infants' manipulations of objects. This can be motivated by a new position and perspective as infants at this age become self-sitters and have new possibilities to explore objects and events, for example, sitting in a chair and playing with an object on a table. This hypothesis is supported by studies surveying infants' locomotion which allow the interpretation that locomotion creates a new level of interaction between the baby and the environment (Bertenthal, Campos and Caplovitz Barrett 1984).

This knowledge infants establish about spatial events does not seem to be induced from experience with language – what is an argument for cognition supporting language learning from the beginning. Language and space are, therefore, likely to converge at the abstract levels of conceptual structures and spatial schemas (Chatterjee 2001: 57). When using a locative preposition, it is assumed that the speaker marks the understanding of a spatial relation (Vorwerg and Rickheit 2000: 9) and the understanding of a preposition means the appropriate spatial relation is being processed.

In the discussion about the nature of the relationship between spatial language and spatial cognition, Johnston and Slobin's study (1979) put forward the idea of a language independent process of categorizing spatial events for young learners. In their study, Johnston and Slobin (1979) examined the acquisition of spatial terms in four languages (English, Turkish, Serbo-Croatian, Italian) and found that children learning different languages acquire spatial terms in a consistent order (e.g., terms for in/on are acquired before front/back). They concluded that the order reflects the way in which underlying spatial concepts are developed independently from language. Children, thus, have to develop a particular spatial concept before they can acquire the related label. The notion of a 'waiting room' (Johnston and Slobin 1979: 543) provides a metaphor, in which the linguistic factors merge with non-linguistic factors in understanding spatial prepositions. According to this metaphor, "each linguistic form has its own waiting room" (Johnston and Slobin 1979: 544). When a child discerns, primarily on non-linguistic grounds, the existence of a given locative notion, she or he will 'receive' the key to the entry door. "The entry is thus determined by conceptual acquisition of the sort generally referred to as COGNITIVE development" (Johnston and Slobin 1979: 544). The child therefore has to figure out a meaning for expressing the concept in 'waiting' (e.g. the corresponding spatial relation) in the language she or he is learning. Only then will the child use this expression.

Later studies (e.g. Sinha, Thorseng, Hayashi, and Plunkett 1999) provided more evidence for a universal development of spatial cognition: Across cultures, young children begin to talk about space at around 16 months (Bowerman 1996) and they are involved in similar spatial events such as putting things in a container or on a surface. These similarities reflect children's shared interests – a view that is also supported by language comprehension studies: Young children understand words for spatial events like containment or support much earlier than, for example, terms for occlusion or proximity (see a summary in Bowerman and Choi 2001; Casasola and Cohen 2002).

3. Language-specific concepts

A contrasting and not less persistent argument in the discussion about the relationship between spatial language and spatial cognition addresses the role that the input language plays in the developmental process of semantic categorization for space. Tomasello (1987), for example, stated that the way children use spatial expressions is not so much due to the underlying universal concepts (as put forward by Johnston and Slobin 1979), but rather to the way adults around them use spatial words. Tomasello (1987) argues against the aforementioned cognitive hypothesis and claims that, if there is a waiting room for UNDER, at the same time there should also be a waiting room for (or a shared room with) the opposite relation OVER. In his study, he observes that several prepositions designating spatial concepts are acquired later than those designated by the corresponding spatial oppositions, for example, OVER versus UNDER. These findings raise a justified question about why concepts for OVER should be different in their complexity (and the waiting rooms take different time) than for the opposite. As Tomasello (1987: 90) puts it: "if the concepts are indeed no more complex than those of the spatial oppositions, their relatively late acquisition must be explained in other than cognitive terms".

The results achieved in Bowerman and Choi (2001; reported also in Bowerman 1996) made Tomasello's argument even more persuasive showing that the meanings of children's early spatial words are language-specific and, therefore, do not entirely derive from nonlinguistic concepts. The authors compared the structuring of spatial categories in young learners (from 2;0 to 3;6) and competent adult speakers of English, Korean and Dutch. These languages differ in the way they categorize dynamic spatial events: While, for example, in English, to put a book in a bag or to put a cassette in its case is categorized as the same relation IN, in Korean, these events are categorized differently: putting a book in a bag is termed NEHTA (put X loosely in or around Y) while putting a cassette tightly into its case is KKITA (put X in a tight-fit relation with Y). Moreover, KKITA also describes a TIGHT-ON-relation like 'putting a pen top on a pen'. After a crosslinguistic comparison of the way children and adult speakers semantically classified different actions (i.e. use of the same word for a set of actions), Bowerman and Choi (2001) reported that children of every age group classified space significantly more like adult speakers of their own language than like same-age children learning the other languages. Thus, two-year-old English learners, the youngest age group in the study, categorized more like adult English speakers, whereas two-year-old Korean learners categorized more like adult Korean speakers. The authors concluded that universal perceptual and conceptual predispositions for space do not shape children's semantic categories directly, but only in interaction with the semantic structure of the language being acquired.

In a subsequent comprehension study by Choi and her colleagues (1999), English- and Korean-learning children's understanding of IN and KKITA respectively was tested. The results confirmed that children are sensitive to the spatial semantics of their target language from at least 18 months of age, i.e. Korean children were sensitive to the difference between TIGHT FIT and LOOSE FIT, whereas English children were more sensitive to the difference between CONTAINMENT and SUPPORT.

This sensitivity to spatial semantics, however, may be constrained to a restricted set of contexts, especially when children are asked to perform a specific relation. Rohlfing (2001; 2006) studied Polish children aged 20 to 26 months in their understanding of the Polish term NA (meaning roughly 'ON' in English). In these studies, different sets of objects in familiar and unfamiliar situations were presented to the participants. Children were then instructed to put, for example, a cup on a table. Rohlfing (2001) confirmed results of earlier studies (Clark 1973) suggesting that in familiar situations, children used the perceptual properties (e.g. horizontal surface) or the functions of the objects as cues for acting out the spatial word given in the instruction. With regard to the influence of the target language on the process of spatial categorization, she argues that even though in some familiar situations, two-year-olds show a good understanding of a spatial term (see also Freeman, Lloyd and Sinha 1980), the lexical knowledge about the relevant spatial term is not fully developed and can barely be transferred to an unfamiliar situation with less geometric or functional cues present (Rohlfing, 2006). Rohlfing (2001) concluded that young children's proficiency in understanding spatial terms is highly situation- and task-dependent.

If the semantic development is not robust at the age of two, then there is a possibility of a period, in which children's semantic categorization of spatial events and understanding of spatial terms is influenced by nonlinguistic factors, particularly in unfamiliar situations. A possible developmental transition from perceptual to semantic knowledge is sketched in McDonough, Choi and Mandler (2003) who investigated spatial categorization for containment in preverbal infants (being raised in either an English or Korean-speaking environment) as well as adult speakers of English and Korean. The question addressed in the study was whether preverbal infants develop fine-grained universal categories for space, which are later shaped according to linguistic influences. The results from the preferential looking experiments (McDonough et al. 2003) suggest that while 9-month-olds perceived a difference between tight and loose containment, the distinction becomes less salient in English adult speakers. In Korean, in contrast, where this difference is semantically encoded, adults remain sensitive to the difference between the two categories of containment. It seems, therefore, that during the preverbal period infants develop a large set of spatial concepts (including tight and loose IN and tight and loose ON), which may be the basis for the notion of semantic universal primitives (Mandler 1997). Some categories distinguished in early infancy may become less salient with language development when the native language does not differentiate them semantically.

With regard to nonlinguistic knowledge influencing children's semantic development, McDonough and her colleagues' study (2003) implicates that some spatial concepts may be acquired earlier in the development (Casasola and Cohen 2002; Casasola, Cohen and Chiarello 2003) and may be helpful in understanding terms for these relations (Mandler 1997). However, according to McDonough and her colleagues (2003), their study cannot tell us the general mechanism by which preverbal spatial categories become coordinated with semantic categories, because they tested only a few of the many different types of relations.

The coordination of the preverbal spatial categories with semantic categories appears dynamic and complex regarding recent research showing that different types of spatial relations may have different developmental courses. Casasola and Cohen (2002; also Casasola 2005) as well as Choi (2003, and Choi et al. 2004) suggested that the sensitivity to the language-specific categories of support (relevant for the term ON) might develop at a different time than those for the containment category (relevant for the term IN). It is reasonable to assume that these differences in developmental pattern may be driven by the more ambiguous geometry and function of a support relationship (Choi 2003).

In sum, it seems that on their way to language, children make use of non-linguistic and linguistic input and progress to an ability to coordinate this knowledge in different tasks and situations. The evidence that infants' concepts change under the influence of other information sources points to a dynamic, interactive information processing, which is used when children acquire spatial words (Bowerman and Choi 2001: 478–479). This is in line with the theory of dynamic systems (e.g. Smith and Thelen 2003), in which there is not a single factor that leads to a particular behavior in children. Language is, therefore, driven by multicausality and interaction of different knowledge sources which make the process "emergent, that is, made at the precise moment from multiple components in relation to the task and to the immediately preceding activity of the system" (Smith and Thelen 2003).

In the next section, I will argue for a newer multicausal view on language development, which highlights the interaction of language and cognition from the beginning of child's development rather than pointing out the influence of language and cognition and discussing language-specific concepts.

4. Current debates about language profiling cognition

4.1. Intersensory redundancy

Current studies about cognitive foundations for language present an intersensory interaction between language and cognition from the beginning of a child's development. Accordingly, in very young infants language already plays a significant role as a perceptual cue and applies to perceptual rather than semantic processes.

Approaches that represent this idea are based on a Gibsonian ecological view on perception. Gibson's ecological theory of perceptual development can be characterized by the interactionist view of perception and action: "Perception guides action; action makes information available for perception" (Gibson and Pick 2000: 21). In other words, children act to discover information, and by discovering information they can act (Miller 2002). Information has to be actively sought, what is achieved by the perceptual system. To describe the mechanisms of the perceptual system for the discovery of information, the notion of attention is important. Especially in infants, rather than in older children, selective attention is most pronounced and gives an initial advantage to the perceptual processing, learning, and memory (Bahrick, Lickliter, and Ross 2004).

It is important to note that according to Gibson's ecological view, perception becomes more efficient during the development. This means that children learn to select the right information that provides a fit between the environment and their knowledge and apply the most useful level of analysis for a particular task (Miller 2002). Later in this chapter, I will argue that the level of analysis becomes more symbolic with the course of child's development. But in the next passages, I will explain some mechanisms of perception and discuss how they might lead to the development of communication.

The Intersensory Redundancy Theory formulated by Bahrick, Lickliter, and Ross (2004) is an approach to explain how selective attention is achieved and how it guides the development of perception and cognition. The concept of amodal information is relevant for this approach. One example is fire, which can be seen, heard and smelled. Thus, the event of fire reaches us by amodal information, that is, "information that is not specific to a single sense modality but is redundant across more than one sense" (Bahrick, Lickliter, and Ross 2004: 99).

In the framework of the Intersensory Redundancy Theory, the basic idea is that stimulus properties that are redundant or amodal reinforce each other, become foreground and attract, thus, the attention. This process promotes earlier processing of redundantly specified properties than of other stimulus properties in early development. Thus, the infant's initial sensitivity to amodal information provides an economical way of guiding perceptual processing to focus on meaningful, unitary events:

"Intersensory redundancy refers to the spatially coordinated and temporally synchronous presentation of the same information across two or more senses and is therefore possible only for amodal properties (e.g., tempo, rhythm, duration, intensity). Thus, the sights and sounds of hands clapping provide intersensory redundancy because they are temporally synchronous, originate in the same place, and convey the same rhythm, tempo, and intensity patterns in vision and audition" (Bahrick, Lickliter, and Ross 2004: 100).

4.2. Redundancy of information guides the development of communication

An example of how intersensory redundancy might lead very young infants towards the development of communication is presented in recent studies about early understanding of pointing. Pointing is defined as referential (deictic) gesture used to reorient the attention of another person so that an object or event becomes the shared focus of attention (Butterworth 2003). In the literature, mostly eye-gaze and pointing as a manual form of deictic gesture have been considered as deictic gestures. In the past, understanding of pointing was proposed as an advanced ability of indicating (Bruner 1975: 271), and most studies have determined understanding a pointing gesture to arise between 9 and 15 months of age (Butterworth 2003; Desrochers, Morissette, and Ricard 1995). However, Deák and his colleagues (2004) found no evidence for a sudden change in understanding pointing around 9–10 months of age suggesting that learning deictic gesture might be a gradual learning process.

Looking at this gradual learning process in an ecological way, Amano, Kezuka, and Yamamoto (2004) studied infants' understanding of pointing gesture not in isolation but combined with adult's eye gaze and showed that the combination (and redundant cues) of eye gaze together with a pointing gesture might be a precursor of more advanced joint attention abilities. The authors report on the ability of 3- and 4-month-olds to follow the pointing gesture: while infants look in the same direction as adults most frequently under the condition of 'pointing with gaze', under the condition of the 'pointing without gaze while maintaining eye contact', they often remained looking at the adult's face. Interestingly, Amano, Kezuka, and Yamamoto (2004) differentiated between pointing done by an experimenter and the mothers. Their findings showed that infants need the combination of eye gaze and pointing gesture more in the case of the experimenter than in the case of the mother. In the latter, children were able to follow the pointing gesture by hand movement alone while the mothers maintained eye contact. This suggests that children paid more attention to an experimenter's face. The question remains whether children perform better in shifting their visual attention due to the fact that in the case of maternal pointing, the face is familiar and they do not pay great attention to it or due to familiarity in mothers' behavior (also their pointing behavior) in general. This finding has a similar implication to what was originally proposed by Hood, Willen, and Driver (1998) for understanding eye-gaze: If infants can focus on a stimulus and are not distracted by a copresentation of a more salient stimulus like a human face, they can show joint attention skills much earlier than reported in literature.

The purpose of the study conducted by Rohlfing, Bertenthal, and Longo (2004) was, thus, to examine whether elimination of the difficulty of disengaging fixation from salient central stimuli like the human hand would allow infants to more easily shift visual attention in the direction of pointing. This study with infants as young as 4.5 months encompassed three presentations of a pointing stimulus:

- a static, in which infants saw a hand waving to attract the infant's attention followed by a hand pointing in one or the other direction
- a dynamic, in which a hand was waving and subsequently forming a pointing gesture which moved in one or the other direction (see forwards pointing in Figure 1)
- a dynamic, in which a hand was waving, subsequently forming a pointing gesture, which moved either to the pointed direction or backwards (see backwards pointing in Figure 1)

Figure 1. Forwards and backwards pointing

The results suggest that the presentation of the stimuli is one crucial component in infants' gaze behavior. The achieved effects were similar to what was found in a study about early understanding of eye-gaze by Ferroni and her colleagues (2000), who showed that it is not the eye gaze that is cueing the shift of attention but rather the motion of the pupils. Rohlfing, Bertenthal, and Longo (2004) found that motion is an important cue for infants, but, as Farroni and her colleagues (2004) already suggested, becomes less important during the development. Accordingly, while motion of a hand rather than a combination of motion and pointing gesture is a sufficient cue to redirect 4.5 month-olds attention, in later development, 6.5-month-olds are more likely to follow a dynamic pointing gesture than just a hand motion. The results suggest, thus, a developmental pattern, according to which infants at the age of 4.5 months respond to the direction of movement; around 6.5 months, however, infants start to also be sensitive to the directionality, i.e. the orientation of the finger, which is a crucial component of the pointing gesture suggesting that at this age, the pointing gesture becomes meaningful.

A similar effect, consisting of motion reinforcing the perception of other communicational cues is reported from studies on other deictic gesture like eye-gaze: Deák and Triesch (2004) argue that motion seems to be important for attention-following. Yet, young infants' gaze-following depends on seeing the adult's head movement rather than the final head pose (Moore, Angelopoulos, and Bennett 1997). In comparison, older infants might use static head pose to infer direction of attention, which is in line with our findings. This suggests a similar developmental pattern, i.e. that the redundancy effect on attention might play a role first in more perceptual, later in the development in more conceptual or even symbolic processes – which will be shown in the next section.

In sum, initially infants appear to infer human action goals from behavioral contacts between body parts and objects, which is a simpler behavioral mechanism (Thoermer and Sodian 2001). Later in the development, the pointing gesture is linked to the referential-intentional nature of human behavior, and language might be an important factor in intentionality attribution (Thoermer and Sodian 2001).

4.3.   Language as a sensory cue

So far, I discussed perceptual information like motion that can be helpful for infants on their way to understand communicative nonverbal behavior. Can the intersensory redundancy principle also account for higher level processes like the acquisition of verbal behavior?

There is empirical evidence showing that infants are more likely to attend to a visual event when it is highlighted by speech (Horowitz 1974; McCartney and Panneton 2005), suggesting that in young infants, language plays a role as one of many possible perceptual cues. Gogate and Bahrick (2001) applied the principle of the intersensory redundancy theory to early acquisition of communication and investigated the speech signal as a help for preverbal infants to remember what they see. Infants saw a novel object, which was moved and labeled synchronously, in which condition the speech signal was reinforced by the movement of the object. Another condition was that infants saw a novel object moving and heard the novel label, in which condition the speech signal was not temporally coordinated with the movement. The authors found that moving an object in temporal synchrony with a label facilitated long-term memory for syllable-object relations in infants as young as 7 months. By providing redundant sensory information (movement and label), selective attention was affected (Gogate and Bahrick 2001). Redundant information can include temporal synchrony, spatial colocation, shared rhythm, tempo, and intensity shifts (Gogate and Bahrick 2001: 220). Gogate and Bahrick (2001) thus argue for the following reference mechanism in learning words (see also Zukow-Goldring 2006): Young infants relate words and objects by detecting intersensory redundancy across the senses in multimodal events. One type of perceptual information can be the sound as it is provided by a person when she or he speaks.

Temporal synchrony and movement seem to constitute two perceptual cues that are ecologically valid: When observing mothers interacting with their children, Gogate, Bahrick, and Watson (2000) found that mothers use temporal synchrony to highlight novel word-referent relations, i.e. they introduced a novel label to their children and moved the new object synchronously to the new label. According to the results achieved in different age groups of children, this phenomenon – observed also cross-culturally (Gogate and Prince 2005) – seems to be very prominent in preverbal children. The decrease in maternal use of temporal synchrony was observed as being well timed with infants' increased lexical abilities starting at around 14 months. At this age, however, children still seem to depend on the movement of the object when inferring the word-referent relation. In mothers of verbal children (21–30 months), less temporal synchrony or object motion was observed suggesting that they adapt to their older children's ability to glean word-referent relations on their own (Gogate, Bahrick, and Watson 2000).

This idea that the presence of a sound signal might help infants to attend to particular units within the action stream was originally proposed and termed acoustic packaging by Hirsh-Pasek and Golinkoff (1996). Hollich and his colleagues (2000) report on literature that considerably supports the notion that infants appear to rely quite heavily on the acoustic system in the phase of perceptual segmentation and extraction (see also Brand and Tapscott 2007). While this segmentation and categorization is going on, Hirsh-Pasek and Golinkoff (1996) argue that children can use this "acoustic packaging" to achieve a linkage between sounds and events (see also Zukow-Goldring, 2006) and to observe that certain events co-occur with certain sounds, like for example a door being opened with the word "open!".

In contrast to Hollich and his colleagues (2000), who suggest that in this phase, in which some event segments may be bracketed be the speech signal, there is "really nothing particularly linguistic about this phase", I propose that there is something linguistic – because socially motivated – in the speech signal. There is considerable support for linguistic differences in how events are packaged differently in different cultures (Bowerman and Choi 2003; Malt et al 2003; Furman et al. 2005). It seems therefore reasonable to assume that the linguistic differences motivated by social needs of the culture will have an impact on how events are presented, highlighted or structured.

In sum, learning and remembering of relationships between sounds and movements of objects can facilitate the discovery of word meaning and is a precursor to lexical comprehension. At this very early stage of communicative development, language provides perceptual information and the meaning of the sound has to be discovered in further development. There is, however, still a debate about whether later in the development, a qualitative change from perceptually driven to processes on a more symbolic level of cognition happens. Hirsh-Pasek and Golinkoff (1996; Golinkoff and Hirsh-Pasek 2006) propose that around their first year of life, infants move beyond prosodic mapping to semantic mapping. Hollich and his colleagues (2000) argue that children, then, begin to use the correlates of prosody, semantics, and even syntactic cues to map individual words to their referents and to establish a more symbolic system of communication and representation, which is marked by the growth of the lexicon. Other research has shown that language as a perceptual cue continues to be present even in lexically advanced children or adults: In acquisition of novel nouns, Goodman, McDonough and Brown (1998) found that information from the linguistic context might help children to choose among multiple possible items for which labels are unknown; in this study, children used the meaning of a familiar verb to limit the possible referent of a novel noun. Similarly, Strohner and his colleagues (2000) reported that if adults are presented with specific linguistic input – for example the definiteness of a noun phrase – the linguistic knowledge helps them to identify the object of reference in a scene and to react appropriately. In opposition to the qualitative change in cognitive processes as proposed by Hirsh-Pasek and Golinkoff (1996), these studies suggest that early prelinguistic sensitivity on an intersensory basis is still present in adults' linguistic competence, what Langacker (1987) calls profiling. According to his linguistic approach, profiling is a cognitive ability for directing attention and creating a reference point. Once the reference point is established, it provides mental access to the background knowledge about things and events. Language competence occurs thus as a build-up rather than a process of maturation.

4.4. Redundancy in symbolic communication

Parents continue to provide redundant information to preverbal children when presenting them relevant events. Yet the nature of the information might change from perceptual to more symbolic. In Schnur and Shatz (1984), for example, it was suggested that gesture had an effect on the children's behavior insofar as children attended more likely to openings preceded by gesture. Gesture, thus, plays a role in attracting children's attention to the interaction, which is fundamental in creating a representation of an event. Zukow-Goldring (2006) suggests that by providing cues, parents educate their children's attention. This education is helpful for further learning. Results achieved in Rowe and Pan (2004) show that mothers' pointing behavior in a book reading context correlated positively with children's vocabulary size. This suggests that pointing helped in attracting children's attention to a picture in a book, so children could map the label onto it and learn the new word more easily. Thus, two assumptions can be drawn from this study: Firstly, maternal nonverbal style (and not only conversational style) seems to correlate with the richness of learning experience in children, and secondly, semantic information relevant for language acquisition is not only provided in the speech channel but can be transferred by gesture or even motion (Goldin-Meadow 1999; Butcher and Goldin-Meadow 2006).

How well mothers adapt their verbal and nonverbal behavior to their children's cognitive and linguistic abilities is specified in a study conducted by Iverson and her colleague (1999). The authors analyzed pointing gestures of English and Italian mothers of 16 to 20 month olds. More specifically, they investigated the semantic content conveyed in pointing and classified it as reinforcing, when the gesture and the co-occured verbal message were redundant, and supplementing, when the information in gesture was significant for the reference resolution. An example for a reinforcing gesture is when a mother points at a ball and says "ball"; an example for a supplementing gesture is when a mother uses a deictic term like "take this" and points at a ball, which gesture clarifies what object she means, because only from her verbal utterance, i.e. without the pointing, it would not be clear which object she specifically refers to.

Iverson and her colleagues (1999) found that mothers' pointing behavior correlates initially with children's verbal behavior and later with children's pointing behavior. Their interpretation is that young children are not able to encode semantic information that is conveyed in gesture only. Thus, in their initial step, mothers reinforce rather than provide additional semantic information by pointing to objects or events. The effect of redundancy is revealed in mothers initial communicative steps: When children are linguistically less advanced, mothers provide the same information in different channels or modalities, in Iverson and her colleagues' study: speech and gesture.

In sum, maternal nonverbal behavior displays a positive effect of cues redundancy in later symbolic development when semantic rather than perceptual information is crucial. In the following, it is of question whether the positive effect of redundancy can be observed not only in the input provided to children, but in young learners themselves.

There is already a large body of psycholinguistic research suggesting that semantic information can be captured completely only by taking into account the interaction of verbal and nonverbal behavior (McNeill and Duncan 2000).

Goldin-Meadow (1999) highlights the role gesture plays in thinking and speaking (see also Kita and Özyürek 2003), reviewing that gesture stands on its own, substituting for speech and clearly serving a communicative function. Gesture and speech are synchronized temporally at another. Even within a single utterance, the gesture and the linguistic segment representing the same information are co-temporal. Such synchrony implies that the speaker is presenting the same meaning in both channels at the same moment and that gesture and speech form a single integrated system (Butcher and Goldin-Meadow 2000).

Unclear remains, how this ability is learned. And does the gesture-speech interaction provide insights into the cognitive communicative processes? Goldin-Meadow (1999) claims that the ability to use gesture and speech together to convey different components of a proposition is a harbinger of the ability to convey those components solely within speech. Arguing for gesture as a precursor to speech, Butcher and Goldin-Meadow (2000) presented results from a longitudinal study. The authors focussed on the role gesture plays in language development. More specifically they evaluated the semantic coherence (combining gesture with meaningful and related speech) and temporal synchrony (producing gesture in synchrony with speech). One obvious implication of their data is that there appears to be a time early in the one-word period when communicative gesture is not yet fully integrated with speech (Butcher and Goldin-Meadow 2000). This disintegration concerns both, the synchrony and the semantic coherence. For each of five tested children, three events converged: gesture-alone combination began to decline and synchronous gesture-speech combination began to increase at just the moment when gesture was first combined in the same utterance with a meaningful word (Butcher and Goldin-Meadow 2000: 248). Butcher and Goldin-Meadow (2000) inferred that the gesture-speech combination allows a child to express two elements of a sentence (one in gesture and one in speech) at a time when the child may not be able to express those elements within a single spoken utterance (Butcher and Goldin-Meadow 2000: 238). Furthermore, the authors observed that children begin producing gesture-speech combinations prior to their first two-word utterances. They conclude that gesture provides the child with an important vehicle for information that is not yet expressed in speech (Butcher and Goldin-Meadow 2000: 254; see also Özçaliskan and Goldin-Meadow 2005 for further syntactic development). Thus, to put it in Goldin-Meadow's (1999) words, gesture may serve as a way-station on the road to language, both over ontogenetic and evolutionary time.

4.5. Evolutionary connection between language and action

Even though the intersensory redundancy theory makes it plausible how an information is attended to and picked up, it does not account for the problem of reference resolution. This means that the theory applied to perceptual information does not explain how this information is processed from an intermodal input to children nor how it becomes meaningful (Malt, Sloman, and Gennari 2003). In other words, it is not obvious why from the variety of signals, children pick up the sequence of phonems and not the melody of the sentences as a speech signal and match it with an object. In this point, the psycholinguistic research offers a better explanation (McNeill 2003). Accordingly, some modalities – more specifically speech and action – work together, because they stem from the same sensomotoric origin (Rizzolatti and Arbib 1998; also Arbib 2002).

In recent neurobiological studies, the interaction of language and action is motivated by their convergence in Broca's area. This region is traditionally considered to be exclusively devoted to speech production. However, as Rizzolatti, Fogassi and Gallese (2001) report, the area was also activated in experiments, in which humans subjects observed hand or arm action. More importantly, it was identified that the activation of this area in action understanding was achieved by the mirror system consisting of mirror neurons. A mirror neuron is a neuron which is activated by both, performing an action and by observing another individual doing a specific action like grasping (Rizzolatti and Craignero 2004). As already stated above, neurobiological studies (Rizzolatti and Arbib 1998; Rizzolatti, Fogassi, and Gallese 2001) constituted an activation of mirror neurons in performance of manual as well as communicative action in primates and humans. Accordingly, the mapping of the observed actions onto one's own motor system is direct, automatic, and does not involve a sophisticated perceptual analysis (Csibra 2005). This mapping is interpreted to provide a social off-line simulation: The observation of an action causes an inner simulation, which mechanism leads to a joint representation of action ontology (Metzinger and Gallese 2003 but see also Prinz, 2003 and Csibra 2005 for criticism). The discovery of the mirror system suggests a strong link between speech and action representation and shows that the mirror system is not limited to hand movements (Rizzolatti, Fogassi, and Gallese 2001) but can be extended to intentional communication (Rizzolatti and Arbib 1998).

There are few but recent empirical studies providing support for the convergence of vocal and actoric system. Concerning the speech production, Ejiri and Masataka (2001) report about rhythmicity of arm movements in infants which are on a transition stage between precanonical to canonical babbling. Their findings based on acoustic analyses suggest that "co-occurrence of rhythmic action and vocal behavior may contribute to the infant's acquisition of the ability to perform the rapid glottal and articulatory movements that are indispensable for spoken language" (Ejiri and Masataka, 2001: 40). A further study, based on these results, investigated a coordination between vocal and motoric development in infancy (Iverson and Fagan 2004). Iverson and Fagan (2004) found that rhythmic vocalizations (consonant-vowel repetitions) were more likely to occur with movement, especially manual activity, rather than without rhythmic movement. The authors conclude that the data points to a link between "more speech-like vocalizations and manual activity that may be a precursor to coordinated manual movements of the sort involved in adult gestures" (Iverson and Fagan 2004: 1063). Indeed, in studies with adults, it was found that motion in form of noniconic movements facilitates the entry into the lexicon for weakly activated word units (Ravizza 2003). A more direct matching between words and visuomotor circuits was found in fMRI studies. The results indicate that listening to action-related sentences activates visuomotor representations of related actions (Tettamanti et al. 2005). Further cross-linguistic studies with adults on communicative movements such as their iconic gestures by Kita and Özyürek (2003) revealed that gestures used to express the same motion events were influenced simultaneously by both, how features of motion events were expressed in each language, and spatial information in the stimulus that was never verbalized. The authors concluded that gestures are generated from spatio-motoric processes that interact online with the speech production process.

Overall, the studies reported here support the view in which the speech process is tightly related to the actoric system. Iverson and Fagan (2004) assume an evolutionary relationship between vocalization and manual activity, and claim that in infants a precursor function to the more coordinated relationship of language and gesture in adults can be observed.

With reference to the intersensory redundancy theory, the convergence of action and language means that not all modalities work together and can provide redundancy of information helpful for the attentional system. Instead, the speech signal seems to create meaningful information particularly well when it is combined with actoric system activities, like motion or communicative motion such as gesture.

5. Conclusions

In this chapter, it was elaborated that primitive meanings are formed already on the perceptual level as preference for certain kind of information. On this level, verbal and actoric systems seem to work particularily efficient in reinforcing each other. As a child grows and experiences more meaningful situations, her or his attention is guided by concepts rather than perceptual preferences. Concepts – as the basis for meaning – are, therefore, more than percepts, and are acquired early for social purposes within social interactions. The influence of language plays a role at a very early stage of development already, because this kind of signal has the power to highlight relevant events. If in different cultures events are packaged differently, it seems reasonable to assume that the linguistic differences will have an impact on how events are presented or structured. This issue, however, remains open for further research and requires closer investigation of how language can structure events and how this is relevant for infants' understanding of events and actions.

The outlined body of research within the theoretical framework of intersensory redundancy contrasts with an abrupt transition from the senso-motoric to the cognitive phase of development as suggested by Piaget. Instead, the outlined research suggests a gradual building-up process starting with early semantic knowledge, which is supported by the perceptual system, and forming linguistic knowledge later in a child's development. In this view, linguistic knowledge is supported and carried by extralinguistic factors (such as sensitivity to movement). It is the goal of cognitive science to identify all the sources that lead to meaning and symbol constitution (Clark 1999).

References

Amano, S., E. Kezuka, and A. Yamamoto
    2004   Infant shifting attention from an adult's face to an adult's hand: a precursor of joint attention. *Infant Behavior and Development* 27: 64–80.
Bahrick, L. E., R. Lickliter, and R. Flom
    2004   Intersensory redundancy gudes the development of selective attention, perception and cognition in infancy. *Current Directions in Psychological Science* 13: 99–102.
Baillargeon, R.
    2004   Infants' physical world. *Current Directions in Psychological Science* 13(3): 89–94.
Barsalou, L. W.
    1999   Perceptual symbol systems. *Behavioral and Brain Sciences* 22: 577–660.
Bertenthal, B. I., J. J. Campos, and K. Caplovitz Barrett
    1987   Self-produced locomotion. An organizer of emotional, cognitive, and social development in infancy. In: R. N. Emde (ed.), *Continuities and Discontinuities in Development,* 175–210. New York: Plenum Press.
Bowerman, M.
    1996   Learning how to structure space for language: a crosslinguistic perspective. In: P. Bloom, M. Peterson, L. Nadel, and M. Garrett (eds.), *Language and Space,* 385–436. Cambridge, MA: MIT Press.
Bowerman, M. and S. Choi
    2001   Shaping meanings for language: universal and language-specific in the acquisition of spatial semantic categories. In: M. Bowerman and S. C. Levinson (eds.), *Language Acquisition and Conceptual Development,* 475–511. Cambridge: Cambridge University Press.
Bowerman, M. and S. Choi
    2003   Space under construction: language-specific spatial categorization in first language acquisition. In: D. Gentner and S. Goldin-Meadow (eds.), *Language in Mind. Advances in the Study of Language and Thought,* 387–427. Cambridge, MA: MIT Press.

Bowerman, M. and S.C. Levinson (eds.)
 2001 Language acquisition and conceptual development. Cambridge: Cambridge University Press.
Brand, R. J. and S. Tapscott
 2007 Acoustic packaging of action sequences by infants. *Infancy* 12(1): 321–332.
Bruner, J. S.
 1975 From communication to language – a psychological perspective. *Cognition* 3(3): 255–287.
Butcher, C. and S. Goldin-Meadow
 2000 Gesture and the transition from one- to two-word speech: when hand and mouth come together. In: D. McNeil (ed.), *Language and Gesture*, 235–257. Cambridge: Cambridge University Press.
Butterworth, G.
 2003 Pointing is the royal road to language for babies. In: S. Kita (ed.), *Pointing: Where Language, Culture, and Cognition Meet*, 9–33. Mahwah, NJ: Lawrence Erlbaum.
Casasola, M. and L. B. Cohen
 2002 Infant categorization of containment, support and tight-fit spatial relations. *Developmental Science* 5: 247–64.
Casasola, M., L. B. Cohen, and E. Chiarello
 2003 Six-month-old infants' categorization of containment spatial relations. *Child Development* 74: 679–693.
Chatterjee, A.
 2001 Language and space: some interactions. *Trends in Cognitive Science* 5/2: 55–61.
Choi, S.
 2003 Language-specific spatial categorization and cognition. Paper presented at the biennial meeting of the Society for Research in Child Development, 24.–27. April, Tampa, Florida.
Choi, S. and M. Bowerman.
 1991 Learning to express motion events in English and Korean: The influence of language-specific lexicalization patterns. *Cognition* 41: 83–121.
Choi, S., L. S. Greenig, E. Wilson, B. Gravis, and G. Hollich.
 2004 Preverbal spatial cognition and language-specific input: Categories of containment and support. Poster presented at the 14th Biennial International Conference on Infant Studies, 5.–8. May, Chicago, USA.
Choi, S., L. McDonough, M. Bowerman, and J. M. Mandler.
 1999 Early sensitivity to language-specific spatial categories in English and Korean. *Cognitive Development* 14: 242–268.
Cibra, G.
 2005 Mirror neurons and action observation. Is simulation involved? Interdisciplines, http://www.interdisciplines.org/mirror/papers/4
Clark, E. V.
 1973 Non-linguistic strategies and the acquisition of word meanings. *Cognition* 3: 161–82.
Clark, A.
 1999 An embodied cognitive science? *Trends in Cognitive Science* 3: 345–351.

Deák, G. O. and J. Triesch
　2004　Origins of shared attention in human infants. In: K. Fujita and S. Itakura (eds.), *Diversity of Cognition*. Kyoto University Press.
Deák, G., Y. Wakabayashi, L. Sepeta, and J. Triesch
　2004　Development of attention-sharing from 5 to 10 months of age in naturalistic interactions. Poster presented at the 14th Biennial International Conference on Infant Studies, 5.–8. May, Chicago, USA.
Desrochers, S., P. Morissette, and M. Ricard
　1995　Two perspectives on pointing in infancy. In: C. Moore and P. J. and Dunham (eds.), *Joint Attention: Its Origins and Role in Development,* 85–101. Hillsdale, NJ: Lawrence Erlbaum Associates.
Ejiri, K. and N. Masataka
　2001　Co-occurrence of preverbal vocal behavior and motor action in early infancy. *Developmental Science* 4: 40–48.
Farroni, T., M. H. Johnson, M. Brockbank, and F. Simion
　2000　nfants' use of gaze direction to cue attention: The importance of perceived motion. *Visual Cognition* 7(6): 705–718.
Farroni, T., S. Massaccesi, D. Pividori, and M. H. Johnson
　2004　Gaze following in newborns. *Infancy* 5(1): 39–60.
Gibson, E. J. and A. D. Pick
　2000　*An Ecological Approach toPperceptual Learning and Development*. Oxford: Oxford University Press.
Gogate, L. J. and L. E. Bahrick
　2001　Intersensory redundancy and 7-month-old infants' memory for arbitrary syllable-object relations. *Infancy* 2: 219–231.
Gogate, L. J., L. E. Bahrick, and J. Watson
　2000　A study of multimodal motherese: The role of temporal synchrony between verbal labels and gestures. *Child Development* 71: 878–894.
Goldin-Meadow, S.
　1999　The role of gesture in communication and thinking. *Trends in Cognitive Science* 3(11): 419–429.
Golinkoff, R.M. and K. Hirsh-Pasek
　2006　Baby wordsmith. *Current Directions in Psychological Science* 15(1): 30–33.
Goodman, J. C., L. McDonough, and N. B. Brown
　1998　The role of semantic context and memory in the acquisition of novel nouns. *Child Development* 69: 1330–1344.
Hespos, S. and E. Spelke
　2004　Conceptual precursors to language. *Nature* 430, 453–456.
Hollich, G., K. Hirsh-Pasek, M. L. Tucker, and R. M. Golinkoff
　2000　The change is afoot: Emergentist thinking in language acquisition. In: P. B. Anderson, C. Emmeche, N. O. Finnemann and P. Voetmann Christiansen (eds.), *Downward Causation,* 143–178. Århus: Aarhus University Press.
Hirsh-Pasek, K. and R. M. Golinkoff
　1996　*The Origins of Grammar: Evidence from Early Language Comprehension*. Cambridge, MA: MIT Press.

Hood, B. M., J. D. Willen, and J. Driver
    1998   Adult's eyes trigger shifts of visual attention in human infants. *Psychological Science* 9: 131–134.
Horowitz, F. D. (ed.)
    1974   *Visual Attention, Auditory Stimulation, and Language Discrimination in Young Infants*. Monographs of the Society for Research in Child Development (Serial No. 158).
Iverson, J. M. and M. K. Fagan
    2004   Infant vocal-motor coordination: Precursor to the gesture-speech system? *Child Development* 75: 1053–1066.
Iverson, J. M., O. Capirci, E. Longobardi, and C. M. Caselli
    1999   Gesturing in mother-child interactions. *Cognitive Development* 14: 57–75.
Johnston, J. R. and D. I. Slobin
    1979   The development of locative expressions in English, Italian, Serbo-Croatian and Turkish. *Journal of Child Language* 6: 529–545.
Kita, S. and A. Özyürek
    2003   What does cross-linguistic variation in semantic coordination of speech and gesture reveal? Evidence for an interface representation of spatial thinking and speaking. *Journal of Memory and Language* 48: 16–32.
Langacker, R. W.
    1987   *Foundations of Cognitive Grammar. Volume 1: Theoretical Prerequisites*. Stanford, California: Stanford University Press.
Malt, B. C., S. A. Sloman, and S. P. Gennari
    2003   Speaking versus thinking about objects and actions. In: D. Gentner and S. Goldin-Meadow (eds.). *Language in Mind. Advances in the Study of Language and Thought* 81–111. Cambridge, MA: MIT.
Mandler, J. M.
    1997   Development of categorization: Perceptual and conceptual categories. In: G. Bremner, A. Slater, and G. Butterworth (eds.), *Infant Development: Recent Advances,* 163–189. Hove, England: Psychology Press.
McCartney, J. S. and R. Panneton, R.
    2005   Four-month-olds' discrimination of voice changes in multimodal displays as a function of discrimination protocol. *Infancy* 7(2): 163–182.
McDonough, L., S. Choi, and J. Mandler
    2003   Understanding spatial relations: Flexible infants, lexical adults. *Cognitive Psychology* 46: 229–259.
McNeill, D.
    2003   Aspects of Aspect. *Gesture* 3: 1–17.
McNeill, D. and S. Duncan
    2000   Growth points in thinking-for-speaking. In: D. McNeill (ed.), *Language and Gesture,* 141–161. Cambridge: Cambridge University Press.
Metzinger, T. and V. Gallese
    2003   The emergence of a shared action ontology: Building blocks for a theory. *Consciousness and Cognition* 12: 549–571.
Miller, P. H.
    2002   *Theories of Developmental Psychology*. New York: Worth Publishers.

Moore, C., M. Angelopoulos, and P. Bennett
 1997 The role of movement in the development of joint visual attention. *Infant Behavior and Development* 2: 109–129.
Needham, A. and R. Baillargeon
 1993 Intuitions about support in 4.5-month-old infants. *Cognition* 47: 121–148.
Özçaliskan, S. and S. Goldin-Meadow
 2005 Gesture is at the cutting edge of early language development. *Cognition* 96: 101–113.
Prinz, W.
 2003 Neurons don't represent. *Consciousness and Cognition* 12: 572–573.
Ravizza, S.
 2003 Movement and lexical access: Do noniconic gestures aid in retrieval? *Psychonomic Bulletin & Review* 10(3): 610–615.
Rizzolatti, G. and M. A. Arbib
 1998 Langauge within our grasp. *Trends in Neuroscience* 21(5): 188–194.
Rizzolatti, G., L. Fogassi, L. and V. Gallese
 2001 Neurophysiological mechanisms underlying the understanding and imitation of action. *Nature Reviews Neurocience* 2: 661–670.
Rizzolatti, G. and L. Craighero
 2004 The mirror-neuron system. *Annual Review of Neuroscience* 27: 169–192.
Rohlfing, K. J.
 2001 No preposition required. The role of prepositions for the understanding of spatial relations in language acquisition. In: M. Pütz, S. Niemeier and R. Dirven (eds.), *Applied Cognitive Linguistics I: Theory and Language Acquisition,* 230–247. Berlin: Mouton de Gruyter.
Rohlfing, K. J.
 2006 Facilitating the acquisition of UNDER by means of IN and ON – a training study in Polish. *Journal of Child Language,* 51–69.
Rohlfing, K. J., M. R. Longo, and B. I. Bertenthal
 2004 Following pointing. Does gesture trigger shifts of visual attention in human infants? Poster presented at 14th Biennial International Conference on Infant Studies, 5.–8. May, Chicago, Illinois.
Rowe, M. and B. A. Pan
 2004 Maternal pointing and toddler vocabulary production during bookreading versus toy play. Poster presented at the 14th Biennial International Conference on Infant Studies, 5.–8. May, Chicago, USA.
Schnur, E. and M. Shatz
 1984 The role of maternal gesturing in conversations with one-year-olds. *Journal of Child Language* 11: 29–41.
Sinha, C., L. Thorseng, M. Hayashi, and K. Plunkett
 1999 Spatial language acquisition in Danish, English and Japanese. In P. Broeder. and J. Murre (eds.), *Language and Thought in Development,* 95–125. Cross Linguistic Studies. Tübingen: Gunter Narr.
Smith, L. B. and E. Thelen
 2003 Development as a dynamic system. *Trends in Cognitive Science* 7: 343–48.

Strohner, H., L. Sichelschmidt, I. Duwe, and K. Kessler
   2000   Discourse focus and conceptional relations in resolving referential ambiguity. *Journal of Psycholinguistic Research* 29: 497–516.

Tettamanti, M., G. Buccino, M. C. Saccuman, V. Gallese, M. Danna, P. Scifo, R. Fazio, G. Rizzolatti, S. R. Cappa, and D. Perani
   2005   Listening to action-related sentences activates fronto-parietal motor circuits. *Journal of Cognitive Neuroscience* 17(2): 273–281.

Thoermer, C. and B. Sodian
   2001   Preverbal infants' understanding of referential gestures. *First Language* 21: 245–264.

Tomasello, M.
   1987   Learning to use prepositions: A case study. *Journal of Child Language* 14: 79–98.

Tomasello, M. and L. Camaioni
   1997   A comparison of the gestural communication of apes and human infants. *Human Development* 40: 7–24.

Vorwerg, C. and G. Rickheit
   2000   Repräsentation und sprachliche Enkodierung räumlicher Relationen. In: C. Habel and C. von Stutterheim (eds.), *Räumliche Konzepte und sprachliche Strukturen*, 9–44. Tübingen: Niemeyer.

Zukow-Goldring, P.
   2006   Assisted imitation: Affordances, effectivities, and the mirror system in early language development. In M. A. Arbib (ed.). *From Action to Language*, 469–500. Cambridge: Cambridge University Press.

4. First utterances

Holly L. Storkel

This chapter traces the development of phonological (individual sounds), lexical (whole-word forms), and semantic (meaning) representations from birth through early school-age. Infants appear to extract regularities in the ambient language that allow them to develop receptive and expressive phonological skills to set the foundation for initial word learning. These skills allow the child to acquire first words, albeit at a somewhat slow rate. However, children also extract regularities from these first words, and this allows them to more rapidly hone in on and store the correct sound sequence and meaning of novel words. These early representations of words are dynamic, changing over the course of development.

1. Introduction

In order to learn a language, a child must learn the grammar of the language including the sounds, rules for combining sounds, words, rules for combining words, morphemes, and rules for combining morphemes. In this chapter, the focus is on learning sounds and words. First utterances typically consist of strings of sounds produced in the absence of a specified meaning, namely babble, followed by single words that may or may not be correctly produced relative to the adult target. To begin to produce first words, the child must create three types of representations: phonological, lexical, and semantic. A phonological representation corresponds to the representation of individual sounds that can be used in multiple words of the language. For example, the phonological representation of "baby" is /b/ /eɪ/ /b/ /i/. The phonological representation determines production accuracy and is partially developed through babble. A lexical representation corresponds to the sound sequence of a word as a whole unit. Continuing the example, the lexical representation of "baby" is /beɪbi/. The lexical representation is accessed to produce or recognize a word. The semantic representation corresponds to the meaning of the word. Thus, the semantic representation for "baby" would be 'a very young child'. The semantic representation is accessed to select a word to express a desired intention or to comprehend the intention of another. To know a word, a child must create both a lexical and a semantic representation and store these in her mental lexicon. Importantly, these three types of representations must be linked to one another so that language expression and comprehension can occur.

Typically developing children appear to rapidly acquire these three types of representations. Infants begin to babble around 6 to 8 months of age, and by 8 to 10 months of age, babbling begins to more closely resemble the sound system of the native language (de Boysson-Bardies and Vihman 1991). Phonological development continues as first words and word combinations are learned with the sound system being mastered by early elementary school (approximately 7–9 years). Lexical and semantic acquisition also is quite rapid. Studies have shown that infants as young as 7.5 months are able to recognize words that they have heard in isolation in fluent speech (Jusczyk and Aslin 1995). Moreover, it is estimated that infants (12–23 months) learn approximately one word per day, toddlers (23–30 months) learn approximately 1.6 words per day, preschool children (30–72 months) learn approximately 3.6 words per day, and school-age children (6–10 years) learn 6.6 to 12 words per day (Bloom 2000).

What skills allow a child to rapidly acquire the phonological, lexical, and semantic representations needed to support first utterances? First, the child must learn to segment a continuous speech stream to identify the words that need to be learned. Second, the child must map the consistency between sound sequences and meanings to acquire the words of the language. The child's early phonological abilities appear to influence this process. Third, the child must recognize regularities or patterns in the native language to become a word learning expert. Finally, a child must continue to refine representations over time as more words are learned.

2. Segmentation

The first challenge an infant language learner faces is segmentation of a continuous speech stream into words. Unlike written language, there are no spaces or reliable pauses between words in spoken language. Moreover, infants hear relatively few words presented in isolation. Even when parents are instructed to teach words to 12-month-old infants, only approximately 20% of words (on average) are presented in isolation with great variability across parents (Aslin, Woodward, LaMendola, and Bever 1996; Woodward and Aslin 1990l). Consequently, a language learner must learn other cues to determine where one word starts and another word ends. Infants appear to develop the ability to use a sophisticated set of cues, including prosodic, phonemic, and phonetic, to support fast and accurate speech segmentation.

2.1. Prosodic cues

Prosodic or suprasegmental cues refer to those cues that are expressed across individual sounds such as pitch and stress (Trask 1997). One cue to word segmentation in English may be word stress. Stress refers to the prominence of a particular syllable in a word such that the stressed syllable is louder, longer, and higher in pitch than the unstressed syllables (Trask 1997). Cutler and Carter (1987) analyzed a corpus of spoken English and found that approximately 90% of content words in English follow a strong-weak (i.e., trochaic) stress pattern. Through a series of studies, Cutler and colleagues demonstrated that English speaking adults use a parsing strategy whereby strong syllables are assumed to indicate the onset of a new word (Cutler and Butterfield 1992; Cutler and Norris 1988; McQueen, Norris, and Cutler 1994).

This ability to use the predominant stress pattern as a cue for speech segmentation appears to emerge around 7.5 months of age. Jusczyk, Houston, and Newsome (1999) used the head turn preference procedure to examine this issue. In this procedure, the infant is seated on the caregiver's lap. Gaze is directed to a center point by a blinking light. Once this center or neutral orientation has been achieved, the infant's gaze is attracted to one side by a flashing light on that side. Once the child orients to the flashing red light, a stimulus is delivered through a speaker in the same location. The stimulus plays in its entirety or is discontinued when the infant's gaze is diverted from the target location for longer than 2 seconds. The infant's looking time is measured for each stimulus as an indicator of how long the infant listened or attended to the auditory stimulus.

Jusczyk and colleagues (1999) familiarized 7.5-month-old infants with two syllable words embedded in meaningful passages. Then, the infants were tested on their recognition of the familiarized words in isolation using the head turn preference procedure. Listening time for the embedded two syllable words when presented in isolation was compared to listening time for unfamiliar (i.e., non-exposed) two syllable words. Results showed that 7.5-month-old infants listened longer to familiarized strong-weak words than to unfamiliar strong-weak words. Thus, infants were able to segment the strong-weak words from the rest of the passage and recognize these words later when presented in isolation. In contrast, 7.5-month-old infants listened longer to only the strong syllable of familiarized weak-strong words. This pattern indicates that infants incorrectly segmented the weak-strong words when presented in the passage. Both patterns together suggest that infants tend to assume that strong syllables indicate the beginning of a new word, leading to correct segmentation of strong-weak words but potentially incorrect segmentation of weak-strong words.

In a follow-up study, Houston, Santelmann, and Jusczyk (2004) demonstrated that 7.5-month-old infants also were able to segment three syllable strong-weak-strong words from continuous speech, but only if the first strong syllable received primary stress. Thus, English-learning infants appear to assume that strong syllables receiving primary stress mark the beginning of a word. Given the predominant pattern of English, this is a relatively useful strategy; however, infants must develop additional strategies to learn words that do not conform to this predominant pattern. In support of this, 10.5-month-old infants do not show the same difficulty segmenting weak-strong words as displayed by 7.5-month-old infants, indicating that older infants rely on more than just stress to segment speech (Jusczyk, Houston et al. 1999).

2.2. Phonemic cues

In addition to regularities in stress patterns, languages also show regularity in the sequencing of phonemes. Phonemes are the basic sound unit of a language and are used to contrast meaning (Trask 1997). Phonotactics refer to the rules that determine which sequences of phonemes are allowed to occur within words in a particular language (Trask 1997). For example, /br/ in English can occur in initial position but not word final position. Infants appear to be sensitive to the phonotactic patterns of their native language by 9 months, preferring to listen to sound sequences that obey the phonotactics of their native language over sound sequences that violate the phonotactics of their native language (Friederici and Wessels 1993; Jusczyk, Friederici, Wessels, Svenkerud, and Jusczyk 1993). Thus, children may mark word boundaries between impermissible phoneme sequences.

Sound sequences also vary in their likelihood of occurrence, termed phonotactic probability. That is, certain phonemes are more likely to occur in certain word positions than other phonemes, termed positional segment frequency. Likewise, certain phonemes are more likely to co-occur together in a particular word position than other phoneme pairs, termed biphone frequency. Like phonotactics, phonotactic probability could be a cue for segmentation. For example, the biphone frequency of two sounds within a word will likely be higher than the biphone frequency of two sounds that occur across a word boundary. Thus, children might mark a word boundary between two sounds that have a low biphone frequency rather than two sounds that have a high biphone frequency. This possibility is strengthened by the fact that children appear to learn the phonotactic probability of their native language by 9 months (Jusczyk, Luce, and Charles-Luce 1994). When presented with lists of monosyllables that contained high probability versus low probability phoneme sequences in English, 9-month-old English learning infants listened longer to the high probability lists than the low probability lists. In contrast, 6-month-old English learning infants showed no such preference.

Direct evidence of infants' ability to use phonotactic probability to aid in segmentation is provided by Mattys and colleagues (Mattys and Jusczyk 2001; Mattys, Jusczyk, Luce, and Morgan 1999). Mattys and colleagues (1999) presented 9-month-old infants with two syllable words that varied in the phonotactic probability of a medial consonant sequence (CVC.CVC) such that some words had a consonant sequence with a high probability of co-occurring within a word and others had a low probability of co-occurring within a word. Results showed that infants listened longer to the two syllable words with high probability internal consonant sequences than low probability internal consonant sequences. This suggests that infants segmented the two syllables as being one word when the medial consonants had a high co-occurrence; whereas they segmented the two syllables into separate words when the medial consonants had a low co-occurrence.

A related concept is transitional probability, the likelihood that a specific sound or syllable will follow another specific sound or syllable. Infants as young as 8-months are able to learn transitional probabilities present in artificial languages from relatively brief exposure to continuous speech (e.g., Aslin, Saffran, and Newport 1998; Saffran, Aslin, and Newport 1996). These studies also used the head turn preference procedure. Infants were familiarized to an artificial language consisting of strings of three syllable words presented in continuous speech. An artificial language was used because it allows precise control over other factors that infants might use to segment the speech stream. The only reliable cue for segmentation in these artificial languages was the transitional probability. Specifically, syllable pairs that occurred within words had high transitional probabilities, whereas syllable pairs that occurred across word boundaries had low transitional probabilities. Following familiarization to the artificial language, infants were presented with three syllable strings that were either words or nonwords in the artificial language. Results showed that infants listened longer to nonwords than words, showing a novelty effect for the nonwords relative to the more familiar words. Thus, infants appeared to extract words from continuous speech based on transitional probabilities.

2.3.   Phonetic cues

To this point, we have primarily been considering phonemes, sounds that are used to contrast meaning (Trask 1997). However, the phonetic realization of a phoneme can vary by context. That is, each phoneme has a variety of different phonetic forms termed allophones (Trask 1997). Knowing the contexts where different allophones of a given phoneme occur may help infants segment speech into words. For example, the aspirated [t] allophone of the phoneme /t/ tends to begin words in English (e.g., "top") and tends not to occur in other contexts (e.g., "stop" or "hot"; Church 1987). Thus, an infant might assume that a new word begins whenever an aspirated [t] is present.

Jusczyk, Hohne, and Bauman (1999) investigated this issue in 10.5-month-old infants using the headturn preference procedure. Infants were familiarized with a word, "nitrate", or a pair of words sharing the same phoneme sequence, "night rate", in isolation. While the two stimuli share the same phonemic sequence, the allophones of the phonemes differ in the single word versus the word pair sequence. For "nitrate", the first /t/ is aspirated, released, and retroflexed and the /r/ is devoiced. For "night rate", the first /t/ is unaspirated and unreleased and the /r/ is voiced. After familiarization with either "nitrate" or "night rate" in isolation, the infants were tested on both items in passages. Results showed that 10.5-month-old infants listened longer to the familiar word (either "nitrate" or "night rate") than to the unfamiliar word presented in the passage, indicating that they were able to distinguish "nitrate" from "night rate" in continuous speech. In contrast, 9-month old infants listened equally to the familiar and unfamiliar words when presented in a passage, suggesting that younger infants confuse phonemically similar words in continuous speech. Taken together, the ability to use allophonic cues for segmentation appears to emerge around 10.5 months.

2.4. Integration of cues

It is clear that infants have a range of useful cues available to segment continuous speech. What remains less clear is how infants integrate or weight these cues, particularly in situations where cues may be in conflict with one another. Johnson and Jusczyk (2001) provide a preliminary examination of this issue by pitting prosodic cues against phonemic cues. In their study, 8-month-old infants were exposed to an artificial language consisting of three syllable words. In the artificial language, prosodic cues indicated one particular segmentation pattern and transitional probabilities indicated a different segmentation pattern due to patterns of syllable occurrence across the entire sample. For example, in the unsegmented stream tibudogolaTUdaropi, the syllable TU could be taken as beginning a word because it is a stressed syllable; however, based on transitional probabilities across the entire sample, TU could be taken as ending the word "golaTU." Infants were familiarized with the artificial language and then tested on sequences that may or may not have been words in the artificial language depending on how the infants segmented the speech stream during familiarization. Results showed that infants segmented the speech stream using stress cues rather than transitional probabilities. This suggests that prosodic cues may be weighted more heavily than phonemic cues in conflicting contexts, but further work is needed to investigate the relative weighting of other cues.

3. First words

As infants are learning the prosodic, phonemic, and phonetic cues needed to segment the speech stream into words, they are also gaining practice producing these same cues in their babble. Infants vocalize almost immediately after birth; however, these first vocalizations typically are not identified as true babble. One commonly used taxonomy identifies five stages of vocalizations (Oller 1980). Stage 1, from birth to 1 month, consists primarily of reflexive vocalizations (e.g., burps, grunts, cries) and quasi-resonant nuclei. Quasi-resonant nuclei refer to vowel-like or syllabic-like consonants that are distinct from reflexive vocalizations. Stage 2, from 2 to 3 months, is characterized by primitive consonant-vowel combinations with a predominant use of back sounds (e.g., velars and uvulars). This is sometimes referred to as the "goo" stage. Stage 3, from 4 to 6 months, is a period of vocal play where the infant increases the range and type of vocalizations used. Variability in production is typical during this stage. Stage 4, from 7 to 9 months, marks the onset of true babbling. Repetition of a given consonant-vowel sequence, namely reduplicated babbling, is common in this stage. Stage 5, from 10 to 12 months, is characterized by varied consonant vowel sequences, such that a given syllable or phoneme may not be repeated. This is often referred to as variegated babbling. The prosodic patterns during this stage match the native language, often leading parents to comment that the child has her own language.

By 12 months of age, the infant's speech production system has taken on many characteristics of the target language. The majority of sounds produced are clearly recognized as belonging to the native language, setting the stage for production of first words which tend to emerge around 10 to 14 months. Productive phonology appears to influence production of first words. Typically developing children learn words composed of sounds that are observed in their babbling (Ferguson and Farwell 1975; Oller, Wieman, Doyle, and Ross 1976; Stoel-Gammon and Cooper 1984; Velleman and Vihman 2002; Vihman, Ferguson, and Elbert 1986; Vihman, Macken, Miller, Simmons, and Miller 1985). These studies have typically focused on naturalistic collection of speech samples with subsequent analysis and comparison of phonology in babble and phonological characteristics of the words attempted and/or learned. For example, Stoel-Gammon and Cooper (1984) examined the consonantal phones used in babbling and compared this to the consonantal phones used in first words by three children who were approximately one year of age at the beginning of the study. Over half the phones observed in babbling were produced in first words. About half of the phones that children babbled but did not produce in first words were non-English sounds that would not be targeted by English words. Likewise, Vihman and colleagues (1985) showed that the distribution of consonants and the syllable structure of first words were identical to that of babble. This finding suggests continuity between babbling and first words.

This association between productive phonology and word learning is observed in children with precocious language development as well as children with delayed language development (Paul and Jennings 1992; Stoel-Gammon and Dale 1988, May; Thal, Oroz, and McCaw 1995; Whitehurst, Smith, Fischel, Arnold, and Lonigan 1991). Specifically, children who know many words tend to produce a greater variety of sounds than children who know few words. Moreover, increasing the expressive vocabulary of a child with an expressive language delay may lead to subsequent improvements in phonological diversity (Girolametto, Pearce, and Weitzman 1997; but see Whitehurst, Fischel et al. 1991).

Experimental studies provide further evidence of the relationship between phonology and first words (Bird and Chapman 1998; Leonard, Schwartz, Morris, and Chapman 1981; Schwartz and Leonard 1982; Schwartz, Leonard, Loeb, and Swanson 1987). In these studies, typically developing children with productive vocabularies of 50 words or fewer were exposed to novel words composed of sounds that the child produced in other words, termed IN sounds, and novel words composed of sounds that the child did not produce in other words, termed OUT sounds. In addition, one of these studies examined sounds that the child had previously attempted in production but never produced accurately, ATTEMPTED sounds (Schwartz et al. 1987). Across these studies, children more readily learned words composed of IN sounds than those composed of OUT or ATTEMPTED sounds when naming was tested. There was no effect of sound production (i.e., IN, OUT, ATTEMPTED) on word learning when comprehension was tested.

Taken together, there appears to be a relationship between productive phonology and the earliest stage of expressive word learning (i.e., 0–50 words or approximately 12–18 months). This has lead some to posit that productive phonology may act as a constraint on word learning (Vihman 1993). Specifically, children may develop phonological templates from their babbling experience and then select words that are similar to these templates, facilitating rapid acquisition of a productive vocabulary (Velleman and Vihman 2002). This rapid acquisition of vocabulary comes at the expense of phonological diversity. Children appear to learn words that are similar to their phonological templates but tend to change the target adult production to better match their phonological templates. This leads to inaccurate production of words relative to the adult target. Thus, at some point, children must abandon their phonological templates to move towards accurate production of words. It is unclear exactly when this occurs, but evidence suggests that it happens by at least 3 years of age. Specifically, Storkel (2004b; 2006) showed that typically developing 3- to 4-year-old children learned words composed of OUT sounds faster than words composed of IN sounds, the reverse effect of that observed at the earliest stage of word learning. Storkel suggested that this reversal may be related to salience. During the earliest stage of word learning, the infant knows few sounds relative to the full sound repertoire of the language. Thus, words containing the few known sounds, IN sounds, are more salient than words containing unknown sounds, OUT sounds. In contrast, preschool children have mastered a larger number of sounds from the full sound repertoire of the language and only a few sounds remain unknown. Consequently, words containing the few unknown sounds, OUT sounds, may be more salient than words containing the many known sounds, IN sounds.

4. Later words: The development of expertise

It has been argued that children learn their first 50 words at a relatively slow pace but once the 50 word threshold has been crossed, the pace of word learning may increase (Fenson et al. 1994; Goldfield and Reznick 1990, 1996). This is referred to as the vocabulary spurt, and it is not without controversy in terms of its timing and even its existence. However, there is evidence that learning words helps children learn how to better learn words. An example of this comes from the work of Linda Smith and colleagues on semantic and syntactic influences on word learning. Smith and colleagues have examined the factors that affect learning of count nouns (as well as other types of words). Count nouns are individuated objects that can be enumerated (Trask 1997). For example, "dog," "girl," "desk," and "glass" are all examples of count nouns. Compare this to mass nouns, which are not individuated objects, such as "water" or "sand" (Trask 1997). In English, count nouns and mass nouns also may be differentiated by syntax. Specifically, count nouns can be preceded by indefinite articles (e.g., "a dog") or numerals (e.g., "one dog") and can be pluralized (e.g., "dogs"); whereas mass nouns can be preceded by quantifiers (e.g., "much water") but not indefinite articles or numerals and can not be pluralized. Another important difference between count and mass nouns as documented by Samuelson and Smith (1999) is that the early count nouns learned by young children tend to share shape. That is, all the objects that could be labeled by a specific count noun tend to be the same shape (e.g., all "dogs" are dog-shaped). If children learned this regularity, then they would only need to see one object that was labeled by a specific count noun, and they could then infer that other objects that were the same shape as the original object would be called by the same name.

Gershkoff-Stowe and Smith (2004) completed a longitudinal study to determine when children learned to attend to shape during word learning. Parents of the participating children were instructed to keep diaries of their children's spoken vocabulary growth. Parents were contacted weekly by phone to determine the number of words their children had learned. Once children started producing some nouns, but fewer than 25 nouns, the experimental task was initiated. This vocabulary size occurred at approximately 16 to 20 months of age. The experimental task was a noun generalization task. Each child was shown an unusual object that was named with the nonsense word "dax." Then the child was shown the trained object and five novel objects that varied in similarity to the trained object (i.e., objects that shared shape, color, or material with the trained object). The experimenter selected the trained object and labeled it again and instructed the child to find another "dax." This exact task was repeated every three weeks until the parent diary showed that the child had learned 75–100 nouns. The question of interest was, "when would children identify the same shaped novel objects as also being called 'dax'"?

Results showed that children's shape choices increased as the size of their vocabulary increased. When children knew between 0–25 nouns, they were equally likely to select novel objects that shared shape as they were to select a novel object that shared another dimension (i.e., color or material or both). This also was true when their productive noun vocabulary was 26–50 words. In contrast, when children had learned 51–100 nouns, they selected novel objects that shared shape more often than objects that shared any other dimension (i.e., color or material or both). Interestingly, the timing of the emergence of a shape bias in the experimental task was tightly linked to a relatively dramatic increase in the learning of real count nouns based on the parent diary. Thus, acquisition of a shape bias, as demonstrated in the laboratory, was correlated with a rapid increase in count noun learning outside the laboratory. This transition point varied by age, from 17 to 23 months, and by the size of the productive noun vocabulary, from 27 to 73 nouns.

Smith, Jones, Landau, Gershkoff-Stowe, and Samuelson (2002) provide further evidence of this link between the emergence of the shape bias and an increase in noun learning through a training study. In this study, 17-month-old children who did not show a shape bias were trained on four shape-based categories. Learning of a shape bias was measured using a generalization task similar to Gershkoff-Stowe and Smith (2004), and vocabulary growth outside the laboratory was tracked using the MacArthur Communicative Development Inventory, a checklist of the words known by toddlers (Fenson et al. 1993). Results showed that the training did promote the early emergence of a shape bias. Importantly, the rate of noun learning outside the laboratory increased dramatically over the training period. Taken together, typically developing toddlers appear to acquire a shape bias by learning words that refer to objects that are similar in shape. In turn, the emergence of the shape bias corresponds to a rapid increase in the rate of noun learning. Thus, children appear to extract regularities from the words they know and use these regularities to facilitate rapid acquisition of new words.

Interestingly, children who demonstrate early delays in word learning do not appear to have acquired a shape bias (Jones 2003). Jones (2003) compared novel name generalization by 2- and 3-year-old children identified as late talkers to that by 2- and 3-year-old children with age-appropriate productive vocabularies. Children identified as late talkers in this study had productive vocabularies below the 30th percentile for their age, a relatively liberal criterion. As expected, children with age-appropriate vocabularies demonstrated a shape bias in the generalization task, selecting novel objects that were the same shape as the trained object. In contrast, children identified as late talkers showed no clear bias in the generalization task, selecting novel objects relatively randomly. Analysis of individual children showed that half of the typically developing children showed a significant shape bias; whereas approximately half of the children identified as late talkers showed a significant texture bias. To conclude, it seems that children who are learning words more slowly than their same aged peers tend not to attend to shape. This does not necessarily mean that the lack of emergence of a shape bias causes vocabulary delays, but does indicate that these two behaviors co-occur with further research needed to examine causal pathways.

Sound based regularities also influence later word learning. As previously discussed, phonotactic probability is the likelihood of occurrence of a sound sequence in a language. Not only does phonotactic probability influence speech segmentation, it also influences word learning. Early studies that examined the influence of phonotactic probability on word learning examined the effect of phonotactic probability when correlated with lexical density. Lexical density refers to the number of words that are phonologically similar to a given word. This is frequently operationally defined as those words that differ by only one phoneme, either a substitution, addition, or deletion in any word position, from a given word (Luce and Pisoni 1998). These two variables are correlated in English with words that have high probability sound sequences tending to have many lexical neighbors and words that have low probability sound sequences tending to have few lexical neighbors (Storkel 2004c; Vitevitch, Luce, Pisoni, and Auer 1999).

Storkel and colleagues have examined the effect of correlated phonotactic probability and lexical density on word learning across a variety of ages and types of words. In these tasks, children are exposed to nonwords that systematically vary in phonotactic probability and lexical density, namely high probability/high density versus low probability/low density. The nonwords are paired with novel or unfamiliar objects with the semantic category of the objects balanced across the two probability/density conditions. The nonword – object pairs are then embedded in a story with accompanying pictures. Learning is measured across exposures to the words, using a picture naming task and/or a referent identification task. In the picture naming task, children are shown the novel objects and asked to produce the appropriate nonword name. In the referent identification task, children hear the nonword and are asked to select the corresponding novel object from a field of choices, varying from 3 to 6.

In this series of studies, Storkel and colleagues showed that children learn high probability/density novel words more rapidly than low probability/density words across a variety of contexts. In particular, phonotactic probability/lexical density influenced word learning by preschool and school-age children when learning nouns (Storkel 2001; Storkel and Rogers 2000). The breadth of this influence was documented further by examining verb learning (Storkel 2003) and homonym learning (i.e., learning a new meaning for a known sequence such as "bat" the animal vs. "bat" the sporting equipment, Storkel and Maekawa 2005; Storkel and Young 2004). In addition, the external validity of these laboratory findings was investigated using existing naturalistic cross-sectional data (Storkel 2004a) and longitudinal data (Maekawa and Storkel 2006). Thus, like semantic regularities, sound regularities also appear to influence word learning.

Storkel and colleagues went on to attempt to differentiate the effect of phonotactic probability from that of lexical density by orthogonally varying both factors (i.e., high probability/high density, high probability/low density, low probability/high density, low probability/low density) in an experimental study of adults and by analyzing a naturalistic corpus of the words known by 16- to 30-month-old children (Storkel 2007; Storkel, Armbruster, and Hogan 2006). Both methods showed a unique effect of phonotactic probability and lexical density. In terms of phonotactic probability, young children and adults learned low probability sound sequences more rapidly than high probability sound sequences. In terms of lexical density, young children and adults learned high density sound sequences more rapidly than low density sound sequences.

Storkel and colleagues posited that phonotactic probability may be critical in triggering new learning. That is, when a sound sequence is heard, one must decide whether the sound sequence is known, entailing retrieval of known information from memory, or novel, entailing the need to learn the new sequence. Because low probability sound sequences are more unique in the language than high probability sound sequences are, detecting the novelty of low probability sound sequences may be faster with learning initiated almost immediately. Storkel and colleagues further suggested that lexical density may be more influential in the creation and retention of new representations in memory. The new lexical representation of a dense word will form associations with many other known words and this may strengthen the new representation, leading to faster learning. In contrast, the new lexical representation of a sparse word will form associations with few other known words. As a result, greater exposure to the sparse word may be required to create a sufficiently detailed representation to support naming or comprehension.

Storkel (2006) also attempted to examine developmental changes in the interaction between phonotactic probability, lexical density and semantic density. Semantic density was defined as the number of words that were meaningfully related to or frequently associated with a given word. Semantic density values were taken from a database developed by Nelson, McEvoy, and Schreiber (1998). Nelson and colleagues presented words to adults and asked them to report the first word that came to mind that was meaningfully related to or frequently associated with the given word. Words reported by two or more participants were counted as semantic neighbors of the target word. As previously discussed, Storkel's analysis of a naturalistic corpus of words known by toddlers showed that more children knew low probability than high probability words, and more children knew words with many lexical neighbors than words with few lexical neighbors. The effect of semantic density was similar with more children knowing words with many semantic neighbors than words with few semantic neighbors. Interestingly, a developmental analysis showed that the effect of phonotactic probability on word learning was relatively constant from 16 to 30 months; whereas the effects of lexical density and semantic density changed over this age range. Specifically, the effect of lexical density decreased as age increased. In contrast, the effect of semantic density increased as age increased. This suggests that the factors that affect word learning may vary across development. Not only do children continue to learn words, they continue to refine how they learn words.

5. Nature of linguistic representation in the mind

Once a child has learned an association between a sound form and a meaning, the child is able to select the appropriate object when the name is heard and produce the appropriate name when the object is seen, in many cases. However, formation of these initial representations and associations is not the end of word learning. Lexical and semantic representations of words are elaborated and refined as the child gains greater experience with a particular word and as the child learns other words that are similar to that word. Thus, the mental representations of words may change with development.

Much evidence suggests that infants can perceive fine differences in auditory stimuli (see segmentation section of this chapter), but recent work suggests that infants have difficulty creating representations of words that capture this fine detail. Werker, Fennell, Corcoran, and Stager (2002) examined infants' ability to learn minimally different words (i.e., two words that differed by only one sound) using a modified habituation paradigm. In this paradigm, the infant is seated on the caregiver's lap. The infant's gaze is directed to a flashing light in the center of the room. Once the infant fixates on the center light, a pretest stimulus consisting of an auditory label and an unusual object is presented for 20 seconds. The infant's looking/listening time is recorded. Then the two test stimuli (e.g., the name "dih" with the object "molecule" and the name "bih" paired with the object "crown") are presented in a random order in blocks of four trials using the same procedure. When the average looking time across a four-trial block decreases to a preset criterion, the habituation phase is discontinued. The logic here is that the infant's habituation to the stimuli indicates familiarity or learning of the stimuli. After habituation, the test phase is initiated. During the test phase, the infant is presented with an object-name pairing that was the same as the habituation phase (e.g., the name "dih" paired with the object "molecule") and an object-name pairing that differed from the habituation phase, namely a switch trial. The switch trial consists of pairing one of the trained labels (e.g., "dih") with one of the trained objects that it was not paired with during habituation (e.g., "crown"). Thus, both the label and the object are familiar but their pairing is novel. Looking/listening time is recorded to determine whether infants detect this novelty.

Results showed that 17- and 20-month-old infants looked/listened longer to switch trials than to same trials, indicating that they recognized the switch. Thus, 17- and 20-month-old children appeared to learn the phonologically similar names. In contrast, 14-month-old infants looked/listened equally to the switch trials and the same trials, indicating that the change in pairings was not recognized. Thus, 14-month-old infants did not appear to learn the phonologically similar names. For the 14-month-olds, there was variability in performance with some infants detecting the switch and others not detecting the switch. Importantly, 14-month-old infants are able to learn two phonologically dissimilar words (e.g., Werker, Cohen, Lloyd, Casasola, and Stager 1998). The ability to learn phonologically similar words appeared to be related to vocabulary size. In Werker and colleagues (2002), infants who knew more words detected the shift, demonstrating evidence of learning the phonologically similar words; whereas, infants who knew fewer words did not detect the shift, suggesting that they had not learned the phonologically similar words. Werker and colleagues (2002) attempted to identify the cross-over point in vocabulary size that best sorted the infants into those who detected the shift/learned phonologically similar words and those who did not. The sharpest cut-offs were observed at expressive lexicons of 25 words and receptive lexicons of 200 words. Thus, learning words appears to help infants learn how to learn words. In this case, learning words appeared to facilitate acquisition of minimally different words.

The fact that infants who know 25 words in production or 200 words in comprehension can learn phonologically similar words suggests that representations of words may contain detailed phonological and semantic information. However, other studies suggest that this may not be the case. Classification studies have been used with preschool and early elementary school children. These tasks ask children to make overt judgments about the similarity among words. In some cases, children are asked to sort words into groups either of the child's making or the examiner's (i.e., identify the words that are like a given word vs. not like a given word). In other cases, children are given a set of three words and asked to either identify the one that does not belong (i.e., odd man out) or identify the two that go together (i.e., create a pair). Results from these paradigms suggest that children have difficulty forming groups based on shared phonemes (e.g., Treiman and Baron 1981; Treiman and Breaux 1982; Walley, Smith, and Jusczyk 1986). The position of the overlap also seems to matter in these classification tasks. Some have found that young children are more successful identifying shared phonemes at the beginnings of words rather than at the ends of words (e.g., Walley et al. 1986); whereas, others show the opposite pattern (e.g., Treiman and Zukowski 1991).

Taken together, these findings lead to the hypothesis that children may not store segmentally detailed information about the entire word form, but rather may store more holistic information about parts of the word form. This position has been formalized by Metsala and Walley as the lexical restructuring model (Metsala and Walley 1998; Walley, Metsala, and Garlock 2003). According to this model, lexical representations are initially holistic but become segmentally detailed across development due to vocabulary growth. This segmental restructuring is argued to be a gradual process that does not occur uniformly across the lexicon. That is, certain words are more likely to be restructured than others. In particular, words that are used frequently, that have resided in the lexicon longer, and that have many lexical neighbors are thought to be restructured earlier than words that are used infrequently, that have recently been added to the lexicon, and that have few lexical neighbors.

Storkel (2002) provides evidence in support of this model. Storkel examined classification by 3- to 5-year-old children of words with many lexical neighbors and words with few lexical neighbors. A sorting task was used where children were told that a character bank (e.g., a bear) had a favorite word and that every time the child heard a word like the bank's favorite word, the child should place a token in the bank. If the word was not like the favorite word, then the child should place a token in a toy trash can. The comparison words for each favorite word varied in the position of similarity: initial consonant-vowel of a consonant-vowel-consonant word (e.g., "tap" and "tan") or vowel-final consonant of a consonant-vowel-consonant word (e.g., "tap" and "map"). In addition, the type of similarity of between the favorite word and the comparison words also varied, including shared phonemes (e.g., "tap" and "tan" where the initial consonants are both /t/), shared manner (e.g., "tap" and "pan" where the initial consonants are both stops), or shared place (e.g., "tap" and "sang" where the initial consonants are both alveolar).

Turning to the results, when the favorite word had many lexical neighbors, children classified comparison words that shared phonemes in the initial or final position as similar to the favorite word. Comparison words that shared either manner or place in either the initial or final position were not judged as similar to the favorite word. This pattern suggests that 3- to 5-year-old children had segmentally detailed representations of the entire word when the word had many lexical neighbors. When the favorite word had few lexical neighbors, children classified comparison words that shared phonemes in initial position, or shared phonemes in final position, or shared manner in final position as similar to the favorite word. The remaining comparison words were not judged as similar to the favorite word. This pattern indicates that 3- to 5-year-old children had segmentally detailed representations of the initial portion of words with few lexical neighbors but holistic representations of the final portion of words with few lexical neighbors. This pattern supports the lexical restructuring model.

Garlock, Walley, and Metsala (2001) provide further support for the lexical restructuring model by examining young children's (i.e., pre-school and kindergarten), older children's (i.e., first and second grade), and adult's word recognition performance in a gating task. In a gating task, words are presented to participants in incrementally longer units with participants being asked to identify the word and rate their confidence in the accuracy of their response. In this study, the first gate corresponded to the first 100 ms of the word. Successive gates increased by 50 ms (e.g., 100 ms, 150 ms, 200 ms, 250 ms, 300 ms, 350 ms, etc.) until the word was played in its entirety. Two dependent variables were calculated: isolation point and total acceptance point. The isolation point was the stimulus duration when a word was first correctly identified. The total acceptance point was the stimulus duration when a word was correctly identified and the confidence rating was high. In this study, results were similar across these two dependent variables. Garlock and colleagues also manipulated the lexical characteristics of the words presented in the gating task. Words varied in age-of-acquisition, number of lexical neighbors, and word frequency.

Results showed that young children, older children, and adults needed more input to recognize later acquired words than earlier acquired words. This difference was smaller for the young children than the older children and adults. This finding supports the hypothesis that earlier acquired words are more likely to have segmentally detailed representations than later acquired words. Turning to the lexical neighbors, older children and adults needed more input to recognize words with many neighbors than words with few neighbors. This supports the hypothesis that words with many neighbors are more likely to have segmentally detailed representations than words with few neighbors due to the competitive effect that neighbors have on recognition. In contrast, young children needed the same amount of input to recognize words with many neighbors and words with few neighbors. Importantly, recognition of sparse words appeared to change more dramatically across age than dense words, suggesting that words with few lexical neighbors underwent lexical restructuring over this age range, whereas lexical restructuring had already occurred for words with many lexical neighbors. Frequency of occurrence minimally affected recognition, suggesting that age-of-acquisition and lexical density may be the critical determinants of lexical restructuring.

Like restructuring of lexical representations, there also is evidence that semantic representations change over time (McGregor, Friedman, Reilly, and Newman 2002). McGregor and colleagues (2002) examined the semantic representations of 5-year-old children. Children were asked to name pictures and then draw and define the same words without pictures. The most frequent type of error made in picture naming was a semantic error where children reported a word that was meaningfully related to the target picture (e.g., "cup" for "water pitcher"). Children's drawings were rated on completeness and accuracy by adults using a 7-point scale. Drawings of words that were named with semantic errors were compared to those of words that were correctly named. Drawings of semantically misnamed objects were rated as less complete and accurate than drawings of correctly named objects. Comparison of definitions of semantically misnamed versus correctly named words showed similar results. Definitions were scored for the number of correct information units. Definitions of semantically misnamed objects contained fewer accurate pieces of information than definitions of correctly named objects. From these two pieces of information, it was possible to hypothesize about the underlying cause of children's semantic errors. For approximately half of the semantic errors, children did not seem to know the word as evidenced by the lowest possible drawing score and a lack of any accurate information in the definition. For slightly less than half of the semantic errors, children appeared to have an impoverished semantic representation as indicated by a moderately accurate drawing and definition. That is, children seemed to know something about the word, but key elements were missing. Very few semantic errors (approximately 10%) resulted from temporary retrieval failures as characterized by incorrect naming but highly accurate and detailed drawings and definitions. Thus, there appears to be a continuum of knowledge for semantic representations from missing to partial to detailed and complete.

6. Conclusions

As detailed in this chapter, children have an amazing ability to extract regularities in the ambient language and then use these regularities to learn language. Children use prosodic, phonemic, and phonetic cues of their native language to segment the speech stream into words between 7.5 and 10.5 months of age. During that same time, children mimic the characteristics of the ambient language in their babbling. These receptive and expressive phonological skills set the stage for word learning. First words in production are initially constrained by the child's phonological system. This constraint eventually diminishes. At the same time, children extract regularities from the words they have learned, such as count nouns share shape, and this learning of regularities further facilitates word learning. Moreover, once a child has created a lexical and semantic representation of a word in memory, these representations are further refined with greater exposure to the word and as other similar words are learned. Taken together, word learning is a dynamic developmental process whereby the relevant cues change over time (Hollich et al. 2000).

Acknowledgment. Preparation of this chapter was supported by NIH grant DC04781; DC08095. Address for Correspondence: Holly L. Storkel, University of Kansas, Department of Speech-Language-Hearing: Sciences and Disorders, Dole Human Development Center, 1000 Sunnyside Ave., Room 3001, Lawrence, KS 66045-7555 USA, hstorkel@ku.edu, www.ku.edu/~wrdlrng/.

References

Aslin, R. N., J. R. Saffran, and E. L. Newport
    1998   Computation of conditional probability statistics by 8-month-old infants. *Psychological Science* 9: 321–324.
Aslin, R. N., J. Z. Woodward, N. P. LaMendola, N. P., and T. G. Bever
    1996   Models of word segmentation in fluent maternal speech to infants. In: J. L. Morgan and K. Demuth (eds.), *Signal to Syntax: Bootstrapping from Speech to Grammar in Early Acquisition* 117–134). Mahwah, N. J.: Lawrence Erlbaum Associates.
Bird, E. K. R. and R. S. Chapman
    1998   Partial representations and phonological selectivity in the comprehension of 13- to 16-month-olds. *First Language* 18: 105–127.
Bloom, P.
    2000   *How Children Learn the Meanings of Words*. Cambridge, MA: MIT Press.
Church, K. W.
    1987   *Phonological Parsing and Lexical Retrieval*. Dordrecht: Kluwer.
Cutler, A. and S. Butterfield
    1992   Rhythmic cues to speech segmentation: Evidence from juncture misperception. *Journal of Memory and Language* 31: 218–236.
Cutler, A. and D. Carter
    1987   The predominance of strong initial syllables in the English vocabulary. *Computer Speech and Language* 2: 133–142.
Cutler, A. and D. G. Norris
    1988   The role of strong syllables in segmentation for lexical access. *Journal of Experimental Psychology: Human Perception and Performance* 14: 113–121.
de Boysson-Bardies, B. and M. M. Vihman
    1991   Adaptation to language: Evidence from babbling and first words in four languages. *Language* 67: 297–319.
Fenson, L., P. S. Dale, J. S. Reznick, E. Bates, D. Thal, and S. Pethick
    1994   Variability in early communicative development. *Monographs of the Society for Research in Child Development* 59.
Fenson, L., P. S. Dale, J. S. Reznick, D. Thal, E. Bates, J. P. Hartung, S. Pethick, and J. S. Reilly
    1993   *The MacArthur Communicative Development Inventories: User's Guide and Technical Manual*. San Diego: Singular Publishing Group.

Ferguson, C. A. and C. B. Farwell
   1975   Words and sounds in early language acquisition. *Language* 51: 419–439.
Friederici, A. D. and J. M. Wessels
   1993   Phonotactic knowledge of word boundaries and its use in infant speech perception. *Perception and Psychophysics* 54: 287–295.
Garlock, V. M., A. C. Walley, and J. L. Metsala
   2001   Age-of-acquisition, word frequency, and neighborhood density effects on spoken word recognition by children and adults. *Journal of Memory and Language* 45: 468–492.
Gershkoff-Stowe, L. and L. B. Smith
   2004   Shape and the first hundred nouns. *Child Development* 75: 1098–1114.
Girolametto, L., P. S. Pearce, and E. Weitzman
   1997   Effects of lexical intervention on the phonology of late talkers. *Journal of Speech, Language, and Hearing Research* 40: 338–348.
Goldfield, B. A. and J. S. Reznick
   1990   Early lexical acquisition: rate, content, and the vocabulary spurt. *Journal of Child Language* 17: 171–183.
Goldfield, B. A. and J. S. Reznick
   1996   Measuring the vocabulary spurt: a reply to Mervis and Bertrand. *Journal of Child Language* 23: 241–246.
Hollich, G. J., K. Hirsh-Pasek, R. M. Golinkoff, R. J. Brand, E. Brown, H. L. Chung, E. Hennon, and C. Rocroi
   2000   Breaking the language barrier: An emergentist coalition model for the origins of word learning. *Monographs of the Society for Research in Child Development*, 65: v–123.
Houston, D. M., L. M. Santelmann, and P. W. Jusczyk
   2004   English-learning infants' segmentation of trisyllabic words from fluent speech. *Language and Cognitive Processes* 19: 97–136.
Johnson, E. K. and P. W. Jusczyk
   2001   Word segmentation by 8-month-olds: When speech cues count more than statistics. *Journal of Memory and Language* 44: 548–567.
Jones, S. S.
   2003   Late talkers show no shape bias in a novel name extension task. *Developmental Science* 6: 477–483.
Jusczyk, P. W. and R. N. Aslin
   1995   Infants' detection of the sound patterns of words in fluent speech. *Cognitive Psychology* 29: 1–23.
Jusczyk, P. W., A. D. Friederici, J. M. Wessels, V. Y. Svenkerud, and A. M. Jusczyk
   1993   Infants' sensitivity to sound patterns of native language words. *Journal of Memory and Language* 32: 402–420.
Jusczyk, P. W., E. A. Hohne, and A. Bauman
   1999   Infants' sensitivity to allophonic cues for word segmentation. *Perception and Psychophysics* 61: 1465–1476.
Jusczyk, P. W., D. M. Houston, and M. Newsome
   1999   The beginnings of word segmentation in English-learning infants. *Cognition Psychology* 39: 159–207.

Jusczyk, P. W., P. A. Luce, and J. Charles-Luce.
   1994   Infants' sensitivity to phonotactic patterns in the native language. *Journal of Memory and Language* 33: 630–645.

Leonard, L. B., R. G. Schwartz, B. Morris, B., and K. Chapman
   1981   Factors influencing early lexical acquisition: lexical orientation and phonological composition. *Child Development* 52: 882–887.

Luce, P. A. and D. B. Pisoni
   1998   Recognizing spoken words: The neighborhood activation model. *Ear and Hearing* 19: 1–36.

Maekawa, J. and H. L. Storkel
   2006   Individual differences in the influence of phonological characteristics on expressive vocabulary development by young children. *Journal of Child Language* 33: 439–459.

Mattys, S. L. and P. W. Jusczyk
   2001   Phonotactic cues for segmentation of fluent speech by infants. *Cognition* 78: 91–121.

Mattys, S. L., P. W. Jusczyk, P. A. Luce, and J. L: Morgan
   1999   Phonotactic and prosodic effects on word segmentation in infants. *Cognitive Psychology* 38: 465–494.

McGregor, K., R. Friedman, R. Reilly, and Newman
   2002   Semantic representation and naming in young children. *Journal of Speech, Language and Hearing Research* 45: 332–346.

McQueen, J., D. Norris, and A. Cutler
   1994   Competition in spoken word recognition: Spotting words in other words. *Journal of Experimental Psychology: Learning, Memory, and Cognition* 20: 621–638.

Metsala, J. L. and A. C. Walley
   1998   Spoken vocabulary growth and the segmental restructuring of lexical representations: Precursors to phonemic awareness and early reading ability. In: J. L. Metsala and L. C. Ehri (eds.), *Word Recognition in Beginning Literacy*, 89–120. Mahwah, NJ: Lawrence Erlbaum Associates, Inc., Publishers.

Nelson, D., C. McEvoy, and T. Schreiber
   1998   The University of South Florida word association, rhyme, and word fragment norms [WWW document]. Retrieved, from the World Wide Web: http://www.usf.edu/FreeAssociation/

Oller, D. K.
   1980   The emergence of speech sounds in infancy. In: G. Yeni-Komshian and K. J. A. and C. A. Ferguson (es.), *Child Phonology*, 93–112. (Vol. 1). New York: Academic Press.

Oller, D. K., L. Wieman, W. Doyle, and C. Ross
   1976   Infant babbling and speech. *Journal of Child Language* 3: 1–11.

Paul, R. and P. Jennings
   1992   Phonological behavior in toddlers with slow expressive language development. *Journal of Speech and Hearing Research* 35: 99–107.

Saffran, J. R., R. N. Aslin, and E. L. Newport
   1996   Statistical learning by 8-month-old infants. *Science* 274: 1926–1928.

Samuelson, L. K. and L. B. Smith
   1999   Early noun vocabularies: Do ontology, category structure and syntax correspond? *Cognition* 73: 1–33.
Schwartz, R. G. and L. B. Leonard
   1982   Do children pick and choose? An examination of phonological selection and avoidance in early lexical acquisition. *Journal of Child Language* 9: 319–336.
Schwartz, R. G., L. B. Leonard, D. M. Loeb, and L. A. Swanson
   1987   Attempted sounds are sometimes not: an expanded view of phonological selection and avoidance. *Journal of Child Language* 14: 411–418.
Smith, L. B., S. S. Jones, B. Landau, L. Gershkoff-Stowe, and L. Samuelson
   2002   Object name learning provides on-the-job training for attention. *Psychological Science* 13: 13–19.
Stoel-Gammon, C. and J. A. Cooper
   1984   Patterns of early lexical and phonological development. *Journal of Child Language* 11: 247–271.
Stoel-Gammon, C. and P. Dale
   1988   Aspects of phonological development of linguistically precocious talkers. Paper presented at the Paper presented at Child Phonology Conference, University of Illinois, Champaign-Urbana.
Storkel, H. L.
   2001   Learning new words: Phonotactic probability in language development. *Journal of Speech, Language, and Hearing Research* 44: 1321–1337.
Storkel, H. L.
   2002   Restructuring of similarity neighbourhoods in the developing mental lexicon. *Journal of Child Language* 29: 251–274.
Storkel, H. L.
   2003   Learning new words II: Phonotactic probability in verb learning. *Journal of Speech, Language and Hearing Research* 46: 1312–1323.
Storkel, H. L.
   2004a   Do children acquire dense neighbourhoods? An investigation of similarity neighbourhoods in lexical acquisition. *Journal of Applied Psycholinguistics* 25: 201–221.
Storkel, H. L.
   2004b   The emerging lexicon of children with phonological delays: Phonotactic constraints and probability in acquisition. *Journal of Speech, Language, and Hearing Research* 47: 1194–1212.
Storkel, H. L.
   2004c   Methods for minimizing the confounding effects of word length in the analysis of phonotactic probability and neighborhood density. *Journal of Speech, Language and Hearing Research* 47: 1454–1468.
Storkel, H. L.
   2007   *Word learning II: Developmental differences in the effects of phonological, lexical, and semantic variables on word learning by toddlers.* Manuscript submitted for publication.

Storkel, H. L.
    2006   Do children still pick and choose? The relationship between phonological knowledge and lexical acquisition beyond 50 words. *Clinical Linguistics and Phonetics* 20:523–529.

Storkel, H. L., J. Armbruster, and T. P. Hogan
    2006   Differentiating phonotactic probability and neighborhood density in adult word learning. *Journal of Speech, Language, and Hearing Research,* 49: 1175–1192.

Storkel, H. L. and J. Maekawa
    2005   A comparison of homonym and novel word learning: The role of phonotactic probability and word frequency. *Journal of Child Language,* 32: 827–853.

Storkel, H. L. and M. A. Rogers
    2000   The effect of probabilistic phonotactics on lexical acquisition. *Clinical Linguistics and Phonetics* 14: 407–425.

Storkel, H. L. and J. M. Young
    2004   Homonymy in the developing mental lexicon. In: L. M. A. Brugos and C. E. Smith (eds.), *Proceedings of the 28th annual Boston University Conference on Language Development,* 577–584. Somerville, MA: Cascadilla Press.

Thal, D. J., M. Oroz, and V. McCaw
    1995   Phonological and lexical development in normal and late talking toddlers. *Applied Psycholinguistics* 16: 407–424.

Trask, R. L.
    1997   *A Student's Dictionary of Language and Linguistics.* London: Arnold.

Treiman, R. J. and Baron
    1981   Segmental analysis ability: Development and relation to reading ability. In: G. E. MacKinnon and T. G. Waller (eds.), *Reading Research: Advances in Theory and Practice,* 159–198. New York: Academic Press.

Treiman, R. and M. Breaux
    1982   Common phoneme and overall similarity relations among spoken syllables: Their use by children and adults. *Journal of Psycholinguistic Research* 11: 569–598.

Treiman, R. and A. Zukowski
    1991   Levels of phonological awareness. In: S. A. Brady and D. P. Shankweiler (eds.), *Phonological Processes in Literacy: A Tribute to Isabelle Y. Liberman,* 67–83. Hillsdale, NJ: Lawrence Erlbaum Associates, Inc.

Velleman, S. and M. Vihman
    2002   Whole-word phonology and templates: Trap, bootstrap, or some of each? *Language, Speech, and Hearing Services in Schools* 33: 9–23.

Vihman, M. M.
    1993   Variable paths to early word production. *Journal of Phonetics* 21: 61–82.

Vihman, M. M., C. A. Ferguson, and M. Elbert
    1986   Phonological development from babbling to speech: Common tendencies and individual differences. *Applied Psycholinguistics* 7: 3–40.

Vihman, M. M., M. A. Macken, R. Miller, H. Simmons, and J. Miller
    1985   From babbling to speech: A re-assessment of the continuity issue. *Language* 61: 397–445.

Vitevitch, M. S., P. A. Luce, D. B. Pisoni, and E. T. Auer
   1999   Phonotactics, neighborhood activation, and lexical access for spoken words. *Brain and Language* 68: 306–311.

Walley, A. C., J. L. Metsala, and V. M. Garlock
   2003   Spoken vocabulary growth: Its role in the development of phoneme awareness and early reading ability. *Reading and Writing: An Interdisciplinary Journal* 16: 5–20.

Walley, A. C., L. B. Smith, and P. W. Jusczyk
   1986   The role of phonemes and syllables in the perceived similarity of speech sounds for children. *Memory and Cognition* 14: 220–229.

Werker, J. F., L. B. Cohen, V. L. Lloyd, M. Casasola, and C. L. Stager
   1998   Acquisition of word-object associations by 14-month-old infants. *Developmental Psychology* 34: 1289–1309.

Werker, J. F., C. T. Fennell, K. M. Corcoran, and C. L. Stager
   2002   Infants' ability to learn phonetically similar words: Effects of age and vocabulary size. *Infancy* 3: 1–30.

Whitehurst, G. J., J. E. Fischel, C. J. Lonigan, M. C. Valdez-Menchaca, D. S. Arnold, and M. Smith
   1991   Treatment of early expressive language delay: If, when, and how. *Topics in Language Disorders* 11: 55–68.

Whitehurst, G. J., M. Smith, J. E. Fischel, D. S. Arnold, and C. J. Lonigan
   1991   The continuity of babble and speech in children with specific expressive language delay. *Journal of Speech and Hearing Research* 34: 1121–1129.

Woodward, A. and R. N. Aslin
   1990, April   Segmentation cues in maternal speech to infants. Paper presented at the International Conference on Infant Studies, Montreal, Quebec, Canada.

5. Discourse acquisition

Clair Pond and Michael Siegal

Often inspired by the framework proposed by Grice (1975), substantial work has been devoted to the extent to which children are capable of following the intended implications of speakers in conversation. In this chapter, we examine children's conversational understanding and proficiency in discourse in terms of their responses on measures designed to determine their ability to detect ambiguous messages and to follow the implications of questions on a range of tasks that concern the ability to distinguish between reality and the phenomenal world of appearances. We proceed to discuss tests of 'explicit' and 'implicit' conversational understanding in terms of children's message processing strategies. Based on their performance on measures of conversational understanding (e.g., such as those that involve "scalar implicatures" and the processing of "garden path sentences"), results point to the development of attentional mechanisms that enable children with increasing age to process conversation as intended and to engage in discourse proficiently.

1. Grice's account of communication

Historically, the nature of communication has been framed in terms of a code model (Shannon 1948; Shannon and Weaver 1949), the basis of which Sperber and Wilson (1995) trace back as far as the writings of Aristotle. Such an account held that communication results from the use of a conventional code into which messages are systematically encoded by speakers into utterances and then decoded by listeners to enable comprehension. Thus discourse proficiency could be reduced to the use and appreciation of standard phonetic-semantic representation pairings. However, such a depiction denies the considerable role of context in utterance interpretation. The situation in which an utterance occurs can be used to assign reference to deictic terms (such as 'you'/'I') as well as to semantically ambiguous expressions. For example, the meaning of the expression 'he was acting as a chair' can vary contextually depending on whether it was said at a conference or in a drama school. Communicative circumstances can also be used to enrich messages. For example, when asked the time, we usually expect an answer that refers to five minute intervals or to a half or quarter hour rather than time in between (2.25 pm rather than 2.26.31) and we assume that a message such as "Can you pass the salt?" amounts to a request for action rather than a yes or no answer that one is capable of salt passing.

The innovation of the work of Paul Grice (1975) was to emphasise the function of intentions within deliberate communication. Grice conceptualised communicative activity in terms of the effect of the expression and recognition of speaker intentions upon the listener's representation of the world. Appreciation of these intentions was considered to provoke listeners to work to realise the exact nature of the intended effect. Grice envisaged communication as an inferential process in which listeners treat utterances as evidence of communicative intentions that can be discovered by a process of active, critical assessment. He depicted comprehension of communicated utterances as a product of rational activity, involving analysis of discourse in accordance with a 'Cooperative Principle' and maxims (or rules) of conversational etiquette. Under Grice's theory, contextual effects arise as the result of maxim-based reasoning under the Cooperative Principle that speakers strive to work together to support the realization of speaker intentions.

To adhere to the Cooperative Principle, speakers and listeners interpret conversation in terms of rules that govern the informativeness, validity, relevance and clarity of their contributions, enabling the participants to draw conclusions beyond those stemming from the literal/semantic 'decoding' of utterances. As characterized by Grice, these rules or maxims of conversation consist of the Maxims of Quantity ('Make your contribution as informative as is required. Do not make your contribution more informative than is required.'), the Maxims of Quality ('Do not say that which you believe to be false. Do not say that for which you lack adequate evidence.'), the Maxim of Relation ('Be relevant.') and the Maxims of Manner ('Avoid obscurity of expression. Avoid ambiguity. Be brief. Be orderly.')

Consider the case where a husband has been informed that his wife is thirsty, to which he replies, "There is a Spar shop over the road." In accordance with the Maxim of Quality, his wife can expect this statement to be accurate (i.e., There actually is a Spar shop over the road), to refer to the chain of Spar shops familiar to her in accordance with the Maxim of Manner, to be relevant to her state of thirst in accordance with the Maxim of Relation, and not to require further expansion in accordance with the Maxim of Quantity (i.e. there is nothing else she ought to be told, such as that the shop is closed until next week). These considerations enable the wife to go beyond the literal/semantic meaning of the utterance, enabling her to infer her husband's intention to indicate that she could quench her current thirst by going over to the shop and purchasing a drink.

However, as Grice pointed out, it is not always possible to accommodate all the maxims satisfactorily. For example, a speaker might be asked a question for which he lacks precise knowledge such as when a school term starts. Wishing to comply with the Maxim of Quantity but not wanting to violate the Maxim of Quality, he might produce an approximate answer, e.g., "sometime in January." Despite satisfying the Maxims of Quality, Relation and Manner, such a statement would fail to fulfill the Maxim of Quantity. However, consideration of the underinformativeness of this utterance in light of the cooperative nature of the exchange would prompt the listener to draw the inference that it was not within the speaker's power to be more informative (i.e., that he did not know the exact start date of the new term). Again, the listener is able to go beyond the basic, semantic meaning of the utterance to infer the speaker's intention to communicate that he did not know the precise start date.

Moreover, there are occasions on which cooperative speakers deliberately violate maxims to exploit the effects on the interpretation of utterances. Consider an example where having been told some frustrating information about a husband's state of tidiness, his wife responds, "Well, he's a man!" Such a phrase would violate the Maxim of Quantity since the wife's statement is not informative – it goes without saying that her husband is necessarily a man. However, by considering such a statement in light of the cooperative nature of the exchange that assumes adherence to the Maxim of Relation, one can infer that the wife intended to emphasise the manly quality of her husband, to communicate that this quality is relevant to her frustration, i.e., men are generally frustrating. Once more, the listener has been enabled to go beyond the basic semantic interpretation to access the speaker intentions.

Sperber and Wilson (1995) point out that the originality of Grice's approach was not in his conception of communication in terms the recognition of speaker intentions, but in his proposal that appreciation of these intentions was all that was necessary to explain utterance comprehension, however this was achieved. Grice argued that an established code was not necessary. To illustrate how communication without coding could occur, imagine a person asking if you would drive him somewhere. In response, you might hold up a half empty wine bottle. There is no standard coded meaning associated with holding up a wine bottle, and indeed if one does concede that there is, it would likely be with offering a drink. However, in this context, such behaviour would provide evidence that you have been drinking, and would allow your communicative partner to infer your intention to convey this message. The listener would then arrive at the inference that you were neither fit nor legal to drive.

Grice's framework permits insight into how it might be that communication is able to extend beyond literal semantics. Appreciation of sarcasm, metaphor and irony requires an explanation for non-literal interpretation – one that involves a consideration of how children come to acquire this sort of proficiency in discourse.

2. Development of children's understanding of the message-meaning distinction

Clearly, children's conversational understanding develops with age. Is this because they suddenly achieve knowledge of the relevant conversational rules? Or is this because they become better able with age to apply an ability that is already 'implicitly' in their possession and that requires attention to when and how it should be used? Some early findings are consistent with the former alternative and seemed to provide evidence that children typically below around 6- or 7-years of age experience difficulty in explicitly distinguishing the intended meaning of a message from the utterance itself by either ignoring the actual message in favour of an accurate paraphrase or ignoring an accurate paraphrase in favour of the actual message.

Olson and Hildyard (1981) reported that, when questioned about a story that had been told concerning children sharing popcorn, 4- to 5-year-olds tended only to recall the intended meaning of speech reported ("Give me some of your popcorn") whereas 7- to 8-year-olds would also recall the exact wording used that gave rise to the implication ("You have more than me"). Similarly, Robinson, Goelman, and Olson (1983) asked 5-year-olds to play a referential communication game in which the speaker had to describe an item that he or she wanted the listener to pick up. Despite correctly rejecting inaccurate paraphrases and accepting verbatim repetitions of ambiguous sentences as what was actually said, children were significantly less likely to correctly reject clarified interpretations of ambiguous instructions. More recently, Lee, Torrance and Olson (2001) found that children younger than 6 to 7 years found it difficult to reject true paraphrases of utterances given in a narrative/story context, when asked to focus on the exact wording of the utterance.

Confusion of message and meaning was also apparent in studies suggesting that children inappropriately focus on the exact wording of messages. Miscione, Marvin, O'Brien, and Greenberg (1978) reported that children below 7 years of age assessed the accuracy of responses based on guessing to indicate knowledge, placing a focus on what was said at the expense of the meaning behind it. In a similar vein, Wimmer, Gruber, and Perner (1984) found that 4- to 6-year-olds evaluated false utterances as lies despite appreciation of the speaker's true beliefs about their statements. Furthermore, Lee, Torrance, and Olson (2001) found that children below 6–8 years have difficulty in accepting true paraphrases of utterances of nursery rhymes when asked to focus on the meaning with the instruction "You don't have to use the same words." As the message-intended meaning distinction is central to Grice's framework in characterizing the ability of speakers to follow the implications of conversation, such evidence points to a situation in which young children fall short of proficiency in discourse.

3. Children's knowledge of the distinction between appearance and reality

Some years ago, Robinson and Whittaker (1986) noted a similarity between children's apparent difficulties with the message-intended meaning distinction and problems reported with their knowledge of the distinction between reality and the phenomenal world of appearances. Comprehension of the appearance-reality distinction indicates appreciation that the real identity of an object does not necessarily correspond to its external appearance – knowledge vital to understanding the nature of the physical and mental world. Typically, in tasks such as those used originally by Flavell, Flavell and Green (1983), children aged 3 and 4 years are shown objects such as a sponge that looks like a rock and are questioned about appearance and reality. For these tasks, children are first given a brief explanation of the terms used to express the distinction in the test questions: "looks like" and "really and truly." Then an object is presented and the children asked test questions in a counterbalanced order concerning the object's appearance ("When you look at this with your eyes right now, does it look like a rock or does it look like a sponge?") and its identity ("What is this really and truly? Is it really and truly a sponge or is it really and truly a rock?"). In response to these questions, 3-year-olds, unlike 4-year-olds, seemed to show little or no knowledge of the distinction between appearance and reality. For example, they claim that a sponge that looks like a rock is either a sponge or a rock in both appearance and reality.

Robinson and Whittaker (1986: 43) likened children's performance on appearance-reality tasks to that on tasks concerning the message-intended meaning distinction. They suggested that young children's difficulty with this distinction arises from problems in conceptualising the dual nature of the relationship between the message and meaning elements in that the message corresponds to appearance and the meaning elements correspond to reality. They argued that a speaker's message needs to be understood "as a stimulus to be interpreted in its own right and also as a representation" of speaker meaning.

However, more recent evidence suggests that 3-year-olds' poor performance on appearance-reality assessments cannot be solely attributed to difficulty in conceptual differentiation, but seems instead to reflect the child's developing acquisition of discourse. Gauvain and Greene (1994) reported that children as young as 2 years who demonstrated poor performance on Flavell et al.'s appearance-reality test questions could distinguish between the appearance and reality of objects in a naturalistic show-and-tell situation. Rice, Koinis, Sullivan, Tager-Flusberg, and Winner (1997) also found that adaptations to task methodology improved performance. In one condition, questions were posed in the context of a deceptive scenario to emphasise involvement of mental states; in another, an exemplar item of appearance was presented alongside an exemplar item of reality to reduce the need for independent mental representation. Both manipulations produced significantly more correct responses. These results are consistent with those of other studies (Gelman and Ebeling 1998; Sapp, Lee, and Muir 2000; Deák, Yen, and Pettit 2001). Indeed the similarity of response patterns for standard appearance-reality task and unrelated-subject but similar discourse structure control questions prompted Deák, Ray, and Brenneman (2003) to suggest that typical performance on appearance-reality tasks might be more representative of the ability to identify speaker intentions in experimental tasks than children's lack of knowledge of an appearance-reality distinction.

A re-examination of preschoolers' responses on measures designed to assess whether they can distinguish lies from mistakes illustrates again the paramount issue of children's ability to identify speaker intentions. To young children lack experience and knowledge of the purpose and relevance of an interviewer's requests, the very asking of a question about lying can imply that there has been a lie rather than a mistake and that this is the correct answer. Under conditions that avoid this assumption, even many 3-year-olds demonstrate an incipient ability to distinguish lies from mistakes (Siegal and Peterson 1998).

4. Clarifying speaker intentions in diverse areas of developmental research

In such disparate subject areas such as number conservation, "theory of mind," and cosmology, investigators have successfully shown that adapting tasks to make the experimenter's intentions more explicit, enhances children's performance on a range of cognitive developmental tests. For example, on conservation tasks, children may be shown two rows of six counters first in one-to-one correspondence and then one row is lengthened and the other shortened so the counters are no longer in correspondence. The children are then asked to say whether there is still the same number of counters as before. By refraining from question repetition (Rose and Blank, 1974) and using a 'naughty' teddy to transform task materials (McGarrigle and Donaldson 1974), investigators have managed to improve young children's performance on number conservation tasks significantly, although age differences still persist. It has been argued that such task manipulations prevent children from introducing mistaken interpretations concerning the experimenter's question intentions. Children might decide that they are being asked the same question a second time because their first response to the question had been wrong, indicating that they should now change their response, or they might think that the question was being asked a second time because something had now changed, so conclude again that they should alter their response.

Similarly, performance on theory of mind tests that examine false-belief understanding has been found to improve following the incorporation of a minor modification to task presentation. False-belief tasks assess the appreciation that someone can possess a mental representation of a situation (a belief) that conflicts with the reality of the circumstances. For example, in an 'unexpected-location' false-belief task (Baron-Cohen, Leslie, and Frith 1985), a story character, Sally, who has placed an object in one location is unaware of its subsequent transfer to another location by a second character, Anne. Sally should thus be seen to hold a false belief regarding the whereabouts of the object and to search unsuccessfully for the object in its original location. However, the question, "Where will Sally (the story character with a false belief) look for the object?" may be interpreted by 3-year-olds who are inexperienced in the purpose and relevance of a speaker's conversation to mean "Where will Sally have to look, or where ought Sally to look, in order to find the object?" In this sense, the test question may be seen to depart from the Maxim of Quantity in that it is inadequately informative. Altering the standard question in this task from "Where will Sally look for ......?" to "Where will Sally look first for ....?" serves to clarify the experimenter's intended meaning, enabling the majority of 3-year-olds to answer correctly (Siegal and Beattie 1991; Yazdi, German, Defeyter, and Siegal 2006).

Related considerations apply in a variety of contexts, including assessments of children's cosmological knowledge (Siegal, Butterworth, and Newcombe 2004; Panagiotaki, Nobes, and Banerjee 2006). In line with such findings highlighting the impact of discourse structure on task responses, young children, particularly at the age of 2 and 3 years, often strive to operate in a manner consistent with Grice's Cooperative Principle. They often display an affirmation bias, a tendency to say 'yes', to yes-no questions even when these are incomprehensible (Fritzley and Lee 2003).

5. Implicit conversational understanding

If children's responses on cognitive developmental tasks often underestimate their conceptual competence in areas such as appearance-reality knowledge, conservation and theory of mind, their ability to conceive of a message as a stimulus to be interpreted in its own right and also as a representation of the speaker's intended meaning requires reconsideration. Ackerman (1993) reports that, when provided with contextual information indicating the intended meaning of a message, children as young as 5 years can take this information on board and represent it separately from information gleaned from a message. He maintains that young children tend to treat messages as reflective of speaker meaning, and to judge the consistency of messages and referents rather than their sufficiency, so that an ambiguous message that precludes specific identification of, but nonetheless allows interpretation in terms of, its intended referent, is deemed adequate. However, he proposes that the focus on message and referent consistency can be disrupted, so that the absence of independent referent identification or the use of a deceptive context can act to direct attention away from the external referent to an internal representation. He proposes that the relation between internal representations and messages are judged in terms of sufficiency, thereby revealing children's potential for proficiency in conversation.

Other evidence that children possess early message-meaning differentiation comes from Reid's (1996) investigation of ambiguity sensitivity in 5- and 6-year-olds. Differentiation of intended-meaning from message-meaning requires the recognition the meaning of a message can be ambiguous if it is consistent with more than one meaning. Reid reports that emphasising the need to evaluate messages improves children's detection of ambiguity. In this investigation, children were presented with a selection of stimuli (pictures of clown faces), differing with relation to some attributes (emotion expression, hat-shape, presence of freckles), and consistent with respect to others (possession of one nose and two eyes). They were asked to select a message referent if it could be identified from the message, or to pick up a card with a large 'X' on it if the referent couldn't be determined. If the set from which participants were asked to select consisted of a happy clown with a square hat and no freckles, a sad clown with a square hat and freckles and a happy clown with a round hat and no freckles, a message referring to "a happy clown with a square hat" would be unambiguous, consistent with only one of the clown faces. However, a message referring to "a clown with a nose and two eyes" would be ambiguous, consistent with all of the clown faces. Children took longer to respond, and did so with less certainty when a message was ambiguous than when it was unambiguous, even when the intended referent was in fact known to them. These findings are consistent with those of Ackerman in suggesting that young children are, at least to some degree, implicitly aware of the message-intended meaning distinction.

In a recent study, Sekerina, Stromswold, and Hestvik (2004) investigated children's ability to match pictures with referents in an ambiguous pronoun task. For example, 4- to 7-year-olds were told, "The boy has placed the box behind him." In this example, the term 'him' could either refer back to the sentence subject and be interpreted as an internal referent (the boy) or to another unidentified character as an external referent (a man). Sekerina, Stromswold and Hestvik created pairs of pictures so that one pictured scene favoured an interpretation in terms of the sentence-internal referent such as an image of two agents, a boy and a man and a box that could be seen behind the boy; the other scene favoured interpretation in terms of an external referent such as an image of two agents, a boy and a man and a box that could be seen behind the man. In response to messages containing ambiguous pronouns, children failed to demonstrate an appreciation of alternative meanings when selecting a picture from a pair. However, when Sekerina et al. used patterns of eye gaze to investigate the allocation of attention to the two referents on ambiguous pronoun tasks, they found a substantial increase in looking time to the external referent compared to that on an internal referent reflexive pronoun control task, pointing to the presence of an implicit sensitivity to alternative interpretations and so the message-meaning distinction.

6. Information processing and conversational understanding

In a performance account of pragmatic development (Surian 1995), it has been proposed that information processing limitations may mask the explicit demonstration of an implicit pragmatic competency. Consistent with this analysis, Musolino and Lidz (2003) investigated the phenomenon of isomorphism – the tendency to interpret ambiguous sentences with negation and quantified noun phrases, such as 'every horse didn't jump over the fence', in a manner consistent with their superficial syntactic structure. Thus in the example given above, the quantified expression 'every', in preceding 'didn't', will take scope over this negation, producing the 'wider' interpretation that no horse jumped over the fence. This interpretation typifies that of children and contrasts with the non-isomorphic interpretation of such sentences typically given by adults. They will normally attribute scope to the negation 'didn't' over the quantified expression 'every' resulting in the 'narrower' reading that not every horse jumped over the fence, giving rise to the implication that some in fact did. Musolino and Lidz (2003, 2006) show that processing demands underpin the extent to which both children and adults provide isomorphic interpretations. They report that even adult listeners overwhelmingly interpret the ambiguous phrase "Two frogs didn't jump over the rock" isomorphically in accordance with its syntactic structure so that the term "two" takes scope over the term "didn't", giving rise to the 'wider' reading that two (particular/definite) frogs didn't jump over the rock. This can be contrasted with the non-isomorphic interpretation in which the term "didn't" takes scope over the term "two", giving rise to the 'narrower' reading that it was not the case that two frogs jumped, and hence the implication that less than two frogs jumped. To reduce processing demands (Horn 1989), Musolino and Lidz then created a positive expectation against which the negative quantified noun phrase could be starkly contrasted as conveyed by the phrase "Two frogs jumped over the fence but two frogs didn't jump over the rock." This modification produced many more non-isomorphic interpretations. The effects of manipulating processing demands on adults' isomorphic interpretations are thus consistent with the effects upon children's interpretations, and would seem to provide strong support for a continuity account of pragmatic development.

Support for a processing demand explanation extends to investigations focusing on the appreciation of scalar implicatures. The 'weaker' terms used in scalar implicatures such as 'some' and 'might' are logically consistent with stronger terms such as 'all' and 'must' but carry pragmatic meanings based on implications in accordance with the Maxim of Quantity. Thus the statement "Some of the dwarfs kissed Snow White" is logically compatible with the statement "All of the dwarfs kissed Snow White" but conveys the pragmatic meaning that "Some though not all the dwarfs kissed Snow White." The implication is that, if a speaker had meant "all," he or she would have informatively said "all."

Studies such as those of Smith (1980), Braine and Rumain (1981) and Noveck (2001) have indicated that children below 7 years of age demonstrate a clear preference for the logical interpretation of scalar terms so that the pragmatic implication of stronger term inapplicability is overlooked. However, Gualmini, Crain, Meroni, Chierchia, and Guasti (2001), Papafragou and Musolino (2003) and Papafragou and Tantalou (2004) have found that adapting tasks to lessen processing requirements, substantially enhances the ability of children aged 3 to 6 years to derive pragmatic interpretations. In such tasks, children have been asked to choose either a pragmatic or logical interpretation of an event or to judge the adequacy of a puppet's description of an event in terms of "some" rather than "all". Under these conditions, many young children have shown to have an adult-like competence (Feeney, Scrafton, Duckworth, and S. J. Handley 2004; Guasti, Chierchia, Crain, Foppolo, Gualmini, and Meroni 2005).

The position that children possess a degree of early proficiency in deriving pragmatic interpretations in discourse is lent further support by research on personal reference pronoun reversals. Personal reference pronouns are special in that their object of reference is not fixed, so that the term 'you' can be used to refer to different people in different contexts and even during simple conversational exchanges in which the speaker and listener exchange roles. Correct production of personal reference pronouns such as 'I', 'You', 'he' or 'she' is performed in accordance with Grice's maxims of Quantity and Manner. However, sometimes reversals occur, in which the pronouns are incorrectly applied so that the speaker might use the term 'I' to refer to the listener or 'you' to refer to him/herself.

Based on a sample of 20-month-olds, Dale and Crain-Thoreson (1993) observed that the frequency of reversal production was consistent with most instances occurring in the context of relatively long or complex utterances. They also noted that reversals were more likely to occur in imitation contexts and to involve reversal of the second person pronoun 'you'. As children who actually produced reversals in fact tended to produce more correct second person pronouns than non-reversers, Dale and Crain-Thoreson (1993: 585) propose that the referential shift required to alternate pronoun direction "presents a substantial processing load," susceptible to impediment from long complex utterances and salient pronoun representations formed in memory during imitation episodes.

Recent work on children's processing of 'garden-path' sentences also underscores the nature of children's early competence in discourse in terms of information processing demands. Consider the sentence Whilst Myrtle ate the chicken laid an egg. The referential ambiguity in this example is due to the phrase 'the chicken', containing the second noun of the sentence. This noun could be interpreted as the object of the verb 'ate' (indicating that the chicken was eaten – a garden-path interpretation) or read as the subject of the verb 'laid' (indicating that the chicken laid an egg). Another example comes from the request "Put the frog on the mat into the box". This sentence could be interpreted to mean that a frog that was already on a mat should be put into the box or that a frog that was not yet on a mat should be first put on the mat and then into the box. The latter is a garden-path interpretation in which sentence processing is consistent with the presence of an initial tendency to process the noun immediately following a verb as its object. When considering a first frog that is not on a mat and a second frog that is already on a mat, this interpretation would lead children to refer to the first frog and to place this frog on a mat before placing it in the box. By contrast, adults parsimoniously choose the second frog that is already on the mat. Trueswell, Sekerina, Hill, and Logrip (1999) analysed the behaviour and eye-movements of 5-year-olds during processing of the 'frog' request. Unlike adults who were able to recognize ambiguity created by the presence of the two frog and to select the appropriate choice from context, children were led down the garden path in failing to identify appropriate sentence referents, indicating a lack of proficiency in this area. However, Meroni and Crain (2003) report that when given an opportunity to plan task responses before being allowed to initiate them, thus extending the processing period, children between the ages of 4 and 6 years of age were able to give contextually appropriate responses and avoid being led down the garden path.

So evidence would appear to support the idea that the child possesses an early understanding of conversational implications, but that the processing demands of certain situations mask this knowledge. Sperber and Wilson (2002) provide an account of the way in which such understanding might form and emerge. Their Relevance Theory account of communication focuses on the role of the Maxim of Relation. They propose that conversational interpretation can be explained entirely in terms of the search for relevance. Sperber and Wilson argue that the focus of this quest emerges as a product of specialised inferential processes built into a subsection of an encompassing Theory of Mind module. The term 'Theory of Mind' here is used broadly to denote the ability to appreciate the mental lives of the self and others. In line with Fodor's (1983) conception of modules, Sperber and Wilson's Theory of Mind module is conceptualised as a fast, focused and automatic processing mechanism, dedicated to making sense of the mental world and impenetrable to the influence of more general cognitive heuristics. Sperber and Wilson propose that processing effort itself plays a part in determining relevance, illustrating how a lack of effort may prevent listeners from computed the implication intended by the speaker. But what does the child need to accomplish in order to process conversation and to acquire mature strategies to engage proficiently in discourse?

7. Processing strategies and executive functioning as a basis for discourse acquisition

The research that we have discussed above suggests that, under optimal conditions, young children do possess an incipient grasp of the implications of conversation. In contexts where alternative interpretations of messages are made clear and they are prompted to attend to these, children show evidence of proficiency in conversation such that they can respond well, though not necessarily at an adult level, on a variety of tasks central to language and cognition. These tasks involve knowledge of the appearance-reality distinction, false belief understanding and scalar implicatures as well as accurate use of the referents of pronouns and of the subjects of garden path sentences. Yet in many circumstances, children's performance does not measure anywhere near that of adults. Children appear to be overly inattentive or to lack the conversational experience or knowledge base to consider more than the literal meaning of a message and thus to overlook the intended implications. In general, young children seem less willing or able than adults to employ skills that oversee their choice of how a message should be interpreted. Such skills concern 'executive functioning' conceptualised as those attention-dependent abilities that enable the coordination, planning and alteration of activities – a cluster of abilities that Bara, Bucciarelli and Colle (2001: 219) consider "allows disengagement from the immediate environment and guides action by internal representations." Given their developing skills in this area, young children may be unable to employ Gricean maxims to interpret conversation as intended and to engage in discourse in a manner that is fully coherent.

Involvement of executive functioning skills would concur with the proposal of Surian (1995) that children's difficulties in processing messages is more accurately seen in terms of performance factors related to attention and effort rather than to a lack of competence, or 'processing capacity' to enable distinguishing between messages and intended meanings. On this account, effort provides the computational resources to communicate effectively. This requires the activation of an attentional system that serves to detect and avoid ambiguity in utterances. In reviewing the pragmatic development literature, Surian (1995) notes that children's accuracy on communication tasks does not correlate significantly with performance on discriminant feature identification tasks in which, for example, children are explicitly asked to attend to, and verbally report, the feature in a set of three that is unique from ambiguous others (Bishop and Adams 1991; Roberts and Patterson 1983; Robinson and Robinson 1978). Consequently, he advocates examining children's ability to identify a speaker's utterance as ambiguous in terms of attention and effort rather than degree of processing capacity. In his investigation, children aged 5 to 9 years were asked to produce utterances directed at listeners that were classified as 'ambiguous' if these did not include the unique discriminant feature, 'contrastive' if the utterances included only this feature, and 'redundant' if the feature was included together with additional ones. With increasing age, children were more likely to produce nonambiguous, redundant messages and, as shown in a dual-task condition in which children had also to finger tap, were able to overcome the attentional demands of tapping while communicating. Thus the relative mental effort demands of a communication task assessing production of ambiguous utterances decreased with age and predicted task success.

Although children's early processing strategies often appear to be based on literal messages rather than intended meaning, Surian's analysis indicates that these strategies are overcome with the development of executive functioning. In this sense, as Siegal and Surian (2004) suggest, discourse acquisition may unfold along the lines proposed by Scholl and Leslie (1999) for the expression of theory of mind reasoning skills. Although Scholl and Leslie view ToM as the product of a specialised module, they do not propose that the resulting proficiency is automatically available; rather they suggest the initial existence of processing biases. Scholl and Leslie are particularly concerned with accounting for the failure of pre-schoolers on assessments of false-belief understanding such as that on 'Sally-Anne' tasks. They suggest that an executive functioning mechanism, the 'Selection Processor', develops as children grow older. This mechanism serves to overrule a default preference for interpreting beliefs as true – one that reflects a state of affairs in which beliefs are usually true and appearance does often provide an accurate clue to reality. Similarly, in the case of children's interpretation of speaker intentions, the evolutionary pressure for the rapid acquisition of language may have created a processing bias to favour initially the literal meaning rather than the intended meaning of messages. Once again it may be the development of executive functioning that assists the child to overcome this processing bias, facilitating access to contextually enriched interpretations based on the appreciation of intended meaning. There are similarities between this model and Sperber and Wilson's (1995, 2002) Relevance theory account of pragmatic reasoning that is centred on Grice's Maxim of Relation. According to the Relevance account, the listener determines speaker intention by searching for relevance in utterance meaning, with search criteria defined in terms of the relative processing effort involved. Sperber and Wilson (1995) suggest that the search starts from the basis of an initial, semantic utterance interpretation, but that as the amount of processing resources available increases, the relative processing effort decreases. With increasing age and experience, children require less effort to process utterances in terms of intended meaning, providing an even greater incentive to derive relevance from conversation.

According to this account, the expression of both pragmatic development and ToM reasoning can be dependent on executive functioning skills, so that modifying tasks to lessen the attentional demands may facilitate performance (Bara, Bucciarelli, and Colle 2001; Sabbagh, Moses and Shiverick 2006; Siegal and Varley 2002). Differences in the attentional demands of tasks can be seen to account for variability in the concurrence of impairments in pragmatics, ToM, and executive functioning skills (Mitchell, Saltmarsh, and Russell 1997). Such an argument would concur with the previously discussed findings reporting demonstration of previously concealed proficiency, on both conversational and more general cognitive tasks when attentional demands are reduced (Siegal and Beattie 1991; Gauvain and Greene 1994; Rice, Koinis, Sullivan, Tager-Flusberg, and Winner 1997; Papafragou and Musolino 2003, in press; Sekerina, Stromswold, and Hestvik 2004; Yazdi, German, Defeyter, and Siegal 2006), suggesting this is the more satisfactory explanation.

Executive functioning skills would to be central in discourse acquisition, but as Miyake, Friedman, Emerson, Witzki, and Howerter (2000) point out, the differentiation and organisation of such competencies requires clarification. Miyake, Friedman, Emerson, Witzki, and Howerter provide support for the existence of three distinct but nevertheless related skills: mental set shifting, information updating and the monitoring and inhibition of prepotent responses. Siegal and Surian (2007) propose that each of these skills can be seen to play a key role as mental set shifting is necessary to enable consideration of alternative utterance interpretations, representations of speaker meaning need to be updated continuously, and prepotent responses need to be inhibited to identify false or ironic utterances. These considerations warrant further study, particularly in regard to children with autism who have often been viewed to have specific difficulties in the pragmatic aspects of language (Tager-Flusberg, 1993). For example, Bara et al. (2001) proposes that the communicative and mental-state appreciation deficiencies often associated with autism can be attributed to an attentional deficit. To remediate these deficiencies, they advocate the use of 'Facilitated Communication' in which a 'facilitator' focuses the individual on a task, by providing physical and psychological support and giving verbal reminders and by presenting task materials in a format that reduce attentional demands. Under these conditions, they report that mute children with autism ranging from 7 to 18 years can perform well on measures of pragmatics and ToM reasoning.

Of course the maturation of executive functioning skills does not provide a complete account of discourse acquisition. For one thing, inferential reasoning ability can be dependent upon subject-specific knowledge. To be sure, Levinson (2000) has argued that some conversational inferences function fairly independently of such specialized knowledge, claiming that 'generalised conversational implicatures' such as the some-all scalar implicature and quantificational implicatures – inferences that the use of fixed number terms imply the inapplicability of larger number terms – are naturally invoked by presence of stable, contrastive elements in the lexicon. However, Chierchia (2004) has challenged this view, claiming that even scalar implicatures are powerfully influenced by context.

Regardless of the degree to which specific knowledge is required to compute implicatures, it is indisputable that many inferences in conversation are contextually bound and their derivation presupposes a consideration of acquired contextual knowledge. For example, a boy may ask his mother whether there are any buttercups in the garden and be told in reply, "All the flowers in the garden are red." A boy who lacks the knowledge that butter-cups are yellow will fail to draw the intended inference that there are no buttercups in the garden, regardless of his communicative competence revealed in other instances. The colour yellow is not integral to the meaning of the term 'buttercup' in the sense that the notion of a buttercup of another colour would be a conceptual impossibility, likened to the idea of a square circle. Thus colour reference is not necessary for an adequate lexical entry for 'buttercup', entailing that dissimilarly coloured flowers should not be naturally invoked as 'contrastive alternates'. Information regarding the colour of buttercups can thus be considered as additionally acquired, circumstantial knowledge, and the contrastive use of this information considered dependent upon subject-specific knowledge acquisition. The accumulation of such knowledge with age permits the extension of inferential reasoning abilities in discourse and the development of conversational understanding.

In sum, evidence suggests that the acquisition of discourse during childhood is not the consequence of a fundamental change in the nature of the communication in which intended meanings cannot be distinguished from the literal message. Reduction of task processing demands has revealed conversational competence at earlier ages. Rather, young children's difficulties on tasks designed to determine their conversational understanding seem best conceptualised in terms of the need to employ executive functioning skills which have an impact upon the expression of intention appreciation and information integration from a knowledge base that increases with age.

However, the work that we have reviewed here is limited to monolingual hearing children despite the fact that children vary enormously in their language backgrounds. For example, early bilingual children who are exposed from birth to two languages appear to have enhanced executive functioning 'switching' skills (Bialystok and Senman 2004). However, further research is required to assess how very early exposure to conversation in more than one language enhances executive functioning skills such that these influence pragmatic development and the course of discourse acquisition. Conversely, there are many cases in which children do not have early access to participation in conversation such as late signing deaf children of hearing parents and nonvocal children with cerebral palsy. Such children seem to have delayed ToM reasoning, if not problems in executive functioning (Courtin and Melot 2005; Dahlgren, Dahlgren Sandberg, and Hjelmquist 2003; Woolfe, Want, and Siegal 2002). However, pragmatic development and discourse acquisition in these groups has scarcely been studied. There remains much to find out.

References

Ackerman, B. P.
    1993   Children's understanding of the relation between referential knowledge and referential behaviour. *Journal of Experimental Child Psychology* 56: 385–411.

Bara, B., M. Bucciarelli and L. Colle
    2001   Communicative abilities in autism: evidence for attentional deficits. *Brain and Language* 77: 216–240.

Bialystok, E. and L. Senman
    2004   Executive processes in appearance-reality tasks: The role of inhibition of attention and symbolic representation. *Child Development* 75: 562–579.

Bishop, D. V. M. and C. Adams
    1991   What do referential communication tasks measure? A study of children with specific language impairment. *Applied Psycholinguistics* 12: 199–215.

Braine, M. D. and B. Rumain
    1981   Development of comprehension of "or": evidence for a sequence of competencies. *Journal of Experimental Child Psychology* 31: 46–70.

Chierchia, G.
    2004   Scalar implicature, polarity phenomena, and the syntax/pragmatic interface. In A. Belletti and L. Rizzi (eds.), *Structures and beyond*. Oxford: Oxford University Press.

Courtin, C. and A.-M. Melot
    2005   Metacognitive development of deaf children: Lessons from the appearance-reality and false belief tasks. *Developmental Science* 8: 16–25.

Dahlgren, S., A. Dahlgren Sandberg and E. Hjelmquist
    2003   The non-specificity of theory of mind deficits: evidence from children with communicative disabilities. *European Journal of Cognitive Psychology* 15: 129–155.

Dale, P. S. and C. Crain-Thoreson
    1993   Pronoun reversals: who, when, and why? *Journal of Child Language* 20: 573–589.

Deák, G. O., S. D. Ray and K. Brenneman
    2003   Children's perseverative appearance-reality errors are related to emerging language skills. *Child Development* 74: 944–964.

Deák, G. O., L. Yen and J. Pettit
    2001   By any other name: When will preschoolers produce multiple labels for a referent? *Journal of Child Language* 28: 787–804.

Feeney, A. S. Scrafton, A. Duckworth and S. J. Handley
    2004   The story of some: everyday pragmatic inference by children and adults. *Canadian Journal of Experimental Psychology* 58: 121–132.

Flavell, J. H., E. R. Flavell and F. L. Green
    1983   Development of the appearance-reality distinction. *Cognitive Psychology* 15: 95–120.

Fodor, J.
   1983   *The Modularity of Mind.* Cambridge, MA: MIT Press.
Fritzley, V. H. and K. Lee
   2003   Do young children always say yes to yes-no questions? A metadevelopmental study of the affirmation bias. *Child Development* 74: 1297–1313.
Gauvain, M. and J. K. Greene
   1994   What do young children know about objects? *Cognitive Development* 9: 311–329.
Gelman, S. A. and K. S. Ebeling
   1998   Shape and representational status in children's early naming. *Cognition* 66: B35–B47.
Grice, P.
   1975   Logic and conversation. Reprinted in Paul Grice 1989 *Studies in the Way of Words* 22–40. Harvard University Press: Cambridge, MA: Harvard University Press.
Gualmini, A., S. Crain, L. Meroni, G. Chierchia and M. T. Guasti
   2001   At the semantics/pragmatics interface in child language. Proceedings of Semantics and Linguistic Theory XI. Ithaca, New York: CLC Publications, Department of Linguistics, Cornell University.
Guasti, M. T., G. Chierchia, S. Crain, F. Foppolo, A. Gualmini and L. Meroni
   2005   Why children and adults sometimes (but not always) compute implicatures. *Language and Cognitive Processes* 20: 667–696.
Horn, L. A.
   1989   *A Natural History of Negation.* Chicago, IL: University of Chicago Press.
Lee, E., N. Torrance and D. R. Olson
   2001   Young children and the say/mean distinction: verbatim and paraphrase recognition in narrative and nursery rhyme contexts. *Journal of Child Language* 28: 531–543.
Levinson, S.
   2000   *Presumptive Meanings.* Cambridge, MA: MIT Press.
McGarrigle, J. and M. Donaldson
   1974   Conservation accidents. *Cognition* 3: 341–350.
Meroni, L. and S. Crain
   2003   How children avoid kindergarten paths. Proceedings of 4th Tokyo Conference on Psycholinguistics. Tokyo, Japan: Hitsuji Shobo.
Miscione, J. L., R. S. Marvin, R. G. O'Brien and M. T. Greenberg
   1978   A developmental study of preschool children's understanding of the words "know" and "guess". *Child Development* 49: 1107–1113.
Mitchell, P., R. Saltmarsh and J. Russell
   1997   Overly literal interpretations of speech in autism: Understanding that messages arise from minds. *Journal of Child Psychology and Psychiatry and Allied Disciplines* 38: 685–691.
Miyake, A., N. P. Friedman, M. J. Emerson, A. H. Witzki and A. Howerter
   2000   The unity and diversity of executive functions and their contributions to complex "frontal lobe" tasks: a latent variable analysis. *Cognitive Psychology* 41: 49–100.

Musolino, J. and J. Lidz
   2003   The scope of isomorphism: turning adults into children. *Language Acquisition* 11: 277–291.

Musolino, J. and J. Lidz
   2006   Why children are not universally successful with quantification. *Linguistics* 44: 817–852.

Noveck, I.
   2001   When children are more logical than adults: experimental investigations of scalar implicature. *Cognition* 78: 165–188.

Olson, D. R. and A. Hildyard
   1981   Assent and compliance in children's language. In W. P. Dickson (ed.) *Children's Oral Communication Skills,* 313–335. New York: Academic Press.

Panagiotaki, G., G. Nobes and R. Banerjee
   2006   Children's representations of the earth: A methodological comparison. *British Journal of Developmental Psychology* 24: 353–372.

Papafragou, A. and J. Musolino
   2003   Scalar implicatures: experiments at the semantics-pragmatics interface. *Cognition* 86: 253–282.

Papafragou, A. and N. Tantalou
   2004   Children's computation of implicatures. *Language Acquisition* 12: 71–82.

Pellicano, E., M. Mayberry and K. Durkin
   2005   Central coherence in typically developing preschoolers: does it cohere and does it relate to mindreading and executive control? *Journal of Child Psychology and Psychiatry* 46: 533–547.

Peterson, C. C. and M. Siegal
   1999   Representing inner worlds: Theory of mind in autistic, deaf, and normal hearing children. *Psychological Science* 10: 126–129.

Peterson, C. C. and M. Siegal
   2000   Insights into theory of mind from deafness and autism. *Mind and Language* 15: 123–145.

Reid, L.
   1996   The effects of focusing children's attention on the literal meaning of the message. *Merrill-Palmer Quarterly* 42: 295–318.

Rice, C., D. Koinis, K. Sullivan, H. Tager-Flusberg and E. Winner
   1997   When 3-year-olds pass the appearance-reality test. *Developmental Psychology* 33: 54–61.

Roberts, R. J. Jr. and C. J. Patterson
   1983   Perspective taking and referential communication: the question of correspondence reconsidered. *Child Development* 54: 1005–1014.

Robinson, E. J., H. Goelman and D. R. Olson
   1983   Children's understanding of the relation between expressions (what was said) and intentions (what was meant). *British Journal of Developmental Psychology* 1: 75–86.

Robinson, E. J. and W. P. Robinson
   1978   The roles of egocentrism and weakness in comparing children's explanations of communicative failure. *Journal of Experimental Child Psychology* 26: 147–160.

Robinson E. and S. J. Whittaker
  1986 Children's conceptions of meaning-message relationships. *Cognition* 22: 41–60.
Rose, S. A. and M. Blank
  1974 The potency of context in children's cognition: An illustration through conservation. *Child Development* 45: 499–502.
Sabbagh, M. A., L. J. Moses and S. Shiverick
  2006 Executive functioning and preschoolers' understanding of false beliefs, false photographs, and false signs. *Child Development* 77: 1034–1049.
Sapp, F., Kang L. and D. Muir
  2000 Three-year-olds' difficulty with the appearance-reality distinction: is it real or is it apparent? *Developmental Psychology* 36: 547–560.
Scholl, B. J. and A. M. Leslie
  1999 Modularity, development and 'theory of mind'. *Mind and Language* 14: 131–153.
Sekerina, I. K. Stromswold and A. Hestvik
  2004 How do adults and children process referentially ambiguous pronouns? *Journal of Child Language* 31: 123–152.
Shannon, C. E.
  1948 A mathematical theory of communication. *Bell System Technical Journal* 27: 379–423 and 623–656.
Shannon, C. E. and W. Weaver
  1949 *The Mathematical Theory of Communication.* Urbana: University of Illinois Press.
Siegal, M. and K. Beattie
  1991 Where to look first for children's knowledge of false beliefs. *Cognition* 38: 1–12.
Siegal, M., G. Butterworth and P. A. Newcombe
  2004 Culture and children's cosmology. *Developmental Science* 7: 308–324.
Siegal, M. and C. C. Peterson
  1998 Children's understanding of lies and innocent and negligent mistakes. *Developmental Psychology* 34: 332–343.
Siegal, M. and L. Surian
  2004 Conceptual development and conversational understanding. *Trends in Cognitive Sciences* 8: 534–538.
Siegal, M. and L. Surian
  2007 Conversational understanding in young children. In: E. Hoff and M. Shatz (eds.) *Handbook of Language Development.* Oxford: Blackwell, 304–323.
Siegal, M. and R. Varley
  2002 Neural systems involved in 'theory of mind'. *Nature Reviews Neuroscience* 3: 463–471
Smith, Carol L.
  1980 Quantifiers and question answering in young children. *Journal of Experimental Child Psychology* 30: 191–205.
Sodian, B.
  1994 Early deception and the conceptual continuity claim. In: C. Lewis and P. Mitchell (eds.) *Children's Early Understanding of the Mind,* 385–401. Hove, UK: Lawrence Erlbaum Associates.

Sperber, D. and D. Wilson
　1995　*Relevance: Communication and Cognition.* Second edition. London: Blackwell Publishing.

Sperber, D. and D. Wilson
　2002　Pragmatics, modularity and mind-reading. *Mind and Language* 17: 3–23.

Surian, L.
　1995　Children's ambiguous utterances: a re-examination of processing limitations on production. *Journal of Child Language* 22: 151–169.

Tager-Flusberg, H.
　1993　What language reveals about the understanding of minds in children with autism. In S. Baron-Cohen, H. Tager-Flusberg and D. J. Cohen (eds.), *Understanding Other Minds: Perspectives from Children with Autism.* Oxford: Oxford University Press.

Trueswell, J. C., I. Sekerina, N. M. Hill and M. L. Logrip
　1999　The kindergarten-path effect: studying on-line sentence processing in young children. *Cognition* 73: 89–134.

Wimmer, H., S. Gruber and J. Perner
　1984　Young children's conception of lying: lexical realism: moral subjectivism. *Journal of Experimental Child Psychology* 37: 1–30.

Woolfe, T., Want, S. C. and Siegal, M.
　2002　Signposts to development: Theory of mind in deaf children. *Child Development* 73: 768–778

Yazdi, A. A., P. German, M. A. Defeyter and M. Siegal
　2006　Competence and performance in belief-desire reasoning across two-cultures: The truth, the whole truth and nothing but the truth about false belief? *Cognition* 100: 343–68.

6. Literacy acquisition and its precursors

Pekka Niemi

Components and processes of literacy acquisition are reviewed. Research has paid most attention to phonological awareness. It has been widely and successfully used in training for reading readiness and remediation of reading difficulties. Training programmes can be made stronger by including explicit teaching of grapheme-to-phoneme correspondences in them. Phonological awareness appears to have at least some causal role in literacy acquisition because effects of preschool training of non-readers sustain until grade 6. Studies commencing from birth or during the first year of life show that there is a predictable path to phonological awareness and literacy acquisition beginning from phoneme discrimination and progressing through acquisition of vocabulary and inflectional morphology. Rapid automatised naming also stands as a potent determiner of literacy development but its own precursors and openness for literacy-relevant training still need to be studied. Orthographies differ markedly with respect to their usability as a means of literacy acquisition. However, an inevitable conclusion is that a sizeable portion of variability in beginning reading ability remains unexplained. One reason probably is that motivational problems occurring concomitantly with reading difficulties play a role to the effect that some pupils become "treatment-resistant readers". Recent efforts to have pre-schoolers to acquire massed practice with grapheme-to-phoneme conversion rules combined with motivational incentives seem therefore particularly promising.

1. Introduction

Slow and inaccurate reading has rapidly become a true handicap for a citizen of a modern society. This development is quite recent. As long as reading and writing compulsory documents occurred fairly seldom in an individual's life, fluent reading for comprehension was not an issue. The past fifty years have meant a decisive shift. Manual labour is disappearing at a breathtaking pace. A worker is expected to read and understand documents and produce them, more often than not with a computer. It is therefore little surprising that deficient literacy skills have become a growing concern. Functional illiteracy refers to poor reading among adults that hampers particularly comprehension and even in countries with high educational standards (see, e.g. Elbro, Møller, and Nielsen 1995). It is to be distinguished from dyslexia, the hallmark of which is poor word reading from grade 1 onwards, often but not always accompanied by poor comprehension skills (e.g. Gough and Tunmer 1986). Dyslexia is characterised by a very slow learning of word decoding skills that sometimes resists even the best of remedial efforts. Causes of dyslexia still remain unknown, at least in part. However, there is no shortage of candidates and their number is rather impressive (see, e.g., Hjelmquist and von Euler 2002). Researchers have paid most attention to those hypothesized causes that are reasonably open to remedial efforts. Reading and spelling being language skills, the search has been directed towards linguistic precursors of problems in literacy acquisition. In this vein, research on literacy acquisition has since 1980's underscored the importance of phonological awareness (PA), also known as phonological sensitivity, as the predictor of beginning reading and spelling. PA refers to a preliterate person's ability to turn the attention away from a spoken word's meaning while deliberately listening to and perceiving its parts, such as syllables and phonemes. PA has been studied in detail for several reasons. Firstly, it comprises a naturally occurring stage in language development as evidenced by language games that children spontaneously play. Secondly, the first signs of PA emerge as early as in 3 to 4 years of age (e.g. Bradley and Bryant 1983). Thirdly, PA is a potent predictor of later reading development across a number of languages that differ widely in terms of orthography and phonology: Danish (Lundberg, Frost, and Petersen 1988), Dutch (de Jong and van der Leij 1999), English (Wagner, Torgesen, and Rashotte 1994), Finnish (Dufva, Niemi, and Voeten 2001) and German (Schneider and Näslund 1993). Fourthly, PA can easily be trained as a part of regular preschool programme (Lundberg, Frost, and Petersen 1988) with positive training results extending throughout the primary school particularly for children at risk for dyslexia (Elbro and Petersen 2004).

Analysing the available literature on phonological awareness would be a formidable task. For example, database PsycINFO gave about 1000 hits for the term at the end of year 2005. The present review therefore considers themes pertinent to the role of PA in literacy acquisition while simultaneously keeping an eye at other important factors that deserve attention. It is suggested that the success of PA is due to its pedagogical usefulness rather than its ability to explain a lion's share of variation in beginning reading. Other factors promoting literacy acquisition are also briefly reviewed. Some of them are cognitive or linguistic in nature such as rapid automatic naming and metacognition. Others have social origins such as letter knowledge and task orientation. Finally, the question is raised whether it is possible to delineate a predictable path from early, even very early language-related skills to beginning reading and spelling. When possible, the review draws on recent cross-linguistic comparisons that underscore the role of the language as a means of literacy acquisition. Presently it is widely recognised that phonologically and orthographically different native languages provide a natural laboratory in which theories of reading acquisition can be tested.

2. Phonological awareness: a definite or partial key to literacy acquisition?

If anything has been thoroughly studied in the context of beginning reading that is phonological awareness. After a slow start in the 1970's, a true research industry has emerged around it. What is more, PA has been studied across a number of languages, both alphabetical and non-alphabetical, and it appears reasonable to conclude that its development is universal across languages (e.g., Anthony and Francis 2005). In the face of such massive evidence, one may start wondering whether less effort would suffice. In fact, it is hard to avoid a heretical thought that certain overdoing is taking place. More than twenty years of devoted research still falls short of explaining a sizeable share of variance in beginning word reading ability by means of PA measured in preliterate children. The correlations typically range from 0.30 to 0.75 (see Kjeldsen, Niemi, and Olofsson 2003). Caution must be exercised, however, with coefficients as high as 0.70. If not explicitly stated otherwise, such strong relationships may be due to the fact that preschool readers are not excluded from the sample. In countries like Finland such a confounding is a real possibility because anything between 20 to 50 % of children are readers before entering grade 1. Caution is also suggested by recent meta-analyses and reviews. Bus and van IJzendoorn (1999) found among 32 intervention studies that PA explained on the average 12 % of the variance in later word-reading skill. Basing on 24 prediction studies, Snow, Martin, and Griffin (1998) reported an average correlation of r = .46, respectively, a result closely paralleling those by Scarborough's (1998; 2002) meta-analyses. The time record for prediction appears to have been set by MacDonald and Cornwall (1995) who observed significant correlations for an unselected group between kindergarten PA and 11 years later collected oral decoding measures (r=.49) and those of spelling (r=.53; n=24). Frost, Madsbjerg, Niedersøe, Olofsson, and Sørensen (2005) have reported a follow-up study of equal time span but with younger participants. However, a reasonable conclusion is that, albeit impressive, the prediction of literacy development on the basis of PA is far from perfect. It appears that its important role in reading acquisition needs qualification.

The emergence of PA in language development means that the child is travelling the path towards being able to read and spell by ear, that is, able to perform phoneme blending and segmentation. With these skills in luggage, the remaining step to full literacy is short. Here different orthographies provide vastly varying challenges. Consider, for example, a young Finn who has learned to hear the sounds of a word. S/he can trust the fact that they reliably coincide with letters when the same word is written. Not surprisingly, s/he usually has a full command of letter names at the time PA makes its debut (e.g. Holopainen, Ahonen, Tolvanen, and Lyytinen 2000). Even children-at-risk who score zero in PA master about half of the alphabet six months before grade 1 (Poskiparta, Niemi, and

Vauras 1999). As a consequence, for Finnish beginning readers the time window is narrow for PA to affect literacy acquisition (Holopainen, Ahonen, and Lyytinen 2001). Cracking the code typically happens within 1 to 4 months after the school entrance. What is more, reading accuracy is nearly perfect. This is evidenced as a high correlation (r=.93) between reading words and non-words during the first months of literacy (Holopainen et al. 2000). The short-lived relevance of PA for literacy acquisition has also been observed in other transparent languages like in Dutch (de Jong and van der Leij 1999) and Latvian (Sprugevica and Høien 2003). All this is in stark contrast with deep, irregular orthographies like Danish and English, in which the beginning reader needs considerably more time to achieve a word reading accuracy above 90% correct (e.g. Seymour, Aro, and Erskine 2003). Accordingly it has been shown that PA remains a longer time a good predictor in English than in transparent orthographies (e.g., Cardoso-Martins and Pennington 2004; Parrila, Kirby, and McQuarrie 2004).

Rate of acquisition of PA seems also to vary between orthographies suggesting that it is learned in the context of some other feats. Mastering simple tasks such as rhyming and onset detection precedes chronologically more demanding phonemic tasks. Among these, blending and deleting phonemes are so close to reading that they typically show a spurt together with beginning reading. The idea of multifactor structure of phonological awareness is attractive from the point of view of skill development. There is recent evidence suggesting that rime awareness and phonological awareness are separable skills (Carroll et al. 2003; Muter et al. 1998). A study of beginning Norwegian readers suggests no less than a three-factor structure, these being phonological sensitivity to rhyme, syllables and phonemes, respectively (Høien et al. 1995). However, evidence is equivocal. In another set of studies based on English language, a single factor solution is typically found (Anthony and Lonigan 2004; Anthony et al. 2002; Lonigan et al. 2000; Stahl and Murray 1994). These conflicting results do not lend themselves to a quick explanation. It would be tempting to speculate that the much more regular Norwegian language results in independent phonological sensitivity factors instead of one global. However, any speculation based on language differences seems to be ruled out due to the fact that American and British results stand in conflict. Be it as it may, the prediction can nevertheless be made that sensitivity to rhyming is predictive of more advanced phonological skills (Anthony and Lonigan 2004).

Some recent findings call into question the idea that PA stands as the most powerful predictor of reading development. Lepola, Salonen, and Vauras (2000) found clearly distinguishable trajectories from preschool to grade 2 with some air of paradox around them. Two sub-groups were of particular interest. A progressive reading career featured a rapid decoding development from very low or no preschool PA up to the best third of readers. A regressive career was characterised by an opposite development from much above average preschool PA, often accompanied by beginning reading, down to the level of lowest third of readers. These profiles remained stable during grades 1 and 2, thus suggesting that they were not due to regression towards the mean.

In conclusion, literacy prognosis based on PA appears to be weaker than usually thought. On the other hand, there is no reason to jettison it. Perhaps a shift of attention is needed, away from general effects towards gains enjoyed by children at risk for serious literacy defects. Training results with pre-school non-readers suggest that these children would be the real beneficiaries (e.g., Lundberg et al. 1988; Schneider et al. 1997). The few published long-term training studies will be reviewed in the following. Then the possibility is considered that PA is a necessary rather than sufficient condition for literacy. Perhaps other factors needed in beginning literacy play an equally prominent role? An obvious candidate, of course, is letter knowledge.

What is more, PA and letter knowledge are skills that children younger than 3 to years do not master. Therefore their own precursors are still largely unknown (Lonigan, Burgess, and Anthony 2000). The section is ended by a review of follow-up studies from the first year of life to literacy acquisition that bear on this question.

3. Long-lasting benefits to children-at-risk?

Longitudinal research extending over several years is needed in order to ascertain whether or not preschool training in PA results in gains that will be maintained over time. Unfortunately, longitudinal training studies are not only time consuming but also expensive, and they are few in number. For example, in their meta-analysis of 32 training studies, Bus and van IJzendoorn (1999) found that the maintenance of the effects was brought up in only 9 of them, with the longest follow-up period being 2 yrs 5 mo. A European database compiled by Schneider and Stengård (1999) lists 144 longitudinal studies of reading development since the 1980's. Of these, only three feature an intervention with a follow-up until grade 3. In an extensive meta-analysis, Ehri, Nunes, Willows, et al. (2001) cited 52 studies resulting in altogether 96 relevant comparisons between treatment and control groups. However, for word reading, only 8 comparisons are reported as "second follow-ups" with delay varying from 7mo to 3 yrs. For spelling this number is 6.

An interim conclusion is that all the above studies fall short of demonstrating effects of PA training that would last throughout the primary school. However, there are a handful of studies with an unusually long follow-up interval. In Australia, Byrne, Fielding-Barnsley and Ashley (2000) observed improved word list reading until grade 5 in an unselected sample. It can be argued, however, that a crucial test is that involving children with a very low level of PA at school entrance. Lundberg (1994) observed sustained training effects until grade 3 among such children-at-risk while following up his original Danish sample (Lundberg et al. 1988). Also in Denmark, Elbro and Petersen (2004) found positive training effects for children with familial risk for dyslexia as late as in grade 7. These effects were significant for word and non-word reading, both in terms of speed and accuracy, and symptomatic for reading comprehension that was not tested in earlier grades. It is noteworthy Elbro and Petersen (2004) reported no observations between grades 3 and 7. Witting (2005) has reported analogous findings in the Swedish-speaking district of Åland in Finland. She found general training effects up to grade 6 on word and sentence reading and specific gains in spelling for children-at-risk identified at the beginning of the preschool.

Byrne et al. (2000) have introduced a dynamic measure of PA that can be applied in the analysis of training effects. "Session of last error" (SLE) refers to the last one in a series of consecutive sessions when the child is still being insecure while choosing items on a worksheet or poster that contain the targeted sound. In other words, "zero" means mastering PA from the beginning while a score equalling the number of sessions stands for clearly less than successful acquisition. It turned out that SLE effectively accounted for variance in reading level in grades 2 and 5 over and above that explained by the post-training score of PA. The fact that SLE predicts later reading level independently of the actual final achievement, suggests that rate of acquisition reflects some fundamental learning potential worth of diagnosing. Thus far this intriguing possibility has not received the attention it deserves.

Some other recent studies suggest that long-term advantage due phonological awareness training may be hard to achieve if training is started after the school entrance. Niemi and Poskiparta (2001) reported that sizeable initial gains disappeared by grade 3 when Finnish readers-at-risk trained in grade 1 were tested with a reading-aloud task. Both speed and accuracy of reading had fallen to the level of the original control group. An additional problem is the lack of transfer of training to reading although PA scores are essentially improved (Olson, 2002). Corroborating evidence comes from a Swedish study of 33 poorly reading 4th graders. After completed training about half of them showed no effect of newly acquired phonological skills on word reading (Gustafson, Samuelsson, and Rönnberg 2000).

4. Not only phonological awareness: The role of letter knowledge

Evidence reviewed so far suggests that a high level of PA is related to later successful literacy acquisition. However, data supporting this have all but almost exclusively been collected at a group level and individual developmental trajectories may look very different. For example, Holopainen et al. (2001) observed low PA scores in preschool for pupils who became accurate readers half a year later. Aro, Aro, Ahonen, et al. (1999) demonstrated the individual variability by means of an intensive time series data. These were collected once a month during 13 months in a training study with 6 pupils whose school entry had been postponed because of underdeveloped social skills and immature group work abilities. The group data reflected well the usual pattern of reading acquisition as a function of increasing PA. However, individual trajectories were different in terms of components of PA and rate of learning to read to the effect that group data did not represent any of individual participants. Observations like these have later led Lyytinen and co-workers (2005) to ask whether the role of PA may have been overrated in explaining reading success or failure. Finnish children typically learn the alphabet early. For example, Lepola et al. (2005) observed that 5 yrs 8 mo old non-readers wrote correctly 7.39/19 letters. In phoneme recognition tests young Finns usually respond by the letter name in question instead of the sound because of the perfect correspondence between the two. Lyytinen et al. (2005) argue that this feat creates a basis for achieving sufficient PA with their combination more often than not resulting in fast reading acquisition. The idea is essentially same as in the phonological linkage hypothesis put forth by Hatcher, Hulme, and Ellis (1994) and Byrne (1998) who argued that explicit teaching of reading should combine learning the alphabet and PA. This observation is far from trivial. Teaching the alphabet alone seems to be a futile enterprise (see Adams 1990: 61–64). While commenting on these early results, Elbro and Scarborough (2004) compared knowing the letter names in the absence of knowledge of grapheme-to-phoneme correspondences with knowing bicycle parts without being able to ride it. Debates concerning the phonological linkage hypothesis make sense in irregular orthographies such as Danish and English. However, there is barely a need to discuss the hypothesis in languages where at least reading is based on reliable G-P conversion rules. German makes a good example of this. What is more, there are orthographies in which the phonological linkage is a necessity that nobody calls into question. In agglutinative languages with perfect or at least predictable G-P conversion rules like Estonian, Finnish and Hungarian, learning to read would be impossible without an explicit G-P linkage. Take the Finnish word for "America", /Amerikka/, that looks easy enough. However, things soon get trickier for the beginning reader. "Americans" would be spelled as /amerikkalaiset/. What about "not even of the Americans", /amerikkalaisistakaan/, with its 20 characters? Typical of agglutinative languages is their morphological richness that easily results in words including more than 20 characters. Needless to say, irregular G-P rules would have devastating effects for literacy acquisition. This risk is effectively alleviated by G-P regularity.

Given the obvious usefulness of mastering G-P rules, one may ask whether it is possible to train them effectively? While being trivial for prospective mainstream readers, the question is crucial for children-at-risk who struggle with phonological recoding. It is obvious that learning of G-P rules cannot be based on "insight" suddenly gained after some teaching. On the contrary, struggling beginning readers are often quite resistant to teaching efforts. The logical way to provide remedy would be massive practice. However, learning would soon to be halted by a lack of motivation that occurs concomitantly with reading and spelling difficulties (e.g. Poskiparta, Niemi, Lepola, et al. 2003).

Computer-assisted training methods have about 30 years' history in the context of reading research. Recently the interest has declined, mainly because transfer to real-life reading seems hard to achieve (see, e.g., Olson 2002). There is one exception deserving attention, however. Drawing on data from a longitudinal study of children with familial risk for dyslexia, Lyytinen, Ronimus, Alanko, et al. (2007) propose a training method that shows great promise in circumventing the above problems. The children in their study have had a history of language problems since the first year of life. In a computer game the trainee makes a choice from among 2–9 written items that matches a simultaneously given auditory item. The written items are balls falling down on the screen and the auditory item is heard through headphones. The participant chooses by clicking the mouse on the relevant orthographic target. The starting level is connecting sounds and letters. After that, the game is gradually made more demanding. Finally the trainee associates difficult pseudoword items with their phonological form. Experience available so far indicates that after a short parental or teacher introduction, the trainee can go on playing independently, usually with an enthusiasm akin to other computer games. The difficulty level can be held within rewarding limits by adjusting the speed and number of falling targets. Initial studies show a significant positive transfer to beginning reading. Tests of eventual long-term gains are in progress.

5. The developmental path to literacy

Not surprisingly, PA and knowledge of the alphabet seem to be the decisive building blocks of beginning literacy. However, studies pertaining to the child's path towards these feats are scarce. Most interesting ones are those that follow the development from the first year of life.

The classical study of Scarborough (1990) is the first linking the mile-stones of language and reading development in a long perspective. She studied three groups of prospective readers. These were 20 children with a familial risk for dyslexia who later became poor readers, 12 children also with a familial risk for dyslexia but who became normal readers, and 20 children with no familial risk but otherwise similar to the dyslexic group. Predictably, the 5 years old prospective dyslexics had a relatively poor letter-sound knowledge and phonemic awareness. Earlier language development, in turn, significantly predicted this outcome. At 2.5 years of age the prospective dyslexics were behind the others in such aspects of spoken language as mean length and syntactic complexity of utterances as well as pronunciation accuracy. At 3 years of age they performed more poorly than others in object naming and receptive vocabulary. Vocabulary differences entered the picture at 3.5 years of age. Importantly, group differences were significantly predicted by previous differences, with early syntactic skills accounting for unique variance still in grade 2 reading ability.

In Finland, Lyytinen and his associates (e.g., 2004) have undertaken an extension of Scarborough's (1990) study. Altogether 107 children with familial risk for dyslexia and their controls (n=93) have been closely followed from birth to first grade that begins in Finland the year when children turn 7 years old. This study is probably the first one that tries to answer prospectively the question of really early signs of dyslexic development. The validity of participant selection was evidenced by the fact that in grade 1 half of the children-at-risk had fallen below the 10th percentile in their reading development relative to the control group. How early were Lyytinen and his associates able to predict this development?

As it turned out, newborn children-at-risk showed a significant tendency to produce a larger cortical response to a rarely occurring auditory vowel length ("kaa" vs. "ka") and, interestingly, consistently in the right hemisphere (Leppänen et al. 1999). At six months, they showed less ability to categorise speech sounds ("ata" vs. "atta") in a head-turning conditioning procedure (Richardson et al. 2003), again a sign of poorly functioning speech discrimination. However, early vocalization as observed by parents did not differ between the groups (Lyytinen et al. 1996) nor did expressive and receptive vocabulary measures between 12 and 30 months of age (Lyytinen and Lyytinen 2004). The first signs of PA as well as related group differences were observed at 3.5 years of age (Puolakanaho et al. 2004). After this point the development towards beginning reading runs the course known from other studies with pseudoword repetition, phoneme identification and rapid serial naming, all measured at 3.5 years of age, being strong predictors of later group differences in reading (Lyytinen et al. 2004).

The above results on early predictors are supported by another set of studies that approaches the problem from a different angle. There is some evidence that awareness of sound patterns in words can be predicted at 4.0 years of age by vocabulary size in late infancy. Evidence comes from Silvén et al. (2004). In that study, children who could read prior to school entrance were compared with their nonreading agemates from their first year of life. Group differences emerged at 2 years of age in expressive vocabulary, while inflectional morphology differentiated well from 3 to 5 years of age. Concomitantly with it, awareness of onset and rhyme showed differences at 4 and 5 years, while phonemic abilities showed robust differences at 5 and 6 years. Taken together, these results suggest that there is a developmental hierarchy in PA and in some measures, either learned previously or to be learned in future, children with differing abilities can well be at the same level of skills or virtually all lack it. The former was shown by Silvén et al. (2004). The latter was demonstrated by de Jong and van der Leij (2003) whose Dutch participants showed significant differences in rhyming ability but no difference at all in tasks requiring phonemic awareness.

6. Slow naming speed and literacy acquisition problems

Because the bulk of literacy research has been conducted in English on English, this language has greatly affected the methods. One consequence has been the emphasis of reading and spelling accuracy at the expense of fluency. Speed measures such as reading aloud, word chains or lexical decision are more seldom used. However, fluency is an integral aspect of learning to read in regular orthographies as convincingly shown by the data of Aro and Wimmer (2003). The Finnish, Finland-Swedish and Spanish first graders read pseudowords and number words at the speed of 2.5 s/item, a fluency that was reached by the Austrian, Dutch and French children in grade 2, and by Scottish children in grade 4.

As the aforementioned data by Lyytinen et al. (2004) and Puolakanaho et al. (2004) showed, naming speed is already at the age of 3.5 yrs associated with further success in literacy acquisition. It refers to the facility that a child shows while naming aloud familiar, overlearned items such as geometric forms, colours, numerals and letters. Its status both as a concurrent and longitudinal predictor of reading difficulty is firmly established (see Wolf, Bowers, and Biddle 2000, particularly Table 1). Rapid naming is obviously confounded with other phonological processes and in this sense it does not differ from other measures used in literacy research. For those aiming at perfect empirical dissociations this may be frustrating. For others the question is rather about whether rapid naming ability adds an independent component to reading acquisition. There is a current debate going on about this issue. Wagner, Torgesen, Rashotte, et al. (1997) showed that individual differences in naming speed were related to initial word-reading ability but the relationship disappeared after that (see also de Jong and van der Leij 1999). On the other hand, Holopainen et al. (2001) observed in a perfectly transparent language, Finnish, that the prediction accuracy of phonological awareness is significant only in grade 1 whereas that of rapid naming ability retained its power still in grade 2. This is in line with Korhonen's (1995) observation that naming problems persist at least into the adolescence.

Two conclusions appear reasonable. First, phonological awareness and rapid naming tap areas of language processing that probably overlap (see, e.g., Schatschneider et al. 2002). Second, if a reader has a deficit in both that is, a so-called double-deficit, s/he is more severely handicapped than one with either deficit alone (e.g. Wolf et al. 2000). The latter observation gives a further possibility to study the relative independence by way of literacy interventions specifically aiming at both deficits. To date such attempts are few. Levy, Bourassa, and Horn (1999) studied second-grader poor readers who had either double-deficit or phonological deficit alone. They were trained to read a word list with the training including onset/rime segmentation, phonemic segmentation, and whole word repetition. Pupils with a double-deficit were slow to learn the words in each training condition, and they were particularly slow with whole words. Other interventions reported have aimed at improved fluency and comprehension among second- and third-graders (Wolf and Katzir-Cohen 2001; Wolf, Miller, and Donnelly 2000), and therefore they do not pertain to literacy acquisition.

7. Two more culprits: metacognition and motivation?

As noted towards the beginning of the chapter, research has not able to explain as much of the variation in beginning reading and writing as desired. Reasons for this are manifold. Some obvious sources are next to impossible to include in studies with a usual scope. Teacher effects suffice as an example of this. When they can be analysed in sufficiently large samples, they prove to be strong (e.g. Lundberg and Linnakylä 1993: 90–91). In a similar vein, there are two more, presently underdiagnosed variables that in part reflect teacher influence in beginning reader's performance. School entrance puts the pupil's motivational resources to a test. Preschool activities are playful and egalitarian whereas school performance, even when not graded, is subject to public evaluative feedback from the teacher. For most pupils such events pass by without causing harm, but for others the stress and even its anticipation may become a burden. It is plausible that pupils with less than average literacy readiness skills are particularly vulnerable because an important asset for successful school performance is the ability to remain concentrated on the task at hand, even in the presence of distractive elements. Poskiparta et al. (2003) found evidence suggesting that this ability deteriorates concomitantly with poor reading development during grades 1 and 2. Prospective poor and average readers did not differ in terms of task orientation in preschool. However, the poor readers significantly more than average readers monitored social cues and resorted in ego-defensive behaviours in school situations, and even in games where performance obstacles were introduced. Another way to examine motivational effects would a prognosis from preschool non-readers' motivation to literacy acquisition. Salonen, Lepola, and Niemi (1998) identified groups of preschoolers with extreme motivational dispositions. An important finding was that task orientation collapsed for the children with a high score in ego-defensive trait-like behaviour when participating in a game with frustrating performance obstacles. In grade 1 task orientation was the strongest predictor of word recognition ability, also when phonological awareness was included. It should be noted, however, that the chicken-and-egg problem is obvious when motivational effects on reading are considered. Be it as it may, preschool task orientation stands as an independent predictor of grade 1 word reading even after phonological awareness and rapid automatised naming ability are controlled (Lepola et al. 2005).

Finally, phonological awareness includes an insight component to the effect that the child understands that words have a form that is, they sound in a special way in addition meaning something. Question can thus be raised whether the ability to go behind the immediately given information is more generally present in literacy acquisition. The relevant measure would be metacognition that is, a child's ability reflect upon his/her cognitive processes such as memory, learning and comprehension. In his reanalysis of existing longitudinal data from preschool to grade 3, Kärnä (2005) showed that the hypothesis gets support. Metacognitive data were collected from preschool non-readers and their contribution to word reading ability in grades 1 to 3 was analysed by means of partial correlations. The variables to be partialled out were phonological awareness and letter knowledge, also measured in preschool. The independent contribution of metacognitive ability to word reading variability was significant albeit not large, varying from 5 to 10 %, with correlations in the range of .20–.30.

8. Conclusions

The state of the art of literacy acquisition seems to point to two directions. On the one hand, the present knowledge is sufficient from the point of view of effective interventions. It probably is justifiable to say that most dyslexics can today be educated to readers. The reason is that two important precursors of reading and spelling ability, phonological awareness and letter knowledge, are common for alphabetic orthographies and very much open for various training approaches. The trainability potential of the third potent predictor, rapid automatised naming, still awaits proper investigation. On the other hand, the dynamics involving various precursors along the path towards competent literacy is heavily dependent on the grapheme-to-phoneme regularity of the orthography. The degree of regularity affects reading development at least up to grade 4, even when very simple reading materials are used (Seymour et al. 2003). As a consequence, the importance of the so-called granularity problem in literacy acquisition has recently been recognised. In irregular orthographies the mapping rules are far more complex than in regular ones because there is no reliable relationship between graphemes and phonemes. Therefore the beginning reader is also forced to used larger units than them as building blocks of word decoding. The first comprehensive treatment of this topic has only recently been published (Ziegler and Goswami 2005). Finally, variability in beginning reading can presently be explained only in part. One reason is that there are struggling readers who are barely helped by any known intervention. These resistant readers are burdened by problems beyond the linguistic and cognitive ones usually associated with dyslexia. Providing them with a decent reading career poses a formidable task for both reading research and profession.

References

Adams, M. J.
    1990   *Beginning to Read. Thinking and Learning about Print.* Cambridge, MA: The MIT Press.
Aro, M., Aro, T., Ahonen, Räsänen, T., Hietala, A., and H. Lyytinen
    1999   The development of phonological abilities and their relation to reading acquisition: Case studies of six Finnish children. *Journal of Learning Disabilities* 32: 457–463, 478.
Aro, M. and H. Wimmer
    2003   Learning to read: English in comparison to six more regular orthographies. *Applied Psycholinguistics* 24: 621–635.
Anthony, J. and D. Francis
    2005   Development of phonological awareness. *Current Directions in Psychological Science* 14: 255–259.
Anthony, J. and C. Lonigan
    2004   The nature of phonological awareness: Converging evidence from four studies of preschool and early grade school children. *Journal of Educational Psychology* 96: 43–55.
Anthony, J., Lonigan, C., Burgess, S., Driscoll, K. Phillips, B., and B. Cantor
    2002   Structure of preschool phonological sensitivity: Overlapping sensitivity to rhyme, words, syllables, and phonemes. *Journal of Experimental Child Psychology* 82: 65–92.
Bus, A. and M. van IJzendoorn
    1999   Phonological awareness and early reading: A meta-analysis of experimental training studies. *Journal of Educational Psychology* 91: 403–414.
Bradley, L. and P. Bryant
    1983   Categorising sounds and learning to read: A causal connection. *Nature* 301: 419–421.
Byrne, B.
    1998   *The Foundation of Literacy. The Child's Acquisition of the Alphabetic Principle.* Hove, UK: Psychology Press.
Byrne, B., Fielding-Barnsley, R., and L. Ashley
    2000   Effects of preschool phoneme identity training after six years: Outcome level distinguished from rate of response. *Journal of Educational Psychology* 92: 659–667.

Cardoso-Martins, C. and B. Pennington
2004 The relationship between phoneme awareness and rapid serial naming skills and literacy acquisition: The role of developmental period and reading ability. *Scientific Studies of Reading* 8: 27–52.
Carroll, J., Snowling, M., Hulme, C., and J. Stevenson
2003 The development of phonological awareness in preschool children. *Developmental Psychology* 39: 913–923.
De Jong, P. and A. van der Leij
1999 Specific contributions of phonological abilities to early reading acquisition: Results from a Dutch latent variable longitudinal study. *Journal of Educational Psychology* 91: 450–476.
De Jong, P. and A. van der Leij
2003 Developmental changes in the manifestation of a phonological deficit in dyslexic children learning to read a regular orthography. *Journal of Educational Psychology* 95: 22–40.
Dufva, M., Niemi, P., and M. Voeten
2001 The role of phonological memory, word recognition, and comprehension skills in reading development: From preschool to Grade 2. *Reading and Writing: An Interdisciplinary Journal* 14: 91–117.
Ehri, L., Nunes, D., Willows, D., Schuster, B., Yaghoub-Zadeh, Z., and T. Shanahan
2001 Phonemic awareness instruction helps children learn to read: Evidence from the National Reading Panel's meta-analysis. *Reading Research Quarterly* 36: 250–287.
Elbro, C. and D. Petersen
2004 Long-term effects of phoneme awareness and letter-sound training: An intervention study with children at risk for dyslexia. *Journal of Educational Psychology* 96: 660–670.
Elbro, C., Möller, S., and E. Nielsen
1995 Functional reading difficulties in Denmark: A study of adult reading of common texts. *Reading and Writing: An Interdisciplinary Journal* 7: 257–276.
Elbro, C. and H. Scarborough
2004 Early intervention. In: T. Nunes and P. Bryant (eds.), *Handbook of Children's Literacy*, 361–381. Dordrecht, The Netherlands: Kluwer.
Gough, P. and W. Tunmer
1986 Decoding, reading, and reading disability. *RASE: Remedial and Special Education* 7: 6–10.
Gustafson, S., Samuelsson, S., and J. Rönnberg
2000 Why do some resist phonological intervention? A Swedish longitudinal study of poor readers in grade 4. *Scandinavian Journal of Educational Research* 44: 145–162.
Frost, J., Madsbjerg, S., Niedersøe, J., Olofsson, Å., and P. Sørensen
2005 Semantic and phonological skills in predicting reading development: From 3–16 years of age. *Dyslexia* 11: 79–92.
Hatcher, P., Hulme, C., and A. Ellis
1994 Ameliorating early reading failure by integrating the teaching of reading and phonological skills: The phonological linkage hypothesis. *Child Development* 65: 41–57.

Hjelmquist, E. and C. von Euler
  2002 *Dyslexia and Literacy*. London. Whurr.
Høien, T., Lundberg, I., Stanovich, K., and I. Bjaalid
  1995 Components of phonological awareness. *Reading and Writing: An Interdisciplinary Journal* 7: 171–188.
Holopainen, L., Ahonen, T., Tolvanen, A., and H. Lyytinen
  2000 Two alternative ways to model the relation between reading accuracy and phonological awareness at preschool age. *Scientific Studies of Reading* 4: 77–100.
Holopainen, L., Ahonen, T., and H. Lyytinen
  2001 Predicting delay in reading achievement in a highly transparent language. *Journal of Learning Disabilities* 34: 401–413.
Kärnä, A.
  2005 Lasten muistia, oppimista ja ymmärtämistä koskevan metakognitiivisen tiedon yhteys dekoodauksen oppimiseen lukutaidon kehityksen alkuvaiheessa. (The relationship of children's metacognitive knowledge of memory, learning and comprehension with learning to decode at the initial stage of reading development.) Unpublished Master's Thesis, University of Turku, Finland.
Kjeldsen, A-C., Niemi, P., and Å. Olofsson
  2003 Training phonological awareness in kindergarten level children: Consistency is more important than quantity. *Learning and Instruction* 13: 349–365.
Korhonen, T.
  1995 The persistence of rapid naming problems in children with reading disabilities: A nine-year follow-up. *Journal of Learning Disabilities* 28: 232–239.
Lepola, J., Poskiparta, E., Laakkonen, E., and P. Niemi
  2005 Development of and relationship between phonological and motivational processes and naming speed in predicting word recognition in grade 1. *Scientific Studies of Reading* 9: 367–399.
Lepola, J., Salonen, P., and M. Vauras
  2000 The development of motivational orientations as a function of divergent reading careers from pre-school to the second grade. *Learning and Instruction* 10: 153–177.
Leppänen., P., Pihko, E., Eklund, K., and H. Lyytinen
  1999 Cortical responses of infants with and without a genetic risk for dyslexia: II. Group effects. *NeuroReport* 10: 901–905.
Levy, B., Bourassa, D., and C. Horn
  1999 Fast and slow namers: Benefits of segmentation and whole word training. *Journal of Experimental Child Psychology* 73: 115–138.
Lundberg, I. and P. Linnakylä
  1993 *Teaching Reading around the World*. Hague, The Netherlands: The International Association for the Evaluation of Educational Achievement.
Lonigan, C., Burgess, S., and J. Anthony
  2000 Development of emergent literacy and early reading skills in preschool children: Evidence from a latent-variable longitudinal study. *Developmental Psychology* 36: 596–613.

Lundberg, I.
   1994   Reading difficulties can be predicted and prevented: A Scandinavian perspective on phonological awareness and reading. In C. Hulme and M. Snowling (eds.), *Reading Development and Dyslexia*, 180–199. London: Whurr.
Lundberg, I., Frost, J., and O.-P. Petersen
   1988   Effects of an extensive program for stimulating phonological awareness in preschool children. *Reading Research Quarterly* 23: 263–284.
Lyytinen, H., Aro, M., Eklund, K., Erskine, J., Guttorm, T., Laakso, M.-L., Leppänen, P., Lyytinen, P., Poikkeus, A-M., Richardson, U., and M. Torppa
   2004   The development of children at familial risk for dyslexia: Birth to early school age. *Annals of Dyslexia* 54: 184–220.
Lyytinen, H., Aro, M., Holopainen, L., Leiwo, M., Lyytinen, P., and A. Tolvanen
   2005   Children's language development and reading acquisition in a highly transparent orthography. In: R. M. Joshi and P. G. Aaron (eds.), *Handbook of Orthography and Literacy*, 47–62. Mahwah, NJ: Erlbaum.
Lyytinen, H., Ronimus, M., Alanko, A., Taanila, M., and A.-M. Poikkeus
   2007   Early identification and prevention of dyslexia. *Nordic Psychology,* 59: 109–126.
Lyytinen, P. and H. Lyytinen
   2004   Growth and predictive relations of vocabulary and inflectional morphology in children with and without familial risk for dyslexia. *Applied Psycholinguistics* 25: 397–411.
Lyytinen, P., Poikkeus, A-M., Leiwo, M., Ahonen, T., and H. Lyytinen
   1996   Parents as informants of their child's vocal and early language development. *Early Child Development and Care* 126: 15–25.
MacDonald, G. and A. Cornwall
   1995   The relationship between phonological awareness and reading and spelling achievement eleven years later. *Journal of Learning Disabilities* 28: 523–527.
Muter, V., Hulme, C., Snowling, M., and S. Taylor
   1998   Segmentation, not rhyming, predicts early progress in learning to read. *Journal of Experimental Child Psychology* 71: 3–27.
Niemi, P. and E. Poskiparta
   2001   Benefits of training in linguistic awareness disspate by grade 3? *Psychology. The Journal of Hellenic Psychological Society* 8: 330–337.
Olson, R.
   2002   Phoneme awareness and reading: From the old to the new millennium. In: E. Hjelmquist and C. von Euler (eds.), *Dyslexia and Literacy,* 100–116. London: Whurr.
Parrila, R., Kirby, J., and L. McQuarrie
   2004   Articulation rate, naming speed, verbal short-term memory, and phonological awareness: Longitudinal predictors of early reading development. *Scientific Studies of Reading* 8: 3–26.
Poskiparta, E., Niemi, P., and M. Vauras
   1999   Who benefits from training in linguistic awareness in the first grade, and what components show training effects? *Journal of Learning Disabilities* 32: 437–446, 456.

Poskiparta, E., Niemi, P., Lepola, J., Ahtola, A., and P. Laine
   2003   Motivational-emotional vulnerability and difficulties in learning to read and spell. *British Journal of Educational Psychology* 73: 187–206.

Puolakanaho, A., Poikkeus, A-M., Ahonen, T., Tolvanen, A., and H. Lyytinen
   2004   Emerging phonological awareness as a precursor of risk in children with and without familial risk for dyslexia. *Annals of Dyslexia* 54: 221–243.

Richardson, U., Leppänen, P., Leiwo, M., and H. Lyytinen
   2003   Speech perception of infants with high familial risk for dyslexia differ at the age of 6 months. *Developmental Neuropsychology* 23: 385–397.

Salonen, P., Lepola, J., and P. Niemi
   1998   The development of first graders' reading skill as a function of pre-school motivational orientation and phonemic awareness. *European Journal of Psychology of Education* 13: 155–174.

Scarborough, H.
   1990   Very early language deficits in dyslexic children. *Child Development* 61: 1728–1734.

Scarborough, H.
   1998   Early identification of children at risk for reading disabilities: Phonological awareness and some other promising predictors. In: B. Shapiro, P. Acardo, and A. Capute (eds.), *Specific Reading Disability: A View of the Spectrum.* 75–119. Timonium, MD: York Press.

Scarborough, H.
   2002   Connecting early language and literacy to later reading (dis)abilities.: Evidence, theory, and practice. In: S. Neuman and D. Dickinson (eds.), *Handbook of Early Literacy Research,* 97–110. New York: The Guilford Press.

Schatschneider, C., Carlson, C., Francis, D., Foorman, B., and J. Fletcher
   2002   Relationship of rapid automatized naming and phonological awareness in early reading development: Implications for the double-deficit hypothesis. *Journal of Learning Disabilities* 35: 245–256.

Schneider, W., Küspert, P., Roth, E., Visé, M., and H. Marx
   1997   Short- and long-term effects of training phonological awareness in kindergarten: Evidence from two German studies. *Journal of Experimental Child Psychology* 66: 311–340.

Schneider, W. and J. Näslund
   1993   The impact of early metalinguistic competencies and memory capacity on reading and spelling in elementary school: Results of the Munich Longitudinal Study on the Genesis of Individual Competencies (LOGIC). *European Journal of Psychology of Education* 8: 273–288.

Schneider, W. and C. Stengård
   1999   Inventory of European longitudinal studies of reading and spelling. Retrieved 2003–08–21 from http://www.psychologie.uni-wuerzburg.de/cost/inventory/htm.

Seymour, P., Aro, M., and J. Erskine
   2003   Foundation literacy acquisition in European orthographies. *British Journal of Psychology* 94: 143–174.

Silvén, M., Poskiparta, E., and P. Niemi
   2004   The odds of becoming a precocious reader of Finnish. *Journal of Educational Psychology* 96: 152–164.

Snow, C., Burns, M., and P. Griffin
 1998 *Preventing Reading Difficulties in Young Children.* Washington, DC: National Academic Press.

Sprugevica, I. and T. Høien
 2003 Early phonological skills as a predictor of reading acquisition: A follow-up study from kindergarten to the middle of grade 2. *Scandinavian Journal of Psychology* 44: 119–124.

Stahl, S. and B. Murray
 1994 Defining phonological awareness and its relatiuonship to early reading. *Journal of Educational Psychology* 86: 221–234.

Wagner, R., Torgesen, J., and C. Rashotte
 1994 Development of reading-related phonological processing abilities: New evidence of bidirectional causality from a latent variable longitudinal study. *Developmental Psychology* 30: 73–87.

Wagner, R., Torgesen, J., Rashotte, C., Hecht, S., Barker, T., Burgess, S., Donahue, J., and T. Garon
 1997 Changing relations between phonological processing abilities and word-level reading as children develop from beginning to skilled readers: A 5-year longitudinal study. *Developmental Psychology* 33: 468–479.

Witting, K.
 2005 Ger en metafonologisk språkleksträning i förskolan effect ännu i årskurs 6? (Does a metaphonological language game training in preschool result in effects still in grade 6?) Unpublished Master's Thesis, Åbo Akademi University, Finland.

Wolf, M., Bowers, P., and K. Biddle
 2000 Naming-speed processes, timing and reading: A conceptual review. *Journal of Learning Disabilities* 33: 387–407.

Wolf, M. and T. Katzir-Cohen
 2001 Reading fluency and its intervention. *Scientific Studies of Reading* 5: 211–239.

Wolf, M., Miller, L., and K. Donnelly
 2000 Retrieval, automaticity, vocabulary elaboration, orthography (RAVE-O): A comprehensive, fluency-based reading intervention program. *Journal of Learning Disabilities* 33: 375–386.

Ziegler, J. and U. Goswami
 2005 Reading acquisition, developmental dyslexia, and skilled reading across languages: A psycholinguistic grain size theory. *Psychological Bulletin* 131: 3–29.

7. Sign language acquisition

Vivian Gramley

Deaf[1] children acquire sign language the same way hearing children acquire spoken language. The stages through which Deaf and hearing children go are the same and occur at approximately the same time; and also the errors they make are comparable. Infants make use of manual "babbling" prior to producing their first words using reduplicated "syllables" and making use of the handshapes and locations which are most frequent in the respective sign language. This is comparable to how hearing children babble, substituting, for example, plosives for fricatives. The first words appear earlier in sign language than in spoken language, namely at about 8.5 months compared to between ten and 13 months for hearing/speaking children. Contrary to belief the majority of early signs are not particularly iconic. The main reason for this can be seen in the advantage of manual or gestural language as opposed to the disadvantages of vocal language. In sign language first words may be recognized and also corrected much earlier than in spoken language due to the overtness of the articulators. A first sign for "bottle" or "pacifier" is counted as a first word for Deaf but not hearing children. Child-directed talk, often referred to as motherese, is used in sign language as well and is not speech specific. Emotional facial expressions are produced consistently and universally by children by one year of age. From early on Deaf children are able to distinguish between communicative and linguistic gestures but are faced with a challenge when acquiring these visual-spatial aspects, the spatial memory demands of co-reference, and the visual attention demands of sign language when engaged in early conversations. The modality qua visual itself seems to plays a minor role in the process of acquiring language.

1. Introduction

Contrary to some people's belief there is not one universal sign language. There is not one sign language that is shared by all deaf people in the world. There are many different sign languages which have evolved independently of each other. They are all very different but also share similar elements. The features that are shared by all sign languages is the existence of a lexicon and grammatical rules. The lexicons and grammatical rules are different for every sign language, comparable to spoken languages. Just like spoken language, sign languages differ in their historical relationships. A well-known example in this respect is the difference between American Sign Language (ASL) and British Sign Language

(BSL). Although both languages are surrounded by the same spoken language, English, these two sign languages are historically very different and mutually unintelligible (Emmorey 2002: 2). French Sign Language and ASL, on the other hand, are more alike due to the influence of French Sign Language on American Deaf people in the eighteenth and early nineteenth centuries, when Laurent Clerc and Thomas Gallaudet, two French teachers of the Deaf, established the first public school for the Deaf in the United States. Nowadays, the two sign languages are clearly distinct languages (Lane 1984) sharing lexical features.

Another mis-belief is that sign languages are made up of pictorial signs, similar to pantomime, and are not as expressive as a spoken language. This is not true. Sign languages have an intricate structure and enable the speakers/ signers to express complex ideas just like speakers of spoken languages do. At times it seems difficult to describe a sign language linguistically because hearing linguists, who usually are the ones who describe sign languages, have to learn not only to look for features in a sign language that they know from spoken languages but recognize and acknowledge that sign languages also use a different modality, namely the visual one.

When taking a closer look at sign languages it becomes obvious that grammatical rules and lexicons are only two general features that sign languages have in common, even though each language has its own set of rules and its own lexicon. Above and beyond this, however, sign languages share the use of movement, handshape, position of the hands, as well as simultaneity. The main difference that can be seen between a signed and a spoken language is its mode. While spoken languages use articulatory organs located in the vocal tract in order to produce sounds, sign languages use a completely different set of articulators, namely the hands and the face. While spoken languages are organized linearly in time, sign languages make use of simultaneity and space. Simultaneity is the expression of more than one lexical and grammatical feature at the same time – meaning that different elements are incorporated in one sign, similar to polysynthetic languages (Bellugi and Klima 1982). Furthermore, spoken languages are perceived with the ear while sign languages are perceived with the eye. Needless to say, spoken languages also employ manual and facial gestures but do not rely solely on these for the transmission of lexical information.

This contribution will show how sign languages are acquired and how we find the similar or even the same types of mistakes in sign languages as we do in spoken languages.

2. Stages of sign language acquisition

When acquiring spoken language all hearing children go through the same stages at more or less the same point in time. It is well-known that there is always considerable variation in age in the actual acquisition process without this being pathological. The first step in language acquisition is the perception of a language. Hearing children start hearing their mother's voiced while still in the womb whereas Deaf children start seeing their mothers' sign for the first time after birth. The fact that infants actually observe and perceive language from the beginning on was shown with the help of *high-amplitude sucking paradigms*, first used by Eimas et al. (1971). "In this task, the infant is given a pacifier which contains a wire attached to a computer which measures the child's rate of sucking" (Ingram 1989: 87). Using this method it is possible to find out whether an infant is able to distinguish between different stimuli presented, e.g. a series of spoken [ba], [ba], [ba] syllables followed by a series consisting of a different syllable (e.g. [pa], [pa], [pa]), i.e. in this case a change between voiced and voiceless stops. In addition to the mere detection of a difference between the stimuli presented the infant is also able to control the amplitude or loudness of the stimuli by increasing the sucking rate (cf. Ingram 1989). It is also known that at this age hearing children react positively when hearing their mothers' voice. At this stage children recognize their mother's voice but do not distinguish between sounds of their mother tongue and foreign sounds. Later, once the child starts producing sounds, according to a universal theory of language acquisition in general and, more specifically, speech production, infants have the ability to produce any and every human sound but will eventually lose this ability and be able to articulate only those sounds that occur in their linguistic environment. It is generally at approximately ten months of age children start using the sounds of their mother tongue only.

What makes the observation of infants' first speech sounds relatively difficult is that they are so very distant from any specific language. Their earliest vocalizations are involuntary crying when they are uncomfortable or hungry (cf. e.g. Lightbown and Spada 2003). Soon they produce not only sounds of displeasure but also of pleasure, such as cooing. Still it takes months before babies start babbling. Even before they start babbling and try to master the phonemic contrasts of their language children begin to develop the articulatory movements needed to produce these distinctions in speech (Cho and O'Grady 1996).

Morford and Mayberry (2000: 112) point out that exposure to language from birth is not the norm for Deaf children. If they are, however, exposed to sign language from birth on, then "[c]hildren's sign language acquisition appears to parallel in many ways the language acquisition process of young children with normal hearing exposed to spoken language input from their parents" (Bonvillian and Patterson 1993: 317). However, when Deaf children acquire language they are faced with a very different situation than hearing children. The set of articulators they have to use is different from that of hearing children; as mentioned above Deaf people do not use their vocal tract but their hands and facial expression in order to communicate. Above and beyond that, sign language itself is perceived through a different channel, namely the visual one. Still, it is assumed that the capacities that underlie language acquisition are not specific for spoken or signed language but rather maturationally controlled and that the psychological, linguistic, and neural mechanisms involved apply to both language systems. Hearing and Deaf children both discover the phonological structure of their mother tongue through babbling. The aspect of manual babbling will be discussed at greater length below. Through "the development of this perceptual-motor connection [...] human infants [are allowed] to discover the units that serve to express linguistic meaning, whether encoded in speech or in sign" (Emmorey 2001: 172).

3. Manual babbling

Deaf children babble before they start producing their first words; however, when they babble they babble with their hands. In hearing children babbling, more technically referred to as "syllabic" or "canonical" babbling "involves vocalizations that exhibit these key properties: (i) use of a reduced subset of possible sounds (phonetic units) found in spoken language [...]; (ii) possession of syllabic organization (well-formed consonant-vowel) (CV) clusters; [...] and (iii) use without any apparent meaning" (Petitto, Holowka, Sergio, Levy and Ostry 2004: 44). This babbling is found to be organized according to rhythm, timing, and stress, as well as reduplications (ibid.). Manual babbling observed by Petitto and Marentette (1991) seemed to be a unique class of hand activities. These manual movements found in Deaf babies growing up in a Deaf environment were found from the age of ten months through fourteen months of age (Pettito and Marentette 1991) showing that babbling does not so much arise to such a high degree from the maturation of the articulatory organs specific to speech (Masataka 2000). These manual movements cannot be found in hearing children growing up in a hearing environment but seem to be unique to Deaf children. In hearing children syllabic repetitions such as "dadada" or "bababa" can be found instead. In analogy cyclic repetitions of movement can be found in Deaf children's babbling. Research has shown that manual babbling is found in Japanese (Masataka 2000) as well as in French Canadian Sign Language (Langue des Signes Québécoise; LSQ) (Pettito 1997), suggesting that babbling may be a universal principle. Further, Pettito and Marentette (1991: 1495) argue that babbling is "the mechanism by which infants discover the map between the structure of language and the means for producing this structure." This means that Deaf children map their manual articulations onto patterns in their visually signed input while hearing children map their vocal articulations onto patterns in auditory speech input. Vocal babbling can be observed in Deaf children, but it is reported to start late, i.e. generally after one year due to the lack of auditory feedback. This babbling also has a very low rate of cyclicity (Oller and Eilers

1988). Hearing children, on the other hand, also make use of manual "babbles" of which the status is not fully clear. However, they do receive visual feedback, i.e. they see grown-ups use nonlinguistic gestures just as they can see their own gestures (Emmorey 2002). They start at about seven months of age and continue past one year (Cormier, Mauk and Repp 1998). Some researchers argue that this babbling is a result of nonlinguistic gestures used in the babies' environment and a mere imitation, whereas others argue that these manual babbles are rooted in the stereotypic rhythmic motor actions that are produced by all infants (Thelen 1991). It has been found that Deaf infants use manual babbles in a more confined space, at a slower velocity, and without leg movement (Meier and Willerman 1995; Pettito and Marentette 1991), which could hint at a more linguistic "function".

In manual and vocal babbling children show preferences for certain signs or phonemes. Hearing children prefer stops (e.g. /b/, /d/, /p/, /t/) over fricatives (e.g. /z/, /s/), which also means that stops are substituted for fricatives. This preference can be found again in children's first words. A similar pattern can be observed in Deaf children, who prefer certain signs, i.e. handshape and locations over others. These frequent locations and handshapes will also dominate the first signs (Petitto and Marentette 1991). Whether babies grow up with sign or spoken language, what they have in common is that they use babbling in order to discover the phonological structure of their language (Emmorey 2002). And because both types of babbling start at more or less the same time, it is suggested that "babbling is not linked to inborn mechanisms for producing speech that may have evolved with our species" (Lieberman 1984), but "that babbling may reflect the maturation of a more general mechanism that maps patterned perceptual input (either auditory or visual) to related motoric output (either vocal or manual)" (Emmorey 2002: 172).

4. Motherese

Child-directed speech is "syntactically and morphologically simplified" (Reilly and Bellugi 1996: 220) and "unswervingly grammatical" (Newport, Gleitman, and Gleitman 1977: 121). Parents consistently modify the language input to their children, i.e. infants and toddlers. Especially for infants, prosody is the most important factor in speech perception, and in spoken language its most salient feature is the melodic contour, which is adjusted to the baby's needs (Masataka 1999). This need for a more differentiated prosody is met in motherese by heightening the pitch and using wider intonation contours (e.g. Garnica 1977). Further, parents have been observed to use shorter and simpler sentences, as well as repetitions and redundancies when communicating with their children (e.g. Snow 1972); also parents use longer pauses, talk more slowly, and add emphatic stress (cf. e.g. Garnica 1977). Independent of the interpretation of these findings, all researchers agree that this modified way of communicating with infants and toddlers serves the wish to communicate with the children (Snow 1972). Studies (Fernald 1985; Werker and McLeod 1989) confirm that infants show more interest in baby-directed talk than in adult-directed speech. A possible explanation lies in the elevated affectiveness of infant-directed speech. In the process of acquiring a first language children react positively towards motherese. The use of child-directed speech comes naturally to most parents when communicating with their infants. It is hypothesized that a more rhythmic type of speech helps children segment what they hear, i.e. detect and discriminate word and clause boundaries (Kemler-Nelson et al. 1989). Other researchers are of the opinion that motherese is employed in order to keep the child's attention. Fernald (1985) found that when given a choice, children prefer child directed speech to adult-directed speech.

Child-directed sign can also be found in Deaf parents signing to their babies. The signs that parents produce for their babies are longer in duration, contain more movement repetitions, and are relatively larger in size (cf. e.g. Holzrichter and Meier 2000;). Mothers, but presumably also fathers, also tend to angle the signs in such a way that the baby can see them better (Masataka 1992, 2000). Holzrichter and Meyer (2000) also suggest that the rhythmic alterations of signs observed in American Sign Language help babies segment the input and detect individual signs. Above and beyond that, the larger and slower movements of the signs are well suited to gaining the babies' attention. In addition, Masataka (2000) found that babies prefer motherese signing over adult-directed signing. The same preference was found in hearing babies who had never previously seen signing. A possible explanation is the pattern of the input – regardless of the input modality. Facial expression in sign languages, e.g. American Sign Language and German Sign Language, is multifunctional serving two purposes: one, to convey affect and, secondly, to convey grammatical morphology, for example, relative clauses, questions, conditional sentences (e.g. Reilly and Bellugi 1996: 221). This multifunctionality, however, puts facial expression in sign language in a conflicting position. Studies have been able to show that Deaf children raised by Deaf mothers are able to exhibit displeasure by furrowing their brows, raising their upper lip, or tightening their lips at the age of approximately seven months (Hiatt, Campos and Emde 1979) and reliably discriminate between happy, angry, and surprised faces (Nelson 1987); at about 10 months of age, these children are able to reliably smile in response to positive stimuli (Hiatt, Campos, and Emde 1979). And at the age of about one year Deaf children are able to consistently associate specific behaviors with affective states, both productively and receptively (Reilly and Bellugi 1996: 222). Only when the child reaches its second birthday do mothers start using linguistic facial expression consistently, as Reilly and Bellugi (1996: 229) found in a study with Deaf mothers and children signing *wh*-questions.

A major difference between hearing and Deaf children when acquiring a language is that hearing children spend a lot of time looking at the objects referred to, pointed at, and named by their parents whereas Deaf children spend a great amount of time looking at their parents when talked to, which leads to an asynchronicity between the linguistic input and the object of reference (Harris 1992; Emmorey 2000). When Deaf children are shown toys or other objects, they first have to look at the parent signing the name of the object and then follow the pointing gestures referring to the object, look back at the parents and get a confirmation for the object referred to. This procedure is much more laborious than with hearing children. Still, there is no observable delay in the acquisition process due to this phenomenon, which can be explained by the nature of motherese.

5. First words

First words are reported to appear earlier in sign language than in spoken language (e.g. Bonvillian, Orlansky, and Novack, 1983; McIntire, 1977; Orlansky and Bonvillian 1985). Some Deaf parents reported about their signing children that they produce their first signs at the age of 8.5 months (Bonvillian, Orlansky, and Novack, 1983), whereas hearing children usually produce their first words at ten to 13 months of age. This putative earlier production of first signs may be due to the notion of counting communicative gestures in the class of lexical signs. Communicative gestures, however, are also found in hearing children who have never been exposed to sign language. Hearing children produce communicative gestures even before they start uttering their first words. The communicative gestures found in hearing children are not counted as first words, however, because they do not resemble adult words (Bates, Benigni, Bretherton, Camaoni, and Volterra 1979). According to Petitto (1992) symbolic gestures and symbolic signs can be differentiated in Deaf children. A child growing up with sign language patting its head for a hat will have this gesture counted as a first word, not so with a hearing child (Caselli 1990). Children who grow up bilingually – with a spoken and a sign language – are reported to sign before they speak (Bonvillian and Folven 1987). Here, however, it is not clear whether these children receive the same amount of spoken and sign input (Emmorey 2002). Modality factors have often been suggested as possible reasons for a reported earlier use of signs in children exposed to sign language early on as opposed to a "later" use of spoken words by hearing children exposed to spoken language (Bonvillian and Patterson 1993). Volterra and Iverson (1995) conclude that the sign advantage may reflect a more general accessibility of the gestural over the vocal modality in all normally developing children.

In addition to this, it is false to assume that the first signs are particularly iconic (Orlansky and Bonvillian 1985); there seems to be no evidence that iconicity at the lexical and morphological level are of any assistance to the acquisition of signs (Rodda 1987: 153). A first assumption about the earlier acquisition of signs than words is founded on the earlier motor development of the hands compared to the articulatory organs of the vocal tract, the larger size of the manual articulatory organs, the child's ability to see his articulatory organs, or even the ability of the parents to directly correct the child's articulation by forming the child's hands (Meier and Newport 1990; Orlansky and Bonvillian 1985). Another possible explanation is that parents recognize first words earlier when signed than when spoken (Meier and Newport 1990). This explanation would not put signs at an advantage but speech at a disadvantage according to Meier and Newport (1990). This gestural advantage can then also be observed in hearing children using deictic gestures at ten months of age on average, which is before they normally produce their first words, even though these pointing gestures are pre-linguistic. In the transition from single words to the two-word stage, children begin by combining a gesture, usually a pointing gesture, with a single word. This development is the same for children acquiring a spoken or signed language (Caprici et al. 2002). Evidence from studies show that "the timing of the one-word stage, in which lexical items are used symbolically, is identical for both sign and speech, indicating that the maturational mechanisms underlying early lexical development are independent of the articulatory and perceptual system of the two modalities" (Emmorcy 2002: 174). They only start to combine lexical signs once they have a vocabulary of about 100 signs, which is at the age of about 18 to 24 months. This stage is followed by the acquisition of morphology. Negation is acquired non-linguistically at the age of about 12 months. The first signs for negating, however, do not appear until the age of about 18 months, without the obligatory accompanying linguistic headshake. This integration, which at the beginning occurs with errors in timing and scope, is used later and correctly only at the age of 26 to 28 months. A similarly late age of acquisition can be observed for the so-called 'puff', which means 'very big/fat'. Some of these adverbial are acquired as late as the age of 4.6 years (Anderson and Reilly 1997, 1998).

6. Baby talk

When hearing children acquire language, they usually are exposed to spoken language from birth on. This ensures a normal acquisition process. The presence of sign language from birth on for Deaf children to acquire sign language is not a given, however. The fact that it is not the norm for Deaf children to be exposed to sign language results in delayed language acquisition. Researchers have looked at the phenomenon of delayed language acquisition and overall results show that Deaf individuals who are exposed to sign language at earlier ages outperform later learners (Mayberry 1993; Mayberry and Eichen 1991; Mayberry and Fischer 1989). Newport (1990) investigated one group Deaf who had been exposed to sign language from early on (native signers) and two groups who started with the acquisition of sign language at later points in time (between the ages of 4 and 6 years and after the age of 12 years). At the time of the study all of the participants had at least 30 years of ASL experience. The participants' use of ASL word order was not affected by the onset of sign language acquisition. What Newport (1990) did find, however, was a gradual decline in the ability to produce and comprehend a variety of ASL morphological structures.

First baby signs, just like the first spoken baby words, are simplified and altered. In spoken language the child might reduce "bottle" to "baba." In sign language the child simplifies the handshape of the sign, for example, signing MOMMY in ASL not with an open "5"-handshape but with an "A"-handshape (fist) instead. In both cases the alteration is a simplification to accommodate the not yet fully controllable motor execution of the vocal tract or the fingers/hands respectively. In sign language it has been observed that in the vast majority of signs the place is signed correctly but only in half the instances do the children use the correct movement, and only in one quarter of the items observed did the children use the correct handshape (Conlin, Mirus, Mauk, and Meier 2000). Children first produce those handshapes which are easy to produce or articulate, easy to perceive, and frequent in use (Boyes Braem 1990). These handshapes include 5, 1, A (fist), B (flat hand with fingers together), C, and O (Emmorey 2002: 175; cf. illustrations). The more difficult handshapes are acquired later. This pattern is comparable to the acquisition of phonemes in spoken languages.

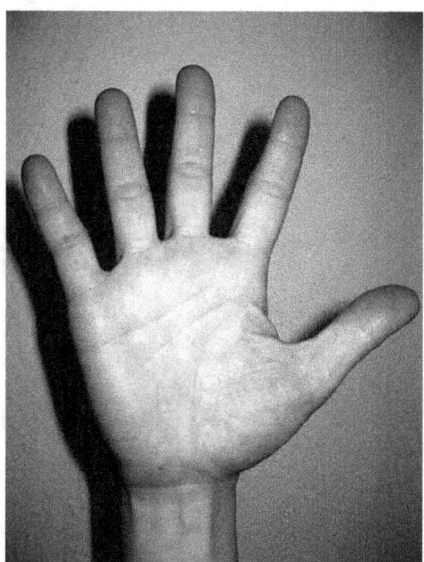
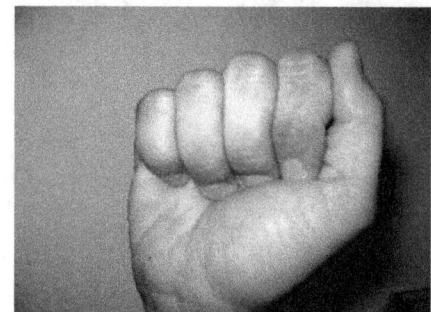

Figure 1. "5" handshape

Figure 2. "A" handshape

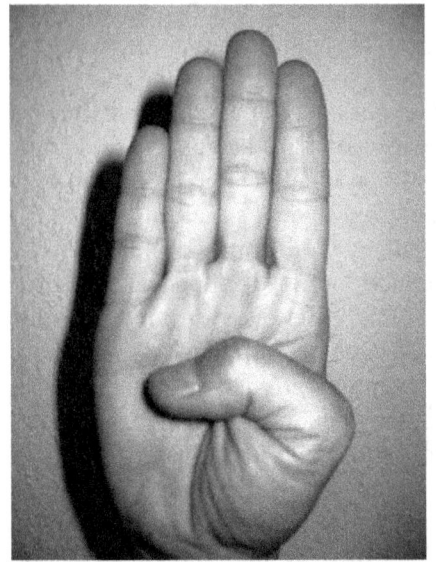

Figure 3. "B" handshape

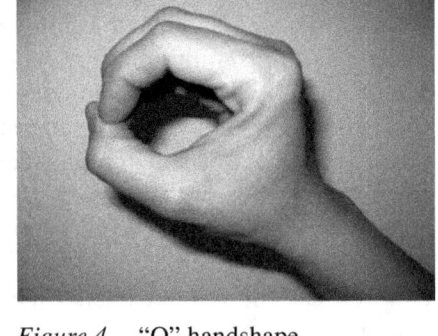

Figure 4. "O" handshape

Figure 5. "1" handshape

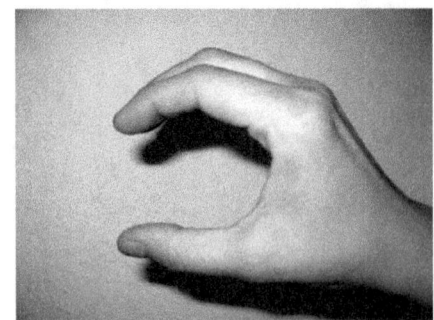

Figure 6. "C" handshape

The pattern of substitution of signs or phonemes in spoken language does not occur randomly. Speaking children substitute stops for fricatives (a process known as "stopping" (Cho and O'Grady 1996), delete final consonants ("dog" becoming "da"), or reduce consonant clusters ("string" becoming "ting"), to name only some phonological processes (ibid.). In sign language children typically replace marked handshapes (e.g. "X") with unmarked handshapes (5 or A, for example), which are easier to produce. Also, one handshape may replace several handshapes (Emmorey 2002: 176). Movement, which is another phonological parameter in sign language, is also altered by children acquiring sign language. Movements are proximalized, which means that children "change which part of their body articulates a movement by substituting an articulator that is closer to (more proximal to) their torso, such as the shoulder, for an articulator that is farther (distal) from their torso, such as the wrist or fingers" (ibid.). A sign that is produced by signing with the hand at the head is instead signed at the chest. A similar pattern can be seen for spoken language, when children devoice voiced consonants, for example.

Boyes Braem (1999) investigated rhythmic patterns in the signing of Deaf early and late learners of Swiss German Sign Language. She points out that as with any learner of a second language – spoken or signed – the learner may have mastered most of the lexicon and the phonological and grammatical rules and still have problems making him-/herself understood. This deficit is oftentimes rooted in the rhythmic abilities exhibited in the second language. Another reason for the reduced intelligibility of second language learners is their inadequate or inappropriate use of grammatical facial expressions. The perception of rhythm usually refers to the perception of some kind of "beat". In spoken language rhythm is established through variations primarily in pitch and duration and, secondarily, in loudness (cf. e.g. Raithel 2004). In sign languages stress or rhythm is not merely of matter of manual components but to a large extent that of facial expression, eye gaze, mouth position and movement, orientation and movement of the head and upper torso. In sign language it has been found that signs have a longer duration than normal when receiving emphatic stress or when they are sentence-initial and function as topics (Liddell 1977). In her study Boyes Braem (1999) found two types temporal prosody marking in Swiss German Sign Language. One is "a temporal balancing of final syntactic phrases which function as P-units [smaller prosodic units] within the sentence and, for larger chunks of certain kinds of discourse, a use of a series of temporally and spatially balanced torso movements […], termed here prosodic D-units [larger prosodic units]" (1999: 204). Wilbur (1999) calls the durational aspect resulting in stress patterns "peak velocity" (247). The acquisition of these larger units has been found to be more difficult for second language learners who tend to transfer prosodic markers more appropriate to their spoken mother tongue resulting in a signed "accent" (Boyes Braem 1999: 204).

7. Syntax and morphology

It is well known that children do not acquire language merely through imitation but that they have an internal system of rules that they apply and that may or may not match the rules that are used by adults. When looking at the mistakes children make while producing language a window opens and allows a look at the nature of the acquisition process (Emmorey 2002: 182).

The acquisition of pronouns, such as "I" and "you", is known to be difficult for hearing children. Pronoun system reference changes, for example, depending on who is speaking. Hearing children, therefore, frequently make errors when using these pronouns and complete the acquisition of personal pronouns at the age of three years. For sign language it could be assumed that the acquisition process would go faster due to the deictic nature of personal pronouns, which are produced by pointing at the respective person ("I" and "you"). But "the performance of deaf children matches that of hearing, both qualitatively and chronologically" (Rodda 1987: 148; cf. also Petitto 1987), not putting the visual modality at an advantage. Children acquiring sign language also tend to make the same pronoun reversals as do children acquiring spoken language. Following Emmorey (2002: 183) children who acquire "ASL pronouns appear to go through three stages: (1) gestural (nonlinguistic) pointing to people and objects (beginning at about 9 months)", which is the same age at which hearing children start using their first nonlinguistic pointing gestures. "(2) pronoun reversal errors may occur and names may be used instead of pronouns (ages 1;6 to 2;0), [and] (3) the correct use of personal pronouns (ages 2;0 to 2;6). Both speaking and signing children begin to use personal pronouns at the same age (around 18 months) and make the same kinds of errors". Petitto (1987; 1993) argues that children acquiring sign language do not recognize a pointing sign as a pronoun or a lexical sign until the age of about 18 months and then may regard it as a lexical sign and not personal pronoun with a shifting function. This may suggest a discontinuity between prelinguistic and linguistic forms (Emmorey 2002: 183).

As discussed above, children are able to produce facial expressions consistently and universally by one year of age (Nelson 1987). As emotional facial expression also seems to appear to be the source of grammaticization in sign language it is an open question whether the ability to produce and comprehend emotional facial expressions is an easier way into the grammatical system of a sign language.

8. Fingerspelling

In German Sign Language fingerspelling is important but plays a more subordinate role within sign language in contrast to ASL. In German Sign Language fingerspelling is used for names that have either not been introduced so far or if, for example, the communication partner does not understand the signed word. In ASL, on the other hand, fingerspelling is not simply a way of representing English orthography but fingerspelled words make up part of foreign vocabulary (Emmorey 2002: 190). Also, ASL signs often are signed starting with the fingerspelled letter of the English word. Fingerspelled input is, however, rarely used with children who acquire sign language naturally. Yet, children acquiring sign language do attempt to use fingerspelled forms even though they cannot yet read or write (Padden 1991). They produce a sign that imitates the adult's movements when fingerspelling (Padden and Le Master 1985). Not until the child is about four years old does it recognize that there is a specific way of moving the hand in order to fingerspell. The early use of fingerspelling by children is therefore without reference to English (or any language's) orthography. Consequently, Padden (1993) concedes that the connection between fingerspelling and English orthography must be consciously established.

A similar problem can be observed in hearing children when they start to learn the grapheme-phoneme correspondence. Children at times tend to make creative spelling attempts based on these correspondences, such as spelling T-R-D-L for the word "turtle" (Read 1975 in Padden 1991).

9. Pidgin sign language acquisition

Finally, it should be mentioned that sign language acquisition as presented in this contribution focuses on first language acquisition, i.e. when children are exposed to Sign Language from birth on. A somewhat different situation arises when looking at sign language acquisition in a not truly Deaf community, as can be seen in the case of Nicaraguan sign language. A Deaf community in Manuaga was discovered when the Sandinistas came to power after the Nicaraguan Revolution. The Deaf members in this discovered community were surrounded by hearing people and consequently, as no provisions had been made for their education or the spread of a standardized sign language, were "home-signers" (Singh 2000: 60), which meant that they did not speak a homogeneous sign language. Each Deaf person had developed his/her own sign inventory enabling him/her to communicate with the hearing people in the immediate environment. The Sandinistas then establish vocational schools for the Deaf, and in this way many Deaf people came into contact with other Deaf people for the first time. The students who did not have signs in common soon developed their own sign system in which there was "no predictable grammar, no pattern to the way the signs fitted together" (Horizon 1997). This shared inventory of signs still being very basic, created by so-called "first generation signers", was the creation of a jargon, the early state of a pidgin (Singh 2000). The second generation signers then unconsciously developed this jargon, grammaticized it, and turned it into a creole language using it fluently and confidently. The differences between first and second generation signers can be seen, among other things, in the fact that first generation signers mainly use an iconic system which is not very well connected; signs are added one after the other without cohesion markers. The signing of the second generation, on the other hand, is very fluent and grammatical. This grammaticality was found to have originated from the children themselves without having had anyone to teach them. Their only role models were the first generation signers.

This example shows that in sign language, as is well-known from spoken language, there is a critical period for language acquisition. At a certain age language, and here specifically sign language, cannot be mastered in a fully fluent way anymore (Singh 2000; Emmorey 2002), thus emphasizing the importance of introducing sign language to Deaf people early on.

10. Conclusion

It can be seen that the acquisition of sign and spoken language does not differ much aside from the modalities used. Children go through comparable acquisitional steps in their language, starting with babbling, which in one case consists of the production of syllabic utterances and in the other case of cyclic movements of the fingers. Then children start to utter the first words, which again they do in a similar way in their language specific modalities. Another phenomenon that can clearly be seen in both language acquisition processes is the supporting use of motherese. Motherese is not unique to spoken languages but seems to be a linguistic universal natural to parents communicating with their children, whether hearing or not. The rhythmical quality, the enlarged size of the signs, and the frequent repetitions are of great help to the child. The processes of simplification can be observed in both acquisitions processes for the production of first words. In spoken language children reduce consonant clusters and adjust their first words according to their articulatory abilities. This pattern can also be observed in children acquiring sign language. They use signs they can produce with relative ease in place of signs which call for more motor control, in this way adjusting their sign production accordingly. The acquisition of syntax and morphology follows approximately the same rules. This means that in both languages children learn to use the pronoun system consecutively and that the overt indexical act of pointing at people in order to refer to them does not aid in the acquisition process. The same holds for the iconicity of signs. Here it is often claimed that it is precisely this iconicity which eases the acquisition process greatly. This, however, has not been found to be true.

Notes

1. The term "Deaf" is capitalized in this article in order to emphasize the fact the there is a Deaf community with its own language, culture, and identity.

References

Anderson, D. E. and J. S. Reilly
    1997   The puzzle of negation: how children move from communicative to grammatical negation in ASL. *Applied Psycholinguistics* 18,4: 411–429.
Anderson, D. E. and J. S. Reilly
    1998   PAH! The acquisition of adverbials in ASL. *Sign Language & Linguistics* 1,2: 117–142.
Bates, E., L. Benigni, L. Bretherton, L. Camaoni, and V. Volterra
    1979   *The Emergence of Symbols: Cognition and Communication in Infancy.* New York: Academic Press.
Bellugi, U. and E. S. Klima
    1982   The acquisition of three morphological systems in American Sign Language. *Papers and Reports on Child Language Development* 21: 1–35.
Bonvillian, J. D. and R. D. Folven
    1987   The onset of signing in young children. In: W. H. Edmondson and F. Karlsson (eds.) *SLR '87: Papers from the Fourth International Symposium on Sign Language Research.* Hamburg, Germany, Signum Press.
Bonvillian, J. D. and F. G. P. Patterson
    1993   Early sign language acquisition in children and gorillas: vocabulary content and sign iconicity. *First Language* 13: 315–338.
Boyes Braem, P.
    1999   Rhythmic temporal patterns in the signing of deaf early and late learners of Swiss German Sign Language *Language and Speech* 42 2–3: 1777–208.
Caprici, O., J. M. Iversen, S. Montanari, and V. Volterra
    2002   Gestural, signed and spoken modalities in early language development: the role of linguistic input. *Bilingualism* 5,1: 25–37.
Caselli, M. C.
    1990   Communicative gestures and first words. In: V. Volterra and C. Erting (eds.) *From Gesture to Language in Hearing and Deaf Children,* 56–67. Springer: Berlin, Germany,.
Caselli, M. C. and V. Volterra
    1990   From communication to language in hearing and deaf children. In: V. Volterra and C. J. Erting (eds.), *From Gesture to Language in Hearing and Deaf Children,* 263–277. Berlin/Heidelberg/New York: Springer,.

Cho, S. W. and W. O'Grady
    1996   Language acquisition: the emergence of a grammar. In: W. O'Grady, M. Dobrovolsky and F. Katamba (eds.), *Contemporary Linguistics. An Introduction*. Longman.

Conlin, K. E., G. R. Mirrus, C. Mauk, and R. P. Meier
    2000   The acquisition of first signs: place, handshape and movement. In: Chamberlain, Charlene, Jill P. Morford and Rachel I. Mayberry (eds.), *Language Acquisition by Eye*, 51–69. Mahwah, N. J./London: Lawrence Erlbaum Associates.

Eimas, P. D., D. K. Oller, P. Jusczyk and J. Vigorito
    1971   Speech perception in infants. *Science* 171: 303–318.

Emmorey, K.
    2001   *Language, Cognition, and the Brain: Insights from Sign Language Research*. Mahwah, N. J.: Lawrence Erlbaum Associates.

Fernald, A.
    1985   Four-month-old infants prefer to listen to motherese. *Infant Behavior and Development*, 8: 181–195.

Fernald, A.
    1989   Intonation and communicative intent in mothers' speech to infants: is the melody the message? *Child Development* 60: 1497–1510.

Garnica, O.
    1977   Some prosodic and paralinguistic features of speech to young children. In: C. E. Snow and C. A. Ferguson (eds.), *Talking to Children: Language Input and Acquisition*, 3–88. Cambridge: Cambridge University Press.

Harris, M.
    1992   *Language Experience and Early Language Development: From Input to Uptake*. Hillsdale, N. J.: Lawrence Erlbaum Associates.

Hiatt, S., J. Campos, and R. Emde
    1979   Facial patterning and infant emotional expression: happiness, surprise and fear. *Child Development* 50: 1020–1035.

Holzrichter, A. S. and R. P. Meier
    2000   Child-directed signing in American sign language. In: C. Chamberlain, J. P. Morford and R. I. Mayberry (eds.), *Language Acquisition by Eye*, 25–40. Mahwah, N. J./London: Lawrence Erlbaum Associates.

Horizon:
    1997   Silent Children, New Language. Produced by Judith Bunting, BBC.

Ingram, D.
    1989   *First Language Acquisition. Method, Description, and Explanation*. Cambridge University Press.

Kemler-Nelson, D. G., K. Hirsch-Pasek, P. W. Jusczyk and K. Wright-Cassidy
    1989   How the prosodic cues in motherese might assist language learning. *Journal of Child Language* 16: 55–68.

Lane, H.
    1983   *When the Mind Hears. A History of the Deaf*. New York: Random House.

Lieberman, P.
    1984   *The Biology and Evolution of Language*. Cambridge, MA: Harvard University Press.

Lightbown, P. M. and N. Spada
  1999   *How Languages Are Learned.* Oxford University Press.
Masataka, N.
  1999   Preference for infant-directed singing in 2-day-old hearing infants of deaf parents. *Developmental Psychology* 35: 4, 1001–1005.
Masataka, N.
  2000   The role of modality and input in the earliest stage of language acquisition: studies of Japanese sign language. In: C. Chamberlain, J. P. Morford and R. I. Mayberry (eds.), *Language Acquisition by Eye,* 3–24. Mahwah, N. J./ London: Lawrence Erlbaum Associates,.
Mayberry, R. I.
  1993   First-language acquisition after childhood differs from second-language acquisition: the case of American sign language. *Journal of Speech and Hearing Research* 36: 1285–1270.
Mayberry, R. I. and E. Eichen
  1991   The long-lasting advantage of learning sign language in childhood: another look at the critical period for language acquisition. *Journal of Memory and Language* 30: 486–512.
Mayberry, R. I. and S. Fischer
  1989   Looking through phonological shape to sentence meaning: the bottleneck of non-native sign language processing. *Memory and Cognition* 17: 740–754.
Meier, R. P. and R. Willerman
  1995   Prelinguistic gesture in deaf and hearing infants. In: K. Emmorey and J. Reilly (eds.), *Language, Gesture, and Space,* 391–409. Hillsdale, NJ: Lawrence Erlbaum Associates,
Nelson, C. A.
  1987   The recognition of facial expression in the first two years of life: mechanisms of development. *Child Development* 58: 890–909.
Newport, E. L.
  1990   Maturational constraints on language learning. *Cognitive Science* 14: 11–28.
Newport, E. L., H. A. Gleitman, and L. R. Newport
  1977   Mother, I'd rather do it myself: some effects and non-effects of maternal speech style. In: C. Snow and C. Ferguson (eds.), *Talking to Children: Language Input and Acquisition.* Cambridge: Cambridge University Press.
Padden, C.
  1991   The acquisition of fingerspelling by deaf children. In: P. Siples and S. Fischer (eds.), *Theoretical Issues in Sign Language Research,* 118–132. Chicago, IL: University of Chicago Press.
Padden, C.
  1993   Early bilingual lives of deaf children. In: I. Parasnis (ed.), *Cultural and Language Diversity and the Deaf Experience,* 99–116. Cambridge: Cambridge University Press.
Padden, C. and B. LeMaster
  1985   An alphabet on hand: The acquisition of fingerspelling in deaf children. *Sign Language Studies* 47: 161–172.
Pettito, L. A.
  2000   The acquisition of natural signed languages: lessons in the nature of human language and its biological foundations. In: C. Chamberlain, J. P. Morford,

and R. I. Mayberry (eds.), *Language Acquisition by Eye*, 41–50. Mahwah, N. J./London: Lawrence Erlbaum Associates.

Pettito, L. A. and P. F. Marentette
1991　Babbling in the manual mode: evidence for the ontogeny of language. *Science* 251: 1483–1496.

Raithel, V.
2004　*The Perception of Intonation Contours and Focus by Aphasic and Healthy Individuals*. Tuebingen: Gunter Narr.

Reilly, J. S. and U. Bellugi
1996　Competition on the face: affect and language in ASL motherese. *Journal of Child Language* 23: 1, 219–239.

Rodda, M.
1987　*Language, Cognition, and Deafness*. Hillsdale, N. J.: Lawrence Erlbaum Associates.

Singh, I.
2000　*Pidgins and Creoles. An Introduction*. London: Arnold.

Snow, C.
1972　Mother's speech to children learning language. *Child Development* 43: 349–365.

Thelen, E.
1991　Motor aspects of emerging speech: a dynamic approach. In: N. A. Krasnegor, D. M. Rumbaugh, R. L. Schiefenbusch, and M. Studdert-Kennedy (eds.), *Biological and Behavioral Determinants of Language Development*, 339–362. Hillsdale, NJ: Lawrence Erlbaum Associates.

Villiers de, J. G. and P. A. de Villiers
1978　*Language Acquisition*. Harvard University Press.

Volterra, V. and J. Iverson
1995　When do modality factors affect the course of language acquisition. In: K. Emmorey and J. Reilly (eds.). *Language, Gesture, and Space*. Mahwah, NJ: Lawrence Erlbaum Associates.

Werker, J. F. and P. J. McLeod
1989　Infant preference for both male and female infant-directed talk: a developmental study of attentional and affective responsiveness. In: *Canadian Journal of Psychology* 43: 230–246.

Wilbur, R. B.
1999　Stress in ASL: empirical evidence and linguistic issues. *Language and Speech* 42, 2–3: 229–250.

III. Adult competence

8. Speaking and listening

Thomas Holtgraves

Language use is intentional behavior. Speakers formulate their utterances with the goal of having their intentions recognized and listeners process a speaker's remarks with the goal of recognizing those intentions. In this chapter I argue that the processes of speaking and listening are based on goals that operate at varying levels of abstraction. There are high-level goals such as face management (Goffman 1967) as well as lower-level goals such as speech act performance. I first discuss the linguistic mechanisms by which speakers can convey their intentions (i.e., perform specific speech acts), and how face management (a concern with the public identities of conversationalists) can affect – and sometimes hinder – this process. I then turn to the listener and discuss the cognitive processes involved in the recognition of the speaker's lower-level goals (i.e., speech acts) and the role played by face management in this recognition process. Finally, I consider some of the obstacles that speakers and listeners must overcome in order to use language successfully.

1. Speaking and listening

Language use is intentional behavior. Speakers formulate their utterances with the goal of having their intentions recognized and recipients process a speaker's remarks with the goal of recognizing those intentions. To do this successfully requires a variety of skills. There is basic linguistic competence, of course – the phonological, morphological, and syntactic competencies that are required to use language. However, to use language to communicate successfully requires much more than linguistic competence (Hymes 1972). One must be able to translate intentions into words and do so in such a way that those intentions will be recognized by the recipient. And recipients must be able to engage in reasoning processes in order to recognize the speaker's intention. And all interactants must be able to do this in such a way so as to avoid offending each other. It is these skills – what is often referred to as pragmatic competence (Bachman 1990) – that is the focus of this chapter.

I assume that language is goal-directed behavior, with the goals existing at varying levels of abstraction. There are high level goals such as face management (Goffman 1967) that are almost always operative, as well as lower level goals (speech acts) that are associated with a single turn or set of turns. I will use the concept of goals as a means of organizing this chapter. I first take the speaker's perspective and consider lower level goals. After a brief review of relevant concepts (illocutionary force) from speech act theory (Searle 1969), I discuss the linguistic mechanisms by which speakers can convey their intentions (and perform speech acts). I then consider high level goals, focusing particularly on the concepts of face management and politeness (Brown and Levinson 1987). I discuss the role played by face management in the construction of conversation turns and how this can affect – and sometimes hinder – the performance of lower level (speech act) goals. I then turn to the listener and discuss the cognitive processes involved in the recognition of the speaker's lower-level goals (speech acts). This is followed by a discussion of the role of high-level goals such as face management in the recognition of the speaker's intention. Finally, in a conclusion section I consider some of the obstacles that speakers and listeners must overcome to use language successfully.

1.1. Speaking

1.1.1. Lower level goals – Speech act production

People typically use their words to do things, to perform certain actions. Conversational turns are used to criticize and compliment, to thank and apologize, and so on. Moreover, speakers usually intend to have their intentions to perform these actions recognized by the listeners. Although there may be times when we want to be deliberately ambiguous (see below), we generally want our addressees to know that they are being thanked, complimented or criticized. This is what Grice (1957) referred to as a reflexive intention, or an intention that is intended to be recognized.

The approach to language that captures this dimension most clearly is speech act theory (Austin 1962; Searle 1969). Although speech act theorists differ on certain points, there is general agreement that speakers are typically performing multiple acts when they use language. At one level they are performing a locutionary act – the uttering of a string of words that constitutes a well-formed utterance with a specifiable sense and reference. The performance of a locutionary act involves the traditional domains of syntax and semantics. At a second level a speaker, by producing a locutionary act, is also performing a specifiable illocutionary act. That is, she is performing a particular action (or speech act) that she intends to have the recipient recognize by virtue of his understanding of the locutionary act. Finally, the performance of an illocutionary act will typically elicit a particular effect in the recipient – this is referred to as a perlocutionary act. A request, for example, may elicit compliance, complaints or crying. Note that although illocutionary and perlocutionary acts are clearly related (i.e., speakers generally intend to bring about a certain perlocutionary effect in their interlocutors), perlocutionary effects can extend far beyond what was intended by the speaker.

The ability to produce and comprehend illocutionary force (or speech acts) is critical for successful language use. This entails, of course, the ability to construct a well-formed, sensible, utterance (the illocutionary act). Although necessary, this capability is not sufficient for successful language use. For example, a computer can be programmed to produce and comprehend grammatical utterances (locutionary acts) but its ability to use these acts in any meaningful way (as illocutionary acts) can still be nil (e.g., Dreyfus 1992). For speakers, the problem is to construct an utterance that will successfully perform a particular speech act, with success being defined as the recipient recognizing the speaker's intention to have that speech act recognized.

To perform speech acts, then, interlocutors must also possess some type of action grammar, a set of rules specifying what actions are allowable in various contexts and how those actions can be performed with language. Thus, one needs to know that language can be used to convey one's commitment to a future course of action (commissives such as threat and promise) and that such commitments are helpful when one's interlocutor is unsure of one's future course of action (e.g., reassure). And one must know that the utterance performing such an action needs to be in the first person future tense. And one should know that directives can be used in an attempt to alter the behavior of the recipient. And so on.

1.1.2. Implicit vs. explicit speech acts.

Speech act performance is complicated by the fact that there is no one-to-one mapping between illocutionary force and a specific utterance. For example, "Shut the door," "Is it possible to have the door shut?" and "It's noisy in here" are all acceptable utterances (in the appropriate contexts) for performing a request that the listener shut a door. One important distinction can be made between explicit and implicit speech acts. Explicit speech acts are relatively clear and direct and include the relevant performative verb, the verb that names the speech act that it performs. Hence, one can perform the act of promising to do the dishes by saying "I promise to do the dishes." Language use would be far less complicated if speech acts could be performed only with performative verbs. However, people often perform speech acts indirectly, with implicit speech acts. These are speech acts that do not contain the relevant performative verb. For example, explicit speech acts such as "I promise to do it" and "I forbid you to do it" could also be performed implicitly with "I guarantee that I'll have it finished tomorrow" and "You are not allowed to do that again," neither of which contain the performative verbs "promise" and "forbid."

What do speakers need to know in order to perform implicit speech acts? Implicit performatives (and explicit performatives as well) typically trade on the felicity conditions that underlie the speech act one is intending to perform.

In a series of studies I assessed how speakers of English typically generate implicit performatives (Holtgraves 2005a). Participants were asked to imagine themselves in various situations and to then indicate how they would perform a particular speech act (request, warn, apologize, etc.) with the stipulation that they could not use the performative verb. For example, if they were to apologize they could not use "apologize" in their utterance. These utterances were then shown to a different group of participants who were asked to indicate what speech act was being performed. Those speech acts that were correctly recognized at a rate exceeding 38 % were then analyzed in terms of their underlying linguistic structure. As expected, most of these implicit performatives were performed by referencing the felicity conditions that underlied the intended speech act. For example, directives (ask, invite, etc.) were typically performed by questioning the recipient's ability to perform a future action (e.g., Do you know the time?; Can you come over for dinner tomorrow night?). These mechanisms have long been studied in terms of indirect requests (Gordon and Lakoff 1975). Expressives (e.g., apologies, thanks) and commissives (e.g., threats, warnings) frequently referenced the speaker's intention to express an internal psychological state or perform a future course of action, respectively.

It is not enough to know the felicity conditions that underlie the performance of a particular illocutionary point (e.g., assertive, directive, commissive, expressive, declarative). This is because many of the speech acts performing the same illocutionary point will have different felicity conditions, with the differing felicity conditions constituting the performance of the different speech acts. For example, some commissives such as "threat" are conditional (e.g., If you x, then I'll y); others such as "promise" are unconditional. Some assertives such as "deny" presuppose the existence of a prior assertion; other assertives such as "guess" do not.

1.1.3. *Particularized implicatures.*

In theory, there are an infinite number of means for performing any particular implicit speech act. Some of these will be particularized implicatures, or utterances that are very indirect and typically entail a Gricean (1975) inference process for their recognition (recognize and reject the literal meaning in favor of an alternative indirect meaning). Perhaps the clearest instance of a speech act performed with a particularized implicature is to perform a request with a negative state remark (Holtgraves 1994). The principle behind a negative state remark is as follows: A speaker can perform a request by asserting or questioning the existence of a negative state if there is some action that the listener can perform to remedy the negative state. The principle yields requests such as "It's noisy in here" and "It's cold in here" as requests to shut a door and turn up a thermostat respectively.

The successful performance of particularized implicatures requires considerable knowledge. A speaker must know what piece of evidence to give in order to instigate an inference process on the part of the listener. Many utterances of this type are performed by violating – often in quite subtle ways – certain conversation maxims such as Grice's (1975) relation maxim (i.e., make your contribution relevant for the exchange of which it is a part). This can be tricky because extreme relevance violations (i.e., abrupt topic changes) may lead to inferences regarding the speaker's emotional stability. The speaker also needs to be aware of the context because it is with reference to the context that so many particularized implicatures are performed. For example, many subtle directives hinge on a status differential. Subtle hints performed by a high status speaker may be missed if performed by a low status speaker (Holtgraves 1994). Speakers must also be aware that if the context provides an easily discernable reason for a violation – such as face management (see below) – then recipients will interpret the violation with that reason in mind.

1.2.1. *Higher level goals – Politeness and face management*

In general, there is a strong tendency for interactants to perform implicit rather than explicit speech acts. Why is this? Clearly, factors other than maximally efficient communication must be at work. Interactants are also attending to an interpersonal dimension, a dimension that is captured well with Ervin Goffman's (1967) concept of face and face-work. According to Goffman (1967), face is the "positive social value a person effectively claims for himself by the line others assume he has taken during a particular contact" (p. 5). Roughly, face is one's public identity, an identity that must be actively managed. Importantly, face can only be given by others (one might claim a particular identity, but it must be ratified by others) and so it is in everyone's best interest to maintain each other's face. This is accomplished by engaging in face-work (Goffman 1971). For example, people generally avoid creating threats to one anthers' face (termed avoidance strategies): they avoid threatening topics, violating another's territory, calling attention to another's faults, and so on. People also engage in approach-based face-work (e.g., greetings, compliments, salutations, etc.) undertaken as a means of affirming and supporting the social relationship.

To be a successful language user, then, a speaker must possess knowledge regarding face management strategies. The specific manifestation of these strategies is captured quite clearly in Brown and Levinson's (1987) politeness theory. This theory is a direct extension of Goffman's analysis of face and face-work; politeness is essentially the linguistic means by which face-work is accomplished. Like Goffman, Brown and Levinson assume face to be quite fragile and subject to continued threat during social interaction. Roughly paralleling Goffman's (1967) avoidance and approach strategies, Brown and Levinson suggested that there are two universal types of face: negative face – or the want to be unrestricted by others – and positive face – or the want to be connected with others[1] The act of merely addressing a remark to someone imposes on that person at some minimal level by requiring a response (hence negative face – or freedom from imposition – is threatened). Disagreements, criticisms, and refusals all threaten (primarily) the recipient's positive face (the desire for closeness with the other). Importantly, the speaker's own face may be threatened by the performance of certain acts. Promises threaten the speaker's negative face (by restricting subsequent freedom) and apologies threaten the speaker's positive face (via an admission of harming the other). Social interaction thus presents a dilemma for interactants. On the one hand, they are motivated to maintain each other's positive and negative face. On the other hand, they are motivated to perform certain speech acts that threaten those very desires. There is thus a fundamental conflict between the lower-level goal of performing certain speech acts and the higher-level goal of managing positive and negative face. This conflict is solved (to varying degrees) by engaging in face-work, or more precisely, by being polite.

So, how exactly do people convey politeness? In the Brown and Levinson model it is deviation from maximally efficient communication (i.e., communication adhering to Grice's (1975) maxims of relation, quantity, quality, and manner) that communicates a polite attitude. There are, of course, many ways this can be accomplished, and Brown and Levinson (1987) organized politeness into five superstrategies. These superstrategies are assumed to be ordered on a continuum of overall politeness, or extent to which face concerns are encoded in the communication. Consider the act of making a request. The least polite strategy is to perform the act without any politeness. To do so is to perform the act bald-on-record, as for example with an imperative ("Shut the door"). These are explicit speech acts that are maximally efficient; they are entirely in accord with Grice's maxims.

The most polite strategy is simply to not perform the act at all. But if the act is performed, then the most polite strategy is to do so with an off-record form. An off-record form (e.g., a negative state remark) can be performed by violating one of Grice's (1975) maxims. Hence, they are particularized implicatures. For example, uttering "It's cold in here" in an obviously cold room violates the quantity maxim (it states the obvious) and hence often functions as a polite request (e.g., to turn up the thermostat). The defining feature of off-record forms is their ambiguity and hence deniability.

Falling between these two extremes are on-record acts with redress emphasizing either positive face or negative face. The former, termed positive politeness, functions via an exaggerated emphasis on closeness or solidarity with the hearer. It is an approach-based politeness. For example, the use of ingroup identity markers (e.g., familiar address forms, slang), jokes, presumptuous optimism

("You'll loan me your car, won't you?") all implicate a view of a relatively close relationship. The latter, termed negative politeness, functions via attention to the recipient's autonomy. It is an avoidance-based politeness. For example, conventionalized indirect forms (e.g., "Could you shut the door?") symbolically give the recipient an "out" and hence are less imposing than a bald on-record form.

Both positively and negatively polite forms are on-record, meaning that the act performed is relatively clear. Still, these strategies represent deviations from maximum communication efficiency. They are, in effect, implicit performatives. For example, although the directive force of "Could you shut the door?" is usually clear, it is performed indirectly (it is an implicit performative) rather than with the imperative. The intent of positively polite strategies is even more clear; many times these forms will include the imperative (and hence be very direct), but the imperative will be embedded within verbal markers of closeness, an embedding that is not necessary and hence violates the quantity maxim (do not say more than is necessary). Research examining this ordering in terms of politeness has received partial support (Holtgraves and Yang 1990; Clark and Schunk 1980). That is, people perceive bald on-record requests to be less polite than positively polite requests, and positively polite requests to be less polite than negatively polite requests.[2]

1.2.2. Contextual determinants of politeness.

What, then, should determine a speaker's level of politeness? Much of a person's politeness can be taken as an indication of how that person perceives the current setting; it reveals one's social cognitions regarding the interpersonal context. Brown and Levinson (1987) proposed that politeness will vary as a function of the weightiness (or degree of face-threat) of the act to be performed (see also Leech 1983 for a consideration of the effects of similar social variables). Weightiness is contextually determined and is assumed to be an additive weighting of the following three variables: the intrinsic (and culturally bound) degree of imposition of the act itself (e.g., asking for a loan of $5 is less imposing than asking for a loan of $500), the power of the hearer relative to the speaker, and the degree of social distance between the interlocutors. More formally, weightiness can be determined with the following formula:

$$W_x = D(S,H) + P(H,S) + R_x$$

where W_x refers to the weightiness of the act in this particular context, $D(S,H)$ refers to the distance between the speaker and hearer, $P(H,S)$ refers to the hearers power in relation to the speaker, and R_x refers to the degree of imposition of the act. Thus, increased weightiness (and hence, in general, greater politeness) occurs as a function of increasing imposition, hearer power, and relationship distance.

A fair amount of research has examined the impact of these variables on politeness (Ambady, Koo, Lee, and Rosenthal 1996; Blum-Kulka, Danet, and Gherson 1985; Brown and Gilman 1989; Holtgraves and Yang 1990; 1992; Lim and Bowers 1991). In general, strong support has been found for the power variable, with most studies demonstrating higher speaker power being associated with less politeness. Fairly consistent support has been found for the imposition variable, with increasing imposition associated with increasing politeness. In contrast, the effects of relationship distance have been more problematic, with some researchers reporting greater politeness as a function of increasing distance (Holtgraves and Yang 1992), and others reporting the exact opposite (Brown and Gilman 1989). These inconsistent results are partly due to a confounding of relationship distance and liking, two variables that are related but conceptually and theoretically distinct (Slugoski and Turnbull 1988).

Politeness provides a mechanism that allows speakers to pursue lower-level goals (performing speech acts) while simultaneously attending to each other's face. This requires speakers to be attentive to the context (e.g., is the recipient my superior or are we equal in status?) and relationship (e.g., how close are we?) in order to formulate utterances with the appropriate level of politeness. This can be tricky. Erring on the side of relationship maintenance might produce an utterance so ambiguous that one's intent is not at all clear. And of course erring on the side of clarity might result in offending one's recipient. But it is not just a question of balancing politeness and clarity. There is also tension between managing one's own face and that of one's interlocutors. To support the hearer's face can sometimes result in threats to one's own face. Apologies, for example, support the face of the offended person but simultaneously threaten the face of the speaker. The skills and knowledge required to be a successful speaker are clearly multifaceted and complex.

2. Listening

The situation for the recipient of an utterance is in many respects a mirror image of the situation for the speaker. Just as the speaker must be capable of performing a locutionary act, the recipient must be capable of comprehending that locutionary act. And similar to the speaker's situation, recognition of the locutionary act is not, by itself, sufficient for successful communication. Moreover, just as the speaker must balance competing concerns in formulating an utterance, so too must recipients have some awareness of these competing concerns in order to comprehend the speaker's meaning.

2.1. Lower level goals – Speech act recognition

Recognition of the speaker's intention is relatively clear when a performative verb is used.[3] However, when implicit performatives are used (and they are obviously used quite often) recognition becomes a little more problematic. Still, there is research suggesting that even with implicit performatives there is a strong tendency for language users to quickly and automatically recognize the speech act being performed (Holtgraves in press; Holtgraves and Ashley 2001). In several studies we had participants read descriptions of situations that were followed by remarks said by one interactant to another interactant. In some conditions the final utterance performed a specific speech act such as "remind" (Don't forget to go to your dentist appointment today). In the control condition the wording was almost identical but did not perform that speech act (e.g., I'll bet you forgot to go to your dentist appointment today). The results strongly supported the on-line activation of illocutionary force. For example, participants were significantly slower at verifying that "remind" had not literally been present in the remark "Don't forgot to go to your dentist appointment today" than in the (control) remark "I'll bet you forgot to go to your dentist appointment today." This suggests that comprehension of the former involved the automatic activation of the concept "remind." Follow-up studies have also demonstrated that illocutionary force forms part of the representation of the utterance in long-term memory (Holtgraves 2007); participants in these studies demonstrated a tendency to falsely recognize and recall nonpresented speech act verbs that characterized the remarks they read earlier.

Although it is clear that language use typically involves speech act recognition, there are many aspects of this process that are not clear. First and foremost, it is not clear *how* illocutionary force is recognized. That is, what type of process is involved in speech act recognition? How, exactly, do language users recognize the speaker's intention when an implicit performative is used? Interestingly, research suggests that the automatic recognition of illocutionary force tends not to occur for nonnative speakers (Holtgraves in press). Hence, this aspect of language use is clearly a feature of pragmatic competence and one that is independent of syntactic and semantic capabilities.

2.1.2. Higher level goals and inferential processing

Many implicit performatives are generalized implicatures that do not require a time-consuming inference process (although, as noted above, the exact nature of this recognition process is not known). However, many implicit speech acts represent particularized implicatures and hence do require a time-consuming inference process. What exactly do language users need to know in order to comprehend particularized implicatures and what is the nature of this process?

In contrast to generalized implicatures, particularized implicatures are heavily dependent on the context, and in fact, cannot be interpreted apart from a context. Hence, language users need to be attentive to various features of the context and their role in conveying a speaker's intention.

One prototypical particularized implicature is to violate Grice's (1975) relation maxim (be relevant). Consider the following example (from Holtgraves 1998a):

> Bob and Al are students in the same history class and Bob has just given a presentation in this class. The following exchange then takes place:
>
> Bob: What did you think of my presentation?
> Al: It's hard to give a good presentation

How is Al's reply to be interpreted? Obviously he is asserting the belief that the act of giving a class presentation is difficult. But most people would probably conclude that he really means something more, the most likely interpretation being that he did not like the presentation. How, exactly, does one arrive at this interpretation? According to Grice (1975), the implicature would be one that makes the utterance a cooperative response, one that would 'fit' in the conversation. This makes perfect sense, but in many instances there are numerous possible interpretations that would fit in the conversation. One approach to this issue is to assume that factors playing a role in language production will play a parallel role in comprehension. Hence, because face management is a major motivator of indirectness, it should play a parallel role in the interpretation of indirectness. More specifically, recipients of a relevance violaton should construct an inference that represents an attempt to explain *why* the relevance violation occurred. Because face management is a major reason for violating conversational maxims, it is reasonable to assume that when faced with such a violation hearers will consider the possibility that the speaker is trying to engage in face management. So, when Al replies "It's hard to give a good presentation", in response to Bob's request for feedback, Bob is likely to infer that Al is engaging in face management. Now, because it is a negative opinion about Bob's presentation that would be face-threatening in this situation, the most likely inference is that Al does not have a positive opinion of the presentation. If the information was positive, there would usually be no need to violate the relation maxim; a positive opinion would not be face-threatening.

Support for this reasoning has been found in several experiments (Holtgraves 1998a; 1999; 2000). In these experiments participants read brief descriptions of situations, each followed by a question-reply exchange (similar to the example provided earlier). The reply always violated the relation maxim, either by completely changing the topic or by providing an excuse for why the requested information might be negative. Participants demonstrated a strong tendency to interpret these replies indirectly. More importantly, they demonstrated a strong tendency to generate a face-threatening interpretation, that the speaker was conveying (indirectly) face-threatening information. Follow-up studies using a reaction time methodology demonstrated that these interpretations occurred when the utterance was comprehended (rather than reflecting a post hoc judgment), and that the inferential process requires a recognition and rejection of the literal reading of the utterance (i.e., a Gricean inference process).

These results provide support for the idea that the specific interpretation given to a relevance violation is guided by beliefs about the reason for the violation. Importantly, it is not being claimed that relevance violations will always be interpreted as conveying negative information, only that if face management is recognized as a motivation for the violation, then the utterance will tend to be interpreted as conveying face-threatening information. Occasionally it might be positive information that is face-threatening. For example, imagine a conversation between two siblings, Mark and John, in which Mark always outperforms John in school, much to John's chagrin. Mark is aware of John's feelings and generally tries to manage John's face. Now, when John asks Mark how he did on his chemistry test, and Mark fails to answer directly (e.g., "Let's go get a pizza"), John will probably interpret the reply as conveying positive information (i.e., he did well on his exam) rather than negative information. In this context it is positive information that may be face-threatening, and so the reply will tend to be interpreted as conveying positive information.

2.1.3. Preference organization and comprehension.

Recognition of a particularized implicature requires the recipient to be very sensitive to the context. Moreover, because the implicature is the product of a reasoning process, recipients should be sensitive to any features of the context that are informative as to the speaker's likely intended meaning. Thus, if face management is recognized as the motive behind a relevance violation, then any contextual information suggesting that face management processes are operative in this context should facilitate recognition of an indirect (face-threatening) meaning.

In our research we have focused on "well" as a marker of dispreferred turns (Holtgraves 2000). In general, the occurrence of "well" at the beginning of an utterance can be interpreted as indicating that the speaker is engaging in face management (Jucker 1993). To refuse a request, decline an offer, and so on are threatening to the other person's face, and the dispreferred marker "well" helps soften this threat (Holtgraves 1992). Moreover, as discourse analysts have argued, discourse markers such as "well" should signal to the recipient that the remark underway is indirect and needs to be interpreted within a context that is not immediately apparent (Jucker 1993). Because of this, the occurrence of the dispreferred marker "well" in a reply should facilitate recognition of a face-threatening interpretation of that reply.

To examine this issue we modified the materials used in our earlier studies of indirect replies (Holtgraves 1998a; 1999). The major change was to manipulate whether the indirect reply contained a "well" marker. One half of the time it did (e.g., Well, I think it's hard to give a good presentation) and one half of the time it did not (e.g., I think it's hard to give a good presentation). As expected, face-threatening interpretations of the replies were more quickly verified when the reply contained a "well" preface than when it did not.

It seems likely that other markers of dispreferred turns will play a role in comprehension similar to that played by a "well" preface. And there is some preliminary evidence that they do. In an earlier study (Holtgraves 1998b; Experiment 3) we had participants listen to (rather than read) question-reply exchanges. In some conditions the reply was briefly delayed (2 sec). Brief delays are a common means of marking a turn as dispreferred, and in these conditions participants were faster at comprehending the reply, relative to replies that were not preceded by a brief delay.

3. Speaker status and comprehending particularized implicatures

Just as face management can play a critical role in utterance interpretation, so too can other contextual variables that play a role in language production play a parallel role in language comprehension. One very important variable in this regard is the speaker's relative status (or power). As noted above, previous research has demonstrated that the greater the status of the recipient, the greater the likelihood that the speaker will use polite (or indirect) request forms (Brown and Levinson 1987; Holtgraves and Yang 1990; 1992). Because of its role in language production, it seems likely that speaker status will play an important role in comprehension. Our research suggests that it does. For example, in our research on the processing of indirect requests (Holtgraves 1994), the status of the speaker moderated the effects of request conventionality. When requests were performed with a conventional form and hence represented a generalized implicature (e.g., Can you shut the door?), the status of the speaker did not play a role in comprehension; these forms were recognized quickly and directly regardless of the status of the speaker. In contrast, when requests were performed with a nonconventional form and hence represented a particularized implicature, comprehension was affected by the status of the speaker. Specifically, participants were faster at comprehending these forms, and did so without need of an inference process, when the speaker was higher rather than equal in status to his conversation partner.

These studies suggest that knowledge that a speaker is high status may circumvent the need for an inference process; a directive interpretation may be activated prior to any activation of the literal meaning of the utterance. Thus, when a speaker is high status, a recipient may be inclined to interpret the speaker's utterances, a priori, as directives (cf., Ervin-Tripp, Strage, Lampert, and Bell 1987). An alternative possibility is that knowledge that a speaker is high status can facilitate an inference process if one is required. Rejection of the literal meaning of an utterance depends, in part, on the possibility that there are alternative interpretations of the utterance (e.g., Sperber and Wilson 1986). People who are high status have the right to issue directives, and hence there exist possible directive interpretations of their utterances. The existence of these interpretations, then, increases the likelihood that the literal meaning will be rejected. Moreover, given that the literal meaning is rejected, knowledge that the speaker is high status can increase the likelihood that a directive interpretation will be adopted.

Regardless of how speaker status impacts the comprehension of speaker meaning, other research suggests that speaker status can influence long-term memory for a speaker's remarks (Holtgraves, Srull, and Socall 1989). In these experiments there was a tendency for the utterances of high status speakers to be recalled as being more assertive (i.e., direct) than identical remarks uttered by an equal status speaker. These results are consistent with research demonstrating the impact of speaker status on comprehension (high speaker status prompts a directive reading, a reading that is then retained in long-term memory).

4. Coordination, culture, and conclusions

The preceding discussion suggests that successful communication is relatively straightforward and almost mechanical. Of course nothing could be further from the truth. Communication does not occur in a vacuum. It is completely contextualized and the context is never exactly the same for the interlocutors. Although most theories of language use stipulate that successful perspective taking is required for language use (e.g., Clark 1985; Krauss and Fussell 1991; Mead 1934; Rommetviet 1974), perspective-taking is often far from perfect. For example, research suggests that interactants often exhibit an egocentric bias, producing and interpreting (at least initially) utterances from their unique perspective, without taking into account the perspective of their interlocutors (Keysar 1998; Keysar, Barr, Balin, and Paek 1998; Keysar and Bly 1995). Hence, speakers may assume they are performing a particular speech act without considering the possibility that the hearer might interpret their utterance as performing a different speech act. Conversely, the hearer might assume their interpretation to be correct without considering the alternative speech acts that the speaker may have intended to perform. Similar mismatches can occur for high level goals as well. A speaker might assume a particular level of politeness is appropriate for a setting without considering possible impolite readings of the remark.

Our research has demonstrated the existence of one systematic perspective-taking bias in language use (Holtgraves 2005b). In these studies participants interpreted replies that functioned as relevance violations. The materials were identical to those used in earlier research (Holtgraves 1998; 1999) except that sometimes participants took the speaker's perspective and indicated what they thought the speaker had intended; other times they took the recipient's perspective and indicated what intention they thought the recipient recognized. In these experiments, participants were far more likely to interpret relevance violations as conveying a negative opinion or disclosure when they assumed the perspective of the hearer than when they assumed the perspective of the speaker. This effect occurred for several different types of utterances. Also, it made no difference whether participants were informed that the requested information was negative. Nor did it make any difference that participants alternated assuming the perspective of the speaker and hearer, a design that should have sensitized them to the possibility that they were interpreting the replies one way when they took the speaker's view and another way when they took the hearer's perspective. Despite these various features of the design, in the end replies were more likely to be interpreted as conveying negative information when participants took the hearer's perspective than when they took the speaker's perspective.

Obviously perspectives will vary across cultures and such differences can represent substantial obstacles to successful cross-cultural communication. For example, although the effects of power, distance, and imposition on politeness may be universal, there are clear cultural differences in what constitutes an imposition and how heavily these variables should be weighted. This can result in cross-cultural misunderstandings. For example, Scollon and Scollon (1981) argue that English-speaking Americans are less polite than Athabaskans because of the former's assumption of greater familiarity. Athabaskans, however, interpret this lack of politeness not in terms of distance but as an assumption of superiority. In terms of weighting, North American speakers weight power and distance less heavily than do South Korean speakers (Holtgraves and Yang 1992). As a result, the politeness levels of South Koreans vary more as a function of the context than the politeness of North Americans. Hence, South Koreans may sometimes perceive a lack of politeness on the part of North Americans and North Americans may sometimes perceive an overly-polite presentation on the part of South Koreans. Clearly, successful cross-cultural communication requires an awareness of relevant contextual variables and possible cross-cultural differences in the role of these variables in social interaction.

Language use is fraught with tension. For the speaker there is always a conflict between lower-level goals (e.g., performing a request, making an apology) and higher-level goals (managing face). And there is tension between different aspects of the higher-level goals as well (e.g., supporting the other's face versus supporting one's own face). Often this delicate balancing act gets played out over a sequence of turns. For example, a speaker might initially err on the side of ambiguity via the use of an implicit performative. Failing to receive confirmation that her meaning is clear she may then restate it and clarify it with the use of an explicit performative (e.g., I'm agreeing with you; I'm promising you). In fact, may times speech acts are performed over a series of turns, with the sequence (rather than single turn) being the result of the higher level goal of face management. For example, people can preface a request with a pre-request, typically a check on the ability condition (e.g., "Are you busy tonight?"). If a negative response is forthcoming then the speaker may forgo performing the intended directive.

Successful language use requires a variety of skills and knowledge above and beyond basic syntactic and semantic competencies. Language users must know what actions can be performed with words and how to go about constructing utterances to perform those actions. And of course this is constrained by the interpersonal dimension of communication – the final form that an utterance takes will reflect the speaker's concern with managing his face and that of his interlocutors. Successful language use requires coordination and greatly facilitating this requirement is the fact that people are both speakers and listeners. The knowledge and skills used in language production can then play a parallel role in language comprehension. Listeners know that speakers will be attempting to perform actions with their words and they will be on the lookout for those actions. Similarly, listeners know that speakers often engage in face management and this awareness plays an important role in any inferential processing undertaken to recover a speaker's meaning. Of course the perspectives of speakers and listeners will never be completely identical. Despite this, human language users are amazingly adept at using language to accomplish their personal and social goals.

Acknowledgment. The writing of this chapter and some of the research reported in this chapter were supported by National Science Foundation grant SBR0131877. Correspondence should be addressed to: Tom Holtgraves, Dept. of Psychological Science, Ball State University, Muncie, IN 47306. Email: 00t0holtgrav@bsu.edu.

Notes

1. There is some debate regarding the cross-cultural validity of this scheme. For example, it had been argued that the desire for freedom from imposition (negative face) may be more characteristic of western, individualistic cultures than of nonwestern cultures (e.g., Fitch and Sanders 1994; Rosaldo 1982).
2. The data have not been entirely consistent with this ordering. In particular, off-record forms are not always perceived as the most polite form.
3. Although the illocutionary act may be clear, there may be ambiguity regarding other aspects of the utterance (e.g., the referents).

References

Ambady, N., F. L. Jasook Koo, and R. Rosenthal.
    1996   More than words: Linguistic and nonlinguistic politeness in two cultures. *Journal of Personality and Social Psychology* 70: 996–1011

Austin, J. L.
    1962   *How to do Things with Words*. Oxford: Claredon Press.

Bachman, L. F.
    1990   *Fundamental Considerations in Language Testing*. Reading, MA: Addison-Wesley Publishing Co.

Blum-Kulka, S., B. Danet, and R. Gherson
    1985   The language of requesting in Israeli society. In: Joseph Forgas (ed.), *Language in Social Situations*, 113–139. New York: Springer-Verlag.

Brown, P. and S. Levinson
    1987   *Politeness: Some Universals in Language Usage*. Cambridge, UK: Cambridge University Press.

Brown, R. and A. Gilman
    1989   Politeness theory and Shakespeare's four major tragedies. *Language in Society* 18: 159–212.

Clark, H. H.
    1985   Language use and language users. In: G. Lindzey and E. Aronson (eds.), *The Handbook of Social Psychology*, 179–232, (3rd ed. Vol. 2). Reading, MA: Addison-Wesley.

Clark, H. and D. Schunk
    1980   Polite responses to polite requests. *Cognition* 8: 111–143.

Dreyfus, H. L.
    1992   *What Computers still can't do: A Critique of Artificial Reason*. Cambridge, MA: MIT Press.

Ervin-Tripp, S., M. Strage, M. Lampert, and N. Bell
    1987   Understanding requests. *Linguistics* 25: 107–143.

Fitch, K. L., and R. E. Sanders
    1994   Culture, communication, and preferences for directness in expression of directives. *Communication Theory* 4: 219–245.

Goffman, E.
    1967   *Interaction Ritual: Essays on Face to Face Behavior*. Garden City, NY: Anchor Books.

Goffman, E.
    1971   *Relations in Public*. New York: Harper and Row.

Gordon, D. and G. Lakoff
    1975   Conversational postulates. In: P. Cole and J. Morgan (eds.), *Syntax and Semantics 3: Speech Acts,* 83–106. New York: Academic Press.

Grice, H. P.
    1957   Meaning. *Philosophical Review* 67: 377–388.

Grice, H. P.
    1975   Logic and conversation. In: P. Cole and J. Morgan (eds.), *Syntax and Semantics 3: Speech Acts,* 41–58. New York: Academic Press.

Hymes, D.
   1972   Models of the interaction of language and social settings. *Journal of Social Issues* 23: 8–28.

Holtgraves, T. M.
   1992   The linguistic realization of face management: implications for language production and comprehension, person perception, and cross-cultural communication. *Social Psychology Quarterly* 55: 141–159.

Holtgraves, T. M.
   1994   Communication in context: Effects of speaker status on the comprehension of indirect requests. *Journal of Experimental Psychology: Learning, Memory, and Cognition* 20: 1205–1218.

Holtgraves, T. M.
   1998a   Interpreting indirect replies. *Cognitive Psychology* 37: 1–27.

Holtgraves, T. M.
   1998b   *Interpreting indirect replies*. Paper presented at International Communication Association Convention, Jerusalem, Israel.

Holtgraves, T. M.
   1999   Comprehending indirect replies: When and how are their conveyed meanings activated. *Journal of Memory and Language* 41: 519–540.

Holtgraves, T. M.
   2000   Preference organization and reply comprehension. *Discourse Processes* 30: 87–106.

Holtgraves, T. M.
   2005a   The production and perception of implicit performatives. *Journal of Pragmatics* 37: 2024–2043.

Holtgraves, T. M.
   2005b   Diverging interpretations associated with the perspectives of the speaker and recipient in conversations. *Journal of Memory and Language* 53: 551–566.

Holtgraves, T. M.
   2007   *Memory for illocutionary force*. (Under review)

Holtgraves, T. M.
   in press a Automatic intention recognition in conversation processing. *Journal of Memory and Language*.

Holtgraves, T. M.
   in press b Second language learners and speech act comprehension. *Language Learning*.

Holtgraves, T. M. and A. Ashley
   2001   Comprehending illocutionary force. *Memory and Cognition* 29: 83–90.

Holtgraves, T. M., T. Srull, and D. Socall, D.
   1989   Conversation memory: The effects of speaker status on memory for the assertiveness of conversation remarks. *Journal of Personality and Social Psychology* 56, 149–160.

Holtgraves, T. M. and J.-N. Yang
   1990   Politeness as universal: Cross-cultural perceptions of request strategies and inferences based on their use. *Journal of Personality and Social Psychology* 59: 719–729.

Holtgraves, T. M. and J.-N. Yang
    1992   The interpersonal underpinnings of request strategies: General principles and differences due to culture and gender. *Journal of Personality and Social Psychology* 62: 246–256.

Jucker, A. H.
    1993   The discourse marker well: A relevance-theoretical account. *Journal of Pragmatics* 19: 435–452.

Keysar, B.
    1998   Language users as problem solvers: Just what ambiguity problem do they solve? In: S. Fussell and R. Kreuz (eds.), *Social and Cognitive Approaches to Interpersonal Communication,* 175–200. Mahwah, N. J.: Erlbaum. (1995).

Keysar, B., D. J. Barr, J. A. Balin, and T. Paek.
    1998   Definite reference and mutual knowledge: A processing model of common ground in comprehension. *Journal of Memory and Language* 39: 1–20.

Keysar, B. and B. Bly
    1995   Intuitions of the transparency of idioms: Can one keep a secret by spilling the beans? *Journal of Memory and Language* 34: 89–109.

Krauss, R. M. and S. R. Fussell
    1991   Perspective taking in communication: Representations of others' knowledge in reference. *Social Cognition* 9: 2–24.

Leech, G.
    1983   *Principle of Pragmatics.* London: Longman.

Lim, T.-S. and J. W. Bowers
    1991   Face-work, solidarity, approbation, and tact. *Human Communication Research* 17: 415–450.

Mead, G. H.
    1934   *Mind, Self, and Society.* Chicago: University of Chicago Press

Rommetveit, R.
    1974   *On Message Structure: A Framework for the Study of Language and Communication.* New York: Wiley

Rosaldo, M. Z.
    1982   The things we do with words: Ilongot speech acts and speech act theory in philosophy. *Language in Society 11:* 203–237.

Scollon, R. and S. Scollon
    1981   *Narrative, Literacy and Face in Interethnic Communication.* Norwood, NJ: Ablex.

Searle, J. R.
    1969   *Speech Acts.* Cambridge, UK: Cambridge University Press.

Slugoski, B. and W. Turnbull
    1988   Cruel to be kind and kind to be cruel: Sarcasm, banter and social relations. *Journal of Language and Social Psychology* 7: 101–121.

9. Writing and reading

Elke Prestin

In the age of globalization, writing and reading have become basic human skills. Although illiteracy is still a considerable problem even in the wealthier parts of the world, nowadays probably most communication world-wide takes place in the written mode (cf. Coulmas 2003). This is why in a handbook on communicative competences, the topic of writing and reading certainly deserves some attention. However, when approached with a broad perspective, the topic is so comprehensive that it can impossibly be dealt with in a single chapter. Therefore, after shortly introducing the various linguistic approaches to writing and reading, I will concentrate on the human competences involved from a mainly psycholinguistic perspective. The most influential models of writing and reading will be discussed, followed by some comments on the demands on cognitive resources they imply. The chapter is closed with an integrated view on writing and reading as interdependent parts of human communication.

1. Linguistic approaches to writing

Within the various fields of linguistics, a lot of research has been done about the topic of 'writing'. The considerable bandwidth of approaches can be attributed to the diversity of the topic itself. In an early attempt to cover the broad meaning, Gelb (1963: 12) defined writing as "a system of human intercommunication by means of conventional visible marks". A more specific account is provided by Coulmas (2003: 1), who distinguishes at least six perspectives on writing, covering

(1) a system of recording language by means of visible or tactile marks;
(2) the activity of putting such a system to use;
(3) the result of such activity;
(4) the particular form of such a result, a script style such as block letter writing;
(5) artistic composition;
(6) a professional occupation.

From a purely linguistic point of view, only meanings (1) to (3) offer genuine fields of research, while (4) could be considered a sub-aspect which specifies the "visible marks" mentioned in (1). Meanings (5) and (6), on the other hand, seem to denominate meta-levels which are based on the socially determined shaping of the various aspects covered by meanings (1) to (4).

While the writing systems are a traditional domain of theoretical linguistics, the production (and comprehension) of written language falls into the realm of cognitive linguistics. The results of these activities are usually investigated by text linguists. Applied linguistics comprises both the latter aspects, which are, at least in part, mutually interdependent. This is why research on writing as a human competence is based upon both process-oriented and product-oriented methods. An overview of the methods of inquiring into text production is supplied by Eigler (1996) and by Bereiter and Scardamalia (1987).

In spite of the diversity of methodical approaches, the development of models has been rather straightforward, with Hayes and Flower's (1980) approach serving as a starting point. An excellent, very detailed description and discussion of the models of writing is presented by Alamargot and Chanquoy (2001). In the following sections, I will give a summary of the most influential approaches.

2. Models of writing as problem solving

The first models of the writing process were based on the notion of writing as a problem-solving task. This approach is accounted for with "the multiple and simultaneous constraints imposed on the writer" (Frederiksen et al. 1990: 89). Among the internal constraints there are "the availability of 'declarative' information in memory, at the conceptual and lexical level", as well as "the availability of 'procedures' for the construction and manipulation of both conceptual and linguistic structures" (Frederiksen et al. 1990: 88). In addition, there are external constraints which "involve mainly the characteristics of the hearer or audience, the genre, the situation of communication, and the purpose of the writer" (Frederiksen et al. 1990: 89). The early models of writing had the objective to give a general account of how writers deal with these constraints.

2.1. Hayes and Flower's (1980) model

The first general model of text production with the focus on problem-solving activities was presented by Hayes and Flower (1980). As figure 1 shows, the writing process in their view consists of planning, translating and reviewing, with contextual information being supplied by the writer's long term memory and the task environment.

In his long term memory, the writer has stored knowledge about various topics and audiences, as well as generalized writing plans which may have the form of story grammars sensu Rumelhart (1975). The task environment provides in its first component, which is called writing assignment, information about the

Writing and reading 227

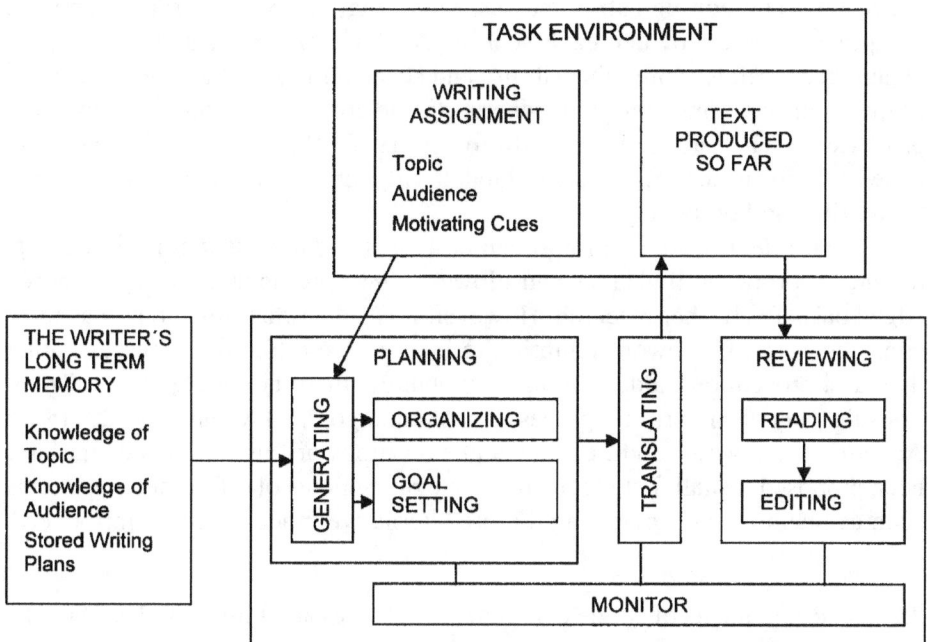

Figure 1. Structure of the writing model; adapted from Hayes and Flower (1980: 11)

actual topic and audience; moreover, there may be "information relevant to the writer's motivation", as Hayes and Flower (1980: 12) note rather vaguely. The second component of the task environment, the text produced so far, is added once the writing process has led to some (intermediate) results. But first the general knowledge stored in long term memory and the actual requirements of the writing assignment have to be integrated. This is achieved in the planning process; more precisely, in its first sub-process called generating. According to Hayes and Flower, the task environment provides memory probes which are used to retrieve relevant items from long term memory. These items have the form of propositions, i.e., they are structures of concepts, relations, and attributes.

The retrieved items may either supply material that is relevant for the topic, or individual criteria by which to judge the text, such as "Better keep it simple," or "I need to write a transition here" (Hayes and Flower 1980: 15). Items of the first kind are passed on to the organizing sub-process where the materials are integrated into a writing plan; items of the second kind are identified by the goal setting process and stored for subsequent use in the translating and editing processes. In the translating process, the material gathered so far is transformed into acceptable written sentences, which are added to the task environment. This text is then examined and improved in the reviewing process, which consists of the reading and editing sub-processes. In editing, various criteria are applied, comprising aspects of language such as spelling, grammar, and accuracy of meaning, as well as comprehensibility and acceptability for the reader. As parts of the monitor component, both generating and editing may interrupt any other processes, such that, as Hayes and Flower (1980: 19) point out, the model in general is not necessarily a stage model with subsequent stages of planning, translating, and reviewing.

With its identification of important processes and representations in writing, the model proposed by Hayes and Flower (1980) provided a widely acknowledged basis for further research. However, it is "clear that this model has to be considered as a framework tempting to identify the different processes, rather than as a procedural model aiming at explaining the functioning and (…) relationships between writing processes" (Alamargot and Chanquoy 2001: 6). Accordingly, several modifications and extensions of this initial account have been proposed. I shall first reconsider some refinements of different components such as planning and reviewing, before alternative models will be introduced.

2.2. Refinements of single components of Hayes and Flower's (1980) model

2.2.1. Planning

As explained above, the planning process in Hayes and Flower's (1980) model consists of the three sub-processes generating, organizing, and goal-setting, with the generating sub-process serving as a link between task environment and long term memory. In their account of the nature of planning in writing, Hayes and Nash (1996) stick to these basic components, but give a slightly different and more detailed explanation of the processes involved. Basically, they conceive of planning as comprising two steps. In the first step, the task has to be represented in what is called the planning environment. This means that in contrast to the former model, which simply presupposed the existence of a writing assignment in the task environment, representing the task is now part of the writing process itself. According to Hayes and Nash, this step includes both "a representation of the desired outcome" and "representations of the resources available for carrying out the task" (Hayes and Nash 1996: 31), with the mode of representation being determined by the respective planning method. For example, planning by abstraction means that topics are represented "by brief names that capture the most important features of the topic" (Hayes and Nash 1996: 35). While this approach is consistent with Newell and Simon's (1972) view on planning, Hayes and Nash propose two further methods: Planning by analogy occurs when the writer accesses former plans on which the current writing plan is then based. Planning by modelling is frequently used when sentences are composed.[1]

Independent of the planning method, the authors generally conceive of a plan as a combination of a goal and certain means to achieve this goal, which may be viewed as "a set of suggestions" (Hayes and Nash 1996: 32) either for how to accomplish the task, or for which additional actions to take, with the latter including actions such as studying literature to gain more information on a topic. In the second step of planning, "the planner tries out alternate goals and/or alternate means for achieving those goals until a satisfactory combination of goals and means is found" (Hayes and Nash 1996: 31). Hayes and Nash (1996) thus provide an account of planning processes that is in its basics derived from Hayes and Flower (1980), but allows for more insights into some of the complexities of writing.

2.2.2. Reviewing

Besides planning, the revision process, which is called reviewing by Hayes and Flower (1980), has also been revised in later publications. Based on the idea that revision is initiated when the writer discovers an incongruity between his goals and the text he has produced so far (cf. Bridwell 1980), Scardamalia and Bereiter (1983) propose the C.D.O. (compare, diagnose, and operate) model. According to the authors, the revision procedure, which is typically applied after each sentence, comprises a cycle of three sub-processes. First, the representation of the text as intended, and the representation of the text as produced[2] are compared. If there is a mismatch, the "diagnose" process seeks the sources of the problem. If the search is successful, the problem can either be solved by changing the plan (in which case the representation of the "text as intended" is affected), or by operating on the text produced so far. In the latter case, the "operation" process is performed, which consists of the selection of a strategy and its application in generating a text change.

However, as Alamargot and Chanquoy (2001: 102) point out, the C.D.O. model "cannot be considered as a real model of revision, but rather, in an educational view, as a technique to help writers to revise". Moreover, Hayes and colleagues (1987) note that the restriction to a comparison of texts and plans may be inadequate. They point out that a reviser may also "evaluate the text against general criteria for texts such as standards of spelling, grammar, and clarity", and "evaluate the plan against criteria he or she believes plans should meet," such as consistency of arguments (Hayes et al. 1987: 179–180). According to the authors, it is different proficiency in this latter respect that causes the superiority of an expert's revision.

Hayes and colleagues themselves embed the various ways of evaluating texts or plans into a process model of revision that basically consists of the five steps task definition, evaluation, strategy selection, selection of procedures, and modification of text and/or plan (cf. Figure. 2).

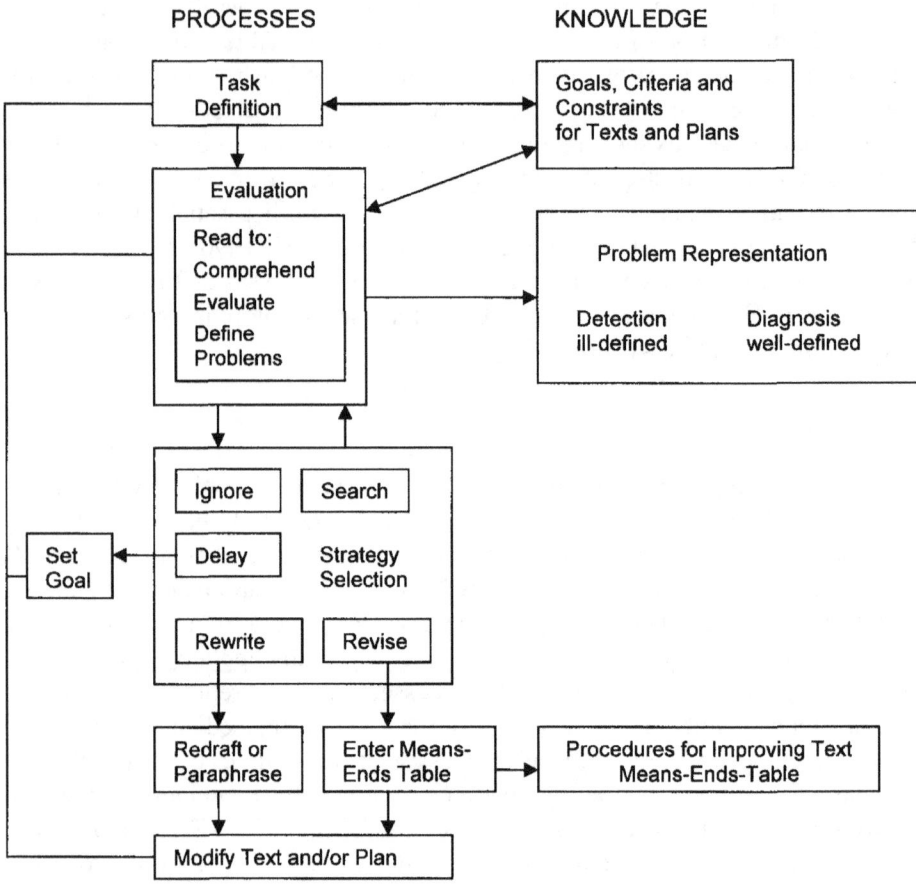

Figure 2. Process model of revision; adapted from Hayes et al. (1987: 185)

Evaluation requires goal-oriented reading, which the authors characterize as an extended form of reading for comprehension, based on the model by Thibadeau, Just and Carpenter (1982). Reading, then, does not only serve as a basis for comparing the produced text with the plans, as in the C.D.O. model. Instead of this, all criteria mentioned above are applied in problem diagnosis: The text is checked for linguistic correctness, and the plan is checked for correspondence with the writer's goals. Accordingly, problems are dealt with either at the text or at the planning level – if they are dealt with at all. Actually, the writer may find the special demand which his text does not meet rather unimportant and decide to ignore the mismatch, or he may delay the effort to deal with it. He may also search for more information before tackling the problem. But if he wants to solve the problem immediately, there are two basic options: He may simply rewrite the critical passage without any deeper analysis, or he may engage in making a diagnosis and then revise either text or plan. This requires a new planning procedure, including a means-ends table in the sense of Newell and Simon (1972).

With their model of revision as a background, Hayes and colleagues compare novice and expert writers. Their empirical findings show that there are considerable differences in task definition, evaluation, and strategy selection. First, only experienced revisers seem to create complex task definitions, including "'global' goals for revision that take into account the purpose of the text in the communication situation" (Hayes et al. 1987: 198). Second, the problem representations created at the evaluation stage "range from spare representations that contain little information" in the case of novices to "richly elaborated diagnoses that offer both conceptual and procedural information about the problem" in the case of experts (Hayes et al. 1987: 211). And finally, novices often deal with text problems by either applying rigid rules or simply deleting those parts they find to be inappropriate, while "experts use a range of procedures that enable them to satisfy a more complex set of goals and constraints" (Hayes et al. 1987: 222).

The comparison of novice and expert writers is a method that has been frequently applied in writing research. While most work in this respect concentrates on single components of text production, Bereiter and Scardamalia (1987) propose a complete model of the writing process which aims at explaining the differences between writers with different levels of competence.

2.3.   Bereiter and Scardamalia's (1987) model

With respect to their model of the writing process (see section 2.1 above), Hayes and Flower (1980: 29) point out that "we do not intend to imply that all writers use all of the processes we have described. Our model is a model of competent writers". The implied idea of different levels of competence in writing is taken up and reflected by Bereiter and Scardamalia (1987; see also Scardamalia and Bereiter 1987), who distinguish two writing strategies. The basic strategy, which even novice writers should master without much effort, is described in the knowledge-telling model (cf. Figure 3).

The authors characterize knowledge telling as "a way to generate text content, given a topic to write about and a familiar genre (factual exposition, personal opinion, instructions, etc.)" (Scardamalia and Bereiter 1987: 143). This means that in contrast to Hayes and Flower's (1980) model, only knowledge of topic (in Bereiter and Scardamalia's terminology: "content knowledge") and stored writing plans ("discourse knowledge") are accessed in long term memory, whereas knowledge of audience or motivational cues do not play a role. The knowledge retrieval via memory probes closely resembles the account Hayes and Flower (1980) gave in their initial model. The retrieved content is tested for

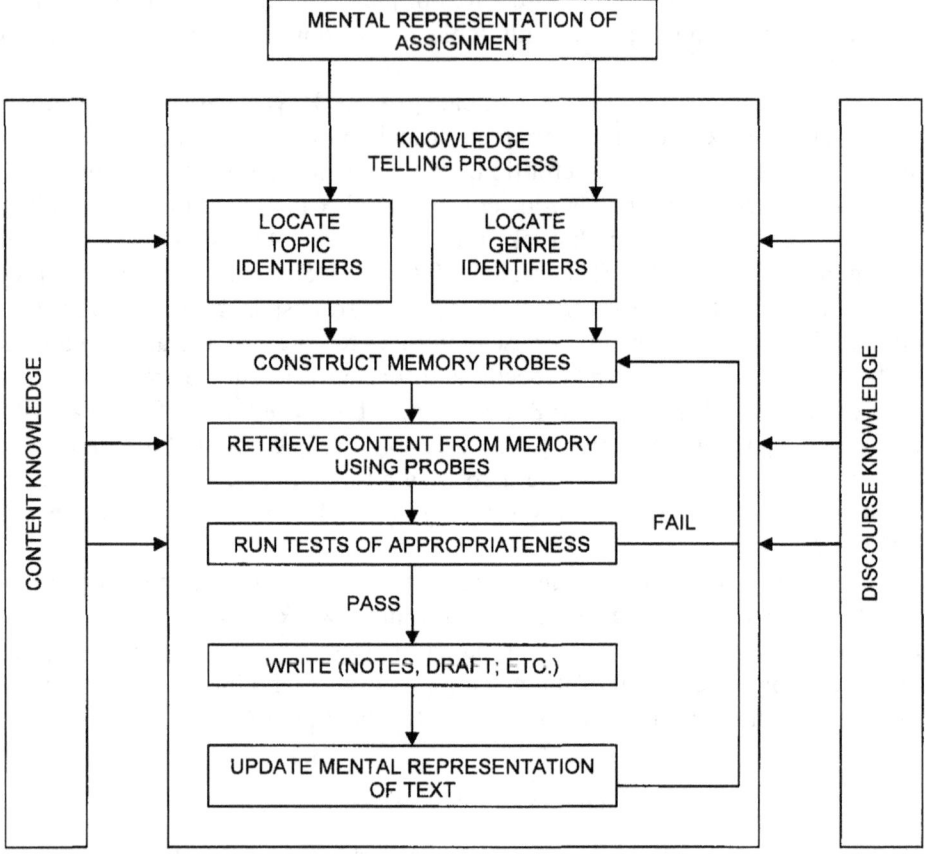

Figure 3. Structure of the knowledge-telling model; adapted from Bereiter and Scardamalia (1987: 8)

appropriateness, which is the only allusion the authors make to reviewing processes – in the knowledge-telling model, then, reviewing concerns pre-text only, and the only strategy of repair seems to be the replacement of the content retrieved. Finally, the content is transformed into writing and the mental representation of the text produced so far is updated accordingly.

While knowledge telling characterizes the very basic abilities a writer must possess, writing as knowledge transforming is a much more complex process (cf. Figure 4).

The components of knowledge-telling are now embedded into a problem-solving context with two interrelated problem spaces: The content space deals with problems of belief and knowledge, while in the rhetorical space, "problems of achieving goals of the composition" (Scardamalia and Bereiter 1987: 11) are addressed.

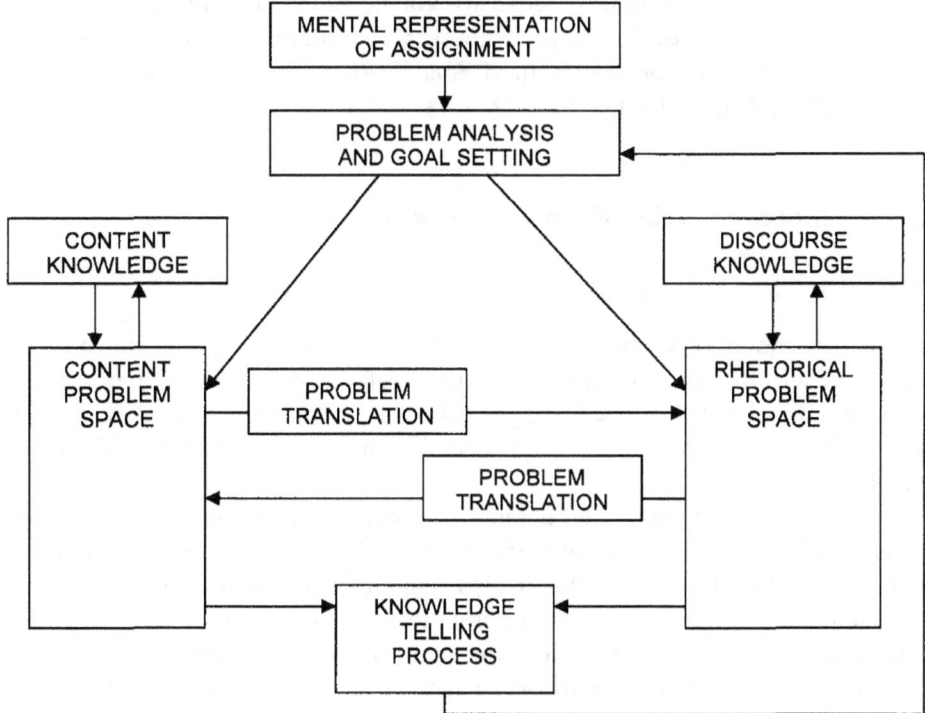

Figure 4. Structure of the knowledge-transforming model; adapted from Bereiter and Scardamalia (1987: 12)

The initial goal-setting, which is based on a problem analysis of the writing assignment, merely serves as the first input for both the content and the rhetorical space. In both spaces, problems then have to be translated into sub-goals which are passed on to the respective other space. For example, "difficulties that are encountered in the rhetorical space, in making a statement clear or convincing, may be translated into sub-goals of generating examples of a concept, (…), arguments against a competing belief, and so on" (Scardamalia and Bereiter 1987: 147). Once submitted to the content space, these sub-goals may lead to elaborations or changes in the writer's belief. The interaction between text processing and knowledge processing explains the fact that writing itself promotes other competences such as reflective and abstract thinking (cf. Molitor-Lübbert 2002: 46). As Bereiter and Scardamalia (1987: 10) put it, in the process of knowledge transforming, "the thoughts come into existence through the composing process itself".

While the models introduced so far provide important insights into some components of the writing process, one problem with problem-solving approaches remains: They give "a high-level, top-down account of writing, focusing on the explicit thinking processes involved rather than the more implicit processes whereby thought is turned into text" (Galbraith and Torrance 1999: 3). This drawback was addressed in the 1990s, when more comprehensive models of writing were developed.

3. More comprehensive models of writing

3.1. Hayes' (1996) model

In his new model of writing, Hayes (1996) wants to present a framework that can "be useful for interpreting a wider range of writing activities than was encompassed in the 1980 model" (Hayes 1996: 1). To achieve this goal, he supplements the task environment with a second component called "the individual" (cf. Figure 5).

The task environment itself is more comprehensive as compared to the previous models. Its first component, the social environment, not only contains the audience and collaborators, but it also includes (though not explicitly mentioned in the diagram) the social-cultural dimension of writing, based on the assumption that "what we write, how we write, and who we write to is shaped by social convention and by our history of social interaction" (Hayes 1996: 5). The text produced so far remains one important aspect of the physical environment, but there, too, a supplement has been made in that the composing medium is also considered.

Regarding the individual, Hayes stresses the influence of motivational factors, stating that writing is determined not only by the writing assignment itself, but also by long-term predispositions and interacting goals, with the course of action being shaped "through a kind of cost-benefit mechanism" (Hayes 1996: 10). Another difference to the 1980 model concerns the cognitive processes, whose components have been fundamentally reorganized: In the place of the reviewing process, there is now a component called text interpretation which is strongly based upon reading activities. The former planning processes are included in the more general reflection process, while translating activities are subsumed by the new and wider component of text production. In his description of long term memory, Hayes (1996) gives a differentiated overview of the relevant classes of information which takes into account, and extends, Bereiter and Scardamalia's (1987) distinction between content problem space and rhetorical problem space. As an additional, and very important, component of his model, Hayes presents an account of the role working memory plays in the writing process. Based upon Baddeley's (1986) general model of working memory, this account includes a phonological loop and a sketchpad which allow for maintaining phonological and visual representations.[3]

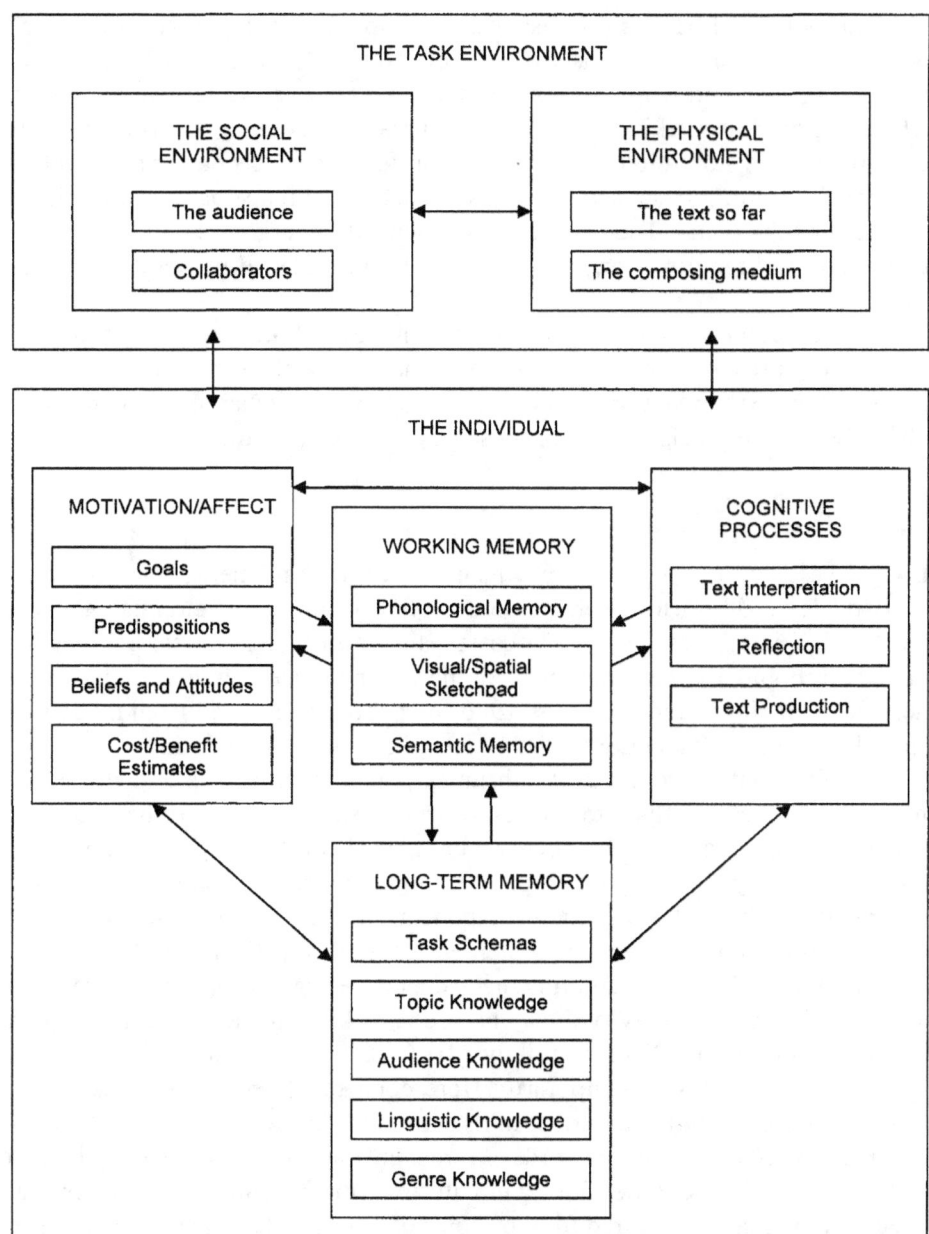

Figure 5. The general organisation of the new model; adapted from Hayes (1996: 4)

Thus equipped, Hayes proposes "a provisional model of text production" which can be summarized as follows (cf. Hayes 1996: 23–24): Cues from the writing plan and from the text produced so far retrieve semantic content, which is stored in working memory. To express this content, a surface form is constructed and stored in the articulatory buffer. When this buffer has reached its capacity limit, the surface form (a sentence or sentence part) is articulated vocally or subvocally. The pretext thus produced undergoes evaluation and is then either written down or, in case of rejection, replaced by another surface form.

Even though Hayes' (1996) model contains several precisions and additions to former approaches, the role of working memory with respect to the various processes of text production remains rather vague (cf. Alamargot and Chanquoy 2001: 18). Some precisions are proposed by Kellogg (1996).

3.2. Kellogg's (1996) model

Like Hayes, Kellogg (1996) adopts the notion of working memory as presented by Baddeley (1986). However, Kellogg explicitly aims at developing an architecture that integrates writing processes and information processing. In his model (cf. Figure 6), the components of the writing process, which are basically derived from Hayes and Flower's (1980) model of writing and from models of speaking (e.g., Bock and Levelt 1994), are all connected to working memory.

The formulation component subsumes planning processes and the transformation of their results into linguistic structures. For writing to be executed, some programming has to be done which depends on the mode of realisation, e.g., handwriting or typing. Both programming and realisation of the message fall into the realm of the execution component. Results of both stages are passed on to the monitoring component, which, in accordance with Hayes et al. (1987), consists of a reading and an editing mechanism. Kellogg (1996) gives a detailed account of how each activity draws back on working memory; the gist of this account can be summarized as follows: (i) In the planning process, the visuospatial sketchpad has to temporarily store conceptual representations. (ii) In translation, the phonological loop, in its short term buffer, has to store the phonological representations of words. Moreover, the phonological loop is also needed for reading activities during monitoring. (iii) Resources from the central executive are mainly required for the choice of words and syntactic structures in translation, and for monitoring processes. Execution, on the other hand, is widely automatized and thus not costly on the central executive – hence the dotted line in figure 6.

The general relationship of writing and cognitive resources is not uncontroversial, however. This is why by way of concluding the discussion of 'writing', a short discussion of this aspect seems to be in order.

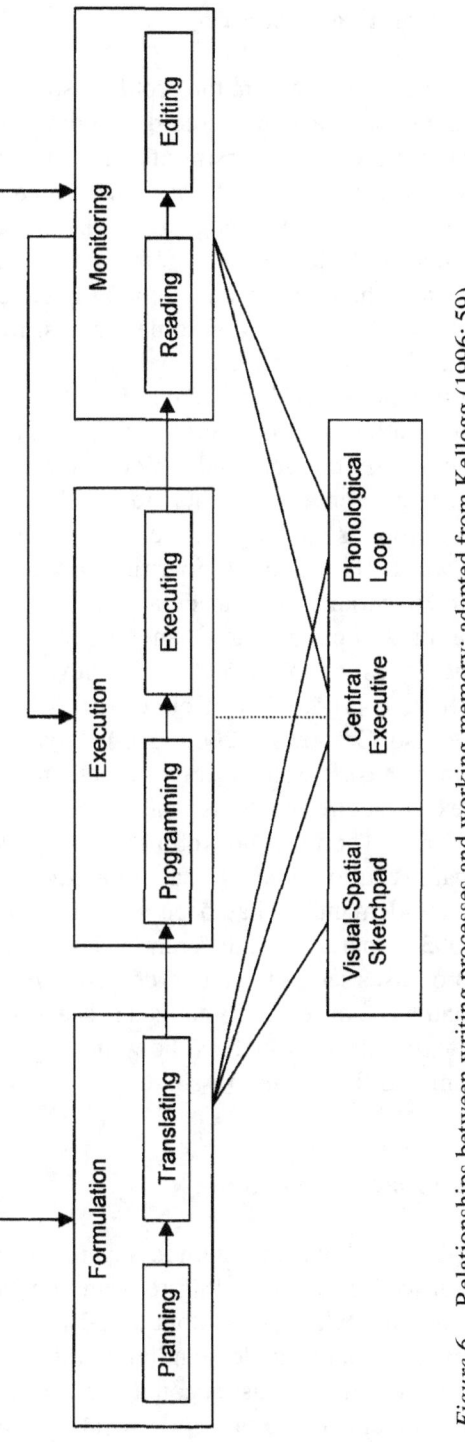

Figure 6. Relationships between writing processes and working memory; adapted from Kellogg (1996: 59)

4. Writing and cognitive resources

As mentioned in section 2 above, within the problem-solving paradigm writing in general is considered as very resource-demanding. Flower and Hayes (1980: 34–40) name three groups of constraints an adult writer must shoulder: First, rather incoherent information has to be transformed "into a highly conceptualized and precisely related knowledge network". Second, conventions of language and style must be followed. And third, the writer's purposes, their sense of the audience, and the interpersonal context have to be considered. As Flower and Hayes (1980: 40) state, "For some writers, this is the straw that breaks the camel's back".[4] A similar view is held by Alamargot and Chanquoy (2001: 1), according to whom "writing is a complex task that needs a coordinated implementation of a large set of mental activities". For example, writers have to delimitate the nature, the goal and the communicative function of the text; establish a precise representation about readers' characteristics and expectations; control the text topic so as to generate or to specify the most relevant ideas; put ideas into words throughout the writing process; sometimes clarify the message, reorganize, modify and articulate ideas, while controlling the whole text coherence (cf. Alamargot and Chanquoy 2001: 1).

Yet it seems to be "questionable whether high-level problem solving is a necessary ingredient of the production of effective text" (Galbraith and Torrance 1999: 4–5; see also Grabowski 2003: 363). Several studies show that when performing routine tasks, writers draw on schemata which include information on, e.g., text structure, contents, and syntactic shaping (cf. Schumacher et al. 1989; Torrance, Thomas, and Robinson 1996). Moreover, Kellogg's (1996) supposition that execution processes, as compared to planning and monitoring, are less resource-demanding has been supported by later experiments (cf. Kellogg 1999, 2003). Therefore, a differentiated approach to the cognitive demands of writing processes seems to be in order: Apparently, both controlled, elaborate activities, and more or less automatized processes are involved in text production, with contextual factors such as the writer's routine with respect to the assignment determining the respective share.

5. Linguistic approaches to reading

In contrast to the English word 'writing' with its several meanings, the notion of reading is less difficult to define. According to Ram and Moorman (1999: 1), reading means "the task that takes as its input a body of text in a natural language and produces as its output an understanding of that text". Ram and Moorman hold that a theory of reading must account for both the processes which reading implies and the understanding of a given text that results from these processes. In that, there is a parallel to the perspectives (2) and (3) on writing Coulmas provides (see section 1 of this chapter).

Regarding the methodical approaches, however, writing research and reading research differ considerably. In writing, the *products* are openly accessible for investigation, whereas in reading, the acquired understanding of a text is a mental entity that can only be indirectly accessed. On the other hand, investigation of *processes* is easier in reading research because the input can be experimentally controlled. This is why empirical reading research is mainly based on on-line methods, even though there are also some off-line measures used to test text comprehension (for an overview and discussion of methodology in reading research, see Kintsch and Rawson 2005: 213–214; Smith 1996). Not surprisingly, then, models of text comprehension tend to be quite detailed in their description of processes. In the next section I will first introduce the components of text comprehension before having a closer look at the various processes involved.

6. Models of text comprehension

6.1. Components of text comprehension

In spite of differences in architecture, recent models of text comprehension agree on the supposition that three components are involved in adult reading (cf. Figure 7). One input is provided by the text itself. To get a mental representation of the text, the reader has to decode the graphic symbols, recognize words and assign them to their roles in phrases and sentences. The results are often supposed to be stored in the form of so-called propositions, a notion that was developed by Kintsch (1974) and has become widely acknowledged since then. Basically, a proposition consists of a predicate and its arguments; e.g., the sentence "Carl likes ice-cream" can be represented as LIKE (CARL, ICE-CREAM), with the capitals indicating that the represented entities are concepts. When organized into higher-order units that reflect the topical structure of the text, these propositions form the text base (cf. Kintsch 1998) which "represents the meaning of the text, as it is actually expressed by the text" (Kintsch and Rawson 2005: 211).

The second input that is crucial for text comprehension is provided by the world and its mental representation. As part of her world-knowledge, the reader has stored abstract schemata representing stereotypical situations (cf. Alba and Hasher 1983), and scripts, which are more specified schemata, representing stereotypical sequences of actions (cf. Abelson 1981). The reader's world-knowledge may also comprise characteristic features of various text types in the sense of van Dijk's (1980) superstructures (e.g., Berkenkotter and Huckin 1995).

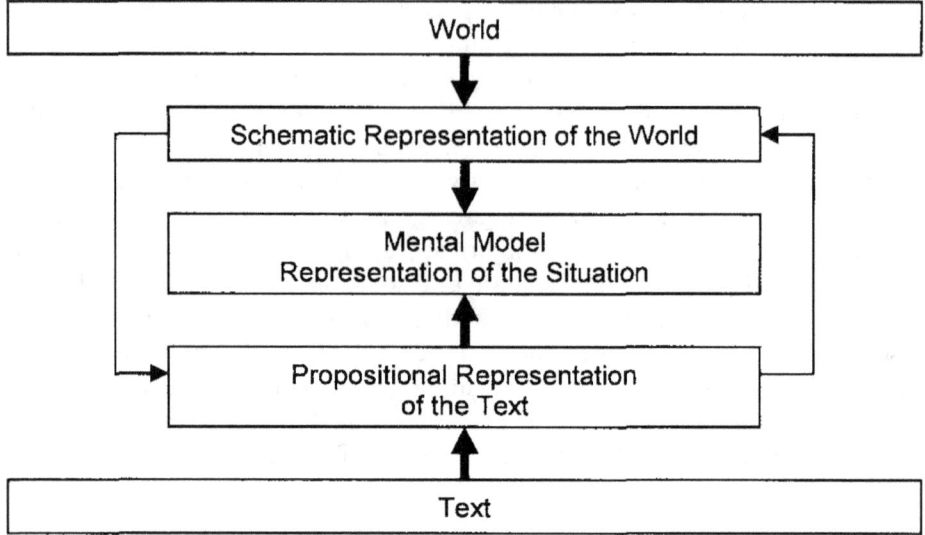

Figure 7. Components of text comprehension; based upon Rickheit, Sichelschmidt, and Strohner (2002: 402)

To gain more than a merely superficial understanding of the text, the reader has to integrate text and world-knowledge by way of building a situation model, i.e., a mental model of the situation described by the text. This wider approach to comprehension goes back to Johnson-Laird (1983), who introduced the notion of mental models, and to van Dijk and Kintsch (1983), who used the term situation model with respect to text comprehension. The situation model comprises a wide range of related information that is either derived from the text, or inferred on the basis of world-knowledge (e.g., Anderson and Pearson 1984). According to Johnson-Laird (1983), at least temporal, spatial, causal, motivational, and person- and object-related information is incorporated. While this notion of a situation model is restricted to a representation of the text world, Rickheit and Strohner (1999) propose an extension to the communicative situation. Text comprehension, then, is also affected by the reader's knowledge of the writer and his goals. As to the mode of representation, there is some consensus that the situation model may include both sets of propositions and integrated information in nonpropositional format (cf. Perfetti, Landi, and Oakhill 2005: 230), which "frequently involves imagery, emotions, and personal experiences" (Kintsch and Rawson 2005: 211).

While until the early 1980s, most researchers more or less equated text comprehension with the construction of a text base, it is now widely acknowledged that a coherent situation model is tantamount to the successful comprehension of a text (e.g., Graesser, Millis, and Zwaan 1997). Therefore, all three components mentioned above (i.e., text base, world-knowledge, and integrated situation model) have to be considered in up-to-date models of text comprehension. There are, however, contradictory opinions as to the interaction of these components. The respective points of view are an important distinguishing feature of the various models.

6.2. Models of the comprehension process: bottom-up vs. top-down

In principle, models of the comprehension process can be divided into bottom-up and top-down approaches. In the bottom-up models, which are closely connected with the name of Walter Kintsch, comprehension is text driven. An early influential theory, which did not yet contain a notion of situation model but was restricted to the construction of a text base, was proposed by Kintsch and van Dijk (1978). On the basis of Kintsch's (1974) theory of propositional representation, they described comprehension as a strictly modular, cyclic process in which the reader first constructs a list of propositions that represent the meaning of the text. These propositions are then in chunks tested for argument overlaps. Only if this does not result in a coherent text base, world-knowledge has to be consulted: The reader infers further propositions which help to complete the text base.

Thorough revision and extension of this early approach led to the construction integration theory (Kintsch 1988, 1998), which is based upon connectionist modelling. In the first phase, a text base is constructed on the basis of explicit and inferred propositions and concepts. In the second phase, world-knowledge is integrated to select those concepts which best fit into the context. In contrast to Kintsch and van Dijk's (1978) approach, the reader is now supposed to build a situation model that may contain more information than the text base alone. However, comprehension is still mainly determined by the text, whereas schemata play a role at the second stage only.

Top-down models, on the other hand, do not distinguish between construction and integration processes. Instead of this, world knowledge is supposed to directly influence the morpho-syntactic, semantic, and pragmatic analysis of the textual input. The probably most important interactive, top-down theory of text comprehension is the theory of mental models (Johnson-Laird 1983, 1989). According to this theory, at a very early stage of comprehension schemata are activated that may determine the further comprehension process. During comprehension (not, as in bottom-up models, at the end of it), propositional information and knowledge-based inferences are integrated into a uniform representation of the situation that can extend the verbal contents of the text. Top-down approaches focus on the fact that reading means not merely the representation, but the construction of meaning (Christmann and Groeben 1996; Groeben 1982), which explains the finding that the same text can be interpreted

242 Elke Prestin

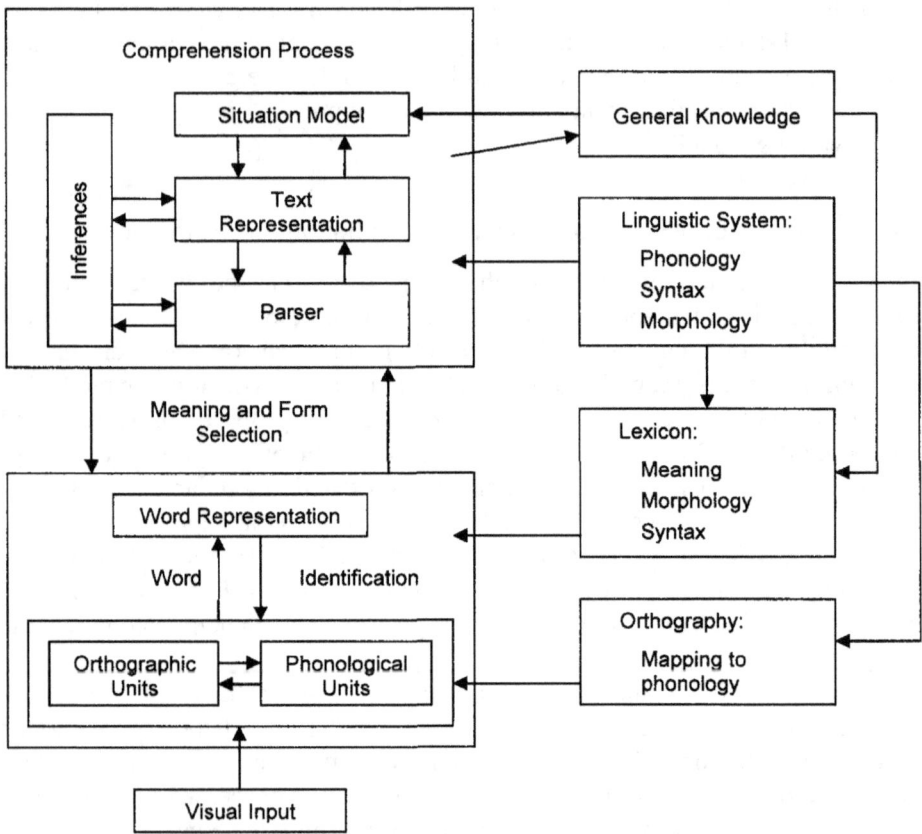

Figure 8. A framework for reading comprehension; adapted from Perfetti, Landi and Oakhill (2005: 229)

differently, depending on the knowledge of the reader and on the context (Anderson et al. 1977).

Nevertheless, altogether the empirical evidence with respect to bottom-up or top-down-processes remains inconclusive (cf. Prestin 2003). This is why recently some researchers have voted for an integrated approach that allows for both kinds of processes (e.g., Rickheit, Sichelschmidt, and Strohner 2002; Rickheit and Strohner 1999). Figure 7 above depicts such an integration, with the arrows pointing in both directions. A general framework for text comprehension that does explicitly not make strong assumptions about the interactions of single units is proposed by Perfetti, Landi, and Oakhill (2005). Their diagram shows in detail the processes involved in reading (cf. Figure 8).

According to the authors, "word identification, parsing, referential mapping, and a variety of inference processes all contribute, interacting with the reader's conceptual knowledge, to produce a mental model of the text" (Perfetti et al. 2005: 228). Provided with this rough overview, we can now have a closer look at some of these processes.

6.3.   Accounts of how processing works at the various levels

6.3.1.   Word level

The first process within reading comprehension depicted in figure 8 is word identification. One issue at this level is the role of phonology, which is often explained in dual route (Coltheart 2005) or dual process (Van Orden and Kloos 2005) approaches. These approaches deal with the question whether understanding individual written words always depends upon prior access to their phonology; in other words, whether the "orthography mapping to phonology" in figure 8 is a necessary process in reading. Dual route or dual process theories deny this and propose a more differentiated model instead. According to this approach, mapping to phonology is restricted to unskilled readers (cf. Van Orden and Kloos 2005: 62), whereas skilled readers have developed a direct access from visual inputs to the mental lexicon.

There is, however, yet another kind of dual-route approaches, which focuses on the role morphology plays in word identification. The basic question here is whether the mental lexicon contains complete words or merely morphemes. In word-centered models (e.g., Schriefers, Zwitserlood, and Roelofs 1991), each word, no matter how complex, is listed in the lexicon, such that word recognition does not require a pre-lexical morphological analysis. In morpheme-centered models (e.g., Taft 1981), on the other hand, the lexicon lists only root morphemes, which are connected to those affixes with which they can be combined. The two approaches are integrated in (morphological) dual-route models (e.g., Chialant and Caramazza 1995; Schreuder and Baayen 1995), according to which the mental lexicon contains both words and morphemes. Word identification, then, can work either via direct access to the stored word or via a pre-lexical morphological analysis.

Independent of the route chosen, lexical access, i.e., the activation of those entries in the mental lexicon that fit the perceptual input, is only one step in word identification. The two other steps, both in listening and reading, are selection and integration: Of all the activated entries, the best candidate has to be selected with the help of co-text and context information; and the syntactic and semantic information that is associated with the lexical entries has to be integrated into further processing (which is called "meaning and form selection" in figure 8). According to autonomous, bottom-up models of word recognition (e.g., Forster 1989), for access and selection processes only two sources of information are relevant, namely the textual input and the mental lexicon. Bottom-up models, however, are faced with the problem that they cannot explain "observable effects of 'higher-level' information on 'lower-level' processing" (Lupker 2005: 40), for example, the word superiority effect (cf. Wheeler 1970). This problem is addressed by interactive models (e.g., Coltheart et al. 2001; Seidenberg and McClelland 1989), which do not strictly distinguish between pre- and post-lexical processes but assume an early interaction of sensory, lexical, syntactic, semantic, and pragmatic information with top-down influences.

6.3.2. Text base level

In figure 8, word identification precedes the actual "comprehension processes" in which a text representation and a situation model are constructed by means of parsing and drawing inferences. With respect to the text representation, or text base, I will mainly draw on Kintsch's (1998) terminology and his notion of propositions explained above. The text base, then, has two levels that are called microstructure and macrostructure. Basically, "the microstructure is constructed by forming propositional units according to the words of the text and their syntactic relationships, and by analyzing the coherence relations among the propositions" (Kintsch and Rawson 2005: 210). The various kinds of possible relations among propositions comprise, e.g., co-reference, logical implication, or cause and effect relationship, with co-reference being the most frequent relation. Among the models of microstructure formation that have been proposed, the construction-integration model by Kintsch (1988, 1998; see section 6.2 above) is widely acknowledged; another connectionist approach is the landscape model (van den Broek et al. 1996).

While the microstructure is built by connecting single propositions, a higher-order organization – the macrostructure – is constructed by considering the global topical structure of the text. To identify this structure, readers frequently draw on "familiar rhetorical schemata" (Kintsch and Rawson 2005: 211); moreover, the importance of a topic within a text can be derived from the degree of repetition of the respective concept label (Surber 2001) or from its occurrence at the beginning of the text or paragraph (Budd, Whitney, and Turley 1995). While these strategies are in principle applicable both in listening and reading comprehension, some other cues for the topical structure are restricted to written texts. Among the latter devices are titles, abstracts, and summaries, as well as layout features such as paragraphs or typeface.

In general, to construct a text base the reader has to build a coherent representation of the text at the local and global level. Therefore, coherence is one of the most important issues in research on text comprehension. In the tradition of van Dijk and Kintsch (1983), local and global coherence strategies (in another terminology: micro and macro strategies; cf. Schnotz, 1996) are distinguished. While local coherence strategies aim at connecting the current input with the input that has been processed directly before, global coherence strategies concern the whole text, including information that is no longer in working memory.

Among the most frequently used coherence strategies both at the local and global level are inferences, i.e., conclusions that have to be drawn because texts are hardly ever completely explicit. To construct a coherent microstructure, readers often have to apply anaphora resolution to establish co-reference, and draw simple bridging inferences. For example, in the sentence, "The courageous fireman entered the house although the roof had already collapsed," a bridging inference is required to make plain that the roof is (or rather: was) part of the house mentioned before. There are, however, many more kinds of inferences, especially when global coherence is concerned. Various taxonomies have been proposed which supply extensive lists of inference-types (e.g., Graesser, Singer, and Trabasso 1994; Zwaan and Radvansky 1998). The demands these inferences make on the reader are summarized by Ram and Moorman (1999: 6–7): "Drawing inferences (…) the reader must draw on the context provided by the text that has been read so far, by the external situation that the reader is in, and by the overarching task that the reader is carrying out. The reader must also draw on background knowledge about the world in general and the reader's past experience".

6.3.3. *Situation-model level*

By integrating text information with relevant world-knowledge as described in the quotation above, the reader forms a situation model of the text that extends the purely text-based macrostructure. Therefore, inferencing is a core process in situation model construction (which is, unfortunately, not expressed in figure 8). However, it is controversial how comprehensive situation models are, i.e., how many inferences readers draw. According to minimalist approaches (e.g., Kintsch and van Dijk 1978; McKoon and Ratcliff 1992), inferences are merely a repair mechanism that is applied when other *local* coherence strategies fail. Consequently, the situation model plays but a minor, if any, role in text comprehension. At the other end of the scale there are maximalist approaches that consider inferences as the indispensable foundation of text comprehension. These approaches coincide with top-down theories (see section 6.2 above), which emphasize the influence of schemata and scripts.

Once again, empirical findings seem to suggest a more differentiated view (cf. Prestin 2003, for a more detailed account). Under some conditions, readers tend to be minimalist, drawing only those inferences that establish textual and, in the case of skilled readers (cf. Perfetti et al. 2005), causal coherence. At other times, readers draw many more inferences than minimally required for a coherent text base (Graesser, Singer, and Trabasso 1994). According to a situated theory of text comprehension (cf. Rickheit and Strohner 1999), the extent of inferencing is influenced by the goals, the knowledge, and the cognitive prerequisites of the reader. Another important criterion is the demand an inference makes on cognitive processing resources. Inferences with little or no cost to resource, such as bridging inferences or mapping pronouns onto antecedents, are more likely to occur than more complex and controlled inferences, such as inferring the exact way in which an action described in the text was performed (Perfetti et al. 2005: 231).

The question of processing is critical because of the limited capacity of working memory (Miller 1956). The so-called reading span, i.e., the capacity of working memory in a reading task as measured by Daneman and Carpenter (1980), is obviously too small to account for more than microstructure building. Yet the construction of a situation model can be a rather elaborate task – a detailed account of the processes involved is provided by Zwaan and Radvansky (1998). (It should be noted, though, that they use a somewhat different terminology that does not distinguish between text base and situation model.) How, then, can situation models be formed without much apparent effort? The answer to this question requires a closer look at the connections between reading and cognitive resources.

7. Reading and cognitive resources

The discrepancy between complex comprehension processes on the one hand and the limitation of working memory on the other hand has been addressed by Ericsson and Kintsch (1995; see also Kintsch, Patel, and Ericsson 1999). They propose to divide working memory into two components: a short-term working memory (STWM) of limited capacity, and a long-term working memory (LTWM). The latter component serves as kind of a connecting link between the reader's short-term memory – which for this purpose can be equated with focus of attention (Kintsch and Rawson 2005: 224) – and her long-term memory, because LTWM contains those items from the long-term memory that are linked to the contents of short-term memory via retrieval structures or cues. In short: "Retrieval structures make available information stored in long-term memory that is directly relevant to the task at hand" (Kintsch and Rawson 2005: 224). Such cues, however, are only existent when the reader has acquired some expertise in the respective domain. Expert comprehension thus appears as a highly automated process, while novices either have to perform effortful searches in long-term memory or settle with a less comprehensive situation model.

Skilled reading, then, entails encreasing automaticity of processes (Perfetti and McCutchen 1987). Conscious reflection only seems to be required when understanding breaks down and automatic repair mechanisms do not succeed (e.g., Schnotz 1996). For example, this may happen when the reader is confronted with novel concepts: In this case a reasoning process has to be started that comprises analogical mapping and, sometimes, problem reformulation (cf. Moorman and Ram 1999). However, it should be kept in mind that reading is a flexible process, with the reader choosing the best comprehension strategy in dependence on the communicative context (cf. Christmann and Groeben 1996; Ram and Moorman 1999). This context may well require some conscious adaptation processes to the external situation in general and the communication partners in particular. In fact, the need for adaptation is inherent both in (skilled) writing and reading, which becomes plain when writing and reading are not regarded as isolated tasks, but as interdependent parts of human communication (cf. Nystrand 1982, 1986).

8. Interaction in writing and reading

According to recent models of writing such as Hayes' (1996) model (see section 3.1 above), writers may draw on their mental representations of the social environment, which comprises, among other things, a representation of the audience. For example, a writer may consider the readers' state of knowledge about the topic and then make his text as informative as required for the audience. But language is more than a means of transporting topic-related informational content. Generally, the writer "has certain intentions and purposes, as well as certain information to convey" (Grabe and Kaplan 1996: 41). These intentions may also concern the interactional function of language, i.e., the expression of attitudes and social relationships (cf. Hyland 2005; Brown and Yule 1993). For example, writers may try to influence the impression the reader gets of their personality through a certain writing style (Ivanic and Weldon 1999). With respect to comprehension, this means that in many cases the reader has to draw on text-external knowledge about the context and the writer to get a comprehensive representation of what is meant (cf. Rickheit and Strohner 1999). Communication, then, works reciprocally: "Writers and readers think of each other, imagine each other's purposes and strategies rightly or wrongly, and write or interpret the text in terms of these imaginations" (Myers 1999: 40).

The aim of communicative homeostasis has been achieved when a text balances the writer's needs for expression and the reader's needs for comprehension (Nystrand 1989; Prestin 2001), which requires some co-ordination. Within applied linguistics, a number of approaches are concerned with how this co-ordination is accomplished. For example, within the framework of implicature theory, Grice (1989) holds that interactants adhere to the co-operative principle with its four maxims of quality, quantity, relevance, and manner, which may serve as a basis for complex reasoning strategies. In their politeness theory, Brown and Levinson (1987) propose that each interactant strives to protect their face and that of the other participant. Face protection is achieved by the use of certain conventional, indirect forms that weaken the face threatening potential of acts such as blaming, requesting, or apologizing.

Even though implicature theory and politeness theory were originally developed to account for conversation, they have been successfully adapted to writing in various studies (e.g., Pateman 1983; Short 1996; for an overview see Myers 1999: 43–44). Yet the application of the notions of co-ordination and co-operation to writing and reading is not uncontroversial. As Dixon and Bortolussi (2001: 1) point out, the supposition that text processing is a form of communication between writer and reader that closely parallels conversation "is inappropriate for many forms of written discourse and for fictional narrative in particular". Dixon and Bortolussi (2001: 6–12) see three classes of problems with what they call the "text-as-communication framework": First, with the author being absent during text comprehension, there is no feedback loop und thus no cooperation between writer and reader. Second, with respect to narratives, the distinction between author and narrator is obscured. And third, even if the author is identifiable, his intentions are difficult to reconstruct. This is why Dixon and Bortolussi (2001: 19) propose to replace the "text-as-communication framework" with a "feature-construction model". In this view, the text is considered as an artifact or stimulus whose generation does not play a role in the comprehension process.

This approach is not meant to be universally applied, however. Actually, the "text-as-communication framework" may be superior whenever there is a "sequence of messages constituting a feedback loop analogous to that which occurs in conversation" (Dixon & Bortolussi 2001: 20), which applies, for example, to exchanges of letters or e-mails. In this respect, the new media offer an important field of research because in chat groups, mailinglists or online discussion groups, the written mode coincides with reciprocity and (at least in the case of chat groups) also with immediacy of communication. The analysis of computer-mediated communication thus promises new insights into writing and reading and their interconnections to oral communication and media competence. But this issue, however interesting, extends the realms of the chapter on hand.

Notes

1. The idea that writers compose sentences mentally before writing them down, with the mental version at the planning stage being "not simpler or less complete" than the written result (Hayes and Nash 1996: 37), is closely connected to the notion of pre-writing or pre-text (cf. Kaufer, Hayes, and Flower 1986; Wrobel 2002).
2. Alamargot and Chanquoy (2001: 103) note that this representation may include what the writer *thinks* he has written, not what he has written actually. This, then, could explain why revising one's own texts is often more difficult than revising texts written by others.

3. An alternative approach is proposed by Grabowski (1996), whose model does explicitly not contain phonological loop and sketchpad.
4. As noted above, Bereiter and Scardamalia (1987) credit only expert writers with following this constraint.

References

Abelson, R. P.
    1981   Psychological status of the script concept. *American Psychologist 7:* 715–729.
Alamargot, D. and L. Chanquoy
    2001   *Through the Models of Writing.* Dordrecht: Kluwer.
Alba, J. and L. Hasher
    1983   Is memory schematic? *Psychological Bulletin* 93: 203–231.
Anderson, R. C. and P. D. Pearson
    1984   A schema-theoretic view of basic processes in reading comprehension. In: P. D. Pearson (ed.), *Handbook of Reading Research*, 255–291. New York: Longman.
Anderson, R. C., R. E. Reynolds, D. L. Schallert, and E. T. Goetz
    1977   Frameworks for comprehending discourse. *American Educational Research Journal* 14: 367–381.
Baddeley, A. D.
    1986   *Working Memory.* Oxford: Oxford University Press.
Bereiter, C. and M. Scardamalia
    1987   *The Psychology of Written Composition.* Hillsdale, NJ: Erlbaum.
Berkenkotter, C. and T. N. Huckin
    1995   *Genre Knowledge in Disciplinary Communication.* Hillsdale, NJ: Erlbaum.
Bock, K. and W. Levelt
    1994   Language production: Grammatical encoding. In: M. A. Gernsbacher (ed.), *Handbook of Psycholinguistics*, 945–984. San Diego, CA: Academic Press.
Bridwell, L. S.
    1980   Revising strategies in twelfth grade students: Transactional writing. *Research in the Teaching of English* 14(3): 107–122.
Brown, P. and S. C. Levinson
    1987   *Politeness: Some Universals in Language Usage.* Cambridge: Cambridge University Press.
Brown, G. and G. Yule
    1993   *Discourse Analysis.* New York: Cambridge University Press.
Budd, D., P. Whitney, and Kandy Turley
    1995   Individual differences in working memory strategies for reading expository text. *Memory and Cognition* 23: 735–748.
Chialant, D. and A. Caramazza
    1995   Where is morphology and how is it represented? The case of written word recognition. In: L. B. Feldman (ed.), *Morphological Aspects of Language Processing*, 55–76. Hillsdale, NJ: Erlbaum.

Christmann, U. and N. Groeben,
    1996   Die Rezeption schriftlicher Texte. In: H. Günther and O. Ludwig (eds.), *Schrift und Schriftlichkeit. Ein interdisziplinäres Handbuch internationaler Forschung. 2. Halbband,* 1536–1545. Berlin/New York: de Gruyter.

Coltheart, M.
    2005   Modeling reading: The dual route approach. In: M. Snowling and C. Hulme (eds.), *The Science of Reading: A Handbook,* 6–23. Malden: Blackwell.

Coltheart, M., K. Rastle, C. Perry, R. Langdon, and Johannes Ziegler
    2001   DRC: A dual-route cascaded model of visual word recognition and reading aloud. *Psychological Review* 108: 204–256.

Coulmas, F.
    2003   *Writing Systems. An Introduction to their Linguistic Analysis.* Cambridge: Cambridge University Press.

Daneman, M. and P. A. Carpenter
    1980   Individual differences in working memory and reading. *Journal of Verbal Learning and Verbal Behavior* 19: 450–466.

Dixon, P. and M. Bortolussi
    2001   Text is not communication: A challenge to a common assumption. *Discourse Processes* 31/1: 1–25.

Eigler, G.
    1996   Methoden der Textproduktionsforschung. In: H. Günther and O. Ludwig, (eds.), *Schrift und Schriftlichkeit. Ein interdisziplinäres Handbuch internationaler Forschung. 2. Halbband,* 992–1004. Berlin/New York: de Gruyter.

Ericsson, K. A. and W. Kintsch
    1995   Long-term working memory. *Psychological Review* 102/2: 211–245.

Flower, L. S. and J. R. Hayes
    1980   The dynamics of composing: making plans and juggling constraints. In: L. W. Gregg and E. R. Steinberg (eds.), *Cognitive Processes in Writing,* 31–50. Hillsdale, N. J.: Erlbaum.

Forster, K.
    1989   Basic issues in lexical processing. In: W. D. Marslen-Wilson (ed.), *Lexical Representation and Process,* 75–107. Cambridge, MA: MIT Press.

Frederiksen, C. H., R. J. Bracewell, A. Breuleux, and A. Renaud
    1990   The cognitive representation and processing of discourse: Function and dysfunction. In: Y. Joanette and H. H. Brownell (eds.), *Discourse Ability and Brain Damage: Theoretical and Empirical Perspectives,* 69–110. New York: Springer.

Galbraith, D. and M. Torrance
    1999   Conceptual processes in writing: From problem solving to text production. In: M. Torrance and D. Galbraith (eds.), *Knowing what to Write: Conceptual Processes in Text Production,* 1–12. Amsterdam: Amsterdam University Press.

Gelb, I. J.
    1963   *A Study of Writing.* Chicago: University of Chicago Press.

Grabe, W. and R. B. Kaplan
    1996   *Theory and Practice of Writing.* London: Longman.

Grabowski, J.
1996 Writing and speaking: Common grounds and differences toward a regulation theory of written language production. In: M. C. Levy and S. Ransdell (eds.), *The Science of Writing. Theories, Methods, Individual Differences, and Applications*, 73–91. Mahwah, NJ: Erlbaum.

Grabowski, J.
2003 Bedingungen und Prozesse der schriftlichen Sprachproduktion. In: G. Rickheit, T. Herrmann and W. Deutsch (eds.), *Psycholinguistik. Ein internationales Handbuch*, 355–368. Berlin/New York: de Gruyter.

Graesser, A. C., K. K. Millis, and R. A. Zwaan
1997 Discourse comprehension. *Annual Review of Psychology* 46: 163–189.

Graesser, A. C., M. Singer, and T. Trabasso
1994 Constructing inferences during narrative text comprehension. *Psychological Review* 101, 371–395.

Grice, H. P.
1989 *Studies in the Way of Words*. Cambridge, MA: Harvard University Press.

Groeben, N.
1982 *Leserpsychologie I: Textverständnis – Textverständlichkeit*. Münster: Aschendorff.

Hayes, J. R.
1996 A new framework for understanding cognition and affect in writing. In: M. C. Levy and S. Ransdell (eds.), *The Science of Writing. Theories, Methods, Individual Differences, and Applications*, 1–27. Mahwah, NJ: Erlbaum.

Hayes, J. R. and L. S. Flower
1980 Identifying the organization of writing processes. In: L. W. Gregg and E. R. Steinberg (eds.), *Cognitive Processes in Writing*, 3–30. Hillsdale, N. J.: Erlbaum.

Hayes, J. R., L. S. Flower, K. A. Schriver, J. F. Stratman, and L. Carey
1987 Cognitive processes in revision. In: S. Rosenberg (ed.), *Advances in Applied Linguistics, Vol. 2: Reading, Writing, and Language Learning*, 176–240. Cambridge: Cambridge University Press.

Hayes, J. R. and J. G. Nash
1996 On the nature of planning in writing. In: M. C. Levy and S. Ransdell (eds.), *The Science of Writing: Theories, Methods, Individual Differences, and Applications*, 29–55. Mahwah, NJ: Erlbaum.

Hyland, K.
2005 *Metadiscourse. Exploring interaction in writing*. London: continuum.

Ivanic, R. and S. Weldon
1999 Researching the writer-reader relationship. In: C. N. Candlin and K. Hyland (eds.), *Writing: Texts, Processes and Practices*, 168–192. London: Longman.

Johnson-Laird, P. N.
1983 *Mental Models: Towards a Cognitive Science of Language, Inference, and Consciousness*. Cambridge, MA: Harvard University Press.

Johnson-Laird, P. N.
1989 Mental models. In: M. I. Posner (ed.), *Foundations of Cognitive Science*, 469–499. Cambridge, MA: MIT Press.

Kaufer, D. S., J. R. Hayes, and L. S. Flower
    1986   Composing written sentences. *Research in the Teaching of English* 20: 121–140.

Kellogg, R. T.
    1996   A model of working memory in writing. In: M. C. Levy and S. Ransdell (eds.), *The Science of Writing: Theories, Methods, Individual Differences, and Applications*, 57–71. Mahwah, NJ: Erlbaum.

Kellogg, Ronald T.
    1999   Components of working memory in text production. In: M. Torrance and G. Jeffery (eds.), *The Cognitive Demands of Writing: Processing Capacity and Working Memory in Text Production*, 43–61. Amsterdam: Amsterdam University Press.

Kellogg, R. T.
    2003   Schriftliche Sprachproduktion. In: T. Herrmann and J. Grabowski (eds.), *Sprachproduktion*, 531–560. Göttingen: Hogrefe.

Kintsch, W.
    1974   *The Representation of Meaning in Memory.* Hillsdale, NJ: Erlbaum.

Kintsch, W.
    1988   The role of knowledge in discourse comprehension: A construction-integration model. *Psychological Review* 95: 163–182.

Kintsch, W.
    1998   *Comprehension. A Paradigm for Cognition.* Cambridge: Cambridge University Press.

Kintsch, W., V. .L. Patel, and K. A. Ericsson
    1999   The role of long-term working memory in text comprehension. *Psychologia* 42: 186–198.

Kintsch, W. and K. A. Rawson
    2005   Comprehension. In: M. Snowling and C. Hulme (eds.), *The Science of Reading: A Handbook*, 209–226. Malden: Blackwell.

Kintsch, W. and T. A. van Dijk
    1978   Toward a model of text comprehension and production. *Psychological Review* 85: 363–394.

Lupker, S. J.
    2005   Visual word recognition: Theories and findings. In: Margaret Snowling and Charles Hulme (eds.), *The Science of Reading: A Handbook*, 39–59. Malden: Blackwell.

McKoon, G. and R. Ratcliff
    1992   Inference during reading. *Psychological Review* 99: 440–466.

Miller, G. A.
    1956   The magical number seven plus or minus two: Some limits on our capacity for processing information. *Psychological Review* 63/2: 81–97.

Molitor-Lübbert, S.
    2002   Schreiben und Denken. Kognitive Grundlagen des Schreibens. In: D. Perrin, I. Böttcher, O. Kruse, and A. Wrobel (eds.), *Schreiben. Von intuitiven zu professionellen Schreibstrategien*, 33–46. Opladen: Westdeutscher Verlag.

Moorman, K. and A. Ram
    1999   Creativity in reading: understanding novel concepts. In: A. Ram and K. Moorman (eds.), *Understanding Language Understanding. Computational Models of Reading*, 359–395. Cambridge, MA.: MIT Press.

Myers, G.
1999   Interaction in writing: principles and problems. In: C. N. Candlin and K. Hyland (eds.), *Writing: Texts, Processes and Practices*, 40–61. London: Longman.
Newell, A. and H. A. Simon
1972   *Human Problem Solving*. Englewood Cliffs, NJ: Prentice Hall.
Nystrand, M.
1982   An analysis of errors in written communication. In: M. Nystrand (ed.), *What Writers Know. The Language, Process and Structure of Written Discourse*, 57–74. New York: Academic Press.
Nystrand, M.
1986   *The Structure of Written Communication. Studies in Reciprocy between Writers and Readers*. Orlando: Academic Press.
Nystrand, M.
1989   A social interactive model of writing. *Written Communication* 6: 66–85.
Pateman, T.
1983   How is understanding an advertisement possible? In: Howard Davies and Paul Walton (eds.), *Language, Image, Media*, 187–204. Oxford: Blackwell.
Perfetti, C. A., N. Landi, and J. Oakhill
2005   The acquisition of reading comprehension skill. In: Margaret Snowling and Charles Hulme (eds.), *The Science of Reading: A Handbook*, 227–247. Malden: Blackwell.
Perfetti, C. A. and D. McCutchen
1987   Schooled language competence: linguistic abilities in reading and writing. In: Sheldon Rosenberg (ed.), *Advances in Applied Linguistics, Vol. 2: Reading, Writing, and Language Learning*, 105–141. Cambridge: Cambridge University Press.
Prestin, E.
2001   Textoptimierung: Von der Verständlichkeit zur Intentionsadäquatheit. In: L. Sichelschmidt and H. Strohner (eds.), *Sprache, Sinn und Situation. Festschrift für Gert Rickheit zum 60. Geburtstag*, 223–238. Wiesbaden: Deutscher Universitäts-Verlag.
Prestin, E.
2003   Theorien und Modelle der Sprachrezeption. In: G. Rickheit, T. Herrmann, and W. Deutsch (eds.), *Psycholinguistik – Ein Internationales Handbuch*, 491–505. Berlin/New York: de Gruyter.
Ram, A. and K. Moorman
1999   Introduction: Toward a theory of reading and understanding. In Ashwin Ram and Kenneth Moorman (eds.), *Understanding Language Understanding. Computational Models of Reading*, 1–9. Cambridge, MA.: MIT Press.
Rickheit, G.
1995   Verstehen und Verständlichkeit von Sprache. In: B. Spillner (ed.), *Sprache: Verstehen und Verständlichkeit*, 15–30. Frankfurt a. M.: Lang.
Rickheit, G., L. Sichelschmidt, and H. Strohner
2002   Gedanken ausdrücken und Sprache verstehen: Psycholinguistik. In: H. M. Müller (ed.), *Arbeitsbuch Linguistik,* 382–402. Paderborn: Schöningh.
Rickheit, G. and H. Strohner
1999   Textverarbeitung: Von der Proposition zur Situation. In: A. Friederici (ed.), *Sprachrezeption*, 271–306. Göttingen: Hogrefe.

Rumelhart, D.
1975 Notes on a schema for stories. In: D. G. Bobrow and A. Collins (eds.), *Representation and Understanding. Studies in Cognitive Science*, 211–236. New York: Academic Press.
Scardamalia, M. and C. Bereiter
1983 The development of evaluative, diagnostic and remedial capabilities in children's composing. In: M. Martlew (ed.), *The Psychology of Written Language: Developmental and Educational Perspectives*, 67–95. New York: Wiley.
Scardamalia, M. and C. Bereiter
1987 Knowledge telling and knowledge transforming in written composition. In Sheldon Rosenberg (ed.), *Advances in Applied Linguistics, Vol. 2: Reading, Writing, and Language Learning*, 142–175. Cambridge: Cambridge University Press.
Schnotz, W.
1996 Lesen als Textverarbeitung. In: H. Günther and O. Ludwig (eds.), *Schrift und Schriftlichkeit. Ein interdisziplinäres Handbuch internationaler Forschung. 2. Halbband*, 972–982. Berlin/New York: de Gruyter.
Schreuder, R. and R. H. Baayen
1995 Modelling morphological processing. In: L. B. Feldman (ed.), *Morphological Aspects of Language Processing*, 131–154. Hillsdale, NJ: Erlbaum.
Schriefers, H., P. Zwitserlood, and A. Roelofs
1991 The identification of morphologically complex spoken words: Continuous processing or decomposition. *Journal of Memory and Language* 30: 26–47.
Schumacher, G. M., B. T. Scott, G. R. Klare, F. C. Cronin and D. A. Lambert
1989 Cognitive processes in journalistic genres. *Written Communication* 6: 390–407.
Seidenberg, M. S. and J. L. McClelland
1989 A distributed, developmental model of word recognition. *Psychological Review* 96: 523–568.
Short, M.
1996 *Exploring the Language of Poems, Plays, and Prose*. London: Longman.
Smith, P. T.
1996 Research methods in the psychology of reading. In: Hartmut Günther and Otto Ludwig (eds.), *Schrift und Schriftlichkeit. Ein interdisziplinäres Handbuch internationaler Forschung. 2. Halbband*, 932–942. Berlin/New York: de Gruyter.
Surber, J. R.
2001 Effect of topic label repetition and importance of reading time and recall of text. *Journal of Educational Psychology* 93: 279–287.
Taft, M.
1981 Prefix stripping revisited. *Journal of Verbal Learning and Verbal Behavior* 20: 263–272.
Thibadeau, R., M. A. Just, and P. Carpenter
1982 A model of the time course and content of reading. *Cognitive Science* 6: 157–204.

Torrance, M., G. V. Thomas and E. J. Robinson
1996 Finding something to write about: Strategic and automatic processes in idea generation. In: M. C. Levy and S. Ransdell (eds.), *The Science of Writing*, 189–205. Mahwah, NJ: Erlbaum.

van den Broek, P., K. Risden, C. R. Fletcher, and R. Thurlow
1996 A 'landscape' view of reading: Fluctuation patterns of activation and the construction of a stable memory representation. In: B. K. Britton and A. C. Graesser (eds.), *Models of Understanding Text*, 165–187. Mahwah, NJ: Erlbaum.

van Dijk, T. A.
1980 *Textwissenschaft: Eine interdisziplinäre Einführung*. Tübingen: Niemeyer.

van Dijk, T. A. and W. Kintsch
1983 *Strategies of discourse comprehension*. New York: Academic Press.

Van Orden, G. C. and H. Kloos
2005 The question of phonology and reading. In: M. Snowling and C. Hulme (eds.), *The Science of Reading: A Handbook*, 61–78. Malden: Blackwell.

Wheeler, D. D.
1970 Processes in word recognition. *Cognitive Psychology* 1, 59–85.

Wrobel, A.
2002 Schreiben und Formulieren. Prätext als Problemindikator und Lösung. In D. Perrin, I. Böttcher, O. Kruse and A. Wrobel (eds.), *Schreiben. Von intuitiven zu professionellen Schreibstrategien*, 83–96. Opladen: Westdeutscher Verlag.

Zwaan, R. A. and G. A. Radvansky
1998 Situation models in language comprehension and memory. *Psychological Bulletin* 123/2: 162–185.

10. Nonverbal communicative competence

Nancy M. Puccinelli

Imagine you are at a party and you can't help but notice that the guest you have just been introduced to seems quite distraught. As you are left alone to continue the conversation, you wonder if you should acknowledge his dour mood by taking on a sympathetic tone or even asking after his well-being. It may be that he has just had a disagreement and he would invite the opportunity to recount the illogical argument of his colleague or perhaps he has recently lost his mother and this evening represents his first effort to venture out and have a good time. Clearly, being able to identify whether or not he will appreciate having his mood acknowledged is critical to the success of this interaction.

As social beings, we frequently find ourselves in situations in which we must be attuned to our own expressions as well as receptive to cues from others. Learning to navigate the complexities of social interaction is challenging, yet critical, to communicative competence. It has been suggested that communicative competence can take two forms: Effectiveness and appropriateness. Effectiveness takes an actor-based perspective as it valorizes empowerment and action (Parks 1994). It has been argued that control over one's own behavior and that of another is key to effective communication. In contrast, appropriateness takes a more observer-based perspective as it valorizes social harmony (Parks 1994). In considering how one can communicate to satisfy one's needs and desires, nonverbal behavior is a key component. Nonverbal behavior's paramount role stems from evidence that the majority of information, especially sensitive information, is communicated nonverbally. This chapter will examine how nonverbal encoding and decoding work separately and in concert to aid individuals in successful communication.

1. Power of nonverbal behavior in interpersonal exchange

Research suggests that nonverbal behavior, such as facial expressions and body movement, communicates more information about what one is thinking or feeling than words. Even conservative estimates of the role of nonverbal behavior suggest that 60 % of what is communicated is done so nonverbally (Burgoon 1994). When nonverbal and verbal cues conflict, nonverbal cues are more likely to be believed. Thus, nonverbal behavior appears to provide unique insights into an individual's thoughts and feelings that are not otherwise accessible (Bonoma and Felder 1977). Research that has examined interactions in which access to nonverbal cues is eliminated, such as over email, finds that people prefer media channels in which nonverbal cues are available (Westmyer, DiCioccio, and Rubin 1998). In addition, they find people with whom they communicate in these channels warmer and more personal. Moreover, when verbal content is unclear, people seem to rely almost exclusively on nonverbal cues. Research looking at the effect of courtroom judges' expectations on jury decisions finds that these expectations can be communicated nonverbally. Specifically, when the instructions for the jury are complex judges' expectations have a greater effect on jury decisions than when the jury receives simplified instructions (Halverson et al. 1997). It seems nonverbal behavior also communicates a great deal about one's competence. Research that had observers evaluate photographs of salespeople were able to predict the most successful salesperson (Walker and Raghunathan 2004). Further, it seems these effects are independent of physical attractiveness. Research finds that nonverbal behavior is a better predictor of how someone will be evaluated than physical attractiveness (Ambady and Rosenthal 1993). Further, in a medical context, doctors' nonverbal cues predict patient compliance better than a doctor's verbal cues (Milmoe, Rosenthal, Blane, Chafetz, and Wolf 1967).

The goal of this chapter is to better understand how communicative competence may be enhanced through an understanding of the role of nonverbal behavior in communication. To this end, the first section will consider what is meant by nonverbal behavior and the behaviors that appear to be the most fruitful for examination. Second, encoding, or the expression of nonverbal behavior, and decoding, or the interpretation of nonverbal behavior, will be considered. Within each of these domains, research that bears on the effectiveness or appropriateness of the communication will be discussed. Finally, the impact of encoding and decoding in concert will be examined in applied contexts.

2. Meaning of nonverbal behaviors

Because of the importance of nonverbal behavior to interpersonal perception, considerable research has sought to understand the meaning of different behaviors. Early research in this area focused on what is now termed "molecular" cues, or discrete actions that are easily coded (e.g., number of smiles, frequency of eye contact, Ambady and Rosenthal 1993; Grahe and Bernieri 2002). Within research on molecular cues, several broad categories of behavior represent the greatest focus of attention (Knapp and Hall 2002): gestures, posture, touching behavior, facial expressions, eye behavior, and vocal behavior (e.g., tone of voice, pauses, and rhythm). While static cues such as age and clothing are also thought to play a role in nonverbal communication (Hulbert and Capon 1972), the lion's share of the research has focused on dynamic cues that are produced during the interaction.

Considering dynamic cues in more detail, several lines of research have identified the signatures for the expression of certain attributes in an interaction. Research suggests, for example, that empathy can be communicated through leaning forward, closer proximity, more eye contact, more openness of arms and body, more direct body orientation, and less eye movement (Hall, Harrigan, and Rosenthal 1995). Dominance seems to be communicated through less smiling, more touching, more frequent initiation of speech, lower likelihood of breaking a mutual glance, more violation of social norms, a more raised head, lowered or frowning brows, and more relaxed, expansive posture (Knapp and Hall 2002). Further, the meaning of nonverbal cues such as these appears to persist across cultures (Elfenbein and Ambady 2002a, 2003).

These prescriptions for communicating specific attributes must be considered with caution, however, as many of the cues that we associate with specific attributes can be spurious. For example, liars appear to exhibit fewer stereotypical cues for lying (such as gaze aversion and fidgeting), compared to non-liars (Mann, Vrij, and Bull 2004). Similarly, cues one may emit to signal confidence may also be misleading as the correlation between the confidence in a statement and its accuracy is zero (Brown 1986). Thus, even non-liars could mislead us with their courage of conviction. Moreover, contextual cues, such as the position of the actor and what the actor is doing can influence judgement of the actor independent of the actor's behavior (Puccinelli et al. 2007).

More recently there has been a shift toward a focus on more "molar" (holistic) judgments of behavior that examine a perceiver's overall impression of an individual based on the individual's nonverbal behavior. For example, rather than asking an observer to count the number of times the actor smiled, the observer might indicate her overall impression of how friendly the actor seemed on a nine-point scale. Researchers find that molar judgments are more accurate and are used more frequently (Ambady and Rosenthal 1993; Grahe and Bernieri 2002). In sum, nonverbal cues can reveal a great deal about what people are thinking and feeling that is both encoded and can be decoded in an interaction.

3. Encoding: The expression of nonverbal behavior

To enable a deeper treatment of nonverbal behavior, we will first consider the process of encoding, or an actor's expression of nonverbal behavior. Examination of encoding tendency is a fairly recent development. In 1980, Howard Friedman developed the Affective Communication Test (ACT) to measure individual differences in one's likelihood to be nonverbally expressive. So, for example, an actor who is more likely to tap their foot when they hear music is would score higher on the affective communication test.

Several factors influence one's encoding and expression of nonverbal behavior. While in some cases this behavior appears conscious and goal-directed, in other cases it seems quite unintended. On the conscious side, it seems that actors can signal greater conviction in a speech using nonverbal cues (e.g., frequent eye contact and low self-touching, Hart and Morry 1996). There also seem to be telling signs that one is seeking to initiate a relationship with a partner. This research finds that the nonverbal cues expressed by unattached men and women during an interaction with an attractive other differ (Simpson, Gangestad, and Biek 1993). More interestingly, they find that the nonverbal behavior of unattached individuals in this interaction differ markedly from those of attached individuals. Thus, given that they are interacting with an attractive partner, one can infer that the difference in behavior between attached versus unattached actors represent cues to initiate a relationship. Finally, research finds that singular expressions, such as anger, are more accurately recognized than compound expressions, such as anger and encouragement. If one's goal is to communicate anger, for example, they are more likely to be understood than if the same angry expression is mixed with a conflicting signal such as an encouraging smile (LaPlante and Ambady 2000). Thus, it seems nonverbal behavior gives people the power to demonstrate conviction, signal the desire to initiate a relationship, or simply communicate how they are feeling.

Less conscious seem to be the effects of personality, gender, culture, and situational context on an actor's expressiveness and encoded behavior. In terms of personality, more sociable, higher self-esteem, and less shy people are more effective at encoding nonverbal cues of agreeableness (Ambady, Hallahan, and Rosenthal 1995). In terms of gender, it seems women will exhibit more positive behavior than their male counterparts (Rafaeli 1989). Culturally, it seems that actors from different cultures exhibit culture-specific cues that enable others to detect their cultural origin. This research had observers look at photographs of Japanese nationals and Japanese Americans and found observers were able to accurately distinguish between the two groups (Marsh, Elfenbein, and Ambady 2003). Japanese Americans may avoid culture specific signals in order to fit in more effectively in the US; however, a Japanese national may seek to retain these cues to maintain inclusion in an in-group. Similarly, for extroverts, expressing nonverbal behavior that signals their agreeableness may facilitate the social connections they need. Extending beyond culture, the immediate environment can also influence encoding. In a study that looked at 11,717 salesperson-customer interactions, the researchers found that salespeople exhibit more positive expressions when wearing a uniform, there are not customers waiting in line, the salesperson is working alone, or the salesperson is serving a male customer (Rafaeli 1989). While these differences in encoding may not be entirely conscious, they may still fill important needs for the actor. In a retail setting, employees may feel a need to be consistent with the professional air of a uniform or be more responsive to male clients who historically have had higher status. Overall, there appear to be a number of factors that affect the nonverbal behavior that one encodes and while not goal directed, may serve important functions for the individual.

The notion that not all behavior is emitted consciously is supported by previous research. It has been suggested that a leakage hierarchy exists such that certain behaviors are more controlled and thus intentional while others are less controlled and unintentional. In particular, researchers find that while facial expression and verbal content are highly controlled by the individual and thus less revealing (overt cues), body movements and tone of voice are less controlled and thus may be highly revealing (covert cues; see Figure 1).

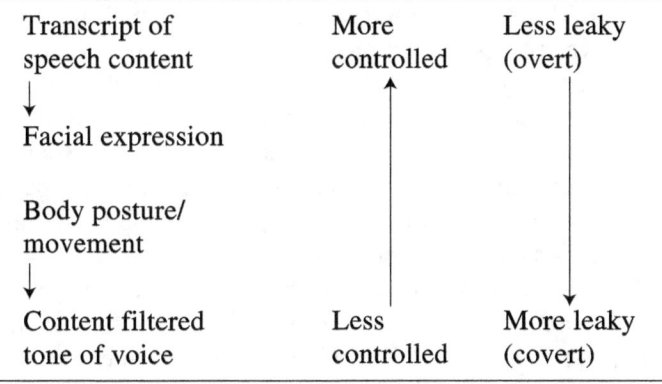

Figure 1. Leakage Hierarchy (Rosenthal and DePaulo 1979a, 1979b)

Evidence finds that while we can control behavior responsible for both overt and covert cues, we typically attend only to regulation of behavior associated with overt cues. Behavior associated with covert cues is then left to be dictated by habit (e.g. tapping your foot when you are nervous, Ekman and Friesen 1969). However, that which one intends to express does not always match what one is truly thinking or feeling. For example, while you might intend to express a desire to help a colleague who has stopped by your office, you secretly wish they would leave as your anxiety builds with a fast approaching deadline. The colleague skilled at reading covert cues may detect your anxiety and be offended you feel he has disturbed you (Puccinelli et al. 2004). Thus, it seems that behavior such as body movements and tone of voice can serve as covert cues to an actor's thoughts and feelings and be responsible for what has been termed the "unintentional display effect" (Bonoma and Felder 1977). That is, the actor may reveal their thoughts or feelings inadvertently.

When an actor's true thoughts and feelings are in conflict with those that the actor intends to communicate, the less controlled, leaky nonverbal behavior may reveal more valid information about how an individual truly feels than more controlled behavior (Ekman and Friesen 1969). That is, the less controlled, leaky nonverbal behavior may be more diagnostic especially in situations in which social desirability or other factors may be constraining the more controlled behavior. As a result, an observer trying to judge if an actor is lying is more likely to detect the liar during a telephone call (through access to cues from their tone of voice) and least likely from a written statement. An interesting study that tested this found that when research assistants assigned to helping a subject actually did not want to help, their covert cues dissuaded some subjects from asking for help (DePaulo and Fisher 1981). Specifically, subjects skilled at decoding covert cues were less likely to ask for help than were subjects with lesser decoding ability. Thus, subjects able to decode the research assistant's covert cues were able to detect the lack of desire to help and so did not seek help. Similarly, individuals who hold a negative appraisal of an interaction partner will display behavior that is critical of the partner nonverbally but not verbally, which in turn appeared to lead to lower self-esteem in the criticized partner (Swann, Stein-Seroussi, and McNulty 1992). The critical partner acts in accordance with social norms that discourage overt criticism but do not suppress their dislike of the partner through more covert cues. As one might expect, this phenomenon has a number of implications for communicative competence. For example, we can imagine a situation in which someone seeks to manage the impression they give to others. If we consider the example at the opening of the chapter of the distraught party guest, we might consider the extent to which he intends to express this negative emotion. It may be that he is smiling in hopes of convincing everyone of his jovial mood, and it is only through his body movements and tone of voice that you discern his true sad state.

4. Encoding competence

Given that behavior may be both intentional and unintentional, the challenge of encoding competence becomes quite formidable. Competent encoding may take the form of enabling actors to achieve their objectives and/or smooth the social interactions. In an effort to understand how encoding competence might be enhanced, it is instructive to consider examples in which actors appear to achieve specific goals through their nonverbal encoding.

The first challenge is assessing encoding ability. While the ACT discussed before measures expressivity, it does not speak to the efficacy of actors or the ability of actors to be accurately interpreted, which would seem necessary for communicative competence. That is, while an individual may self-report that they are expressive; people around them may not be able to recognize the meaning of their expressions. Therefore, while actors may believe they smile a lot when they are happy, the ACT does not enable us to assess the degree to which observers are able to detect the actor's mood of happiness, but rather just the actor's subjective assessment of the actor's likelihood of emitting the behavior.

However, other research has found ways in which encoding skill may be reliably measured. It finds that competent encoders can signal task competence and social skill. Certain nonverbal behavior can communicate competence in a task and enable the actor to be more influential, e.g., well-moderated tone of voice and rapid speech (Driskell, Olmstead, and Salas 1993). Moreover, signaling task competence appears to be more effective for increasing one's status in a group than displaying dominance cues (e.g., loud, tense voice, and knitted brows). Interestingly, the circumstances that lead one to enact nonverbal behavior that signals competence are different for men and women. While women emit cues that signal competence when speaking with a superior, men are more likely to signal competence when speaking with a peer (Steckler and Rosenthal 1985). Finally, good encoders appear to be able to signal their social skill nonverbally through the gestures they use and the time they spend talking (Gifford, Ng, and Wilkinson 1985).

There is also evidence that encoding ability has real-world benefits. It seems good encoders can lead interviewers to hire them in spite of a weak resume (Kinicki, Lockwood, Hom, and Griffeth 1990) and poor verbal quality of responses to interviewer questions (Rasmussen 1984). Specifically, candidates that were more expressive (i.e., held more eye contact, smiled more, and gestured more) were judged more positively (Rasmussen 1984). Further, once hired, good encoders appear to be able to command better treatment from supervisors (Naquin and Paulson 2003) and serve clients better (Ambady, Koo, Rosenthal, and Winograd 2002) through their nonverbal behavior. Naquin and his colleagues find that more assertive employees are able to get fairer treatment from a superior. Similarly, Ambady and her colleagues (2000) find that therapists who smile, nod, and frown less seem to help patients improve their physical and cognitive functioning, whereas therapists who engage in negative behavior cause a decline in patient functioning.

Much of the work summarized above would seem to represent examples of nonverbal behavior that were both effective and appropriate. That is, the behavior that enables people to achieve their objectives would do so because the behavior was also appropriate to the setting. One piece of research, however, looked at encoding behavior strictly enacted to be appropriate and smooth the interaction. Work on politeness theory (Brown and Levinson 1987) has examined ways in which speech is often altered so as to couch a communication, such as a request, to attenuate the impact of the communication on the listener – in essence to be more appropriate and allow a smoother interaction in spite of the request. For example, instead of saying, "Pass the salt," one might instead say, "Could I please trouble you to pass the salt?" More recently, it has been found that such politeness strategies are also implemented nonverbally (Ambady et al. 1996). The researchers examined other-orientation (e.g., the degree to which the person was attentive), affiliation (e.g., the degree to which the person was open), and circumspection (e.g., the degree to which the person was indirect). They found that while used somewhat differently within each cultural group, each of these politeness strategies was used by both American's and Korean's as politeness strategies to smooth interactions.

Before leaving the topic of encoding competence, it is also worthwhile to note the concept of emotional labor (Hochschild 1983). While the focus of this chapter is on ability, that is the ability to effectively and appropriately encode nonverbal behavior to achieve one's goals, it must also be recognized that such skillful encoding excises a cost for the actor. Specifically, the effort that is often necessary to express positive affect that is effective and appropriate in a given situation may be exerting for the actor. Early work in this area considers the example of flight attendants and the tremendous challenge of expressing positive affect in the face of a long flight, disgruntled passengers, and sleep deprivation. Not surprisingly, emotional labor has been linked to job satisfaction, emotional exhaustion, and well-being (Glomb, Kammeyer-Mueller, and Rotundo 2004). Moreover, it seems that employees from cultures in which emotion regulation is less common (e.g., the US) may face even more significant challenges than those coming from a culture characterized by more emotion regulation (e.g., France, Grandey, Fisk, and Steiner 2005). Thus, as we consider ways in which communicative competence may be enhanced through more effective and appropriate encoding, we must consider both personal limits as well as those that may derive from socialization.

5. Decoding competence: Interpreting the behavior of others

Relative to encoding, considerably more research has looked at decoding competence or ability to accurately interpret the behavior of others. Some of the earliest work in this area developed a measure, the Profile of Nonverbal Sensitivity (PONS), to assess an individual's accuracy in interpreting nonverbal cues. Further, it seems that different cues (covert vs. overt) not only communicate different information, but different people appear to be skilled at reading each, as measured by subtests of the PONS. Someone can be accurate at reading overt cues, covert cues, neither, or both (Rosenthal, Hall, DiMatteo, Rogers, and Archer 1979). More recently, a measure using still photographs and expressions of positive and negative emotions has been developed to measure an observer's ability to detect positive and negative emotion expressed either overtly or covertly (Nowicki and Duke 1994). It should be noted that at the base of each of these measures is the intentional enactment of a specific emotion or situation. The accuracy of the observer is determined by the degree of correspondence between the enacted emotion or situation and the observer's interpretation.

There are also many instances in which we would like to have observers interpret the behavior of actors in a real-world setting. For evaluating real interactions, many researchers use judgment studies in which short video clips of an actor's behavior are recorded and shown to naïve observers. To assess observer accuracy, observers' ratings are correlated with one of a number of other sources of converging evidence. For example, for assessing accuracy in judging personality characteristics, converging evidence may take the form of a self-report by the actor, agreement with people who know the actor or consensus with a larger group of observers. Judgment studies have been found to be very reliable and an accurate means for assessing emotion or personality from nonverbal behavior. Further, while we might expect that observers would need to observe a great deal of nonverbal behavior to make an accurate judgment; this does not appear to be the case. Research finds that observers can make remarkably accurate judgments from a thin slice of behavior in the form of a 30-second clip (Ambady and Rosenthal 1993). Thus, measures for assessing competence in decoding ability are quite well-developed and may represent a useful starting point for assessing one's communicative competence.

As with encoding ability, there are a number of moderators of decoding ability that include personality of the observer, sex of the observer, characteristics of the actor, and the setting judgment (Hall and Andrzejewki 2007). In terms of personality, people who score high on self-monitoring seem to be better decoders. Surprisingly, those who are better decoders are not more extraverted and may even be less sociable (Ambady, Bernieri, and Richeson 2000; Ambady et al. 1995). Yet among children, higher sociometric status is predicted by better decoding ability (Edwards, Manstead, and MacDonald 1984). That is, more popular children appear to be characterized by better decoding ability. In terms of sex of the observer, the finding that women are better at decoding is well-documented (Ambady et al. 1995; Rosenthal et al. 1979). In terms of characteristics of the actor, research finds that observers are able to more accurately interpret nonverbal behavior of someone from their same ethnic group compared to that of someone in a different ethnic group (Elfenbein and Ambady 2002a). Finally, in terms of occupational setting, it seems that better teachers, clinicians and law enforcement officers are better at accurately decoding nonverbal behavior (Mann et al. 2004; Rosenthal et al. 1979). Police officers reporting considerable experience interviewing suspects were more likely to detect a liar. Further, you might expect an experienced police officer to have awareness of this skill based on his experience yet, it turns out that such decoding skill is difficult to judge in one's own self and is best judged by a supervisor or spouse (Rosenthal et al. 1979). Finally, the task the actor is engaged in as well as the position of the actor relative to the observer impacts accurate perception (Puccinelli et al. 2004). Many of the explanations for these results have centered around skill development that has emerged through socialization to serve specific communication objectives. For example, it may be important to discern subtle cues to one's affect in someone else in your ethnic group to achieve in-group acceptance. In the case of occupational advantages, this may be explained by self-selection that is fostered by experience.

Given the utility of accurate decodings, research has naturally looked at methods for improving decoding ability. Unfortunately, efforts at training to improve decoding skill have met with dismal results (Ambady and Gray 2002; Bernieri, Gillis, Davis, and Grahe 1996; Gillis, Bernieri, and Wooten 1995; Grahe and Bernieri 2002). Perhaps this is why law enforcement personnel, such as FBI and CIA agents, are not more skilled than college students (Ekman and O'Sullivan 1991). Further, it seems thinking too long about one's interpretation of nonverbal behavior may actually impair an observer's accuracy. In research looking at the effect of mood on accuracy, Ambady and Gray (2002) find that sad observers are less accurate than neutral observers. They propose and find support for a deliberative information-processing explanation. Specifically, it seems sad subjects engage in more deliberative processing of nonverbal behavior and this over-analysis not only takes longer but is also less accurate (Ambady and Gray 2002).There also appear to be some contextual factors that influence decoding and decoding ability. For example, research finds that decoders under stress may be more likely to base their judgment on their first impression (Srinivas and Motowidlo 1987). Raters made to do a stressful exercise showed less dispersion in evaluations of a videotaped target compared to raters made to do a non-stressful exercise. Given that first impressions are typically more accurate, this may represent a strategy for improving accuracy. Thus, consistent with Ambady and Gray (2002), a more heuristic processing style that relies on first impressions, appears more accurate.

As one might expect, the general implications of decoding ability are quite positive. Decoding skill is associated with a number of aspects of workplace performance such as IQ and interpersonal skill as well as the ability to diagnose patients effectively (Halberstadt and Hall 1980; Hall and Andrzejewki 2007; Harrigan and Rosenthal 1986). People who are more interpersonally sensitive are perceived as more effective leaders, have more satisfied subordinates, and are evaluated as more successful (Elfenbein and Ambady 2002b; Riggio, Riggio, Salinas, and Cole 2003). Further, research suggests that decoding ability plays a key role in rapport development between a service provider and client (Hall et al. 1995). Perhaps this decoding ability enables service providers to adapt their behavior in response to the client's behavior more effectively (Spiro and Weitz 1990). Research looking at adaptive selling suggests that service agents who self-report adapting their behavior to customers are more effective sales agents, as indicated by a generally positive relationship between adaptive selling and sales performance (Park and Holloway 2003).

However, as suggested earlier, different aspects of behavior may reveal different types of information, some of it unintentional. Research suggests that there are at least some instances when decoding ability may be disadvantageous. For example, research finds that one's sexual orientation can be discerned from nonverbal cues (Ambady, Hallahan, and Conner 1999) and yet we can imagine contexts in which an actor may wish to conceal this information and respond negatively to explicit recognition of this attribute. The ability to accurately decode less controllable covert cues (e.g., body movement) opposed to more controllable nonverbal overt cues (e.g., facial expressions) has been termed by researchers "eavesdropping" ability (Rosenthal and DePaulo 1979a). As the label would suggest, this is a somewhat invasive practice on the part of the observer that can have negative ramifications. Research finds that people skilled at eavesdropping, or decoding of covert cues to what one is thinking or feeling, report experiencing more difficulty in social relationships (e.g. are less popular and seen to have less social understanding, Rosenthal and DePaulo 1979a). More recently, this finding was replicated in an organizational setting. Employees skilled at eavesdropping on negative emotions were evaluated more negatively by both supervisors and peers (Elfenbein and Ambady 2002b; Tickle-Degnen and Puccinelli 1999). Further, this effect appears to be exacerbated by the predisposition of the actor to experience negative emotions. Research finds that when eavesdroppers are paired with someone prone to experience negative affect, both the actor and the observer experience a more negative interaction (Puccinelli and Tickle-Degnen 2004). On the flipside, it seems people may appreciate having covert positive emotions detected. Employees skilled at eavesdropping on positive emotions were evaluated more positively by supervisors and peers. Thus, it seems while we might be eager to share our secret joy from a recent success, we prefer to conceal our disappointment with a recent failure.

Evidence also suggests that the effect of eavesdropping may be moderated by occupational setting. Eavesdropping clinicians were rated higher by supervisors in a pediatric rehabilitation setting, lower in a psychiatric rehabilitation setting, and the same in a physical rehabilitation setting relative to clinicians less skilled at detecting covert cues (Tickle-Degnen 1998). This research suggests that in the pediatric setting, where the young patients may be less able to communicate using speech and controllable overt cues, less controlled covert cues may provide important clues for diagnosis and treatment. However, in a psychiatric context, where patients work to adapt to everyday life, it may be important to respect a patient's self-presentation goals and respond only to the controlled overt cues. Thus, it may be important to consider the situational context of the actor before responding to specific nonverbal cues of the actor. If we consider our example of the distraught guest, we might try to discern if the negative affective state is being expressed through his face, which may signal a desire to have the negative mood recognized, or through his body movements, which may be unintentional, making it unwise to comment on it.

6. Nonverbal communication competence in the real world

In applying work on encoding and decoding to the real world, it seems important to consider skills in these areas in concert. In reality, there are myriad behaviors and reactions to behaviors that can take place during a single interaction that affect the subjective experience of the actors and the interaction's outcomes. While specific nonverbal behaviors in a negotiation, for example, can signal dominance, deference, and equality (Soldow and Thomas 1984), it seems impossible to conceive of a given negotiation strictly in terms of specific behaviors. Further, the exchange of nonverbal cues in a negotiation appear critical to establishing trust and rapport as well as reaching an optimal outcome (Drolet and Morris 2000; Naquin and Paulson 2003). On a project team, nonverbal exchange is a key predictor of whether that team member is seen as contributing to the project. In teams that interfaced electronically, actual contribution predicted perception of a group member's contribution; while in face-to-face interactions, liking predicted perception of a group member's contribution (Weisband and Atwater 1999). In a retail context, it seems customers engage in tell tale cues signaling their objectives in a sales or service encounter (Kirmani and Campbell 2004). Customers may be "goal seekers" and attempt to use the salesperson to help them achieve their goals or they may be "persuasion sentries" and seek to avoid marketing persuasion at all costs. It would seem critical for salespeople in these settings to be attuned to these cues when serving customers.

Nonverbal behavior also has a significant impact on the dynamics of interpersonal exchange. Several streams of research find that the behavior of one actor in an interaction affects the behavior of their interaction partner. Interestingly, the nature of this effect seems to depend on the type of behavior encoded by the actor. Sometimes an actor's behavior can lead to a Pygmalion effect whereby their partner will conform to the expectations of the actor while at other times it will take the form of emotional contagion whereby the affective state of an actor is spread to the partner.

Evidence of a Pygmalion effect is well-documented. Robert Rosenthal's early work in this area found that if teachers were told a student was an "early bloomer" the student performed better (Rosenthal 1991; Rosenthal and Jacobson 1992). Further investigation found that the teacher would give off subtle nonverbal cues of encouragement that would lead the student to do better. This effect has been replicated across age groups and in a wide range of educational and business contexts. There is also evidence to suggest that this effect may be stronger under certain circumstances. Research finds a stronger effect among men, when the leader and subordinate are in a military environment and if the expectations for the subordinate had been especially low (Dvir, Eden, and Banjo 1995; McNatt 2000). The effect of sex may be explained in part by a difference in the response of men versus women to feedback. This research finds that while men are more productive and satisfied when they received negative feedback in a positive tone of voice; women were more productive and satisfied when they received feedback that was positive in a negative tone of voice (LaPlante and Ambady 2000). Thus, as we think about the Pygmalion effect with respect to communicative competence we might consider the typical objectives of a teacher or a squadron leader. To the extent that they hope that their students and subordinates will perform well, expectations for this may lead their nonverbal behavior to make this a self-fulfilling prophecy.

A second way in which nonverbal behavior affects the dynamics of interaction is through emotional contagion. Elaine Hatfield (1994) was among the first to document that the affective state of one individual can be communicated to an interaction partner in such a way that the partner actually experiences the same affective state. Emotional contagion has been observed in the work place, retail settings and even among members of professional sports teams. Research finds that the mood of supervisors not only affects the mood of their employees but also influences employee coordination and employee effort exerted to achieve organizational goals (Sy, Côté, and Saavedra 2005). In a retail context the mood of sales staff appears to extend to customers and not only makes customers feel better but increases the time the customer spends in the store, the customers willingness to return, and the customer's tendency toward positive word of mouth (Tsai and Huang 2002). Finally, it seems certain individuals may be more susceptible to emotional contagion than others. For example, in the case of the professional sports team, older, more committed players appear more likely to catch the mood of their teammates (Totterdell 2000). Linking emotional contagion to communicative competence, we might be able to imagine a situation in which it would be effective to bring others to your mood state to more clearly appreciate your point of view. Along similar lines, emotional contagion may form the critical foundation for rapport building that enables smoother interactions. So while it may not seem appropriate to inflict your mood on another, your inclination to catch the mood of an interaction partner could be advantageous.

Thus it seems nonverbal communicative competence is best conceived of as a dynamic process of encoding and decoding that sits within the larger scheme of dialogue and natural interaction. While focusing specifically on the communication of emotion, researchers have begun discussing a new intelligence, that of emotional intelligence. First introduced by Peter Salovey (Salovey, Hsee, and Mayer 1993) and popularized by Daniel Goleman (1995), emotional intelligence (EI) encompasses the entire spectrum from the encoding of emotion, and restraint in encoding when necessary, to the sensitive decoding of behavior in others. It has been established that EI is distinct from other personality measures and may predict life satisfaction and job performance (Law, Wong, and Song 2004). Further, it has been argued that emotional intelligence may be as critical as technical knowledge to the success of a firm.

In summary, nonverbal behavior clearly plays a critical role in being a competent communicator. How effectively people encode their needs and signal their strongest attributes has a significant impact on their ability to achieve their goals. Similarly, the ability to accurately decode and appropriately respond to the cues of others is also key to this process. Focusing on these specific skill sets are a good starting point for understanding their role in the more complex exchange that is social interaction and the processes, such as the Pygmalion effect and emotional contagion that occur there.

References

Ambady, N., F. J. Bernieri., and J. A. Richeson
   2000   Toward a histology of social behavior: Judgmental accuracy from thin slices of the behavioral stream. *Advances in Experimental Social Psychology 32:* 201–207.
Ambady, N. and H. M. Gray
   2002   On being sad and mistaken: Mood effects on the accuracy of thin-slice judgments. *Journal of Personality and Social Psychology* 83(4): 947–961.
Ambady, N., M. Hallahan, and B. Conner
   1999   Accuracy of judgments of sexual orientation from thin slices of behavior. *Journal of Personality and Social Psychology* 77(3): 538–547.
Ambady, N., M. Hallahan, and R. Rosenthal
   1995   On judging and being judged accurately in zero-acquaintance situations. *Journal of Personality and Social Psychology* 69(3): 1–12.
Ambady, N., J. Koo, F. Lee and R. Rosenthal
   1996   More than words: Linguistic and nonlinguistic politeness in two cultures. *Journal of Personality and Social Psychology* 70(5): 996–1011.
Ambady, N., J. Koo, R. Rosenthal, and C. H. Winograd
   2002   Physical therapists' nonverbal communication predicts geriatric patients' health outcomes. *Psychology and Aging* 17(3): 443–452.
Ambady, N. and R. Rosenthal
   1993   Half a minute: Predicting teacher evaluations from thin slices of nonverbal behavior and physical attractiveness. *Journal of Personality and Social Psychology* 64(3): 431–441.

Bernieri, F. J., J. S. Gillis, J. M. Davis, and J. E. Grahe
  1996   Dyad rapport and the accuracy of its judgment across situations: A lens model analysis. *Journal of Personality and Social Psychology 71*(1): 110–129.
Bonoma, T. V. and L. C. Felder
  1977   Nonverbal communication in marketing: Toward a communicational analysis. *Journal of Marketing Research 14*(May): 169–180.
Brown, P. and S. C. Levinson
  1987   *Politeness. Some Universals in Language usage.* New York NY: Cambridge University Press.
Brown, R.
  1986   *Social Psychology* (2 ed.). New York: The Free Press.
Burgoon, J. K.
  1994   Nonverbal signals. In:: M. L. Knapp (ed.), *Handbook of Interpersonal Communication,* 229–285 (2nd ed.). Thousand Oaks: Sage.
DePaulo, B. M. and J. D. Fisher
  1981   Too tuned-out to take: The role of nonverbal sensitivity in help-seeking. *Personality and Social Psychology Bulletin 7*(2): 201–205.
Driskell, J., E., B. Olmstead, and E. Salas
  1993   Task cues, dominance cues, and influence in task groups. *Journal of Applied Psychology 78*(1): 51–60.
Drolet, A. L. and M. W. Morris
  2000   Rapport in conflict resolution: Accounting for how face-to-face contact fosters mutual cooperation in mixed-motive conflicts. *Journal of experimental social psychology 36*(1): 26–50.
Dvir, T., D. Eden, and M. L. Banjo
  1995   Self-fulfilling prophecy and gender: Can women be pygmalion and galatea? *Journal of Applied Psychology 80*(2): 253–270.
Edwards, R., A. S. R. Manstead, and C. J. MacDonald
  1984   The relationship between children's sociometric status and ability to recognize facial expressions of emotion. *European Journal of Social Psychology 14*(2): 235–238.
Ekman, P. and W. V. Friesen
  1969   Nonverbal leakage and clues to deception. *Psychiatry 32*(1): 88–106.
Ekman, P. and M. O'Sullivan
  1991   Who can catch a liar? *American Psychologist 46*(9): 913–920.
Elfenbein, H. A. N. and Ambady
  2002a   On the universality and cultural specificity of emotion recognition : A meta-analysis. *Psychological Bulletin 128*(2): 203–235.
Elfenbein, H. A. and N. Ambady
  2002b   Predicting workplace outcomes from the ability to eavesdrop on feelings. *Journal of Applied Psychology 87*(5): 963–971.
Elfenbein, H. A. and N. Ambady
  2003   When familiarity breeds accuracy: Cultural exposure and facial emotion recognition. *Journal of Personality and Social Psychology 85*(2): 276–290.
Gifford, R., C. F. Ng, and M. Wilkinson
  1985   Nonverbal cues in the employment interview: Links betweeen applicant qualities and interviewer judgements. *Journal of Applied Psychology 70*(4): 729–736.

Gillis, J. S., F. J. Bernieri, and E. Wooten
   1995   The effects of stimulus medium and feedback on the judgment of rapport. *Organizational Behavior and Human Decision Processes 63*(1): 33–45.

Glomb, T. M., J. D. Kammeyer-Mueller, and M. Rotundo
   2004   Emotional labor demands and compensating wage differentials. *Journal of Applied Psychology 89*(4): 700–714.

Goleman, D. C.
   1995   *Emotional Intelligence.* NY: Bantam Books.

Grahe, J. E. and F. J. Bernieri
   2002   Self-awareness of judgment policies of rapport. *Personality and Social Psychology Bulletin 28*(10): 1407–1418.

Grandey, A. A., G. M. Fisk, and D. D. Steiner
   2005   Must "service with a smile" be stressful? The moderating role of personal control for American and French employees. *Journal of Applied Psychology 90*(5): 893–904.

Halberstadt, A. G. and J. A. Hall
   1980   Who's getting the message? Children's nonverbal skill and their evaluation by teachers. *Developmental Psychology 16*(6): 564–573.

Hall, J. A. and S. A. Andrzejewki
   2007   Psychosocial correlates of interpersonal sensitivity: A meta-analysis. Unpublished manuscript.

Hall, J. A., J. A. Harrigan, and R. Rosenthal
   1995   Nonverbal behavior in clinician-patient interaction. *Applied and Preventive Psychology 4*(1): 21–37.

Halverson, A. M., M. Hallahan, A. J. Hart and R. Rosenthal
   1997   Reducing the biasing effects of jedges' nonverbal behavior with simplified jury instruction. *Journal of Applied Psychology* 82(4): 590–598.

Harrigan, J. A. and R. Rosenthal
   1986   Nonverbal aspects of empathy and rapport in physician-patient interaction. In: P. D. Blanck, R. Buck and R. Rosenthal (eds.), *Nonverbal Communication in the Clinical Context,* 37–73. London: The Pennsylvania State University.

Hart, A. J. and M. M. Morry
   1996   Nonverbal behavior, race, and attitude attributions *Journal of Experimental Social Psychology 32*(2): 165–179.

Hatfield, E.
   1994   Mechanisms of emotional contagion. II. Emotional experience and facial, vocal, and postural feedback. In: E. Hatfield, J. Cacioppo and R. L. Rapson (eds.), *Emotional contagion* 48–78.

Hochschild, A.
   1983   *The Managed Heart: The Commercialization of Human Feeling.* Berkeley, CA: University of California Press.

Hulbert, J. and N. Capon
   1972   Interpersonal communication in marketing: An overview. *Journal of Marketing Research IX:* 27–34.

Kinicki, A. J., C. A. Lockwood, P. W. Hom, and R. W. Griffeth
   1990   Interviewer predictions of applicant qualifications and interviewer validity: Aggregate and individual analyses. *Journal of Applied Psychology 75*(5): 477–486.

Kirmani, A. and M. C. Campbell
  2004 Goal seeker and persuasion sentry: How consumer targets respond to interpersonal marketing persuasion. *Journal of Consumer Research 31*(3): 573–582.
Knapp, M. L. and J. A. Hall
  2002 *Nonverbal Communication in Human Interaction* (5th ed.). London: Thomas Learning, Inc.
LaPlante, D. and N. Ambady.
  2000 Multiple messages: Facial recognition advantage for compound expressions. *Journal of Nonverbal Behavior 24*(3): 211–224.
Law, K. S., C.-S. Wong, and L. J. Song
  2004 The construct and criterion validity of emotional intelligence and its potential utility for management studies. *Journal of Applied Psychology 89*(3): 483–496.
Mann, S., A. Vrij, and R. Bull
  2004 Detecting true lies: Police officers' ability to detect suspects' lies. *Journal of Applied Psychology 89*(1): 137–149.
Marsh, A. A., J. A. Elfenbein, and N. Ambady
  2003 Nonverbal "accents": Cultural differences in facial expressions of emotion. *Psychological Science 14*(4): 373–376.
McNatt, D. B.
  2000 Ancient pygmalion joins contemporary management: A meta-analysis of the result. *Journal of Applied Psychology 85*(2): 314–322.
Milmoe, S., R. Rosenthal, H. T. Blane, M. E. Chafetz, and I. Wolf
  1967 The doctor's voice postdictor of successful referral of alcoholic patients. *Journal of Abnormal Psychology 72*(1): 78–84.
Naquin, C. E. and G. D. Paulson
  2003 Online bargaining and interpersonal trust. *Journal of Applied Psychology 88*(1): 113–120.
Nowicki, S. and M. P. Duke
  1994 Individual differences in the nonverbal communication of affect: The diagnostic analysis of nonverbal accuracy scale. *Journal of Nonverbal Behavior 18(1)*.
Park, J.-E. and B. B. Holloway
  2003 Adaptive selling behavior revisited: An empirical examination of learning orientation, sales performance, and job satisfaction. *Journal of Personal Selling and Sales Management 23*(3): 239–251.
Parks, M. R.
  1994 Communicative competence and interpersonal control. In: M. L. Knapp (ed.), *Handbook of Interpersonal Communication*, 589–618 (2nd ed.). Thousand Oaks: Sage.
Puccinelli, N. M.
  2006 Putting your best face forward: The impact of customer mood on salesperson evaluation. *Journal of Consumer Psychology 16*(2): 156–162.
Puccinelli, N. M. and L. Tickle-Degnen
  2004 Knowing too much about others: Moderators of the relationship between eavesdropping and rapport in social interaction. *Journal of Nonverbal Behavior 28*(4): 223–243.

Puccinelli, N. M., L. Tickle-Degnen and R. Rosenthal
   2003   Effect of dyadic context on judgements of rapport. Dyad task and partner presence. *Journal of Nonverbal Behavior* 47(4).

Puccinelli, N. M., L. Tickle-Degnen and R. Rosenthal
   2004   Effect of target position and target task on judge sensitivity to felt rapport. *Journal of nonverbal Behavior* 28(3), 211–220.

Rafaeli, A.
   1989   When clerks meet customers: A test of variables related to emotional expressions on the job. *Journal of Applied Psychology* 74(3): 385–393.

Rasmussen, K. G.
   1984   Nonverbal behavior, verbal behavior, resume credentials, and selection interview outcomes. *Journal of Applied Psychology* 69(4): 551–556.

Riggio, R. E., H. R. Riggio, C. Salinas, and E. J. Cole
   2003   The role of social and emotional communication skills in leader emergence and effectiveness. *Group Dymnamics: Theory, Research, and Practice* 7(2): 83–103.

Rosenthal, R.
   1991   Teacher expectancy effects: A brief update 25 years after the pygmalion experiment. *Journal of Research in Education* 1(1): 3–12.

Rosenthal, R. and B. M. DePaulo
   1979a   Sex differences in accommodation in nonverbal communication. In: R. Rosenthal (ed.), *Skill in Nonverbal Communication: Individual Differences*, 68–103. Cambridge, MA: Oclgeschlager, Gunn and Hain.

Rosenthal, R. and B. M. DePaulo
   1979b   Sex differences in eavesdropping on nonverbal cues. *Journal of Personality and Social Psychology* 37(2): 273–285.

Rosenthal, R., J. A. Hall, M. R. DiMatteo, P. L. Rogers, and D. Archer
   1979   *Sensitivity to Nonverbal Communication: The Pons Test*. Baltimore: Johns Hopkins University.

Rosenthal, R. and L. Jacobson
   1992   *Pygmalion in the Classroom* (2 ed.). New York: Irvington Publishers, Inc.

Salovey, P., C. K. Hsee, and J. D. Mayer
   1993   Emotional intelligence and the self-regulation of affect. In: D. M. Wegner and J. W. Pennebaker (eds.), *Handbook of Mental Control. Century Psychology Series*, 258–277. Englewood Cliffs, NJ: Prentice-Hall.

Simpson, J. A., S. W. Gangestad, and M. Biek
   1993   Personality and nonverbal social behavior: An ethological perspective of relationship initiation. *Journal of Experimental Social Psychology* 29(5): 434–461.

Soldow, G. F. and G. P. Thomas
   1984   Relational communication: Form versus content in the sales interaction. *Journal of Marketing* 48(1): 84–93.

Spiro, R. L. and B. A. Weitz
   1990   Adaptive selling: Conceptualization, measurement, and nomological validity. *Journal of Marketing Research* 27(1): 61–69.

Srinivas, S. and S. J. Motowidlo
   1987   Effects of raters' stress on the dispersion and favorability of performance ratings. *Journal of Applied Psychology* 72(2): 247–251.

Steckler, N. A. and R. Rosenthal
   1985   Sex differences in nonverbal and verbal communication with bosses, peers and subordineates. *Journal of Applied Psychology* 70(1): 157–163.
Swann, W. B., A. Stein-Seroussi, and S. E. McNulty
   1992   Outcasts in a white-lie society: The enigmatic worlds of people with negative self-conceptions. *Journal of Personality and Social Psychology* 62(4): 618–624.
Sy, T., S. Côté, and R. Saavedra
   2005   The contagious leader : Impact of the leader's mood on the mood of group members, group affective tone, and group processes. *Journal of Applied Psychology* 90(2): 295–305.
Tickle-Degnen, L.
   1998   Working well with others: The prediction of students' clinical performance. *The American Journal of Occupational Therapy* 52(2): 133–141.
Tickle-Degnen, L. and N. M. Puccinelli
   1999   The nonverbal expression of negative emotions: Peer and supervisor responses to occupational therapy students' emothonal attributes. *The Occupational Therapy Journal of Research* 19(1): 18–39.
Totterdell, P.
   2000   Catching moods and hitting runs: Mood linkage and subjective performance in professional sport teams. *Journal of Applied Psychology* 85(6): 848–859.
Tsai, W.-C. and Y.-M. Huang
   2002   Mechanisms linking employee affective delivery and customer behavioral intentions. *Journal of Applied Psychology* 87(5): 1001–1008.
Walker, R. E. and R. Raghunathan
   2004   Nonverbal cues-based first impressions: What can static images of salespersons tell us about their success at selling? In: M. F. Luce and B. Kahn (eds.), *Advances in Consumer Research,* 198–199. (Vol. 31). Austin, TX: Association of Consumer Research.
Weisband, S. and L. Atwater
   1999   Evaluating self and others in electronic and face-to-face groups. *Journal of Applied Psychology* 84(4): 632–639.
Westmyer, S. A., R. L. DiCioccio, and R. B. Rubin
   1998   Appropriateness and effectiveness of communication channels. *Journal of Communication* 48(3): 27–48.

11. Media competence

Daniel Perrin and Maureen Ehrensberger-Dow

Children call their grandparents to thank them for new clothes, teenagers send each other photos of themselves with their mobile phones, and brides-to-be email their mothers' website addresses for them to preview wedding dresses: every generation has its preferred tools for conveying information. Media such as the telephone (Hutchby 1991) and the internet (Crystal 2001) encourage, facilitate, impede, or hinder certain types of communication and language use: primarily verbal or primarily non-verbal, spoken or written, spontaneous or planned, face-to-face or apart, personal or business, informal or formal, public or private, as senders, receivers, or in alternating roles. How people communicate depends very much on the medium that they choose to bridge the gap across space and time. Within the range of what is technically possible, people can use a medium more or less skillfully, appropriately, or purposefully.

This chapter examines such media competence – specifically, in terms of language use. It defines and links the terms "media" and "competence" (section 1); infers from sample discussions the specific language competence involved in medially-transmitted communication (section 2); explains the methodology of research into media competence with examples of journalistic processing of discussions and producing media texts (section 3); presents an overview of research into appropriate and successful language use in medially-transmitted public communication (section 4); and identifies current gaps in the general area of research into media competence (section 5).

1. Media and competence – basic concepts

In communication, a medium can be anything that contributes to someone being able to convey something to someone else – even the air that carries the sound waves of speech. Here it seems sensible, however, to define the term more narrowly and understand media as technical equipment for communication or, even more precisely, as technical equipment for the production, storage, reproduction, and transmission of signs. This definition of media would still encompass all technical communication aids including, for instance, a post card, a corporate intranet, or an auditorium's sound system. With such a broad use of the term, any deeper understanding of a particular area of language application is difficult – since technical media are part of every form of communication except non-amplified speech and signing.

A more focused definition refers primarily to journalistic media: the technical means used to produce and publish communication for the public under economic conditions. Journalistic media characterize an autonomous, socially relevant area of language application. The concept of journalistic media is specified communicatively, socio-politically, and economically. "Publish" means to distribute outside of the production context to a wide circle of recipients personally unknown to the sender; "communication for the public" contributes to establishing a general public in societies whose relationships extend past direct contacts such as within a village; and "economic conditions" signify the pressure and the opportunity to create value in a technical process based on the division of labor.

Nevertheless, the borders between public and private communication are becoming blurred because of media convergence. This phenomenon results from the technical developments from digitization and networking that allow texts from several sign systems to be conveyed with a single technical device for various sensory channels. Media have developed interdependently and fused together in the form of computers, the universal communication device. A networked computer can process anything digital: for example, all visual and auditory signs. It can tap into libraries and radio programs or act as a typewriter, game console, and telephone. It can be both receiver and sender in the internet, with push and pull offers. As a push-medium, it sends offers of communication to an individual or any number of addressees anywhere in the world-wide web, instantly. As a pull-medium, it has offers of communication stored in the network so that people with official permission or other interested parties can access them according to personal preference.

The former strict separation between personal and journalistic media has thus disappeared, so personal and public communication have also become more closely meshed. For example, someone who reads, hears, or sees an interesting news item on the computer can make a comment on it and forward both to a friend with the computer; previously, an alternate communication channel would have had to be used. Nonetheless, people communicate differently with familiar and selected recipients than with unfamiliar and incalculable masses. The analytical distinction between personal and public communication thus continues to be justified despite media convergence – particularly concerning the inter-relationships between language, media, and competence. Personal and public communication conveyed through media differ in one important respect, namely in terms of the relation of senders to recipients. For this reason, they draw on fundamentally different competences of media specific language use.

Competence here is understood as the individually-determined, socially-influenced, and socially-formative cognitive capacity to solve specific problems in an effective and appropriate way within the framework of specific expectations. Media-specific language competence refers to the capacity to use language in a socially appropriate way and apply it successfully to meet one's own communication objectives (and those of other relevant concerned parties) in interpersonal, organizational, and public settings. People with a sufficient degree of media competence work incrementally at five levels: a) appropriately assessing themselves, their communication partners, situations, and tasks, b) weighing their own views against how they presume others view things, c) planning and carrying out offers of communication, d) sensibly monitoring the actions of other participants, and e) drawing conclusions that feed into continual planning. Personal and public communication conveyed through media differ primarily in d) and e). The following section explores these in more detail.

2. Types of media competence

Appropriate and successful language use in communication conveyed through media presupposes three types of competence: a) underlying self, social, and subject competences that play a role in every instance of communication; b) topic-specific subject competence; and c) event-related competence, determined by the social event in which communication takes place. Social events are complex, temporally and spatially determined and limited patterns of behavior that certain groups use to solve certain problems and that mark certain forms of communication: complex patterns of language used to solve communication problems (Keppler 1994; Luckmann 1986), such as a family discussion at the dinner table or a business call. The precise form of communication is highly dependent on the use of media and signs and the corresponding competences for media-specific language use.

How social events, communication forms, media use, and ultimately competences for media-specific language use interact is demonstrated in the following examples of discussions in private and professional life (2.1). A more in-depth example, a CEO doing a television interview, illustrates the interaction between basic competences and form-specific competence (2.2). Finally, a shift in perspective to the journalistic production of a television interview highlights typical possibilities and conflicts inherent in social events in terms of competent media-specific language use (2.3).

2.1. Media competence in everyday situations

A consultation on the phone, a business call, a discussion between parents and children as they watch television, a flirt while watching a movie in a theater, an e-mail message to a friend, an entry in a blog – these are all examples of communication forms. Each of these discussion types involve typical participants who solve typical problems with typical media and language resources and thereby employ certain competences. As is explained in more detail below, participants can a) carry out real-time discussions through a medium, such as in a consultation on the phone or a business call; b) talk face-to-face but be stimulated by previous or simultaneous use of media, as an audience; and c) initiate or respond to discussions by sending or leaving messages through media with potentially unrestricted access.

a) In a consultation on the phone, listening is of primary importance for the advice giver: not just for the verbal message, but also to understand the prosodic and paralinguistic signs and signals such as pauses and intonation, voice and breath quality. Added to this are the abilities to empathize, to treat the other person's comments respectfully, to indicate this paraverbally and verbally, and of course in general the ability to communicate with others about problems and possible solutions using nothing but spoken language. By contrast, business calls across cultural boundaries require experience with culture-specific discourse conventions in addition to listening skills, quick decisions, and assertiveness through spoken language. Common to all telephone discussions is that usually one of the participants triggers the contact, that both or all of the participants organize the course of the discussion together by resorting to standard patterns and formulations, such as for the beginning and end of the discussion, and that participants have to limit themselves to auditory input (Luke and Pavlidou 2002).

b) Anyone who watches television with their children is familiar with another media-influenced form of communication: audience talk while viewing. Such discussions contribute significantly to cognitive and emotional development and to understanding media content (Klemm 2000). The adults follow the video action, interpret children's comments, verbally respond briefly but helpfully to individual children's emotional and cognitive difficulties, if possible during pauses, and mediate any quarrels. A flirt during a movie, also a type of audience talk, requires the ability to ascertain the approachability of the partner, to stimulate the latter with physical proximity without overly disturbing the social surroundings, to follow the story on the screen, and to make such pithy, pointed comments related to the shared experience that it can be assumed the partner feels attracted and involved. The shared feature of all audience talk is multitasking: following the medially-conveyed experience, including the comments and concerns of the social surroundings, and contributing purposefully to the discussion at hand.

c) Transcending the problems of both space and time, computer-mediated communication such as email, newsgroups, and weblogs allow people to initiate or respond to discussions instantaneously. Since these are disembodied forms of communication, however, they do not demand instantaneous reception or provide immediate feedback. Although email can be quite speech-like, often making use of typeface features, punctuation, and devices like so-called emoticons to compensate for a lack of paralinguistic cues (Baron 2000), it differs in the extent of its potential for distribution to an unintended, unknown audience. A technical problem with a provider's server or an accidental click of a button can be all it takes for a message to be sent to the wrong person or people. Contributors to open weblogs, by contrast, intend their messages to be read by the public: Schlobinski and Siever (2005) estimate that by January 2005 there were about 8 million "bloggers" and that 30 % (50 million) of all US internet users may visit weblogs. Despite its speed and apparent transience, all forms of computer-mediated communication are characterized by their potential for distribution and permanence, thanks to ever-increasing storage capacity, access, and logging of texts in interconnected computer networks.

In addition to the capacity to access and use media tools, media competence involves various types of competence that allow people to simultaneously process different types of input at various levels, understand the limitations and potential of specific types of media, and communicate appropriately for the particular task at hand. The following sections deal with how basic competences and media-specific language competence interact.

2.2. Media competence in media situations

"… ah, um, our wor- …work-… um.. valued employees …" Anyone who talks like this to the television camera in the morning runs the risk of experiencing the same discomfort that evening while watching the interview on TV, knowing it might be seen by hundreds of thousands of viewers including customers, colleagues, and supervisors who could refer to it later. A media appearance, whether for print or on-line media, for radio or television, represents a threefold burden for media laypersons (Perrin 2006a). First, people often appear in the media acting as representatives of an organization, a particular group, or a subject area, although the expectations of their employers, professional colleagues, and interest groups can diverge wildly from their own. Role conflicts are inevitable. Second, any work with media professionals is heavily influenced by the industrial production routines of the media enterprise. There is always a rush. And third, through the microphone and camera, people are exposed indirectly and put on full display to a diffuse, dispersed public that receive only an excerpt of the whole appearance in the media item, can hardly ask questions, but probably still form an opinion within a few seconds. The social event of the media interview takes place in the center of this triangle of communication task, production routines, and public opinion making.

Media-specific language use is based on various types of basic competence: on self-competence, for instance, in handling personal values and emotions and on social competence in dealing with other people's perceptions, roles, groups, and social processes. A CEO being interviewed, for example, employs various competences before and during the social event of a television interview, in order to:

- perceive, reflect on, and expand on personal values, abilities, and skills (What impression do I want to make? Can I handle a cross-examination by communication pros? Can I spontaneously convey complex ideas? How can I become more courageous, more quick-witted?)
- handle emotions and symptoms of stress, anxiety, or stage fright (How can I make positive use of my tension? How can I stay calm and focused when someone is trying to rush me? What can I do if my hands start shaking? How can I sleep well before the media appearance?)
- perceive the other people's behavior and assess how others perceive one's own behavior (What effect does my enthusiastic shop-talk have on the television producers? How can I recognize that? Do I notice when I speak too quickly and my voice rises?)
- handle groups and group dynamics (How should I play the part of an expert in a round-table discussion or podium? How can I recognize whether and how hierarchies are forming? How do I deal with assigned hierarchical levels and how can I change group constellations?)
- perceive and help organize large-scale individual and social processes (How do I set topics? How do I structure relationships? How, for whom, and according to which measure do I increase my value? How do I get into and out of crises?)
- negotiate roles (Who assigns which role to whom? How does the discussion partner, the interviewer, do this before, during, and after the discussion? How can I recognize the attempt to assign roles? How do I develop my own role?)

Above and beyond these basic types of competence, such a CEO will also employ competences for media-specific language use that he might need only for discussions, or only for television interviews or live television interviews, or even only for controversial, conflict-laden live television interviews – different types of competence precisely for certain types of media-influenced communication forms. Before and during an interview the CEO would employ such competences in order to:

- assess the framework of discourse (Who publicly sets which topics at present, and who defends which positions? Where does my discussion partner, the journalist, the editors or producers, and/or the audience probably stand in this discourse framework – and where do I stand?)

- respond appropriately to an encounter and help organize the framework (Will a discussion take place? Do I take part myself or does someone else from my side? When, how, and where should an interview take place, if I have a part in these decisions?)
- be prepared for the announced topic and other possible topics and for the expected form of topic management by the journalist (What are the facts about the designated topic and other current topics that the journalist could tie into my role? How should I respond? What should I not respond to? What arguments should I use?)
- construct a suitable model of the discussion partner and other possible addressees and continually adapt it while monitoring the discussion (What does the journalist or the discussion partner want to achieve with their contribution? Which institution, organization, position, or interest group do they represent? What reaction can they trigger in the various addressees of the media item?)
- listen attentively, respond to questions, keep own objectives in view, and make an appropriate impression on the various addressees (What is the interviewer saying, and what does the interviewer mean by it? How does the journalist want to include my statement after the discussion? What do the interviewer's questions and behavior say about the planned media item?)

After the interview, the journalist might produce a media item that provides a frame for parts of the discussion. In another variant of the television interview, the discussion is transmitted live, in real-time, and incorporated into a program of public communication. Here, too, the audience does not simply see the discussion itself but rather a well-designed reconstruction of the discussion: with light and camera angles, sound levels, picture inserts, moderator input, and overall program context all carefully planned. Even a live interview is journalistically structured well beyond the guidance of the discussion by the interviewer. All of this represents the work that goes into a television interview from the perspective of the journalists, the producers, the media enterprise, and the whole system of public, medially-transmitted communication. People with certain roles are at work here, media professionals who also employ their competences for media-specific language use. They rely on them continually to overcome typical conflicts.

2.3. Media competence in media production

Anyone working in journalistic mass media production is subject to conflicting expectations with respect to their role. In the interest of the media enterprise, journalists should achieve high impact at low cost but in the public interest still address socially relevant topics in a nuanced way. Or they have to be ready to respond to the unexpected every day while working within rigid production structures. Such conflicting demands lead to problems in balancing the elements of journalistic text production outlined in (a) to (f) below, all of which assume corresponding competences (Perrin 2004).

(a) *Limiting the topic.* Which topic and which aspect of a topic should I choose, and how much detail should I go into?

In an item about a new airport terminal, journalists pick up on the loudest voices in the current discussion about the airport and focus on the high costs in economically tight times. They could also have developed the topic further and included other positions in their report, which might have presented the new terminal as an anti-cyclical long-term investment, for example. This would have prolonged the media production and incurred more expense, though, which would have led to a conflict with (f).

(b) *Finding sources.* How seriously do I look into a situation with respect to reliable sources, and how should I reproduce them?

In the item about the airport terminal, a building site manager comments extensively about the complexity of the construction details, giving the impression of unreasonable structural expenditures. The journalists could have had the site manager or other protagonists indicate where and how costs would be saved over the long-term with the buildings under discussion. However, this would have deprived the item of a gripping hypothesis: conflict with (c).

(c) *Establishing and formulating own position.* Which perspective should I assume; what is my hypothesis on the topic?

An item on reductions in social benefit payments for single parents includes an excerpt of an interview that makes it clear that the official responsible does not know the price of diapers, milk, or bread. The journalist frames the excerpt with the criticism that anyone making decisions about cuts in social benefits should know what the cost of living is. The journalist could have assumed a more neutral position, but this would have taken the advocacy sting out of the item: conflict with (e).

(d) *Guiding the role play.* How much space do I give to the facts of the matter I have researched, to the sources I have asked, and to myself, and how do I link things together?

In the item on social benefits, the journalist supports her interpretation of the matter with an interview excerpt. The portrayed official indicates that he has little idea about how expensive life is for the people whose benefit levels he has to decide upon. The journalist could have kept the interview more open, with fewer leading questions, or reproduced other excerpts from it, but this would have weakened her position: conflict with (c).

(e) *Establishing relevance for the audience.* What previous knowledge of which audience do I want to tie into; which expectations do I want to fulfill; and what effect do I want to achieve?

In an item on the hostage release from a Moscow concert hall, for example, the media professionals have a suitable expert explain the physical difficulties the Moscow authorities had to deal with when they flooded the hall with stun gas. The media producers could also have presented this explanation to their lay audience with didactic means such as animated graphics. However, this would have been beyond the scope of a short item in a news broadcast: conflict with (f).

(f) *Holding to space and time restrictions.* How do I treat my topic adequately with the resources at hand, in the prescribed space, and in the prescribed time?

In the item on the Moscow hostage release, the media professionals decide to be satisfied with a rather ponderous statement from an expert who is not in top form. There is no time to rehearse because the camera team has another assignment. Perhaps the expert could have been prompted for a better formulation, but this would have detracted from the authenticity of the source's comment: conflict with (b).

This close-up zoom from selected discussions (2.1.), to a television interview (2.2.), and from there to conflicts for media professionals (2.3.) has demonstrated that whereas basic competences also allow appropriate and successful action in many areas other than media and language use, the specific types of competence are oriented to certain topics, roles, media, and communication forms in social events. Media competence encompasses general, topic-specific, and event-specific abilities that together make it possible to solve tasks appropriately and effectively with medially-transmitted communication. These abilities are cognitively determined in the individuals concerned, thus a part of people's retrievable and usable knowledge about themselves, others, and the world. The abilities are socially influenced and influential, developing as individuals deal with themselves, others, and the world and having repercussions on their surroundings.

Researching media competence, accordingly, means relating observed cognitive and social practices to measures of their appropriateness and effectiveness (Deppermann 2004).

3. Researching media competence in newsrooms

Which media-specific language use is appropriate for a task and its social surrounding and leads to success in that context depends, on the one hand, on the use of language itself and, on the other, on what is considered appropriate and successful. Competence is thus a term related to norms. Empirical research on competences does not assume such norms as given but rather establishes evidence of them with the norm providers in the area of study. For an investigation of media competence in journalistic settings, possible norm providers include the public, professional organizations, media houses, and production teams. Such communities – and their individual participants – can set language norms either explicitly such as with editorial guidelines or implicitly by tacit modeling and reproduction in everyday behavior. For example, since no-one speaks loudly in an open-plan office, the norm holds that people do not speak loudly in an open-plan office. Practices and norms thus interact with each other (for a basic review, see Giddens 1984; for an example with journalistic offices, see Wyss 2004).

Both the practices and the norms have to be determined when media-specific language competences are being investigated using standards of empirical research. Media linguistics is a branch of applied linguistics that concerns itself with the area of journalistic text production, using four approaches (Perrin and Ehrensberger 2007) to investigate the language products themselves (3.1.) as well as language use as a cognitive (3.2.), social (3.3.), or cognitive-social activity (3.4.). One method from each of the four approaches is outlined below and illustrated with an empirical research project that works primarily with this method.

3.1. Investigating language products with version analysis

Version analysis is a linguistic approach for obtaining and analyzing data that tracks language features in intertextual chains. Version analysis indicates how language functions and structures change when statements are incorporated into media items and successively revised at several processing levels such as those of correspondents, news agencies, editors, and producers, or when media report several times successively on the same topic. One example of the usefulness of version analysis is to track how the significance or meaning of a quote can change after it is taken out of its interview context and incorporated into a new text on its own. Text and discourse analyses of individual media items and their precursors in the production flow form the basis for comparing various versions of texts.

In another application of version analysis, Dor (2003) relied on it as the key method in his study of newspaper headlines. He examined the features that characterize headlines considered successful by editorial staff, using the case of the popular Israel newspaper Ma'ariv. From email correspondence between copy editors and the senior editor in chief, Dor reconstructed the development of 134 headlines that appeared between 1996 and 1998. He analyzed the semantic and pragmatic differences between headlines that were rejected and those that were accepted. Using empirically derived criteria, Dor (2003: 716) illustrated that the "art of headline production" was a case of optimizing relevance for the reader.

A relevance optimized headline is easy for the reader to understand because it is kept short, clear, unambiguous, and highly readable; in addition, it triggers expectations in the reader because it makes the topic sound new and interesting. Part of the optimization is that the headline contains newsworthy names and concepts, refers to established facts, and does not rely on unknown presuppositions. According to Dor's results, optimizing the relevance of headlines in this sense is also part of the media-specific language competence of people working at a newspaper's news-desk.

What version analysis cannot do, however, is provide information about whether journalists make conscious decisions when recontextualizing excerpts; whether some practices are typical for certain media with certain target readerships and audiences; and whether practices and associated problems in the production and editorial process are discussed and negotiated or not. To investigate these sorts of questions, methodical access to cognitive practices is required.

3.2. Investigating cognitive practices with progression analysis

Progression analysis is a multi-method linguistic approach for obtaining and analyzing data that addresses the text production process directly as a cognitively-based activity and indirectly as a socially-based activity. For example, what exactly does a journalist do and why does he do it when he removes a comment from a source text and incorporates into his own text? With progression analysis, data about such a writing process can be obtained at three levels and related to each other: before writing begins the work situation is established with interviews and participant observation; during the actual writing all movements are measured with computer-supported recordings; and after the writing process, the repertoire of writing strategies is inferred through event-specific retrospective verbal protocols.

Progression analysis was the key method used in a case study of media text construction by Sleurs, Jacobs, and van Waes (2003). They examined how Dutch corporate press releases and the quotes they contain are constructed. As part of a larger investigation, they recorded in detail how a 26-year-old writer in a PR agency produced a single press release for a corporate client and what explanations he offered for his actions. The data support the hypothesis that PR writes use pseudo-quotes and preformulations of text so that media journalists can take over as much as possible directly from the press release. In order to avoid alienating media journalists, the writer in the case study also takes care that the quotes do not sound too much like advertising or promotion. For this reason, he formulates quotes to sound more neutral – or he attributes quotes to a more credible or neutral source, such as a customer of his client's company or an analyst. In addition, the writer attempts to place his client's company in a positive light; he thus tries to meet the expectations of people in the media at the same time as those of his clients. Overall, Sleurs et al. conclude that the structure and function of quotes in press releases are more complex than previous research has indicated. Writing journalistically acceptable and attractive quotes proves to be a good working strategy for the writer in the case study and in general might be part of media-specific language competence in PR.

"Might be" ... in fact, progression analysis deals with practices of the individual language users under study. If the question of interest, however, is how a whole discourse community such as the news staff of a media enterprise produce texts, then progression analysis has to be combined with methods that allow more direct inferences to be made about social practices – about what normally happens in a particular setting.

3.3. Investigating social practices with variation analysis

Variation analysis is a linguistic approach for obtaining and analyzing data that indicates the special features of the language of certain discourse communities. For example, what do news staff from one newsroom do with the individual comments of an interviewed person compared to what they usually do with such comments and to what another newsroom usually does in such situations? Upon investigation, it becomes apparent that the language in such a situation differs from the language of the same participants in other situations or from the language of other language users. Critical discourse analysis (CDA), a variant of variation analysis, also seeks markers of ideologies that are expressed in the language of a community – markers like hidden political judgments or social stereotypes (Fairclough 1995).

Variation analysis was the key method for Choi (2002) in a study of how language is used in the media to pursue ideological objectives. The corpus consisted of Washington Post and China Daily articles about the collision between an American and a Chinese aircraft above the South China Sea that occurred on April 1, 2001. Choi examined the choice of lexis, syntactic and semantic structures, focal points, and the use of indirect quotations. The choice of lexis seemed significant: the China Daily described the American plane as a spy aircraft, implying illegal activity, whereas the Washington Post referred to it as a surveillance plane, implying legitimate monitoring. Furthermore, the verb form that China Daily used ("bumped into") implied agency on the part of the American plane whereas the Washington Post's choice stressed the accidental nature of the incident ("collided with"). Linguistic resources are adapted to suit the conflicting interests of the political forces that dominate where the articles are produced. According to Choi's findings, therefore, the use of linguistic resources to supply recipients with politically opportune frameworks for interpretation is part of media-specific language competence.

Although variation analysis gains breadth compared with an approach like progression analysis, it suffers from a lack of depth. Variation analysis cannot determine why and at whose request the members of a newsroom frame an event with linguistic choices that conform politically and whether this happens consciously or not – despite many CDA studies inferring language users' thoughts directly from linguistic choices. Some depth of analysis could be regained with an approach that considered not only the text products like variation analysis, and not only the strategies and ideas of individual text producers like progression analysis, but rather the institutionalized discussions and discourse about language use of a whole newsroom. One such approach, metadiscourse analysis, is explained in the next section.

3.4. Investigating cognitive-social practices with metadiscourse analysis

Metadiscourse analysis is a linguistic approach for obtaining and analyzing data to determine the socially and individually anchored (language) awareness within discourse communities. Metadiscourse analysis investigates communication through communication and language. For example, at their regular staff meetings how does a newsroom team discuss the ideas they share about acceptable ways of dealing with interview excerpts? Which language practices do they approve of and which do they reject? What source of norms is referred to? Analyzing metadiscourse reveals how rules about language use in a discourse community are consciously negotiated and applied. Linguistic techniques for analyzing verbal communication form the basis for metadiscourse analysis.

Metadiscourse analysis was the key method for Häusermann (2007) in his study of original soundbites and their interpretation. He was interested in the practical possibilities of editing soundbites appropriately for radio scripts, of reflecting on how to incorporate them, and of putting them in a suitable context for interpretation. He analyzed not only the language use, but also the meta-communication of the media staff when things did not work according to plan. This meta-communication allows inferences to be made about the language awareness of the people under study. The analysis tracks the production phases of original soundbites: recording, editing, and then incorporating them. For the recording phase, Häusermann found that journalists and sources usually work together: journalists are able to obtain media-appropriate statements by guiding their informants and re-recording if attempts are less than successful at first. In doing so, though, they influence and distort the soundbite. In the phase when the soundbite is incorporated into a script, the relationship between the journalist and the informant can change. For example, the journalist might act as a cooperative partner during the recording but then put the jointly produced soundbite into a critical context, thereby purposefully recontextualizing differently. Recognizing, questioning, indicating, or avoiding such practices is, according to

Häusermann, part of the media-specific language competence of media professionals. According to him, recognizing and questioning these practices is also part of the competence of all media users.

Cognitive and social language practices can be systematically determined with the four approaches outlined above with their linguistic and linguistically-based interdisciplinary methods. The findings allow theoretically and empirically supported conclusions to be drawn about what participants actually do with language in medially-transmitted communication – and what they want to do and should do. In turn, these findings lay a foundation to describe types of media-specific language competence – in the sense of Hymes' (1972) framework of different types of communicative competence. These range from the actual competences of individual language users (e.g. Sleurs et al. 2003) and competences strived for by institutions (e.g. Dor 2003; Choi 2002) to potential competences that would be possible with the help of advice and training (e.g. Dor 2003; Häusermann 2007) and ideal competences that are justified as desirable from a general theoretical perspective (e.g. Häusermann 2007). Such knowledge about media-specific language competence is outlined in the next section, using journalistic text production as an example.

4. Research questions and findings

This section provides a systematic overview of specific research questions and findings in the area of appropriate and successful media-specific language competence in the context of journalist text production. The research is first categorized in terms of variously complex settings for language use (4.1.), then language functions (4.2.), and finally linguistic structures (4.3.). Each subsection addresses issues that can be dealt with insightfully from that particular perspective – mostly theory-driven issues but also practice-driven questions of appropriate and successful language use in journalism, such as interview strategies for questioning and answering.

4.1. The perspective of setting

The next four subsections outline four approaches to media language that differ according to the setting of the language use: a) interpersonal, b) inter-situational, c) intertextual, and d) intersemiotic. The description of these settings becomes more complex from one level to the next, and each level builds incrementally on the previous one.

a) *Interpersonal setting.* Communicative language use is interpersonal in that it is directed to other people. The beginnings of journalistic communication are also discussions, although the participants are aiming beyond their immediate communication situation, and are oriented not only to their discussion partner but also to the media audience. The theoretical question of interest for linguistics at this interface of interpersonal setting and media competence is how interview participants can address their contributions appropriately for different target audiences. Natural, easily accessible data for such investigations are available in media interviews, where microphones, cameras, and recordings belong to the field of activity itself and are not artificial intrusions by researchers. From the point of view of practice, the question arises as to how media interviews manage to address all of the relevant target audiences at the same time. Media linguistics can employ tools from discourse linguistics to identify and consider the language competence that interviewers and interviewees use to establish a relationship with multiple target audiences – for example, the use of loaded questions.

A loaded question is a complex contribution to a discussion that consists of a claim or observation plus a question designed to elicit an answer that also indicates acceptance of the claim or question. In this area, Bucher (2000) as well as Clayman and Heritage (2002) examine the relationship between questions and claims in loaded questions. Clayman (1993) identifies strategies that politicians use to react to loaded questions by reformulating the questions into a form that they find acceptable whereas Harris (1991) finds that politicians use strategies such as changing the topic after a loaded question, forgetting the question, or frankly refusing to give an answer. Ekström (2001) discusses the process of editing loaded questions out of interview recordings for television news, and Roth (2005) highlights the practice by interviewers before elections to spring surprise questions on candidates in order to make them appear ignorant.

b) *Inter-situational setting.* Even things that seem fleeting and spontaneous in journalistic media are inter-situational and done deliberately: with calculable effort and expenditure, for a pre-determined time frame or space, with the simplest possible access for an unknown audience far away from the production situation. Texts for media items are therefore usually produced in written form even if they are later presented in spoken form. The theoretical question of interest for linguistics at this interface of inter-situational setting and media competence is how writers produce their texts, whether alone or sharing authorship. This can be easily determined at journalistic workstations: writing processes here are predictably short and integrated into computer systems, which simplifies following the text development step-by-step. From the point of view of practice, the question arises as to how journalistic contributions can be produced under economical production conditions, with multiple authors, and in a media- and task-specific interplay of spoken and written modes. Media linguistics can employ tools from writing research to identify and consider the corresponding language competence – for example the writing strategies of experienced media professionals.

A writing strategy is an established, conscious, and thus articulable idea of how decisions are to be made during writing in order that there is a greater probability that the writing process or text product takes on the intended form and fulfills the intended function. Examples of research into writing strategies include studies by Wolf and Thomason (1986) and Laakaniemi (1987) on strategy-oriented approaches of writing coaches in newsrooms; by Androutsopoulos (2000) on writing strategies of writers of fanzines; by Dor (2003) on writing strategies and news headlines; by Perrin (2001; Perrin and Ehrensberger 2006) on the differences between experienced and inexperienced journalists; by Perrin (2004; 2006b) on expanding repertoires of journalistic writing strategies in consulting projects; by Ruhmann and Perrin (2002) on typical journalist conflicts of interest during writing; and by Sleurs et al. (2003) on a PR writer's writing strategies for dealing with quotes.

c) *Intertextual setting.* Journalistic text production transmits societal discourse, thus basically draws on discussions and fixed offers of communication. This recourse to intertextuality occurs in journalistic communication through several steps according to its own domain-specific rules about dealing with sources. The theoretical question of interest for linguistics at this interface of intertextual setting and media competence is how societal discourse functions; that is, how discourse communities communicate about certain topics over time and space and pick up on previous contributions to those topics. Items in journalistic media support such discourse and also record it for analysis at a later date. From the point of view of practice, the question arises as to how discourse can be conveyed from sources to audience in a journalistically appropriate and economically acceptable way. Media linguistics can employ tools from text linguistics to identify and consider the corresponding language competence with which media professionals create, simulate, and blur intertextuality – for example by clustering items or intensifying them with quotes.

Clustering is a term to describe the linguistic activity of preparing a media contribution as a non-linear compilation of intertextually linked texts within a perceptual field. Intensifying is used to describe a linguistic activity whereby utterances are (re-)constructed to lead to a main claim having public appeal. A quote is a unit in a media item that is represented as a faithful replication of a source's utterance. An example of research into clustering is Bucher's (1996) study, which shows it to be a text design strategy in daily newspapers, with a text cluster arising from several individual items such as reports and comments or from an individual item that is comprised of sub-sections, boxes, tables, etc. clustered together. Lugrin (2001) also investigates text clusters in terms of differences between them in a prestige and a tabloid newspaper. Burger (2001) considers quotes in television news broadcasts; Marinos (2001) examines the authenticity of reported speech in newspaper reports; Ekström (2001) describes how the same utterances from politicians can be subject to completely different journalistic intentions in various television news items; and Häusermann (2007) and Sleurs et al. (2003) discuss quotes in PR texts that are invented and formulated in such a way that they intensify a journalistic focus.

d) *Intersemiotic setting.* The symbolic system of language, whether spoken or written, is always intersemiotically integrated in media items: language never occurs as language alone. The various forms of journalistic media permit and demand their own links between language and other symbolic systems. This has repercussions for the use of language. The theoretical question of interest for linguistics at this interface of intersemiotic setting and media competence is how language interacts with other symbolic systems. The technology of each medium allows its own interaction of symbolic systems and the dramaturgy demands it: print with its script and still pictures; television with moving pictures; and radio with the background noise of the reported events. From the point of view of practice, the question arises as to how signs from several systems can be coordinated with each other. Media linguistics can employ tools from semiotics to identify and consider the corresponding language competence with which media items can be illustrated, scripted, sound-tracked, and linked – for example the gap between spoken text and pictures, the text/image divide.

The text/image divide refers to the divergence between the meaning of verbal utterances and simultaneously perceptible images in media items. Some examples of relevant research include Jucker (2003) on media convergence that lets print, radio, and TV items appear to be special cases of hypermedia; Quinn (2005) on the general problems of multimedia reporting; Ballstaedt (2002) on text-image design; and Huth (1985) and Oomen (1985) on functions of images in television news. Renner (2001) discusses the metaphor of "shears" to describe the text/image divide. He differentiates among strong and weak confirmation, contradiction, and lack of reference between text and image, and recognizes them to be functional in various ways for the four genres of documentary film, reportage, explanatory film, and essay. The metaphor of a zipper in place of shears is offered by Holly (2005) as an alternate view of the relationship between text and image.

4.2. The perspective of function

This section outlines four approaches to media language that differ according to the function of language: a) referential, b) cognitive, c) interactive, and d) social-constitutive. The description of these settings becomes more complex from one level to the next, and each level builds incrementally on the previous one.

a) *Referential function.* Language usually refers to things outside itself: it relates to non-verbal phenomena and labels things in the world. Every form of communication makes use of this labeling, the primary function of language. However, as the term suggests, journalistic news is concerned with conveying new information. It has to be able to refer quickly to things that have not been labeled previously. The theoretical question of interest for linguistics at this interface of referential function and media competence is what linguistic utterances mean in everyday life. Linguistic inquiry focuses on the meaning of words and complex linguistic units, on logical connections of meaning, on hierarchies of meaning, and on themes. In journalistic media, it discovers that attempts to make meaning public are ongoing, rapid, and routine. From the point of view of practice, the question arises as to how it is possible to regularly report about current events and often about unfamiliar things with well-known signs and symbols. Media linguistics can employ tools from semantics to identify and consider the corresponding language competence with which media professionals quickly and routinely link what is familiar to what is new – for example with metaphors.

Metaphors transpose the meaning of a sign from a familiar field to a new field that is then perceived as similar. Research into the use of metaphors in the media can be found in Settekorn (2001) on metaphor transfers between journalism and advertising as well as between sports and economic reporting; Burger (2004) on metaphors in intertextual journalist text production; Zinken (2003) on the connection between metaphors and ideology in the Polish press at the collapse of communism; Kobozeva (2005) on metaphors in the Russian press; Koller (2004a; 2004b) on metaphors in media items about women in management positions; Dirks (2005) on metaphors in press commentaries about peace demonstrations; Stenvall (2003) on the use of metaphors by international news agencies in reporting about terrorism; Peck MacDonald (2005) on metaphors in journalist reports about hormone therapies; Johnson and Suhr (2003), Johnson, Culpeper, and Suhr (2003), and Toolan (2003) on metaphors in media items that have political correctness as a main or secondary theme.

b) *Cognitive function.* The use of language requires and generates cognitive processes: by speaking or writing, people express thoughts in the form of language and then by understanding language, thoughts are triggered. In journalistic communication, though, language production is disconnected from language comprehension. The media professionals cannot directly track what the chosen linguistic devices trigger in their audience. The theoretical question of interest for linguistics at this interface of cognitive language function and media competence is how language is processed in the mind, how a language user's previous knowledge contributes to understanding texts, and how this knowledge can be activated. Journalistic communication, with its practically unknown addressees, has to build on basic assumptions of general prior knowledge. From the point of view of practice, the question arises as to how news journalism can report in an illuminating and attractive way. Media linguistics can employ tools from psycholinguistics to identify and consider the corresponding language competence with which media professionals strive for such features of quality – like framing, establishing coherence, and comprehensibility.

Framing refers to the representation or interpretation of an extract of reality in terms of cognitively and socially anchored patterns of interpretation. Coherence is the capacity of an understood text to connect together through additional thoughts it triggers. Comprehensibility is determined by all of the features of a text that are suitable for influencing how addressees understand that text. Some examples of research into framing are studies by Fang (2001) on framing politically sensitive events in Chinese newspapers and by Lind and Salo (2002) on framing feminism in American radio news. On the subject of coherence, Dorenbeck (1997) examines a newsmagazine's "strategy" of leaving coherence gaps open at critical points for the audience to fill as they like; Eggs (1996) discusses multi-stranded, associative argumentation in newspaper commentaries; and Perrin (1999) identifies coherence problems in patching together agency news reports. Finally, comprehensibility has been considered by Lutz and Wodak (1987) in their comparisons of various versions of the same news; by Hardt-Mautner (1992) with radio news; by McAdams (1993) in terms of the readability of newspaper texts; and by Bucher (2005) for journalism in general.

c) *Interactive function.* Cognitive change favors interactive change: when knowledge changes, behavior can change. Communication aims for such effects. People do things with language so that something happens; they communicate purposefully. Participants in a communication situation can pursue the same objectives – or complementary or exclusory objectives. The theoretical question of interest for linguistics at this interface of pragmatic language function and media competence is how verbal and non-verbal activities interact, what intentions language users have, and how meaning is negotiated in communication. In journalistic communication the intended actions and conflicts of various actors overlap systematically: those of the media professionals, the sources, the target audience, and the broader public. From the point of view of practice, the question arises as to how to make an offer of communication available to the public and at the same time sell it. Media linguistics can employ tools from pragmatics to identify and consider the corresponding language competence with which media professionals choose and dramaturgically prepare their topics – for example storytelling.

Storytelling consists of designing an offer of communication as a story, with typical text roles, scenes, action, and perspectives. There are many examples of research into journalistic storytelling: Tuchman (1976) discusses news journalism as telling stories, similar to Schudson (1982), Bennett, Gresset, and Haltom

(1985), Redd (1991), Pietilä (1992), Püschel (1992), Kunelius (1994), Jaworski and Connell (1995), Hickethier (1997), Ekström (2000), and Ungerer (2000). Le (2004) examines journalistic self-positioning and the dramaturgical function of text actors in editorials; Hartley (1982), Fiske (1987) and Roth (2002) investigate the dramaturgical representation of interviewees in radio; Koller (2004a) that of business women in media items; Spranz-Fogasy (2003) of managers; Ekström (2001) of politicians; Burger (1996) of the lay public; and Kleinberger (2004) of the lay public and experts. Luginbühl (2004) focuses on authenticity in television news, similarly to Coupland (2001) with a television news review; Jacobs (1996) on storytelling and crises; and Jaworski, Fitzgerald, and Morris (2003) on storytelling when reporting about future events.

d) *Social-constitutive function.* Finally, communication has a social-constitutive function: people can establish common ideas and discourse communities with language and, conversely, the chosen language indicates which discourse community people belong to. Journalistic communication translates between the languages of communities, such as between the languages of text actors and addressees. By doing so it overcomes social differences – and at the same time consolidates them. The theoretical question of interest for linguistics at this interface of social language function and media competence is how communities differ in their languages and language variants and how language use changes – also under the influence of journalistic media. From the point of view of practice, the question arises as to how to reliably reach different addressees with linguistic means while at the same time defining a unique profile in the market and committing audience, sources, and advertising clients over the long-term. Media linguistics can employ tools from sociolinguistics to identify and consider the corresponding language competence with which media professionals commit their target groups – so-called audience design.

Audience design refers to tailoring a media item for certain target groups: a) adjusting to the expectations, prior knowledge, and receptiveness of addressees; b) using a different style from other offers in the market; and c) contributing to the commitment of users. Research into audience design in journalist media has been carried out by Bell (1984; 2001), who examines the conflict between adaptation to the norms of the market and an independent profile in the market; by Selting (1983), who discusses a radio moderator's practice of purposefully using different linguistic styles for different tasks and with different discussion partners – using high register in discussions with experts and the proximity of dialect in discussions with persons affected by an issue; by Schwitalla (1993), who views the changes of journalistic genres as a consequence of audience design; by Roeh (1982), who considers the repercussions of audience design on the content of journalistic news; and by Schudson (1982) and Cameron (1996), who explore the political background of audience design.

4.3. The perspective of structure

The following subsections outline four approaches to media language that differ according to the structure of the verbal utterances: a) sound, b) word, c) sentence, and d) text. The description of these structures become more complex from one level to the next, and each level builds incrementally on the previous one.

a) *Sound structure.* Language connects the smallest possible units that distinguish meaning: sounds, letters, characters, and elements of signs that people can produce and convey and that they can perceive as systematically different. Journalistic communication has to limit itself to technically transmitted signs – at present to visible and audible signs. The theoretical question of interest for linguistics at this interface of sound structure and media competence is how auditory features of language contribute to comprehension. Individual sound segments and their articulation are of interest, as is prosody, the supra-segmental sound of language. In the spoken language of journalistic media, articulation and prosody are intended to be as widely accepted as possible. From the point of view of practice, the question arises as to how to structure the auditory component of media items, including the sound of spoken language. Media linguistics can employ tools from phonetics and phonology to identify and consider the corresponding language competence with which media professionals speak effectively – for example prosodic phrasing.

Prosodic phrasing is the linguistic phenomenon of a speaker using prosodic means to emphasize the semantic and pragmatic structure of an utterance. Prosodic means include broad patterns such as intonation curves as well as emphasis with loudness, pitch, or duration. For example, Bell (1982; 1991) discusses the differences in the spoken English of newscasts in six New Zealand radio stations that target audiences from various social levels by choosing appropriate linguistic means. Schubert and Sendlmeier (2005) examine the sound features of newscast language that is positively judged by test audiences in listening trials, finding that one of the key features is the division of the news text into sensible sections with the aid of breaks. Bergner and Lenhart (2005) ascertain similarities in prosodic arrangement between radio news of a public and private station, allowing producer-independent generalizations to be made about genre-specific patterns. The point of a "prescriptive notation" for radio news is explored by Marx (2005): written advice about prosody should make it simpler to say news texts as comprehensibly as possible, so that the semantic and pragmatic structure and thereby the meaning and understood more easily.

b) *Word structure.* Language combines meaningfully distinctive units into meaningful units: linguistic symbols that stand for specific details in the world. The details, their perception by the language user, and communication requirements change over time, so language users create new words, some of which establish themselves in the language community. The theoretical question of interest for linguistics at this interface of word structure and media competence is how new words form, spread, change, and disappear. Journalistic media are especially interesting in this context for three reasons: they constantly create new words to meet their own needs, they spread language to many other users, and their media products allow methodologically simple access to the language output. From the point of view of practice, the question arises as to which types of words suit media tasks. Media linguistics can employ tools from morphology to identify and consider the linguistic devices with which media professionals are recognized in public discourse, talk about new things concisely in a way that is easily remembered, and relieve communication of the duress of creativity – for example by using idioms, on the one hand, or coinages, on the other.

An idiom consists of a group of words in a specific order that has a set meaning as a whole. For example, the idiom "give something the green light" means something different from the sum of the meanings of the individual words. Thus, idioms do not operate according to the composition principle. By contrast, a spontaneous coinage or neologism is a word that is made up or applied spontaneously in a concrete situation and relies on users being able to deduce its particular meaning from its components or the context. Some examples of relevant research include Burger (1999) on idioms in the press and Burger (2004) on idioms in intertextual chains of journalistic text production. Sawitzki (2001) examines neologisms in German newsmagazines, and Holly (2002) does so in columns written by a well-known German author, Elke Heidenreich, for the German woman's magazine "Brigitte". Peck MacDonald (2005) considers word choice and sentence structure in sensationalist popular science articles; and Jesensek (1998) discusses the function of coinages as catchwords in political press commentaries.

c) *Sentence structure.* Language, whether spoken or written, is represented linearly, one symbol after the other. In terms of meaning, the symbols form cross-connections, networks, and hierarchies. Symbols for actors and actions combine into propositional units that are linearly represented as sentences. Journalistic communication verbalizes the propositions densely and in portions as appropriate to the product templates and target group models. The theoretical question of interest for linguistics at this interface of sentence level and media competence is what sentences are – how they are linked internally and with each other. The use of sentence structures change over time, but even at any particular point in time the possible patterns are used differently with various intentions and for various tasks. In journalistic language use this can be easily traced. From the point of view of practice, the question arises as to how sentences and chains of sentences can be formed so that addressees can quickly understand the key message. Media linguistics can employ tools from syntax to identify and consider the language competence with which media professionals create sentence structures specific to the task at hand – for example, condensing and portioning information.

Condensing information is the linguistic process of conveying as much information as possible with the fewest possible signs. Portioning information refers to dividing linguistic utterances into units that are easy to process cognitively. An example of research into sentence structure in journalism is Jucker's (1992) study that shows that the sentence structures in British daily newspapers are more similar within a section of the paper than between different sections or editorial offices. Biber (2003) identifies the presence of condensed nominal phrases in newspapers; Mardh (1980) discusses "headlinese", the structural characteristics of headlines on the title pages of English newspapers; Kniffka (1980) examines headlines and formulations of leads in American dailies; Bell (1991) considers the omission of the definite article in certain types of apposition; and Perrin (2005) describes which strategies journalists use to condense their source's utterances. The functions of the beginnings of sentences in German news articles are examined by Schröder (2001), and Cotter (2003) considers the function of the connectors "and" and "but" in the newspaper language of the 20th century. Specifically addressing the technique of portioning, Häusermann (2005) explains that the technique helps in the editing of illogical or confusingly structured complex sentences. After editing, sentences convey information step-by-step with clear links.

d) *Text structure.* Ultimately, linguistic complexes form meaningful units: texts that deal with a certain topic and embody certain intended actions. For recurring topics and intentions in recurring communication situations, text patterns or genres develop. Journalistic communication makes use of such patterns and constantly breaks out of them as it strives for market share and media evolve. The theoretical question of interest for linguistics at this interface of text level and media competence is what makes a text a text and which patterns develop from this in language use, even in the rapid, industrial pace of journalistic media. From the point of view of practice, the question arises as to how to make text processing simpler by using text patterns while still appearing autonomous. Media linguistics can employ tools from text linguistics to identify and consider the language competence with which media professionals use and break away from familiar patterns – the strategic variation of text patterns such as genres.

A text genre is a socially determined pattern for texts in a particular setting and with a certain function and/or structure. Genre change is the continuous evolution of a genre as it used over a longer period of time. Text pattern variation is the purposeful adaptation and development of text patterns in the sense of audience design. Some examples of research in this area include Adam's (2001) analysis of journalistic genres; Ljung's (2000) examination of the repertoire of genres in English-language quality newspapers; Grosse's (2001) study of the development of genres in journalism; Östman and Simon-Vandenbergen's (2004) investigation into text genre mixing and change; Bell's (2003) discussion of genre change in informative journalism; Ungerer's (2000) arguments about new media changing newspaper reporting; Van Dijk's (1988a) overview of the various text structures of 250 newspaper reports from 100 countries on the same event; studies by Lorda (2001) and Moirand (2001) about journalistic texts that do not fit into any of the usual genres of today; and Kropf's (1999) criticism of the so-called pyramid model of journalistic news and his proposal of a new "docking" model for radio news that can be completely understood upon first hearing.

From setting through to function and structure, this section has opened up a system of language use and competence and filled it for one particular area of the media, that of journalistic text production. It has shown that structural features of language (4.3) depend on the functions of that language (4.2) in certain settings (4.1). A quote from an interview becomes a headline condensed in the practices of the organizationally, institutionally, and socially linked participants, whereby the practices are influenced by structures such as norms and resources but also have a reverse effect on them. For example, the norm that competent interviewers of a particular television station do not preformulate answers for ineloquent interviewees might only hold until an interviewer otherwise considered competent and exemplary does so with conviction.

This is a very broad view of things. For practical reasons, the individual empirical approaches can seldom take a broad enough view to be able to vividly yet firmly grasp the complex construct "media competence". At this point, the issue of blank spots or current gaps in research in this area needs to be addressed.

5. Current gaps in research into media competence

Media competence clearly involves being able to access and make appropriate use of various types of individual, institutional, and media-specific language competence as the setting demands. As yet, few studies have managed to investigate media competence in all its complexity. An example of an investigation that attempts to address various types of language competence in a complex setting is Perrin, Schanne, and Wyss's (2005) research project on language policy, norms, and practices in the Swiss national radio and television broadcasting company. The project is part of a national research program on language competence and diversity in Switzerland, a country of about 7 million people and four national languages. The public broadcaster, in a monopoly position, has the mandate that its programs contribute to an understanding of, integration of, and communication between the country's linguistic and cultural communities. The outcomes of the project are consultations, coaching, and training of the media professionals working in the company – all measures to improve their media-specific language competence. Beforehand, it is necessary to determine how the Swiss national broadcasting company does, should, and could deal with language. This is done in the four research modules outlined below.

- Module A traces the development of the explicit and implicit external language policy expectations of the Swiss broadcaster, using document analysis and thematic interviews. Consistencies and contradictions become discernible in the demands on the overall institution, its enterprise units, and its programs.
- Module B reconstructs actions and reactions, interpretations and reasons of the broadcaster's management and those of their leading media outlets, using document analysis and thematic interviews. Organizational-hierarchical internal rules and resources for language use in programs and broadcasts become identifiable.
- Module C investigates text production practice for the most important information broadcasts in German and French with process and product analysis. The institutional, organizational, and individually motivated strategies and practices of media professionals as well as traces of their actions become recognizable in the language of the programs.
- Module D uses discourse analysis to investigate the quality control follow-up communication in the editorial offices of the leading news programs in German and French: Tagesschau and téléjournal. The language awareness that the Swiss company's language professionals and trainers bring to broadcasting becomes evident in such communication.

The practical complexities of research into media competence become particularly apparent in certain settings. When media competence refers to the capacity to use language appropriately and successfully in medially-transmitted communication, then this competence is not just part of an individual – but part of a socially integrated individual. In order to reconstruct the repertoire of competences at someone's disposal or that someone could or should have available, then research must investigate the practices of the individuals under study in complex, social settings – for sufficiently long and in enough depth. A field of applied linguistics that understands itself to be "dealing with practical problems of language and communication that can be identified, analyzed or solved" (AILA 2006) cannot avoid expanding its previous boundaries in order to tackle practical, relevant questions about media-specific language competence.

The preceding sections provide examples of the type of research that is being done in the area of media competence. Despite much systematic study of media-specific language use in variously complex settings (interpersonal, inter-situational, intertextual, inter-semiotic), of functions of media-specific language (referential, cognitive, interactive, socially-constitutive), and of media-specific language structures (sound, word, sentence, text), some serious gaps remain.

The first main gap primarily concerns the "competence" in media competence. In order to more easily handle an integrative, competence-oriented project such as that in the public broadcasting company described above, applied linguistics needs more solid, (inter-)disciplinary knowledge about the interconnections between language and other semiotic systems; language products and processing; production and reception processes; cognitive-individual and social practices; public and personal communication; scientific, systematic knowledge and practical, experiential knowledge; knowledge creation and transfer; as well as quantitative and qualitative methods. The mission of applied linguistics to address questions in their practical complexity basically includes all areas of language use and all research areas in the field. The gaps in knowledge are particularly disadvantageous with respect to medially-transmitted communication, though, because it is so important in daily life and business, in private and public, and will quickly become even more important.

A second gap concerns the "media" in media competence and is based directly on the pace of development of media technology. Digitization, networking, and media convergence are quickly opening up new technical possibilities for medially-transmitted communication. The subject of interest is developing far faster than research can track it. Street television, for example, where "peripheral groups juggle power relations and subvert the conventions of television" (Renzi 2005) by broadcasting their own ideas of television via the internet, can concern avant-garde media makers and users for years before the topic also appears in linguistic research. Counter-examples do exist, such as Crystal's (2001) treatment of language and the internet, which was written and distributed quite early on, and the internet site www.mediensprache.net that presents research news about language use in the (new) media. As early as August 2006, for instance, there was already a link to an on-line publication with contributions about the language of Chinese, German, English, Italian, Polish, Portuguese, Russian, Swedish, and Spanish weblogs (Schlobinski and Siever 2005) – although nothing yet on the topics of podcasting or talking over the internet using VoIP (Voice over Internet Protocol).

As Van Dijk (1988b: 23) observed about two decades ago: "The field [of mass media discourse analysis] is only 20 years young, with most of its substantial work having been done in the last decade. For many levels and dimensions of analysis, we still lack the theoretical instruments. Thus, we still know little about the precise structures and processes of media discourse." For media practitioners, those words must seem rather guarded. Journalists who prepare new topics for publication every day or sales staff who have to understand and explain the navigation logic of new models of mobile phones every week (with media competence in terms of practical, on-the-job experience with media) should be able to expect a couple of good ideas from a field that has been considering the topic for a number of years now. On the other hand, recognizing complex interconnections (media competence as a theoretical construct for understanding and communicating appropriately with media) requires a certain degree of distance.

A few years after the first, enthusiastic studies about the language of email messages appeared, Dürscheid (2005: 94), for example, determined that there were only a small number of linguistic features typical of email communication and that they usually occur only if the sender uses the reply and quote functions of the email program. Even what until now has been considered typical about the telephone can be called into question, since it may soon dissolve in general media convergence. Many mobile communication devices and laptop computers have built-in cameras and programs that allow people to "phone" via the internet and with pictures. Children may soon be chatting to their grandparents face-to-face despite being in different geographical locations, and brides-to-be may be able to model their wedding dresses live from distant cities to get their mothers' opinion. Media technology comes and goes, just like the telegraph, the fax machine, and the DOS computer with its dial-up analog modem. For the concept of media competence, the key issue is one's position on the scale between personal and public communication.

References

Adam, J.-M.
    2001   Genres de la presse écrite et analyse de discours. *SEMEN* 13: 7–14.
AILA
    2006   What is AILA. Retrieved 2.09.06, from http://www.aila.info/about/index.htm
Androutsopoulos, J.
    2000   Non-standard spellings in media texts: The case of German fanzines. *Journal of Sociolinguistics* 4(4): 514–533.
Ballstaedt, S.-P.
    2002   Schreibstrategien zum Medienwechsel. Text-Bild-Design. In: D. Perrin, I. Boettscher, O. Kruse, and A. Wrobel (eds.), *Schreiben. Von intuitiven zu professionellen Schreibstrategien*, 139–150. Wiesbaden: Westdeutscher Verlag.
Baron, N. S.
    2000   *Alphabet to Email. How Written English Evolved and Where It's Heading.* London/New York: Routledge.
Bell, A.
    1982   Radio: The style of news language. *Journal of Communication* 32(1): 150–164.

Bell, A.
1984 Language style as audience design. *Language in Society* 13(2): 145–204.
Bell, A.
1991 *The Language of News Media*. Oxford: Blackwell.
Bell, A.
2001 Back in style. reworking audience design. In: P. Eckert and J. R. Rickford (eds.), *Style and sociolinguistic variation*, 139–169. Cambridge: Cambridge University Press.
Bell, A.
2003 A century of news discourse. *International Journal of English Studies* 3: 189–208.
Bennett, B. L., L. A. Gresset, and W. Haltom
1985 Repairing the news. A case study of the news paradigm. *Journal of Communication* 35(2): 50–68.
Bergner, U. and H. Lenhart
2005 Analyse von Hörfunknachrichten am Beispiel zweier Sender. Eine sprechwissenschaftlich-empirische Studie. In: N. Gutenberg (ed.), *Schreiben und Sprechen von Hörfunknachrichten. Zwischenergebnisse sprechwissenschaftlicher Forschung*, 41–119. Frankfurt am Main: Lang.
Biber, D.
2003 Compressed noun-phrase structures in newspaper discourse. In: J. Aitchison and D. M. Lewis (eds.), *New media language*, 169–181. London: Routledge.
Bucher, H.-J.
1996 Textdesign – Zaubermittel der Verständlichkeit? Die Tageszeitung auf dem Weg zum interaktiven Medium. In: E. W. B. Hess-Lüttich, W. Holly, and U. Püschel (eds.), *Textstrukturen im Medienwandel*, 31–59. Frankfurt am Main: Lang.
Bucher, H.-J.
2000 Geladene Fragen. Zur Dialogdynamik in politischen Fernsehinterviews. Retrieved 16.12.04, from http://www.medienwissenschaft.de/forschung/geladene_fragen/start.html
Bucher, H.-J.
2005 Verständlichkeit. In: H. J. Kleinsteuber, B. Pörksen, and S. Weischenberg (eds.), *Handbuch Journalismus und Medien*, 464–470. Konstanz: UVK.
Burger, H.
1996 Laien im Fernsehen. Was sie leisten – wie sie sprechen – wie man mit ihnen spricht. In: B. U. Biere and R. Hoberg (eds.), *Mündlichkeit und Schriftlichkeit im Fernsehen*, 41–80. Tübingen: Narr.
Burger, H.
1999 Phraseologie in der Presse. In: N. Bravo Fernandez, I. Behr, and C. Rozier, (eds.), *Phraseme und typisierte Rede*, 77–89. Tübingen: Stauffenburg.
Burger, H.
2001 Das Zitat in den Fernsehnachrichten. In: D. Möhn, D. Roß, and M. Tjarks-Sobhani (eds.), *Mediensprache und Medienlinguistik. Festschrift für Jörg Hennig*, 45–62. Frankfurt am Main: Lang.
Burger, H.
2004 Phraseologie (und Metaphorik) in intertextuellen Prozessen der Massenmedien. In: Christine Palm Meister (ed.), *EUROPHRAS 2000. Internationale*

Tagung zur Phraseologie vom 15.–18. Juni 2000 in Aske/Schweden, 5–13. Tübingen: Stauffenburg.

Cameron, D.
1996   Style policy and style politics: A neglected aspect of the language of the news. *Media, Culture and Society* 18: 315–533.

Choi, D.
2002   *A Critical Discourse Analysis on Different Representations of the Same Event in the Media*. Essen: LAUD Linguistic Agency.

Clayman, S. E.
1993   Reformulating the question. A device for answering/not answering questions in interviews and press conferences. *Text* 13: 159–188.

Clayman, S. E. and J. Heritage
2002   *The News Interview. Journalists and Public Figures on the Air*. Cambridge: Cambridge University Press.

Cotter, C.
2003   Prescription and practice. Motivations behind change in news discourse. *Journal of Historical Pragmatics* 4(1): 45–74.

Coupland, N.
2001   Stylization, authenticity, and TV news review. *Discourse Studies* III(4): 413–442.

Crystal, D.
2001   *Language and the Internet*. Cambridge: Cambridge University Press.

Deppermann, A.
2004   "Gesprächskompetenz" – Probleme und Herausforderungen eines möglichen Begriffs. In: M. Becker-Mrotzek and G. Brünner (eds.), *Analyse und Vermittlung von Gesprächskompetenz*, 7–14. Frankfurt am Main: Verlag für Gesprächsforschung.

Dirks, U.
2005   Pressekommentare zur größten Friedensdemonstration vor dem Irakkrieg (2003) aus transkultureller Perspektive – Eine Dokumentarische Gattungsanalyse. In: C. Fraas and M. Klemm (eds.), *Mediendiskurse – Bausteine gesellschaftlichen Wissens*, 286–308. Frankfurt: Lang.

Dor, D.
2003   On newspaper headlines as relevance optimizers. *Journal of Pragmatics* 35: 695–721.

Dorenbeck, N.
1997   Zweifelhafte Wegweiser. Pragmatische Charakteristika und kommunikative Strategie der SPIEGEL-Story. *Sprache und Literatur* 80: 83–95.

Dürscheid, C.
2005   E-Mail – verändert sie das Schreiben? In: T. Siever, P. Schlobinski, and J. Runkehl (eds.), *Websprache.net. Sprache und Kommunikation im Internet*, 85–97. Berlin: de Gruyter.

Eggs, E.
1996   Formen des Argumentierens in Zeitungskommentaren – Manipulation durch mehrsträngig-assoziatives Argumentieren? In: E. W. B. Hess-Lüttich, W. Holly, and U. Püschel (eds.), *Textstrukturen im Medienwandel*, 179–209. Frankfurt am Main: Lang.

Ekström, M.
2000   Information, storytelling and attractions: TV journalism in three modes of communication. *Media, Culture and Society* 22(4): 465–492.

Ekström, M.
2001   Politicians interviewed on television news. *Discourse and Society* 12(5): 563–584.

Fairclough, N.
1995   *Media Discourse*. London: Arnold.

Fang, Y.-J.
2001   Reporting the same events? A critical analysis of Chinese print news media texts. *Discourse and Society* 12(5): 585–613.

Fiske, J.
1987   *Television Culture. Popular Pleasures and Politics*. London: Methuen.

Giddens, A.
1984   *The Constitution of Society*. Cambridge: Polity Press.

Grosse, E.-U.
2001   Evolution et typologie des genres journalistiques. Essai d'une vue d'ensemble. *SEMEN* 13: 15–36.

Hardt-Mautner, G.
1992   *Making Sense of the News. Eine kontrastiv-soziolinguistische Studie zur Verständlichkeit von Hörfunknachrichten*. Frankfurt am Main: Lang.

Harris, S.
1991   Evasive action. How politicians respond to questions in political interviews. In: P. Scannell (ed.), *Broadcast Talk,* 76–99. London: Sage.

Hartley, J.
1982   *Understanding News. Studies in Communication*. London: Methuen.

Häusermann, J.
2005   *Journalistisches Texten. Sprachliche Grundlagen für professionelles Informieren (2 ed.)*. Konstanz: UVK.

Häusermann, J.
2007   Zugespieltes Material. Der O-Ton und seine Interpretation. In: Harun Maye, Cornelius Reiber, and Nikolaus Wegmann (eds.), *Original/Ton. Zur Mediengeschichte des O-Tons*. Konstanz: UVK.

Hickethier, K.
1997   Das Erzählen der Welt in den Fernsehnachrichten. Überlegungen zu einer Narrationstheorie der Nachricht. *Rundfunk und Fernsehen* 45(1): 5–18.

Holly, W.
2002   "Klare und normale Sprache" als sozialer Stil. Zu Elke Heidenreichs 'Brigitte'-Kolumnen. In: I. Keim and W. Schütte (eds.), *Soziale Welten und kommunikative Stile,* 363–378. Tübingen: Niemeyer.

Holly, W.
2005   Zum Zusammenspiel von Sprache und Bildern im audiovisuellen Verstehen. In: D. Busse, T. Niehr, and M. Wengeler (eds.), *Brisante Semantik. Neuere Konzepte und Forschungsergebnisse einer kulturwissenschaftlichen Linguistik,* 353–373. Tübingen: Niemeyer.

Hutchby, I.
1991   *Conversation and Technology: From the Telephone to the Internet*. Oxford: Polity.

Huth, L.
1985   Bilder als Elemente kommunikativen Handelns in den Fernsehnachrichten. *Zeitschrift für Semiotik* 7(3): 203–234.

Hymes, D.
1972   On communicative competence. In: J. B. Pride and J. Holmes (eds.), *Sociolinguistics*, 269–293. Harmondsworth: Penguin.

Jacobs, R. N.
1996   Producing the news, producing the crisis. Narrativity, television and news work. *Media, Culture and Society* 18: 373–397.

Jaworski, A. and I. Connell
1995   Telling journalistic stories. *Zeszyty Prasoznawcze* 36(1–2): 49–73.

Jaworski, A., R. Fitzgerald, and D. Morris
2003   Certainty and speculation in news reporting of the future: the execution of Timothy McVeigh. *Discourse Studies* 5(1): 33–49.

Jesensek, V.
1998   Zur Leistung der okkasionellen Lexik im politischen Pressekommentar. In: B. Kettemann, M. Stegu, and H. Stöckl (eds.), *Mediendiskurse. verbal-Workshop Graz 1996*, 133–140. Frankfurt am Main: Lang.

Johnson, S., J. Culpeper, and S. Suhr
2003   From "politically correct councillor" to "Blairite nonsense": disourses of "political correctness" in three British newspapers. *Discourse and Society* 14(1): 29–47.

Johnson, S. and S. Suhr
2003   From "political correctness" to "politische Korrektheit": discourses of "PC" in the German newspaper Die Welt. *Discourse and Society* 14(1): 49–68.

Jucker, A. H.
1992   *Social Stylistics. Syntactic Variation in British Newspapers*. Berlin/New York: de Gruyter.

Jucker, A. H.
2003   Mass media communication at the beginning of the twenty-first century. *Journal of Historical Pragmatics* 4(1): 129–148.

Keppler, A.
1994   *Tischgespräche. Über Formen kommunikativer Vergemeinschaftung am Beispiel der Konversation in Familien*. Frankfurt am Main: Suhrkamp.

Kleinberger, U.
2004   Mediale Einbettung von Textsorten und Texten. Am Beispiel von Laien und Experten in der Wirtschaftsberichterstattung am Fernsehen und im Internet. *Medienwissenschaft Schweiz* 2: 109–115.

Klemm, M.
2000   *Zuschauerkommunikation. Formen und Funktionen der alltäglichen kommunikativen Fernsehaneignung*. Frankfurt am Main: Lang.

Kniffka, H.
1980   *Soziolinguistik und empirische Textanalyse. Schlagzeilen und Leadformulierungen In: amerikanschen Tageszeitungen*. Tübingen: Niemeyer.

Kobozeva, I. M.
2005   Identification of metaphors in the political discourse of mass media: a pragmatic approach. In: W. Kallmeyer and M. N. Volodina (eds.), *Perspektiven*

auf Mediensprache und Medienkommunikation, 145–158. Mannheim: Institut für Deutsche Sprache.

Koller, V.
2004a   Businesswomen and war metaphors: "Possessive, jealous and pugnacious"? *Journal of Sociolinguistics* 4(1): 3–22.

Koller, V.
2004b   *Metaphor and Gender in Business Media Discourse*. Basingstoke: Palgrave Macmillan.

Kropf, T.
1999   Von den Schwierigkeiten mit dem klassischen Nachrichten-Aufbau – oder: Ein "Andock-Modell" als Alternative zum "Pyramiden-Modell". *Publizistik* 44(2): 200–216.

Kunelius, R.
1994   Order and interpretation: A narrative perspective on journalistic discourse. *European Journal of Communication* 9: 249–270.

Laakaniemi, R.
1987   An analysis of writing coach programs on American daily newspapers. *Journalism Quarterly* 2–3(64): 567–575.

Le, E.
2004   Active participation within written argumentation: metadiscourse and editorialist's authority. *Journal of Pragmatics* 36(4): 601–629.

Lind, R. A. and C. Salo
2002   The framing of feminists and feminism in news and public affairs programs in U.S. electronic media. *Journal of Communication* 52(1): 211–228.

Ljung, M.
2000   Newspaper genres and newspaper English. In: F. Ungerer (ed.), *English Media Texts – Past and Present*, 131–149. Amsterdam: Benjamins.

Lorda, U. C
2001   Les articles dits d'information: la relation de déclarations politiques. *SEMEN* 13: 119–134.

Luckmann, T.
1986   Grundformen der gesellschaftlichen Vermittlung des Wissens: Kommunikative Gattungen. In: F. Neidhardt, R. M. Lepsius, and J. Weiß (eds.), *Kultur und Gesellschaft*, 191–211. Opladen: Westdeutscher Verlag.

Luginbühl, M.
2004   Staged authenticity in TV news. An analysis of Swiss TV news from 1957 until today. *Studies in Communication Sciences* 4(1): 129–146.

Lugrin, G.
2001   Le mélange des genres dans l'hyperstructure. *SEMEN* 13: 65–96.

Luke, K. K. and T.-S. Pavlidou (eds.)
2002   *Telephone Calls: Unity and Diversity in Conversational Structure across Languages and Cultures*. Amsterdam: Benjamins.

Lutz, B. and R. Wodak
1987   *Information für Informierte. Linguistische Studien zu Verständlichkeit und Verstehen von Hörfunknachrichten*. Wien: Verlag der Österreichischen Akademie der Wissenschaften.

Mardh, I.
1980 *Headlinese. On the Grammar of English Front Page Headlines*. Lund: CWK Gleerup.

Marinos, A.
2001 *"So habe ich das nicht gesagt!" Die Authentizität der Redewiedergabe im nachrichtlichen Zeitungstext*. Berlin: Logos.

Marx, U.
2005 Entwicklung und Begründung einer präskriptiven Notation von Hörfunknachrichten und Vergleich mit empirisch deskriptiver Analyse. In: Norbert Gutenberg (ed.), *Schreiben und Sprechen von Hörfunknachrichten. Zwischenergebnisse sprechwissenschaftlicher Forschung*, 121–193. Frankfurt am Main: Lang.

McAdams, K. C.
1993 Readability reconsidered. A study of reader reactions to fog indexes. *Newspaper Research Journal* 1: 50–59.

Moirand, S.
2001 Du traitement différent de l'intertexte selon les genres convoqués dans les évènements scientifiques à caractère politique. *SEMEN* 13: 97–118.

Oomen, U.
1985 Bildfunktionen und Kommunikationsstrategien in Fernsehnachrichten. In: G. Bentele and E. W. B. Hess-Lüttich (eds.), *Zeichengebrauch in Massenmedien. Zum Verhältnis von sprachlicher Information in Hörfunk, Film und Fernsehen*, 155–191. Tübingen: Niemeyer.

Östman, J.-O. and A.-M. Simon-Vandenbergen
2004 Media discourse – extensions, mixes, and hybrids (special issue), introduction. *Text* 24(3): 303–306.

Peck MacDonald, S.
2005 The language of journalism in treatments of hormone replacement news. *Written Communication* 22: 275–297.

Perrin, D.
1999 Woher die Textbrüche kommen. Der Einfluß des Schreibprozesses auf die Sprache im Gebrauchstext. *Zeitschrift für Deutsche Sprache* 2: 134–155.

Perrin, D.
2001 *Wie Journalisten schreiben. Ergebnisse angewandter Schreibprozessforschung*. Konstanz: UVK.

Perrin, D.
2004 Journalistisches Schreiben – Coaching aus medienlinguistischer Perspektive. In: K. Knapp, G. Antos, M. Becker-Mrotzek, A. Deppermann, S. Göpferich, J. Grabowski, M. Klemm, and C. Villiger (eds.), *Angewandte Linguistik. Ein Lehrbuch*, 255–275. Tübingen: Francke.

Perrin, D.
2005 "Den Leuten die Sachen verdichten" – Kreativ schreiben unter Druck. In: K. Ermert and O. Kutzmutz (eds.), *Wie aufs Blatt kommt, was im Kopf steckt. Beiträge zum Kreativen Schreiben,* 34–54. Wolfenbüttel: Bundesakademie für kulturelle Bildung.

Perrin, D.
2006a Coaching im Umgang mit Medien. In: Eric Lippmann (ed.), *Coaching*, 201–214. Heidelberg: Springer.

Perrin, D.
    2006b   Verstanden werden. Vom doppelten Interesse an theoriebasierter, praxisgerichteter Textberatung. In: H. Blühdorn, E. Breindl, and U. Hermann Waßner (eds.), *Text – Verstehen. Grammatik und darüber hinaus*, 332–350. Berlin: de Gruyter.

Perrin, D. and M. Ehrensberger
    2007   Progression analysis: Tracing journalistic language awareness. In: M. Burger (ed.), *L' analyse linguistique des discours des médias : théories, méthodes en enjeux. Entre sciences du langage et sciences de la communication et des médias*. Québec: Nota Bene.

Perrin, D. and M. Ehrensberger-Dow
    2006   Journalists' language awareness: Inferences from writing, *Revista Alicantina de Estudios Ingleses* 19: 319–343.

Perrin, D., M. Schanne, and V. Wyss
    2005   *SRG SSR idée suisse – Sprachpolitik, Sprachnorm und Sprachpraxis am Beispiel der SRG SSR* (Forschungsgesuch an den Schweizerischen Nationalfonds zur Förderung der wissenschaftlichen Forschung, Programm NFP 56). Winterthur: Institut für Angewandte Medienwissenschaft.

Pietilä, V.
    1992   Beyond the news story: News as discoursive composition. *European Journal of Communication* 7: 37–67.

Püschel, U.
    1992   "guten abend und die welt hält den atem an." Berichte nach Skripts in den Fernsehnachrichten über den 19. August 1991 in Moskau. In: Joachim Dyck (ed.), *Rhetorik. Ein internationales Jahrbuch. Band 11: Rhetorik und Politik*, 67–84. Tübingen: Niemeyer.

Quinn, S.
    2005   *Convergent Journalism. The Fundamentals of Multimedia Reporting*. Frankfurt am Main: Lang.

Redd, T. M.
    1991   The voice of time. The style of narration in a newsmagazine. *Written Communication* 2(8): 240–258.

Renner, K. N.
    2001   Die Text-Bild-Schere. Zur Explikation eines anscheinend eindeutigen Begriffs. *Studies in Communication Sciences* 1(2): 23–44.

Renzi, A.
    2005   Power, hegemony and the language of tactical street television. In: Book of abstracts for the international conference *Language in the Media: Representations, identities, ideologies*, 12th–14th September 2005, University of Leeds.

Roeh, I.
    1982   *The Rhetoric of News in the Israel Radio. Some Implications of Language and Style for Newstelling*. Bochum: Brockmeyer.

Roth, A. L.
    2002   Social epistemology in broadcast news interviews. *Language in Society* 31: 355–381.

Roth, A. L.
    2005   "Pop Quizzes" on the campaign trail. *The Harvard International Journal of Press/Politics* 10(2): 28–46.

Ruhmann, G. and D. Perrin
2002   Schreibstrategien in Balance. Was Wissenschaftler von Journalistinnen lernen können. In: D. Perrin, I. Boettcher, O. Kruse, and A. Wrobel (eds.), *Schreiben. Von intuitiven zu professionellen Schreibstrategien*, 129–138. Wiesbaden: Westdeutscher Verlag.

Sawitzki, I.
2001   Zu okkasionellen Wortbildungen in der Pressesprache. Dargestellt an Substantiven in den Magazinen Focus, Spiegel und Stern. In: Jörg Meier and Arne Ziegler (eds.), *Deutsche Sprache in Europa. Geschichte und Gegenwart. Festschrift für Ilpo Tapani Piirainen zum 60. Geburtstag*, 385–400. Wien: Edition Praesens.

Schlobinski, P. and T. Siever
2005   Sprachliche und textuelle Merkmale in Weblogs. Ein internationales Projekt. *Networx* 46. Retrieved August 11, 2006, from http://www.mediensprache.net/networx/networx-46.pdf

Schröder, T.
2001   Im Vorfeld. Beobachtungen zur Satzstruktur in Zeitungsnachrichten. In: U. Breuer and J. Korhonen (eds.), *Mediensprache – Medienkritik*, 129–144. Frankfurt am Main: Lang.

Schubert, A. and W. Sendlmeier
2005   Was kennzeichnet gute Nachrichtensprache im Hörfunk? Eine perzeptive und akustische Analyse von Stimme und Sprechweise. In: Walter Sendlmeier (ed.), *Sprechwirkung – Sprechstile in Funk und Fernsehen*, 13–70. Berlin: Logos.

Schudson, M.
1982   The politics of narrative form: The emergence of news conventions in print and television. *Deadalus* 4: 97–112.

Schwitalla, J.
1993   Textsortenwandel in den Medien nach 1945 in der Bundesrepublik Deutschland. Ein Überblick. In: B. U. Biere and H. Henne (eds.), *Sprache in den Medien nach 1945*, 1–29. Tübingen: Niemeyer.

Selting, M.
1983   Institutionelle Kommunikation. Stilwechsel als Mittel strategischer Interaktion. *Linguistische Berichte* 86: 29–48.

Settekorn, W.
2001   Tor des Monats – Tor zur Welt. Zum Metapherngebrauch in Massenmedien. In: D. Möhn, D. Roß, and M. Tjarks-Sobhani (eds.), *Mediensprache und Medienlinguistik. Festschrift für Jörg Hennig*, 93–110. Frankfurt am Main: Lang.

Sleurs, K., G. Jacobs, and L. Van Waes
2003   Constructing press releases, constructing quotations: A case study. *Journal of Sociolinguistics* 7(2): 135–275.

Spranz-Fogasy, T.
2003   Kommunikationsstilistische Eigenschaften gesellschaftlicher Führungskräfte im Spiegel der Presse. In: S. Habscheid and U. Fix (eds.), *Gruppenstile. Zur sprachlichen Inszenierung sozialer Zugehörigkeit*, 171–187. Frankfurt am Main: Lang.

Stenvall, M.
    2003   An actor or an undefined threat? The role of "terrorist" in the discourse of international news agencies. *Journal of Language and Politics* 2(2): 361–404.

Toolan, M.
    2003   Le politiquement correct dans le monde français. *Discourse and Society* 14(1): 69–86.

Tuchman, G.
    1976   What is news? Telling stories. *Journal of Communication* 26(6): 93–97.

Ungerer, F.
    2000   News stories and news events: A changing relationship. In: F. Ungerer (ed.), *English media texts – past and present*, 177–195. Amsterdam: Benjamins.

Van Dijk, T. A.
    1988a   *News Analysis. Case Studies of International and National News in the Press*. Hillsdale/London: Erlbaum.

Van Dijk, T. A.
    1988b   *News as Discourse*. Hillsdale/London: Erlbaum.

Wolf, R. and T. Thomason.
    1986   Writing coaches. Their strategies for improving writing. *Newspaper Research Journal* 3(7): 43–59.

Wyss, V.
    2004   Journalismus als duale Struktur: Grundlagen einer strukturationstheoretischen Journalismustheorie. In: M. Löffelholz (ed.), *Theorien des Journalismus. Ein diskursives Handbuch (2. überarb. Aufl)*, 305–320. Opladen: Westdeutscher Verlag.

Zinken, J.
    2003   Ideological imagination: intertextual and correlational metaphors in political discourse. *Discourse and Society* 14(4): 507–523.

IV. Competence training

12. Communication training[1]

Annette Lepschy

This contribution proposes a system of categories which helps to discern teaching and learning methods aimed at developing communicative competence. On the basis of a definition of "conversation" and a task-oriented operationalisation of "communicative competence," methods of communicative teaching and learning processes will be divided, according to their didactic functions, into representation methods on the one hand and reviewing methods on the other. Finally, activating and receptive representation methods and reflective and analytical review methods will be discussed in view of their didactic efficiency.

Objective of this contribution. Communication trainers are generally faced with the problem of having to review the complexities of conversations in a very short space of time and to identify and interpret structures, processes, problems and dysfunctions in a manner that will allow them to suggest alternative procedures for improvement. The trainer is charged with the task to create a didactically efficent structure for each individual communication training. This structure must reflect the rationale of correlation between the interlocutory act, the learning targets, and the methods employed (see also Gutenberg 1996: 35–36).[2] The aim of this article is to provide an overview over those learning and teaching methods that are most conducive to developing communicative competence. The teaching and learning methods presented here will first be systematized according to their didactical function and then discussed. As a basis for this discussion, the subject conversation – at the modification and improvement of which all these methods are always aimed – will first be briefly outlined and the learning target communicative competence operationalised.

1. Subject-matter and learning target

1.1. Conversation

According to Becker-Mrotzek and Meier (1999: 19), conversation means "verbal and non-verbal human acts aimed at mutual understanding. Understanding here must be understood in the broad sense of establishing common meanings for practical goals" ["das auf Verständigung zielende sprachliche und nichtsprachliche Handeln von Menschen. Verständigung ist dabei in einem weiten Sinne als das Herstellen gemeinsamer Bedeutung für praktische Ziele zu verstehen."].[3] These practical goals are directed towards coming to terms with reality as expressed in diverse social forms and structures. In this sense, conversations can be conceived as actions aimed at mutual understanding "with a view to making a common cause or to acting in common for a certain cause" ["mit dem Ziel, etwas zur gemeinsamen Sache zu machen bzw. etwas gemeinsam zur Sache zu machen"] (Geißner 1988: 45). It can thus be assumed that conversation partners that aim at mutual understanding wish to communicate in a meaningful and efficient manner. Conversations can furthermore be characterised as situationally controlled, intentional and mutual acts aimed at reaching mutual understanding. In other words, communicative action always happens in a social and individual context that determines and controls every single interaction.

The specific social and individual structure in which the actors use language is called speech situation (Pawlowski 2005: 27–28). As acts aimed at mutual understanding, conversations are dynamic processes marked by the alternation of the speaking and the listening roles, and in which the interlocutors try to achieve a common purpose. Communication processes exhibit situation-related phase or sequence progressions and negotiation procedures. These progressions and procedures follow sequential rules and principles and can be controlled by specific speech actions.

1.2. Conversation-control tasks

The speech situation and the process structure of a conversation are the two factors the improvement of conversation abilities focuses on. In order to understand the importance of these two factors, one needs to take a closer look at the tasks interlocutors have to fulfil as regards the control of speech situation and process. Only on the basis of a description of these tasks, can one appreciate the communicative skills that are required to participate successfully in conversations.

1.2.1. *Situation control*

In conversations, one central task for the participants to reach mutual understanding is to find a common ground. A speech situation, being a constellation of social and individual conditions, is never static. The interlocutors keep the situation in a constant state of flux by relating it to themselves through subjective perceptions and evaluations. Speech situations are always the result of individual assessments and interpretations.

The mutual intent in a conversation, to "make a common cause" (Geißner 1988: 45), confronts the interlocutors with the problem of creating a mutual situational understanding in spite of possibly diverging assessments. Accordingly, before engaging in a conversation, the individual needs to look into the specific conditions of the situation by examining his own assessments of the speech situation and by contrasting and comparing them with the anticipated assessments of the conversation partners (see Pawlowski 2005: 27–50). For this purpose, he must on the one hand understand the interdependence of the influencing factors of a speech situation and their controlling powers, and he must on the other hand put himself in the situation of the conversation partners in order to know their possible assessments of the situation. The basic skill required here is perspective-taking.

1.2.2. Process control

The design of the current communication process confronts the participants with further control tasks. As to the control of the communication process, the following partial tasks are assigned to the conversation partners (Lepschy 1997: 167–186):[4]

Organisation of conversations: The participants must regulate the organisation of the conversation, i.e., they must organise the conversation and make sure it proceeds in a well-ordered fashion, both in terms of the total process and in terms of turn-taking.

Management of topic: The participants need to deal with the topic of the conversation. Dealing with the topic in terms of both content and intention includes all issues which the participants think relevant to the topic and on which they have agreed to focus on currently.

Design of relationships: The participants need to design their relationships. They need to establish and maintain relationships, and, if need be, resolve conflicts. Design of relationships also includes that the conversation partners act according to their situational role, i.e., that they keep the balance between social expectations and individual notions.

1.3. Learning target communicative competence[5]

In communication trainings, the focus is invariably on enhancing and developing the communicative competence of the participants. The learning target communicative competence has two dimensions: to start with, communicative competence aims at taking the participants from an intuitive problem awareness to an analytical one. Secondly, it endeavours to create a greater individual scope for interaction. These two dimensions include the capacity to interpret social norms and expectations in and for speech situations. To be able to react flexibly to situations, problems and conversation partners, means not to re-enact rigid, pre-established patterns, but to control communication processes consciously and in knowledge of action alternatives. Based on of the above task breakdown, the learning target communicative competence can be thus operationalised:[6]

Communicatively competent can be called who is able to take currently necessary decisions in specific speech situations and who can (re)act adequately in speech. He or she needs to be in a position to organise the conversation in accordance with the situation, to deal with the topic in a goal-oriented manner, and to create a co-operative relationship.

In this process, communicative competence is always both an expression and an awareness of personal and social identity; it also includes verbal skills (e.g., reasoning, informing, listening, structuring of processes) that should be developed and improved in equal parts in communication trainings.

2. Methods in teaching and learning processes

In the following, the methods that will help to understand and work on communicative competence, will be introduced and discussed. Teaching and learning methods in the field of oral communication mean those procedures that systematically enable and further the widening of the scope for interaction.

The methods discussed below are constituents of diverse concepts and show, both in terms of their provenance and purpose and in terms of their application in communication seminars, no systematic consistency. They have their origin and their fields of application as much in psychology, specifically in group dynamics,[7] and in economic education,[8] didactics and teaching methods,[9] speech science (*Sprechwissenschaften*)[10] and speech education (*Sprecherziehung*),[11] as in recent years in applied discourse analysis.[12]

In spite of some dissent between some methodological approaches,[13] the following pages will attempt to introduce a largely coherent, interdisciplinary methodological concept and include a critical assessment of the diverse methods as to their efficiency for communication trainings.

2.1. Didactic functions as differentiating criteria for methods

Accepting that the main focus of communication trainings is on how conversation partners can improve and control the communication process while taking into account all specific conditions, one can discern two types of methods or practices that differ in their didactic function in the teaching and learning process. Didactic function here describes the action goals teachers and learners pursue at different stages of the teaching and learning process.

1. First of all, the communication reality of the participants must be represented in the process
   a) in order to obtain reviewing material
   b) in order to implement and rehearse in the communication reality the action alternatives that have been developed.

Methods integrating a given communication reality into the teaching and learning process in order to work on them and translate the resulting action alternatives into communicative action, will be called representation methods.

2. Communication reality needs to be reviewed
    a) in order to apprehend it in a first step (perception) and
    b) to comprehend it, analytically and conceptually, in a second step (apperception).

These steps are prerequisite for the development of action alternatives. They are essential for the improvement of interaction behaviour as they turn a more or less intuitive problem awareness into a reflective and systematic approach.

Methods that help perceive and apperceive the individual communication reality and produce action alternatives, will be called reviewing methods.

2.2. Representation methods

Representation methods have been defined as procedures that incorporate a particular communication reality and its pertinent problems (allowing for the specific teaching and learning situation) into the teaching and learning process. The manner of representing a communication reality in a teaching and learning process can be carried out in various ways. In the following, activating and receptive methods will be distinguished.

2.2.1. Activating methods of representation

Activating methods of representation are geared towards producing interactions in which conversations can be experienced and explored.[14] These methods are simulations (role play), games and exercises. Here, in the form of real-life simulations and structured interaction exercises, experiences, perceptions and analytical results are implemented, experienced, retraced and reproduced. It will be assumed that even within the context of a seminar authentic conversations will be produced that reflect everyday communication problems and behavioural patterns of the participants.

2.2.1.1. Simulated conversations

By integrating parts of the communicative reality into the workshop process that will provide convincing illustrations of typical communcation problems, simulated conversations fulfil the didactic function of representation. There are numerous publications on simulated conversation (see, e.g., Schützenberger 1976; Keim 1992b; Sader 1986; Kochan 1980, van Ments 1985) but there is no single definition. Here, simulated conversations will be understood as interactions that currently possess an "as-if-character" (Mann 1956: 227; quoted in Sader 1986: 15). Simulated conversations are characterised by reconstructive/imitative and constructive/creative interactions. Simulations are reconstructive/imitative because they "simulate a reality given by the situation or action of a play and thereby make a designed representation of reality accessible in the experience of the play" [weil sie eine "durch die Spielsituation oder Spielhandlung vorgegebene Realtität simulieren und damit Spielrealität als gestaltetes Abbild von Realität erfahrbar machen"] (Keim 1992b: 134). The simulation represents, in a prototypical and model-like manner, slices of reality – in particular, typically difficult situations, personal and conflict constellations, and their verbal and nonverbal patterns. Participants in a simulation reconstruct these patterns and will draw on them during representations. Simulations are constructive/creative because their progression is dynamic and because in the course of the representation a new reality will be produced that cannot be predicted.[15]

Participants do not reproduce prefashioned dialogues; they have to perform, in a mutual process of impromptu speech and attentive listening behaviours, current and novel acts of communication. The individual interpretation of accepted behavioural patterns and the shaping of the simulated situation makes the specific communication process unique and unreproducible. For that reason, we can here also speak of a real, authentic communication process.[16] A simulation produces its own reality which, due to the specific seminar context, naturally differs from other communications in other contexts.

In practice, simulations can be realised in a variety of ways (see Becker-Mrotzek and Brünner 1999: 73–75). Their main difference lies in the manner in which the "as-if character" is being handled, i.e., how the setting (process and situation) is defined and which goals of action and cognitive interests are being pursued in the simulation.

As a rule, highly structured simulations will attribute determined roles to participants, including definite character traits of the parts to be played and instructions on how to behave during the conversation.[17] This type of simulation corresponds to traditional models of role theory, in which an ascribed role automatically implicates a set of conventional behavioural patterns which are then acted out in the conversation. Assessment here aims at identifying the deviations from traditional role models and role behaviours.

One shortcoming of this kind of simulation is that it often leaves participants uncertain about if and in what manner they can bring their own ideas, solutions and issues into play. As a complete denial of identity is impossible, this uncertainty can never be completely eliminated and instances of incoherence may be the consequence. The clash between instructions and individual behaviours may result in unauthentic acts and turn simulations into spectacles with game-show character.[18] There are other simulations in which the situation, or more specifically the group constellation (superior–assistant; client–salesperson), and the problem under revision will be specified; the interpretation of the roles and the presentation of the problem is left in the hands of the participants. In this case, the actors are required to relate the interpretation of their assumed role to their personal identity. That is to say, the simulation necessitates from the communicators to attune their personal and social identities in the interpretation of their roles – just as in "real life." It is by this very process that the scope for possible action is widened. At this point it needs to be emphasized again that simulations do not intend to represent the participant's reality congruently in all its dimensions (see Becker-Mrotzek 1994: 252). Simulations can, however, be distinguished in terms of their contiguity with the participants' professional communication reality. There is no categorically work-unrelated simulation, there are only work-unrelated simulations in terms of a specific seminar group. The more participants recognise their professional reality in the simulated situation, the greater will be the proximity to everyday communication. Without this, the communctication training will lose its essential attribute of participant-orientation. Reality-unrelated simulations first of all fall short of acknowledging the participants' professional reality and identity. The key question in the processes of selection and execution is whether participants can identify with the situation and their assigned role, or, more precisely, whether a simulation provides motivation for action. Secondly, an inadequate introduction to the situation will lead to problems that may compromise the efficency of simulated conversations. The use of simulations requires a high degree of transparency. It has to become clear that a simulated conversation is a tool that helps resolve communcation problems in an authentic and participant-oriented way. If the framework of such simulations can be made transparent, participants will, as a rule, engage with the process. They will also not be tempted to focus on incidental concerns by either justifying or apologizing for their behaviour or by constantly emphasizing that in real-life situations they would act differently.

Learning transfer is the chief goal of simulations (see Keim 1992b: 134). The experiences, knowledge and models for action alternatives gained in a simulation need to be correlated with the individual communication reality. It is not the simulation itself that will ensure a lasting benefit for the participants, but it is first and most of all the subsequent discussion, and the assessment of alternative strategies for interaction, that may initiate behavioural changes. This cannot be achieved by the simulation alone, but needs to be supported by subsequent evaluation and reflection in the form of feedback and analysis.

2.2.1.2. Structured communication xxcersises

Structured communication exercises have been, for the main part, adopted for communication trainings from group dynamics. In structured communication exercises, the focus is on specific aspects, functions and problems of communication processes in order to work on them individually (see also Rechtien 1999:

195; Neumann and Heß 2005: 55–56). Structured exercises may also concentrate on assigned and limited problems.[19] Furthermore, and in contrast to simulations, structured exercises do not include a prepared social setting that reflects a particular communication reality. Frequently, they are marked by deliberate alienation in order to bring communication phenomena and problems into relief. This reduction of communicative complexity is meaningful where single aspects and partial phenomena need to be delineated.

Intending to foster pertinent abilities and skills, structured exercises may be aimed at both the plane of cognitive and emotive capacity for reflection and at the instrumental plane of language and speaking performances. The controlled dialogue is one example of a structured exercise, which focusses on the single aspect of listening (see, e.g., Antons 2000: 87–91).

If structured communication exercises are not being interpreted with the help of adequate analytical methods, the relevance of the exercise for everyday communication reality will not become apparent to the participant. If this is happens, one may suspect that the instructors have used structured exercises "as panaceas for their own disorientation, and their lack of control and competence" ["als rettende Allheilmittel gegen die eigene Disorientiertheit, den mangelnden Durchblick und die ungenügende Handlungskompetenz"] (Antons-Volmerg 1989: 22). This is why structured communication exercises should be used sparingly and in a didactically effective and goal-oriented fashion.

2.2.2. Receptive methods of representation

Receptive methods of representation are characterized by their focus on the mental reconstruction of written records of communication reality. Among these are case studies and transcript analyses.

2.2.2.1. Case studies

Case studies are set and prototypical situation descriptions in which the situation will be considered from different angles, the problem identified, and, if need be, classified and its structure hierarchized (Is it, for instance, a managerial problem? If it is, can the difficulties be located at the level of lacking or inadequate communication, or, instead, at the level of structural organisation?). Case studies may vary in their degree of detail. They range from rather general situation descriptions to detailed accounts of the personalities of those involved, their motivations and behaviours. Frequently, they also include background information about the problem and interaction context of the described situation (e.g., about the company, its hierarchy, personnel structure etc.).

Through this analytical approach, case studies particularly assist perspective-taking. In order to be able to understand the complexity of a given situation and identify the structure of the problem, the participants need to reconstruct and understand different points of view. The didactic efficiency of case studies depends on the extent of the real-life changes that are effected by the interpretation of the situation description (see Keim 1992: 134–136). Case studies may lead to inconclusive and learning-inefficient discussions a) if the proposed cases are not participant-, problem-, and goal-oriented and b) if the subsequent analysis is not structured to that effect. This method has its obvious limitations in that speaking about a situation cannot replace acting in a situation and taking the currently necessary decisions.

2.2.2.2. Transcripts[20]

For some time now, discourse-analytically oriented communication trainings have been using transcripts of authentic conversations as their preferred method of representation (Becker-Mrotzek and Brünner 2004: 40–42, and 1999). Transcripts are written reconstructions of conversations. Each workshop is preceded by a more or less extensive phase of investigation, in which conversations from everyday working life are first taped and subsequently transcribed. These transciptions are the basis for analysis and development of action alternatives in the workshop.[21] In the teaching and learning process, the basis for an interpretation of the individual communication reality is thus its written form. Discourse-analytically oriented communication trainers prefer this representation method (see, e.g., Fiehler 1995: 148) because, in their opinion, material culled form "natural communication situations" ["natürlichen Kommunikationssituationen"] (Becker-Mrotzek/and Brünner 1992: 16) represents authentic communication and is better suited for teaching and learning processes.

One flaw, however, of this method is that the time-consuming production of transcripts generates a considerable time-gap between the actual situation and the training, and an emotional distance from the communication event. Experience has also shown that seminars cannot provide a complete analysis of the transcripts. There is always the danger of deviating from the relevant questions and getting lost in the analysis of details that only skirt the participants' vital communication problems and that cannot provide viable alternatives for action (see also Keseling 1992: 157).

2.2.3. A comparison of representation methods

Simulations and structured exercises ensure a high degree of emotional involvement because the communicators do not just (re)construct their communicative actions mentally – as they would in case studies or in the analysis of transcripts – but actually create and experience them as participants. Because the participants experience themselves as real actors and with all their senses, this total immersion is much closer to the actual communication reality. Just as in their communication reality, they must make current decisions and account for them. Through the reactions of their conversation partners they immediately experience the effects and consequences of their actions.

Unlike the experience of interaction in a simulation or in a structured exercise, the representation of communicative reality by means of case studies or transcripts creates an emotional detachment from the situation which may help develop action plans regardless of the situation or personal involvement. In contrast to simulations and excerises, participants here may distance themselves from the communicative event, adopt, as it were, a third-party view, without committing to specific roles, positions or behavioural patterns. Depending on the learning group, case studies and transcripts may offer "soft" access to simulated conversations, since they may lower resistance against simulations. Resistance is usually connected with the pressure of expectations that they must deliver a "perfect communicative performance." In practice, after the simulation, participants often feel disappointed with their performance ("Now, with hindsight, I know how I could have done it better/differently."). Because of the limitations of time, only very few get another opportunity to repeat the conversation and try alternative behaviours. While in simulations decisions always "have to be taken under pressure of time and often spontaneously" ["immer unter Zeitdruck und oftmals ad-hoc"] (Buddensieck 1992: 19), participants studying cases or transcripts have extensive opportunity to weigh the pros and cons of individual decisions. They can diagnose problem structures and action patterns and premeditate and structure alternative courses for action. Premeditated structures may then be be practiced in a simulation to provide experience-oriented learning.

Activating and receptive methods differ with respect to communicative activity on the one hand, and limitation to exclusively cognitive action plans on the other. Due to the inherent dynamics of a communicative action, opinions, emotions and attitudes tend to change during the interaction with a partner in a specific situation. Participants gain hands-on experience of the fact that conversations are current events, the outcome of which is determined by how the participants manage in to achieve mutual understanding in immediate interaction, and where current decisions must constantly be made that effect the development of the conversation.

In addition, activating methods of representation are employed subsequent to analyses of communication realities. By implementing and testing the results of analyses in a sanction-free environment, they help effect the transfer of action alternatives and problem solutions to interactions. As a result, the expansion of the scope for interaction will be assisted and consolidated.

When adult persons become sensitised to and aware of longstanding automatisms[22] and communicative patterns, these methods prove to be imperative because there is no other environment in which new behaviours can be tested without fear of the consequences or of sanctions. Testing new behavioural patterns means naturally adapting them to one's own repertory and thereby to gain in confidence (see Rechtien 1999: 195). Structured excercises help acquire and test communicative skills particularly on the instrumental level, e.g., in excersises focussed on attentive listening behaviour, comprehensibility, questioning techniques, or reasoning. The activating representation method of controlled dialogue, for instance, provides important insights into how conversation partners respond to one another, or rather, how difficult it may be to relate to the conversation partner in one's own contributions. At the same time, the exercise improves listening ability and so acquires, as it were, the status of a synthesising method for the application of communicative skills.

In comparison with simulations and case studies, structured exercises have, through focus on specific points and problems, the advantage of taking the pressure of a complex communication event and its multiple factors and aspects off the participants. Participants often feel overburdened by this complexity and are left with the impression of being unable to effect any changes in their communicative behaviour. Structured exercises realise at least partial achievements and so contribute substantially to the motivation of participants in a workshop process. At the same time, the reintegration of results into the totality of a communicative situation may prove difficult, since it demands a high level of transfer performance, which not all participants feel up to. Learning transfer can only be achieved if the transferability of knowledge and skills to the actual work situation can be made manifest and ensured (see von Rosenstiel 1995: 66).

Case studies and transcript analyses are not suited to consolidate and test communicative action alternatives. They do contain certain transfer aspects in that participants enact set situation descriptions or transcribed conversations in their minds and talk them through with others in order to diagnose causes and find solutions for the problems that have been identified. These blueprints for action alternatives are, however, limited to cognitive planning and are therefore no methods to test the enhanced communication skills in practice.

2.3.   Review methods

The communication reality represented in the teaching and learning situation is subject to reviewing. In revision, reflective and analytical methods can be applied.

Analytical reviewing methods for communication will be understood to be systematic methods with which conversations can be analysed in terms of its components, factors, processes and negotiation procedures. Communicative actions and processes are broken down into their constituents. The observations are comprehended through apperception, i.e. conceptually.

Analytical methods need to be distinguished from reflective methods. In comparison with analytical methods, reflection, in the sense of cogitation on one's own actions, thoughts, sensations and those of others, includes a considerably higher degree of self-experience, and focusses more closely on the subjectivity of observations and evaluations of communication processes. Reflective methods particularly aim at producing context sensitivity by attempting to increase the awareness of individual and group behaviour and by focussing on currently produced communicative effects. In contrast to analytical methods and by encouraging immediate feedback on observed communicative behaviour, reflection proceeds on the basis of subjective evaluations. This is the sense in which the term "reflective" needs to be understood.

On the basis of reflective and/or analytical reviewing, action alternatives will be jointly developed by instructors and students in a functional, and task- and problem-oriented manner, and then allocated and tried out.

While standard communication trainings often only present a collection and a listing of communication tips, which, however, have little or no connection with the particular conversation-type functions and situational needs, it is the explicit claim of speech-scientifically and discourse-analytically oriented communication trainings to develop action alternatives from reflective and analytical reviewing, since only in that manner a rationale for particular alternatives can be substantiated.

2.3.1. *Reflective review method: feedback*

Feedback can be defined as a subjective, individual, immediate, and, in general, verbal response from one person to another, making explicit how a behaviour in a specific situation was perceived and what its effects were. This method is called reflective because feedback favours a subjective response to communication processes. Feedback answers questions such as: What am I doing when I am talking to others? What effect does this have on my conversation partners and how do they experience this situation? Feedback helps review the "processes of coding, transmission and decoding" ["Kodierungs-, Übermittlungs- und Dekodierungsvorgänge"] (Rechtien 1999: 202) by giving a feedback recipient information about "whether the result of a message reflects our intentions, and if not, for what reasons" ["ob das Ergebnis einer Mitteilung dem entspricht, was wir beabsichtigten bzw. wenn nicht, woran dies liegen kann"] (Rechtien 1999: 202). On the one hand, feedback needs to be distinguished from offhand commentaries on the interactions of others (see Rechtien 1999: 183). On the other hand and unlike analytical and psychotherapeutic procedures, it is a structured and controlled process of self-experience that becomes effective in interactions.

Therefore, we can speak of feedback only if it follows specific rules. Especially in contrast to psychotherapeutic methods, feedback is no study of causes for a specific communicative behaviour. Feedback does not aim at discovering repressed complexes or unresolved conflicts that may be the cause for a certain behaviour, but it is a "theory- and indicator-oriented, intentional behaviour aiming at changes in a group process or its members" ["ein theorie- und indikationsbezogenes, absichtsvolles Verhalten, das darauf gerichtet ist, Veränderungen im Prozess einer Gruppe oder ihrer Mitglieder zu bewirken"] (Voigt and Antons 1987: 30). Feedback trains the perceptional sensitivity for interactions and communication processes and initiates a confrontation of self-image and other-image from which a problem awareness for indivdiual communicative action emerges.

The particular efficency of feedback with regard to creating communicative action alternatives lies in its capacity of showing that there are no communication behaviours that are unequivocally right or wrong. Feedback just measures situational effects the perception of which may vary considerably (see Geißner 1982: 43). To focus on the individual, subjective and emotional aspects of communication is the outstanding feature of the feedback method. Precisely because it is confined to the persons involved, and to the feedbacker in particular, there cannot be any claim to universal validity, accuracy or truth. Feedback, therefore, is not a diagnostic or critical instrument that can discern and assess effective and ineffective communication.

In trainings, feedback is used to support the learning process, since in real-life situations the behavioural pattern of explicit and intentional feedback never or rarely occurs. Precisely for that reason feedback may produce resistance, since feedback recepients often feel confused and disoriented by the variety of effects that other participants and the instructor specify in their feedbacks. Simultaneously, participants tend to book communication trainings expecting to receive patent expert guidelines and directions for correct and successful communication behaviour.

To most people, feedback appears to be an unusual way to communicate, "since in our society feedback is thought to be unorthodox, improper, rude or even taboo. [...] Usually, feedback is not given for fear of hurting, insulting or simply because 'it's not done'" ["da Rückmeldungen in unserer Gesellschaft in den meisten Fällen als ungewöhnlich, ungebührlich, unhöflich oder gar als Tabu gilt (...) Oft wird Feedback gar nicht gegeben, aus Angst zu verletzen, zu beleidigen oder 'weil man es nicht tut'"] (Rechtien 1999: 203).

In communication trainings, therefore, feedback often carries out a double function. On the one hand, it functions as a reflective method for communicative behaviour; simultaneously, it supports the ability to accept and give criticism and thus is a hands-on method for acquiring communicative compentence. From an interactionist point of view it thereby particularly improves the individual's ambiguity tolerance and thus makes an important contribution to the individual's ability to deal with criticism and conflicts in conversations (see Slembek 1996: 323; 1998: 57–61).

2.3.2. Analytical review methods

Analytical review methods are repeatable observations and reconstructions of communicative behaviour that are structured by categories. The methodological need to analyse communicative behaviour arises from the didactic requirement that a controlled improvement of communication processes can only be initiated if the pertinent problems have been identified and analysed. In order to exceed the "tips and advice" level, the development of well-founded communicative action alternatives requires an analytical problem description. Analytical methods aim at a cognitive, disinterested description and awareness of communication processes. As a rule, the analysis involves a greater emotional dissociation from the aspect in focus; in contrast to feedback, a communication in which the analyst himself is not involved can also be the object of the analysis. Analytical methods can be used for both situation and process analyses.

2.3.2.1. Situation analysis

Speech situation analysis has its background in speech science, and it has been operationalised as an analytical instrument for communications by Geißner (1988: 72). With the help of so-called speech situation factors, this device measures the set of individual and social preconditions under which communication in general, and conversations in particular, happen. It highlights the reciprocity in which individual communicators find themselves with their social context. Since speech situations are no fixed, unchangeable constellations, but are, on the one hand, constantly reconstituted, and constantly reassessed and reinterpreted by the communicators on the other, the analysis of the preconditions of the event is elemental to any analysis of interaction.

The speech situation model is an analytical device that serves, with the help of conditional factors in the form of questions, to analyse a speech situation (see Geißner 1988: 72). Among the factors constituting a speech situation are the conversation target and motive, the constellation of conversational partners with their roles and role expectations, topic, language and the temporal and local conditions.

The analysis of motives and goals (Why and Wherefore) of conversations is requisite because it reveals the functions that communications have in social structures. By broaching the issue of situation evaluations, it can help detect potential "hidden agendas" and goal conflicts. Since in a conversation individuals with different backgrounds meet, the social structure of relationships in personal constellations needs to be analysed, which will generally surface as a complex texture of role expectations. It is also essential to analyse the differing parts of social and personal identity that are expressed in a communication. The topic analysis (What about) is intimately connected with the goal analysis. The main point here is to examine the relation between the focussed topics and the goal of the conversations. The focussed topics are the partial subject-matters that the participants have accepted and deemed relevant to the context. Likewise, the analysis attempts to bring out how communicative intentions (What and How) are verbalised. Can typical, problematic or common uses of language and speech be identified in specific communication situations? And what may be the reasons for such uses? Which effects do these uses have?

Furthermore, a situation analysis will look at the temporal and spacial conditions (Where and When) in which a communication takes place. In this connexion, the structural conditions and the possibilities to initiate change need to be examined. Participants carry out the analysis both from their own point of view and from that of their partners, since only perspective-taking will reveal diverging situation evaluations. This twofold analysis by means of the speech situation model creates an awareness for the complexity of the speech situation and potentially diverging situation evaluations. This is the basis for a conceivably necessary reorientation before or during the conversation. Speech situation analysis contributes to determine opportunities to modify speech situations. Modifications may include time and place, corrections of goals or a readjustment of role interpretations and role attitudes.

2.3.2.2. Process analysis

Process analysis examines the interactive procedures applied in conversations in terms of the tasks participants have to perform in order to control the process. The following task levels are the object of a process analysis: organisation of conversation, management of topic, and the design of relationship in a conversation.[23] Didactically, process analysis aims at answering the following questions:

Organisation of conversations:
– What do participants need in order to organise the conversation in terms of both the total process and in terms of the organisation and co-ordination of turn-taking?
– Did the participants organise the conversation? Were there marked transitions between the individual phases of the conversation, e.g., the opening and the middle phases?
– How can the participants ensure the intentional and content-oriented development of the currently focussed topics considered relevant for the subject under discussion?
– Were rules introduced to ensure a well-ordered process?
– Were current speakers able to finish their turn, and, if not, were interruptions dealt with adequately?

Management of topic:
- Did the conversation goal become apparent, i.e., did the speakers determine it?
- Did the speakers manage to structure the topic of the conversation?
- Were issues and problems sufficiently explicated to keep everyone on the same level of information (e.g., by asking questions, active listening, summaries)?
- Did the interlocutors make arrangements and record results?
- In what way did the speakers deal with the argumentation and the objections of their partners?
- Were personal interests made explicit?
- Was the conversation terminated at a moment appropriate for both goal and topic?

Design of relationship:
- How did the participants establish their relationship (e.g., greetings)?
- How did the speakers manage to maintain their relationship throughout the conversation, e.g., in case of misunderstandings or disagreement?
- How did the participants deal with aggressive behaviour or strategic reasoning?

In communication trainings, such a list of questions proves to be a helpful tool in the systematic analysis and evaluation of simulations and role plays with a clear focus on the development of action alternatives. There is always one follow-up question: What would have been the alternative options for action in this situation, or this phase or that sequence of the conversation?

Depending on the conversation type or the situation (negotiation, conflict talk, counselling or information interview), further analytical questions may be required. In this context, it is extremely helpful if the trainer has a high standard of field compentence, i.e., knowledge and background information about the individual speech situations.

The implementation of process analysis requires the introduction of analytical categories. Didactically, this can be defined as an instructive method – as opposed to reflective methods – where the instructor provides analytical categories. In teaching and learning processes it is critical that analytical results and categories are translated back into questions that ensure problem orientation and the forming of problem hierarchies (e.g.: Which problems in what field of responsibility are typical of conflict talks, negotiations, or sales talks?). On the one hand, the analysis aims at discovering problem typifications and problem structures in order to resolve them. On the other hand, it serves to analyse communicative requirements by attempting to establish the requirements that have to be met by the participants on different task levels in different conversation types.

Process analysis, the analysis of the actual progression of a conversation, is, methodologically, the most complex and, up to date, one of the least satisfactorily resolved tasks in communication workshops. The principal reason for this is that linguistic methods of analysis and their categories are not easily transferred to teaching and learning environments. The application of process analytical methods to teaching and learning processes requires more manageable and simplified analytical rasters, with which the process of conversations can be analysed in a didactically meaningful way, i.e., a way that serves to generate action alternatives that can be worked on. Micro-analyses concerned with individual phenomena need to be reintegrated into the totality of the process. The tools of analytical differentiation must be flexible and able to generate problem hierarchies. Constant reference to the totality of the process is necessary, since the focus of communication seminars is on the specific communication problems of the participants. The aim of such seminars is not a complete micro-analysis, but the identification of problems specific to certain individuals and conversation types so as to offer solutions. The specific density of the analysis must meet the requirements of the group, the schedule and of other circumstances in which the seminar takes place.

The greatest dissent between speech scientific and discourse analytical approaches surfaces precisely with regard to this question. In seminars that prefer a speech scientific approach, analytical methods clearly come second to reflective methods such as feedback.[24] On the whole, speech educators are sceptical about applying process analytical methods. One of the reasons for this scepticism lies in the fact that learning processes in the field of oral communication can only be initiated through a high degree of individual participation and self-experience. The second reason is that most of the problems connected with the didactic implementation of process analysis still remain unresolved. Speech educators prefer to use reflective methods in their seminars. But these methods are, to some extent, also guided by a set of specific criteria, which is attested to by the observation catalogues used for evaluation in speech scientifically-oriented seminars. Bartsch (1987), for instance, distinguishes observation criteria that pertain to surface structure (e.g., visual, acoustic, language) and criteria that pertain to deep structure (e.g., topic relatedness, argumentation; signals for opinions/positions; signs of social or intellectual creativity). Bartsch (1988) also proposes a phase structure model for non-person oriented conversations, which includes a phasing proposal for problem-solving conversations. A descriptive analytical model serving to identify and analyse speech actions and their communicative effects, has also been developed by Bartsch and Pabst-Weinschenk (2004: 127). This model, however, is restricted to single speech actions or conversational steps. In Geißner, assessment aids for process observations can also be found, but they have been tailored to primarily suit phenomena of group dynamics (see, e.g., 1982: 111–112). Their application is specifically geared towards what he calls the elementary forms of rhetorical communication, i.e., (dispute-)resolving and conflict conversations (also see Gutenberg 1979). Additionally, Geißner introduces an analytical instrument for documentation, the conversation process sociograph ("Gesprächsverlaufssoziogramm"). This formal raster for process observation should be employed "if a group ought not simply be left to their own devices, or if the skills in giving and receiving feedback have not yet been sufficiently developed" ["wenn eine Gruppe nicht nur ihren eigenen Fähigkeiten überlassen werden soll, oder wenn die Fähigkeiten im Feedback (geben und nehmen) noch nicht weit genug entwickelt sind"] (Geißner 1982: 107). On the one hand, the conversation process sociograph can provide a quantitative analysis of the conversation process by measuring the distribution of contributions by individual participants. It can also be used to record comments on the quality of the contributions "by marking down a participant's constructive or disruptive interventions" ["Markierung gruppendienlicher oder -störender TN-Interventionen"] (Geißner 1982: 107).[25] This method does, however, not include categories for a systematic analysis of conversation processes.

In discourse-analytically oriented communication trainings, teaching heavily relies on transcript-based process analyses. Becker-Mrotzek only gives a few general hints on how process analyses could be didactically operationalised in discourse-analytically oriented seminars (e.g., Becker-Mrotzek and Brünner 1999: 42–46).

2.3.3. *A comparison of reflective and analytical review methods*

Feedback is an intervention controlled by the trainer: the instructor initiates and builds in feedback as a methodological part of the training. The trainer's feedback must not, however, be mistaken for expert feedback; instead, it must be on par with the feedback of the participants. Employing analytical methods, on the other hand, requires expert knowledge. To be able to apply specific analytical categories, the participants need to be first instructed by their trainer.

While analysis inevitably needs expert knowledge, it is precisely the participants' everyday knowledge and competencies that make feedback so effective. Consequently, analysis cannot replace feedback; conversely, feedback is not a layperson's substandard form of analysis.

In contrast to analytical methods, feedback is not an instrument that claims to describe communicative reality regardless of individual and temporal aspects. Rather, it is an expression of an individual and immediate response by one person to the communicative behaviour of another. It mirrors perceptions back to the actor (also see Slembek 1996: 323). Reflective reviewing by feedback thus produces individual, personal and situational insights. As communication is always situational, feedback cannot be repeated: it is a one-off and only valid for the currently described situation and the observed communication process.

This distinguishes feedback clearly from analytical methods that use specific rasters which can be applied to, and independent of, a variety of situations and which, to a certain degree, back up their claim for objectivity.

Analysis may yield insight into structures of specific conversation types such as conferences, team meetings, appraisal interviews, and their processes and offer more tightly structurally focussed options for the development of action alternatives.

Both the review models described above should not be regarded as rivalling methods, but as useful complements to one another. While analysis integrates a portion of social structural actuality into the seminar and thus counterbalances the impending danger of a communication "island" ("It's all different in the real world anyway"), feedback successfully emphasizes the situational aspect of interactions and their effects. Both kinds of experience are necessary to the remodeling of communicative behaviour.

3. Outlook

This contribution has attempted to systematize and describe, according to their didactic functions, teaching and learning methods primarily applied by speech educators and discourse analysts. The performance of the methods here presented does however not depend on the school from which they hail; in the first place, it depends on their effective integration into the didactic conception of the seminar and on the reflection of the learning target. For the development of distinct discourse analytically and speech scientifically oriented teaching and learning conceptions (and also to mark off this approach from psychological ones), this would imply to overcome the stereotyped prejudices against the other method. The choice of method should be determined by didactic function.

Methods of representation and review methods need to be viewed as integral parts of communication trainings. Both activating and receptive methods of representation and reflective and analytical review methods should be looked on not as competing but as complementary with regard to the learning target, i.e., the widening of the participants' scope for communicative action.

In the choice of procedure, one should keep in mind that communication must be taught and experienced on multiple levels. The methods must provide learning through practice, emotional motivation through self-experience, cognitive acquisition of knowledge through communication, and the acquirement of instrumental skills. This can be ensured by a diligently balanced alteration of methods. Specifically, the development of a didactic inventory for conversation analysis and of synthesizing methods appears to be a central future task for applied linguistics.

Notes

1. This contribution is a revised and extended version of Lepschy 1999.
2. The question whether communicative competence can be taught and learnt at all, is discussed elsewhere; e.g., Gutenberg 1988; Antos 1992; Fiehler 1999.
3. All quotations in this text are from German sources. Hereafter, the original German text will be given in square brackets, following the translation.
4. See, in particular, Schwitalla (1979) and his thoughts on dialogue control.
5. For the definition of "communicative competence" see also Hymes 1987, Becker-Mrotzek and Brünner 2004: 29, Fiehler and Schmitt 2004: 114, Hartung 2004: 47.
6. In educational literature these abilities are often called core qualifications ("Schlüsselqualifikationen"): among these are abilities like creativity, problem resolving, the ability to deal with criticism and conflicts, the capacity for teamwork (see Kaiser 1992: 62, and Keim 1992b: 144).
7. See, mainly, Antons (1992) who can be called a classic in the field of group dynamic exercises; Rechtien (1999) provides a good overview over the taxonomy and the history of group dynamics.
8. See, e.g., Keim (1992a).
9. Here also, only an exemplary reference, Meyer, H. (1989).
10. In Germany, *Sprechwissenschaft* (speech science), is an application-oriented discipline that studies oral communication. Its four fields of study include: rhetorical communication, aesthetic communication (art of speaking, theatre), therapy (logopedics), and voice and speech coaching. *Sprechwissenschaft*, as the theory, and *Sprecherziehung* (speech education) as the didactics and methodology of oral communication, are dialectically interrelated. See Geissner 1992 and 1988; see also Gutenberg 2001, 18–19; Lüschow 1991: 7 and Pabst-Weinschenk 2004, 261–263.
11. Conceptually independent conversation theories can be found, first of all, in Geißner and his theory and practice of rhetorical communication (et al. 1982). Bartsch and Pabst-Weinschenk propose their approach of co-operative dialogue rhetorics, which they have specifically developed with regard to topical conversations like negotiations (2004: 122–125); see also the overview in Gutenberg/Herbig (1992).
12. See, e.g., Fiehler and Sucharowski (1992); Bliesener and Brons-Albert (1994).
13. The main differences are between speech science and applied discourse analysis, particularly with regard to the application of simulated conversations and transcripts. See the discussion in the following chapters on transcript analysis and on simulations. On these differences, see also Lepschy 2004: 277–286, and Lepschy 1995.
14. In the concept elaborated here, psychotherapeutic methods, which aim at a change in the psychic setup, will not be considered. In contrast to therapeutic methods, the methods described here do not aim at a change in the individual psyche. Through the awareness of the effects of language and speech, they wish to initiate a change in communicative attitudes and actions. For the differences between communication trainings and psychotherapeutic concepts, see Keseling 1992.
15. See Bliesener's conflicting opinion: "Role play is a communication process in which the common requisites and consequences of actions are suspended and replaced by secondary ones. Therefore, one may call the special framework of

communication in role plays 'artificial'" ["Das Rollenspiel ist ein Kommunikationsprozess, bei dem die üblichen Voraussetzungen und Folgen von Handlungen gekappt und durch sekundäre ersetzt sind. Wenn man will, kann man diesen besonderen Rahmen der Kommunikation in Rollenspielen als 'künstlich' bezeichnen"] (Bliesener 1994, 15).
16. See also, for a similar assessment, Friedrich (1994, 10): "Reality and simulation will remain incongruent for the simple fact that simulation is its own reality, its own actuality with its own rules" ["Realität und Simulation sind deshalb nicht in völlige Übereinstimmung zu bringen, weil die Simulation selbst eine eigene Realtität, eine eigene Wirklichkeit mit eigenen Gesetzen darstellt"]. Other discursive analysts emphasize that they cannot call simulations authentic (see, above all, Bliesener and Brons-Albert 1994). This is one of the major quarrels between discourse analysts and speech scientists, which I feel unable to reconcile. In this case, I defend a position which contradicts that of the discourse analysts.
17. See, e.g., the collection of role plays in Birkenbihl 1988.
18. In these instances, in effect, one must question whether the performers are able to generate "authentic" motivations for action.
19. These include, e.g., dealing with perceptions, listening and comprehension (controlled dialogue), decision making, problem resolving in groups, dealing with prejudices, norms, co-operative vs. competitive behaviour etc. Collections of exercises can be found in, e.g., see Antons 2000; Francis and Young 1996; Dießner 2005; Pawlowski, Lungershausen, and Stöcker 1985; Geißner 1982.
20. The significance of transcripts in communication trainings is another "bone of contention" in discussions between discourse analysts and speech scientists. I think that in future one should not discuss the method itself, but its didactic function in the training.
21. On this, see, Fiehler's criticism of so-called "patterns of disapproval" that frequently are the basis for reflection in communication trainings: "The stated objective of the discussions (between teacher and learner, A. L.) is for trainer and participant to pinpoint difficult, ineffective or wrong behaviours of the interlocutors and suggest better and more effective ways that the participants are supposed to actualise in future conversations" ["Erklärtes Ziel der Besprechungen ist, dass Trainer und Teilnehmer gemeinsam problematische, ineffektive, falsche Verhaltensweisen der Gesprächsteilnehmer herausarbeiten und bessere, effektivere Möglichkeiten aufzeigen, die von den Teilnehmern dann in späteren Gesprächen realisiert werden sollen"] (1999: 21).
22. For the deautomatization and reautomatization of communicative actions in trainings, see Schwandt 2005: 97–106.
23. This taxonomy is meant as a proposal for an effective handling of the inherently complex communication process.
24. Many speech educators even dismiss these methods by pointing out that communication classes are not linguistic foundation courses. It seems to me, however, that this displays more of a reservation concerning linguistic competition than well-grounded misgivings about analytical methods.
25. In this context, see Geißner's criticism of the so-called "thermostat feedback" ["Thermostat-Feedback"] (1996, 290).

References

Ammon, U., N. Dittmar, and K. Mattheier (eds.)
    1987   *Soziolinguistik. Ein internationales Handbuch zur Wissenschaft von Sprache und Gesellschaft, Band 1.* Berlin/New York: De Gruyter.
Antons, K.
    2000   *Praxis der Gruppendynamik* Göttingen/Toronto/Zürich: Hogrefe.
Antons-Volmerg, K.
    1989   Nachdenkliches zu einem scheinbar abgekühlten Dauerbrenner. *Gruppendynamik* 12: 11–28.
Antos, G.
    1992   Demosthenes oder: Über die "Verbesserung der Kommunikation". Möglichkeiten und Grenzen sprachlicher-kommunikativer Verhaltensänderungen. In: R. Fiehler and W. Sucharowski (eds.), *Kommunikationsberatung und Kommunikationstraining. Anwendungsfelder der Diskursforschung,* 52–67. Opladen: Westdeutscher Verlag.
Bartsch, E.
    1987   Gesprächstechniken und -methoden als Grundlagen für Verhandlungen und Konferenzen. Universität Duisburg (unveröffentl. Seminarpapier)
Bartsch, E.
    1988   The organisation of intercultural negotiation modes within a communication model. In: J. Lehtonen (ed.), *Speech in the Future and the Future of Speech,* 85–104. Jyväskyla:: Universita of Jyväskyla.
Bartsch, E.
    1990   Grundlagen einer "Kooperativen Rhetorik". In: Hellmut Geißner (ed.), *Ermunterung zur Freiheit. Rhetorik und Erwachsenenbildung,* 37–50. (Sprache und Sprechen 23/24) Frankfurt am Main: Reinhardt.
Bartsch, E. (ed.)
    1994   *Sprechen – Führen – Kooperieren in Betrieb und Verwaltung,* (Sprache und Sprechen 29), München: Reinhardt.
Bartsch, E. and M. Pabst-Weinschenk
    2004   Gesprächsführung. In: M. Pabst-Weinschenk (ed.), *Grundlagen der Sprechwissenschaft und Sprecherziehung,* 122–133. München: Ernst Reinhardt.
Becker-Mrotzek, M.
    1994   Gesprächsschulung für Mitarbeiter und Mitarbeiterinnen öffentlicher Dienstleistungsunternehmen auf linguistischer Basis. In: E. Bartsch (ed.), *Sprechen – Führen – Kooperieren in Betrieb und Verwaltung,* 240–254 (Sprache und Sprechen 29), München: Reinhardt.
Becker-Mrotzek, M. and G. Brünner (eds.)
    2004   *Analyse und Vermittlung von Gesprächskompetenz.* Frankfurt am Main: Peter Lang.
Becker-Mrotzek, M. and G. Brünner
    2004   Der Erwerb kommunikativer Fähigkeiten: Kategorien und systematischer Überblick. In: M. Becker-Mrotzek and G. Brünner (eds.), *Analyse und Vermittlung von Gesprächskompetenz,* 29–46. Frankfurt am Main: Peter Lang.

Becker-Mrotzek, M. and G. Brünner
1999   Simulation authentischer Fälle (SAF). In: G. Brünner, R. Fiehler, and W. Kindt (eds.), *Angewandte Diskursforschung, Band 2: Methoden und Anwendungsbereiche,* 72–80. Wiesbaden: Westdeutscher Verlag.
Becker-Mrotzek, M. and G. Brünner
1992   Angewandte Gesprächsforschung: Ziele – Methoden – Probleme. In: R. Fiehler and W. Sucharowski (eds.), *Kommunikationsberatung und Kommunikationstraining. Anwendungsfelder der Diskursforschung,* 12–23. Opladen: Westdeutscher Verlag.
Becker-Mrotzek, M. and C. Meier
1999   Arbeitsweisen und Standardverfahren der Angewandten Diskursforschung. In: G. Brünner, R. Fiehler, and W. Kindt (eds.), *Angewandte Diskursforschung, Band 2: Methoden und Anwendungsbereiche,* 18–45 Wiesbaden: Westdeutscher Verlag.
Birkenbihl, M.
1988   *Train the Trainer. Kleines Arbeitshandbuch für Ausbilder und Dozenten.* Landsberg am Lech: Verlag Moderne Industrie.
Bliesener, T.
1994   Authentizität in der Simulation. In: T. Bliesener and R. Brons-Albert (eds.), *Rollenspiele in Kommunikations- und Verhaltenstrainings,* 13–32. Opladen: Westdeutscher Verlag.
Bliesener, T. and R. Brons-Albert (eds.)
1994   *Rollenspiele in Kommunikations- und Verhaltenstrainings,* Opladen: Westdeutscher Verlag.
Brinker, K. and S. F. Sager
1996   *Linguistische Gesprächsanalyse. Eine Einführung.* Berlin: Erich Schmidt.
Brünner, G., R. Fiehler and W. Kindt (eds.)
1999   *Angewandte Diskursforschung, Band 2: Methoden und Anwendungsbereiche.* Wiesbaden: Westdeutscher Verlag.
Buddensieck, W.
1992   Entscheidungstraining im Methodenverbund – Didaktische Begründung für die Verbindung von Fallstudie und Simulationsspiel. In: H. Keim (ed.), *Planspiel, Rollenspiel, Fallstudie,* 9–23. Köln: Wirtschaftsverlag Bachern.
Dahmen, R. (ed.)
1979   *Erziehung zur politischen Mündigkeit,* Otzenhausen.
Dießner, H.
2005   *Neue gruppendynamische Übungen. Kreatives Kommunikationsmanagement. Basis Arbeitsbuch.* Paderborn: Junfermann.
Domsch, M., E. Regnet, and L. von Rosenstiel (eds.)
2003   *Führung von Mitarbeitern. Fallstudien zum Personalmanagement.* Stuttgart: Schaeffer-Poeschel.
Domsch, M., E. Regnet, and L. von Rosenstiel (eds.)
1995   *Führung von Mitarbeitern. Handbuch für erfolgreiches Personalmanagement.* Stuttgart: Schaeffer-Poeschel.
Dyck, J., W. Jens, and G. Ueding (eds.)
1980   *Rhetorik. Ein internationales Jahrbuch,* Bd. 1. Tübingen: Max Niemeyer

Fiehler, R.
1999 Kann man Kommunikation lehren? Zur Veränderbarkeit von Kommunikationsverhalten durch Kommunikationstrainings. In: G. Brünner, R. Fiehler and W. Kindt (eds.), *Angewandte Diskursforschung, Band 2: Methoden und Anwendungsbereiche*, 18–35. Wiesbaden: Westdeutscher Verlag.

Fiehler, R. and R. Schmitt
2004 Die Vermittlung kommunikativer Fähigkeiten als Kommunikation. Kommunikationstrainings als Gegenstand der Gesprächsanalyse. In: M. Becker-Mrotzek and G. Brünner (eds.), *Analyse und Vermittlung von Gesprächskompetenz*, 113–136. Frankfurt am Main: Peter Lang.

Fiehler, R. and W. Sucharowski (eds.)
1992 *Kommunikationsberatung und Kommunikationstraining. Anwendungsfelder der Diskursforschung.* Opladen: Westdeutscher Verlag.

Francis, D. and D. Young
1996 *Mehr Erfolg im Team.* Hamburg: Windmühle.

Friedrich, G.
1994 Begründungshandlungen in echter und simulierter Unterrichtskommunikation. In: T. Bliesener and R. Brons-Albert, (eds.), *Rollenspiele in Kommunikations- und Verhaltenstrainings*, 91–128. Opladen: Westdeutscher Verlag.

Geißner, H.
1979 Zur Lage der Sprechwissenschaft in der Bundesrepublik Deutschland. *Studium Linguistik* 7, 77–85

Geißner, H.
1982 *Sprecherziehung. Didaktik und Methodik der mündlichen Kommunikation.* Frankfurt am Main: Scriptor

Geißner, H.
1988 *Sprechwissenschaft. Theorie der mündlichen Kommunikation.* Frankfurt am Main: Scriptor

Geißner, H. (ed.)
1990 *Ermunterung zur Freiheit. Rhetorik und Erwachsenenbildung*, (Sprache und Sprechen 23/24) Frankfurt am Main: Reinhardt.

Geißner, H.
1996 "Linien ziehen im Fließenden" (W. Dilthey): Vom Oberflächen- zum Tiefenfeedback. In: S. Lemke and S. Thiel (eds.), *Sprechen – Reden – Mitteilen. Prozesse allgemeiner und spezifischer Sprechkultur,* 290–299. (Sprache und Sprechen Bd. 32) München/Basel: Ernst Reinhardt

Gutenberg, N.
1979 Gespräch und Interesse – Skizze eines Prozessmodells für Klärungs- und Streitgespräche. In: R. Dahmen (ed.), *Erziehung zur politischen Mündigkeit*, 91–129. Otzenhausen.

Gutenberg, N. (ed.)
1988 *Kann man Kommunikation lehren?*, (Sprache und Sprechen, Bd. 19) Frankfurt: Scriptor

Gutenberg, N.
1996 Grundzüge einer Methodenlehre der Sprecherziehung. In: S. Lemke and S. Thiel (eds.), *Sprechen – Reden – Mitteilen. Prozesse allgemeiner und*

spezifischer Sprechkultur, 35–42. (Sprache und Sprechen Bd. 32) München/ Basel: Ernst Reinhardt.

Gutenberg, N.
2001   *Einführung in die Sprechwissenschaft und Sprecherziehung.* Frankfurt am Main: Peter Lang.

Gutenberg, N. and A. Herbig
1992   Kommunikationspädagogische Konzepte in Sprechwissenschaft und Sprecherziehung. In: R. Fiehler and W. Sucharowski (eds.), *Kommunikationsberatung und Kommunikationstraining,* 370–380. Opladen: Westdeutscher Verlag.

Hartung, M.
2004   Wie lässt sich Gesprächskompetenz wirksam und nachhaltig vermitteln? Ein Erfahrungsbericht aus der Praxis. In: M. Becker-Mrotzek and G. Brünner (eds.), *Analyse und Vermittlung von Gesprächskompetenz,* 47–66. Frankfurt am Main: Peter Lang.

Hymes, D.
1987   Communicative competence. In: U. Ammon, N. Dittmar, and K. Mattheier (eds.), *Soziolinguistik. Ein internationales Handbuch zur Wissenschaft von Sprache und Gesellschaft, Band 1,* 219–229. Berlin/New York. De Gruyter.

Kaiser, F.-J.
1992   Der Beitrag partizipativer Methoden Fallstudie, Rollenspiel und Planspiel zur Vermittlung von Schlüsselqualifikationen. In: H. Keim (ed.)1992a *Planspiel, Rollenspiel, Fallstudie. Zur Praxis und Theorie lernaktiver Methoden,* 62–90. Köln: Wirtschaftsverlag Bachem.

Keim, H.(ed.)
1992a   *Planspiel, Rollenspiel, Fallstudie. Zur Praxis und Theorie lernaktiver Methoden.* Köln: Wirtschaftsverlag Bachem.

Keim, H.
1992   Kategoriale Klassifikation von Plan-, Rollenspielen und Fallstudien. In: H. Keim (ed.) 1992a, *Planspiel, Rollenspiel, Fallstudie. Zur Praxis und Theorie lernaktiver Methoden,* 122–151. Köln: Wirtschaftsverlag Bachem.

Keseling, G.
1992   Praktische Gesprächsanalyse. In: R. Fiehler and W. Sucharowski (eds.), *Kommunikationsberatung und Kommunikationstraining. Anwendungsfelder der Diskursforschung,* 143–160. Opladen: Westdeutscher Verlag.

Kochan, B. (ed.)
1980   *Rollenspiel als Methode sozialen Lernens.* Bodenheim: Athenaeum.

Lehtonen, J. (ed.)
1988   *Speech in the Future and the Future of Speech,.* Jyväskyla: Universita of Jyväskyla.

Lemke, S. and S. Thiel (eds.)
1996   *Sprechen – Reden – Mitteilen. Prozesse allgemeiner und spezifischer Sprechkultur,* (Sprache und Sprechen Bd. 32) München/Basel: Ernst Reinhardt.

Lepschy, A.
2004   Angewandte Gesprächsforschung. In: M. Pabst-Weinschenk (ed.), *Grundlagen der Sprechwissenschaft und Sprecherziehung,* 277–286. München: Ernst Reinhardt.

Lepschy, A.
1999 Lehr- und Lernmethoden zur Entwicklung von Gesprächsfähigkeit. In: G. Brünner, R. Fiehler, and W. Kindt (eds.), *Angewandte Diskursforschung, Band 2: Methoden und Anwendungsbereiche*, 50–71. Wiesbaden: Westdeutscher Verlag.

Lepschy, A.
1997 Ein analytisches und didaktisches Modell für die Situations- und Prozesssteuerung in Gesprächen. In: M. Pabst-Weinschenk, R. W. Wagner, and C. L. Naumann (eds.), *Sprecherziehung im Unterricht*, 159–173. (Sprache und Sprechen Bd.33) München/Basel: Ernst Reinhardt.

Lepschy, A.
1995 Zum Verhältnis von Sprechwissenschaft und linguistischer Gesprächsforschung. Ein Kooperationsversuch. *Sprechen* I, 4–23.

Lüschow, F.
1991 Einleitung: Überlegungen zu einer axiomatischen Sprechwissenschaft. In: F. Lüschow and M. Pabst-Weinschenk (eds.), *Mündliche Kommunikation als kooperativer Prozeß*. 2–15. Frankfurt am Main/Bern/New York/Paris: Peter Lang

Lüschow, F. and M. Pabst-Weinschenk (eds.)
1991 *Mündliche Kommunikation als kooperativer Prozeß*. Frankfurt am Main/Bern/New York/Paris: Peter Lang.

Mann, J. H.,
1956 Experimental evaluations of role-playing. *Psychological Bulletin* 53: 227–234.

Meyer, H.
1989 *UnterrichtsMethoden*. Bd. 1 und 2, Frankfurt am Main: Skriptor.

Neumann, E. and S. Heß
2005 *Mit Rollen spielen*, Bonn: managerSeminareVerlag.

Pabst-Weinschenk, M. (ed.)
2004 *Grundlagen der Sprechwissenschaft und Sprecherziehung*, München: Ernst Reinhardt.

Pabst-Weinschenk, M.
2004 Fachgeschichte: Von der Sprecherziehung zur Sprechkunde und Sprechwissenschaft. In: M. Pabst-Weinschenk (ed.), *Grundlagen der Sprechwissenschaft und Sprecherziehung*, 254–263. München: Ernst Reinhardt.

Pawlowski, K.
2005 *Konstruktiv Gespräche führen*, München: Ernst Reinhardt Verlag.

Pawlowski, K.
1980 Partnerzentriertes Sprechen als Dialogstrategie. Zur Theorie und Didaktik der Rhetorik. In: J. Dyck, W. Jens and G. Ueding (eds.) *Rhetorik. Ein internationales Jahrbuch*, Bd. 1. 70–88. Tübingen: Max Niemeyer.

Pawlowski, K., H. Lungershausen, and F. Stöcker
1985 *Jetzt rede ich. Ein Spiel- und Trainingsbuch zur praktischen Rhetorik*. Wolfsburg.

Rechtien, W.
1999 *Angewandte Gruppendynamik*. München: Beltz.

Rosenstiel, L. von
1995   Entwicklung und Training von Führungskräften. In: M. Domsch, E. Regnet and L. von Rosenstiel (eds.), *Führung von Mitarbeitern. Handbuch für erfolgreiches Personalmanagement*, 55–82. Stuttgart: Schaeffer-Poeschel.

Sader, M.
1986   *Rollenspiel als Forschungsmethode*. Opladen: Westdeutscher Verlag.

Schützenberger, A.
1976   *Einführung in das Rollenspiel*, Stuttgart: Klett-Cotta.

Schwandt, B.
2006   Kommunikation lernen. *Sprechen* 44/45, 97–106.

Schwitalla, J.
1979   *Dialogsteuerung in Interviews. Ansätze zu einer Theorie der Dialogsteuerung mit empirischen Untersuchungen von Politiker-, Experten- und Starinterviews in Rundfunk und Fernsehen*. München: Hueber.

Slembek, E.
1998   Feedback als hermeneutischer Prozess, In: E. Slembek and H. Geißner (eds.), *Feedback. Das Selbstbild im Spiegel der Fremdbilder*, 55–72. St. Ingbert: Röhrig Universitätsverlag.

Slembek, E.
1996   Kritik oder Feedback in der Arbeit mit Gruppen. In: S. Lemke and S. Thiel (eds.), *Sprechen – Reden – Mitteilen. Prozesse allgemeiner und spezifischer Sprechkultur*, 322–329. (Sprache und Sprechen Bd. 32) München/Basel: Ernst Reinhardt.

Slembek, E. and H. Geißner (eds.)
1998   *Feedback. Das Selbstbild im Spiegel der Fremdbilder*. St. Ingbert: Röhrig Universitätsverlag.

Van Ments, M.
1985   *Rollenspiel: effektiv*, München: Ehrenwirth.

Voigt, B. and K. Antons
1987   Systematische Anmerkungen zur Intervention in Gruppen. *Gruppendynamik* 18, 29–46.

13. Coping with the needs of presentation

Mike Allen, Nancy Burrell, and John Bourhis

This chapter focuses on influence of presenter's level of anxiety about communication on the perceptions of competence and effectiveness by message receivers. The first part of the chapter outlines the impact such anxiety about communication by the communicator generates in the perceptions of message receivers. The next part of the chapter focuses on the techniques used to diminish the level of anxiety felt by the communicator. The final part of the chapter considers the impact of such anxiety about social interaction as it may impact on the development of anti-social (criminal) sexual behaviors. The last part of the chapter is intended as a exemplar of one impact that anxiety about communication and the corresponding impact on lack of competence may contribute to a variety of social problems. Other persons have written about how the relationship of communication anxiety to low levels of communication competence contribute to a number of important social interactions (medical treatment, HIV risk behavior, employment, etc.,) (Allen, Emmers-Sommer, and Crowell 2002; Ayres, Ayres, and Sharp 1993; Richmond, Heisel, Smith, and McCroskey 1998).

Many people when communicating face the challenge of overcoming the level of anxiety or fear felt about interacting or speaking with other persons. Often, the level of anxiety felt about public speaking is one of the top fears or phobias experienced by individuals, 25% of all individuals experience a high degree of terror involving public speaking (Sharp 1992). One of the reasons that so much research exists on this issue becomes reflected in the ease a researcher can find significant numbers of persons afflicted with this fear. The history of the research on issues related to communication anxiety represent one of the oldest in the quantitative social sciences (Dow 1937; Knower 1937). Any experienced instructor teaching fundamental communication skills will attest to the negative consequences on competent communication that anxiety produces (Ayres and Hopf 1993). The diminished view of the competence of the communicator by the message receivers and the undermining of the effectiveness of the message comprise one of the immediate outcomes (Allen 1989; Allen and Bourhis 1996).

1. Goals of the competent presenter

The communicator generally has a goal or outcome sought which serves as the basis for the presentation. For example, common goals in public communication are: (a) informational, (b) persuasion, and (c) ceremonial. Informational goals are present when the individual wishes the audience to learn about some person, process, or object. Informational outcomes desire that an audience should learn something and/or demonstrate improved understanding. Persuasion goals involve the formation, change, or reinforcement of some type of attitude, belief, or value. Persuasive messages serve to promote some type of evaluation consistent with the goal of the communicator so that as a result of the message the conclusion offered by the communicator becomes adopted or shared by the listeners. Ceremonial goals typically are communications that are part of established social rituals. Common rituals involving the need for presentations are awards ceremonies, funerals, retirements, weddings, and graduations. The ceremonial communicator provides a message consistent with the emotions and themes that share purpose and meaning behind the events necessitating the ceremony. These goals may not be exclusive and in many instances are combined both for larger and more localized instances.

One goal for any communication is that the communicator wants to be evaluated as competent by the message receivers. The general term, "credibility" refers to the evaluation that a group of message receivers make of a message source (Cronkhite and Liska 1980). A credible source constitutes a person providing a message that should be believed. Credibility of the source is not a property inherent in the communicator but instead constitutes an evaluation by an audience about the source of the message. A source may be credible for one set of individuals and not credible to another set of audiences. For example, U.S. President George W. Bush by some is viewed as a very credible source about the success of the U.S. led coalition in the occupation and transformation in Iraq, however, other persons would not accept any statement by the U.S. President as credible.

Generally, the measurements of credibility reveal two important factors or characteristics: (a) expertise and (b) trust. Expertise refers to the evaluation made of the communicator about the level of confidence in the knowledge or competence in the subject matter. An expert communicator has some specialized knowledge that the audience does not possess and therefore offers a more informed opinion. For example, a virologist would probably be more liked viewed as an expert on issues of avian flu than even a well respected football coach. The expert's opinion is one that is more likely to be accurate and possess higher accuracy. The evaluation of the audience would generally grant more credibility to the expert communicator.

Trust reflects the evaluation message receivers make about the honesty, integrity, and general believability of the communicator. A communicator may provide the truth but when not believed sends a message of little value to the audience. Trust can reflect an evaluation of the communicator based on the current message or the kinds of past experience the audience has with the communicator. Often, the speaker may indicate a prior relationship and refer to a series of messages that were viewed as honest and believable. Conversely, a communicator with a history of misleading, incomplete, or dishonest messages may find it difficult to communicate effectively with an audience, regardless of the level of expertise.

The evaluations are not universal but instead reflect a relationship that the audience believes exists between the speaker, the audience, and the topic of the message. For example, ex-U.S. President Bill Clinton may receive high evaluations on trust when speaking about ways to promote world peace but elicit extremely low levels when he refers to his strong and monogamous relationship with his wife. Similarly, a nuclear physicist may be viewed as an expert when providing information about any potential weapons of mass destruction program in North Korea but not have expertise when offering advice on baking a cake. The audience applies a set of social logic to evaluate the credibility of the communicator.

Evaluations made by the audience consider the past relationship, if any, that exist between the audience, topic, and communicator. However, for many speakers, no historical pattern exists and the speaking situation may be the first situation or encounter with the communicator. The evaluation of competence may largely become reflected or based on that message. The impact that variations in the credibility of the communicator on persuasiveness of a message are well established and point to the desirability of a communicator generating and maintaining high levels of evaluations of credibility (Allen and Stiff 1989, 1998; Allen et.al. 2002).

2. Importance of appearing confident

Communication situations are often important for the communicator. The impact of importance is to provide the potential for the communicator to be nervous or apprehensive about the process or act of communicating. The consequences of performing poorly provide the basis for nervousness about the upcoming communication.

The term the authors prefer is communication apprehension, however, the term across the disciplines has many manifestations and applications. In theatre the term is stage fright, in speech the term is public speaking anxiety, for relational scholars the term is shyness, in music and athletic the "performance anxiety" is the term used. Virtually all fields considering performance use a term to indicate how anxiety about competence in the activity becomes impacted by the emotional responses to the event.

Many different measurement devices and assumptions exist about how to measure this anxiety. The consensus seems to be building that the apprehension reflects a situational basis related to the number of persons with which the person is communicating (Levine and McCroskey 1990). One original consideration was whether the construct was an enduring personality characteristic or trait or reflected an anxiety specific to the situation and changing over time. A meta-analysis (Booth-Butterfield 1989) indicates a high average correlation, $r = .70$, between trait and state measures.

The term spans cultures and boundaries. Research across cultures and geographic boundaries provides a great deal of evidence that the concepts of anxiety about communication interfering with the ability to demonstrate competence are widespread if not universal. The ability does differ across cultures, largely due to social issues and how important or likely communication in the various methods exists (Bourhis, Tkachuk, and Allen 1993).

The results of nervousness are well documented. The physiological effects are related to increases in heart rate, blood pressure, and palmar sweat (Allen 1989; Beatty 1984). The general reaction is that of a panic or a fear to some type of situation. The physiological effects are in response to some type of fear or panic reaction. However, when this reaction is visible or can be viewed by persons the reaction is negative. The attribution made by persons witnessing the communication usually involves some type of reduced influence of the communicator (Allen and Bourhis 1996).

This emotional feeling is noticed and labeled in children as early as five years old (Comadena and Prusank 1988). The development of avoidance of communication situations due to unpleasant sensations emerges at a very early age. The impact of communication anxiety on the development of basic speaking skills at an early age has been demonstrated (Garrison and Garrison 1979). Whether the genesis of the anxiety originates from the genetics or the environment (or some combination) remains a topic under investigation (Beatty, Heisel, Hall, Levine, and La France 2002; Beatty, McCroskey, and Heisel 1998; Berquist, Bourhis, and Allen 1992). However, whatever the underlying cause, the evidence does indicate that the effects of communication apprehension can be reduced.

The consequences of the feelings of fear become manifested in reduced level of effective performance. What happens is that an audience for the message begins to question the reasons for this reaction. Many of the reactions, sweating, shaking, inability to look up, indicate reactions of flight or a desire not to communicate. Many of these same reactions are similar to cues that persons use to determine whether a person is telling the truth. Put simply, the impact of behaviors associated with high levels of anxiety is to create the impression that the speaker is not telling the truth.

Judgments by the audience are not usually that severe. The impact of the behaviors is to undermine the view of the communicator as someone with a great deal of confidence when delivering the message. The impact of this view that the person if fearful leads to an examination of why a person should be anxious.

A person that is confident, an expert, and someone worthy of trust should not exhibit behaviors more consistent with a person that is lying or misleading. The person appears to lack competence in the act of communicating and appears to not feel comfortable.

Situations where there exist multiple persons communicating about some topic where a choice is required positions puts the anxious communicator at a disadvantage. The confident person (confident but not over confident or arrogant) becomes someone viewed as higher in trust and more expert. Therefore that person is more likely to be considered as presenting a superior set of options. The communicator faces the challenge of appearing confident and in control without appearing arrogant. Anxiety that is manifested undermines the positive evaluation of the communicator by exhibiting behavior associated with deceit and lying.

The impact of this anxiety is a decreased level of communication competence. Persons with higher levels of anxiety will communicate less frequently and with less duration (Allen and Bourhis 1996). The quality of the message diminishes as these signs of anxiety increase.

Persons reporting higher levels of anxiety experience less success in educational settings from grade school to college (Bourhis and Allen 1992). This should not be surprising given the pedagogy of most classrooms teaching fundamental skills like reading and math. Reading is often taught by having each person in the classroom reading a portion of a text with an instructor publicly stopping and correcting a person. The impact of this method is the introduction of stress and the desire for avoidance of the exercise. The fear of poorly communicating and the impact of public embarrassment by an instructor would lead to avoidance and reduced competence due to stress.

Mathematics instruction where a student is sent to the front of the classroom may generate similar fears. The need to avoid the setting due to fear and the paralysis that takes place when the person is required to communicate becomes a serious issue. What happens is that the person's inability to communicate effectively becomes interpreted instead in terms as a lack of competence on the actual subject matter. In this sense, the apprehension or fear functions to reduce the perceptions of competence held by the person making an evaluation.

A student with a fear about communication may be less likely to raise a hand and ask a question for clarification. A student fearing negative evaluation may not participate in classroom exercises or venture to express an answer that becomes viewed as something unacceptable. The result of this fear is a student that never has questions answered.

Cures or treatments exist that minimize the impact of anxiety on presentation. There are principally three methods of reducing anxiety felt about communication events (Allen, Hunter, and Donohue 1989). The basic three methods are: (a) Skills training, (b) cognitive modification, and (c) systematic desensitization. Each technique offers a different view about why persons experience anxiety about communication. Based on the analysis, each of the methods then offers specific recommendations about how to reduce the level of fear felt. The following sections discuss in detail each of the methods and how undertaking the procedures will reduce fear.

The research demonstrates that all three methods of reducing communication apprehension are successful. The findings also strongly suggest that the impact of the methods in combination are additive. What this means is that not only can someone reduce levels of anxiety using the methods described but that using a combination of all the methods maximizes the amount of reduction. The methods should not be viewed in isolation, it may very well be possible to combine the methods in a manner that reinforces or serves to address many of the underlying causes of the anxiety.

3. Skills training to diminish anxiety

Not surprisingly, knowing how to do something properly reduces the level of anxiety that a person experiences. The underlying theory or argument in favor of using skills training reflects the belief that anxiety stems from the expectation about the performance of any task. A person expected to give a speech should feel anxiety if there exists a lack the training necessary to give a good speech. Advocates for skills training believe in the need for confidence borne out of experience and training. The anxiety reflects no underlying psychological issue, anxiety is simply a manifestation of a lack of skill. Anxiety about the task represents a relatively rational reaction to the need to undertake an important task without appropriate preparation. Training and skill development remove the underlying reason for the fear. If a person is prepared and knows how to do something, then the fear of failure caused by lack of preparation should not take place.

The solution becomes relatively easy. One takes a public speaking class or participates in some training to provide the expertise necessary to succeed. Dale Carnegie (1955) was famous for his argument in this book about the need for confidence in speaking. Carnegie believed that the primary failure of a speaker stemmed from a lack of training. Anxiety felt about communication stemmed from this lack of knowledge. Carnegie's approach emphasized building vocabulary, making outlines, doing research on the topic of the presentation, and then practicing and practicing this presentation.

Dale Carnegie was a very successful trainer in public speaking. Carnegie believed that if you developed the necessary skills, then you would be a successful speaker. He first focused on content, a speaker should know the material. A speaker cannot speak unless the content of the communication is known and fully understood by the communicator. The emphasis was on using personal experience of the communicator, supplemented with appropriate research, to make sure that the communicator knew as much about the material as reasonably possible. Good preparation for a communication involved effort prior to the communication to gain knowledge. Carnegie then believed in organizing the material, the material is not random, thoughts should be focused and organized to provide effectiveness for the audience. Therefore, organizational schemes and outlining play an essential role in preparation. Finally, a speaker should practice, practice, practice, the presentation, in front of a mirror, in front of family and friends, as well as simply alone. Practice provides focus and increases confidence in the ability to communicate the content.

Confidence comes from the certainty that proper preparation exists to handle the challenge of communication. The event is important and the outcomes are never known fully in advance, but good and complete training means the communicator expects success. Research validates the effectiveness of skills training to reduce anxiety about communication (Allen, Bourhis, Emmers-Sommer, and Sahlstein 1998; Allen, Hunter, and Donohue 1989).

4. Using cognitive modification to reduce anxiety

Another approach to reducing anxiety argues that the problem of public speaking anxiety stems from "bad" thoughts. Generating thoughts of failure, humiliation, and embarrassment because of poor communication would cause negative emotional feelings. The feeling of anxiety represents an emotional manifestation of those images about the event. Another implication of this thinking is the "self-fulfilling prophecy" because the thoughts or thinking about the outcome contribute to that outcome coming true.

If the outcome envisioned is negative, a person is more likely to make that image come true. Cognitive modification approaches hold the converse, envisioning an image that is positive and encouraging increases the probability of that outcome. The key is that the ability to translate the image about performance into the competence of actual behavior.

The technique for improving this image is often called "visualization." The technique is very popular in the athletic community among athletes experiencing anxiety about a particular outcome. Listening to audiotapes on headsets that are tapes of images (all positive) that provide a vision of accomplishment and success. One of the most convenient and effective methods of reducing the impact of negative anxiety is to visualize. Thinking about what a good public speaking effort would look and sound like contributes to the actual success. For example, the tape starts with the introduction and asks the person to imagine how the words are said and the positive response of the audience. The audiotape expects the listener to visualize the appropriate method of generating the kind of response that a communicator ought to generate from an audience. The focus of the thinking becomes what a realistic and successful outcome should look like.

The research conducted by Ayres and Hopf (1989, 1990, 1991, 1992) demonstrates a large set of research findings dedicated to an exploration and understanding of this particular method of communication anxiety reduction. The research demonstrates that the positive impact of using visualization to reduce anxiety. Ayres and Hopf (1993) in their book, *Coping with Speech Anxiety*, provide a great description of the technique. Book stores commonly sell self-help tapes, CDs, or even DVDs that contain directions and exercises to reduce the level of communication anxiety. The tapes provide a means of warming up or focusing prior to the event to permit the individual to reduce anxiety and improve performance. Visualization is not a perfect technique, but the research does demonstrate that reductions in anxiety take place when persons participate in visualization. The decline in communication apprehension corresponds to more positive evaluations of competence for the communicator (Allen 1989).

5. Using systematic desensitization to reduce anxiety

A final method of dealing with anxiety and trying to reduce this involves dealing with emotional connections a person has to a stimulus. The technique, known as systematic desensitization, focuses on changing the emotional reaction that a person experiences when faced with some communication event. The assumption is that the individual has learned an emotional reaction that manifests in increased physiological reaction (blood pressure rises, heart rate quickens, etc). The psychological reaction creates a physiological reaction that is similar to a panic response to some stimulus. Basically, the stimulus of a communication event (like a public speech, a classroom presentation, a conversation with some significant other) creates a reaction. The reaction can particularly be acute if the interaction or presentation involves some important evaluation.

Various advertisements exist for drugs for people to use when they are experiencing "social anxiety." The use of the medication changes or prevents the reaction of the body, essentially a form of chemical relaxation. The overwhelming majority of individuals do not require medical assistance to treat communication anxiety. However, the underlying rationale for the treatment is the same as systematic desensitization, changing the underlying emotional response of a person to a stimulus.

The systematic desensitization technique typically emphasizes relaxation and can feature biofeedback where a person learns to control physiological reactions to the stimulus. The technique teaches the individual to become less sensitive to the stimulus. The argument runs that the physiological reaction is what inhibits performance, that biological reaction prevents the person from responding competently (being frozen with fear is one way of putting it). A person learning to control the physiological reaction permits the underlying skill and talent of the person to become manifested in performance.

The technique has a person controlling the physiological reaction by employing various means of relaxation. The connection between psychological (or emotional) and the physiological implies that a change in the emotion or a change in the associated physiological responses means an improvement in the outcome. The physiological response inhibits appropriate behavior, the exhibition and existence of nervousness makes the person unable to follow whatever appropriate behavioral routine exists. Systematic desensitization provides an option of regaining control over the physiological and the emotional. Regaining that control means that the person can utilize the behavioral routines and exhibit competence in communication.

This technique requires that a person learn to control the reactions that they feel in response to a stimulus. A number of these approaches suggest breathing exercises and muscle relaxation techniques designed to reduce the feeling of fear and anxiety that create the physiological reactions. The idea of breathing, of muscle relaxation, of the conscious lowering of blood pressure provides the means a person uses to change the physiological state in order to control the responses of the body to the stimulus.

The technique is not dissimilar from watching actors/actresses before a performance that go through various behavioral routines to focus and become prepared to perform. Athletes will go through relaxation routines involving music, tapes, napping, or other various techniques to gain control over the physiological reactions so that the performance is not hindered. Basically, every person has a routine that they enact in order to deal with the coming challenge, the focus for each individual should be the establishment of the routine or preparation so that focus can be gained and insight into how the person will simply focus and succeed at the particular event.

A person before an important event becomes excited, the key is mastering that excitement in generating productive energy focused that helps the person succeed in the task. Energy devoted to negative emotional responses becomes unproductive and inhibits desirable outcomes. Basically, the body and mind devote energy to sustaining and enacting the anxiety responses. The result of the energy, however, is not something productive, the energy is going to sustain a response that most persons would rather avoid.

A person should also avoid negative physiological stimuli. For example, lots of coffee and smoking cigarettes increases the physiological processes of the person. Using a lot of stimulants before a presentation, particularly if the person has a tendency to be nervous, may make a person jittery and more emotional. The key is that the stimuli, food, alcohol, tobacco, etc, all play a role in changing the physiological reactions of the individual. That is why so many of the methods mention various exercises directed at bringing a kind of synchrony or harmony between mind and body about the event or the challenge that focus on feelings of peace and serenity.

The focus remains on dealing with the physiological reactions and finding methods of handling them in a manner that reduces the anxiety. Equally important is avoiding situations and substances that increase the emotional reaction/ physiological reaction to the situation. The focus on remembering to breathe and to simply relax the muscles remains a simple but successful set of advice to give to communicators. Research does indicate that the technique is successful in reducing feelings of anxiety (Allen, Hunter, and Donohue 1989) and raising the perception of competence in communication (Allen 1989).

6. Communication anxiety, low communicative competence, and sexual offenses

One consideration of why persons engage in violent or coercive sexual practices (rape, pedophilia, incest) may be a lack of communicative competence. The question of why some persons engage in a series of anti-social sexual acts continues to receive a lot of attention. The recognition that no magic bullet or simple single underlying cause for this outcome appears reasonable to maintain. The question is whether one part of this situation involves issues related to communicative competence.

Malamuth suggests that anti-social sexual behaviors may be in part a function of the lack of communication skills. Rather than viewing the problem as the result of a single or dominant cause, Malamuth proposes that the emergence of this kind of personality should be considered the result of a combination of several factors in various combinations. One of the factors represents the ability to form and sustain interpersonal relationships. If a male is unable to form and sustain relationships, then the risk of developing a preference for anti-social sexual relations increases. The lack of communicative competence serves to reduce the number of potential options that exist, the fear of rejection, the inability to express one's self to another person represents a real anxiety producing situation that has a person "play it safe" and not engage another person.

A meta-analysis does indicate that convicted male sexual offenders exhibit less social skills than corresponding male nonoffenders populations (Emmers-Sommer et. al. 2004). What this suggests is that the communication competence of sexual offenders is simply less and the possibility of formation of satisfying social relationships becomes reduced. The empirical question is whether the lower social skills and anti-social sexual behavior are the outcomes of some other mutual factor or whether the lack of social skills in part creates the behavior.

The lack of social skills would mean that the person would feel justifiably a great deal of fear in engaging other persons. The lack of social skills reduces the probability of successful interaction with another person. The person is going to have difficulty in finding, initiating, and sustaining relationships. The resulting failures should create a person more likely to feel like a social outcast and the associated feelings of alienation. The person would tend to avoid situations in which failure is higher and the implications of the failure involve a fundamental threat to their face. Appearing embarrassed or acting awkwardly around someone that a person would like to impress provides an incentive to avoid such interactions.

Many persons respond to this claim when applied to pedophiles by pointing out how pedophiles often develop an ability to communicate successfully with children. However, the choice to communicate with children indicates the selection of an audience that is less discerning and able to filter and evaluate the messages. Essentially, the sexual predator is selecting an audience that is less likely to negatively evaluate the problems in the communication skills of the speaker/writer. This impact is similar to persons in a foreign country speaking an unfamiliar language, very often children are viewed as more desirable because they appear less threatening and provide a greater feeling of safety.

One alternative would be the reliance on sexually explicit materials as a means of accomplishing sexual gratification when the availability of other sources do not exist. Given the high incidence of use of sexual materials by those convicted of sexual crimes, the consideration of alternatives should not be surprising. The problem is that the content of the material does not advise or represent socially beneficial relationships and can be interpreted as communicating a message about the desirability of anti-social sexual behaviors. But what is important is that the frequency of use of the materials does not differ, instead it is the function of the materials. The materials for the convicted sexual offender are consumed prior to engaging in behavior. Consider that the degree of physiological arousal triples when the content of the material is matched to the crime that the person was convicted of. Basically, what is happening is that the material is serving a different use for that person then the rest of the population.

The underlying question turns on why the material serves as a behavioral prompt. However, the person has fewer social skills and therefore relies on the media as a prompt. The lack of competence in social communication provides a basis for the acquisition of social role models for behavior, in this case dysfunctional one.

Obviously, anti-social sexual behavior is not simply the result of low competence in social skills. However, the lack of social skills probably provides one contributory factor in the development of a behavioral routine that ultimately becomes severely dysfunctional. The challenge is what would have happened instead if the person possessed the level of social skills fundamentally necessary to appear competent.

One consideration is whether identification and remediation remains possible. An entire set of literature considers addressing this type of anxiety on the basis of teaching dating skills to heterosexual males. Whether such skills training would have impact on reducing anti-social sexual behavior at this point has not received any attention. The impact of the potential interventions to reduce various sexual offensives on the basis of improving communicative competence of individuals provides an intriguing idea. However, the goal must be prevention and probably not remediation. Providing social skills training to already convicted sexual offenders may not be prudent or wise without a guarantee in other reorientation.

The goal of this section was to provide an example of how low levels of competence in communication may play a role in behaviors not normally associated with lack of communication skill. This section proposes simply a reconsideration of how the fundamental lack of competence may contribute various social dysfunctions. What probably happens is that low skill in communication, when combined with other environmental and social conditions, may generate a series of other outcomes. What this suggests is that the role of communication competence may be far larger as a general process than more persons realize.

7. Conclusions

The challenge of formulating and presenting a successful communication provide a real challenge to almost any individual. Even the most experienced and confident person will, on occasion, experience some sense of uncertainty or apprehension about an upcoming important communication. Part of the success requires not allowing those feelings of anxiety to interfere with the demonstration of competence.

The problem with anxiety about communication is that a person can be terrified and not appear to others as even slightly nervous. A person experiences anxiety at a psychological and physiological level and may or may not manifest observable behaviors of that feeling. When the manifestation of that fear in observable behaviors occurs the impact is usually a reduction in the perception of competence. The observed anxiety makes the communicator less likely to achieve the goals sought in the audience.

Fortunately, the impact of chronic anxiety is treatable and can be reduced using a variety of methods, alone or in combination. The view of the underlying condition is typically more like a phobia experienced by a person rather than a personality trait. Phobias are unreasoned fears held by a person that can be addressed through a variety of methods. One can learn to master a fear of snakes, heights, or even mimes. The mastery of that fear permits a confrontation and successful practice in that situation.

The example provided about sexual offenses should give some indication of the potential for how the anxiety about communication creates consequences in a variety of circumstances. The ongoing research program that considers the relationship of communication anxiety, communication competence and other social outcomes provides some evidence for concern. The feelings of alienation, loneliness, and depression that contribute to drug addiction and suicide may be in part involve these relationships. The continuation of research to explore and define these connections continues.

Many communicators develop a ritual or a method of preparation that provides a system for challenging the energy necessary for making a successful presentation. Given the impact of this anxiety occurs at a young age, the need for identification and remediation may need to start earlier in the life of an individual. Given the importance of competence in communication, removing a barrier to that process should remain a fundamental consideration of educational institutions. The key is not the avoidance of the generation of emotion or energy but instead the productive use of that energy in the creation of a message that reflects the competence of the communicator.

References

Allen, M.
  1989   A comparison of self report, observer, and physiological assessments of public speaking anxiety reduction techniques using meta-analysis. *Communication Studies* 40: 127–139.
Allen, M., L. Adamski, M. Bates, M. Bernhagen, A. Callendar, M. Casey, A. Czerwinski, L. Decker, G. Howard, B. Jordan, E. Kujawski, K. May, P. Olson, A. Parenteau, S. Reilly, J. Schmidt, S. Stebnitz, S. Thau, M. Tollefson, D. Zindler, and C. Zirbel
  2002   An examination of timing of communicator identification and level of source credibility on perceptions of credibility and attitude. *Communication Research Reports* 19: 46–55.
Allen, M. and J. Bourhis
  1996   The relationship of communication apprehension to communication behavior: A meta-analysis. *Communication Quarterly* 44: 214–226.
Allen, M., J. Bourhis, T. Emmers-Sommer, and E. Sahlstein
  1998   Reducing dating anxiety: A meta-analysis. *Communication Reports* 11: 59–56.
Allen, M., D. D'Alessio, and K. Brezgel
  1995   A meta-analysis summarizing the effects of pornography II: Aggression after exposure. *Human Communication Research* 22: 258–283.
Allen, M., D. D'Alessio, and T. Emmers-Sommer.
  1999   Reactions to criminal sexual offenders to pornography: A meta-analytic summary. In: M. Roloff (ed.), *Communication Yearbook* 22, 139–169. Thousand Oaks, CA: Sage Publications.

Allen, M., D. D'Alessio, T. Emmers, and L. Gebhardt
 1996 The role of educational briefings in mitigating effects of experimental exposure to violent sexually explicit material: A meta-analysis. *Journal of Sex Research* 33: 135–141.

Allen, M., T. Emmers, L. Gebhardt, and M. Giery
 1995 Pornography and rape myth acceptance. *Journal of Communication* 45(1): 5–26.

Allen, M., T. Emmers-Sommer, and T. Crowell
 2002 Couples negotiating safer sex behaviors: A meta-analysis of the impact of conversation and gender. In: M. Allen, R. Preiss, B. Gayle, and N. Burrell (eds.), *Interpersonal Communication Research: Advances through meta-analysis,* 263–280. Mahwah, NJ: Lawrence Erlbaum.

Allen, M., J. Hunter, and W. Donohue
 1989 Meta-analysis of self-report data on the effectiveness of public speaking anxiety treatment techniques. *Communication Education* 38: 54–76.

Allen, M. and J. Stiff
 1989 Testing three models for the sleeper effect. *Western Journal of Speech Communication* 53: 411–426.

Allen, M. and J. Stiff
 1998 An analysis of the sleeper effect. In: M. Allen and R. Preiss (eds.), *Persuasion: Advances through Meta-analysis,* 175–188. Cresskill, NJ: Hampton Press Inc.

Ayrcs, J. and T. Hopf
 1989 Visualization: Is it more than extra attention? *Communication Education* 38: 1–5.

Ayres, J. and T. Hopf
 1990 The long-term effect of visualization in the classroom: A brief research report. *Communication Education* 39: 75–87.

Ayres, J. and T. Hopf
 1991 Visualization: The next generation. *Communication Research Reports* 8: 133–140.

Ayres, J. and T. Hopf
 1992 Visualization: Reducing speech anxiety and enhancing performance. *Communication Reports* 5: 1–10.

Ayres, J. and T. Hopf
 1993 *Coping with Speech Anxiety.* Norwood, NJ: Ablex.

Ayres, J., D. Ayres, and D. Sharp
 1993 A progress report on the development of an instrument to measure communication apprehension in employment interviews. *Communication Research Reports* 10: 87–92.

Beatty, M.
 1984 Physiological assessment. In: J. Daly and J. McCroskey (eds.), *Avoiding Communication: Shyness, Reticence, and Communication Apprehension,* 95–106. Beverly Hills, CA: Sage.

Beatty, M., A. Heisel, A. Hall, T. Levine, and B. La France
 2002 What can we learn from the study of twins about genetic and environmental influences on interpersonal affiliation, aggressiveness, and social anxiety?: A meta-analytic study. *Communication Monographs* 69: 1–18.

Beatty, M., J. McCroskey, and A. Heisel
  1998 Communication apprehension as temperamental expression: A communibiological paradigm. *Communication Monographs* 65: 197–219.
Berquist, C., J. Bourhis, and M. Allen
  1992 *Like father, like sons and daughters: Predicting communication apprehension in families.* Paper presented at the Speech Communication Association Convention, Chicago, Illinois.
Booth-Butterfield, S. R.
  1989 The relationship between state and trait communication anxiety. *Communication Research Reports* 6: 19–25.
Bourhis, J. and M. Allen
  1992 Meta-analysis of the relationship between communication apprehension and cognitive performance. *Communication Education* 41: 68–76.
Bourhis, J. and M. Allen
  1993 The needs of the apprehensive student. In: L. Hugenberg, P. Gray, and D. Trank (eds.), *Teaching and Directing the Basic Communication Course*, 71–76. Dubuque, IA: Kendall/Hunt Publishing Co.
Bourhis, J. and M. Allen
  1998 The role of videotaped feedback in the instruction of public speaking: A quantitative synthesis of published empirical literature. *Communication Research Reports* 15: 256–261.
Bourhis, J., T. Tkachuk, and M. Allen
  1993 *A comparison of and commentary on cross-cultural communication apprehension research: A preliminary assessment.* Paper presented at the Speech Communication Association Convention, Chicago, Illinois.
Bourhis, J., M. Allen, and I. Bauman
  in press Communication apprehension: Issues to consider in the classroom. In: B. Gayle, R. Preiss, N. Burrell, and M. Allen (eds.), *Classroom Communication and Instructional Practices: Advances through Meta-Analysis*. Mahwah, NJ: Lawrence Erlbaum.
Bradford, L., M. Allen, and K. Beisser
  2000 Meta-analysis of intercultural communication competence research. *World Communication*, 29: 28–51.
Carnegie, D.
  1955 *Public Speaking and Influencing Men in Business*. New York, NY: Association Press.
Cronkhite, G. and J. Liska
  1980 The judgment of communicant acceptability. In: M. E. Roloff and G. R. Miller (eds.), *Persuasion: New Directions in Theory and Research,* 101–140. Beverly Hills, CA: Sage.
Comadena, M. and D. Prusank
  1988 Communication apprehension and academic achievement among elementary and middle school students. *Communication Education* 37: 270–277.
Cooper, E. and M. Allen
  1998 A meta-analytic examination of the impact of student race on classroom interaction. *Communication Research Reports* 15: 151–161.

Dow, C.
   1937   A personality study of college speakers. Unpublished Master's thesis, Massachusetts State College.

Emmers-Sommer, T., M. Allen, J. Bourhis, E. Sahlstein, K. Laskowski, W. L. Falato, J. Ackerman, M. Erian, D. Barringer, J. Weiner, J. Corey, J. Krieger, G. Moramba, and L. Cashman
   2004   A meta-analysis of the relationship between social skills and sexual offenders. *Communication Reports* 17: 1–10.

Garrison, J. and K. Garrison
   1979   Measurement of oral communication apprehension among children: A factor in the development of basic speech skills. *Communication Education* 28: 119–128.

Huxman, S. and M. Allen
   2004   Scientists and storytellers: The imperative pairing of qualitative and quantitative approaches in communication research. In: S. Iorio (ed.), *Qualitative Research in Journalism: Taking it to the Streets,* 175–192. Mahwah, NJ: Lawrence Erlbaum.

Knower, F.
   1937   A study of speech attitudes and adjustments. *Quarterly Journal of Speech,* 23: 130–203.

Levine, T. and J. C. McCroskey
   1990   Measuring trait communication apprehension: A test of rival measurement models of the PRCA–24. *Communication Monographs* 57: 62–71.

Preiss, R. and M. Allen
   in press   Understanding and using meta-analysis. In: R. Preiss, B. Gayle, N. Burrell, M. Allen, and J. Bryant, in press. *Mass Media Effects Research: Advances through Meta-Analysis.* Mahwah, NJ: Lawrence Erlbaum.

Preiss, R., M. Allen, and B. Gayle
   in press   Test anxiety and study skills. In: B. Gayle, R. Preiss, N. Burrell, and M. Allen. (eds.), *Classroom Communication and Instructional Practices: Advances through Meta-Analysis.* Mahwah, NJ: Lawrence Erlbaum.

Preiss, R., L. Wheeless, and M. Allen
   1991   The cognitive consequences of receiver apprehension: An empirical review. In: M. Booth-Butterfield (ed.), *Anxiety, Cognition, and Social Behavior,* 155–172. Newbury Park, CA: Sage.

Richmond, V., A. Heisel, R. Smith, and J. McCroskey
   1998   The impact of communication apprehension and fear of talking with a physician and perceived medical outcomes. *Communcation Research* 15: 344–353.

Sharp, D.
   1992   Conquer your fear of public speaking. *Reader's Digest* 141(844): 127–132.

14. Training of writing and reading

Eva-Maria Jakobs and Daniel Perrin

Even if all of the users of this handbook skip over this chapter, the text would nevertheless still have been appreciated by some readers: at the least it has been carefully read by those who wrote it and revised it. Writing and reading processes intermesh during writing and editing: authors read source texts, their own developing texts, and the comments and revision suggestions from their co-authors. Being able to write, therefore, always means being able to read. Poor readers find it difficult to monitor text quality and identify weaknesses. Difficulties are intensified when facts have to be researched and source texts have to be understood and processed. Reading, thus, is part of all writing processes, and in source-based text production reading is twice as important. Because of this, it is surprising that so little attention has been paid to reading in the teaching of writing. Education and training tend to focus either on writing or reading competence; programs that systematically relate writing and reading as a complex combination of skills are rare.

The present chapter deals with this type of training. It defines and links the basic terms "writing", "reading", and "training" (section 1), locates reading and writing processes in text production (section 2), provides a detailed review of methodology (section 3) and the state of research into the interface of writing, reading, and training (section 4), and finally identifies gaps in the current research (section 5). The chapter focuses on the reading and writing processes of adults involved in text production, mostly professionally, in domains such as science, technology, administration, and public communication. As examples of a case study, details of a training and consulting project in a journalistic editorial office are provided throughout the chapter.

1. Basic concepts: Writing, reading, and training

Writing refers to the activity of language users encoding thoughts in permanent form; that is, as visible signs on some kind of material or storage device with suitable tools and according to set rules. This occurs in processes. The writing process is a predominantly purposeful, mental, and material procedure to produce a written text. Both individual and communication objectives can be pursued. For example, epistemic writing relieves thought processes; transcribed thoughts can be examined and organized, such as by brainstorming with mind maps. Mnemonic writing uses transcriptions as aids for remembering, such as the classic shopping list. Finally, a text is also accessible to other people, in other places, and at other times. Writing detaches thoughts from the author and the production situation and allows communication over time and space, with known and unknown readers (Ludwig 2005: 11–21).

Reading refers to the activity of language users understanding written signs. They interpret these signs according to rules and establish an idea of what a text could mean, guided by both the signs and their own world knowledge. Reading also takes place in processes, predominantly purposeful processes that create mental representations from physical representations. In written communication, reading is the counterpart of writing: people perceive an offer of communication by reading a text. Reading can occur in isolation from writing, but communicative reading processes often include minor writing processes, such as when people make notes about a text they are reading. Conversely, every writing process includes reading processes, since people always read parts of what they have just written. For this reason, it makes sense to address reading whenever text production is being trained (Freiman 2005).

Training in the everyday sense of the word can refer to practice, instruction, educational courses, or various kinds of professional or personal development, in brief, to measures that maintain and improve certain abilities and skills. The scientific definition of the term refers primarily to didactic methods and applied psychology. Under this definition, trainings are understood to be teaching and learning events in which a trainer professionally and methodically guides trainees within the conflicting poles of the individuals themselves, their roles, and the setting by: clarifying their starting position; setting goals; acquiring the means to reach their goals; and expanding their repertoires of competences (Lippmann 2006: 28–30). Training thus extends the individually-determined, socially-influenced, and socially-influential competences or cognitive capacities in order to allow specific problems within the framework of specific expectations to be solved in an appropriate and effective way. In text production training, the focus is on writing tasks – and interlinked processes of writing and reading.

2. Reading processes within writing processes

Studies on text production show that reading processes more or less systematically accompany the entire process of text development. The type and purpose of reading vary, contingent on the stage of text development and on the related text (Jakobs 1997). Depending on the related text, two types of reading processes can be differentiated: production-oriented reading, to monitor the developing text product (section 2.1), and source-oriented reading, to understand texts being referred to that are written by other authors (section 2.2).

2.1. Production-oriented reading while writing

Reading processes are not explicitly mentioned in early models of text production (such as those of Hayes and Flower 1980; Bereiter 1980; and De Beaugrande 1984) and at most are just implied when models refer to writers resorting to knowledge that is either present before writing begins or that emerges during the writing process and can be modified.

Other approaches, especially more recent ones, emphasize the value and diverse functions of reading in text production and the close interconnectedness of writing and reading processes (e.g. Bracewell and Frederiksen 1982; Ludwig 1983; Nelson Spivey 1990; Flower et al. 1990; Rau 1994; Jakobs 1999). In general, such approaches view reading as an important part of the ongoing monitoring of what has already been written and as a basis for additional decisions about production (Jakobs and Molitor-Lübbert 1994; Hayes 1996). This occurs at all levels, including graphomotoric functioning, formulation, intermediate products, and text versions.

- Graphomotoric level: writers follow the appearance of characters on the recording surface and, in a scarcely conscious monitoring process of visual feedback loops, check the graphomotoric realization of linguistic expressions. People see what they write, just as they listen while they speak, and can immediately detect and rectify motor errors and slips.
- Formulation level: writers read formulated chunks of texts and check them for grammatical, semantic, and logical coherence. In periods of difficulty formulating passages, re-reading can encourage new ideas on how to continue (reactivation re-reading; cf. Rau 1994) and help assess before writing them down whether draft formulations would fit with what has already been written (evaluative re-reading; cf. Rau 1994). Finally, re-reading aloud produces a sound pattern that provides important indications about linguistic violations (Keseling 1988: 233).
- Intermediate product level: writers read what they have already written in order to heighten their awareness of it before continuing (reading to comprehend vs. reading to evaluate; Hayes et al. 1987) and then to correct discrepancies between the current and intended form (Molitor-Lübbert 1984) and/or to encourage ideas for the next stages of work (Keseling 1988). Re-reading intermediate products is especially important for bottom-up oriented writers – those writers who start writing with only vague ideas of the text purpose, content, and structure and then use the text production process to clarify them (Molitor 1987: 404).
- Text version level: writers re-read the current version of the text they have just written in order to gain a new overall idea of the sense, meaning, and structure of it before they revise the text as a whole. This function of re-reading is important, for example, when an author wants to understand written comments from a co-author and incorporate them into the text.

Re-reading one's own text version before a general revision in order to understand it intellectually and to be able to incorporate comments from a co-author is a borderline case of production-oriented reading. The writing process is abandoned, the text is approached from a new angle, and preparations are made for a new type of creative process. This holds even more for cases when an author optimizes the existing text of another author (Schriver 1989) or when people rewrite their own texts for a different target readership (Sauer 1997). Such variations from production-oriented reading are closely related to source-oriented reading, discussed below.

2.2. Source-oriented reading while writing

Texts often develop intertextually, related to and supported by source texts (Selzer 1993, Jakobs 1999). So-called source reading encompasses all reading processes that are focused on such source texts. For quite a while, research neglected this aspect of reading in writing. Many experimental designs purposely excluded production circumstances in which writers could or had to resort to other texts. In the 1990s, the situation changed: Hayes (1996) included source reading in his cognitively- and socially-anchored model of text production. In his and similar models, source reading aims at and realizes mental representations of the contents of the text, a sense of the author, and the text as a physical entity.

Before and along with general models, there have been specific approaches to and models of source reading, including that of Nelson Spivey (1990) on cognitive-constructive processes in source reading; Ludwig (1983) on source reading from a pedagogical standpoint; Rouet et al. (1996) and Jakobs (1995, 2003) on source reading in scientific text production; Perrin (2001) and Sleurs, Jacobs, and Van Waes (2003) on source reading in journalism and public relations; and Kretzenbacher (1990), Endres-Niggemeyer and Schott (1992) and Keseling (1993) on source reading in summarizing texts. Keseling, for example, shows that the ability of writers to differentiate between important and unimportant source comments, relate texts to each other appropriately, and ultimately apply the information from source texts productively to a writing task depends mainly on their age, writing experience, and reading ability.

Exactly how source reading is embedded in the writing process depends on the task that a writer has to accomplish (Jakobs 1999). The task-dependent factors in writing and reading processes include:

- where source reading takes place in the writing process; for example: before, during, or after formulating content;
- how source reading combines with other activities in text production; for example with copying and citing;

- which source texts are included in source reading and what content is focused on;
- what level of depth and critical distance is employed; for example, whether the reading is tied to evaluation or to elaboration.

In addition, the purpose and profile of source reading depend on the phases that a text production process goes through (Jakobs 1999):

- In the initial stages of text production, writers explore the area: they read up on the topic and gain an overview of the field. Depending on their prior knowledge, the reading process can be rather unfocused and general. A typical strategy of exploratory reading is scanning. The reading attitude is rather neutral, with the reader open to arguments and various standpoints.
- In the course of treating a topic, reading becomes more focused, selective, and restrictive. Source reading, treatment of the topic, and preliminary attempts at formulation influence each other reciprocally. As a text takes form, the perspective on the topic can change, which demands a focused and thorough re-reading of the source texts. Comparing positions requires reading at the highest level of critical-constructive understanding.
- Integrative actions such as citing and reviewing sources frequently necessitate renewed source reading. The linguistic reproduction of content requires discerning re-reading. Quoting directly requires form-oriented reading as well, with the goal of generating as exact a representation of the linguistic surface of the source text passage as possible, even including details such as typing mistakes in the source.

Just as general text production tasks and processes have a determining influence on source reading, source reading has an effect on the whole text production process, the text product, and ultimately on the text production setting. The process of embedding information from a source in a text, the care, the finesse, the reflection – in short, the quality of the source reading influences how previous discourse is used in text production. It can be critical, by questioning and evaluating various positions, or creative, by conceiving and recognizing new connections, or reproductive, by marked and unmarked copying, or manipulative, by distorting the sense of a message. This reproduction in a new contribution to the discourse on a topic ultimately changes the social environment and the conditions for future text production intentions.

To illustrate the interrelationships between reading, writing, and training, an in-depth examination of text production trainings in journalism is made here and at the end of the following sections. In this domain of journalism, text production with source reading is an essential element of professional life – journalistic text production is systematically determined as collaborative re-production in intertextual chains (Figure 1). Under economic conditions, media professionals with various responsibilities work in teams to create media items from texts and other excerpts of reality they are aware of. Their texts quickly become source texts for the next processing level in the production chain (the dashed line in Figure 1). The media professionals also communicate directly with sources and audiences, and sources, such as interviewed politicians, can themselves be part of the audience for a media item (the dotted lines in Figure 1).

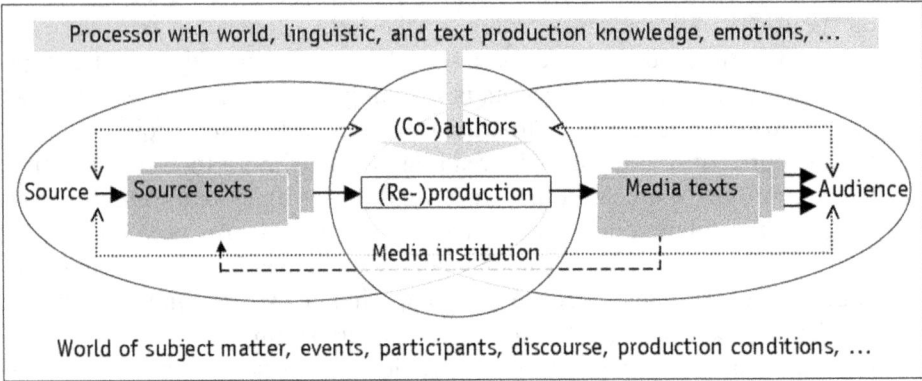

Figure 1. Journalistic text (re-)production as a socially- and cognitively-governed activity (Perrin 2006a: 87).

In such a network of cross-references, the social setting – or more precisely, the mental representation of it in the minds of the text producers – determines how any particular previous contribution to the discourse from a source is incorporated into a new text. Conversely, the new text product can have an effect on the social setting, such as when a politician thinks that his comments have been distorted in a newspaper article and as a result refuses to give journalists from that paper any more interviews. This example, selected from one of the many domains of professional text production, demonstrates that text production competence includes the ability to read purposefully: not just the source texts but also the new text being written. This insight has consequences for the methodology of empirically-based text production trainings, discussed in the next section.

3. Methods

Scientifically-based trainings require systematic knowledge at two levels: knowledge about conveying information and knowledge about the topic, in this case, about text production. At the level of conveying information, trainers have to carry out and guide educational processes that are suitable to expand their trainees' repertoires of competences in a targeted way. At the level of subject matter, trainers have to provide theoretically and empirically sound knowledge. If they do not want to put their trainees at the mercy of unquestioned opinions, then they have to know the basic patterns of text production, be able to recognize individual patterns of behavior, discover successful variants, identify deviations from the ideal in their trainees' text production behavior, and decide on appropriate intervention measures with which their trainees can purposefully expand their repertoires of strategies (Fiehler 2002; Johnston 2003). Two groups of methods are applicable in this context: methods of knowledge transfer (section 3.1) and methods of knowledge creation (section 3.2).

3.1. Methods of knowledge transfer

Whereas in school children learn reading and writing as new skills, professional text production trainings are oriented to adults with previously established competence in written communication (Fiehler and Schmitt 2004: 132). The educational experience of training is essentially oriented to retraining or "learning anew", and not to new learning. Trainees, guided by their trainers, have to learn to recognize and evaluate established routines, develop new routines, and thereby break open, expand, and increase the flexibility of their repertoires. Put succinctly, they have to de-automate and re-automate their patterns of solving problems. In contrast to new learning, such retraining is only possible through conscious monitoring, analysis, and practice (Becker-Mrotzek and Brünner 2004; Lambertini and Ten Thije 2004): by practicing examples in simulated situations in training sessions and repeating them in actual situations outside of the training context (Fiehler 2002: 33–34). This framework determines the (a) objectives and (b) forms of teaching and learning in text production trainings.

(a) With their intentional, consciously triggered teaching and learning processes, both teachers and learners pursue goals: they strive to elaborate competences. The learners should understand and convince themselves that a certain type of behavior is sensible for certain purposes, since they are supposed to implement, retain, and maintain that solution pattern (Becker-Mrotzek and Brünner 2004); the learners should work on constantly developing certain abilities. With these competences, they can subsequently solve problems of varying degrees of complexity. To do so, the corresponding resources have to be made available (Perrin, Dörig and Vervoort 2005: 43).

– These competences represent abilities people have to cope with certain demands and solve problems in dealing with matters of fact, with other people, and with themselves (Euler and Reemtsma-Theis 1999). Subject competence, the competence to deal with world matters or things, consists in connection with text production trainings of recognizing functions and forms of texts and text production processes and of being able to produce suitable text products with suitable processes in specific situations (Antos 1995; Schoonen and De Glopper 1996; Steinhoff 2003; Hyland 2003). Social competence, oriented to other people, allows people to assess other participants (and an audience) in a communication situation and to produce a communication offer in an addressee-appropriate way (Hyland 2001; Schriver 1992). Finally, with self-competence people can focus their emotions (Brand and Powell 1986; McLeod 1987; Brand 1989; Hayes 1996; Herrmann, 2006) and especially their motivation (Charney, Newman, and Palmquist 1995; Bruning and Horn 2000; Pajares 2003; Hidi and Boscolo 2006) on a text production task.

- The problems that have to be overcome in practice and in the preparatory learning situation can have various degrees of complexity (Dörig 2003: 548–574). An example of a normally simple problem is the power supply for a portable computer on commuter trips: one of the bits of experience that those who read and write on their jobs have is that computers need power, batteries discharge, and electrical outlets are often lacking. To solve this problem, it suffices to take along an additional charged battery as a replacement or to keep the energy requirements of the computer low, for example by dimming the screen (although that makes reading more difficult). Examples of complex problems, by contrast, include overcoming writing blocks (Rose 1984; Keseling 2004) or balancing the conflicting demands of sources, clients, co-authors, and addressees in text production. In much research into text production, experts have been found to differ from novices in that the former can solve such complex problems in a routine way (Rouet et al. 1996; Sharples 1996; Torrance 1996; Beaufort 2000, 2005; Perrin 2001).

- To overcome complex problems, three resources are required to various degrees: knowledge, methods, and attitudes (Dörig 1994). Learning targets for knowledge focus on the information about a subject, for example knowledge about usual sources and text genres (Schoonen and De Glopper 1996; Hyland 2003). Learning targets for methods focus on the implementation of what has been learned with suitable abilities and skills, the writing skills (Jeffery and Underwood 1996; Tapper 2000; Uppstad and Wagner 2006). Finally, learning targets for attitudes focus on things like sensitivity to communication cultures (Surma 2000), interest in sources and addressees, readiness to listen in research discussions, and the care in attributing borrowed utterances and formulations to sources; put simply, on the level of attentiveness for communicative processes (Fiehler 2002: 34).

(b) Teaching and learning are directed to increasing certain types of subject, social, and self-competence on the basis of knowledge, methods, and attitudes. The choice of educational arrangement thus depends on the learning targets. This arrangement, be it a consultation, coaching, or training session, is basically determined by the form of teaching and learning in terms of control, social context, and type of interaction (Perrin, Dörig and Vervoort 2005: 45).

- The control form describes who regulates the teaching and learning process more: the teacher or the learner. Processes that are strictly controlled by the teacher are managed collectively: the teacher determines the processes for an entire group. Such training sessions can convey information such as which features are of central importance for a certain text genre, which strategies and techniques experienced and inexperienced professional colleagues use (Fiehler 2002: 32; Rijlaarsdam et al. 2005: 127), or how quality of text production can be ensured in an organization. However, the abilities to produce texts of a certain genre, to avoid writing blocks, or to engage in constructive, institutionalized criticism of texts all require individual practice and the establishment of a professional attitude to production. These abilities result from learning alongside learners' individual insights and experience, questions and initiatives, self-assessments and assessments from others (Hansen 2003; Fiehler and Schmitt 2004: 132; Lalouschek 2004).
- The social form describes whether people learn on their own or in groups. Those who learn individually, for example, by systematically reflecting on their own writing practices (Bräuer 2000; Varner and Peck 2003), have the greatest possible degree of independence in shaping processes. Learning in groups, by contrast, allows social competence to develop the ability to learn, work, and act with others. For instance, the abilities to constructively criticize texts and conversely to respond appropriately to criticism can only develop if people in an learning situation have the opportunity to give other people feedback and respond to other people's comments. Dealing with others while learning in groups also promotes dealing with the subject matter itself: the educational material is clarified by people questioning and explaining it (Bliesener 2004: 177).
- The interaction form describes whether a group communicates directly with each other or whether communication is technically transmitted over time and space. Being physically present in a learning situation, such as in a training group, fosters direct social interaction but demands that teachers and learners come together at one location at the same time. Distance learning, by contrast, does not require that people physically move except to access some kind of learning platform, such as a book and desk or a computer with an internet connection. Distance learning also allows social interaction. In synchronous distance learning, learners communicate at the same time over

the phone, via videoconferences, or with chat programs. In asynchronous distance learning there is a time delay but learners can choose when they want to communicate by email, in internet forums, and on websites. Internet-based training of writing relies on distance learning (Tench 2006).

Educational arrangements like trainings are therefore determined by both the targets and the appropriate form of teaching and learning. For example, subject competence is in the forefront of text production trainings: trainers impart expertise and trainees work in groups (Bünting, Bitterlich, and Pospiech 1996; Trappen 2002; Lalouschek 2004; Klemm 2004; Segev-Miller 2004). With text production coaching, participants often work individually with their coaches and focus more on targets concerning self- and social competence (Wolf and Thomason 1986; Zaslow 1991; Begovich 1993; Baldwin and Chandler 2002; Hansen 2003). Another type of training, supervision and organizational development, is oriented to whole communities (Dysthe 2002; Mönnich 2004). Writing therapy is committed to objectives beyond communication success (Salovey and Haar 1990; Greenhalgh 1999; Pizarro 2004). A complex arrangement, which often includes both trainings and coaching, is text consulting (Ortner 2004; Klemm 2004; Perrin 2006b).

An example of a complex teaching and learning arrangement is a newsroom consulting project with integrated text production coaching and trainings (Perrin 2006b). The project was carried out from 1999–2001, both as a service contract and as an ethnographic case study, and involved 180 writers and editors of the print edition and 14 of the on-line edition of the highest-circulation Swiss quality newspaper (Tages-Anzeiger). The client's objectives were to increase the quality of the newspaper and to improve its image. It was agreed to cooperate at four levels of organizational text production in order to: a) establish a basic mutual appreciation of the commission; b) develop a mission statement and guidelines as a measure of the quality to be strived for; c) measure the repertoires of text production strategies in the newsroom against the guidelines and expand them as needed; and d) cyclically review the whole procedure by checking the end product, the printed newspaper. This plan called for methods of knowledge transfer, especially at the level of c). On the other hand, it presupposed knowledge about text production in general and about text production in the specific situation at hand. What was also needed therefore were methods to create this knowledge.

3.2. Methods of knowledge creation

Text production trainings as professional development for people who write as part of their jobs are oriented to trainees who already have so much competence in reading and writing that they have been managing fine professionally until now. If trainers want to claim to be experts in text production – and not only experts in guiding learning processes – then they have to be able to offer and create knowledge about text production that extends beyond the trainees' practical knowledge and professional experience and is also verifiable (Olson 1987; Fiehler and Schmitt 2004: 132). What is required is systematically created knowledge as well as suitable methods to create such knowledge: not only methods from text production research that examine the finished product, but also those that record the production process in as many of its dimensions as possible, and from several perspectives.

Completely product-based methods include all types of text analysis procedures. Special variants are analyses of typos or slips of the typewriter key (Berg 2002) and of handwriting features (Baumann 2004). If several versions of a developing text are examined, more can be inferred in investigations about the production process than if only the final product is considered (Becker-Mrotzek 1992; Grésillon 1995; Van der Geest 1996b). The big advantage of product-based methods is that data collection does not disturb the production process or change the conditions under investigation. Because of the intrusiveness of most data collection methods, the natural production of text done by hand or with typewriters has hardly ever been registered.

By contrast, when texts are produced in electronic work settings it is also possible to trace the process of text production without any perceptible change in the writing situation: every keystroke can be recorded and the development of the text can be reconstructed step-by-step (Severinson-Eklundh 1994; Bergmann and Meier 2000; Severinson-Eklundh and Kollberg 2003; Strömqvist et al. 2006). After every text production process, authors can report in verbal protocols what they were doing and thinking. This can also be done during writing, but then the research procedure has a strong influence on the text production situation (Pitts 1982; Smagorinsky 1994, 2001; Levy, Marek, and Lea 1996; Janssen, Van Waes, and Van den Bergh 1996). Finally, it is possible to investigate discussions between writers who are producing a text together (Levin and Wagner 2006). Multi-method approaches consider the object of study from several of these perspectives and thus provide more dimensions to reconstruct text production than single-method approaches do (Beaufort 1999; Sleurs et al. 2003; Dor 2003; Perrin 2006c).

One such multi-method approach, progression analysis, was used in the Tages-Anzeiger consulting project introduced in section 3.1 (Perrin 2006b). With the agreement of the staff members, a computer program recorded all of the work done at all of the workstations in the newsroom. Writing processes recorded in such a way can be presented systematically and evaluated or even played back as a film. One possible way to represent these is with a so-called progression graph. It shows how a writer moves through the developing text with the computer cursor. The writing steps over time are shown on the horizontal axis, and the spatial sequences in the text product are indicated by the vertical axis. A line from the upper left to the lower right represents a writing process without any backward jumps in the text; a jump upwards or downwards in the graph indicates that the writer jumped backwards or forwards (by scrolling up or down the screen) to make a change in the previously written text. For example, the progression graph of a short title that an editor wrote in eleven attempts shows a lot of movement (see Figure 2).

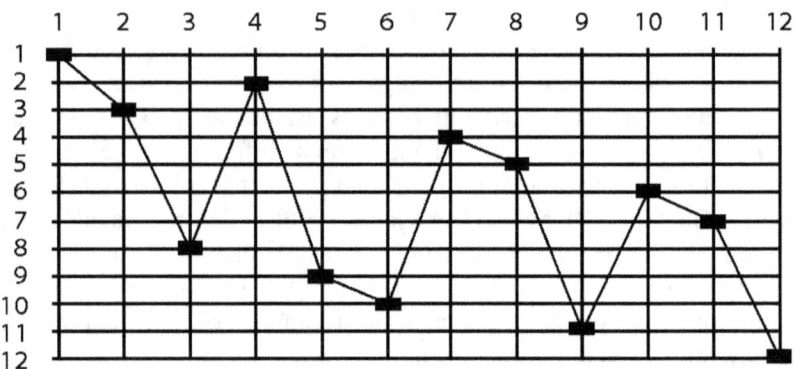

Figure 2. A progression graph indicates the sequence of revisions in a writing process (Perrin 2001: 33).

In the consulting project, the editors and writers were able to review their writing processes in the form of progression graphs or videos in real-time or time-lapse mode. They viewed these with the consultant, watching how the text developed on the computer screen and commenting continuously on what they had done while writing and why they had done it. Recordings were made of these event-supported retrospective verbal protocols. Of course, a retrospective verbal protocol cannot be interpreted as a faithful reproduction of the considerations that a writer actually made during the writing process. Rather, stimulated by observing their own writing behavior, writers mention some of the considerations they could have made while writing in comparable situations: considerations based on their accessible knowledge about language, about language use, and in particular about text production. In the excerpt below from a verbal protocol, the editor explains how he formulated a title so that it was exactly the right length and "immediately" indicated the relevance of a text.

> "It is too long, so I go and just take out 'crash'. Then I take out another word, because it's still too long. There isn't much room on this page." – "Now I just have the title 'Insulation examined'. But something else has to be added, so it's immediately clear what it's about." (translation from the German protocol)

Such considerations and text production movements can be related to the text product, the amount of work involved, the writers' expectations of themselves, and the expected quality specified by the newspaper in its guidelines. This editor, like others, failed to allocate time carefully enough and so often came under pressure towards the end of the production process – and of the text. This diagnosis lent itself to an intervention with training techniques for text planning. Individual coaching was called for when successful and experienced journalists wanted to break out of production routines that had proven reliable but become too boring for them. With team coaching and organizational development sessions, groups improved the production processes that were based on division of labor, such as updating previously uploaded on-line news reports. Diagnosed problems thus determine the teaching and learning arrangements and the topics or, in the case of trainings, the training fields.

4. Training fields – research questions and findings

Text production training is directed to certain text production tasks that presuppose certain competences in written communication. Systematic knowledge about written communication has been elaborated in the field of linguistics. A perspective on the information about text production training can therefore follow from the linguistic-pragmatic insight that language structures are trained through use and depend on the language functions in the settings where the language is used. Text production tasks and trainings can be differentiated according to their relationship to the text production setting (section 4.1), function (section 4.2), and structure (section 4.3).

4.1. Training and text production settings

Text production is embedded in more comprehensive verbal and non-verbal settings: in situations, social events, and projects. These settings influence text genres and their re-production, and thus the reading and writing of them. This is apparent in diachronic analyses such as in the history of writing. For certain types of recurring text production situations in domains such as universities, business, or journalism, patterns of text production have developed along with corresponding educational activities. Some examples of research into this area are: Ludwig (2005) on the history of writing and the interface of writing with reading, speaking, and listening; Russell (2002) on the history of writing at universities; Chin (1994) on the notion of context in writing research; Gunnarsson (1997) on writing processes from a socio-linguistic standpoint; Landis (2003) on writing and reading as social and cultural practices; Björk et al. (2002) and Kruse (2006) on teaching academic writing at universities; and Ruhmann and Perrin (2002) on the similarities and differences between scientific and journalistic writing as a starting point for writing training sessions.

The most important setting for written text production for most adults is the workplace. Text production there is a component of other activities, the text producers are integrated in a community that is based on the division of labor, and texts are closely related to other texts in an on-going discourse. Examples of research include: Spilka (1993), Van der Geest (1996a), and Jakobs (2005a) who provide an overview of writing in the workplace; Schneider (2002), who describes writing in the workplace as an activity that is influenced by the organization but is also reactive and influences the organization; Selzer (1993), who discusses the intertextuality of writing processes in the workplace; O'Hara et al. (2002), who consider writing in everyday life as an evaluation of multiple sources; and Melenhorst, Van der Geest et al. (2005), who offer observations about how professionals take notes. As well, Henry (2000) identifies cultures at writing workplaces; Flower and Ackerman (1994) present strategies for professional writing; Gunnarsson (1997) explains the interplay of written and oral communication in the workplace; Henry (1995) talks about ghostwriting in the military; Pogner (2003) analyzes writing produced in cooperative work between engineers; and Zhu (2005) focuses on social writing in various cultures. Jakobs (2005b) describes domain and context related problems of writing at work.

In cultures with institutionalized schools, people learn about writing before they arrive at the workplace. A second, task-specific writing socialization process takes place in professional life and in the workplace. High school and university graduates either have to acquire product and process patterns on their own or they are taught them, which often happens in trainings. Schools and universities can also prepare their students for the move to the writing setting of the workplace. Some relevant research includes: Dysthe (2002) on professors as imparters of academic text culture; Surma (2000) on professional writing as the object of research and university education; Tapper (2000) on the preparation of university graduates in communication as an employee; Beaufort (2000) on writing socialization in the conflicts between objectives and roles in a non-profit organization; Parks (2001) on retraining as a part of the writing socialization for nurses who change language communities after they finish their medical training; Becker-Mrotzek (2004) on the acquisition of writing skills using the example of operating instructions; and Ongstad (2005) on writing socialization in institutions, as well as Jakobs and Schindler (2006) on writing socialization in the field of engineering.

In the modern world, writing workplaces are computer workplaces. The plasma consistency of texts on a computer screen makes it possible to constantly revise them, and the network infrastructure simplifies access to stored knowledge and encourages cooperative work in spatially and temporally stretched communication situations. Research has been carried out by Spinnen (1992) on the influence of the writing tool, especially the computer, on writing; Bolter (1991) on the development of writing right up to writing hypertext on the computer; Schmitz (2003) on text production with new media; Gabel-Becker and Wingert (1989) and Van Waes and Schellens (2003) on writing on the computer versus writing by hand; Williamson and Pence (1989) and Jakobs and Molitor-Lübbert (1994) on scientific text production on the computer; Bangert-Drowns (1993) and Van Waes (1994) on computers in writing education; Wolfe (2002), Melenhorst et al. (2005), Palaigeorgiou et al. (2006) and Rodriguez and Severinson-Eklundh (2006) on making notes and annotating texts on the computer; Severinson-Eklundh (1992) and Price (1999) on outlining and processing ideas on the computer; Reece and Cumming (1996) on dictating with a speech recognition computer program; McGee and Ericsson (2002) on MS Word correction aids; and Dürscheid (2005) on email writing and the reply function as a significant difference from letter writing.

Whereas text production is simply an important part of supplying services and material goods in many professional fields, it is actually an element of the net product itself in professional fields of communication: professional communicators generate nothing but attempts at communication, such as written texts. Text production trainings at the workplace or in educational institutions represent a key component of guided socialization in these communication fields, which is professionalized late (Perrin 2006b). In any case, there is little distinction made between training and coaching in the professional discourse in the field. Coaching is customarily used to refer to many forms of teaching and learning activities that are part of or accompany professional life. Some examples are given in: Ruffner (1981), an empirical approach to assessing journalistic writing; Wolf and Thomason (1986) and Laakaniemi (1987a, 1987b), on how writing coaches and trainers work in newsrooms; Coulson and Gaziano (1989), on the assessment of writing coaches by journalists; Begovich (1993), on writing coachings in small editorial offices; Chin (1994), on the notion of context in writing research and its application in journalism education; and Perrin (2003), on investigating journalistic writing strategies as a part of the preparation for training and coaching sessions.

In the consulting project with the Tages-Anzeiger editorial staff mentioned in section 3.2, the consultant and the client first established a joint understanding of their collaboration. They agreed that the consultant would accompany the editorial office in organizationally anchoring quality management for text production as a circular process. This involved locating and including the relevant people, defining the desired quality of the text production, measuring the current quality level, optimizing the text production processes – and re-considering the standard of the desired quality with new experience. In addition, a mutual understanding of journalist text production was negotiated. It was understood to be as not only an individual task but also an organizational, institutional, and social task: a division of labor at the interface of cognitive and social practices in which problems were to be solved and decisions to be made constantly at various, sometimes conflicting levels. For example, journalists are supposed to reach a broad audience at low cost, in the interests of the media company, while at the same time prepare socially relevant topics in an nuanced way, in the interests of the public. Defusing or resolving such conflicts in expectations with more functional texts and production processes was the objective of the consulting process and its integrated trainings.

4.2. Training and text production function

Independent of the domain and research orientation, certain basic functions have been ascribed to writing: it simplifies thinking, as well as the retention and rendering of information. A writer can capture thoughts in order to examine them in more depth right then, to remember them later, or to make them accessible to others. In every case, writing makes a permanent record of thoughts. Depending on the perspective, thinking can be seen as a supply process for writing, or writing (and reading) can be considered a supportive process for thinking. Relevant research includes: Hermanns (1988) on the "heuristic function" of writing, or "writing as thinking"; Molitor-Lübbert (1996) on writing as a linguistic and mental process; Molitor-Lübbert (2002) on the cognitive basis of writing; Ortner (1995, 2000) for an overview of the relationship between writing and thinking; Ortner (2002) on the conditions that encourage ideas while writing; Ruhmann (2003) on the relationship between thinking, speaking, and writing in process-oriented writing centers at universities; and Smiley (1999) on writers' intentions and insights while reading and revising their own stories.

The connection between writing and thinking is exploited by educational approaches in which writing is done to learn. Ordering things, writing them down, reading them, and reformulating while writing all encourage in-depth consideration of concepts and their associations, of mental representations, and of the material to be learned. Text production helps writers clarify their thoughts and process them, first physically and then mentally. Some examples of research in this area are: Ackerman (1993), with his critical discussion of the "the promise of writing to learn"; Bräuer (1998, 2004), with an overview of writing to learn; Molitor-Lübbert (1998) on the relationship between writing, learning, and media technology; McCarthy Young (1998) on written processing of historical documents as a means of socialization for history students; Varner and Peck (2003) on writing of learning journals in management education; and Klein (1999) on cognitive processes in writing to learn.

In writing to convey information, text producers orient themselves to their intended readers, who will read their records in other locations and at other times. Such texts represent attempts at communication that can work if they correspond to the competences of the addressees. The text producers must therefore learn to read their texts with the eyes of the addressees. In professional text production, this relationship to the audience often develops collaboratively. For example, Hyland (2001) discusses audience-appropriate writing of scientific texts; Burrough-Boenisch (1999) reviews strategies used in reading scientific texts in various subject areas and cultures and the consequences of these insights for writing such texts; Gutenberg (2002, 2005) outlines the considerations made by radio editors to write news texts in a way that the newscaster can present them appropriately for the target audiences; Marx (2005) proposes a transcription system for newscasters that marks prosodic features such as accent and intonation; Dor (2003) examines the factors journalists consider in trimming their headlines to their readership; and Sleurs et al. (2003) presents a PR writer's rationale for focusing and inventing quotes to attract audience.

In the Tages-Anzeiger newsroom consulting project described in section 3.2, text producers fulfill various functions to meet the expectations of various parties. These functions can be grouped into those that 1) present a topic, 2) include text protagonists that are interesting to their public, 3) introduce the writer's own position, 4) assign speaking roles and moderate the discussion, 5) establish a relationship with the audience, and 6) observe the economically-determined production constraints of space, time and costs. These functions can contradict each other. For example, writers who stop doing research as soon as they can outline the essentials of a topic save time and can present their knowledge in little space or broadcast time. By contrast, those who isolate and differentiate contradictions do better justice to a complex topic but need more space and time, a conflict between functions 1) and 6). If writers incorporate direct quotes into a text, they might have to present the utterances to the sources for authorization, which risks production delays. Writers who want to avoid this problem by incorporating the utterances as indirect speech forfeit authenticity, a conflict between functions 6) and 4). As explained in more detail in Ruhmann and Perrin (2002), decisions at certain points in the production sequence can neutralize conflicts. Trainings thus can profit from models of text production structure.

4.3. Training and text production structure

Text production proceeds as a process in time. A text production process can be defined as the totality of all of the production steps between the perception of a writing assignment and the submission of the text product to the addressees or the next higher production authority. The individual activities have various degrees of complexity, ranging from finding the global sense to physical control over the writing tool. For effective trainings, it is crucial that text production processes are pattern-governed. Research into such regularities includes: Alamargot and Chanquoy (2001), with an overview of writing models; Ludwig (2005), with a hierarchical model of writing instruction and learning separated into writing letters (handwriting lessons), writing words (spelling), writing sentences (stylistics), writing texts, producing documents, and producing written communication; Levy and Ransdell (1996), about "writing signatures", procedural basic patterns that recur in a particular individual's writing processes; Van Waes and Schellens (2003), about such basic patterns or "writing profiles" of experienced writers; and Antos (1995), on the function of sample texts and text production patterns in learning to write.

Phase models of the text production process basically assume that different activities predominate during different time periods in the process. Most of the newer models describe the process as incremental, increasing at every level. Both far-reaching decisions such as those concerning topic planning and local actions such as correcting a typing mistake are possible at any time but not equally probable at all times and not equally functional at all times. Furthermore, phases can overlap each other and recur cyclically. For example, Levy and Ransdell (1995) discuss the change in cognitive effort for text planning, creation, and revision during the course of the writing process, and Severinson-Eklundh (1994) describes linear and non-linear sections of writing processes, meaning those with little or much back and forth movement in a developing text.

Three phases of text production are strongly supported in the academic discourse on writing research and education: planning, formulation, and revision. They can be traced to earlier models, such as that of Hayes and Flower (1980). At that time, writing processes were investigated with simple tasks in experimental settings. However text production in situ, for example as an activity in professional life, also includes understanding and determining a sensible task as well as interfaces to evaluate the text product. Relevant research has been carried out by Keseling (1992) on planning in the pauses while writing and speaking; Hayes and Nash (1996) on planning while writing; Van der Geest (1996a) on text planning from the perspective of professional writers; Wrobel (1997) on modelling formulation processes; Wrobel (2002) on "mental pretext", a cognitively-produced but not yet transcribed idea of a formulation; Baurmann and Ludwig (1985) and Rau (1994) for an overview of revision in the writing process; Sommers (1980) and Flower et al. (1986) on revision strategies used by students; Van den Bergh, Rijlaarsdam, and Breetvelt (1994) on the relationship between the revision process and text quality; Severinson-Eklundh and Kollberg (2001) on revision patterns used by various authors; and Allal, Chanquoy, and Largy (2004) on revision in writing education.

Just as the text production process can be divided into phases, the whole process can be interpreted as one of many stages in a superordinate pattern of text production. Professional abstracting, for example, represents such a process pattern: a previously written text is summarized for later users. Abstracting is a type of text generation which involves a lot of reading and thinking but relatively little actual formulation. Consequently, abstractors have a correspondingly wide repertoire of reading strategies at their disposal. They read to establish a mental representation of the original text, to ascertain suitable passages for the formulation of the abstract, to get ideas for how to start the abstract, or to find a text passage that they cannot quite remember exactly. Endres-Niggemeyer and Schott (1992), for example, discuss reading and writing for abstracting; Melenhorst et al. (2005) make observations about the various practices of professional reviewers in note-taking while reading on-screen; and Galbraith (1996) explores how inexperienced writers produce drafts of texts.

Psychologically-anchored and experimental writing research is heavily focused on individual writers. However, such approaches fall short for knowledge creation and transfer. Professional writing is always based on division of labor, integrated in other processes that are also based on division of labor. In these processes, several authors work on a text at almost the same time or in succession, consciously referring to each other. Examples of research in this area include: Bracewell (2003) on collaborative writing as an activity at the workplace; Bauer and Hammer (1996) on feedback during the production of journal articles and effect of feedback on the texts; Pogner (2003) on the function of collaborative writing when engineers work together; Wolfe (2005) on non-verbal communication during collaborative text planning by a group of students; Berg (2002) on typographical errors that authors and other proofreaders miss and that then appear in journal articles; Bell (1984) on journalistic practices in news editing; and Dor (2003) on collaborative writing of newspaper headlines in a newsroom where the chief editor makes written comments to copy editors about their suggestions and then the editors revise their headlines.

In the ethnographic case study mentioned in section 3.2. (Perrin 2006b), the Tages-Anzeiger consulting project, the comparison between experienced and inexperienced writers resulted in task-specific good practice models for whole writing processes and specific phases. One such practice by experienced journalists consists of first mapping out the main message and text organization and then writing the text in the order it is to be read, as much as possible without jumping back and forth or moving text blocks around. Extensive revisions under time pressure usually lead to text rifts: there is too little time to gain distance from the mental representations of old versions of the text. This and other production patterns were justified in trainings and practiced as variants instead of familiar patterns. Various methods, such as the "stage technique" and the "typo test", helped participants improve their writing performance (outlined in Perrin and Rosenberger 2005). The stage technique, for the formulation phase of text production, can be summarized as: "to get back into your text after a break, just read the last two sentences, not the whole text from the beginning; this will help you formulate smooth transitions." The typo test, for the revision phases, is: "change the general appearance of your text (e.g. font type and size, line width and spacing), then print it out and go somewhere else to proofread it; this will help you recognize problems you did not see in the familiar layout and at the familiar place." Such interventions are based on empirical insights concerning the interaction of writing and reading process in natural text production. However, they still fall too short.

5. Unexplored areas

Whereas it is now possible to track writing movements on the computer screen without disturbing natural writing processes, reading processes can only be assessed in a very indirect way. From certain writing movements, it can be assumed that authors revise their texts in certain locations. Following eye movements as well, so-called eye-tracking, has only been possible in laboratory settings until now (Andersson et al. 2006). Empirically solid analyses of the interaction between reading and writing processes during text production are definitely lacking for trainings (Wrobel 2000: 468). There is also little empirically-supported information available as to how cognitive and social influences intermesh in writing – and in learning how to write. As Rijlaarsdam et al. (2005: 149) put it: "Learning-to-write theories are an open field". But even where more knowledge is available, such as the area of conversational analysis research, there is a lack of educationally concise models and visualizations of linguistic concepts (Becker-Mrotzek and Brünner 2004: 43). Finally, since educational offerings such as trainings can only resort to fragmentary parts of relevant knowledge, there is obviously also a lack of studies on the success of transfer of such knowledge in the applied fields (Fiehler 2002: 18; Hartung 2004).

Investments to determine practically applicable knowledge about text production would be worthwhile in two ways: for practical purposes – but especially for linguistics itself. In trans-disciplinary contact with non-academic subjects, linguistics can recognize which parts of texts language users identify as problematic, how they handle language, and how they reflect on their cognitive and social practices of language use. Language awareness becomes tangible, a linguistic research field of topical interest. Applied linguistics can ultimately profit from text consulting and text production trainings not only at the level of the knowledge they generate within the discipline itself but also at a meta-level. In academic-political terms, it is of importance what linguistic laypeople want to know about language and consequently where opportunities exist for knowledge transfer. Since applied research is increasingly justified by its broad acceptance, authors should not be the only ones to read their own texts.

References

Ackerman, J.
    1993   The promise of writing to learn. *Written Communication* 10(3): 334–370.
Alamargot, D. and L. Chanquoy
    2001   *Through the Models of Writing*. Dordrecht: Kluwer Academic Publishers.
Allal, L., L. Chanquoy, and P. Largy (eds.)
    2004   *Revision: Cognitive and Instructional Processes* (Vol. 13). Dordrecht: Kluwer Academic Publishers.
Andersson, B., J. Dahl, K. Holmqvist, J. Holsanova, V. Johansson, H. Karlsson, *et al.*
    2006   Combining keystroke logging with eye-tracking. In: L. Van Waes, M. Leijten, and C. Neuwirth (eds.), *Writing and Digital Media*, 166–172. Amsterdam: Elsevier.
Antos, G.
    1995   Mustertexte und Schreibprozeduren. Standardisiertes Schreiben als Modell zur Aneignung von Schreibprozeduren. In: J. Baurmann and R. Weingarten (eds.), *Schreiben. Prozesse, Prozeduren, Produkte. Eine Hinführung zur Schreibforschung*, 70–84. Opladen: Westdeutscher Verlag.
Baldwin, C. and G. E. Chandler
    2002   Improving faculty output: The role of a writing coach. *Journal of Professional Nursing* 18(1): 8–15.
Bangert-Drowns, R. L.
    1993   The word processor as an instructional tool. A meta-analysis of word processing in writing instruction. *Review of Educational Research* 1(63): 69–93.
Bauer, T. N. and L. B. Hammer
    1996   Help received during the journal article writing process: The outcomes of quality and quantity. *Journal of Social Behaviour and Personality* 11(2): 213–224.
Baumann, M.
    2004   Diagnose und Schrift II (Editorial zum Heft "Diagnose und Schrift II: Schreibfähigkeiten"). *Osnabrücker Beiträge zur Sprachtheorie* 67: 5–8.
Baurmann, J. and O. Ludwig
    1985   Texte überarbeiten. Zur Theorie und Praxis von Revisionen. In: D. Boueke and N. Hopster (eds.), *Schreiben. Schreiben lernen*, 254–276. Tübingen: Narr.
Beaufort, A.
    1999   *Writing in the Real World. Making the Transition from School to Work*. New York: Teachers College.
Beaufort, A.
    2000   Learning the trade: A social apprenticeship model for gaining writing expertise. *Written Communication* 17(2): 185–223.
Beaufort, A.
    2005   Adapting to new writing situations. How writers gain new skills. In: E.-M. Jakobs, K. Lehnen and K. Schindler (eds.), *Schreiben am Arbeitsplatz*, 201–216. Wiesbaden: Verlag für Sozialwissenschaften.

Becker-Mrotzek, M.
    1992   Wie entsteht eine Bedienungsanleitung? Eine empirisch-systematische Rekonstruktion des Schreibprozesses. In: H. P. Krings and G. Antos (eds.), *Textproduktion. Neue Wege der Forschung*, 257–280. Trier: Wissenschaftlicher Verlag.

Becker-Mrotzek, M.
    2004   *Schreibentwicklung und Textproduktion. Erwerb der Schreibfertigkeit am Beispiel der Bedienungsanleitung*. Randolfzell: Verlag für Gesprächsforschung.

Becker-Mrotzek, M. and G. Brünner
    2004   Der Erwerb kommunikativer Fähigkeiten: Kategorien und systematischer Überblick. In: M. Becker-Mrotzek and G. Brünner (eds.), *Analyse und Vermittlung von Gesprächskompetenz*, 29–46. Frankfurt am Main: Lang.

Begovich, R. S.
    1993   Planning and implementing writing coach programs at small newspapers. Unpublished dissertation, Ball State University, Muncie, Indiana.

Bell, A.
    1984   Good copy – bad news. The syntax and semantics of news editing. In: P. Trudgill (ed.), *Applied Sociolinguistics*, 73–116. London: Academic Press.

Bereiter, C.
    1980   Development in writing. In: L. W. Gregg and E. R. Steinberg (eds.), *Cognitive Processes in Writing*, 73–93. Hillsdale, NJ: Erlbaum.

Berg, T.
    2002   Slips of the typewriter key. *Applied Psycholinguistics* 23(2): 185–207.

Bergmann, J. R. and C. Meier
    2000   Elektronische Prozessdaten und ihre Analyse. In: U. Flick, E. Von Kardoff, and I. Steinke (eds.), *Qualitative Forschung. Ein Handbuch*, 429–437. Reinbek: Rowohlt.

Björk, L., G. Bräuer, P. Stray Jorgensen, and L. Rienecker (eds.)
    2002   *Teaching Academic Writing in Higher Education*. Amsterdam: University Press.

Bliesener, T.
    2004   Kooperatives synchrones Lernen mit Multimedia in Telegruppen. In: U. Schmitz (ed.), *Linguistik lernen im Internet*, 177–191. Tübingen: Narr.

Bolter, J. D.
    1991   *Writing Space. The Computer, Hypertext, and the History of Writing*. Hillsdale: Erlbaum.

Bracewell, R. J.
    2003   Tasks, ensembles, and activity. Linkages between text production and situation of use in the workplace. *Written Communication* 20(4): 511–559.

Bracewell, R. J. and J. D. Frederiksen
    1982   Cognitive processes in composing and comprehending discourse. *Educational Psychologist* 17(3): 146–164.

Brand, A. G.
    1989   *The Psychology of Writing. The Affective Experience*. New York: Greenwood.

Brand, A. G. and J. L. Powell
1986   Emotions and the writing process. A description of apprentice writers. *Journal of Educational Research* 79(5): 280–285.
Bräuer, G.
1998   *Schreibend lernen*. Innsbruck: Studienverlag.
Bräuer, G.
2000   *Schreiben als reflexive Praxis: Tagebuch, Arbeitsjournal, Portfolio*. Freiburg im Breisgau: Fillibach.
Bräuer, G.
2004   *Schreiben(d) lernen. Ideen und Projekte für die Schule*. Hamburg: Körber.
Bruning, R. and C. Horn
2000   Developing motivation to write. *Educational Psychologist* 35(1): 25–37.
Bünting, K.-D., A. Bitterlich, and U. Pospiech
1996   *Schreiben im Studium. Ein Trainingsprogramm*. Berlin: Cornelsen Scriptor.
Burrough-Boenisch, J.
1999   International reading strategies for IMRD articles. *Written Communication* 16(3): 296–316.
Charney, D., J. H. Newman, and M. Palmquist
1995   "I'm just no good at writing". Epistemological style and attitudes toward writing. *Written Communication* 12(3): 298–329.
Chin, E.
1994   Redefining "context" in research on writing. *Written Communication* 11(4): 445–482.
Coulson, D. and C. Gaziano
1989   How journalists at two newspapers view good writing coaches. *Journalism Quarterly* 2: 435–440.
De Beaugrande, R.-A.
1984   *Text Production: Toward a Science of Composition*. Norwood: Ablex.
Dor, D.
2003   On newspaper headlines as relevance optimizers. *Journal of Pragmatics* 35: 695–721.
Dörig, R.
1994   *Das Konzept der Schlüsselqualifikationen. Ansätze, Kritik und konstruktivistische Neuorientierung auf der Basis der Erkenntnisse der Wissenspsychologie* (Vol. 1541). Hallstadt: Rosch Buch.
Dörig, R.
2003   *Handlungsorientierter Unterricht – Ansätze, Kritik und Neuorientierung unter bildungstheoretischer, curricularer und instruktionspsychologischer Perspektive*. Stuttgart/Berlin: WiKu.
Dürscheid, C.
2005   E-Mail – verändert sie das Schreiben? In: T. Siever, P. Schlobinski, and J. Runkehl (eds.), *Websprache.net. Sprache und Kommunikation im Internet*, 85–97. Berlin: de Gruyter.
Dysthe, O.
2002   Professors as mediators of academic text cultures. An interview study with advisors and master's degree students in three disciplines in a Norwegian university. *Written Communication* 19(4): 493–544.

Endres-Niggemeyer, B. and H. Schott
1992   Ein individuelles prozedurales Modell des Abstracting. In: H. P. Krings and G. Antos (eds.), *Textproduktion. Neue Wege der Forschung*, 281–310. Trier: Wissenschaftlicher Verlag.

Euler, D. and M. Reemtsma-Theis
1999   Sozialkompetenzen? Über die Klärung einer didaktischen Zielkategorie. *Zeitschrift für Berufs- und Wirtschaftspädagogik* 95: 168–198.

Fiehler, R.
2002   Kann man Kommunikation lehren? Zur Veränderbarkeit von Kommunikationsverhalten durch Kommunikationstrainings. In: G. Brünner, R. Fiehler, and W. Kindt (eds.), *Angewandte Diskursforschung* (Vol. 2), 18–35. Radolfzell: Verlag für Gesprächsforschung.

Fiehler, R. and R. Schmitt
2004   Die Vermittlung kommunikativer Fähigkeiten als Kommunikation. Kommunikationstrainings als Gegenstand der Gesprächsanalyse. In: M. Becker-Mrotzek and G. Brünner (eds.), *Analyse und Vermittlung von Gesprächskompetenz*, 113–136. Frankfurt am Main: Lang.

Flower, L. S. and J. Ackerman
1994   *Writers at Work. Strategies for Communicating in Business and Professional Settings*. Orlando: Harcourt Brace.

Flower, L. S., J. R. Hayes, L. Carey, K. A. Schriver, and J. F. Stratman
1986   Detection, diagnosis, and the strategies of revision. *College Composition and Communication* 1: 16–55.

Flower, L. S., V. Stein, J. Ackerman, M. J. Kantz, K. McCormick, and W. C. Peck
1990   *Reading to Write. Exploring a Cognitive and Social Process*. New York: Oxford University Press.

Freiman, M.
2005   Writing/Reading: Renegotiating Criticism. *TEXT* 9(1), http://www.griffith.edu.au/school/art/text.

Gabel-Becker, I. and B. Wingert
1989   Schreiben am Computer und mit anderen Schreibwerkzeugen. Ein Erfahrungsbericht. *Literatur und Erfahrung* 20: 3–34.

Galbraith, D.
1996   Self-monitoring, discovery through writing and individual differences in drafting strategy. In: G. Rijlaarsdam, H. Van den Bergh, and M. Couzijn (eds.), *Theories, Models and Methodology in Writing Research*, 121–144. Amsterdam: Amsterdam University Press.

Greenhalgh, T.
1999   Writing as therapy. Effects on immune mediated illness need substantiation in independent studies. *British Medical Journal* 319: 270–271.

Grésillon, A.
1995   Über die allmähliche Verfertigung von Texten beim Schreiben. In: W. Raible (ed.), *Kulturelle Perspektiven auf Schrift und Schreibprozesse. Elf Aufsätze zum Thema Mündlichkeit und Schriftlichkeit*, 1–36. Tübingen: Narr.

Gunnarsson, B.-L.
1997   The writing process from a sociolinguistic viewpoint. *Written Communication* 14(2): 139–188.

Gutenberg, N.
2002 Schreiben und Sprechen in den Rundfunknachrichten – Skizze eines Forschungsprojekts. In: L.-C. Anders, A. Biege, I. Bose, and C. Keßler (eds.), *Aktuelle Facetten der Sprechwissenschaft. Bericht über das Ehrenkolloguium zum 65. Geburtstag von Eberhard Stock*, 65–78. Frankfurt am Main: Lang.

Gutenberg, N. (ed.)
2005 *Schreiben und Sprechen von Hörfunknachrichten. Zwischenergebnisse sprechwissenschaftlicher Forschung.* Frankfurt am Main: Lang.

Hansen, J.
2003 Introduction: Writers as evaluators. Self-evaluation enables writer's growth. *Reading and Writing Quarterly* 19(4): 321–328.

Hartung, M.
2004 Wie lässt sich Gesprächskompetenz wirksam und nachhaltig vermitteln? Ein Erfahrungsbericht aus der Praxis. In: M. Becker-Mrotzek and G. Brünner (eds.), *Analyse und Vermittlung von Gesprächskompetenz*, 47–67. Frankfurt am Main: Lang.

Hayes, J. R.
1996 A new framework for understanding cognition and affect in writing. In: C. M. Levy and S. Ransdell (eds.), *The Science of Writing. Theories, Methods, Individual Differences, and Applications*, 1–28. Mahwah: Erlbaum.

Hayes, J. R. and L. S. Flower
1980 Identifying the organization of writing processes. In: L. W. Gregg and E. R. Steinberg (eds.), *Cognitive processes in writing*, 3–30. Hillsdale: Erlbaum.

Hayes, J. R., L. S. Flower, K. A. Schriver, J. F. Stratman, and L. Carey
1987 Cognitive processes in revision. In: S. Rosenberg (ed.), *Advances in Applied Psycholinguistics. Reading, Writing, and Language Learning* (Vol. 2), 176–240. Cambridge: Cambridge University Press.

Hayes, J. R. and G. J. Nash
1996 On the nature of planning in writing. In: C. M. Levy and S. Ransdell (eds.), *The Science of Writing. Theories, Methods, Individual Differences and Applications*, 29–56. Mahwah: Erlbaum.

Henry, J.
1995 Workplace ghostwriting. *Journal of Business and Technical Communication* 9(4): 425–445.

Henry, J.
2000 *Writing Workplace Cultures. An Archeology of Professional Writing.* Carbondale: Southern Illinois University Press.

Hermanns, F.
1988 Schreiben als Denken. Überlegungen zur heuristischen Funktion des Schreibens. *Der Deutschunterricht* 40/4: 69–81.

Herrmann, F. (ed.)
2006 *Unter Druck. Die journalistische Textwerkstatt. Erfahrungen, Analysen, Übungen.* Opladen: VS Verlag für Sozialwissenschaften.

Hidi, S. and P. Boscolo (eds.)
2006 *Motivation and Interest in Writing.* Amsterdam: Elsevier.

Hyland, K.
2001   Bringing in the reader. Addressee features in academic articles. *Written Communication* 18(4): 549–574.
Hyland, K.
2003   Genre-based pedagogies. A social response to process. *Journal of Second Language Writing* 12(1): 17–29.
Jakobs, E.-M.
1995   Text und Quelle. Wissenschaftliche Textproduktion unter dem Aspekt Nutzung externer Wissensspeicher. In: E.-M. Jakobs, D. Knorr, and S. Molitor-Lübbert (eds.), *Wissenschaftliche Textproduktion mit und ohne Computer*, 91–112. Frankfurt am Main: Lang.
Jakobs, E.-M.
1997   Lesen und Textproduzieren. In: E.-M. Jakobs, and D. Knorr (eds.), *Schreiben in den Wissenschaften*, 75–90. Frankfurt am Main: Lang.
Jakobs, E.-M.
1999   *Textvernetzung in den Wissenschaften. Zitat und Verweis als Ergebnis rezeptiven, reproduktiven und produktiven Handelns.* Tübingen: Niemeyer.
Jakobs, E.-M.
2003   Reproductive writing – writing from sources. *Journal of Pragmatics* 35(6): 893–906.
Jakobs, E.-M.
2005a Writing at work. In: E.-M. Jakobs, K. Lehnen, and K. Schindler (eds.): *Schreiben am Arbeitsplatz*, 13–40. Wiesbaden: Verlag für Sozialwissenschaften.
Jakobs, E.-M.
2005b Texte im Beruf. Schreiben, um verstanden zu werden? In: H. Blühdorn, E. Breindl, and U. H. Waßner (eds.), *Text – Verstehen. Grammatik und darüber hinaus*, 310–326. Berlin: de Gruyter.
Jakobs, E.-M. and S. Molitor-Lübbert
1994   *Wissenschaftliches Schreiben als Balanceakt – Mit Computer (k)eine Kunst?* Saarbrücken: Universität des Saarlandes.
Jakobs, E.-M. and K. Schindler
2006   Wie viel Kommunikation braucht der Ingenieur? Ausbildungsbedarf in technischen Berufen. In: C. Efing and N. Janich (eds.), *Förderung der berufsbezogenen Schreibkompetenz. Befunde und Perspektiven*. Paderborn: Eusl.
Janssen, D., L. Van Waes, and H. Van den Bergh
1996   Effects of thinking aloud on writing processes. In: C. M. Levy and S. Ransdell (eds.), *The Science of Writing. Theories, Methods, Individual Differences and Applications*, 233–250. Mahwah: Erlbaum.
Jeffery, G. and G. Underwood
1996   The role of working memory in the development of a writing skill. Learning to co-ordinate ideas within written text. In: G. Rijlaarsdam, H. Van den Bergh, and M. Couzijn (eds.), *Theories, Models and Methodology in Writing Research*, 268–282. Amsterdam: Amsterdam University Press.
Johnston, B.
2003   Teaching and researching critical academic writing: scrutiny of an action research process. *Educational Action Research* 11(3): 365–388.

Keseling, G.
1988   Textmuster und Klangstrukturen als Grundlage von Bewertungen beim Schreiben. In: W. Brandt (ed.), *Sprache in Vergangenheit und Gegenwart*, 219–236. Marburg: Hitzerroth.

Keseling, G.
1992   Pause and intonation contours in written and oral discourse. In: D. Stein (ed.), *Cooperating with Written Texts. The Pragmatics and Comprehension of Written Texts*, 31–66. Berlin: Mouton de Gruyter.

Keseling, G.
1993   *Schreibprozess und Textstruktur. Empirische Untersuchungen zur Produktion von Zusammenfassungen.* Tübingen: Niemeyer.

Keseling, G.
2004   *Die Einsamkeit des Schreibers. Blockaden und Schwierigkeiten bei der schriftlichen Textproduktion.* Opladen: VS Verlag für Sozialwissenschaften.

Klein, P. D.
1999   Reopening inquiry into cognitive processes in writing-to-learn. *Behavioural Science* 11(3): 203–270.

Klemm, M.
2004   Schreibberatung und Schreibtraining. In: K. Knapp, G. Antos, M. Becker-Mrotzek, A. Deppermann, S. Göpferich, J. Grabowski, M. Klemm, and C. Villiger (eds.), *Angewandte Linguistik. Ein Lehrbuch*, 120–142. Tübingen: Francke.

Kretzenbacher, H. L.
1990   *Rekapitulationen. Textstrategien der Zusammenfassung von wissenschaftlichen Fachtexten.* Tübingen: Narr.

Kruse, O.
2006   The origins of writing in the disciplines. Traditions of seminar writing and the Humboldtian ideal of the research university. *Written Communication* 23(3): 331–352.

Laakaniemi, R.
1987a   An analysis of writing coach programs on American daily newspapers. *Journalism Quarterly* 2–3(64): 567–575.

Laakaniemi, R.
1987b   Letter from the coach. *Newspaper Research Journal* 3: 53–58.

Lalouschek, J.
2004   Kommunikatives Selbst-Coaching im beruflichen Alltag. Ein sprachwissenschaftliches Trainingskonzept am Beispiel der klinischen Gesprächsführung. In: M. Becker-Mrotzek and G. Brünner (eds.), *Analyse und Vermittlung von Gesprächskompetenz*, 137–158. Frankfurt am Main: Lang.

Lambertini, L. and J. D. Ten Thije
2004   Die Vermittlung interkulturellen Handlungswissens mittels der Simulation authentischer Fälle. In: M. Becker-Mrotzek and G. Brünner (eds.), *Analyse und Vermittlung von Gesprächskompetenz*, 175–198. Frankfurt am Main: Lang.

Landis, D.
2003   Reading and writing as social, cultural practices. Implications for literary education. *Reading and Writing Quarterly* 19(3): 281–307.

Levin, T. and T. Wagner
  2006   In their own words: Understanding student conceptions of writing through their spontaneous metaphors in the science classroom. *Instructional Science* 34(3): 227–278.
Levy, C. M., J. P. Marek, and J. Lea
  1996   Concurrent and retrospective protocols in writing research. In: G. Rijlaarsdam, H. Van den Bergh, and M. Couzijn (eds.), *Theories, Models and Methodology in Writing Research*, 542–556. Amsterdam: Amsterdam University Press.
Levy, C. M. and S. Ransdell
  1995   Is writing as difficult as it seems? *Memory and Cognition* 23(6): 767–779.
Levy, C. M. and S. Ransdell
  1996   Writing signatures. In: C. M. Levy and S. Ransdell (eds.), *The Science of Writing. Theories, Methods, Individual Differences and Applications*, 127–148. Mahwah: Erlbaum.
Lippmann, E.
  2006   *Coaching*. Heidelberg: Springer.
Ludwig, O.
  1983   Der Schreibprozess. Die Vorstellungen der Pädagogen. In: K. B. Günther and H. Günther (eds.), *Schrift, Schreiben, Schriftlichkeit. Arbeiten zur Struktur, Funktion und Entwicklung schriftlicher Sprache*, 191–210. Tübingen: Niemeyer.
Ludwig, O.
  2005   *Geschichte des Schreibens* (Vol. 1: *Von der Antike bis zum Buchdruck*). Berlin: de Gruyter.
Marx, U.
  2005   Entwicklung und Begründung einer präskriptiven Notation von Hörfunknachrichten und Vergleich mit empirisch deskriptiver Analyse. In: N. Gutenberg (ed.), *Schreiben und Sprechen von Hörfunknachrichten. Zwischenergebnisse sprechwissenschaftlicher Forschung*, 121–193. Frankfurt am Main: Lang.
McCarthy Young, K.
  1998   Writing from primary documents. A way of knowing in history. *Written Communication* 15(1): 25–68.
McGee, T. and P. Ericsson
  2002   The politics of the program MS Word as the invisible grammarian. *Computers and Composition* 19(4): 453–470.
McLeod, S.
  1987   The affective domain and the writing process. *College Composition and Communication* 38(4): 426–435.
Melenhorst, M., T. Van der Geest, and M. Steehouder
  2005   Noteworthy observations about note-taking by professionals. *Journal of Technical Writing and Communication* 35(3): 317–329.
Molitor, S.
  1987   Weiterentwicklung eines Textproduktionsmodells durch Fallstudien. *Unterrichtswissenschaft* 4: 396–409.
Molitor-Lübbert, S.
  1984   *Kognitive Prozesse beim Schreiben*. Tübingen: Deutsches Institut für Fernstudien an der Universität.

Molitor-Lübbert, S.
1996 Schreiben als mentaler und sprachlicher Prozeß. In: H. Günther and O. Ludwig (eds.), *Schrift und Schriftlichkeit. Ein interdisziplinäres Handbuch internationaler Forschung* (Vol. 2), 1005–1027. Berlin: de Gruyter.

Molitor-Lübbert, S.
1998 Schreiben und Lernen im Licht der Neuen Medien und Informationstechnologie. In: H. G. Klinzing (ed.), *Neue Lernverfahren*, 205–221. Tübingen: Dgvt.

Molitor-Lübbert, S.
2002 Schreiben und Denken. Kognitive Grundlagen des Schreibens. In: D. Perrin, I. Boettcher, O. Kruse, and A. Wrobel (eds.), *Schreiben. Von intuitiven zu professionellen Schreibstrategien*, 33–46. Westdeutscher Verlag: Westdeutscher Verlag.

Mönnich, A.
2004 Gesprächsführung lernen. Welche impliziten Konzeptualisierungen des Kommunikationslernens sind in Methoden zur Entwicklung der Gesprächsfähigkeit zu finden? In: M. Becker-Mrotzek and G. Brünner (eds.), *Analyse und Vermittlung von Gesprächskompetenz*, 87–113. Frankfurt am Main: Lang.

Nelson Spivey, N.
1990 Transforming texts. Constructive processes in reading and writing. *Written Communication* 7(2): 256–287.

O'Hara, K. P., A. Taylor, W. Newman, and A. J. Sellen
2002 Understanding the materiality of writing from multiple sources. *International Journal of Human-Computer Studies* 56(3): 269–305.

Olson, L. D.
1987 Recent composition research is relevant to newswriting. *Journalism Educator* 42(3): 14–18.

Ongstad, S.
2005 Enculturation to institutional writing. In: T. Kostouli (ed.), *Writing in Context(s). Textual Practices and Learning Processes in Sociocultural Settings*, 49–68. Amsterdam: Elsevier.

Ortner, H.
1995 Die Sprache als Produktivkraft. Das (epistemisch-heuristische) Schreiben aus der Sicht der Piagetschen Kognitionspsychologie. In: J. Baurmann and R. Weingarten (eds.), *Schreiben. Prozesse, Prozeduren und Produkte*, 320–342. Opladen: Westdeutscher Verlag.

Ortner, H.
2000 *Schreiben und Denken*. Tübingen: Niemeyer.

Ortner, H.
2002 Schreiben und Wissen. Einfälle fördern und Aufmerksamkeit staffeln. In: D. Perrin, I. Boettcher, O. Kruse, and A. Wrobel (eds.), *Schreiben. Von intuitiven zu professionellen Schreibstrategien*, 63–82. Wiesbaden: Westdeutscher Verlag.

Ortner, H.
2004 Der Sprachbegriff in der Schreibberatung. In: A. Linke, H. Ortner, and P. R. Portmann-Tselikas (eds.), *Sprache und mehr. Ansichten einer Linguistik der sprachlichen Praxis*, 305–322. Tübingen: Niemeyer.

Pajares, F.
 2003 Self-efficacy beliefs, motivation, and the achievement in writing. A review of the literature. *Reading and Writing Quarterly* 19(2): 139–158.

Palaigeorgiou, G. E., T. D. Despotakis, S. Demetriadis, and I. A. Tsoukalas
 2006 Synergies and barriers with electronic verbatim notes (eVerNotes): note taking and report writing with eVerNotes. *Journal of Computer Assisted Learning* 22(1): 74.

Parks, S.
 2001 Moving from school to the workplace: disciplinary innovation, border crossings, and the reshaping of a written genre. *Applied Linguistics* 22(4): 405–438.

Perrin, D.
 2001 *Wie Journalisten schreiben. Ergebnisse angewandter Schreibprozessforschung.* Konstanz: UVK.

Perrin, D.
 2003 Progression analysis (PA): Investigating writing strategies at the workplace. *Journal of Pragmatics 35*(6): 907–921.

Perrin, D.
 2006a *Medienlinguistik.* Konstanz: UVK [=UTB 2503].

Perrin, D.
 2006b Verstanden werden. Vom doppelten Interesse an theoriebasierter, praxisgerichteter Textberatung. In: H. Blühdorn, E. Breindl, and U. Hermann Waßner (eds.), *Text – Verstehen. Grammatik und darüber hinaus*, 332–350. Berlin: de Gruyter.

Perrin, D.
 2006c Progression analysis: An ethnographic, computer-based multi-method approach to investigate natural writing processes. In: L. Van Waes, M. Leijten, and C. Neuwirth (eds.), *Writing and Digital Media*, 175–181. Amsterdam: Elsevier.

Perrin, D., R. Dörig and P. Vervoort
 2005 Hypermedia-Lerntext gestalten. Lehrmitteldesign im Schnittfeld von Didaktik und Linguistik. In: D. Perrin and H. Kessler (eds.), *Schreiben fürs Netz. Aspekte der Zielfindung, Planung, Steuerung und Kontrolle*, 41–64. Wiesbaden: Verlag für Sozialwissenschaften.

Perrin, D. and N. Rosenberger
 2005 *Schreiben im Beruf. Wirksame Texte durch effiziente Arbeitstechnik.* Berlin: Cornelsen Pocket Business.

Pitts, B. J.
 1982 Protocol analysis of the newswriting process. *Newspaper Research Journal* 4: 12–21.

Pizarro, I.
 2004 The efficacy of art and writing therapy. Increasing positive mental health outcomes and participant retention after exposure to traumatic experience. *Art Therapy* 21(1): 5–12.

Pogner, K.-H.
 2003 Writing and interacting in the discourse community of engineering. In: D. Perrin (ed.), *The Pragmatics of Writing. Journal of Pragmatics. Special Issue 35/6*, 855–867.

Price, J.
    1999   *Outlining Goes Electronic*. Stamford: Ablex/Greenwood.
Rau, C.
    1994   *Revisionen beim Schreiben. Zur Bedeutung von Veränderungen in Textproduktionsprozessen*. Tübingen: Niemeyer.
Reece, J. E. and G. Cumming
    1996   Evaluating speech-based composition methods. Planning, dictation and the listening word processor. In: C. M. Levy and S. Ransdell (eds.), *The Science of Writing. Theories, Methods, Individual Differences, and Applications*, 361–380. Mahwah: Erlbaum.
Rijlaarsdam, G., M. Braaksma, M. Couzijn, T. Janssen, M. Kieft, H. Broekkamp, et al.
    2005   Psychology and the teaching of writing in 8000 and some words. *BJEP Monograph Series II, Number 3: Pedagogy – Teaching for Learning* 1(1): 127–153.
Rodriguez, H. and K. Severinson-Eklundh
    2006   Visualizing patterns of annotation in document-centered collaboration on the web. In: L. Van Waes, M. Leijten, and C. Neuwirth (eds.), *Writing and Digital Media*, 131–144. Amsterdam: Elsevier.
Rose, M.
    1984   *Writer's Block. The Cognitive Dimension*. Carbondale: Southern Illinois University Press.
Rouet, J. F., M. Favart, D. Gaonac'h, and N. Lacroix
    1996   Writing from multiple documents. Argumentation strategies in novice and expert history students. In: G. Rijlaarsdam, H. Van den Bergh, and M. Couzijn (eds.), *Theories, Models and Methodology in Writing Research*, 44–60. Amsterdam: Amsterdam University Press.
Ruffner, M.
    1981   An empirical approach for the assessment of journalistic writing. *Journalism Quarterly* 1: 77–82.
Ruhmann, G.
    2003   Präzise denken, sprechen, schreiben. Bausteine einer prozessorientierten Propädeutik. In: K. Ehlich and A. Steets (eds.), *Wissenschaftlich schreiben – lehren und lernen*, 211–231. Berlin: de Gruyter.
Ruhmann, G. and D. Perrin
    2002   Schreibstrategien in Balance. Was Wissenschaftler von Journalistinnen lernen können. In: D. Perrin, I. Boettcher, O. Kruse, and A. Wrobel (eds.), *Schreiben. Von intuitiven zu professionellen Schreibstrategien*, 129–138. Wiesbaden: Westdeutscher Verlag.
Russell, D.
    2002   *Writing in the Academic Disciplines. A Curricular History* (2nd ed.). Carbondale: Southern Illinois University Press.
Salovey, P. and M. D. Haar
    1990   The efficacy of cognitive-behavior therapy and writing process training for alleviating writing anxiety. *Cognitive Therapy and Research* 14(5): 513–526.
Sauer, C.
    1997   Visualisierung inbegriffen. Textüberarbeitung und Textgestaltung. In: E.-M. Jakobs and D. Knorr (eds.), *Schreiben in den Wissenschaften*, 91–106. Frankfurt am Main: Lang.

Schmitz, U.
   2003   Schreiben und neue Medien. In: U. Bredel, H. Günther, P. Klotz, J. Ossner, and G. Siebert-Ott (eds.), *Didaktik der deutschen Sprache* (Vol. 1), 249–260. Paderborn: Schöningh.
Schneider, B.
   2002   Theorizing structure and agency in workplace writing. An ethnomethodological approach. *Journal of Business and Technical Communication* 16(2): 170–195.
Schoonen, R. and K. De Glopper
   1996   Writing performance and knowledge about writing. In: G. Rijlaarsdam, H. Van den Bergh, and M. Couzijn (eds.), *Theories, Models and Methodology in Writing Research*, 87–107. Amsterdam: Amsterdam University Press.
Schriver, K. A.
   1989   Evaluating text quality. The continuum from text-focused to reader-focused methods. *IEEE transactions on professional communication* 32(4): 238–255.
Schriver, K. A.
   1992   Teaching writers to anticipate readers' needs. A classroom-evaluated pedagogy. *Written Communication* 2(9): 179–208.
Segev-Miller, R.
   2004   Writing from sources: The effect of explicit instruction on college student's processes and products. *L1-Educational Studies in Language and Literature* 4(1): 5–33.
Selzer, J.
   1993   Intertextuality and the writing process. In: Rachel Spilka (ed.), *Writing in the workplace. New research perspectives*, 171–180. Carbondale: Southern Illinois University Press.
Severinson-Eklundh, K.
   1992   The use of "idea processors" for studying structural aspects of text production. In: A.-C. Lindeberg, N. E. Enkvist, and K. Wikberg (eds.), *Nordic Research on Text and Discourse – Nordtext Symposium 1990*, 271–287. Abo: Abo Academy Press.
Severinson-Eklundh, K.
   1994   Linear and nonlinear strategies in computer-based writing. *Computers and Composition* 11: 203–216.
Severinson-Eklundh, K. and P. Kollberg
   2001   Studying writers' revision patterns with s-notation analysis. In: T. Olive and C. M. Levy (eds.), *Contemporary Tools and Techniques for Studying Writing*, 89–104. Dordrecht/Boston/London: Kluwer Academic Publishers.
Severinson-Eklundh, K. and P. Kollberg
   2003   Emerging discourse structure: computer-assisted episode analysis as a window to global revision in university students' writing. In: D. Perrin (ed.), *The Pragmatics of Writing. Journal of Pragmatics. Special Issue 35/6*, 869–891.
Sharples, M.
   1996   An account of writing as creative design. In: C. M. Levy and S. Ransdell (eds.), *The Science of Writing. Theories, Methods, Individual Differences and Applications*, 127–148. Mahwah: Erlbaum.

Sleurs, K., G. Jacobs, and L. Van Waes
   2003   Constructing press releases, constructing quotations: A case study. *Journal of Sociolinguistics* 7(2): 135–275.
Smagorinsky, P.
   1994   Think-aloud protocol analysis. Beyond the black box. In: P. Smagorinsky (ed.), *Speaking about Writing. Reflections on Research Methodology*, 3–19. Thousand Oaks: Sage.
Smagorinsky, P.
   2001   Rethinking protocol analysis from a cultural perspective. *Annual Review of Applied Linguistics* 21: 233–245.
Smiley, J.
   1999   What stories teach their writers. The purpose and practice of revision. In: J. Checkoway (ed.), *Creating Fiction. Instruction and Insights from Teachers of the Associated Writing Programs*, 244–255. Cincinnati: Story Press.
Sommers, N.
   1980   Revision strategies of student writers. *College composition and communication* 31: 378–388.
Spilka, R. (ed.)
   1993   *Writing in the Workplace. New Research Perspectives*. Carbondale: Southern Illinois University Press.
Spinnen, B.
   1992   "– unser Schreibzeug arbeitet mit an unseren Gedanken". Anmerkungen zum Computerschreiben. *Sprache im technischen Zeitalter* 121: 41–52.
Steinhoff, T.
   2003   Wie entwickelt sich die wissenschaftliche Textkompetenz? *Der Deutschunterricht* 55(3): 38–47.
Strömqvist, S., K. Holmqvist, V. Johansson, H. Karlsson, and Å. Wengelin
   2006   What key-logging can reveal about writing. In: K. Sullivan and E. Lindgren (eds.), *Computer Key-Stroke Logging and Writing: Methods and Applications*, 45–72. Dordrecht/Boston/London: Kluwer Academic Publishers.
Surma, A.
   2000   Defining professional writing as an area of scholarly activity. *TEXT* 4(2), http://www.griffith.edu.au/school/art/text.
Tapper, J.
   2000   Preparing university students for the communicative attributes and skills required by employers. *Australian Journal of Communication* 27(2): 111–130.
Tench, R.
   2006   Supporting writing. The role of evaluation in VLE design. *Zeitschrift Schreiben*, http://www.zeitschrift-schreiben.eu.
Torrance, M.
   1996   Is writing expertise like other kinds of expertise? In: G. Rijlaarsdam, H. Van den Bergh, and M. Couzijn (eds.), *Theories, Models and Methodology in Writing Research*, 3–9. Amsterdam: Amsterdam University Press.
Trappen, S.
   2002   Repertoires öffnen. Ein Rhethorik-Modell für Schreibtrainings. In: D. Perrin, I. Boettcher, O. Kruse, and A. Wrobel (eds.), *Schreiben. Von intuitiven zu professionellen Schreibstrategien*, 169–182. Wiesbaden: Westdeutscher Verlag.

Uppstad, P. H. and A. K. H. Wagner
   2006   Approaching the skills of writing. In: L. Van Waes, M. Leijten, and C. Neuwirth (eds.), *Writing and Digital Media*, 221–238. Amsterdam: Elsevier.

Van den Bergh, H., G. Rijlaarsdam, and I. Breetvelt
   1994   Revision process and text quality. An empirical study. In: G. Eigler and T. Jechle (eds.), *Writing. Current Trends in European Research*, 133–147. Freiburg: Hochschul Verlag.

Van der Geest, T.
   1996a   Professional writing studied. Authors' accounts of planning in document production processes. In: M. Sharples and T. Van der Geest (eds.), *The New Writing Environment. Writers at Work in a World of Technology*, 7–24. London: Springer.

Van der Geest, T.
   1996b   Studying 'real life' writing processes. A proposal and an example. In: C. M. Levy and S. Ransdell (eds.), *The Science of Writing. Theories, Methods, Individual Differences, and Applications*, 309–322. Mahwah: Erlbaum.

Van Waes, L.
   1994   Computers and writing. Implications for the teaching of writing. *Odense Working Papers in Language and Communication* 6: 41–61.

Van Waes, L. and P. J. Schellens
   2003   Writing profiles: the effect of the writing mode on pausing and revision patterns of experienced writers. In: D. Perrin (ed.), *The Pragmatics of Writing. Journal of Pragmatics. Special Issue 35/6*, 829–853.

Varner, D. and S. R. Peck
   2003   Learning from learning journals. The benefits and challenges of using learning journal assignments. *Journal of management education* 27(1): 52–77.

Williamson, M. M. and P. Pence
   1989   Word processing and student writers. In: B. K. Britton and S. M. Glynn (eds.), *Computer Writing Environments. Theory, Research and Design*, 93–127. Hillsdale: Erlbaum.

Wolf, R. and T. Thomason
   1986   Writing coaches. Their strategies for improving writing. *Newspaper Research Journal* 3(7): 43–59.

Wolfe, J.
   2002   Annotation technologies: A software and research review. *Computers and Composition* 19(4): 471–497.

Wolfe, J.
   2005   Gesture and collaborative planning. A case study of a student writing group. *Written Communication* 22(3): 298–332.

Wrobel, A.
   1997   Zur Modellierung von Formulierungsprozessen. In: E.-M. Jakobs and D. Knorr (eds.), *Schreiben in den Wissenschaften*, 15–24. Frankfurt/Berlin: Lang.

Wrobel, A.
   2000   Phasen und Verfahren der Produktion schriftlicher Texte. In: G. Antos, K. Brinker, W. Heinemann, and S. F. Sager (eds.), *Text- und Gesprächslinguistik. Ein internationales Handbuch zeitgenössischer Forschung* (Vol. 1), 458–472. Berlin/New York: de Gruyter.

Wrobel, A.
2002 Schreiben und Formulieren. Prätext als Problemindikator und Lösung. In: D. Perrin, I. Boettcher, O. Kruse, and A. Wrobel (eds.), *Schreiben. Von intuitiven zu professionellen Schreibstrategien*, 83–96. Wiesbaden: Westdeutscher Verlag.

Zaslow, R.
1991 Managers as writing coaches. *Training and Development* 45(7): 61–64.

Zhu, Y.
2005 *Written Communication across Cultures. A Sociocognitive Perspective on Business Genres*. Amsterdam: Benjamins.

V. Language therapy

15. Developmental dyslexia: A developmental neurolinguistic approach

Virginia W. Berninger, William Nagy, Todd Richards, and Wendy Raskind

This chapter is organized around seven themes pertinent to understanding developmental dyslexia. The first theme is the historical origin of the concept of developmental dyslexia, which is contrasted with other reading disorders. The second theme is the biological basis of this developmental disorder – genetic and neurological. The third theme is the language basis of developmental dyslexia, which is best understood within a theoretical framework that (a) distinguishes among levels of language, (b) takes into account functional systems, and (c) models language in relationship to working memory components. The fourth theme is the instructional basis of developmental dyslexia and the role the language learning device may play in learning written as well as spoken language. The fifth theme is the nature-nurture interaction perspective that integrates the biological and behavioral bases of written language learning and illustrates the plasticity of the human brain that does respond to reading and writing instruction. The sixth theme concerns definitional issues, which are currently not fully resolved and have implications for research, clinical, and educational practice. Developmental dyslexia expresses itself behaviorally not only as a reading disorder but also as a writing disorder, the nature of which changes over the course of development as students interact with changing curriculum requirements. The seventh theme is theoretical issues in linguistics that are relevant to understanding developmental dyslexia, including phonological, morphological, and orthographic word forms, mapping relationships among them and their parts (triple word form theory), and the relationship of syntax to working memory.

1. Historical origin of the term dyslexia

Neurologists initially reported cases of *acquired dyslexia* in which normal readers lost normal reading ability due to stroke, brain injury, or disease. Towards the end of the 19th century and at the beginning of the 20th century, neurologists (e.g., Orton 1937) first observed that otherwise normal children sometimes struggled to learn to read and called this condition *developmental dyslexia* (for a review of the early medical reports of developmental dyslexia, see Shaywitz 2003, Chapter 2). At the same time, psychologists began conducting experimental studies of the reading process (e.g., Huey 1908). By the middle of the 20th century, basic knowledge of the psychology of reading had been translated into scientifically supported pedagogy for teaching children to read (e.g., Bond and Tinker 1967; Gates 1947; Gray 1956). Unfortunately this knowledge gleaned from research and clinical practice was not transmitted in many teacher training programs and did not get widely implemented in practice. However, clinics for applying this knowledge to diagnostic assessment were established in many teaching hospitals and universities. It was no longer thought that children of normal intelligence who did not learn to read easily were necessarily mentally retarded. Rather, those children were thought to have a condition called dyslexia (if the professionals who assessed them were medically oriented) or a reading disability (if the professionals who assessed them were educationally oriented).

During the 1960s, national concern with civil rights emerged in the United States and led to federal legislation that guaranteed children with educational handicapping conditions the right to appropriate assessment and instruction in public schools. One kind of educationally handicapping condition covered in the federal legislation, which was enacted in 1975, was learning disability – unexpected difficulty, despite normal intelligence, in learning to read, write, do math, understand oral language, and/or use oral language. Although the most frequently identified learning disability involved reading disability, the term dyslexia was not used in either the diagnostic or treatment planning process mandated by the legislation in the United States. Although the term dyslexia is often used by professional organizations that further knowledge of this learning disorder, the term is not widely used in the schools in the United States. Nor were diagnostic and treatment processes for reading disability always informed by scientific research, much of which has been done since the federal law for educationally handicapping conditions was initially enacted (e.g., see McCardle and Chhabra 2004). See Johnson and Myklebust (1967) and Kirk and Kirk (1971) for additional early history of the field of learning disabilities in the United States.

2. Differentiation from other reading disorders

Dyslexia is not the only kind of reading disability observed in school age children, regardless of whether it is called dyslexia, specific reading disability (indicating that development is normal except for reading), or learning disability. Children with mental retardation (all areas of development fall outside the normal range), pervasive developmental disorder (two or more areas of development are outside the normal range), and primary language disability (receptive and/or expressive language are outside the normal range) also struggle in learning to read. Likewise, children with a variety of neurogenetic syndromes like fragile X, Downs, Williams, autism etc., with substance-abuse related conditions like fetal alcohol syndrome, or with brain injury or disease may struggle in learning to read. The diagnosis of dyslexia presupposes that none of these other medical conditions is accounting for the unexpected difficulty in learning to read. Preschool oral language status does not predict reading achievement during the school years or diagnostic classification associated with reading disability; thus, it is important that children with early history of oral language problems be carefully monitored and assessed during the school years (Aram, Ekelman, and Nation 1984; Bishop and Adams 1990; Catts, Fey, Zhang, and Tomblin 1999). Many factors should be taken into consideration in predicting expected reading levels during the school age years (Catts, Fey, Zhang, and Tomblin 2001).

3. Genetic basis

The methods of genetics research are rapidly advancing. For an introduction to this technical field for non-geneticists, with a focus on developmental dyslexia, see Thomson and Raskind (2003) or Gayán et al. (2005). Although considerable behavioral research on dyslexia subtypes exists (e.g., Manis, Seidenberg, Doi, McBride-Chang, and Petersen 1996), genetics research has not been focused on subtypes of dyslexia; rather, the research on the genetics of this complex developmental disorder has typically treated all individuals with reading disability as if they belonged to the same population or has investigated the genetic basis for specific measures of the behavioral expression of the underlying genetic disorder (referred to as phenotypes, subphenotypes, or endophenotypes).

Heritability. Dyslexia is more prevalent in some families than others (Pennington and Lefly 2001). However, simply demonstrating that a trait tends to occur frequently in a family does not constitute evidence that it is genetic. Geneticists conduct heritability analyses of twin pairs – monozygotic ("identical"; share all their genes) and dizygotic ("fraternal"; share, on average, half their genes, just like other siblings) or aggregation analyses of nuclear and extended family members to address the issue of whether a specific behavioral trait may have a genetic basis, and, if so, to what degree it is likely to be heritable (genetic) versus environmental in origin. The conclusion based on both the twin heritability studies (e.g., Olson 2004; Olson, Datta, Gayan, and DeFries 1999) and the family aggregation studies (e.g., Hsu et al. 2002; Raskind et al. 2000) is that developmental dyslexia does indeed have a genetic basis and is heritable, with about 50% of the variance, on average, attributable to genetic factors (e.g., Olson, Forsberg, and Wise 1994).

Analyses of genetic mechanisms of inheritance. Segregation analyses (e.g., Chapman, Raskind, Thomson, Berninger, and Wijsman 2003; Wijsman et al. 2000) evaluate alternative mechanisms of transmission in families of the specific behavioral phenotype (measurable behavior associated with a disorder like dyslexia). This information is used in linkage analyses to pinpoint which chromosome (and site on that chromosome) may contain a gene that contributes to the phenotype.

Linkage analyses for dyslexia. Like other complex disorders, it is likely that many genes can contribute to developmental dyslexia. To date, linkage of dyslexia or phenotypes associated with dyslexia (behavioral measures) has been found for at least 13 regions on 10 chromosomes (reviewed in Fisher and DeFries 2002 and Raskind et al. 2005). The two most consistently replicated regions for dyslexia are on chromosomes 6 (e.g., Cardon et al. 1994; Cardon et al. 1995; Grigorenko et al. 1997; Gayan et al. 1999; Fisher et al. 1999) and 15 (e.g., Smith et al. 1983; Grigorenko et al. 1997; Schulte-Körne et al. 1998; Chapman et al. 2004) and the presumed genes at these locations are referred to as DYX2 and DYX1, respectively. Our group has replicated chromosome 15 linkage (Chapman et al. 2004) and reported novel linkage sites for reading fluency – chromosome 2 for rate of phonological decoding (Raskind et al. 2005) and chromosome 13 for rate of real word reading (Igo et al. 2006). There are also failures to replicate linkage to the various locations (e.g., Chapman et al. 2005; Petryshen et al. 2000), which may indicate that different research groups focused on the genetics of dyslexia may be studying different relative mixes of different kinds of developmental dyslexia; hence, definitional issues are of critical importance to scientific advances, a topic emphasized later in this chapter.

Genes. Recently, candidate genes have been proposed for the developmental dyslexia susceptibility loci DYX1 on chromosome 15 (*DYX1C1*; Taipale et al. 2003), DYX2 on chromosome 6 (*KIAA0319* and *DCDC2*; Cope et al. 2005; Meng et al. 2005; Schumacher et al. 2006) and DYX5 on chromosome 3 (Hannula-Jouppi et al. 2005). However, these results have not been consistently replicated and it is unclear what relationship changes in these genes have to major subtypes of developmental dyslexia. Much research remains to be done on the genetic basis of developmental dyslexia.

4. Neurological basis

During the first two decades of *in vivo* brain imaging, differences between developmental dyslexics and good readers have been well documented at many different levels of neural substrate (Berninger and Richards 2002), ranging from *structural neuroanatomy* (Eckert et al. 2005; Hynd, Semrud-Clikeman, Lorys, Novey, and Eliopulos 1990; Leonard et al. 1993; Pennington et al., 1999), to *white matter tracts* (Klingberg et al. 1999, 2000), to neuro*chemical changes* (Rae et al. 1998), to PET and rCBF (Flowers, Wood, and Naylor 1991; McCrory, Frith, Brunswick, and Price 2000; Rumsey et al. 1992), to *spatially sensitive fMRI BOLD activation* (Booth, Burman, Meyer, Gitelman, Parrish, and Mesulam 2003; Eden, Van Meter, Rumsey, and Zeffiro 1996; Paulesu et al. 2001; Shaywitz et al. 1998, 2002; Temple et al. 2001), to *temporally* sensitive *MEG* (Cornelissen et al. 1998; Helenius, Salmelin, Service, and Connolly 1999) or *MSI* (Simos et al. 2002, 2005; Simos, Breier, Fletcher, Forman et al. 2000; Simos, Papanicolaou et al. 2000; Simos, Breier, Fletcher, Bergman, and Papanicolaou 2000), to ERPs (Breznitz 2002; Molfese 2000; Molfese, Molfese, Key, Modglin, Kelley, and Terrell, 2002). The neural signature of dyslexia is remarkable similar across different languages (Paulesu et al. 2001) even though some brain differences have been reported for normal readers associated with differences in the orthographies of language (regularity of correspondences between written and spoken words) (e.g., Tan, Liu, Perfetti, Spinks, Fox, and Gao 2001).

Most, but not all, of these imaging studies were done with adults. Some studies compared children and adults on the same task to understand how the brain may change over development while performing the same task, which is easily performed by both the children and the adults (Booth, MacWhinney, Thulborn, Sacco, Voyvodic, and Feldman 2000; Turkeltab, Gareau, Flowers, Zeffiro, and Eden 2003). In contrast, our research group studied disabled and good readers in middle childhood when the brain is still responsive to reading instruction (Aylward et al. 2003; Corina et al. 2001; Richards et al. 1999, 2000, 2002, 2005, 2006, in press).

Based on the studies done to date on adults and children, considerable knowledge has accrued about where the brain architecture of dyslexics and good readers differs (especially on the left): posterior word form areas, superior temporal and parietal regions, and frontal regions (especially on the left) and cerebellum (e.g., Pugh et al. 2000; Shaywitz et al. 1998). However, exactly where functional activation occurs depends on which tasks the participants are asked to perform while their brains are scanned (Berninger and Richards 2002).

These studies have also shown that just because a developmental disorder has a genetic and/or neurological basis, it does not follow that it is not responsive to environmental input. The brain is an organ uniquely designed for interacting with the environment. All the treatments used in our imaging research (Berninger 2000 for children scanned in Richards et al. 1999 and 2000; Berninger, Nagy et al. 2003, for children scanned in Richards et al. 2002, 2006b, and Aylward et al. 2003; and Berninger and Hidi, 2006, 2006a, for Richards et al. 2005, 2006) that showed change and normalization of dyslexics on specific fMRI language tasks were designed to teach to all levels of language (subword, word, and text) close in time to create connections across levels of language and overcome working memory inefficiencies in dyslexia (Berninger et al. 2007; Byrne et al. 2002; Swanson 1999, 2000). Others have used different treatments and fMRI tasks both with adults (Eden et al. 2004) and children (Shaywitz et al. 2004; Simos et al. 2002; Temple et al. 2000, 2003) and also showed the plasticity of the brain of children with dyslexia in response to language-based treatments.

5. Language basis

Paradigm shift. The dominant causal model throughout most of the 20th century attributed developmental dyslexia to a visual perceptual disorder that led to reversals. Considerable scientific research led to a paradigm shift during the last two decades of the 20th century and the consensus now is that dyslexia is a language disorder and the causal mechanisms are primarily (if not exclusively) phonological (e.g., Morris et al. 1998; Stanovich 1986; Wagner and Torgesen 1987; Vellutino and Scanlon 1987) and not due to a general auditory deficit (Mody, Studdert-Kennedy, and Brady 1997).

Levels of language. The lay concept of language is that it is a unitary construct that can be contrasted with other unitary constructs such as attention, memory, cognition (thinking) and so on. One of the major contributions of linguistics has been the development of schemes for discussing the complexities of language, including the levels at which it can be analyzed, ranging from phonology to morphology to syntax to semantics to text discourse (e.g., Whitaker, Berninger, Johnston, and Swanson 1994). This notion of levels of language is relevant to understanding the different kinds of reading and writing disabilities that occur. One kind of reading disability affects only the decoding or recognition of single written words – text comprehension is spared once an adequate level of decoding proficiency is attained. However, another kind of reading disability affects both word recognition (probably because of problems in semantic access as well as phonological decoding) and reading comprehension at the sentence and text levels (Berninger, in press). Although a phonological causal mechanism may explain the first kind of reading disability, additional levels of language are undoubtedly involved in explaining the second kind of disability (see Butler and Silliman 1994; Catts and Kamhi 2005; Wallach and Butler 1994; Scarborough 2001).

Functional systems. The same brain regions may participate in different systems that orchestrate together in time to accomplish different language goals (Luria 1970). Reading and writing are complex skills that draw on many different component processes and the functional organization of these processes in the brain changes over time (Berninger and Richards 2002). Developmental dyslexia affects individuals differently, depending on their stage of reading or writing development and expectations placed on their functional reading or writing systems for accomplishing academic tasks imposed by the changing school curriculum across the grades. For example, when the task is to learn strategies for pronouncing written words, the orthographic and phonological processes in the functional reading system must work together. If either of these processes is impaired in an individual, the functional system for oral reading will not develop in typical fashion. However, if the goal is to gain meaning from words and read text with understanding, then morphological and syntactic processes may play a greater role in the functional system. When the goal becomes to generate written text, many processes not involved in interpreting text may be called upon, for example, transcription (handwriting and spelling) and text generation (for generating ideas and translating them into language).

Working memory. The brain mechanism that coordinates the multiple processes involved in reading and writing is working memory, which stores words, has a phonological loop for maintaining words in active memory and learning new words, and an executive system for self-regulation of its processes (Baddeley 2002; Baddeley and Della Sala 1996; Baddeley, Gathercole, and Papagano 1998). Working memory contributes uniquely to both reading comprehension and written composition (Swanson 1999, 2000; Swanson and Berninger 1995, 1996). The phenotype for dyslexia can be characterized in terms of the components of working memory all of which have a phonological component; the impaired phonology explains their phonological decoding deficits, and the underdevelopment of specific components of working memory interferes with the overall efficiency of working memory and explains the fluency problems of dyslexics (Berninger et al. in press).

6. Instructional basis

Home environment. Biological variables are not the only influence on learning to read and write. Educational level of parents and home literacy experiences also influence children's emergent written language skills before and during formal schooling (Adams 1990). Experiential deficits may result in brain differences related to written language learning as much as biological deficits do (Eckert, Lombardino, and Leonard 2001).

School curriculum. During the 1970's and 1980's pendulum swings in the educational philosophy emphasized meaning (discourse level of language) and deemphasized phonology (subword and word levels of language). As a result, many children in general education did not develop adequate decoding skills for unknown words, which in turn, compromised their reading comprehension. In addition, meta-analyses showed that special education for students with learning disabilities has not been effective in raising student learning outcomes (e.g., Bradley, Danielson, and Hallahan 2002; Lyon et al. 2001) especially in reading (McCray, Vaughn, and Neal 2001; Vaughn, Moody, and Schumm 1998). Thus, curriculum casualities or curriculum disabilities are another source of reading disabilities, but it is often not just the curriculum per se but also teacher knowledge in implementing curriculum that contributes to inadequate student learning of written language.

Teacher knowledge. Low achievement in both general and special education may be due to inadequate preservice training in the psychology and pedagogy of reading and writing. Currently, many preservice teacher training programs advocate philosophical approaches (e.g., constructivism) that are not consistent with what research in developmental science and educational science during the past three decades has shown – namely the effectiveness of explicit instruction in general (Mayer 2004) and in particular for reading (to bring language processes into conscious awareness, Mattingly 1972). There is a myth that explicit instruction is drilling skill, but see, Bear, Ivernizzi, Templeton, and Johnston (2000) and Berninger, Nagy et al., (2003) for examples of explicit instruction for developing linguistic awareness in reflective ways that are intellectually engaging.

In addition, preservice teachers are not given sufficient coursework in linguistics, or taught how this knowledge of language is relevant to teaching reading and writing (Moats 2000). First of all, they need to have a clear understanding of the alphabetic nature of the writing system. Spelling units, typically one or two letters in length, generally represent speech sounds called phonemes in a predictable manner. It has been well established that knowledge of the alphabetic principle can explain the acquisition of one and two syllable words of Anglo-Saxon origin that occur with high frequency in reading materials in the lower elementary grades (for reviews see Balmuth 1992; Ehri, Nunes, Stahl, and Willows, 2001; Rayner, Foorman, Perfetti, Pesetsky, and Seidenberg 2001). Grasping the alphabetic principle requires the ability to analyze spoken words into their constituent phonemes, which can be especially difficult for students with dyslexia. Both phonological awareness activities (manipulating phonemes in spoken words) and articulatory awareness activities (becoming aware of motor movements of the mouth) have been found effective in teaching dyslexics to apply alphabetic principle to the word decoding process; however, phonological awareness activities alone are sufficient for most dyslexics (Wise, Ring, and Olson 1999). Nevertheless, including articulatory awareness training in a comprehensive reading intervention may have some benefit for children with both dyslexia and attention deficit disorder (e.g., Torgesen et al. 2001), but further research is needed on this topic.

Knowledge about the importance of phonological processes in early word decoding has become more widespread, but teachers are likely to know less about how other levels of language are relevant to learning written words. In particular, teachers need to understand that our writing system is morphophonemic. Much of the apparent unpredictability of American spelling disappears when morphology is taken into consideration – that is, different forms of the same root word maintain the same spelling despite changes in pronunciation. For example, the spelling of *sign* maintains the form of the root also found in *signature*. Knowledge of morphology is critical to the acquisition of the *longer, more complex written words* that occur with high frequency in reading materials from mid-elementary school through high school and college (Carlisle 2004; Carlisle and Stone 2004; Carlisle, Stone, and Katz 2001; Nagy, Anderson, Schommer, Scott, and Stallman 1989; Nagy, Osborn, Winsor, and O'Flahavan 1994). From fourth grade on, students encounter in their school texts an increasing number of complex words in terms of sound-letter relations and internal structure (i.e., syllabic or morphemic structure) (Carlisle 2000; Carlisle and Fleming 2003; Nagy and Anderson 1984).

Instructional needs transcend phonology and morphology. Students who earlier struggled with mastering alphabetic principle, because of difficulties in phonological processing (Liberman, Shankweiler, and Liberman 1989), face additional challenges in learning to recognize specific words automatically: (a) creating and linking precise phonological and orthographic representations in long-term memory (Ehri 1992; Perfetti 1992), and (b) encountering low frequency written words frequently enough (White, Power, and White 1989). Students who were earlier taught phonics and may have learned letter-sound correspondences in alphabetic principle, word family patterns (e.g., -at in pat, bat, etc), and syllable types (e.g., open and closed, vowel teams, silent e, r-controlled, and -le) need to learn additional strategies for dealing with the complexity in English orthography (Nagy et al. 1994; White, Power, and White 1989), especially in content-area texts, which may have spellings unique to word origin (Anglo-Saxon, Latinate, or Greek), complex word structures, and unfamiliar, low frequency words.

To summarize, teachers are often not adequately prepared conceptually or pedagogically for the linguistic issues involved in teaching reading and writing. This lack of teacher knowledge can contribute as much as biological factors to the observed reading and writing disabilities of dyslexics.

7. Nature-nurture interactions and the language learning device

Chomsky first proposed the language learning device as a biologically based mechanism that governs the acquisition of oral language. With the emergence of the field of child language in the 1970's and 1980's, there was an increasing recognition of the role of social interaction with adults and other children in learning oral language. The recent research on combining brain imaging with instruction in written language (see Richards et al. 1995, in press, for reviews) points to nature-nurture interactions in learning written language – the brain is not an independent variable that causes language learning in and of itself but rather is also a dependent variable that changes in response to language input from the environment. The time has come to reexamine the role of the language learning device in light of this new nature-nurture interaction perspective in neuroscience, with special emphasis on its role in written language acquisition as well as oral language acquisition.

Recent developments in working memory research suggest that the time-sensitive phonological loop of working memory may be an important component of the language learning device (e.g., Baddeley et al. 1998). Children initially learn oral language by naming visual objects, that is, attaching phonological codes for whole words to the objects. Later, during early schooling, they learn written words by naming them, that is, attaching phonological codes for letters and whole words to the written words. This phonological loop may also play a role in second language learning as children coordinate phonological codes across two languages. Developmental dyslexics are often impaired in phonological loop processes (e.g., Berninger et al. in press), which may explain their difficulties in second language learning (Ganschow and Sparks 2000). To summarize, the phonological loop may play a role in first language learning (oral language), written language, and second language learning (oral and written language).

We suspect that dyslexics who have a double deficit in phonological awareness and rapid automatic naming (Wolf and Bowers 1999) may have combined impairment in two components of working memory – word storage and phonological loop: the phonological awareness deficit stems from imprecise phonological word form storage, which interferes with analysis of phonemes in the phonological word form; and the rapid naming deficit stems from impairment in the temporally sensitive phonological loop, which interferes with the rate of coordinating orthographic and phonological codes during the naming process. Some dyslexics may also have a deficit related to the third component of working memory – supervisory attention that underlies the rapid switching of attention or mental set, as assessed by the rapid alternating switching task for naming letters and digits (Berninger et al. in press; Wolf 1986).

Children with language learning disability, which is often confounded with dyslexia in studies of reading disabilities, may also have severe impairment in their language learning device that interferes first with oral language development and subsequently with written language development and/or second language learning. Like the children Chall (1983) described who first have difficulty in learning to read and then in using reading to learn, these children first have difficulty learning aural/oral language and then in using both aural/oral and written language to learn (see Berninger, 2006 in press). More research is needed on the language learning mechanism from a nature-nurture perspective and in regard to its role in written language learning, its relationship to the phonological loop of working memory, and its contribution to the etiology of language learning disability.

8. Definitional issues

Exclusionary criteria. Because professionals could not agree on how to define what a learning disability is (inclusionary criteria), the federal law for educationally handicapping conditions defined learning disability on the basis of what it is not, that is, criteria for excluding children from services under the learning disability category: Learning disability is not due to mental retardation, sensory acuity or motor impairment, lack of opportunity to learn, or cultural difference. These exclusionary criteria are confusing because children with mental retardation are disabled in their learning. Sometimes children with learning disabilities also have sensory and/or motor anomalies. Sometimes, because of curriculum issues and inadequate preparation of teachers about language as already discussed, students with learning disabilities do lack adequate opportunity to learn. Sometimes children with cultural or language difference also have learning disabilities that stem from biological influences. Another source of confusion stems from the federal law not explicitly mentioning *dyslexia* as a diagnostic category or a category for qualifying children for special services (Berninger, in press). Thus, many educators tell parents (and apparently believe) that dyslexia does not exist. This resistance to acknowledging that dyslexia exists is very hurtful to families that are affected across multiple generations with severe reading disabilities. Although the exact scenarios vary across English-speaking countries, all are plagued with similar challenges resulting from definitional confusion. All are struggling with the challenges of serving not only biologically based dyslexia (Lyon et al. 2003) but also English language learners in the large waves of immigration all the English-speaking countries are encountering. Are the etiologies and effective treatments the same or different for dyslexics, English language learners, children from low income homes, and children whose parents have little formal education? Resolving these issues may be the most pressing research problems, which have both practical and scientific significance.

Inclusionary criteria based on phenotypic, behavioral expression. Thus, in our research program we have operationalized and differentiated three specific learning disabilities that occur with sizable frequency in the school age population (Berninger 2006, in press): dyslexia (Berninger 2001), language learning disability (Berninger and O'Donnell 2004), and dysgraphia (Berninger 2004). Dyslexics have unusual difficulty in learning to pronounce and spell written words that is unexpected (Lyon, Shaywitz, and Shaywitz 2003). We document unexpected based on their measured verbal intelligence, which is an index of metalinguistic competence in (a) accessing via the executive function system representations in semantic memory that link cognitive structures with the language structures, and (b) using decontextualized language to express that accessed knowledge (Berninger in press). See Snow, Cancino, Gonzales, and Shriberg (1989) for discussion of the relationship of decontextualized language and literacy learning. Individuals with language learning disability first have difficulty learning oral language and once they do acquire it have difficulty using oral language to learn written language and using teacher's decontextualized oral instructional language to learn academic knowledge; that is, they have difficulty with using decontextualized language to verbally mediate and self-regulate the learning process (possibly because of inefficiencies in their language learning device) (Berninger in press). In the case of the language learning disabled, we use nonverbal intelligence rather than verbal intelligence to document that their reading and writing problems are unexpected; verbal intelligence is not used as a gauge of expected written language achievement because it is lowered by the nature of their language learning disability. Dysgraphics have unusual difficulty in learning to write letters and/or spell words that is not related to their reading ability; verbal intelligence predicts their spelling but not handwriting abilities (Berninger in press).

Hallmark phenotypic, behavioral indicators. Dyslexics have unexpected difficulty in accuracy and/or rate of oral reading (on lists without context clues and often in passages with context clues) and in written spelling. These problems with written words are associated with not only discrepancy from Verbal IQ but also three hallmark processing deficits – orthographic, phonological, and rapid automatic naming (integrating orthographic and phonological codes quickly in time) (Berninger, Abbott, Thomson, and Raskind 2001). Dyslexics also show impairment in the phonological processes associated with the components of working memory – storage of phonological word forms, time-sensitive phonological loop, and inhibition and switching attention related to phonological processes (Berninger et al. 2006). The language learning disabled, in contrast, often do not show discrepancy from Verbal IQ (which is lowered due to their deficits in general metalinguistic competence) and have significant problems in word recognition (probably because of impaired semantic access) even after they learn age-appropriate phonological decoding and in reading comprehension. They have the same associated processing problems as the dyslexics but in addition have severe morphological and syntactic impairment (Berninger in press). Dysgraphics show early indicators of impaired letter writing and orthographic problems (coding written words into working and long-term memory); their impaired handwriting is often more related to orthographic than fine motor problems (Berninger 2004).

Developmental changes in phenotypic, behavioral expression. Underlying biological factors may express themselves differently across schooling as the curriculum requirements change. Dyslexics initially have difficulty in naming letters and attaching sounds (phonemes) to them. Next, they have difficulty in phonological decoding of written words (sounding out the phonemes that go with sequential graphemes in left to right sequence). Decoding often remains a slow, effortful process for dyslexics who struggle in acquiring automatic decoding and word recognition. Once they have learned to decode accurately, their oral reading fluency problems become apparent – slow rate and disjointed, uncoordinated oral productions that do not reflect the prosody of spoken language (e.g., Wolf 1986); while their silent reading comprehension is typically age-appropriate at this developmental phase, they may need a longer time than peers to read text. However, they often have persisting spelling problems that may interfere with development of written composition skills in the middle school and high school years. Students with language learning disability show the same developmental changes as those with dyslexia but in addition typically struggle with reading comprehension and written composition throughout schooling. Their written syntax tends to be less mature than age peers (Scott 2002); and underdeveloped syntactic skills may explain their reading comprehension problems.

Dysgraphics first show slower development of letter writing skills. Once they can form legible or somewhat legible letters, they may not be able to write them automatically (quickly and without effort). This underdeveloped letter writing automaticity then interferes with the amount and quality of their written composition in the upper grades. In addition, executive function problems interfere with their ability to plan, review, and revise their written compositions in the upper grades and require instruction aimed at both writing specific genres of discourse and executive functions (e.g., Wong 2000). Because dysgraphics may have significant difficulty in keeping up with the written assignments that become increasingly complex across grade levels and require integration of reading and writing (Altemeier, Jones, Abbott, and Berninger 2006), they may begin to look reading disabled when their underlying problem originally was in writing.

9. Assessment and diagnostic classification issues

Because the federal legislation for learning disabilities in the United States does not provide clear, science-supported guidelines for differential diagnosis, not only dyslexia but also language learning disability and dysgraphia are seldom diagnosed appropriately. As summarized in Figure 1, p. 408, our research over the past two decades suggests that children who have only orthographic problems are likely to develop dysgraphia (e.g., Abbott and Berninger 1993), those

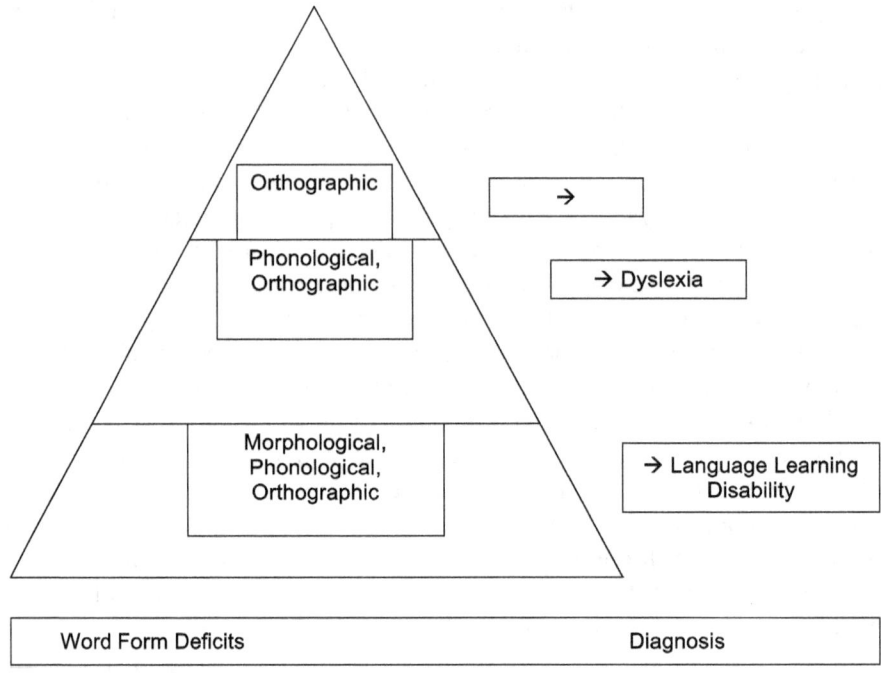

Figure 1. Theoretical model of relationship between diagnostic classifications and triple word form theory.
Process Assessment of the Learner-Second Edition, Copyright © 2007 by Harcourt Assessment, Inc. Reproduced with permission. All rights reserved.

who have phonological and orthographic problems are likely to develop dyslexia (Berninger et al. 2001), and those who have morphological/syntax, phonological, and orthographic problems are likely to develop language learning disability (Berninger and O'Donnell 2004). Others have called attention to the common problems in phonology in dyslexics and oral language impaired individuals (e.g., Bishop and Snowling 2004; Goulandris, Snowling, and Walker 2000). We also find a common phonological deficit as shown in Figure 1, but have observed a deficit in morphological and syntactic awareness that differentiates them and may explain why the dyslexics show Verbal IQ-reading achievement discrepancies affecting the reading and spelling of words but the language learning disabled do not (Berninger in press). All three kinds of specific learning disabilities affecting written language acquisition are associated with orthographic processing problems. Because of the insufficient attention given to definitional and diagnostic issues, these three specific learning disabilities affecting written language may be confounded in samples used in research on dyslexia. The lack of a consensus on precise definition and diagnosis may hinder scientific progress as well as service delivery.

10. Instructional issues

Programs for explicit instruction in word decoding that draw upon alphabetic principle and morphological structure have been developed by Henry (1988, 1989, 1990, 1993, 2003 and Lovett and colleagues (e.g., Lovett 1999; 2000; Lovett, Lacerenza, and Borden 2000). Both programs require children to manipulate units of phonology, orthography, and morphology. Both programs combine explicit instruction and strategy instruction and practice, which a metaanalysis showed was the most effective approach for improving reading achievement (Swanson 1999).

Henry's program (Henry 1990, 2003) focuses on reading and spelling words from different etymological backgrounds – words of Anglo-Saxon, Romance and Greek origins; for each word origin, students are taught linguistic units in written words (i.e., letter-sound correspondences, syllable types, morphemes). Before receiving such instruction, 3rd, 4th, and 5th graders had letter-sound knowledge but little knowledge of syllable or morpheme patterns; the 3rd and 5th graders who received the morphophonemic training linked to word origin improved significantly more in reading and spelling than those who received only basic phonics (Henry 1988, 1989, 1993). Lovett (e.g., Lovett 1999; Lovett et al. 2000) validated methods to improve the word-reading skills of students with reading disabilities: PHAB/DI (direct instruction in sound analysis, blending skills, and letter-sound correspondences) and WIST (four word identification strategies: using analogy, seeking the part of the word you know, attempting variable vowel pronunciations, and peeling off affixes) and Combined PHAB/DI and WIST (PHAST) (Phonological and Strategy Training Program). Clinical studies showed positive gains in reading both trained and untrained (transfer) words (Lovett 2000).

However, teaching low frequency words can help students read content-area texts beginning in the 4th grade (Stahl and Nagy 2005). Analysis of the printed materials used in schools showed that there are more than 88,000 "distinct" words in texts through ninth grade. About half of the word types in printed text through ninth grade occur once in a billion words of text or less, but at least 60% of these can be broken down into parts whose meanings give clues that would allow the student to infer meaning of the word with some help from context (e.g., *abnormality, dreariness, dynamism, elaboration, emplacements, unutterable*). Likewise, for every word a student learns, there are between one and three related words that should be understandable to the student (Nagy and Anderson 1984). Thus, students with reading and writing disability also need explicit instruction in word formation processes and inferring word meaning from context (Bauman, Edwards, Boland, Olejnik, and Kame'enui 2003). Phonics may be necessary for beginning decoding instruction but it is not sufficient for advanced reading and writing skills as students with dyslexia progress through the grades.

An instructional issue that has not been given sufficient attention by practitioners or researchers is syntactic awareness (Demont and Gombert 1996) and its role in interpreting sentences to facilitate comprehension of written text. Yet another issue that has only begun to be investigated (e.g., Connor, Morrison, and Katch 2004) is the differing needs of dyslexics and typically developing children in their relative needs for teacher-directed explicit language instruction and for self-generated, self-regulated learning.

11. Theoretical issues

Triple word form theory. Studies that integrated treatment and brain imaging provided support for this theory, according to which learning to read and spell depends on establishing phonological, orthographic, and morphological representations of words and their parts and creating mental models (mental maps) of their interrelationships. Both unique neural signatures for the three word forms – phonological, orthographic, and morphological – in good readers (Richards et al. 2005, 2006b) and cross-over effects in dyslexics following treatment (Richards et al. 2005) were observed in our studies: Individuals who received *morphological treatment* showed significant changes in *phoneme mapping* during brain scans, whereas individuals who received *phonological treatment* showed significant changes in *morpheme mapping* during brain scans. Richards et al. (2002) showed that for dyslexics morphological awareness training improved efficiency (rate) of phonological decoding and led to greater metabolic efficiency in neural processing during phonological judgment while the brain was scanned than did training in only phonological awareness. In addition, structural equation modeling of phenotypes in the family genetics study of dyslexia showed that a second-order factor modeled on indicators of each word form factor predicts reading and spelling outcomes better than the first-order factors based on single word forms alone (Berninger et al. 2006). The benefits of Wolf et al.'s (2003) RAVO training for the reading disabled may be related to the way it integrates phonological, orthographic, and vocabulary (morphological) training.

Mapping relationships among phonology, morphology, and orthography. In the initial work on triple word form theory, we used a standard paradigm in fMRI research in which a target task is compared to a control task to identify the brain activation that is unique to the target task rather than the control task. For example, we compared a morphological task (comes-from judgment) to a synonym judgment task to identify processing specific to the morphological word form compared to semantic judgments. An example of a morphological judgment item was to decide whether *builder* comes from *build* (yes) or whether *corner* comes from *corn* (no); in some cases a common spelling pattern (e.g., er) functions as a morpheme and sometimes it does not. An example of a synonym/semantic judgment item was to decide whether two words (e.g. *baby* and *infant* or *mother* and *father*) mean the same thing. One of the morphological tasks used word pairs that involved a phonological shift from the base word to the derived word (e.g. Does national come from nation?), and one of the morphological tasks used word pairs that did not involve a phonological shift (e.g., Does lovely come from love?). The phonological task required judgments about the phoneme alternations in English (Venezky 1970, 1999), that is, whether a grapheme (single letter or letter group) in pink in each word in a pair of pseudowords could stand for the same phoneme. For example, could the letter o in pink in the pseudoword wode stand for the same sound as the letters ow in pink in the pseudoword smow or the letters oo in pink in the pseudoword toop? The control task was a letter-string matching judgment (deciding whether two letter strings matched exactly) to control for letter processing. The orthographic task was deciding whether each word in a pair of words, both of which were pronounced like a real word, were correctly spelled; the same control task was used as for the phonological task to control for letter processing apart form orthographic word form. The results were reported in Richards et al. (2006).

Additional comparisons were conducted between each of the target tasks compared to each other (Richards et al. 2005) rather than for the target task compared to the control task (Richards et al. 2006). These analyses, which have implications for whether unique brain activity is associated with each of the word forms as children create mental models of the relationships among the word forms, showed that dyslexics differed from good reading controls on the morphological task with phonological shifts but not the morphological task without phonological shifts (Richards et al. 2005). Tables 1 and 2 illustrate this novel approach to data analyses in which different target tasks are directly compared to each other, after controlling for contrasts with control tasks, rather than comparing them only to control tasks. First, regions of reliable activation are identified based on group maps at time 1 and verified for reliability in individual controls (good readers) across two time points (see column 1 of Table 1). Next, dyslexics are compared to the controls at time 1 to identify for specific task comparisons the regions where dyslexics underactivated compared to controls (see columns 2 and 3 of Table 1) or activated where controls did not (Table 2). As shown in these tables, dyslexics differ from good readers both in their underactivation and overactivation compared to good readers. Finally, changes in brain activation in individual dyslexics from time 1 (see columns 2 and 3, Table 1 r column 2, Table 2) to time 2 (see columns 4 and 5, Table 1 or columns 3 and 4 Table 2) are analyzed and brain activation in dyslexics at time 2 is compared to controls at time 2 to evaluate whether normalization has occurred.

Word forms. Prior research reported unique activation associated with phonological and orthographic processing in children (Gabrielli 2001) and with phonological (Crossen et al. 1999) and orthographic (Crossen et al. 1991; Dehaene, Le Clec'H, Poline, Bihan, and Cohen 2002; and Demonet et al., 2002) processing in adults. We analyzed our results (Table 3) to evaluate how, as children during middle childhood create mapping relationships between each of the three word forms with the other word forms, specific brain regions may emerge as uniquely associated with a specific word form; see Richards et al. (2005) for regions that are common to two of the word forms (but not the third one) and may be involved in creating maps that relate the word forms.

Phonological word form. Table 3 summarizes our findings showing that good readers in middle childhood uniquely activate 20 brain regions during phoneme mapping (phonological word form task), regardless of whether this task was compared to either of the morphological tasks or the orthographic task; these good readers appear to have mastered the phonological stage of spelling development. In contrast, dyslexics activated only two of the same regions for phonological word form (see Table 3).

Orthographic word form. Unique activation was associated with orthographic mapping (orthographic word form) compared to the other word forms in right inferior frontal gyrus (triangularis region) in good readers. This region has been shown to have structural MRI differences between dyslexics and controls during middle childhood (Eckert et al. 2003) that are related to orthographic skill. Orthographic, but not morphological, treatment was associated with reliable change and normalization in right inferior frontal gyrus (Richards et al. 2006; also see Table 1). This finding is consistent with research on spelling development (Templeton and Bear 1992), in which the orthographic stage precedes the morphological stage. An alternative explanation for the brain responsiveness to orthographic treatment is that dyslexics receive treatment focused mainly on their phonological deficits and do not receive sufficient instruction in orthographic awareness. Hence, child dyslexics were responsive to the novel orthographic treatment when provided in the research study on spelling. The treatment in this study (Berninger and Hidi 2006) did not emphasize phonological awareness or morphological-phonological connections as Berninger, Nagy et al. (2003) did for reading; if it had, the children may have been more responsive to the morphological treatment and showed more changes in phoneme mapping regardless of treatment. However, further research is needed as to whether the phoneme mapping problems of dyslexics in middle childhood must be fully remediated before dyslexics benefit from orthographic spelling treatment at a stage when good readers are entering the orthographic stage of spelling development. In another combined treatment and fMRI study (Berninger et al. 2007; Richards et al. in press) we trained phonological awareness to improve spelling of dyslexics during middle childhood.

Morphological word form. No clear patterns emerge for unique activation for the morphology task without phonological shift (see Table 3). However, when morpheme mapping with phonological shifts was compared to either phoneme mapping or orthographic mapping, unique activation occurred in two frontal regions (superior and middle) and in three posterior regions associated with visual processing (see Table 3). Taken together, these findings suggest that during middle childhood children are beginning to create maps of how morphology and phonology are interrelated rather than representations of morphological word form alone. This interpretation is consistent with Nagy's programmatic research showing that morphological awareness begins to emerge during middle childhood (e.g., Nagy et al. 2003, in press) but continues to develop through high school (e.g., Nagy et al. 1989) – that is the morphological stage of spelling is the last to develop.

Developmental changes in mapping relationships among the word forms. A recent fMRI functional connectivity study during phoneme mapping (Stanberry et al. 2006) showed that . when seed points were set in right and left IFG and right cerebellum (regions of structural MR differences between child dyslexics and good readers, Eckert et al. 2003), adult dyslexics and good readers differed in the spatial extent of temporal functional connectivity (co-activation of other brain regions) emanating from these regions; right inferior frontal gyrus was temporally connected to the posterior word form regions where orthographic processing occurs (Stanberry et al. 2006). Changes in the relationship of fMRI activation in the left and right inferior frontal gyrus were associated with improvement in phonological decoding that requires integration of orthographic and phonological codes (Richards et al. 2006b). Heilman, Voeller, and Alexander (1996) proposed that the right cerebellar-left inferior frontal gyrus pathway may be part of the phonological loop of working memory. Unique left IFG and right cerebellum activation was associated with phoneme mapping during middle childhood (see Table 1). Further research is needed on the relationship among the phonological, orthographic, and morphological word forms within working memory architecture (storage, phonological loop, supervisory executive function) at different stages of reading and spelling development (early childhood, middle childhood, adolescence, and adulthood) in good readers and dyslexics.

Syntax and working memory. Although the dyslexics we study have morphological and syntactic skills that are on average at about the population mean (Berninger et al. 2006), the language learning disabled we have assessed tend to have morphological and syntactic skills that are significantly below the population mean (Berninger and O'Donnell 2004). It is not known whether the severe impairment in morphosyntactic processes, which is related to reading comprehension (Nagy et al. 2003, 2006), causes the working memory inefficiencies that further impede development of reading comprehension, or working memory inefficiencies associated with reading disability (Swanson and Siegel 1999) cause the syntactic processing problems (due to difficulties in storing the accumulating word strings without grammatical structures to integrate them) (Berninger in press). Also see Montgomery (2003) for further discussion of these issues in children with selective language impairment. Further research on the role of syntactic awareness in development of written language in typically developing readers and writers as well as dyslexics, language learning disabled, and dysgraphics is sorely needed. Such research should be grounded in current scientific knowledge of functional language systems (for listening, speaking, reading, and writing) and working memory (Berninger and Richards 2002).

Contributions of multidisciplinary research teams. Scientific advances in understanding developmental dyslexia and related disorders of written language depend on increasing collaboration among psychologists, linguists, neuroscientists, and geneticists. These four disciplines are represented on our team and the co-authorship of this chapter reflects, in respective order, these relevant disciplines for understanding and treating developmental dyslexia.

Acknowledgement. Grants P50 33812 and R01 HD25858 from the National Institute of Child Health and Human Development (NICHD), USA, supported preparation of this chapter and much of the research discussed in it.

References

Abbott, R. and V. Berninger
   1993   Structural equation modeling of relationships among developmental skills and writing skills in primary and intermediate grade writers. *Journal of Educational Psychology* 85(3): 478–508.

Adams, M. J.
   1990   *Beginning to Read: Thinking and Learning about Print.* Cambridge, MA: MIT Press.

Altemeier, L., J. Jones, R. Abbott, and V. Berninger
   2006   Executive factors in becoming writing-readers and reading-writers: Note-taking and report writing in third and fifth graders. *Developmental Neuropsychology* 29: 161–173.

Aram, D., B. Ekelman, and J. Nation
   1984   Preschoolers with language disorders: 10 years later. *Journal of Speech and Hearing Research* 27: 232–244.

Aylward, E., T. Richards, V. Berninger, W. Nagy, K. Field, A. Grimme, A. Richards, J. Thomson, and S. Cramer
   2003   Instructional treatment associated with changes in bran activation in children with dyslexia. *Neurology* 61: 212–219.

Baddeley, A.
  2002   Is working memory still working? *European Psychologist* 7: 85–97.
Baddeley, A. and S. Della Sala
  1996   Executive and cognitive functions of the prefrontal cortex. *Philosophical Transactions: Biological Sciences* 351 (1346): 1397–1403.
Baddeley, A., S. Gathercole, and C. Papagno
  1998   The phonological loop as a language learning device. *Psychological Review* 105: 158–173.
Balmuth, M.
  1992   *The Roots of Phonics. A Historical Introduction.* Baltimore: York Press.
Bauman, J., E. Edwards, E. Boland, S. Olejnik, and E. Kame'enui
  2003   Vocabulary tricks: Effects of instruction in morphology and context on fifth grade students' ability to derive and infer word meanings. *American Educational Research Journal* 40: 447–494.
Bear, D., M. Ivernizzi, S. Templeton, and F. Johnston
  2000   *Words their Way Word Study for Phonics, Vocabulary, and Spelling Instruction* (2nd ed.). Upper Saddle River, NJ: Merrill.
Berninger, V. W.
  2000   Dyslexia: the invisible, treatable disorder: The story of Einstein's ninja turtles. *Learning Disabilities Quarterly* 23: 175–195.
Berninger, V.
  2001   Understanding the lexia in dyslexia. *Annals of Dyslexia* 51: 23–48.
Berninger, V.
  2004   Understanding the graphia in dysgraphia. In: D. Dewey and D. Tupper (eds.), *Developmental Motor Disorders: A Neuropsychological Perspective,* 328–350. New York: Guilford.
Berninger, V.
  in press   Defining and differentiating dyslexia, dysgraphia, and language learning disability within a working memory model. To appear in E. Silliman and M. Mody (eds.), *Language Impairment and Reading Disability-Interactions among Brain, Behavior, and Experience.* Guilford Press.
Berninger, V.
  2006   A developmental approach to learning disabilities. In: I. Siegel and A. Renninger (eds.), *Handbook of Child Psychology,* Vol. IV, *Child Psychology and Practice,* 420–452. New York: John Wiley & Sons.
Berninger, V.
  (2007)   *Process Assessment of the Learner II User's Guide.* San Antonio, TX: Harcourt/PsyCorp.
Berninger, V., R. Abbott, F. Billingsley, and W. Nagy
  2001   Processes underlying timing and fluency of reading: Efficiency, automaticity, coordination, and morphological awareness. In: M. Wolf (Ed.) *Dyslexia, Fluency, and the Brain,* 383–414. Extraordinary Brain Series. Baltimore: York Press.
Berninger, V., R. Abbott, J. Thomson, and W. Raskind
  2001   Language phenotype for reading and writing disability: A family approach. *Scientific Studies in Reading* 5: 59–105.
Berninger, V., R. Abbott, J. Thomson, R. Wagner, H. L. Swanson, and W. Raskind
  2006   Modeling developmental phonological core deficits within a working mem-

ory architecture in children and adults with developmental dyslexia. *Scientific Studies in Reading*, 10: 165–198.

Berninger, V., A. Dunn, S. Lin, and S. Shimada
2004   School evolution: Scientist-practitioner educators creating optimal learning environments for ALL students. *Journal of Learning Disabilities* 37: 500–508.

Berninger, V. and S. Hidi
2006   Mark Twain's writers' workshop: A nature-nurture perspective in motivating students with learning disabilities to compose. In S. Hidi and P. Boscolo (eds.). *Motivation in Writing*, (159–179). Dordrecht, The Netherlands: Kluwer Academic Publishers.

Berninger, V., W. Nagy, J. Carlisle, J. Thomson, D. Hoffer, S. Abbott, R. Abbott, T. Richards, and E. Aylward
2003   Effective treatment for dyslexics in grades 4 to 6. In B. Foorman (ed.), *Preventing and Remediating Reading Difficulties: Bringing Science to Scale*, 382–417. Timonium, MD: York Press.

Berninger, V. and L. O'Donnell
2004   Research-supported differential diagnosis of specific learning disabilities. In: A. Prifitera, D. Saklofske, L. Weiss, and E. Rolfhus (eds.), *WISC-IV Clinical Use and Interpretation. Scientist-Practitioner Perspectives,* 189–233. San Diego, CA: Academic Press.

Berninger, V. and T. Richards
2002   *Brain Literacy for Educators and Psychologists.* San Diego: Academic Press (Elsevier Imprint).

Berninger, V., W. Winn, P. Stock, R. Abbott, K. Eschen, C. Lin, N. Gracia, M. Anderson-Youngstrom, H. Murphy, D. Lovitt, P. Trivedi, J. Jones, D. Amtmann, and W. Nagy
in press   Tier 3 specialized writing instruction for students with dyslexia. *Reading and Writing. An Interdisciplinary Journal.* Printed Springer On Line. May 15, 2007.

Bishop, D. and C. Adams
1990   A prospective study of the relationship between specific language impairment, phonological disorders, and reading retardation. *Journal of Child Psychology and Psychiatry and Allied Disciplines* 31: 1027–1050.

Bishop, D. V. M. and M. J. Snowling
2004   Developmental dyslexia and specific language impairment: Same or different? *Psychological Bulletin* 130: 858–886.

Bond, G. and T. Tinker
1967   *Reading Difficulties. Their Diagnosis and Correction.* New York: Appleton-Century-Crofts.

Booth, J., D. Burman, J. Meyer, D. Gitelman, T. Parrish, and M. Mesulam
2003   Relation between brain activation and lexical performance. *Human Brain Mapping* 19: 155–169.

Booth, J. R., B. MacWhinney, K. R. Thulborn, K. Sacco, J. T. Voyvodic, and H. M. Feldman
2000   Developmental and lesion effects in brain activation during sentence comprehension and mental rotation. *Developmental Neuropsychology* 18: 139–69.

Bradley, R., L. Danielson, and D. Hallahan
  2002   *Identification of Learning Disabilities. Research to Practice.* Mahwah, NJ: Lawrence Erlbaum.
Breznitz, Z.
  2002   Asynchrony of visual-orthographic and auditory-phonological word recognition processes: An underlying factor in dyslexia. *Journal of Reading and Writing* 15: 15–42.
Butler, K. and E. Silliman
  2002   *Speaking, Reading, and Writing in Children with Language Learning Disabilties.* Mahwah, NJ: Lawrence Erlbaum Associates, Inc.
Byrne, B., C. Delaland, R. Fielding-Barnsley, P. Quain, S. Samuelsson, T. HØien, R. Corley, J. DeFries, S. Wadsworth, E. Willcutt, and R. Olson
  2002   Longitudinal twin study of early reading development in three countries: Preliminary results. *Annals of Dyslexia* 52: 4–73.
Cardon, L. R., S. D. Smith, D. W. Fulker, W. J. Kimberling, B. F. Pennington, and J. C. DeFries
  1994   Quantitative trait locus for reading disability on chromosome 6. *Science* 266: 276–279.
Cardon, L. R, S. D. Smith, D. W. Fulker, W. J. Kimberling, B. F. Pennington, and J. C. DeFries
  1995   Quantitative trait locus for reading disability: correction. *Science* 268: 1553.
Carlisle, J. F.
  2000   Awareness of the structure and meaning of morphologically complex words: Impact on reading. *Reading and Writing: An Interdisciplinary Journal* 12: 169–190.
Carlisle, J.
  2004   Morphological processes that influence learning to read. In A. Stone, E. Silliman, B. Ehren, and K. Apel (eds.), *Handbook of Language and Literacy: Development and Disorders,* 318–339. New York: The Guilford Press.
Carlisle, J. F. and C. A. Stone
  2004   The effects of morphological structure on children's reading of derived words. In E. Assink and D. Santa (eds.), *Reading Complex Words: Cross-Language Studies.* Amsterdam: Kluwer.
Carlisle, J. F., C. A. Stone, and L. A. Katz
  2001   The effects of phonological transparency n reading derived words. *Annals of Dyslexia* 51: 249–274.
Carlisle, J. F. and J. Fleming
  2003   Lexical processing of morphologically complex words in the elementary years. *Scientific Studies of Reading* 7: 239–253.
Catts, H., M. Fey, X. Zhang, and J. Tomblin
  1999   Language basis of reading and reading disabilities. *Scientific Studies of Reading* 3: 331–361.
Catts, H., M. Fey, X. Zhang, and J. Tomblin
  2001   Estimating the risk of future reading difficulties in kindergarten children: A research based model and its clinical implications. *Language, Speech, and Hearing Services in Schools* 32: 38–50.

Catts, H., and A. Kamhi (eds.)
  2005   *The Connections between Language and Reading Disabilities.* Mahwah, NJ: Lawrence Erlbaum Associates.
Chall, J.
  1983   *Stages of Reading Development.* New York: McGraw Hill.
Chapman, N., R. Igo, J. Thomson, M. Matsushita, Z. Brkanac, T. Hotzman, V. Berninger, E. Wijsman, and W. Raskind
  2004   Linkage analyses of four regions previously implicated in dyslexia: confirmation of a locus on chromosome 15q. *American Journal of Medical Genetics (Neuropsychiatric Genetic)* 131B: 67–75. and *American Journal of Medical Genetics Supplement* 03174 9999:1 (2004).
Chapman, N., W. Raskind, J. Thomson, V. Berninger, and E. Wijsman
  2003   Segregation analysis of phenotypic components of learning disabilities. II. Phonological decoding. *Neuropsychiatric Genetics* 121B: 60–70.
Cohen, L., S. Lehericy, F. Chhochon, C. Lemer, S. Rivaud, and S. Dehaene
  2002   Language-specific tuning of visual cortex? Functional properties of the visual word form area. *Brain* 124: 1054–1069.
Connor, C., F. Morrison, and L. Katch
  2004   Beyond the reading wars: Exploring the effect of child-instruction interactions on growth in early reading. *Scientific Studies of Reading* 8: 305–336.
Cooke, A., E. B. Zurif, C. DeVita, D. Alsop, P. Koenig, J. Detre, J. Gee, M. Pinango, J. Balogh, and M. Grossman
  2002   Neural basis for sentence comprehension: grammatical and short-term memory components. *Human Brain Mapping* 15: 80–94.
Cope, N., D. Harold, G. Hill, V. Moskvian, J. Stevenson, P. Holmans, M. Owen, M. O'Donovan, and J. Williams
  2005   Strong evidence that KIAA0319 on Chromosome 6p is a susceptibility gene for developmental dyslexia. *American Journal of Human Genetics* 76: 581–591.
Corina, D. P., T. L. Richards, S. Serafini, A. L. Richards, K. Steury, R. D. Abbott, D. R. Echelard, K. R. Maravilla, and V. W. Berninger
  2001   fMRI auditory language difference between dyslexic and able-reading children. *Neuroreport* 12: 1195–1201.
Cornelissen, P., P. Hansen, J. Hutton, V. Evangelinou, and J. Stein
  1998   Magnocelluar visual function and children's single word reading. *Vision Research* 38: 471–482.
Crosson, B., S. Rao, S. Woodley, A. Rosen, J. Bobholz, A. Mayer, J. Cunningham, T. Hammeke, S. Fuller, J. Binder, R. Cox, and E. Stein
  1999   Mapping of semantic, phonological, and orthographic verbal working memory in normal adults with functional magnetic resonance imaging. *Neuropsychology* 13: 171–187.
Dehaene, S., H. G. LeClec, J. B. Poline, D. Bihan, and L. Cohen
  2002   The visual word form area: A prelexical representation of visual words in the fusiform gyrus. *Brain Imaging* 13: 321–325.
Demonet, J., F. Chollet, S. Ramsay, D. Cardebat, J. Nespoulous, R. Wise, A. Rascol, and R. Frackowiak
  1992   The anatomy of phonological and semantic processing in normal subjects. *Brain* 115: 1753–1768.

Demont, E. and J. Gombert
  1996   Phonological awareness as a predictor of recoding skills and syntactic awareness as a predictor of comprehension skills. *British Journal of Educational Psychology* 66: 315–332.
Eckert, M. A., C. M. Leonard, T. L. Richards, E. H. Aylward, J. Thomson, J., and V. W. Berninger
  2003   Anatomical correlates of dyslexia: frontal and cerebellar findings. *Brain* 126: 482–494.
Eckert, M., C. Leonard, M. Wilke, M. Eckert, T. Richards, A. Richards, and V. Berninger
  2005   Anatomical signatures of dyslexia in children: unique information from the manual and voxel based morphometry brain measures. *Cortex* 41. 304–315.
Eckert, M., L. Lombardino, L., and C. Leonard
  2001   Planar asymmetry tips the phonological playground and environment raises the bar. *Child Development* 72: 98–1001.
Eden, G., K. Jones, K. Cappell, L. Gareau, F. Wood, T. Zeffiro, N. Dietz, J. Agnew, and L. Flowers
  2004   Neurophysiological recovery and compensation after remediation in adult developmental dyslexia. *Neuron* Volume 44 (3): 411–422.
Eden, G. F., J. W. Van Meter, J. W. Rumsey, J. Maisog, and T. A. Zeffiro
  1996   Functional MRI reveals differences in visual motion processing in individuals with dyslexia. *Nature* 382: 66–69.
Ehri, L., S. Nunes, S. Stahl, and D. Willows
  2001   Systematic phonics instruction helps students learn to read: Evidence from the National Reading Panel's meta-analysis. *Review of Educational Research* 71: 393–447.
Fisher, S. E., A. J. Marlow, J. Lamb, E. Maestrini, D. F. Williams, A. J. Richardson, D. E. Weeks, J. F. Stein, and A. P. Monaco
  1999   A quantitative-trait locus on chromosome 6p influences different aspects of developmental dyslexia. *American Journal Human Genetics* 64: 146–156.
Fisher, S. E. and J. C. DeFries
  2002   Developmental dyslexia: genetic dissection of a complex cognitive trait. *Nat Rev Neuroscience* 3: 767–80.
Flowers, L., F. Wood, and C. Naylor
  1991   Regional cerebral blood flow correlates of language processes in reading disability. *Archives of Neurology* 48: 637–643.
Gabrielli, J.
  2001   Disrupted neural responses to phonological and orthographic processing in dyslexic children: an fMRI study. *Neuroreport* 12: 299–307.
Ganschow, L. and R. L. Sparks
  2000   Reflections on foreign language study for students with language learning problems: research, issues, and challenges *Dyslexia* 6: 87–100.
Gates, A.
  1947   *The Improvement of Reading, 3rd edition.* New York: Macmillan.
Gathercole, S. E. and A. D. Baddeley
  1989   Evaluation of the role of phonological STM in the development of vocabulary in children: A longitudinal study. *Journal of Memory and Language* 28: 200–213.

Gayan, J., S. D. Smith, S. S. Cherny, L. R. Cardon, D. W. Fulker, A. M. Brower, R. K. Olson, B. F. Pennington, and J. C. DeFries
    1999   Quantitative-trait locus for specific language and reading deficits on chromosome 6p. *American Journal Human Genetics* 64: 157–164.

Gayan, J., E. G. Willcutt, S. E. Fisher, C. Francks, L. R. Cardon, R. K. Olson, B. F. Pennington, S. D. Smith, A. P. Monaco, and J. C. DeFries
    2005   Bivariate linkage scan for reading disability and attention-deficit/hyperactivity disorder localizes pleiotropic loci. *Journal of Child Psychology and Psychiatry* 46: 1045–56.

Gray, W.
    1956   *The Teaching of Reading and Writing*. Chicago: Scott, Foresman.

Goulandris, N., M. Snowling, and I. Walker
    2000   Is dyslexia a form of specific language impairment? A comparison of dyslexic and language impaired children as adolescents. *Annals of Dyslexia* 50: 103–122.

Grigorenko, E. L., F. B. Wood, M. S. Meyer, L. A. Hart, W. C. Speed, A. Shuster, and D. L. Pauls
    1997   Susceptibility loci for distinct components of developmental dyslexia on chromosomes 6 and 15. *American Journal Human Genetics* 60: 27–29.

Hannula-Jouppi, K, N. Kaminen-Ahola, M. Taipale, R. Eklund, J. Nopola-Hemmi, H. Kaariainen, and J. Kere
    2005   The axon guidance receptor gene ROBO1 is a candidate gene for developmental dyslexia. *PLoS Genetics* 1: 467–474.

Harris, A.
    1961   *How to Increase Reading Ability, 4th edition*. New York: Longsman.

Heilman, K. M., K. Voeller, and A. W. Alexander
    1996   Developmental dyslexia: a motor-articulatory feedback hypothesis. *Annals of Neurology* 39: 407–12.

Helenius, P., R. Salmelin, E. Service, and J. Connolly
    1999   Semantic cortical activation in dyslexic readers. *Journal of Cognitive Neuroscience* 11: 535–550.

Henry, M. K.
    1988   Beyond phonics: Integrated decoding and spelling instruction based on word origin and structure. *Annals of Dyslexia* 38: 259–275.

Henry, M. K.
    1989   Children's word structure knowledge: Implications for decoding and spelling instruction. *Reading and Writing: An Interdisciplinary Journal* 2: 135–152.

Henry, M.
    1990   *Words. Integrated Decoding and Spelling Instruction Based on Word Origin and Word Structure*. Austin, TX: Pro-Ed.

Henry, M. K.
    1993   Morphological structure: Latin and Greek roots and affixes as upper grade code strategies. *Reading and Writing: An Interdisciplinary Journal* 5: 227–241.

Henry, M.
    2003   *Unlocking Literacy. Effective Decoding and Spelling Instruction*. Baltimore: Paul H. Brookes Publishing.

Horwitz, B., J. M. Rumsey, and B. C. Donohue
1998   Functional connectivity of the angular gyrus in normal reading and dyslexia, *Proceedings National Academy of Sciences. USA* 95: 8939–44.

Hsu, L., E. Wijsman., V. Berninger, J. Thomson, and W. Raskind
2002   Familial aggregation of dyslexia phenotypes: Paired correlated measures. *American Journal of Medical Genetics/Neuropsychiatrics* 114: 471–478.

Hynd, G., M. Semrud-Clikeman, A. Lorys, E. Novey, and D. Eliopulos
1990   Brain morphology in developmental dyslexia and attention deficit disorder/hyperactivity. *Archives of Neurology* 47: 919–926.

Huey, E. B.
1908   *The Psychology and Pedagogy of Reading*. Macmillan, New York. Reprinted by MIT Press. Cambridge, MA, 1968.

Igo, R. P. Jr., N. H. Chapman, V. W. Berninger, M. Matsushita, Z. Brkanac J. Rothstein, T. Holtzman, R. Abbott, K. Nielsen, W. H. Raskind, and E. M. Wijsman
2006   Genomewide scan for real-word reading subphenotypes of dyslexia: Novel chromosome 13 locus and genetic complexity. *American Journal of Medical Genetics/Neuropsychiatric Genetics*141B: 15–27.

Johnson, D. and H. Myklebust
1967   *Learning Disabilities*. New York: Grune & Stratton.

Kirk, S. and D. Kirk
1971   *Psycholinguistic Learning Disabilities: Diagnosis and Remediation*. Chicago: University of Chicago Press.

Klingberg, T., M. Hedehus, E. Temple, T. Salz, J. D. Gabrieli, M. E. Moseley, and R. A. Poldrack
2000   Microstructure of temporo-parietal white matter as a basis for reading ability: evidence from diffusion tensor magnetic resonance imaging [see comments]. *Neuron* 25: 493–500.

Klingberg, T., C. J. Vaidya, J. D. Gabrieli, M. E. Moseley, and M. Hedehus, M.
1999   Myelination and organization of the frontal white matter in children: a diffusion tensor MRI study, *Neuroreport* 10: 2817–21.

Leonard, C.
2001   Imaging brain structure in children. *Learning Disability Quarterly* 24: 158–176.

Leonard, C. M., K. K. Voeller, L. J. Lombardino, M. K. Morris, G. W. Hynd, A. W. Alexander, H. G. Andersen, M. Garofalakis, J. C. Honeyman, J. Mao et al.
1993   Anomalous cerebral structure in dyslexia revealed with magnetic resonance imaging [see comments]. *Archives Neurology* 50: 461–9.

Lovett, M. W.
1999   Redefining and remediating the core deficits of developmental dyslexia: Lessons from remedial outcome research with reading disabled children. In: R. Klein and P. McMullen (eds.), *Converging Methods for Understanding Reading and Dyslexia*. Cambridge: MIT Press.

Lovett, M. W., L. Lacerenza, and S. L. Borden
2000   Putting struggling readers on the PHAST track: A program to integrate phonological and strategy-based remedial reading instruction and maximize outcomes. *Journal of Learning Disabilities* 33: 458–476.

Luria, A. R.
1970   *The Working Brain*. New York: Basic Books.

Lyon, G. R., J. Fletcher, S. Shaywitz, B. Shaywitz, J. Torgesen, F. Wood, A. Schulte, and R. Olson
    2001   In: C. Finn, A. Rotherham, and C. Hokanson (eds.), *Rethinking Learning Disabilities. In Rethinking Special Education for a New Century,* 259–287. Washington, D.C. The Fordham Foundation.

Lyon, G. R., S. Shaywitz, and B. Shaywitz
    2003   A definition of dyslexia. *Annals of Dyslexia* 53: 1–14.

Manis, F., M. Seidenberg, L. Doi, McBride-Chang and A. Petersen, A.
    1966   On the basis of two subtypes of developmental dyslexia, *Cognition* 58: 157–195.

Mattingly, I. G.
    1972   Reading, the linguistic process, and linguistic awareness. In J. F. Kavanagh and I. G. Mattingly (eds.), *Language by Ear and by Eye: The Relationship between Speech and Reading,* 133–147. Cambridge, MA: MIT Press.

Mayer, R.
    2004   Should there be a three-strikes rule against pure discovery learning. *American Psychologis* 59: 14–19.

McCardle, P. and V. Chhabra
    2004   *The Voice of Evidence in Reading Research.* Baltimore: Paul H. Brookes.

McCray, A. D., S. Vaughn, and L. V. I. Neal
    2001   Not all students learn to read by third grade: Middle school students speak out about their reading disabilities. *Journal of Special Education* 35: 17–30.

McCrory, E., U. Frith, N. Brunswick, and C. Price
    2000   Abnormal functional activation during a simple word repetition task: A PET study of adult dyslexics. *Journal of Cognitive Neuroscience* 12: 753–62.

Meng, H. Y., S. D. Smith, K. Hager, M. Held, J. Liu, R. K. Olson, B. F. Pennington, J. C. DeFries, J. Gelernter, T. O'Reilly-Pol, S. Somlo, P. Skudlarski, S. E. Shaywitz, B. A. Shaywitz, K. Marchione, Y. Wang, M. Paramasivam, J. J. LoTurco, G. P. Page, J. R. Gruen
    2005   DCDC2 is associated with reading disability and modulates neuronal development in the brain. *Proceedings of the National Academy of Sciences of the United States of America* 102: 17053–17058.

Moats, L.
    2000   *Speech to Print. Language Essentials for Teachers.* Baltimore: Paul H. Brookes Publishing Co.

Mody, M., M. Studdert-Kennedy, and S. Brady
    1997   Speech perception deficits in poor readers: Auditory processing or phonological coding? *Journal of Experimental Child Psychology* 64: 199–231.

Molfese, D.
    2000   Predicting dyslexia at 8 years of age using neonatal brain responses. *Brain and Language* 72: 238–245.

Molfese, D., V. Molfese, S. Key, A. Modglin, S. Kelley, and S. Terrell
    2002   Reading and cognitive abilities: Longitudinal studies of brain and behavior changes in young children. *Annals of Dyslexia* 52: 99–120.

Montgomery, J. W.
    2003   Working memory and comprehension in children with specific language impairment: What we know so far. *Journal of Communication Disorders* 36: 221–231.

Morris, R., K. Stuebing, J. Fletcher, S. Shaywitz, G. R. Lyon, D. Shakweiler, L. Katz, D. Francis, and B. Shaywitz
    1998   Subtypes of reading disability: Variability around a phonological core. *Journal of Educational Psychology* 90: 347–373.

Nagy, W. E. and R. Anderson
    1984   How many words in printed school English? *Reading Research Quarterly* 19: 304–330.

Nagy, W. E., R. C. Anderson, M. Schommer, J. Scott, and A. Stallman
    1989   Morphological families and word recognition. *Reading Research Quarterly* 24: 262–282.

Nagy, W., V. Berninger, R. Abbott, K. Vaughan, and K. Vermeulin
    2003   Relationship of morphology and other language skills to literacy skills in at-risk second graders and at-risk fourth grade writers. *Journal of Educational Psychology* 95: 730–742.

Nagy, W., V. Berninger, and R. Abbott
    2006   Contributions of morphology beyond phonology to literacy outcomes of upper elementary and middle school students. *Journal of Educational Psychology*, 98: 134–147.

Nagy, W., J. Osborn, P. Winsor, J. O'Flahavan
    1994   Structural analysis: Some guidelines for instruction. In: F. Lehr and J. Osborn (eds.), *Reading, Language, and Literacy,* 45–58. Hillsdale, NJ: Lawrence Erlbaum Associates.

Olson, R.
    2004   SSSR, environment, and genes. *Scientific Studies in Reading* 8: 111–124.

Olson, R., H. Datta, J. Gayan, and J. C. DeFries
    1999   A behavioral-genetic analysis of reading disabilities and component processes. In: R. Klein and P. McMullen (eds.), *Converging Methods for Understanding Reading and Dyslexia,* 133–151. Cambridge, MA: MIT Press.

Olson, R., H. Forsberg, and B. Wise
    1994   Genes, environment, and the development of orthographic skills. In: V. W. Berninger (ed.), *The Varieties of Orthographic Knowledge I: Theoretical and Developmental Issues,* 27–71. Dordrecht, the Netherlands: Kluwer Academic Press.

Orton, S.
    1937   *Reading, Writing, and Speech Problems in Children.* New York: Norton.

Paulesu, E., J. F. Demonet, F. Fazio, E. McCrory, V. Chanoine, N. Brunswick, S. F. Cappa, G. Cossu, M. Habib, C. D. Frith, and U. Frith
    2001   Dyslexia: cultural diversity and biological unity. *Science* 291: 2165–7.

Pennington, B. F., P. A. Filipek, D. Lefly, J. Churchwell, D. N. Kennedy, J. H. Simon, C. M. Filley, A. Galaburda, M. Alarcon, and J. C. DeFries
    1999   Brain morphometry in reading-disabled twins. *Neurology* 53: 723–9.

Pennington, B. and D. Lefly
    2001   Early reading development in children at family risk for dyslexia. *Child Development* 72: 816–833.

Petryshen, T. L., B. J. Kaplan, M. F. Liu, and L. L. Field
    2000   Absence of significant linkage between phonological coding dyslexia and chromosome 6p23–21.3, as determined by use of quantitative-trait methods: confirmation of qualitative analyses. *American Journal Human Genetics* 66: 708–14.

Pugh, K., W. Mencl, B. Shaywitz, S. Shaywitz, R. Fulbright, R. Constable, P. Skudlarski, K. Marchione, A. Jenner, J. Fletcher, A. Liberman, D. Shankweiler, L. Katz, C. Lacadie, and J. Gore
  2000   The angular gyrus in developmental dyslexia: Task-specific differences in functional connectivity within posterior cortex. *Psychological Science* 11: 51–56.
Rae, C., M. A. Lee, R. M. Dixon, A. M. Blamire, C. H. Thompson, P. Styles, J. Talcott, A. J. Richardson, and J. F. Stein
  1998   Metabolic abnormalities in developmental dyslexia detected by 1H magnetic resonance spectroscopy, *Lancet* 351: 1849–52.
Raskind, W.
  2001   Current understanding of the genetic basis of reading and spelling disability. *Learning Disability Quarterly* 24: 141–157.
Raskind, W., L. Hsu, J. Thomson, V. Berninger, and E. Wijsman
  2000   Family aggregation of dyslexic phenotypes. *Behavior Genetics* 30: 385–396.
Raskind, W., R. Igo, N. Chapman, V. Berninger, J. Thomson, M. Matsushita, Z. Brkanac, T. Holzman, M. Brown, and E. Wijsman
  2005   A genome scan in multigenerational families with dyslexia: Identification of a novel locus on chromosome 2q that contributes to phonological decoding efficiency. *Molecular Psychiatry* 10: 699–711.
Rayner, K., B. Foorman, C. Perfetti, D. Pesetsky, and M. Seidenberg
  2001   How psychological science informs the teaching of reading. *Psychological Science in the Public Interest* 2: 31–74.
Richards, T., E. Aylward, V. Berninger, K. Field, A. Parsons, A. Richards, and W. Nagy
  2006a   Individual fMRI activation in orthographic mapping and morpheme mapping after orthographic or morphological spelling treatment in child dyslexics. *Journal of Neurolinguistics* 19: 56–86.
Richards, T., E. Aylward, W. Raskind, R. Abbott, K. Field,. A. Parsons, A. Richards, W. Nagy, M. Eckert, C. Leonard, and V. Berninger
  2006b   Converging evidence for triple word form theory in child dyslexics. *Developmental Neuropsychology*, 30: 547–589.
Richards, T., V. Berninger, E. Aylward, A. Richards, J. Thomson, W. Nagy, J. Carlisle, S. Dager, and R. Abbott
  2002   Reproducibility of proton MR spectroscopic imaging: Comparison of dyslexic and normal reading children and effects of treatment on brain lactate levels during language tasks. *American Journal of Neuroradiology* 23: 1678–1685.
Richards, T., V. Berninger, W. Nagy, A. Parsons, K. Field, and A. Richards
  2005   Brain activation during language task contrasts in children with and without dyslexia: Inferring mapping processes and assessing response to spelling instruction. *Educational and Child Psychology* 22(2): 62–80.
Richards, T., V. Berninger, W. Winn, S. Stock, R. Wagner, A. Muse, and K. Maravilla
  in press fMRI activation in children with dyslexia during pseudoword aural repeat and visual decode: Before and after instruction. *Neuropsychology*.
Richards, T., D. Corina, S. Serafini, K. Steury, S. Dager, K. Marro, R. Abbott, K. Maravilla, and V. Berninger
  2000   Effects of phonologically-driven treatment for dyslexia on lactate levels as measured by proton MRSI. *American Journal of Radiology* 21: 916–922.

Richards, T., S. Dager, D. Corina, S. Serafini, C. Heidel, K. Steury, W. Strauss, C. Hayes, R. Abbott, S. Kraft, D. Shaw, S. Posse, and V. Berninger
    1999   Dyslexic children have abnormal chemical brain activation during reading-related language tasks. *American Journal of Neuroradiology* 20: 1393–1398.

Rumsey, J. M., P. Andreason, A. J. Zametkin, T. Aquino, A. C. King, S. D. Hamburger, A. Pikus, J. L. Rapoport, and R. M. Cohen
    1992   Failure to activate the left temporoparietal cortex in dyslexia. An oxygen 15 positron emission tomographic study. *Archives Neurology* 49: 527–34.

Scarborough, H.
    2001   Connecting early language and literacy to later reading (dis)abilities: Evidence, theory, and practice. In: S. Neuman and D. Dickson (eds.), *Handbook for Research in Early Literacy*, 97–110. New York: Guilford Press.

Schulte-Körne G, T. Grimm, M. M. Nothen, B. Muller-Myhsok, S. Cichon, I. R. Vogt, P. Propping, H. Remschmidt
    1998   Evidence for linkage of spelling disability to chromosome 15. *American Journal Human Genetics* 63: 279–82.

Schumacher J, H. Anthoni, F. Dahdouh, I. R. Konig, A. M. Hillmer, N. Kluck, M. Manthey, E. Plume, A. Warnke, H. Remschmidt, J. Hulsmann, S. Cichon, C. M. Lindgren, P. Propping, M. Zucchelli, A. Ziegler, M. Peyrard-Janvid, G. Schulte-Korne, M. M. Nothen and J. Kere
    2006   Strong genetic evidence of DCDC2 as a susceptibility gene for dyslexia. *American Journal of Human Genetics* 78: 52–62.

Scott, C.
    2002   A fork in the road less traveled: Writing intervention based on language profile. In: K. Butler and E. Silliman (eds.), *Speaking, Reading, and Writing in Children with Language Learning Disabilities*. Mahwah, New Jersey: Lawrence Erlbaum.

Shaywitz, S.
    2003   *Overcoming Dyslexia*. New York: Alfred A. Knopf.

Shaywitz, B. A., S. E. Shaywitz, B. A. Blachman, K. R. Pugh, R. K. Fulbright, P. Skudlarski, et al.
    2004   Development of left occipitotemporal systems for skilled reading in children after a phonologically-based intervention. *Biological Psychiatry* 55(9): 926–933.

Shaywitz, B. A., S. E. Shaywitz, K. R. Pugh, W. E. Mencl, R. K. Fulbright, P. Skudlarski, R. T. Constable, K. E. Marchione, J. M. Fletcher, G. R. Lyon, and J. C. Gore
    2002   Disruption of posterior brain systems for reading in children with developmental dyslexia. *Biological Psychiatry* 52: 101–10.

Shaywitz, S. E., B. A. Shaywitz, K. R. Pugh, R. K. Fulbright, R. T. Constable, W. E. Mencl, D. P. Shankweiler, A. M. Liberman, P. Skudlarski, J. M. Fletcher, L. Katz, K. E. Marchione, C. Lacadie, C. Gatenby, and J. C. Gore, J. C.
    1998   Functional disruption in the organization of the brain for reading in dyslexia, *Proceedings of the National Academy of Sciences* 95: 2636–2641.

Siegel, L.
    1989   Why we do not need intelligence scores in the definition and analysis of learning disabilities. *Journal of Learning Disabilities* 22: 514–518.

Simos, P. G., J. M. Fletcher, E. Bergman, J. I. Breier, B. R. Foorman, E. M. Castillo, et al.
    2002   Dyslexia-specific brain activation profile becomes normal following successful remedial training. *Neurology* 58(8): 1203–1213.

Simos, P. G., J. I. Breier, J. M. Fletcher, E. Bergman, and A. C. Papanicolaou
    2000   Cerebral mechanisms involved in word reading in dyslexic children: a magnetic source imaging approach. *Cerebral Cortex* 10: 809–16.

Simos, P. G., J. I. Breier, J. M. Fletcher, B. R. Foorman, E. Bergman, K. Fishbeck, and A. C. Papanicolaou
    2000   Brain activation profiles in dyslexic children during non-word reading: a magnetic source imaging study. *Neuroscience Letters* 290: 61–5.

Simos, P. G., J. M. Fletcher, E. Bergman, J. I. Breier, B. R. Foorman, E. M. Castillo, R. N. Davis, M. Fitzgerald, and A. C. Papanicolaou
    2002   Dyslexia-specific brain activation profile becomes normal following successful remedial training. *Neurology* 58: 1203–13.

Simos, P., J. Fletcher, B. Foorman, D. Francis, E. Castillo, R. Davis, M. Fitzgerald, P. Mathes, C. Denton, and A. Papanicolaou
    2005   Brain activation profiles during the early stages of reading acquisition, *Journal of Child Neurology*

Simos, P. G., A. C. Papanicolaou, J. I. Breier, J. M. Fletcher, J. W. Wheless, W. W. Maggio, W. Gormley, J. E. Constantinou, and L. Kramer
    2000   Insights into brain function and neural plasticity using magnetic source imaging. *Journal Clinical Neurophysiology* 17: 143–62.

Smith, S. D., W. J. Kimberling, B. F. Pennington, H. A. Lubs
    1983   Specific reading disability: identification of an inherited form through linkage analysis. *Science* 219: 1345–7.

Snow, C., H. Cancino, P. Gonzales, and E. Shriberg
    1989   Giving formal definitions: An oral language correlate of school literacy. In: D. Bloome (ed.), *Literacy in Classrooms,* 233–249. Norwood, NJ: Ablex.

Stahl, S. and W. Nagy
    2005   *Teaching Word Meaning.* Mahwah, NJ: Lawrence Erlbaum.

Stanberry, L., T. Richards, V. Berninger, R. Nandy, E. Aylward, K. Maravilla, P. Stock, and D. Cordes
    2006   Low frequency signal changes reflect differences in functional connectivity between good readers and dyslexics during continuous phoneme mapping. *Magnetic Resonance Imaging* 24: 217–229.

Stanovich, K.
    1986   Matthew effects in reading: Some consequences of individual differences in the acquisition of literacy. *Reading Research Quarterly* 21: 360–407.

Swanson, H. L.
    1999   *Interventions for Students with Learning Disabilities. A Meta-Analysis of Treatment Outcomes.* New York: Guilford.

Swanson, H. L.
    2000   Working memory, short-term memory, speech rate, word recognition and reading comprehension in learning disabled readers: Does the executive system have a role? *Intelligence* 28: 1–30.

Swanson, H. L. and V. Berninger
1996   Individual differences in children's writing: A function of working memory or reading or both processes? *Reading and Writing. An Interdisciplinary Journal* 8: 357–383.
Swanson, L. and L. Siegel
2001   Learning disabilities as a working memory deficit. *Issues in Education* 7: 1–48.
Swanson, H. L. and V. Berninger
1995   The role of working memory in skilled and less skilled readers' comprehension. *Intelligence* 21: 83–108.
Taipale M, N. Kaminen, J. Nopola-Hemmi, T. Haltia, B. Myllyluoma, H. Lyytinen, K. Muller, M. Kaaranen, P. Lindsberg, K. Hannula-Jouppi, and J. Kere
2003   A candidate gene for developmental dyslexia encodes a nuclear tetratricopeptide repeat domain protein dynamically regulated in brain. *Proceedings of the National Academy of Sciences of the United States of America* 100: 11553–11558.
Tan, L. H., H. L. Liu, C. A. Perfetti, J. A. Spinks, P. T. Fox, and J. H. Gao
2001   The neural system underlying Chinese logograph reading. *NeuroImage* 13: 826–846.
Temple, E., R. A. Poldrack, G. K. Deutsch, S. Miller, P. Tallal, M. M. Merzenich, J. D. E. Gabrieli
2003   Neural deficits in children with dyslexia ameliorated by behavioral remediation: Evidence from fMRI. *Proceedings of the National Academy of Sciences* 100: 2860–2865.
Temple, E., R. A. Poldrack, A. Protopapas, S. Nagarajan, T. Saltz, P. Tallal, M. M. Merzenich, and J. D. E. Gabrieli
2000   Disruption of the neural response to rapid acoustic stimuli in dyslexia: Evidence from functional MRI. *Proceedings of the National Academy of Sciences, USA* 97: 13907–13912.
Temple, E., R. A. Poldrack, J. Salidis, G. K. Deutsch, P. Tallal, M. M. Merzenich, and J. D. Gabrieli
2001   Disrupted neural responses to phonological and orthographic processing in dyslexic children: an fMRI study. *Neuroreport* 12: 299–307.
Templeton, S. and D. Bear (eds.)
1992   *Development of Orthographic Knowledge and the Foundations of Literacy*, 307–332. Hillsdale, NJ: Lawrence Erlbaum Associates.
Thomson, J., and W. Raskind
2003   Genetic influences on reading and writing disabilities. In: H. L. Swanson, K. Harris, and S. Graham (eds.), *Handbook of Learning Disabilities*, 256–270. New York: Guilford.
Torgesen, J.
2004   Learning disabilities: An historical and conceptual overview. In: B. Wong (ed.), *Learning about Learning Disabilities*, 3rd Ed., 3–40. San Diego: Academic Press (Elsevier).
Torgesen, J., A. Alexander, R. Wagner, C. Rashotte, C., K. Voeller, T. Conway, and E. Rose
2001   Intensive remedial instruction for children with severe reading disabilities: Immediate and long-term outcomes from two instructional approaches. *Journal of Learning Disabilities* 34: 33–58.

The_SLI_Consortium
   2002   A genomewide scan identifies two novel loci involved in specific language impairment. *American Journal of Human Genetics* 70: 384–398.

Turkeltaub, P. E., L. Gareau, D. L. Flowers, T. A. Zeffiro, and G. F. Eden
   2003   Development of neural mechanisms for reading. *Nature Neuroscience* 6: 767–73.

Vaughn, S., S. Moody, S., and J. Schumm
   1998   Broken promises: Reading instruction in the resource room. *Exceptional Children* 64: 211–225.

Vellutino, F. and D. Scanlon
   1987   Phonological coding, phonological awareness, and reading ability. Evidence from a longitudinal and experimental study. *Merrill Palmer Quarterly* 33: 321–363.

Venezky, R.
   1970   *The Structure of English Orthography.* The Hague: Mouton.

Venezky, R.
   1999   *The American Way of Spelling.* New York: Guilford.

Wagner, R., J. Torgesen
   1987   The nature of phonological processing and its causal role in the acquisition of reading skills. *Psychological Bulletin* 101: 192–212.

Wallach, G. and K. Butler
   1994   *Language Learning Disabilities in School-Age Children and Adolescents. Some Principles and Applications.* Needham Heights, MA: Allyn and Bacon.

Whitaker, D., V. Berninger, J. Johnston, J., and L. Swanson
   1994   Intraindividual differences in levels of language in intermediate grade writers: Implications for the translating process. *Learning and Individual Differences* 6: 107–130.

White, T., M. Power, and S. White
   1989   Morphological analysis: Implications for teaching and understanding vocabulary growth in diverse elementary schools: Decoding and word meaning. *Journal of Educational Psychology* 82: 283–04.

Wijsman, E., D. Peterson, A. Leutennegger, J. Thomson, K. Goddard, L. Hsu, V. Berninger, and W. Raskind
   2000   Segregation analysis of phenotypic components of learning disabilities I. Nonword memory and digit span. *American Journal of Human Genetics* 67: 31–646.

Wise, B., J. Ring, and R. Olson
   1999   Training phonological awareness with and without explicit attention to articulation. *Journal of Experimental Child Psychology* 72: 271–304.

Wolf, M.
   1986   Rapid alternating stimulus naming in the developmental dyslexias. *Brain and Language* 27: 360–379.

Wolf, M. (ed.)
   2001   *Dyslexia, Fluency, and the Brain* (especially the preface on the seven dimensions of time). Timonium, MD: York Press.

Wolf, M., and P. Bowers
   1999   The double-deficit hypothesis for the developmental dyslexias. *Journal of Educational Psychology* 91: 415–438.

Wolf, M., B. O'Brien, K. Adams, T. Joffe, J. Jeffrey, M. Lovett, and R. Morris
   2003   Working for time: Reflections on naming speed, reading fluency, and intervention. In: B. Foorman (ed.), *Preventing and Remediating Reading Difficulties. Bringing Science to Scale.* Baltimore: York Press.

Wong, B. Y. L.
   2000   Writing strategies instruction for expository essays for adolescents with and without learning disabilities. *Topics in Language Disorders* 20(4): 29–44.

Table 1.

Regions of Reliable Activation in Controls (Good Readers) from Time 1 to Time 2 for Four Sets of Contrasts between Specific Kinds of Morpheme, Phoneme, and Orthographic Mapping (Column 1) and Concordance or Divergence of Dyslexic Brain Activation in These Regions Before (Columns 2 and 3) and After (Columns 4 and 5) Alternative Spelling Treatments. (Yes=significant activation > 50; No=significant activation > 50 IND=*Indeterminate* indicates that both dyslexic treatment groups did not show the same brain response – significant activation or insignificant activation at time 1. See text for abbreviations of regions.)

Mapping Contrast	Time 1 Orthographic Treatment	Time 1 Morphological Treatment	Time 2 Orthographic Treatment	Time 2 Morphological Treatment
Morpheme Mapping w/o Phono Shift>				
Morpheme Mapping with Phono Shift				
R IPG	no	no	no	no
Phoneme Mapping				
L Ling	yes	yes	no[c]	no[c]
Orthographic Mapping				
R PrC	yes	yes	no[b,c]	yes
L MFO	no	no	no	no
R MFO med	no	no	no	no
R Rec	no	no	no	no
R Cun	yes	yes	n, o[b,c]	yes
L Cun	yes	yes	yes	yes
R Ling	yes	yes	no[c]	no[c]
L SOG	yes	yes	yes	yes
R MOG	yes	yes	yes	yes
L MOG	yes	yes	no[c]	no[c]
R Fus	yes	yes	no[c]	no[c]
R SPG	yes	yes	no[c]	no[c]
L SPG	ind	ind	no	no
R IPG	yes	yes	yes	no[b,c]
R Ang	yes	yes	no[b,c]	yes
L Ang	yes	yes	no[c]	no[c]
R Precun	yes	yes	no[b,c]	yes
L Precun	yes	yes	no[c]	no[c]
R MTG	yes	yes	no[c]	no[c]
L MTG	ind	ind	no	no
R ITG	yes	yes	no[b,c]	yes

Morpheme Mapping with Phono Shift>				
Morpheme Mapping w/o Phono Shift none				
Phoneme Mapping				
R IFG oper	no	no	no	no
L SFG med	no	no	yes[a, b]	no
L MFO med	no	no	no	no
R Ins	ind	ind	no	no
L Mid Cing	no	no	yes[a, c]	no
L Pos Cing	no	no	no	no
R Calc	no	no	no	no
R Ling	yes	yes	no[b]	no[b]
R SupraM	no	no	no	no
R Precun	ind	ind	no	no
L Precun	no	no	no	no
R ITG	no	no	no	no
Orthographic Mapping				
R PrC	ind	ind	no	no
L SFO	no	no	no	no
L SFG med	yes	yes	no[b, c]	yes
R *MFO med*	no	no	no	no
L *MFO med*	no	no	no	no
R *Mid Cing*	no	no	no	no
R *Calc*	yes	yes	yes	no[b, c]
R *Cun*	yes	yes	no[b]	no[b]
L *Cun*	yes	yes	yes	yes
L *SOG*	yes	yes	no[b, c]	yes
L *MOG*	yes	yes	yes	yes
R *PosC*	yes	yes	no[b]	no[b]
L *PosC*	no	no	no	no
R SPG	ind	ind	no	no
L SPG	no	no	no	no
R Precun	yes	yes	no[b]	no[b]
L Precun	ind	ind	no	no
Phoneme Mapping >				
Morpheme Mapping w/o Phono Shift				
L PrC	ind	ind	yes	yes
R SFG	no	no	yes[a, c]	no
L *SFG*	ind	ind	yes	yes
L *MFG*	yes	yes	yes	yes

L MFO	no	no	no	no
L IFG oper	ind	ind	yes	yes
R IFG tri	no	no	no	no
L IFG tri	ind	ind	yes	no
R IFO	no	no	no	no
L IFO	no	no	no	no
R SuppMA	ind	ind	yes	yes
L SuppMA	ind	ind	yes	yes
R SFG med	no	no	yes[a]	yes[a]
L SFG med	ind	ind	yes	yes
L Ins	no	no	no	no
L Ling	no	no	no	no
L SOG	ind	ind	yes	no
R MOG	ind	ind	yes	no
R Fus	no	no	no	no
L Fus	no	no	yes[a,b]	no
L SPG	no	no	yes[a,b]	no
L IPG	no	no	yes[a,b]	no
L Ang	no	no	yes[a,b]	no
L ITG	ind	ind	yes[a,b]	no
R cereb crus 1	no	no	yes[a,b]	no
R cereb crus 2	ind	ind	yes	yes
R cereb_ 6	ind	ind	yes	no
L cereb_6	ind	ind	yes	yes
R cereb 7b	ind	ind	yes	no
Morpheme Mapping with Phono Shift				
L PrC	yes	yes	yes	yes
R SFG	no	no	no	yes[a,b]
L SFG	ind	ind	yes	yes
R MFG	ind	ind	yes	yes
L MFG	yes	yes	yes	yes
R MFO	no	no	no	no
L MFO	no	no	no	no
L IFG oper	ind	ind	yes	yes
R IFG tri	no	no	yes[a,b]	no
L IFG tri	no	no	yes[a,b]	no
R IFO	no	no	no	no
L IFO	no	no	yes[a,b]	no
R SuppMA	ind	ind	yes	yes
L SuppMA	no	no	yes[a]	yes[a]
R SFG med	no	no	no	yes[a,b]
L SFG med	no	no	no	no
L Ins	no	no	yes[a,b]	no

R Mid Cing	no	no	no	no
L Calc	no	no	no	no
L Ling	no	no	no	no
L SOG	yes	yes	yes	no[b,c]
L IOG	ind	ind	no	no
R Fus	no	no	yes[a,b]	no
L Fus	no	no	yes[a,b]	no
R SPG	no	no	no	no
L SPG	no	no	no	no
R IPG	ind	ind	no	no
L IPG	no	no	no	no
L SupraM	no	no	no	no
R Ang	ind	ind	no	no
L Ang	ind	ind	no	no
R Precun	no	no	no	yes[a,b]
L Precun	no	no	no	no
R MTG	no	no	yes[a,b]	no
L ITG	no	no	no	no
R cereb crus 1	no	no	yes[a,b]	no
R cereb crus 2	no	no	no	no
L cereb crus 2	no	no	yes[a,b]	no
R cereb 6	no	no	yes[a,b]	no
Orthographic Mapping				
L PrC	yes	yes	yes	yes
R SFG	ind	ind	no	yes
L SFG	yes	yes	no[b,c]	yes
R SFO	no	no	no	no
L SFO	no	no	no	no
R MFG	yes	yes	no[b,c]	yes
L MFG	yes	yes	yes	yes
L MFO	no	no	no	no
L IFG oper	yes	yes	no[c]	no[c]
L IFG tri	ind	ind	yes	no
L IFO	no	no	no	no
R SuppMA	yes	yes	no	no
L SuppMA	yes	yes	no[b,c]	yes
L Cun	yes	yes	yes	yes
L Ling	ind	ind	yes	yes
R SOG	yes	yes	yes	yes
L SOG	yes	yes	yes	yes
R MOG	yes	yes	yes	yes
L MOG	yes	yes	yes	yes
R IOG	yes	yes	yes	no[b,c]
R Fus	ind	ind	yes	yes

L Fus	yes	yes	yes	no[b,c]
R SPG	ind	ind	no	no
L SPG	no	no	no	no
R IPG	yes	yes	yes	no[b,c]
L IPG	ind	ind	no	no
L SupraM	yes	yes	no	no
R Ang	yes	yes	yes	no[b,c]
L Ang	yes	yes	yes	no[b,c]
R Precun	yes	yes	no[c]	no[c]
L Precun	ind	ind	no	no
R MTG	ind	ind	no	no
L MTG	yes	yes	no[c]	no[c]
R ITG	yes	yes	no[c]	no[c]
L ITG	yes	yes	no[b,c]	yes
R cereb crus 1	yes	yes	yes	yes
R cereb crus 2	ind	ind	yes	no
R cereb 6	yes	yes	yes	yes
L cereb 6	yes	yes	yes	no[b,c]
R cereb 7b	ind	ind	no	no
R cereb 8	yes	yes	no[c]	no[c]
L cereb 8	ind	ind	yes	yes
Orthographic Mapping >				
Morpheme Mapping w/o Phono Shift				
R IFO	no	no	no	no
R SFG med	ind	ind	no	no
L *Ling*	ind	ind	no	yes
L *Fus*	no	no	yes[a,b]	no
Morpheme Mapping with Phono Shift				
R SFG	no	no	no	no
R MFG	no	no	yes[a,b]	no
R IFG tri	no	no	yes[a,b]	no
L IFG tri	no	no	yes[a,b]	no
R IFO	no	no	no	no
R SuppMA	no	no	yes[a]	yes[a]
R SFG med	no	no	yes[a,b]	no
R Ins	no	no	no	yes[a,b]
L Ins	no	no	no	no
R Ant Cing	no	no	no	no
L Calc	no	no	no	no
L Ling	no	no	no	yes[a,b]
R IPG	no	no	no	no
R ANG	no	no	yes[a,b]	no

Phoneme Mapping				
R IFG oper	ind	ind	no	no
R IFG tri	no	no	no	no
R Ins	ind	ind	no	no
R ITG	no	no	no	no

[a] Normalization because previously inactivated region activates.
[b] Treatment-specific finding because only one treatment leads to normalization.
[c] Denormalization because prior to treatment but not after treatment dyslexics activated a region good readers did.
Key: superior frontal gyrus (SFG), middle frontal gyrus (MFG), inferior frontal gyrus (IFG) (tri=trinangularis; oper= operculum; orb=orbital);, MFO= middle frontal orbital cortex, orbital frontal (Orb), supplementary motor area (SuppMA), precentral gyrus (PreC), anterior cingulate (Ant Cing), posterior cingulate (Pos Cing), superior temporal gyrus (STG), middle temporal gyrus (MTG), inferior temporal gyrus (ITG), fusiform gyrus (FG), lingual gyrus (Ling), PosC=postcentral gyrus, SPG=superior parietal gyrus; IPG= inferior parietal gyrus; Ang=angular gyrus, SupraM=supramarginal gyrus, Ins=insula, SOG-superior occipital gyrus; MOG= middle occipital gyrus;, Calc=calcarine, Rec= rectus; Precun=precuneus, Cun=cuneus; thalamus, and cerebellum (cereb)

Table 2. Deactivation (Deact) of Brain Regions at Time 2 Following Alternative Spelling Treatments in which Both Dyslexic Treatment Groups But Not Controls Activated at Time 1.

Mapping Contrast	Both Treatment Groups But Not Controls Activated at Time 1	Orthographic Treatment Group Time 2	Morphological Treatment Group Time 2
Morpheme Mapping w/o Phono Shift >			
Morpheme mapping with phono shift	R PrC	no change	deact[b,c]
Phoneme Mapping	R Cereb	deact[a]	no change
	L Cereb	deact[b]	deact[b]
	Verm	deact[b]	deact[b]
Orthographic Mapping	L PrC	no change	deact[b,c]
	R SFG	no change	deact[b,c]
	F MFG	deact[b]	deact[b]
	R_SFG Med	deact[b]	deact[b]
	L_SFG Med	deact[b]	deact[b]
	R_Calc	deact[a]	no change
	R_SOG	no change	no change
	R_IOG	deact[b,c]	no change
	L Fus	deact[b]	deact[b]
	R PosC	deact[b]	deact[b]
	L PosC	deact[b]	deact[b]
	R ParaC	deact[b]	deact[b]
	L ParaC	deact[b]	deact[b]
	R STG	deact[a]	deact[a]
	L ITG	deact[b]	deact[b]
	R Cereb	deact[a]	no change
	Verm	deact[b]	deact[b]
Morpheme Mapping with Phono Shift >			
Morpheme Mapping w/o Phono Shift		none	
Phoneme Mapping	L_Cerb	deact[b]	deact[b]
	R_Cereb	deact[a]	deact[a]
	Verm	deact[a]	deact[a]
	Verm	deact[b]	deact[b]
Orthographic Mapping	R_SFG	no change	deact[b,c]
	L_SFG	deact[b]	deact[b]
	R_MFG	deact[b]	deact[b]
	R_SFG_Med	no change	deact[b,c]
	L_Calc	deact[b,c]	no change
	R_Ling	deact[a]	no change

		R_SOG	no change	no change
		R_MOG	no change	no change
		R_IOG	deact[b]	deact[b]
		L_IOG	deact[b]	deact[b]
		R_Fus	deact[b]	deact[b]
		L_Fus	deact[b]	deact[b]
		R_Ang	deact[b]	deact[b]
		R_Put	deact[b]	deact[b]
		R_STG	deact[b]	deact[b]
		R_MTG	deact[b]	deact[b]
		R_ITG	no change	deact[b,c]
		L_ITG	deact[b]	deact[b]
		L_Cerb	deact[b]	deact[b]
		R_Cereb	deact[b,c]	no change
Phoneme Mapping >				
Morpheme Mapping w/o Phono Shift	L MOC	no change	no change	
Morpheme Mapping with Phono Shift	LMOC	no change	no change	
Orthographic Mapping	R_PrC	deact[b]	deact[b]	
	R_IFG_Tri	deact[b]	deact[b]	
	R_Calc	no change	no change	
	L_Calc	no change	no change	
	R_Cun	no change	no change	
	R_Ling	no change	deact[b,c]	
	L_IOG	deact[b,c]	no change	
	L_PosC	deact[b]	deact[b]	
	L_Cereb	deact[b,c]	no change	
Orthographic Mapping >				
Morpheme Mapping w/o Phono Shift	none			
Morpheme Mapping with Phono Shift	none			
Phoneme Mapping	none			

[a] Deactivation of previously activated region is not evidence of normalization because controls were activated at time 2 even though they were not at time 1.
[b] Normalization because region previously activated only in dyslexics is now deactivated.
[c] Treatment-specific responding because normalization (see footnote b) occurred for only one of the alternative treatments.
Key: superior frontal gyrus (SFG), middle frontal gyrus (MFG), inferior frontal gyrus (IFG) (tri=trinangularis; oper= operculum; orb=orbital);, MFO= middle frontal oribtal cortex, orbital frontal (Orb), supplementary motor area (SuppMA), precentral gyrus (PreC), anterior cingulate (Ant Cing), posterior cingulate (Pos Cing), superior temporal gyrus (STG), middle temporal gyrus (MTG), inferior temporal gyrus (ITG), fusiform gyrus (FG), lingual gyrus (Ling), PosC=postcentral gyrus, SPG=superior parietal gyrus; IPG= inferior parietal gyrus; Ang=angular gyrus, SupraM=supramarginal gyrus, Ins=insula, SOG-superior occipital gyrus; MOG= middle occipital gyrus;, Calc=calcarine, Rec= rectus; Precun=precuneus, Cun=cuneus; thalamus, and cerebellum (cereb)

Table 3. Uniquely Activated Brain Regions for Phonological, Orthographic, and Morphological Word Forms Compared to Each of the Other Word Forms in Good Readers (Regions Also Activated by Dyslexics Bolded)

Phonological Word Form (Phoneme Mapping)	**L PrC, R SFG, LSFG, LMFG, LMFO, LIFG oper, LIFG tri, LIFO, R SuppMA, LSuppMA, L Ling, L SOG, R Fus, L Fus, LSPG, LIPG, L Ang, LITG, R cereb crus 1, R cereb crus 2**
Orthographic Word Form (Orthographic Mapping)	R IFG tri (but not compared to morphological task without phoneme shift – only morphological task with phoneme shift and phoneme mapping)
Morphological Word Form (Morpheme Mapping – No Phonological Shift)	None
Morphological Word Form (Morpheme Mapping + Phonological Shift)	None compared to morpheme mapping without phonological shifts but compared to both phoneme mapping and orthographic mapping: L SFG med, LMFO med, R Calc, R Precun, and L Precun

Key: superior frontal gyrus (SFG), middle frontal gyrus (MFG), inferior frontal gyrus (IFG) (tri=trinangularis; oper= operculum; orb=orbital);, MFO= middle frontal orbital cortex, orbital frontal (Orb), supplementary motor area (SuppMA), precentral gyrus (PreC), anterior cingulate (Ant Cing), posterior cingulate (Pos Cing), superior temporal gyrus (STG), middle temporal gyrus (MTG), inferior temporal gyrus (ITG), fusiform gyrus (FG), lingual gyrus (Ling), PosC=postcentral gyrus, SPG=superior parietal gyrus; IPG= inferior parietal gyrus; Ang=angular gyrus, SupraM=supramarginal gyrus, Ins=insula, SOG-superior occipital gyrus; MOG= middle occipital gyrus;, Calc=calcarine, Rec= rectus; Precun=precuneus, Cun=cuneus; thalamus, and cerebellum (cereb)

16. Language disorders

Martina Hielscher-Fastabend

Acquired language and communication impairments can result from brain damage of various neurological etiology. Of course, the most intriguing disorder concerning language skills in adults is aphasia. Aphasia has to be contrasted to other language and speech problems caused by brain damage, for example lesions of the right hemisphere or frontal lobes on the one hand and the dysarthrias and speech apraxia on the other hand. Usually, patients suffering from aphasia have problems with auditory/oral language as well as with written language in perception and production. Quite often problems are more severe in the productive than in the perceptive mode. But depending on the area and extent of the lesion site, some patients may be able to speak but not write or vice versa, and some patients have even more severe problems with auditory comprehension than with reading or with language production.

This chapter first gives a short introduction followed, second, by an overview on the basic brain mechanisms of language functions. In the third part we begin with the traditional classification of aphasia which is closely related to neurobiological questions of lesion site. This general section is followed by the neurolinguistic approach and a communicative perspective to describe symptoms, diagnostic tools and therapeutic methods.

1. Aphasia and other acquired language disorders

Modern Classification schemata like the ICF (*International Classification of Functioning, Disability and Health*), given by the World Health Organization (WHO 2001) do not only focus on aspects of the "impairment" (lesions in specific brain areas causing specific language disorders), "disability" (resulting activity limitation, communicative difficulties, behavior which is no longer optimal but deficient from normal and healthy language use and communication), and "handicap" (participation limitation, for example the loss of employment or social isolation) of patients suffering from language disorders. The individual and situational "resources" (e.g. non-verbal communicative competences, help from the family) vs. "barriers" (e.g. social isolation, depression) in leading a responsible and self-dependent life are parameters in the classification scheme enhancing or decreasing the problem for the patient (cf. Davis, 2007). As will be shown in this article, the planning of therapeutic and rehabilitative programs strongly relies on both of these aspects, (1) the components of changed skills and language processes, and (2) the individual, situational and social coping potential. This calls for adequate diagnostic tools for both of these domains, which is not yet the case. An impairment orientation still dominates scientific research, diagnosis, and therapy.

This article focuses on the impairment of and coping with language functions in terms of *aphasia*. Aphasia is defined as an impairment of the ability to produce and comprehend oral as well as written language as a result of a neural lesion of the adult brain with a sudden onset, typically as a result of a stroke. In this way aphasia is often called a "multimodality deficit" (cf. Davis 2007, p. 2). Some common language problems can be sketched as very typical to describe most aphasic patients even if the individual patterns of impairments, handicaps and coping behavior show a wide variety. Several syndromes of aphasia are common to label specific patterns of functional disorders as a consequence of lesions in different brain regions involved in processes of speech production on one hand or on phonological comprehension and lexical-semantic processes on the other hand. No matter how divergent these specific classifications may have been (cf. section 3.1), all approaches agree at least on the relevant modalities and on a set of relevant symptoms in aphasic speech production, some of which will be defined in short before the characterization of the main syndromes will be given:

Most patients show severe problems in word finding and naming functions, even if other symptoms have faded and their communicative ability would be in the normal range. Typically, we find signs of aphasic productions in spontaneous speech which refer to word production in terms of *'paraphasias:'* i.e a word that is substituted for the obviously correct one; if the target word is *knife*, *"cutter"* would be called a 'semantic paraphasia', /maif/ would be called a 'phonematic paraphasia', and *"life"* would be in a semantic as well as in a phonematic relation to the target word. If no phonological similarity to the target word can be observed or if the expression depicts no semantically correct term in the language, they are called phonematic or semantic neologisms.

Sentence production is often described in terms of *'agrammatic' vs.' paragrammatic'* style: The typical features of agrammatic speech are short sentences and phrases, containing mainly content words (nouns and verbs, mostly not inflected infinite or progressive forms) in a telegraphic style with elliptical phrases and incomplete sentences. Grammatical elements are typically missing. – The typical features of paragrammatic speech are quite unobtrusive at first if not especially long and complex in their sentence structures, often with repeated constituents, sometimes with a shrinking of two sentence structures. Function words are quite normal or even more frequent in relation to content words but often wrongly used or placed. Verbs and nouns are often not correctly inflected.

Several characteristics concern the informativeness of speech. *Echolalia* means the repetition of words and phrases which are used by the communication partner in an identical or very similar imitative way and is shown by patients often without understanding the meaning of these utterances. *Automatic speech* as a category label for several phenomena can vary in its adequacy in communication. In aphasic utterances we find a high frequency of set phrases which are used not always appropriately and quite often in the same way. Stereotypes are used quite adequate in the communicative context, but they are frequently produced without variation. We also find invariable structures with some patients which do not fit semantically nor syntactically in the communicative context and which are not expected by the communication partner (THERAPIST: "Would you like to have a cup of tea?" PATIENT: "Oh, well, come in come out"). Furthermore, *recurring utterances* may consist of repetitions of meaningless syllables ("dododo", "tantantan") or neologisms ("bandi, bandi, bandi"), of words or short phrases ("well well well"; "come in come out") but some patients use their automatized expressions with very informative prosodical variation.

Besides these few parameters of aphasic speech production, a differential description of production and comprehension problems for sound, word, sentence, and text level will be given in the following sections. Isolated problems of naming (anomia) or of written language skills (alexia/agraphia) will be discussed briefly. The more peripheral problems of speech planning (apraxia of speech) and articulation (dysarthria) will be sketched in a short review. And finally, some impairments of higher order language and communicative functions (cognitive dysphasias) will be presented due to the fact that these "syndromes" have gained growing attention in the last ten years.

Usually, aphasia is a result of damage to specific cortical structures, typically in the left cortical hemisphere. Lesions in several other parts of the brain can also result in problems with language functions and communication, which are often more difficult to differentiate from what is defined as 'normal' functioning. Problems of planning and executing speech and articulation can result if the primary and secondary motor cortex or specific areas in the left insula cortex are involved.

Before the typical impairments of the various language skills of various neurological syndromes can be described, a short introduction to relevant cortical structures and their functions for language processing is given, followed by a paragraph on modern psycholinguistic and clinically relevant models for language comprehension and production.

2. Language functions and brain centers

One of the most surprising things about the neo-cortex of higher mammals is the large number of distinct cortical areas in the sensory and motor systems. The best analyzed example may be the primary visual cortex and the many more cortical areas devoted to vision. The generalization of results from studies on rhesus monkeys and humans is that the visual areas of the ventral stream are more concerned with identification of what things are, and the dorsal stream areas are concerned with localization and where things happen. The auditory and somato-sensory cortex similarly have a large number of separate cortical areas, though apparently not quite as many as the visual system. For instance, the 'homunculus' in the primary motor and sensory cortex has been famous since the work of Penfield and Rasmussen (1950). The special functions of many of the areas are known, but others are not. But beyond the many strictly sensory and motor areas, much of the cortex cannot yet be assigned to one function or another. The remaining areas of the cortex are traditionally called the multimodal association or tertiary cortex. It is these tertiary or multimodal association cortical areas that have reached their maximum size in the higher apes and humans and seem to be intimately involved in language function. It has also been shown that these areas of the brain are last to complete in ontogenetical development. In fact, it is suggested that myelination of the angular gyrus region of the parietal lobe in man is not be complete before the age of twenty years, and some frontal structures develop not before the age of fourteen or fifteen years (cf. Frackowiak 2004, Toga and Mazziotta 2000).

The most distinctive higher cortical function is the production and comprehension of language. Human language includes the comprehension and production of sounds, words, phrases, sentences, and texts. It is defined by the central aspect of communication of abstract ideas. These functions rely on the neural mechanisms of the primary and secondary auditory, visual, and motor cortex, but they include many more areas and functions. The multimodal association cortex is distinct in its location and connections from primary (i.e., motor, visual, auditory, somato-sensory) cortex and the secondary cortex which is immediately adjacent to and highly connected with the primary cortex areas.

In a brief historical review of our modern understanding of the cortical representation of language functions and lesion syndromes the most obvious functional localization is the specificity of the left hemisphere for language function in most people. Usually, the language specific centers of the brain are located in the left hemisphere. A dominance for language functions is found in the right hemisphere only in a very small number of people, or even both hemispheres seem to be equally responsible for language comprehension (approx. 2% each, e.g. Huber, Poeck, and Weniger 2002). Most of these persons are left-handed, but even 76% of left-handers seem to have a dominance for language in their left hemisphere (Pujol, Deus, Losilla, and Capdevila 1999).

Early phrenologists like Franz-Josef Gall (1758–1828) were first to postulate a clear association of brain regions and higher cognitive functions. The discovery that language function is lateralized was made by Paul **Broca** in the 1860's. He described (1960/1863) two patients who suddenly lost the ability to speak. Lesions were found in the left inferior frontal lobe at the bottom of the third frontal gyrus, a region of the brain which is called Broca's area today and which is marked in relation to Brodmann's (1909) historical mapping of the cerebral cortex as areas 44 and 45 (Figure 1). Only few years later Carl **Wernicke** described patients with lesions in the left temporal lobe and a predominant language comprehension deficit known today as Wernicke's aphasia. He presented a quite sophisticated view of various language functions which may be impaired selectively in different patients (Wernicke, 1874). Typically, lesions are found in the left auditory association cortex (Brodmann area 22), which seems to be important for associating sounds and stimuli of other modalities (i.e., learning names, linking phonological word forms to semantic concepts).

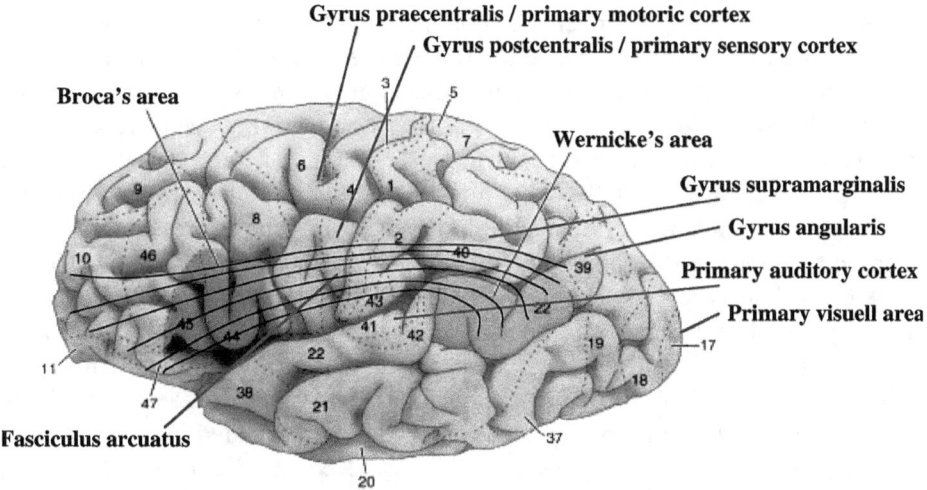

Figure 1.

In modern psycho- and neurolinguistics the central speech area, which is assumed to serve language functions such as the production and reproduction of sounds, words, and grammatical phrases in expressive language, requires cortico-cortical connections between auditory and intermodal association areas (BA 22, 39, 40) on one hand, and between the auditory and motor association cortex (Broca's area; BA 44, 45) on the other hand. The connections involve white matter pathways through the parieto-frontal operculum known as the arcuate fasciculus. It should be stressed that each site within the central speech area functions by virtue of its connections to other speech-related cortical (and subcortical) areas.

Another cortical area related to language function is concerned with written language. Usually, reading and writing are learned several years after a child has extensive language experience in the auditory and vocal modality. The written language system is, therefore, added onto pre-existing intermodal associations. As one might expect, a more posterior representation of written language skills than auditory language skills has been isolated in the parieto-occipital region of the language dominant hemisphere, namely between visual association areas of the occipital lobe and the temporal intermodal association areas. In fact, certain lesions in the gyrus angularis and adjacent structures can impair reading and/or writing skills while leaving auditory language skills intact. In contrast, lesions of auditory-intermodal association areas typically impair both reading and auditory comprehension since the auditory associations are supposed to support written language functions.

The right hemisphere (as the non-dominant hemisphere in most people) has been negotiated for a long time because functions were not as easily demonstrable as in the left hemisphere. Lesion studies of the right hemisphere often show more diffuse disabilities making them more difficult to verbalize. Lesions in the right parietal lobe, specifically the angular and supra-marginal gyri, usually give rise to deficits in the manipulation of spatial concepts (e.g. spatial disorientation, inability to draw three dimensional figures, neglect of the left side of the body; cf. Bisiach 1999). Other not so striking difficulties, for example the ability to comprehend emotional stimuli, prosody, or facial expressions, are also seen with lesions in the right hemisphere (Gainotti 1999). In a very ambitious work on typical syndromes of prosodic disabilities Ross (1981, 2000) has tried to find parallels between syndromes of language impairment for lesions in the left hemisphere and syndromes of prosodic impairment in the right hemisphere (The Aprosodias). This very interesting approach was documented by single case studies, but the syndrome predictions were not replicated in its initial specificity (e.g. Baum and Pell, 1999; Johnston, van Reekum, Oakes, and Davidson 2006; Wildgruber et al. 2004, 2005; Williams, Harrison, Shenal, Rhodes, and Demaree 2003). A current view sees right hemispheric processing connected to specialized functions of the right amygdala, a structure in the center of the temporal lobe which builds a system that serves emotional processing and memory functions. The right hemisphere may serve to analyze situational cues, facial, prosodic and even verbal material in regard to their basic connotation and emotional relevance (cf. Ross, Homan, and Buck 1994; Davis 2007). But not only emotional aspects of language are processed by the right hemisphere. Several functions of the right hemisphere at least in language comprehension have been shown in numerous lesion studies as well as in psycholinguistic and neuroimaging studies (cf. Beeman and Chiarello 1998; Joanette and Brownell 1990).

The frontal lobes are last in their ontogenetic development and they are least explicitly described in their specific function so far. But in the last years several interesting projects have shed light on the functions of the frontal lobes (cf. Toga and Mazziotta 2000). Some researchers discuss for instance the syndrome of an executive control disorder (Knight and D'Esposito 2003), which concerns 'action planning', 'problem solving', and 'flexibility in cognitive and behavioral reactions' (BA 9, 46). Lesions of adjacent sites in the lateral prefrontal areas (BA 44, 45) have been shown to be important for higher functional processes in language and communication, too (Ardila 1987; Beeson & Ardila 1999). Some areas in the left-lateral prefrontal lobe are proposed to be involved during language comprehension in context (Ferstl and von Cramon 2001, Maguire, Frith, and Morris 1999) and they may serve a special role for inference processes (Ferstl, Guthke, and von Cramon 2002).

In summary, the traditional localistic view of the cortical representation of language functions postulates a central speech area, represented usually in the left hemisphere that consists of a receptive and auditory word association region (BA 22, or Wernicke's area), connected to the adjacent areas in the parieto-occipital lobe as well as connected via the arcuate fasciculus to a speech production, word-sequencing region in the frontal lobe (BA 44, 45 or Broca's area).

But, many problems shine of with this neat and simple picture of language centers and functions in the recent debate on language functions, impairments, and recovery. Today's view of localization, lesion, and function is not as strict anymore as it used to be and several additional areas have been found to be involved in language comprehension. Only two prominent examples will be given here in order to document the complexity of language processing and associated brain regions.

Adjacent to the central speech area posteriorly to BA 22 are groups of cells which are more concerned with auditory-intermodal, visual-symbolic processing and other, less well-defined symbolic manipulation. Especially the temporo-parieto-occipital area, the gyrus angularis (BA 39) is suggested to be involved in written language processing. But acquired disorders of reading show quite different patterns associated even with heterogeneous lesion sites (cf. Coslett 2003).

The gyrus supramarginalis (BA 40) seems to be involved in phonological encoding and lexical-semantic access. Other temporal regions beneath Wernicke's area in the gyrus temporalis medius and inferior play a role in naming and word finding deficits in anomic aphasia. But the specific localizations may differ between individuals (cf. Bookheimer 2002).

These results show the problems of all lesion studies as well as of modern neuro-imaging concerning the individual variation of localizations, which depends on individual development, on brain mapping methods, and on experimental tasks. Several authors stress the network character of cognitive structures and functions, for example see Susan Bookheimer (2002), who discusses three lines of fMRI research on the extent of organization and division in the adult brain. She discusses the role of the left inferior frontal lobe in semantic processing, the organization of categories of objects and concepts in the temporal lobe, and the role of the right hemisphere in comprehending contextual and figurative meaning. Her results challenge some commonly held notions of functional modularity in the language system. However, most neuroimaging techniques try to identify localizations, specific structures, and functional areas. Only some alternative brain mapping techniques identify patterns of neurophysiological correlates of cognitive processes, as it is the case in coherence analysis of EEG-data (Weiss and Müller 2003).

3. Aphasia

Aphasia is defined as an impairment of the ability to produce and comprehend oral as well as written language with its onset after language development is completed (at least in most aspects). Some additional criteria are said to be important for the definition by many authors:

1. The impairment will usually affect *all four modalities* (listening, speaking, reading and writing) and *all linguistic functions* (lexical access, morphological and phonological encoding, sentence syntax and semantics, text processing). – This general postulate will be discussed in more detail in sections 3.2 and 3.3, because modern aphasiology focuses on symptom oriented analysis of the individual impaired functions. Depending on the area and extent of the damage, a person suffering from aphasia may be quite successful in speaking but not in writing, or vice versa, or may display any of a variety of other deficiencies in reading, writing, naming, sentence production and comprehension. The specific pattern of relatively spared vs. relatively impaired functions is very important for the individual diagnosis and for adequate therapy.

2. In the classical view *the impairment's onset is of an immediate nature*, as caused by a stroke, traumatic brain injury, or by other sudden head injuries – indeed, in about 80 % of all classically defined aphasias the patients suffer from stroke (Caplan 1987; Davis 2007; Huber, Poeck and Weniger 2002). Several classical definitions even restricted the label "aphasia" to these CVA (cerebrovascular accident) etiologies of language impairment, because the complete aphasic syndrome may only occur when occlusions or stenoses of the associated artery causes damage or stop the blood flow in the entire territory supplied. – But slowly developing diseases, as in the case of a brain tumor, infections, or degenerative neurological disorders play an important role in modern aphasia research. These etiologies do not typically correspond to classical brain areas, and lesions of different etiology may cause different impairments of neuronal structures and may therefore cause different symptoms and restitution processes (cf. Fawcett, Rosser, and Dunnett 2004; Hillis 2004).

3. The impairment's *onset is in the adult speaker* or in adolescence, when language acquisition is largely completed (cf. Hécaen 1976, 1983). – But, of course, many children suffer from severe head injuries with language impairments, even when language acquisition is not completed (Paquier and van Dongen 1996). It has not been defined homogenously yet, if these children have to be classified as 'aphasic', and there is not much systematic research on 'aphasic syndromes' (Paquier and van Dongen 1991; van Dongen, Paquier, Creten, van Borsel, and Catsman-Berrevoets 2001) and the progress of these children in their long-term language or second language acquisition (Dennis 2000).

Some additional aspects have to be mentioned in order to describe aphasia from a differentially perspective. *The neural disorder is a specific deterioration of language functions.* The classical view stresses that aphasia is not a result of peripheral disorders, that means, the language problems are neither depending on some forms of hearing loss or recognition deficit (agnosia) on the input side nor on speech programming (apraxia) or execution (dysarthria) (cf. Davis 2007, p. 4). Depending on the lesion site and size, other cognitive functions can coordinately be impaired, as the ability to calculate, mental inferences and problem solving, and attention and memory functions. But in general, intellect and conceptual thinking is hold to be intact in these patients.

Another important point is that *aphasic symptoms change* over time. Depending on the underlying impairment, aphasic symptoms seem to fluctuate in some cases and phases of the disease. Especially following a stroke aphasic symptoms often show a high degree of fluctuation and recovery in the acute phase (up to six weeks following the stroke) and some amount of spontaneous recovery in the post-acute phase (up to one year following stroke). Its degree of fluctuation in the acute phase depends on parameters of cerebral blood flow and diaschisis, on early restitution processes in the neuronal structures depending on mechanisms of neuronal plasticity. The neurobiological mechanisms underlying these functions are discussed in great detail in the recent literature (cf. Baron and Marchal 2000; Hallett 2000; Fawcett, Rosser, and Dunnett 2004; Stein, Brailowsky, and Will 1995, 2000). In addition, fluctuation and severity of aphasic symptoms depend on overlapping neuropsychological disorders, e.g. attention, apraxia, and general psychogenic causes as for example depression (Davis 2007).

In spontaneous recovery the aphasic symptoms will be reduced in the acute phase and to a limited amount in the post-acute phase even without therapy. The impact of several relevant prognostic factors have been discussed in the literature for spontaneous recovery, which include the size and the site of the lesion, the type of aphasia, the age at onset, general health constitutions of the patient and a supportive social environment (cf. Davis 2007). Other factors, for example gender, handedness or intelligence seem to have no clear impact on progress. Still a reliable prognosis of the individual's spontaneous restituation and reorganization processes remains difficult. Systematic therapy of aphasia enhances these processes (cf. Basso 2003). The degree of progress has been shown to be significantly higher for aphasic patients who received specific language therapy in many group studies (cf. Robey 1998; Schoonen 1991) as well as in single-case designs (cf. Robey 1994). But even these methodologically well structured meta-analyses do not meet all evaluation standards of clinical outcome research, as Greener, Enderby, and Whurr have critically commented in the Cochrane Database (2006). Further systematic therapy evaluation programs will have to be conducted – and financed! Even so we have convincing evidence for specific methods to be more effective for treating patients with specific symptoms which we will discuss in more detail in the following sections.

The traditional approach to explain and describe aphasia is a syndrome classification associating regions of cortical lesions to specific language functions and impairments (Benson and Ardila 1996; Hedge 2006; Davis 2007). The most common approach to classification in western societies will be sketched in section 3.1. The following section 3.2 outlines a neurobiological view on recovery and treatment of aphasia, which is closely connected to this syndrome classification. In section 3.3 a second tradition in aphasiology is presented, which focuses on a systematic investigation of the miscellaneous impairment samples of small groups and single aphasic patients. This approach has promoted a more precise knowledge of the processes which are involved in the production, perception, and storage of oral and written language, at least on the word level. The logic of systematic individual case studies can already be found in the work of early "aphasiologists" coming from neurological research at the end of the nineteenth century such as Wernicke (1874; rep. 1974). The single subject approach has been developed further, so that finely grained single case studies and multiple single case studies with specific methodological designs even allow for theoretically relevant hypotheses about 'normal' language processes. The very systematic and acclaimed work done, for instance, by Shallice (1988) and by Ellis & Young (1988) has stimulated the neuropsychological and neurolinguistic research tradition as well as diagnostic and therapeutic methods up to this day. In the section 3.3 the communicative view of aphasia will be presented in a short overview and I will discuss consequences of the latest WHO principles for aphasia therapy.

3.1. Aphasic symptoms and syndromes

Aphasia has always been subdivided into more specific categories by many authors since the ancient work of Paul Broca (1863/1960) and Carl Wernicke. (1874/1974). The first syndrome descriptions by these two famous aphasiologists of the nineteenth century sketched two very different forms of aphemia/ aphasia at similar times without direct contact about their neurological work in

Paris and Berlin. Both authors postulated specific localizations in the human brain for the impaired and non-disturbed functions and defined their observed impairments as syndromes (the *'localizationist view'*). In this tradition, patterns of impaired language functions are usually defined as aphasic syndromes in relation to specific brain lesions, but the categories were not always defined and labeled in the same way (cf. Benson and Ardila 1996; Goodglass 1988; Leischner 1987). Several classification systems have been co-existing throughout the twentieth century which have been introduced in different research traditions.

In the Anglo-American tradition Norman Geschwind (1965) is often cited to have revived the interest in the anatomical localization of aphasic symptoms after a period of a more holistic view of brain functions based on the ideas of John Hughlings Jackson (1874), an early opponent of Broca's localization view. Pierre Marie (1853–1944), a French neurologist, and Henry Head (1861–1940), an English neurologist, both opposed the idea of strict anatomic localization of brain functions. In addition, they assumed that some level of conceptual or symbolic impairment accompanies aphasia. In a similar way, Kurt Goldstein (1878–1965), a German neurologist of the Gestalt school, proposes that higher mental function is organized into a unitary whole, so that language cannot be impaired without affecting other mental processes. Even Aleksandr Luria (1902–1977), the famous Russian neuropsychologist, took a moderate view and avoided a strict localizationist approach to his differentiated classification of aphasic patterns. (cf. Hegde 2006; Basso 2003). Of course, the debate goes on, as Hegde resumes, and for example Caplan (1992) argues that the classical syndrome approach may hold for primary aphasic syndromes, whereas the holistic approach points to more diffuse and complex forms of language disorders, which he calls secondary aphasias.

In the tradition of classification approaches we have today the global distinction between fluent and non-fluent aphasia in the simplest form, or a classification of four main syndromes and some special forms. There are two large test batteries designed not only to select and describe aphasic patients, but with an explicit intention to classify them according to these forms: first, the Boston Diagnostic Aphasia Examination (BDAE) (Goodglass and Kaplan 1972, revised and extended by Goodglass, Kaplan and Barresi 2001), and secondly, the Western Aphasia Battery which was introduced by Kertesz and Poole (1974) as a modification of the BDAE. In Germany, the Aachener Aphasie Test (AAT) (Huber, Poeck, Weniger, and Willmes 1983) is based on a similar model of aphasic syndromes and gives statistical support for the individual patient's classification. But one main problem of these tests – or even of the idea of classifying aphasic patients – showed up in several studies (Wertz, Deal, and Robinson 1984; Ferro and Kertesz 1987) questioning the comparability of classifications and distinctions between tests.

In spite of this methodological problem and several additional limitations of the clinical syndromes approach, I will now give an overview of the main syndromes with a description and some examples of the typical patterns of impaired and spared functions as they are commonly described.

Fluent vs. non-fluent aphasia. Current classifications distinguish at least between fluent and non-fluent forms of aphasia. Fluent aphasia has been first described as a form of aphasic language problem associated with lesions more posterior to the central fissure and non-fluent forms with anterior or very extended lesions of the whole central speech area by Benson (1967). This rough classification seems to be even useful in the acute stage of aphasia following stroke (Biniek 1993). Fluent speech production is usually defined as having a normal to enhanced speech rate with no extended pauses, with sentences and phrases of normal length and complex syntax, usually with a high frequency of function words and automatic or idiomatic phrases. A typical example would be the answer of patient M. B. to the question *"Do you remember how you came to the hospital?"*

> Patient example 1
> *Well, it may be my broth .. my sister came and he found me lying on the f. on the flower . on the floor. And then, oh well, maybe an umb. an ambulace . don't know.*

Non-fluent aphasia is usually described as having an effortful, slow und hesitant speech production, a low speech rate and reduced, often elliptical and not completed utterances, which miss function words and the typical filler phrases to maintain communication. A typical example would be the answer of patient P. N. to the same question as above:

> Patient example 2
> *At home ... call my husband, and then ... nothing. Hospital ... here. Susan ... tell me ... stroke.*

But even a distinction between 'fluency' and 'non-fluency' is not a very clearly defined category. Critical research on reliability of fluency classifications is documented by Gordon (1998) and Wittler (2007). The heterogeneity of patients' speech patterns is just one of the problems for a fluency dimension classification. Not all patients can be classified unambiguously as fluent or nonfluent because of mixed parameters. Just for the acute phase, Wittler shows very heterogeneous patterns and courses of development in the symptom structure questioning the classification for acute aphasia. Besides, the concept of fluency is often ill-defined, which means that ratings and rater judgments do not rely on the same parameters in different studies. Wittler (2006) were able to show a quite low reliability of inter-rater judgements for speech probes of aphasics. But she found judgments to be highly predictable by two general factors underlying the classification of fluent and nonfluent aphasia in the acute stage: a grammar factor (sentence length, completeness, ratio of function words to content words) and a speech factor (frequency, syllables per minute, pause durations). Based on this, one might expect "fluency" to be a useful construct, but this is only the case if it is well defined and quantified by more specific parameters.

The classical view of aphasic 'standard syndromes' differentiates between the following four syndromes: anomic aphasia, Wernicke's aphasia, Broca's aphasia, and global aphasia, and some forms appearing less frequently: conduction aphasia, transcortical motor, and sensory aphasia. In addition, there are isolated symptoms of more peripheral difficulties as in central word deafness, or of special problems with the written language system as in agraphia and alexia (Benson and Ardila, 19996; Huber, Poeck, and Weniger, 2002). Clinically and neurophysiologically, aphasia syndromes fall into two major categories: first, those depending on lesions of the central speech area (Wernicke's area, Broca's area and the cortex which overlies the arcuate fasciculus) and secondly, those of the adjacent associated cortex (frontal, parietal and posterior temporal). The most severe type of aphasia is a result of a huge extended lesion of the whole perisylvian area, called global (or total) aphasia.

In *global aphasia* language production is most severely impaired, but also comprehension is very problematic. Spontaneous speech is slow, hesitant and the aphasic's language production needs heightened effort, mostly in which the articulation is very indistinct. Repeating is also difficult for the global aphasics as well as naming and all written language modalities. The stereotypic language automatisms and the so-called 'recurring utterances' are also striking in many patients suffering from global aphasia. Above and beyond that, they often produce phonological paraphasias and neologisms, as well as semantic paraphasias, which differ very much from the target word. As a consequence, communication with these patients is heavily impaired. Some authors further differentiate in a) a mutistic style, without any speech production as it is quite common in the first days following stroke, b) an iterative style, which is characterized by fluent but neologistic utterances or repetitive phrases, i.e. recurring utterances, c) a neologistic style with mainly vast phonological paraphasias and few phonological variations, and d) a stereotyped style, characterized by a small set of set phrases which is repeated and may be interrupted by meaningful words only occasionally (Huber, Poeck, and Weniger 2002).

Patients with global aphasia are usually additionally challenged due to a considerable hemiparesis of their right arm and leg as a result of extended lesions in the frontal, parietal, and temporal lobes, which typically affect relevant areas in the primary and secondary motor cortex, too. Global aphasia without hemiparesis has been discussed as an uncommon stroke syndrome since years (e.g., Ferro, 1983) which has now been shown to have heterogeneous underlying impairments, language profiles, and recovery patterns depending on the specific lesion site (Hanlon et al., 1999).

The two most distinct syndromes of the central speech area are Broca's aphasia (which has also been called motor, expressive, or verbal aphasia) and Wernicke's aphasia (which has also been called sensory or receptive aphasia). Both syndromes have in common deficits in repetition tasks and in confrontation naming. Patients are unable to repeat a short sentence without errors and they often fail when asked to name an object, picture, or scene with a single word or a short phrase. But the type of mistakes differs between the two aphasic syndromes.

Patients with *Broca's aphasia* have a labored and non-fluent speech. They talk in an elliptical, and sparse format in spontaneous speech referred to as 'agrammatism'. Historically, Broca's area is located in the inferior part of Brodmann area 44 and 45 in the dorsal part of the left frontal lobe. Vascular lesions which result in Broca's aphasia often involve the frontal operculum, lower motor cortex, lateral striatum, and subcortical white matter.

Patient example 3
Well ... Monday . Tuesday ...Peter .. come home. And then ... pho . telephone. Peter ... take car ... St. John's ho . hopital.

Agrammatism can be roughly characterized by three components (cf. Harley 2001): first, a sentence construction deficit with problems of arranging words to form complex and complete sentences. Secondly, function words and bound inflectional morphemes are performed poorly and below average. Free syntactic morphemes are often omitted, verbs are not or not correctly inflected, and grammatical objects are not or not correctly marked for case or number. These two problems of syntactic and morphological sentence production of typical agrammatic speech are found in the language production of many Broca's aphasics, but the specific patterns vary (Badecker and Caramazza 1985; Caramazza and Hillis 1989). A third component, a sentence comprehension deficit typically with problems on non-generic word order sentences (passives, topicalized accusative sentences, and subordinate clauses) has been proposed by several authors (Caramazza and Zurif 1976; Schwartz, Saffran and Marin 1980). But the pattern of sentence processing problems, again, is not as uniform (cf. Berndt, Mitchum and Haendiges 1996) as some authors have predicted (for example Grodzinsky 1995a,b;). As a consequence there is an ongoing debate between different groups of researchers if it makes sense to speak of a syndrome of 'agrammatism' (cf. Caplan 2001; Zurif and Pinango 1999; Zurif 2001).

Most linguistic research on Broca's aphasia has, of course, tackled the phenomenon of sentence processing disorders however some important further problems have to be mentioned. Pronunciation of single words is often phonologically impaired but improves with repetition as long as word combinations do not exceed about three items. Patients often show additional apraxia of speech and/or dysarthria because motor cortex areas and subcortical areas are frequently impaired, too. Associated with these problems a hemiplegia of the right body parts (arm and leg) is quite common. Finally, the group of patients suffering from Broca's aphasia is quite concerned and aware of their communication deficits. This frequently results in a secondary depression.

In contrast, patients with *Wernicke's aphasia* are quite unconcerned, often euphoric with fluent but often paraphasic and somehow meaningless speech. Lesions seen in these patients are typically in the posterior superior and middle gyrus of the left temporal lobe. Historically, Wernicke's area is located in the posterior part thirds of Brodmann area 22.

Patient example 4
Oh well, my woman, my sister, see, she is going to go to come in. Found me living [=lying] on the floor. He [=she] is crying, shouts 'Oh dear, what is going and going on?' And then two doctor come into time coming here. As you know, he . she's coming in at eight, nine, ten o'clock. And here I am!

The fluent language production style of Wernicke's aphasia with incorrect function words and bound inflectional morphemes, with mainly correct and complex sentence structures, which sometimes seems to shrink two different structures or doubles sentence parts has been called paragrammatic style (cf. de Bleser 1987; Butterworth and Howard 1987). Phonology is impaired in most patients, resulting in many phonematic paraphasias or even phonematic jargon. In addition, or sometimes in the course of restitution of phonology, semantic paraphasias or neologisms can be found in these patients. These semantic paraphasias do not always have a clear meaning relation to the target word. Phonematic problems may result of lesions with an extension to parietal structures (gyrus supramarginalis), whereas semantic paraphasias may result of lesions with an extension to temporal structures (gyrus temporalis medius, gyrus angularis) (cf. Binder 2003).

Patients have a highly impaired comprehension for the specific meaning of words and sentences, but they are quite capable of inferring the communicative content. Processes of repetition tasks can be problematic because these patients may not understand what is wanted of them, they may not perceive the words correctly, and they may have problems with the production process. Reading and writing is often very problematic for these patients.

Dysarthria or hemiplegia of the right body part, arm and leg, is usually not present (or transient).

The last important syndrome of the central speech area is *conduction aphasia* (which was also called repetition aphasia or afferent-motoric aphasia). Patients with this syndrome have relatively good comprehension and fluent spontaneous speech production. They have most difficulties, however, repeating words and sentences. Although they do understand most utterances, repetition gets increasingly worse, the longer and the more complex a target sentence is. Patients are usually aware of their mistakes. This special repetition problem has been found in patients with lesions of the parietal lobe (area 40), or of the posterior superior temporal lobe sparing Wernicke's area, or of the posterior insula (Geschwind 1965; cf. Axer et al. 2001).

Of the aphasias resulting from lesions outside the central speech area a*nomic aphasia* (also called *amnestische Aphasie*, verbal amnesia, anomia, semantic or mild aphasia) is the most common type. It is often due to a discrete vascular lesion of the parietal lobe close to the angular gyrus or above it. It has also been reported in association with lesions of the left pulvinar region of the thalamus. Lesions in the posterior inferior temporal lobe have also been described with anomic aphasia. This means that this syndrome may have the most imprecise cortical lesion association and it develops from more severe forms of aphasia in the process of restitution and rehabilitation. In addition, this type of aphasia may also be seen in diffuse dementias, metabolic encephalopathy or brain tumors in any location (Damasio 1995).

Patients showing symptoms of anomic aphasia have fairly normal comprehension but have great difficulty finding the correct name or word. Paraphasias do not differ very much in their meaning. Patients might call a wristwatch an "alarmclock" (semantic paraphasia) or use a circumlocution like "the thing you tell time with". Syntax is for the most part normal and complex. Nor can any problems with function words be observed and grammatical forms are mainly preserved for production and perception of sentences and texts. Problems with cohesive means in text comprehension are common and speech production is often not very informative, as it consists of many function words, set phrases, and stereotypes.

Anomic aphasia is often seen in the absence of any other striking neurological defects. But, depending on the specific lesion site, some patients show symptoms of additional written language problems, acalculia, neglect, or asymbolia.

The *transcortical syndromes of aphasia* are marked by very good language repetition and specific problems in production and/or comprehension of language. Since Lichtheim (1885) it has been proposed to result from a form of 'isolation of the speech area' (Goldstein 1948; Geschwind et al. 1968) with unimpaired formal language functions.

Mixed transcortical aphasia is the most severe form of transcortical aphasia with impaired production and comprehension. It has been labelled 'isolation syndrome' because formal language knowledge and lexical-semantics seem to be disconnected in these patients.

Transcortical-sensory aphasia (TSA) has been described as having impaired auditory comprehension with intact repetition and fluent spontaneous speech, which often shows patterns of mistakes as seen in Wernicke's aphasia. Sentences can be repeated correctly even if they have not really been understood. In addition, naming and word comprehension are impaired in most patients. Lesions are proposed to concern the temporo-occipital white matter and a disconnection of the Wernicke area from representational areas for lexical-semantic processing. This widely accepted 'disconnection model' (Lichtheim 1885; Goldstein 1948; Geschwind, Quadfasel, and Segarra 1968) assumes a bidirectional disconnection between phonological processing and lexical-semantic representations, presumed to be located more posteriorly (Heilman et al. 1981; Kertesz, Sheppard and MacKenzie 1982) in the temporo-parietal junction, the fusiform gyrus, or in parietal or even in frontal lobe structures (e.g. Berthier, 2001; Berthier et al., 1991). In a very interesting study on transiently induced TSA by electrical interference during routine cortical function mapping in six seizure patients Boatman et al. (2001) show a high coincidence of areas associated with both, phonological and lexical-semantic processing, and only some areas, which seem to be involved in phonological processing. Results are interpreted in terms of a *"one-way disruption between left hemisphere phonology and lexical-semantic processing"* (Boatman et al., 2001, p. 1634), revising the original simple model of isolated centers for the different functions. This sophisticated experimental study suggests TSA to reflect impaired access from phonological encoding to lexical-semantic knowledge, not an impairment of the lexical-semantic system itself, as naming is spared with specific lesion sites induced in this experiment.

Transcortical-motor aphasia (TMA) is characterized by spared repetition and comprehension relative to spontaneous speech production. It has been associated with lesions adjacent to Broca's area and with areas of the supplementary motor cortex (Ruben and Kertesz 1983; Huber Poeck and Weniger 2002) in the frontal lobe of the left hemisphere. In more recent studies (Hanlon et al. k1999), lesions in subcortical structures and the white matter have shown language impairments similar to symptoms of TMA, too. Some of these patients start with global aphasia (without hemiplegia) or Broca's aphasia (Lichtheim, 1885) and often have a quite good prognosis.

Acquired *dyslexias* (Coslett 2003) and *dysgraphias* (Ellis & Young, 1996) following brain damage can appear together with aphasia, but these impairments are also documented in isolation of severe general language impairments. Several patterns of functional disorders of the reading and writing processes are described in the literature, and will be discussed in more detail in the following section 3.3.

Problems of the syndrome approach are manifold.

1. Even with modern brain-imaging techniques the specific localizations of functions and syndrome patterns remain at least imprecise and often heterogeneous. We have some good notion today of which components of language processing are assisted roughly by which brain locations, but much more research especially on behavior in the undamaged brain is necessary in order to isolate neuronal nets serving specific cognitive functions.

2. The definition of aphasic syndromes can be helpful in order to communicate a short and rough picture of the typical language impairments and difficulties of a patient, but several authors have been able to show that the classification is not very reliable (Benson and Ardila 2006). A patient's classification depends strongly on factors such as the research tradition of the clinician, on the definition of the syndrome's obligatory and facultative symptoms and on the tests used to classify the patients.

3. Testing and classification are highly interrelated. Aphasia tests, like the *Boston Diagnostic Aphasia Battery*, the *Western Aphasia Battery*, or the *Aachener Aphasie Test* give normative data and specific hints for the classification of the aphasic syndrome. However, there are several methodological problems with aphasia classifications. First, the classification cannot be more reliable or valid than the test used for classification. Secondly, the syndrome correlates with the severity of aphasia and aphasic symptoms. In the course of recovery not all symptoms change similarly at the same time, so that patterns of symptoms change and a considerable degree of syndromal variation is documented in the course of the first year following the stroke (for example Poeck, Huber, and Willmes, 1989). Thirdly, several patients show patterns of symptoms which make a classification very difficult, because these patterns do not follow the classical description, for example, fluent speech with many paraphasias and morpho-syntactic problems as in Wernicke's aphasia, but relatively good preserved language comprehension.

4. In this context we can ask for the general validity of the classification scheme. How many patients can be identified clearly in regard to belonging to a specific aphasic syndrome. Statistical data vary around only 60% to 80%, mainly depending on the classification scheme and test that is used by the researchers, and depending on each patient's etiology. Syndromes are formulated based on patient descriptions suffering from stroke. Syndromes are often understood in terms of vascular areas belonging to specific branches of the brain arteries. In the case of aphasia these are specific territories of the arteria cerebri media. Similar circumscribed lesions have been documented for bullet wounds or tumors. Other etiologies like encephalitis, dementia, or other degenerative disorders will seldom result in similarly clear defined patterns.

5. The last critical question which will be discussed in this context asks for aspects that can be derived as a consequence for theory and therapy. Do we know how to treat an aphasic patient, if we have a classification of his symptoms distinguishing between a global, a Broca's, or a Wernicke's aphasia? The answer is a definite no. Of course, some earlier reviews on aphasia therapy (Chapey, 1994) have given quite helpful approaches on how to treat the typical problems of, for example, a patient with Broca's aphasia showing agrammatism, phono-

logical and phonetic paraphasias, or a patient with Wernicke's aphasia suffering from a severe comprehension problem, phonological paraphasias and neologisms and some morpho-syntactical mistakes. But these articles can only be a first guideline for planning therapy. This approach may allow for a first orientation, but it will not replace further detailed testing of the deficits and the remaining functions in each modality and on each language structural level, nor the communicative consequences, handicaps, and alternative aids.

We will need much more explicit knowledge about the dependencies between the aphasic symptoms, their underlying lesion sites, reorganizing principles, and helpful therapeutic tools and intervention strategies to verify the clinical relevance of this classification. Some recent research in this tradition will be outlined in the following section.

3.2. A neurophysiological perspective on recovery in aphasia

The neurobiological perspective of aphasia and its recovery includes three main research traditions concerned with, first, the research on brain plasticity and neurological recovery, secondly, diagnostic methods to document individual and group changes in neurophysiological activity, and thirdly, therapeutic means to minimize lesion size by increasing, e.g., neuronal sprouting, restitution, and reorganization processes of the neuronal tissue.

Research and modeling of neurobiological recovery focuses on the possibilities to minimize lesion sites and to enhance processes of neuronal restitution and reorganization. We know today that brain plasticity allows recovery even in the adult brain – a hypothesis that is not new but which has been rejected by one of its famous inventors, Ramon y Cajal (1928). After a decade of research on neuronal regeneration in animals and human y Cajal concluded that there is no possibility for regeneration of neurons in the brain and spinal cord. This pioneer work on plasticity of the famous researcher who held the Nobel Price was tremendously influencing our concepts of the adult brain, so that it took half a century, before neuronal plasticity became a topic for research again (Masland, Portera-Sanchez, and Toffano 1987) and today it is clear, that the brain is not only capable of reorganizing itself, but is in fact constantly doing so, as has been shown for learning processes (cf. Hallett 2000). Stein, Brailowsky, and Will (1995) discuss the most common hypotheses on the functional recovery mechanisms until the early nineteen-nineties. For the language functions these hypotheses can be formulated as follows: First, we do not use the power of our huge brain with millions of neurons and billions of synapses, therefore we have free capacity for language functions, if the original areas are damaged. Secondly, other tissue than the original region can take over functions of language processing and will be reorganized. Thirdly, the brain's functional representations are highly redundant, which means that we have a kind of 'backup copy' for all important language functions in additional regions of the brain. These copies can replace the original structures destroyed. Fourthly, the brain serves similar functions to the ones that have been destroyed; we learn to serve the same targets, for example comprehend and speak words by using cognitive strategies that rely on different mechanism – perhaps of right hemisphere comprehension processes – than the original ones. Fifthly, the brain is handicapped by only transient functional disorders, which can result from decreased blood flow in areas which are functionally associated to the lesion area, but which have the potential to recover. This effect of 'diaschisis' has often been replicated by modern blood flow brain mapping techniques showing transiently reduced blood flow in even quite distant regions from the lesion site, which will be normalized if adequate input will stimulate the secondarily affected neural nets.

Each of these ideas has more or less good explanatory power and for each of the underlying brain mechanisms recent brain mapping studies have documented at least some evidence for these hypotheses by exploring changes in cerebral blood flow and metabolic alterations as well as in electro-physiological activity. But recovery processes after a lesion in the CNS and particularly after a stroke remain very difficult to predict in individual cases (Chollet and Weiller 2000). They depend on the etiology, size, and site of the lesion and further studies are needed in order to correlate characteristics of the initial damage to the resulting recovery of function.

Diagnostic methods to document the course of recovery are manifold today. Mazziotta and Frackowiak (2000) as well as Toga and Mazziotta (1996) give an excellent overview and discuss the advantages and limitations of documenting the course of the cortical rehabilitation process with modern brain mapping methods, which include x-ray computed tomography (CT), magnetic resonance imaging (MRI, fMRI), positron emission tomography (PET), single photon emission computed tomography (SPECT), helical computed tomography (CTA), electroencephalography (EEG), magnetoencephalography (MEG), and transcranial magnetic stimulation (TMS) as the most common ones today. The different methods each provide information about only one or very few aspects of underlying anatomy, cerebral physiology, and pathophysiology, e.g. brain structure, cerebral blood flow, electrophysiological activity, perfusion, or metabolism. Accordingly, the methods will be used as best diagnostic methods for different disorders, e.g. acute trauma, atrophy, epilepsy, aneurysms, ischemic states or hemorrhages, neoplasms, and affective disorders. In addition, some methods are better suited than others in order to examine particular sites in the brain, for example cortical areas and deeper structures in the midbrain or in the brainstem. As it has been outlined before, a stroke is the most common cause for aphasia. Lesions caused by acute or chronic strokes will be detected best by means of CT scans in the case of hemorrhages, and by MRI, PET or SPECT in the case of ischemic states.

And most of these common methods are either exact in the local dimension or in the time dimension, so that only few methods can detect differences of brain functions depending for example on specific language tasks which are conducted by the patient at the time of the measurement. These methods have been mainly fMRI (detecting local perfusion changes at specific sites) and EEG-scans (measuring relative electric activity on a cortical network; evoked potentials: EPs). The most exact data will be acquired with pre- or intra-operative mappings (TMS) which are used today by surgical therapy, for example for epilepsy or tumor resection.

Therapy of the neurobiological lesion may have increasing chances in aphasia therapy in the future. Although the efficacy of aphasia treatment has been demonstrated in general (cf. Schoonen 1991; Robey 1998), the very fact that this demonstration continues to be controversial (cf. Greener, Enderby, and Whurr 2006) shows that traditional language treatment of aphasia, despite its effectiveness, remains unsatisfactory. But what are the contributions of neurology today?

Neurologists are able to increase cerebral blood flow particularly in the acute phase, which means within several hours for a lysis. They use specific pharmacologic agents to modulate neuroreceptors in relevant functional networks, e.g. for memory, motoric functions, and even for language functions (e.g. in the lexical network, Howard et al. 1992). In addition, factors that impede a patient's recovery can be reduced, for instance treating post-stroke depression that occurs in about 50% of people with aphasia (Chollet and Weiller 2000; Small 1994). But there are many variables involved in the case of each patient, such as age and mode of therapy; which impact on the processes of restitution and reorganization is not really understood Wineburgh and Small (2004). Moreover, limited knowledge about neurophysiology and anatomy restricts treatment. It is usually directed at the external manifestations of the damaged structure rather than at the damaged structure itself. Thus, we attempt to reactivate knowledge or to (re-)educate the patient to regain lexical access and syntactical structures rather than looking at the brain's potential to reinstantiate language functions. A third issue evaluates the goals of treatment that are used in current approaches and social care. The best of modern aphasia treatments try to make small restorative or compensatory changes in language behavior. Patients are often frustrated and disappointed because they do not see rapid changes and sometimes not even the right ones. Conversely, some neurologists will not accept these minor gains. For example Wineburgh and Small (2004) do believe that it might be possible in some future to cure aphasia – which is a very high-set goal compared to our modern success rates.

Some recent studies on animal models have successfully been used in order to provide information about brain's plasticity and restituation or reorganization of damaged cortical tissue (Xerri et al. 1998; Nudo et al., 2000). Of course, these studies did not show effects on language rehabilitation, but gave explicit information about the tremendous amount of reorganization in the cortical tissue of the damaged somato-sensory and motor cortex. It seems to be possible at least for small regions, that the surrounding area will overtake functions and restitute most of the impaired processes in the course of several months following the lesion. This model has been formulated in a similar way by Robertson and Murre (1998). They postulate, that lesion size will have important consequences for therapy, with extended lesions requiring therapy which aims at compensation and recruitment of remote areas, e.g. in the right hemisphere, and with small circumscribed lesions requiring therapy which aims at restitution and extension of functions to adjacent areas.

Aphasia treatment may comprise two complementary factors in the future. Biological interventions will have to stimulate or repair the injured brain area, and speech and language treatment will be provided to retrain the new circuitry and integrate it with the preserved, existing tissue. Tissue transplantation and electronic prostheses are not yet viable, but may be in the future (Spice and Srikameswaran, 1998). Tissue transplantation using neural stem cells might also have a promising role if we can cause new brain structure to develop in the area that is damaged by a stroke. Work in neural prostheses using cortical electrode grids is also in progress around the world. Pharmacotherapy has not yet fulfilled its promise for aphasia treatment (cf. Whineberg and Small 2004; Small 1994). Although many studies of aphasia pharmacotherapy have been conducted, only few are well-designed and reliable quasi-experiments (e.g. Huber et al. 1997) which show that language therapy can profit when it is accompanied by specific drugs. Pharmacotherapy alone has not been shown to have any effect on the specific recovery of language.

Finally, we will have to face the problem, that aphasia therapy which may on one hand help to alter lesioned tissue may on the other hand bear a risk of harming the patient other than prolonging recovery and heightening costs. An aphasia treatment that has the potential to change the brain for the better is likely to have the same potential to change it for worse. This radical concept (cf. Wineburgh and Small 2004) has been studied to a limited degree in the motor system with the notion that some patients develop a "learned nonuse" of a paretic extremity due to behavioral habits that minimize the use of the extremity. A recent approach in aphasia therapy is based on this assumption called *Constraint Induced Communicative Therapy* (Pulvermüller, Neininger, Elbert, et al. 2001).

Several studies on modeling language, learning and aphasia in artificial neural networks in language and aphasia provided data that suggest that providing the wrong training to a network can lead to failures in the learning process (Harley 2001; Elman 1993; McCloskey and Cohen 1989). Harris and Small (1998) conclude that it seems likely that damaged, transplanted and/or pharmacologically altered natural neural networks will require significant attention to what is the best kind of training. From a neurobiological perspective, aphasia treatments will have to be evaluated in terms of both benefit and detriment to the biological and behavioral recovery of brain circuits for language. Consequently, we will need even more explicit knowledge about components of human language functions, language learning, stimulation and access, about its biology, and about the effects of particular treatments and the didactic of therapy.

3.3. A clinical neurolinguistic perspective on aphasia

Our knowledge about language functions has grown tremendously in the last 25 years, but still many questions and problems are left unsolved. Modeling aphasic language processing is nearly always based on highly underspecified theories and models of unimpaired 'normal' processing, which is a problematic approach in itself, because we think of the impaired language processing patterns merely in terms of the normal processes minus a specific damaged function. According to a modern view of neural networks serving several functions and of lesions resulting in complex reorganization processes for higher order functions this might not be the best approach at all, but it is at least the best we have today.

As was said before, all modalities of language processing are impaired in aphasia: the language production and the understanding of verbal as well as of written language for words and sentences. But patients differ in their individual pattern of relatively impaired and spared functions. Different pathological mechanisms will require specific therapeutic procedures and materials based on a functional approach. Today, quite fine grained analyses of the components of processing are discussed. The traditional models are concerned with either lexical-semantic processing of single words, or with phrase and sentence production and perception. These two levels of language processing will be discussed separately in the next two sections, each beginning with a theoretical perspective followed by questions of specific diagnostic tools and therapeutic methods.

3.3.1. *Processing of single words in aphasia*

The traditional work on models for lexical-semantic processing in auditory perception and reading, in oral production and writing is based on early psycholinguistic work done by Morton in the nineteen-sixties. Many later versions of 'boxes-and-arrow' models refer back to this basic model. Early tachistoscopic psycholinguistic experiments by Morton (1969, 1979) gave evidence for significant criticism of the historical serial search models of word recognition. Morton introduced the basic idea of parallel processing for all possible memory traces representing word forms in a visual and an auditory input memory system. Every written or spoken word has its own simple feature counter, called a 'logogen', corresponding to it. Both input systems are further connected with semantic representations in the cognitive system. When a written or spoken word is presented, every logogen accumulates evidence for its presentation until for one of them the individual excitation threshold level is reached. It will then activate the cognitive system and can pass on activation to the phonological or written output form. Morton's ideas have been taken up euphorically in neuropsychology and clinical linguistics, because this model gave an excellent theoretical frame for the description of dissociations between language functions in single neurological patients. The tradition of defining isolated cognitive functions based on double dissociations in patients has been postulated first by Teuber in the nineteen-fifties for selective impairments of verbal and visual memory span in the medial left and right temporal lobe (cf. Warrington and Shallice 1969). This modular functional approach was applied to clinical neurolinguistics for instance by Shallice (1988) and by Ellis and Young (1988, 1996), who brought together material from many patients whose language behavior seemed to reflect impairment on specific routes or to specific representational levels. In the following years numerous additional case studies have been reported adding evidence for dissociations of buffers, lexical representations, and cognitive semantic systems as well as for routes of access and direction of influences. A model will be sketched briefly similar to the one Harley (2001: 395) presented as a conclusion of the current state of the art (see Figure 2).

One of the central questions refers to the number of lexical modules which have to be differentiated. In his earliest psycholinguistic experiments Morton (1969, 1979) found modality specific priming as well as missing interferences between input and output logogens. Because of these results he changed his former unitary logogen system and defined the classical four forms of auditory and visual input logogens as well as spoken (and written) output forms. Additional support from lesion studies (e.g. Shallice, McLeod, and Lewis 1985; Shallice, Rumiati, and Zadini 2000; Warrington and Shallice 1969, 1979) and brain mapping studies (e.g. Petersen et al. 1989; Petersen and Savoy 1998) suggested that these four representational levels and further buffers and pathways are indeed separated. This means that it would be too simplified to speak of one unified 'lexicon' as it is assumed for example in the model given by Levelt (1989).

On the other hand, Levelt's model formalizes the production process at least as a two-level process, first accessing the words lemma before composing the word form by morphological and phonological encoding and syllabification. The lemma will provide information about a word's syntactic gender, countability, and word class (Levelt, Roeloffs, and Meyer 1999). But where can we locate a lemma representation in the original model of lexical processing? Harley (2001) suggests to put it modality specific prior to the phonological output lexicon, but also suggests that it is involved in all (spoken) language production tasks. In the recent years it has been discussed in detail if we need the lemma-

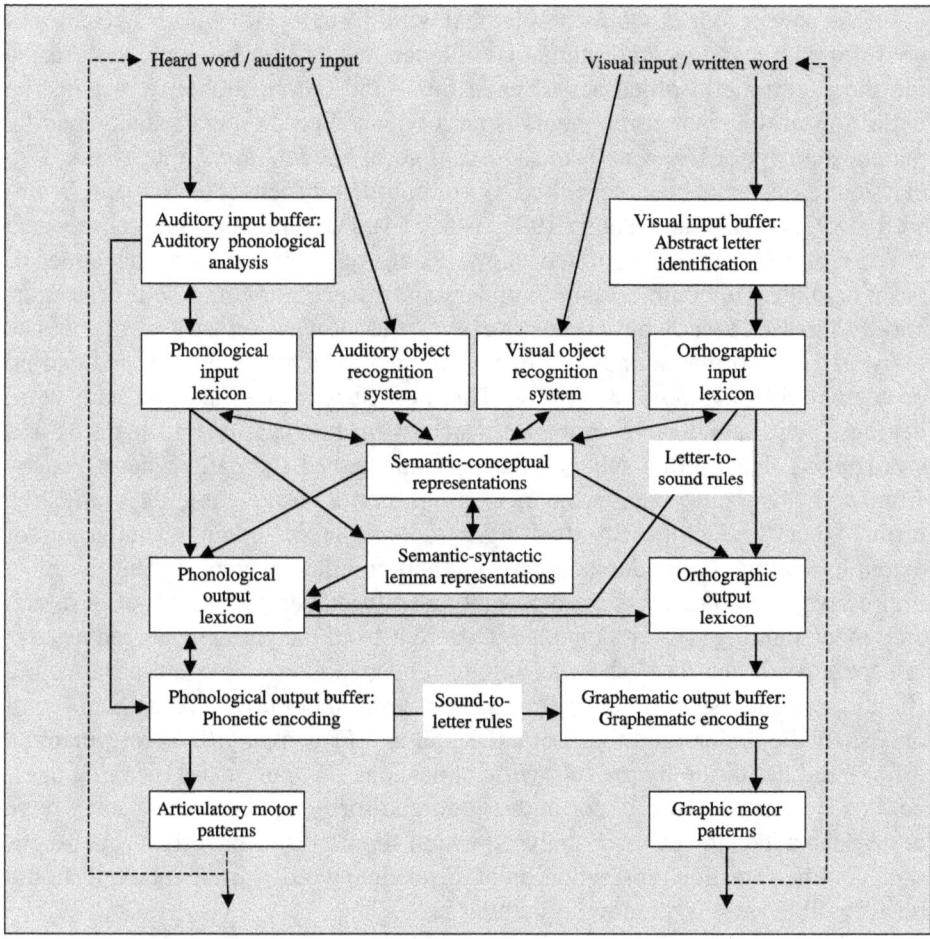

Figure 2. Modular description of spoken and written word comprehension and production, model similar to Ellis and Young (1996) and Harley (2001).

level in modeling language production at all, and where it may play a role in the comprehension processes. Some theoretical approaches question the two stage lexicalization process (Caramazza 1997), because some patients seem to have access to phonological forms without correct knowledge of lemma level information as gender and word class. These authors suggest to model lexical access in production as well as in perception as an interaction between a semantic network (features and semantic concepts), a syntactic network (gender, word class, countability), and a phonological network, which does not make it necessary, to access lemma information before phonological encoding. Lemma information may be passed by in specific contexts and may be not an obligatory level in the production process – at least not for specific patients.

If we accept four modalities of lexical word form representations because of neurolinguistic and psycholinguistic evidence, we will further have to describe the more peripheral processes of each input and output modality. Again, the definition of different components is largely based on dissociations in specific patient descriptions. Let us take the example of the auditory input route. Two classical cases have been described by Hemphill and Stengel (1940) and Bramwell (1897, cf. Ellis and Young 1996: 146; 154). Hemphill and Stengel reported the case of a 34-year-old man who showed signs of deafness as a consequence of brain damage. He could no longer understand speech nor could he repeat utterances addressed to him, but his hearing of pure tones was perfectly normal and he registered the normal sounds of his environment. He spoke fluently and had no problems with reading and writing. This patient was classified as 'pure word deafness' with a selective problem of accessing language sound patterns and word forms. He, among others, can be contrasted to the patient described by Bramwell (1897), a young woman who suffered a stroke some days after the birth of her third child. She had signs of aphasia for complex material, for example reading and understanding long and complex sentences. But the most impressive impairment was the dissociation between hearing sounds of birds etc. and understanding spoken language. Different from the patients labeled as having 'pure word deafness' she was able to repeat spoken words and phrases, but she did not understand their meaning. She wrote them down, read them – and only then she understood the content. Kohn and Friedman (1986) formulated a differential definition by the following conditions for 'pure word meaning deafness': (1) When a word is not understood auditorily, it nonetheless must have undergone adequate acoustic analysis, which should result in correct oral repetition. (2) The semantic representation of the critical word must be intact, it should be accessible from written input without problems.

Patients suffering from 'word meaning deafness' show a good auditory perception for sounds and noises in general, but they seem to have specific problems understanding spoken language, which was defined as a specific problem accessing the semantic representation from an auditory input lexicon. Patients suffering from 'pure word deafness' have problems at an earlier stage in the input process. These patients might show specific problems with a left hemisphere 'phonetic speech mode' of perception (Mann & Libermann, 1983). Some authors have also documented evidence for a specific auditory perception problem with short frequency shifts in the latter patients, which seems to be a specific capacity of left hemisphere structures and which is, of course, especially important for analyzing speech. Patients with a 'pure word deafness' do profit from a reduced speech rate and perform better on lexical decision tasks, repetition and comprehension (cf. Ellis and Young 1996: 154).

A modular comprehension model which can account for these deficits will have to integrate at least the following levels of language perception and comprehension: (1) a general auditory analysis of acoustic features, (2) a phonological analysis allowing sequences of phonological entities to be memorized for a short time (phonological input buffer), and (3) an access to the lexical word form, which is represented in the 'mental lexicon' for phonological word forms, maybe similar to the lexeme level representation in Levelt's model (1989). From this lexicon a modality specific access to (4) the meaning representation of a word in the cognitive system has to be assumed, maybe mediated by a lemma representation (see above), which should be thought as independent from modality, perception or production.

Representational levels (3) and (4) of the auditory comprehension process can be seen as accessing and processing word forms and word meaning stored in long-term memory, whereas the results of analyses (1) and (2) are thought of as representations composed in working memory, especially in the auditory buffer. This buffer has been defined most explicitly by Baddeley (1995) in his general version of the working memory with a central executive and the two 'slave systems', the 'articulatory loop', and the 'visuo-spatial sketchpad' for visual/written information. The examples given above may illustrate the clinically based formulation of a modular version of the language perception processes. In a similar vein, the whole multi-modal word comprehension and production model can be justified.

We have to take a closer look at the central 'cognitive system' now, which has been discussed quite heterogeneously in the past. The first author who proposed a dual-code hypothesis was Paivio (1971). It has been suggested by several authors that we have at least one semantic representation of word meanings, which captures the perceptual characteristics of a concept, the *perceptual code*, and a *verbal code* representing the abstract, non-sensory aspects of a concept. For instance, Warrington and Shallice (1984), and Bub, Black, Hampson, and Kertesz (1988) argue for different semantic representations belonging to modality specific (visual, verbal, motoric etc.) and/or category specific (animate/inanimate, abstract/concrete) conceptual semantic systems. Riddoch and Humphreys (1987), or Caramazza, Hillis, Rapp and Romani (1990) on the other hand, give alternative explanations in selective access problems which might explain patients' dissociations between semantic knowledge for these different domains. Caplan (1992) saw the results from patient studies and priming experiments as evidence at least for the separation of verbal and visual conceptual systems. Similarly, Harley (2001) gives the following parsimonious interpretation of the clinical data.

> *At present, the most likely explanation is that they [the word meanings] are decomposed into semantic features, some of which might be fairly abstract. Initial contact with the conceptual system is probably made through modality-specific stores The meanings of words can be connected together to form a propositional network which is operated on by schemata (in comprehension [...]) and the conceptualizer (in production [...]).* (Harley 2001: 392)

Semenza (1999) gives a more critical summary of the manifold results and stresses the dependencies between task demands, results, parameters of the defining model, and interpretation, similar to the arguments given by Caramazza et al (1990). Each of the results given by many researchers and clinicians might be modeled in a separated stores model as well as in a single store network model, representing single concepts through features which are each more or less close to the input modality or abstract knowledge.

Depending on the definition of the different stores and buffers, now, it has to be decided on the 'arrows' between 'boxes'. Some theorists have chosen the easiest solution: they think of a straight feed-forward processing approach and do not discuss the option of feed-back, at all. Ellis and Young are very specific in their definition of feed-back in their model (1988, 1996). Figure 2 largely adopts this more interactive view, assuming that even more connections between moduls might be bidirectional.

Aphasic patients show a wide spectrum of impairments on most of the levels represented by the multi-modal word processing model given above. Do we need such a finely grained analysis only for psycholinguistic interests, or is it also necessary for clinical neurolinguistic diagnostics and therapy? We argue for the relevance of this kind of experimental testing of capacities because aphasic patients often show dissociations between different modalities and modes in language processing. Specific deficits in word comprehension and in naming have to be addressed as well as the written modalities, for which again very heterogeneous patterns have been documented. Several authors speak of the central forms of acquired dyslexia and dysgraphia (or alexia and agraphia to differentiate them from childhood forms), which fall into three main forms, (1) the deep dyslexia/dysgraphia, which is the most sever form and uses the route through activating the concept in the semantic system. No peripheral routes of grapheme-phoneme- or phoneme-grapheme-conversion are possible for these patients. And (2), the surface dyslexia/dysgraphia is characterized by using these routes quite efficiently but often without knowledge of the semantics of what is read or written. These patients regularize words while reading and/or writing, because they apply 'phonem-grapheme-conversion rules', which very often does not give the correct spoken output or spelling. And (3), phonological dyslexia/dysgraphia which uses the lexical word forms for reading and writing. This results in fewer regularizations in these patients. Again, they often do not have access to the meaning of written forms and show phonological and visual errors. A peripheral form is called 'letter-by-letter reading' or writing. These patients show difficulty in identifying single letters and have to put them together laboriously in order to form the whole word. Other forms of peripheral disorders have been identified which defined the early processes in reading and the late processes in writing (cf. Ellis & Young, 1996). These specific syndromes are not observed very frequently, but many patients show more or fewer deficits and spared competences on different routes which have to be assessed thoroughly for an adequate therapy.

Several *diagnostic tools* have been published in the recent fifteen years providing assessment materials for a finely grained psycholinguistic description of the specific pattern of functions for a patient. A comprehensive screening or test has to measure the components of language production and perception for spoken and written words. We have a wide range of tools today in different countries and in different languages which allow for such descriptions. In English the first battery aiming at a differential diagnosis was PALPA (*Psycholinguistic Assessments of Language Processing in Aphasia*; Kay, Lesser, and Coltheart 1992). With this screening the authors filled a gap for specific competences. The test battery consists of tasks which assess auditory processing, reading and spelling, picture and word semantics, as well as sentence comprehension. The authors suggest the combination of PALPA with additional screenings, for example for conceptual knowledge and sentence production, in order to gain a comprehensive pattern of the patient's behavior. But, despite the high importance of such batteries for the identification of dissociations a very controversial discussion came up with PALPA and similar screenings concerning the following critical aspects:

1. Most screenings do not provide norms which allow to say if a patient is really deviant on a specific scale or how severely impaired he is.
2. The relative amount of differences between competences of different modules and routes which would allow a quantification of a reliable 'dissociation' is not defined.
3. The usual test criteria of objectivity, reliability or validity are rarely addressed.
4. The administration of the whole screening takes very long, which in turn means that in practice only parts will have to be used for a single patient, which should be the most relevant ones. But which are the most relevant ones? No exact instructions have been given, assisting the therapists to choose the relevant parts of the battery.

These formal arguments (cf. discussion in the journal *Aphasiology* Vol. 10, 1996) were considered for further developments resulting in somewhat revised and test psychologically proofed screening batteries. Recently, Swinburn, Porter, and Howard (2004) have published the *Comprehensive Aphasia Test* which integrates tests for word and sentence processing as well as disability ratings. Martin, Schwartz, and Kohen (2006) suggest a multi-measurement approach based on a semantic measurement battery (including the *Peabody Picture Vocabulary Test*, Dunn and Dunn 1981 and the *Pyramids and Palm Trees Test*, Howard and Patterson 1992) and a phonological measurement battery together with the *Philadelphia Naming Test* (Roach et al. 1996). In Germany, the *LeMo battery* has been published by de Bleser et al. (2004) which gives some norms and pieces of advice in order to rate degree of severity for each task. *LeMo* applies tasks and word lists for all possible language functions on the level of word processing using the different routes, buffers, and lexical stores discussed in the model given above. In addition, it considers linguistic aspects of the material such as varying word frequencies, complexity and word class.

In the logic of the clinical neurolinguistic approach we have to base *therapy of impaired word processing* (comprehension, access and naming disorders in the oral or written modality) on a specific description of the impaired representations and routes of our model. A review on case studies based on psycholinguistic models for specific competences (naming therapy, auditory comprehension, reading and writing, sentence production and comprehension) has been presented by Lesser and Milroy (1993). Several therapy-studies have been published recently giving evidence of a higher efficiency, if therapy was individually designed to change the specific impairment and use preserved abilities (for example Nettleton and Lesser 1991; Nickels and Best 1996a,b).

Most aphasics show problems in *oral naming* and accessing the adequate words in spontaneous speech. Therapy for naming disorders has been described with a phonological focus (e.g. name repetition, rhyme judgments, using pictures and naming with phonemic cuing) or a semantic focus (e.g. word-picture matching amongst semantic associates, semantic judgments, category sorting). The advantages of a model-based therapy for naming disorders has been first documented by Howard et al. (1985). They concluded from their results that phonological and semantic cueing were both efficient, but the relative success depends on the specific difficulties patients exhibit. In addition, only semantic cues and facilitation tasks showed longer lasting and generalizing effects on retrieval competences. But for instance Howard et al. (2006) found most facilitation effects on the lemma level for retrieving the word form, which led them to a revision of the former idea of the importance of semantic facilitation, at least for conceptual semantic cues.

Many studies have addressed the question of which cues are best for which patients. Nickels (2002) gave a general detailed overview and evaluation of single case studies as well as group studies on naming therapy. The patients differed in the degree of severity of impairment on the conceptual semantic level, on the level of phonological word form or lemma, or on even more peripheral levels of phonemic sequencing and storing in working memory for the actual production. Cueing and facilitation strategies included conceptual and contextual cues, lexical-semantic cues, phonological cues, and also gesture cues. All of these facilitations and treatments have been shown to be efficient with noun retrieval (Drew and Thompson 1999; Pashek 1997; Raymer and Thompson 1991). Only few therapy-studies have been conducted on verbs, for instance by Rodriguez et al. (2006), or Raymer and Rothi (2001), who compare two different approaches to verb retrieval: the classical semantic-phonologic cueing aiming at a direct restoration of the processes in the temporal structures and pairing gestures with phonological forms, which might be seen as a vicariative method (Rothi 1995) that might be especially helpful for the retrieval of verbs, because of the assumed localization of verb semantics and gesture knowledge, both in the inferior frontal cortex. But the results did not clearly support this assumption. In a similar way, we find several studies which are not very clear in the resulting postulates for therapy what make a formulation of specific evidence based standards for therapy often problematic.

Therapy for *auditory word comprehension* has been rarely described and tested in single case or group studies yet. Some early concepts for reactivating auditory processing and accessing phonological word forms have been described by Luria and tested clinically by Naeser et al. (1986) or Gielewski (1989), working on phonemic discrimination by using rhyming words and sets of minimal pairs. Clark (1979) used the priming effect of facilitating context sentences, in order to reactivate the appropriate word form. Similarly most recent studies used reactivation strategies typically with patients in the acute or post-acute phase. For patients with long lasting problems in comprehension (severe global aphasia, word deafness, persistent jargon aphasia) a quite negative prognosis is usually given, and the focus in treatment is on strategies of how to circumvent the problem and improve communication disorders in the family.

Reactivation of semantic representations by auditory word forms has been shown for patients in the post-acute phase (Behrman and Liberthal 1989) as well as for the chronic stage (Byng 1988) with a good success. These studies applied techniques of picture-word matching, finding or looking up definitions especially for abstract word meanings or games, using guessing for defined concepts.

Therapy for *reading and writing* may be the most frequently explored for aphasic patients as well as for other neurological disorders. It is based on the prediction of impaired vs. spared functional routes in the two main syndromes mentioned above. Deep dyslexia is usually the most severe form of dyslexic disorders and accompanied by deep dysgraphia. Therapy aims at re-teaching or reactivating grapheme to phoneme-conversion rules if possible. Else, it may help the patient to relearn some of the most important words for daily needs (Mitchum and Berndt, 1991; Bachy-Langedock and de Partz 1989). Patients being classified as surface dyslexic (and dysgraphic) use just these GP-conversion rules (PG-conversion rules) extensively, but they have few knowledge about grapheme cluster sound patterns and word specific spelling. Scott and Byng (1988) suggested to teach a surface dyslexic patient a whole word strategy. Computer-assisted methods to present words with very short presentation time may improve especially lexical access to visual graphemic word forms.

3.3.2. Processing of sentences and phrase structures in aphasia

Aphasic descriptions of sentence production deficits so far have been formulated in terms of agrammatism and paragrammatism, with the agrammatic style being a defining characteristic of the syndrome of Broca's aphasia and the paragrammatic style as a defining characteristic of Wernicke's aphasia. We have described agrammatic speech production as a reduced, slowed, and telegraphic style, which is typically limited to content words (mainly nouns, some verbs). The mean phrase length is usually not longer than three words. Even repetition of longer sentences and phrases is impaired for most Broca's aphasics. Grammatical morphemes and function words (articles, conjunctions, prepositions, copula, and auxiliary verbs) are often omitted. In some languages even inflections are occasionally omitted (English: *"he go"* omitting the inflection for 3rd person singular; *"I pay yesterday"* omitting the past tense inflection). In higher inflecting languages patients produce simple verb forms, which have not to be varied according to person etc. (German: *"Brot kaufen"* using the infinitive for a telegraphic utterance). Apart from these problems in language production the comprehension of sentences is impaired for many patients, too. The sentence comprehension deficit typically occurs with problems on non-generic word order sentences (passives, topicalized accusative sentences, and subordinate clauses) (cf. Caramazza and Zurif 1976; Schwarz, Saffran, and Marin 1980). But the pattern of sentence processing problems is not as uniform as theory might predict (cf. Berndt, Mitchum, and Haendiges 1996).

These three criteria are not present in each patient with Broca's aphasia and/or with an agrammatic style. Badecker and Caramazza (1985) were amongst the first authors to describe in great detail the different patterns of agrammatic speech production. Variation was shown to be dependent on lesion site, material, and the production task (Caramazza and Hillis 1989; Höhle 1995), as well as on differences in compensatory patterns and strategies to cope with the deficits (Kolk and Heeschen 1992; Schade and Hielscher 1998). Similarly, several reports of single case studies have documented 'dissociations' between these three components of agrammatism (e.g. Goodglass and Menn 1985; Caplan, Baker, and Dehaut 1985; Schwartz, Linebarger, Saffran, and Pate 1987; Heeschen and Schegloff 1999) and a huge variability for each of these domains (Miceli et al. 1989; Saffran, Berndt, and Schwartz 1989).

A comprehensive view on agrammatic language production and comprehension in different languages has been given by the work of Menn and Obler (1990). Another important review on cross-linguistic studies on grammatical impairment has been provided by Bates, Wulfeck, and MacWhinney (1991) and Wulfeck, Bates, and Capasso (1991).

Many different theoretical explanations have been formulated presented as an overview for instance by Davis (2007). Only few theoretical positions try to explain paragrammatism characterized by fluent speech, many errors in the use of function words and syntactic inflections, repetitions and errors in sentence structures (Butterworth and Howard 1987; Harley 1990). A very good historical view on both concepts is presented by de Bleser (1987). Here only the the most recent hypotheses on agrammatism (and paragrammatism) which are of importance for therapeutic approaches today will be presented. These hypotheses are based on different sentence production (and comprehension) models.

One of the first psycholinguistic models for language production was presented by Garrett (1984). He bases the stages of his model on observations of naturally occurring speech errors. The stages of sentence planning identified his model are defined as follows:

1. Inferential cognitive processes work on the *message level representation;* it consists of the basic concepts which a speaker wishes to talk about.
2. Logical, semantic, and syntactic processes build up the *functional level representation;* it defines lexical elements and the thematic roles, the argument structure of the verb.
3. Syntactic and phonological processes fill in the slots for the *positional level representation*; at this level the sentence syntactic form is specified and phonological forms are filled in for content words, function words and inflectional morphemes are marked at this level.
4. Regular phonological processes specify in more detail the *phonetic level representation*;
5. Word coding processes transform this representation into an *articulatory representation*.

The entire model remained very underspecified, for instance with respect to the specific sentence planning, how syntactic structures are created and how the exact form of the elements is defined. But this model gives a first adequate differentiation between the relative stages of syntactic planning and it has been taken as a reference model for the study of the breaking down of sentence-production processes in agrammatic speech (for example by Caplan, 1985). Several authors (Kean 1977; Lapointe 1983) have proposed that agrammatic speech is based on specific problems with "closed class" elements of a language (i.e. function words, inflectional morphemes), which would be modeled as an impairment on the positional level and/or at the phonetic representation. Others, again, stress the problems agrammatic speakers have with verbs (Miceli et al. 1984), which would be an impairment on the positional level, mainly. A different hypothesis assumes problems on an even higher level of production for the mapping processes which assign objects to thematic roles. This would point to problems between the functional and the positional level. This problem is assumed to hold for perception (Linebarger et al. 1983; Linebarger 1990) as well as for production processes (Schwartz 1987; Schwartz et al. 1994). In this way, the model given by Garrett has been developed further and has been validated by neurolinguistic data, even as many details of processes remain underspecified.

More recently, Levelt (1989) and his colleagues formulated the syntactical and phonological encoding processes for words and sentences in greater detail based on a vast amount of empirical evidence and presented a computational model called WEAVER++ (Levelt et al. 1999). First hypotheses and descriptions of agrammatic symptoms and paragrammatism are based on this psycholinguistic approach today (Schade and Hielscher 1998; van de Sandt and Visch-Brink 2003).

Aside from these psycholinguistic models, there are approaches based in the tradition of generative grammar to formulate theoretical hypotheses for the agrammatic symptoms. Grodzinsky (1986, 1990, 1995) postulated a deficit in co-indexing grammatical elements on the deep and surface structure. This *"trace deletion"*-hypotheses allows for strong predictions for agrammatic patterns of production and comprehension processes. According to this assumption agrammatic patients loose the ability to correctly assign traces to moved constituents. Consequently, they will have to guess by chance on the subject and object of passive sentences and questions in English and several other languages. Grodzinsky (1989, 1995a) conducted several studies on the comprehension of passive structures and relative clauses. But the basic assumption for a default-strategy of interpreting subjects and objects in passive sentences was not always replicated in further studies (Druks and Marshall 1995; Berndt et al. 1996; Beretta and Munn 1998).

The most recent approach in this tradition is the *"tree pruning hypothesis"* (Friedman and Grodzinsky 1997; Friedman 2002) which postulates that agrammatic patients have underspecified nodes in the syntactical tree representation of sentences. Most common are underspecifications of the complementizer, tense, or agreement. The hierarchy of the tree is assumed to be cut off at the point of the underspecified tree information, allowing no higher syntactical structure to be used correctly. This hypothesis was validated in several case studies and it has been used successfully for some therapy studies and predictions of generalization effects of treated to untreated materials (Thompson et al. 2006). But it is again an approach which holds for only a small part of agrammatic behavior.

A third general methodological tradition has been applied to agrammatism by interactive activation models (Stemberger 1984; Dell 1986; Schade 1999). Stemberger compares agrammatic speech errors with normal production errors. Added lesions or noise to this model resulted in agrammatic speech patterns, i.e. the omissions of low frequency words in Stemberger's production network. The model suggested by Schade (1999) describes the production of nominal phrases showing the tendency to a reduced form of NPs. These networks aim at modeling specific symptoms each, they are not capable of explaining all different symptoms and patterns of agrammatism, yet.

An application of interactive activation models on paragrammatism has been formulated by Harley (1990) and by Schade (1999). Harley modeled errors involving misconstructed grammatical frames in terms of excessive substitutions. Schade proposed the activation of different patterns for the sentence structure which stay activated because of reduced lateral inhibition at the level of phrase structure representations. In addition, reduced feedback processes between layers can be assumed enhancing the chance for mal-constructed utterances to be brought to articulation. Problems of reduced feedback in the production system have been connected to paragrammatic style in classic model by Butterworth and Howard (1987), too. But this model proposed many modules which work on production copies for each process level. The underlying idea of reduced control seems to be very plausible but it is simulated much easier and more elegantly in interactive-activation models.

Finally, a somewhat different question addressed an early discussion between Heilbronner (1906), describing agrammatism as the primary impairment, and Goldstein (1913) or Isserlin (1922) who saw agrammatic symptoms as a secondary, perhaps 'compensatory' deficit because of primary 'articulatory' deficits. This second compensatory view has been discussed in various approaches with the recent one formulated by Kolk and Heeschen in the nineteen-nineties. This so called '*adaptation hypothesis*' (Kolk and Heeschen, 1990; Kolk et al. 1985) has two central basic ideas: first, elliptical expressions are used extensively in order to prevent the production system from overtaxing, and second, planning shorter and easier utterances can be seen as a kind of adaptation by the aphasic person to his changed capacities. If agrammatism and paragrammatism are indeed two sides of the same coin, as Kolk and Heeschen proposed in 1992, then we have to model the same underlying deficits which are modified by an intact feedback system in the agrammatic speaker, which is absent in the paragrammatic speaker. Changing the task (Höhle, 1995) or the communicative situation (Heeschen and Schegloff 1999) influences the amount of feedback, so that agrammatic speakers tend to change (back) to a paragrammatical style with a higher amount of substitutions instead of omissions and more complex and complete sentence structures.

Diagnostic methods for sentence production in communication, picture description, or in sentence completion tasks as well as sentence comprehension tasks are integrated in the most traditional aphasia batteries (*BDAE, WAB, AAT* as mentioned above). Sentence comprehension is traditionally examined by the *Token Test* and further variations (DeRenzi and Vignolo 1962; DeRenzi and Faglioni 1978). But in order to test specific syntactic knowledge, several screenings were published or proposed in the literature. Two tests are quite commonly used in English. The first is the *Functional Auditory Comprehension Task (FACT)* published by LaPointe and Horner (1978) as a measure of the comprehension of commands, which vary in length, vocabulary level, and syntactic complexity.

The *Auditory Comprehension Task for Sentences (ACTS,* Shewan 1981) gives a measure for comprehension in a picture matching task using 21 sentences of varying sentence length and complexity. Several subtests of more comprehensive tests can be used, too, for instance from *PALPA* (Kay, Lesser, and Coltheart 1992) or from the *Comprehensive Aphasia Test* (Swinburn et al. 2004).

The *therapy for sentence processing* has to be based on a specific description of the impaired components in the sentence comprehension and/or production processes. The basic components of each functional treatment use the critical linguistic structures in sentence-picture matching tasks, in simple questions in spontaneous speech, in picture descriptions, in sentence completion, or sentence verification tasks. But therapy implies more then providing the aphasic with the adequate linguistic material or with the critical structural knowledge.

In general, we find many programs and methods documented in the literature (cf. Chapey 2001; Basso 2003). But only few of these approaches are sufficiently evaluated, yet. The following overview sketches only briefly some most important lines in the traditional therapy for grammatical impairments. We can differentiate between more *explicit* rule-based learning programs which teach the patients about rules or structures on the one hand and more *implicit* learning programs aiming at an automatic reinstallation of syntactic structures on the other hand. A second dimension refers to a *production* or *comprehension* topic in the therapy, and a third dimension can be defined according the *grammatical complexity and correctness* or *communicative function* of the target utterances.

An early program to increase the syntactic correctness, variety and complexity of agrammatic utterances was introduced by Nancy Helm-Estabrooks (1981). The original *HELPSS*-Program was recently revised by Helm-Estabrooks and Nicholas (2000) and is now known as the *Sentence Production Program for Aphasia (SPPA)*. The program trains sentences of increasing complexity. Each sentence type is stimulated by a kind of eliciting story-completion format and gives hierarchical stimulation accompanied by a picture. It is indicated for patients with good sentence comprehension and about low to moderate production competences. The program is evaluated in several single case and small group studies which show quite good efficacy, but only little stimulus or response generalization (cf. Helm-Estabrooks and Albert 1991).

Another well documented line of therapy targets sentence comprehension and production problems between the functional level and the positional level in mapping lexical entries onto the thematic roles defined by verb slots. *Mapping therapy* has been shown to be quite successful for patients with this problem. Several single case studies and small group studies were published showing success in comprehension, and most studies show success in production as well, even if production has not been trained explicitly. Generalization effects were found in several studies, too.

Closely related are therapy concepts working at the level of the verb. These approaches aim at using the verbs with their complements and train verb recall and predicate-object relations. Empirical results given by Marshall, Pring, and Chiat (1998), or Marshall (1999a,b) show improvement for patients in sentence production after a therapy aiming at verb-related tasks even without explicit production training. In several case studies Schneider and Thompson (2003) obtained similar results for trained material. But in most studies generalization effects were poor. Eventually a specific question arises when we ask with which verbs and structures to begin with. It may be interesting to start with the more complex verb structures, if possible, because a generalizing effect may be expected only from complex to easy material.

A linguistic therapy which is designed to train specific syntactic structures is based on the trace deletion hypothesis and the tree-pruning account for agrammatism. Cynthia Thompson has conducted several studies on a *linguistic specific treatment (LST)* (Thompson and Shapiro 1994) and *treatment of underlying forms (TUF)* (Thompson and Shapiro 2005) of movement-structures in wh-questions and some other complex sentence structures. Most patients profited from this treatment for the trained sentence type, but generalization to other movement structures was not obtained. Following the logic of a tree-pruning deficit in agrammatism it should help to train higher functional nodes in the tree, assuming them to help with problems in lower functions, for example training the COMP structure should result in a generalizing effect on tense, not the reverse. First promising results have been given by Thompson et al. (2006).

Some programs have been suggested for the therapy of severely handicapped patients with agrammatism which do not aim at using correct syntactic forms, but at enhancing production and utterance length in general. Such concepts were described for instance with the *REST* program (*reduced-syntax-therapy*) by Schlenck, Schlenck, and Springer (1995), with a program called *MODAK (multimodal activation program)* by Lutz (1997), and similar with the *response elaboration training RET* by Kearns (1985, 2005), all of these programs aiming at the communicative competence of the patients by increasing utterance length and flexibility of response options.

3.4. A communicative perspective on aphasia

A third perspective on questions of the aphasic disorder and an adequate therapy focuses the communicative perspective, which has been widely neglected in the biological and in the neurolinguistic chapters before. Aphasia therapy is concerned with training and reactivating specific words, phrases and sentences, but this perspective received increasing criticism in the last years (Simmons-Mackie 2001; Lyon 1998). *Functional language skills* have been proposed to be of high importance for the generalization of improvements from language therapy into communicative contexts in real life situations. The recent position that has been taken for example by Kagan et al. (2001), or Lyon (1998) emphasizes the need to approach treatment from a social communication-integration standpoint. This is in line with the new WHO *Classification of Function, Disability and Health* (ICF) (World Health Organization, 2001). Two patients with the same type of severity of aphasia may have very different outcomes and social and communicative needs and success depending on barriers and social support from family, friends and therapeutic organizations.

So what then are the goals of aphasia therapy? Elman (2005) sees the central goal for speech and language therapy in teaching communication and conversational skills especially for relevant social situations, in order to improve the overall quality of life of the aphasic person. A competent adult speaker uses most language functions automatically. He is able to use language in communication in parallel with other cognitive tasks, like driving a car, watching TV, or going for a walk. One common aspect for adult speakers suffering from language disorders resulting from brain damage is a loss of this ease and automation remaining even after most symptoms have vanished and the daily communication seems to be quite normal. Other problems may arise for aphasic patients in their abilities to cope with the new situation, the impairment, and a new identity (Gatehouse and Clark 2007; Pound 2007). Again this leaves the question of what the primary goals for aphasia therapy are from a communicative perspective.

Patients' goals for their rehabilitation of language and communicative functions vary greatly, depending on the individual situation, the residual competences, facilitators and barriers. Patients and therapists do not always agree on realistic and primary goals for language therapy, but goals should be always discussed and validated from time to time (Cairns 2007; Byng, Cairns, and Duchan 2002).

The classical approaches to communication and conversation have drawn attention to language use in a more complex setting. Linguistically they focus on parameters of text comprehension and production (cf. Armstrong 2000), use of metaphoric language (for example Tompkins 1990) and different pragmatic means (Zaidel, Kasher, Soroker, and Batori 2002). Going one step further, conversational behavior analyses can be applied to the aphasic's communicative situations, as for instance Copeland (1989) applied speech act theory to elicited conversation. With this step Lesser and Milroy (1993: 319–323) describe five very important changes in the perspective on aphasic language use. In short, these changes are

1. conversation analysis as a bottom-up procedure starts with minimum prior imposition on analytic categories,
2. pragmatic competence is frequently said not to be not impaired in aphasic

persons, but it is in many aspects of conversational ability (pauses, repair strategies etc.),
3. a successful conversation has to be treated as a collaborative process between the aphasic person and his communicative partner,
4. conversational behaviors and utterances are analyzed and interpreted in their sequential context,
5. the label of 'appropriacy' and correctness of aphasic utterances are replaced by the label of success or failure of the communication.

Next to cognitive factors social aspects of the communicative competence play a major role in the success of reintegration of the aphasic person into occupational life. Only first programs have been developed in order to integrate these patients into an occupational context (Johnson 1998). Designing the process of reintegration has to be based not solely on language and communication therapy, it needs a problem solving approach (Hielscher-Fastabend and Richter 2004) in order to define the barriers and handicaps as well as possible strategies and facilities to reach the goals that have to be formulated as precisely as possible in order to make them testable.

Diagnostic methods can be divided to apply to the different levels of communicative competences and processes. Methods concerning the level of text and utterances have been published by Gardner and Brownell (1986), adapted by Zaidel et al. (2002). Both are applied to access competences in aphasic patients as well as in right hemisphere patients and patients with damage of the frontal lobes.

Methods and schedules assessing the functional communicative ability of the patient have been first proposed by Taylor Sarno (*FCP Functional Communication Profile*, 1969), a relatively broad and undifferentiated rating, which can be applied quickly and is used not only by therapists but also by relatives and other care persons. In a similar way the *CETI (Communicative Effectiveness Index)* given by Lomas et al (1989), checks with concrete questions the everyday communicative abilities. Several protocols have been developed in order to allow a standardized observation and evaluation of communicative adequacy and conversational strategies (for example the *Pragmatic Protocoll* designed by Prutting and Kirchner, 1983, 1987).

The *Amsterdam-Nijmegen Everyday Language Test* (*ANELT*, Blomert, Kean, Koster, and Schokker 1994) uses role playing to get explicit information about the patients' verbal and nonverbal competences and limitations

The approach formulated by Gerber and Gurland (1989) goes one step beyond the assessment of the patient's communicative behavior, as it documents the sequences in communication of the aphasic with the therapist and with a close relative or friend. This *Assessment Protocol of Pragmatic Linguistic Skills* (*APPLS*) describes conversation as collaborative and analyses for instance breakdown-repair sequences in the aphasic conversation. Further it tries to identify problems with contextual relevance, presuppositional referencing, topic maintenance and shift, as well as turn-taking. The authors propose several therapeutic possibilities depending on possible conversational problems that haven been found with the protocol. Lesser and Milroy (1993) formulate a checklist of conversational abilities, which has to be applied to communication observed. Five sections were defined: (1) Turn-taking, (2) repair, (3) embedding of sequences, (4) routines, and (5) discourse markers. This is an excellent approach, but we know today that ratings of the complex variables by the therapist or even by relatives or aphasics will lack reliability at least what makes it difficult to interpret.

Some assessment procedures do not rely on purely observational schedules but ask the patient to answer questions about communicative skills, to perform in role playing situations or some real life situations in a standardized way. The first comprehensive schedule was the *CADL (Communication Abilities of Daily Living)* published by Holland first in 1980 and has been revised only recently (Holland, Frattali, and Fromm 1998). It asks the patient to perform a wide range of communicative behavior, but it includes some items on text and utterances, too. The *Functional Assessment of Communication Skills for Adults (ASHA FACS)* was published by Frattali et al (1995) and requires direct observation of the aphasic's behavior in social communication, communication of basic needs, daily planning, and reading, writing and number concepts. It has been designed for the American Speech-Language-Hearing Association (ASHA) and can be used as a reliable tool in the evaluation of rehabilitation programs. But both, the CADL as well as the ASHA FACS do not describe the patients pragmatic competences in a linguistic way as to allow detailed planning of an adequate therapy.

Despite of all positive aspects of the different batteries and protocols we have to conclude that to this day we miss an adequate, comprehensive and valid method for accessing communicative competences of people with aphasia.

Therapy of the communicative abilities has many facets, which cannot be discussed here in detail. In their introduction to the previously published second Aphasia Therapy File Byng and Duchan (2007) summarize the overarching themes of the chapters, which focus on communicative and psycho-social aspects of language therapy and give several important topics for communication-oriented therapy.

The first problem is to define appropriate goals for both the patient and the therapist. This seems to be critical for the outcome as well as for the relationship between the person with aphasia and the therapist (Cairns et al 2007).

The therapy has to involve the family and other relevant persons into relevant situations to ensure that the communication skills being learned in therapy will be applied in day-to-day life afterwards. In addition, it will be of assistance for the relatives of aphasic persons to learn to cope with often difficult communicative situations (Simpson 2007).

Therapy of language and communication often implies changes in the aphasic patients identity (Gatehouse and Clark 2007). Speech and language therapists are often involved in this process of coping and changing identity, which influences the whole therapeutic setting (Pound 2007), the definition of roles (McVicker and Winstanley 2007), and the communicative style and learning approach (Montagu and Marshall 2007).

The evaluation of the therapy has not only to reflect the language competences and how patients 'perform' on language and communication tasks. Conversely, and in addition, it always has to reflect the outcome from the perspective of the patient, too.

Special settings for communicative therapy have been described in the literature. One of its most famous approaches has been the *PACE* therapy (*Promoting Aphasics' Communicative Effectiveness* by Davis and Wilcox 1985), which has been adapted and integrated into numerous other concepts over years. A recent approach of a very intensive communicative therapy based on the idea of constraint-induced mechanisms is published by Pulvermüller et al. (2001; Meinzer et al. 2004, 2005). The chances and problems of group therapy and the role of the therapist has to be reflected in this context. Finally, augmented communication and communication aids for severely handicapped aphasic patients have been developed in the last years, which may provide an additional chance for functional communication.

References

Alexander, M. P.
    1997   Aphasia: Clinical and anatomical aspects. In: T. E. Feinberg and M. J. Farah (eds.), *Behavioral Neurology and Neuropsychology* 133–149. New York: McGraw Hill.

Alexander, M. P.
    2003   Transcortical motor aphasia: A disorder of language production. In: M. D'Esposito (ed.), *Neurological Foundations of Cognitive Neuroscience,* 165–173. Cambridge MA: Bradford MIT Press.

Armstrong, E.
    2000   Aphasic discourse analysis: The story so far. *Aphasiology* 14: 875–892.

Axer, H., A. G. v. Keyserlingk, G. Berks, and D. G. v. Keyserlingk
    2001   Supra- and infrasylvian conduction aphasia. *Brain and Language* 76: 317–331.

Bachy-Langedock, N. and M.-P. de Partz
    1989   Coordination of two reorganization therapies in a deep dyslexic patient with oral naming disorders. In: X. Seron and G. Deloche (eds.), *Cognitive*

Approaches in Neuropsychological Rehabilitation, 211–248. Hillsdale NJ: Lawrence Erlbaum.

Badecker, W. and A. Caramazza
1985   On considerations of method and theory governing the use of clinical categories in neurolinguistics and cognitive neuropsychology: The case against agrammatism. *Cognition* 20: 97–125.

Baron, J. C. and G. Marchal
2000   Functional imaging in vascular disorders. In: J. C. Mazziotta, A. W. Toga, and R. S. J. Frackowiak (eds.), *Brain Mapping: The Disorders*, 299–315. San Diego, USA: Academic Press.

Basso, A.
2003   *Aphasia and Its Therapy.* New York: University Press.

Bates, E., B. Wulfeck, and B. MacWhinney
1991   Cross-linguistic research in aphasia: An overview. *Brain and Language* 41, 123–148.

Baum, S. R. and M. D. Pell
1999   The neural basis of prosody: Insights from lesion studies and neuroimaging. *Aphasiology* 13: 581–608.

Beeman, M.
1998   Coarse semantic coding and discourse comprehension. In: M. Beeman and C. Chiarello (eds.), *Right Hemisphere Language Comprehension: Perspectives from Cognitive Neuroscience,* 255–284. London: Lawrence Erlbaum Associates.

Beeman, M. and Chiarello, C. (eds.)
1998   *Right Hemisphere Language Comprehension. Perspectives from Cognitive Neuroscience.* Mahwah NJ: Lawrence Erlbaum.

Behrmann, M. and T. Lieberthal
1989   Category-specific treatment of a lexical-semantic deficit: a single-case study of global aplasia. *British Journal of Disorders of Communication* 24: 281–299.

Benson, D. F.
1967   Fluency in aphasia. Correlation with radioactive scan localization. *Cortex* 3: 373–394.

Benson, D. F. and A. Ardila
1996   *Aphasia: A Clinical Perspective.* New York and Oxford: Oxford University Press.

Beretta, A. and A. Munn
1998   Double-agents and trace-deletion in agrammatism. *Brain and Language* 65: 404–421.

Berndt, R. S., C. C. Mitchum, and A. N. Haendiges
1996   Comprehension of reversible sentences in "agrammatisms": A meta-analysis. *Cognition* 58: 289–308.

Berthier, M. L., S. E. Starkstein, and R. Leiguarda
1991   Transcortical aphasia. *Brain* 114: 1409–1427.

Binder, J. R.
2003   Wernicke Aphasia: A disorder of central language processing. In: M. D'Esposito (ed.), *Neurological Foundations of Cognitive Neuroscience,* 175–238. Cambridge: Bradford MIT Press.

Biniek, D.
   1993   *Akute Aphasie*. Stuttgart: Thieme.

Bisiach, E.
   1999   Unilateral neglect and related disorders. In: G. Denes and L. Pizzamiglio (eds.), *Handbook of Clinical and Experimental Neuropsychology*, 479–495. Hove: Psychology Press.

Blanken, G.
   1990   Formal paraphasias: A single case study. *Brain and Language* 38: 534–554.

Blomert, L., M. L. Kean, C. Koster, and J. Schokker
   1994   Amsterdam-Nijmegen Everyday Language Test: Construction, reliability, and validity. *Aphasiology* 8: 381–407.

Boatman, D., B. Gordon, J. Hart, O. Selnes, D. Miglioretti, and F. Lenz
   2000   Transcortical sensory aphasia: revisited and revised. *Brain* 123: 1634–1642.

Bonilha, L., D. Moser, C. Rorden, G. C. Baylis, and J. Fridriksson
   2006   Speech apraxia without oral apraxia: Can normal brain function explain the physiopathology? *Neuroreport* 17: 1027–1031.

Bookheimer, S.
   2004   Functional MRI of language: New approaches to understanding the cortical organization of semantic processing. *Annual Review of Neuroscience* 25: 151–188.

Broca, P.
   1960   Remarks on the seat of the faculty of articulate language, followed by an observation of aphemia. In: G. von Bonin (ed.), *Some Papers on the Cerebral Cortex*, 49–72. Springfield, IL: Charles C. Thomas.

Bub, D., S. Black, E. Hampson, and A. Kertesz
   1988   Semantic encoding of pictures and words: Some neuropsychological observations. *Cognitive Neuropsychology* 5: 27–66.

Butterworth, B. and D. Howard
   1987   Paragrammatism. *Cognition* 26: 1–37.

Byng, S.
   1988   Sentence processing deficits: Theory and therapy. *Cognitive Neuropsychology* 5: 629–676.

Byng, S., D. Cairns, and J. Duchan
   2002   Values in practice and practicing values. *Journal of Communication Disorders* 35: 89–106.

Byng, S. and J. Duchan
   2007   Describing therapies for aphasia. In: S. Byng, J. Duchan, and C. Pound (eds.), *The Aphasia Therapy File*, 1–13, (Volume 2). Hove, UK: Taylor and Francis Psychology Press.

Cairns, D.
   2007   Controlling language and life: Therapy for communication and identity in a bilingual speaker. In: S. Byng, J. Duchan, and C. Pound (eds.), *The Aphasia Therapy File*, 15–34, (Volume 2). Hove, UK: Taylor and Francis Psychology Press.

y Cajal, R.
   1928   *Degeneration and Regeneration of the Nervous System*. London: Oxford University Press.

Caplan, D.
  1985   Syntactic and semantic structures in agrammatism. In: M.-L. Kean (ed.), *Agrammatism*, 125–152. New York: Academic Press.
Caplan, D.
  1987   *Neurolinguistics and Linguistic Aphasiology. An Introduction.* Cambridge, UK: Cambridge University Press.
Caplan, D.
  1992   *Language. Structure, Processing, and Disorder.* Cambridge, MA: MIT Press.
Caplan, D.
  2001   Points regarding the functional neuroanatomy of syntactic processing: A response to Zurif (2001). *Brain and Language* 79: 329–332.
Caplan, D., C. Baker, and F. Dehaut
  1985   Syntactic determinants of sentence comprehension in aphasia. *Cognition* 21: 117–175.
Caramazza, A.
  1997   How many levels of processing are there in lexical access? *Cognitive Neuropsychology* 14: 177–208
Caramazza, A. and A. E. Hillis
  1989   The disruption of sentence production: Some dissociations. *Brain and Language* 36: 625–650.
Caramazza, A., A. E. Hillis, B. C. Rapp, and C. Romani
  1990   The multiple semantics hypothesis: Multiple confusions? *Cognitive Neuropsychology* 7: 61–189.
Caramazza, A. and E. B. Zurif
  1976   Dissociation of algorithmic and heuristic processes in language comprehension: Evidence from aphasia. *Brain and Language* 3: 572–582.
Chapey, R.
  1992   Functional communication assessment and intervention: some thoughts on the state of the art. *Aphasiology* 6: 85–94.
Chapey, R. (ed.)
  2001   *Language Intervention Strategies in Adult Aphasia and Related Neurogenic Disorders* (fourth edition). Baltimore: Lippincott Williams and Wilkins.
Chollet, F. and C. Weiller
  2000   Recovery of neurological function. In: J. C. Mazziotta, A. W. Toga, and R. S. J. Frackowiak (eds.), *Brain Mapping: The Disorders*, 587–597. San Diego, USA: Academic Press.
Clark, H.
  1979   Responding to indirect speech acts. *Cognitive Psychology* 11: 430–477.
Copeland, M.
  1989   Assessment of natural conversation with Broca's aphasics. *Aphasiology* 3: 391–196.
Coslett, H. B.
  2003   Acquired dsylexia: A disorder of reading. In: M. D'Esposito (ed.), *Neurological Foundations of Cognitive Neuroscience*, 109–127. Cambridge MA: Bradford MIT Press.
Crary, M. A., R. T. Wertz, and J. L. Deal
  1992   Classifying aphasias: Cluster analysis of Western Aphasia Battery and Boston Diagnostic Aphasia Examination results. *Aphasiology* 6: 29–36.

Crinion, J., E. A. Warburton, M. A. Lambon-Ralph, D. Howard, and R. J. S. Wise
   2006   Listening to narrative speech after aphasic stroke: The role of the left anterior temporal lobe. *Cerebral Cortex* 16: 1116–1125.

Damasio, H.
   1998   Neuroanatomical correlates of the aphasias. In: M. Taylor Sarno (3rd ed.) *Acquired Aphasia*, 43–70. San Diego: Academic Press.

Davis, G. A.
   2007   *Aphasiology. Disorders and Clinical Practice* [second edition]. Boston MA: Allyn and Bacon.

Davis, G. A. and M. J. Wilcox
   1985   *Adult Aphasia Rehabilitation: Applied Pragmatics.* San Diego: Singular.

De Bleser, R.
   1987   From agrammatism to paragrammatism: German aphasiological traditions and grammatical disturbances. *Cognitive Neuropsychology* 4: 187–256.

De Bleser, R., J. Cholewa, N. Stadie, and S. Tabatabaie
   2004   *LeMo: Lexikon modellorientiert. Einzelfalldiagnostik bei Aphasie, Dyslexie und Dysgraphie.* München, Jena: Elsevier; Urban und Fischer.

Dell, G.
   1986   A spreading activation theory of retrieval in sentence production. *Psychological Review* 93: 283–321.

Dennis, M.
   2000   Developmental plasticity in children: the role of biological risk, development, time and reserve. *Journal of Communication Disorders* 33: 321–332.

DeRenzi, E. and P. Faglioni
   1978   Normative data and screening power of a shortened version of the Token Test. *Cortex* 14: 41–49.

DeRenzi, E. and L. A. Vignolo
   1962   The token test: A sensitive test to detect receptive disturbances in aphasics. *Brain* 85: 665–678.

Drew, R. L. and C. K. Thompson
   1999   Model-based semantic treatment for naming deficits in aphasia. *Journal of Speech, Language, and Hearing Research* 42: 972–989.

Dronkers, N. F.
   1996   A new brain region for coordinating speech articulation. *Nature* 384(6605): 159–161.

Druks, J. and J. C. Marshall
   1995   When passives are easier than actives: Two case studies of aphasic comprehension. *Cognition* 55: 311–331.

Duffau, H., L. Capelle, N. Sichez, D. Denvil, M. Lopes, J.-P. Sichez, A. Bitar, and D. Fohanno
   2002   Intraoperative mapping of the subcortical language pathways using direct stimulations. *Brain* 125: 199–214.

Dunn, L. M. and L. M. Dunn
   1981   *Peabody Picture Vocabulary Test* (rev. ed.). Circle Pines, MN: American Guidance Service.

Ellis, A. W. and A. W. Young
　1996　　Human Cognitive Neuropsychology (augmented edition) [first edition 1988]. Hove: Lawrence Erlbaum.
Elman, R. J.
　2005　　Social and life participation approaches to aphasia intervention. In: L. L. LaPointe (ed.), *Aphasia and Related Neurogenic Language Disorders*, 39–50. New York: Thieme.
Ferro, J. M.
　1983　　Global aphasia without hemiparesis. *Neurology, 33*, 1106.
Ferro, J. M. and A. Kertesz
　1987　　Comparative classification of aphasic disorders. *Journal of Clinical and Experimental Neuropsychology* 9: 365–375.
Ferstl, E. C., T. Guthke, and D. Y. von Cramon
　2002　　Text comprehension after brain injury: left prefrontal lesions affect inference processes. *Neuropsychology* 16: 292–308.
Ferstl, E. C. and D. Y. von Cramon
　2001　　The role of coherence and cohesion in text comprehension: An event-related fMRI study. *Cognitive Brain Research* 11: 325–340.
Frackowiak, R. S. J., K. J. Friston, C. D. Frith, R. J. Dolan, and J. C. Mazziotta
　2003　　*Human Brain Function*. San Diego: Academic Press.
Frackowiak, R. S. J. (ed.)
　2004　　*Human Brain Function*. Second edition. Oxford: Elsevier Science.
Frattali, C. M., C. K. Thompson, A. L. Holland, C. B. Wohl, and M. M. Ferketic
　1995　　*Functional Assessment of Communication Skills for Adults* (ASHA FACS). Rockvill, MD: American Speech-Language-Hearing Association.
Freedman, M., M. P. Alexander, and M. A. Naeser
　1984　　Anatomic basis of transcortical motor aphasia. *Neurology, 34*, 409.
Friedman, N.
　2002　　Question production in agrammatism: The tree pruning hypothesis. *Brain and Language* 80: 160–187.
Friedman, N. and Y. Grodzinsky
　1997　　Tense and agreement in agrammatic production: Pruning the syntactic tree. *Brain and Language* 56: 397–425.
Gatehouse, C. and L. Clark
　2007　　Reassembling language and identity: A longitudinal programme involving psycholinguistic and social approaches in the life of a young man with aphasia. In: S. Byng, J. Duchan, and C. Pound (eds.), *The Aphasia Therapy File*, 35–57. Hove, UK: Taylor and Francis Psychology Press.
Gainotti, G.
　1999　　Neuropsychology of emotions. In: G. Denes and L. Pizzamiglio (eds.), *Handbook of Clinical and Experimental Neuropsychology*, 613–634. Hove: Psychology Press.
Gardner, H. and H. H. Brownell
　1986　　*Right Hemisphere Communication Battery*. Boston: Psychology Sevice, Veterans Administration Medical Center.
Garrett, M. F.
　1984　　The organization of processing structure for language production: Applications to aphasic speech. In: D. Caplan, A. R. Lecours, and A. Smith

(eds.), *Biological Perspectives on Language*, 172–193. Cambridge, MA: MIT Press.

Gerber, S. and G. B. Gurland
    1989   Applied pragmatics in the assessment of aphasia. *Seminars in Speech and Language* 10: 263–288.

Geschwind, N.
    1965   Disconnection syndromes in animals and man. *Brain* 88: 237–294 and 585–644.

Geschwind, N., F. A. Quadfasel, and J. M. Segarra,
    1968   Isolation of the speech area. *Neuropsychologia*, 6, 327–340.

Gielewski, E. J.
    1989   Acoustic analysis and auditory retraining in the remediation of sensory aphasia. In: C. Code and D. Muller (eds.), *Aphasia Therapy*, 138–146. (second edition). London: Cole and Whurr.

Goodglass, H.
    1988   Historical perspectives on concepts of aphasia. In: F. Boller and J. Grafman (eds.), *Handbook of Neuropsychology*, 51–63. Amsterdam: Elsevier.

Goodglass, H.
    1993   *Understanding Aphasia*. San Diego: Academic Press.

Goodglass, H. and L. Menn
    1985   Is agrammatism a unitary phenomenon? In: M.-L. Kean (ed.), *Agrammatism*, 1–26. Orlando, FL: Academic Press.

Gordon, J. K.
    1998   The fluency dimension in aphasia. *Aphasiology* 12: 673–688.

Greener, J., P. Enderby, and R. Whurr
    2006   Speech and language therapy for aphasia following stroke (Cochrane Review). In: *The Cochrane Database of Systematic Reviews* 1. Oxford.

Grodzinsky, Y.
    1986   Language deficits and the theory of syntax. *Brain and Language* 27: 135–159.

Grodzinsky, Y.
    1989   Agrammatic comprehension of relative clauses. *Brain and Language* 31: 480–499.

Grodzinsky, Y.
    1990   *Theoretical Perspectives on Language Deficits*. Cambridge, MA: MIT Press.

Grodzinsky, Y.
    1995a   A restrictive theory of agrammatic comprehension. *Brain and Language* 50: 27–51.

Grodzinsky, Y.
    1995b   Trace deletion, Q-roles, and cognitive strategies. *Brain and Language* 51: 469–497.

Hallett, M.
    2000   Therapeutics and recovery of function: Plasticity. In: J. C. Mazziotta, A. W. Toga, and R. S. J. Frackowiak (eds.), *Brain Mapping: The Disorders*, 569–586. San Diego, USA: Academic Press.

Hanlon, R. E., W. E. Lux, and A. W. Dromerick
    1999   Global aphasia without hemiparesis: language profiles and lesion distribution. *Journal of Neurology, Neurosurgery and Psychiatry* 66: 365–369.

Harley, T. A.
1990 Paragrammatism: Syntactic disturbance or breakdown of control? *Cognition* 34: 85–91.
Harley, T. A.
2001 *The Psychology of Language: From Data to Theory*. Hove, GB: Psychology Press, Taylor and Francis.
Hartley, L. L.
1995 *Cognitive-Communicative Abilities Following Brain Injury: A Functional Approach*. San Diego: CA.: Singular Publishing Group, Inc.
Hartje W. and K. Poeck (eds.)
2002 *Klinische Neuropsychologie*. Stuttgart: Thieme Verlag.
Hècaen, H.
1976 Acquired aphasia in children: Revisited. *Neuropsychologia* 21: 581–587.
Hècaen, H.
1983 Acquired aphasia in children and the ontogenesis of hemispheric functional specialization. *Brain and Language* 3: 114–134.
Heeschen, C. and E. A. Schegloff
1999 Agrammatism, adaptation theory, conversation analysis: On the role of so-called telegraphic style in talk-in-interaction. *Aphasiology* 13: 365–405.
Hegde, M. N.
2006 *A coursebook on aphasia and other neurogenic language disorders* (third edition). New York: Thomson Learning.
Heidler, M.-D.
2006 *Kognitive Dysphasien*. Frankfurt: Peter Lang.
Heilman, K. M., Rothi, L., McFarling, D., and Rottman, A. L.
1981 Transcortical sensory aphasia with relatively spared spontaneous speech and naming. *Archives of Neurology* 38: 236–239.
Helm-Estabrooks, N.
1981 *Helm Elicited Language Program for Syntax Stimulation (HELPSS)*. Chicago: Riverside.
Helm-Estabrooks, N. and M. L. Albert
1991 Using the process approach to generate treatment programs. In: N. Helm-Estabrooks and M. L. Albert (eds.), *Manual of Aphasia Therapy*, 147–174. Austin, TX: Pro-Ed.
Helm-Estabrooks, N. and M. Nicholas
2000 *Sentence Production Program for Aphasia*. Austin TX: Pro-Ed.
Herbert, R., W. Best, J. Hickin, D. Howard, and F. Osborne
2003 Combining lexical and interactional approaches to therapy for word finding deficits in aphasia. *Aphasiology* 17: 1163–1186.
Hillis, A. B.
2004 Acquired aphasic syndromes. *Journal of Neurology, Neurosurgery, and Psychiatry* 75: 942–946.
Hodges, J. R.
2003 Semantic Dementia: A disorder of semantic memory. In: M. D'Esposito (Ed.), *Neurological Foundations of Cognitive Neuroscience*, 67–87. Cambridge, MA: Bradford MIT Press.

Höhle, B.
1995   *Aphasie und Sprachproduktion. Sprachstörungen bei Broca- und Wernicke-Aphasikern.* Opladen: Westdeutscher Verlag.
Holland, A. L., C. M. Frattali, and D. Fromm
1998   *Communication Activities in Daily Living* (CADL), second edition. Austin, TX: Pro-Ed.
Howard, D. and K. Patterson
1992   *Pyramids and Palm Trees.* Bury St Edmunds, UK: Thames Valley Test Company.
Howard, D., K. Patterson, S. Franklin, V. Orchard-Lisle, and J. Morton
1985   Treatment of word retrieval deficits in aphasia. A comparison of two therapy methods. *Brain* 108: 817–829.
Howard, D., J. Hickin, T. Redmond, P. Clark, and W. Best
2006   Re-visiting "semantic facilitation" of word retrieval for people with aphasia: Facilitation yes but semantic no. *Cortex,* 42: 946–962.
Huber, W., K. Poeck, D. Weniger, and K. Willmes
1983   *Aachener Aphasie Test (AAT).* Göttingen, Hogrefe.
Huber, W., K. Poeck, and D. Weniger
2002   Aphasie. In: W. Hartje and K. Poeck (eds.), *Klinische Neuropsychologie,* 93–173. Stuttgart: Thieme.
Huber, W., K. Willmes, K. Poeck, B. van Vleymen, and W. Deberdt
1997   Piracetam as an adjuvant to language therapy for aphasia: A randomized double-blind placebo-controlled pilot study. *Archives of Physiology and Medicine* 78: 245–250.
Humphreys, G. W. (ed.)
1994   *Cognitive Neuropsychology and Cognitive Rehabilitation.* Hove, UK, Lawrence Erlbaum Associates, Publishers.
Joanette, Y. and H. H. Brownell (ed.)
1990   *Discourse Ability and Brain Damage.* New York: Springer.
Johnson, R.
1998   How do people get back to work after severe head injury? A 10 year follow-up study. *Neuropsychological Rehabilitation* 1: 61–79.
Johnston, T., C. M. van Reekum, T. R. Oakes, and R. J. Davidson
2006   The voice of emotion: an fMRI study of neural responses to angry and happy vocal expressions. *Social Cognitive and Affective Neuroscience* 1: 242–249.
Kagan, A., S. E. Black, J. F. Duchan, N. Simmons-Mackie, and P. Square
2001   Training volunteers as conversation partners using "Supported Conversation for Adults with Aphasia" (SCA): A controlled trial. *Journal of Speech, Language, and Hearing Research* 44: 624–638.
Kay, J., R. Lesser, and M. Coltheart
1992   *Psycholinguistic Assessments of Language Processing in Aphasia (PALPA).* Hove, UK: Lawrence Erlbaum.
Kaplan, E., H. Goodglass, and S. Weintraub
1983   *Boston Naming Test.* Philadelphia: Lea and Febinger.
Kean, M.-L.
1977   The linguistic interpretation of aphasic syndromes: Agrammatism in Broca's aphasia. *Cognition* 5: 9–46.

Kearns, K. P.
1985 Response elaboration training for patient initiated utterances. In: R. H. Brookshire (ed.), *Clinical Aphasiology* 15: 196–204. Minneapolis: BRK.

Kearns, K. P.
2005 Broca's aphasia. In: L. L. LaPointe (ed.), *Aphasia and Related Neurogenic Language Disorders*, 117–141. New York: Thieme.

Kertesz, A.
1982 *Western Aphasia Battery.* Orlando: Grune and Stratton.

Kertesz, A., A. Sheppard, and R. MacKenzie
1982 Localization in transcortical sensory aphasia. *Archives of Neurology*, 39, 475–478.

Knight, R. T. and M. D'Esposito
2003 Lateral prefrontal syndrome: a disorder of executive control. In: M. D'Esposito (ed.), *Neurological Foundations of Cognitive Neuroscience*, 259–279. Cambridge MA: Bradford MIT Press.

Kolk, H. H. J. and C. Heeschen
1990 Adaptation symptoms and impairment symptoms in Broca's aphasia. *Aphasiology* 4: 221–231.

Kolk, H. H. J. and C. Heeschen
1992 Agrammatism, paragrammatism and the management of language. *Language and Cognitive Processes* 7: 89–129.

Kolk, H. H. J., M. J. F. van Grunsven, and A. Keyser
1985 On parallelism between production and comprehension in agrammatism. In: M.-L. Kean (ed.), *Agrammatism*, 165–206. New York: Academic Press.

Lamb, S.
1999 *Pathways of the Brain: The Neurocognitive Basis of Language.* Amsterdam and Philadelphia: John Benjamins.

LaPointe, L. L.
1983 Some issues in the linguistic description of agrammatism. *Cognition* 14: 1–39.

LaPointe, L. L. and J. Horner
1978 The functional auditory comprehension task (FACT): Protocol and test format. *FLASHA Journal*: 27–33.

Leischner, A.
1987 *Aphasien und Sprachentwicklungsstörungen.* (second edition). Stuttgart: Thieme.

Lesser, R. and L. Milroy
1993 *Linguistics and Aphasia: Psycholinguistics and Pragmatic Aspects of Intervention.* New York: Longman Publishing.

Levelt, W. J. M.
1989 *Speaking. From Intention to Articulation.* Cambridge, MA: MIT Press.

Levelt, W. J. M., A. Roelofs, and A. S. Meyer
1999 A theory of lexical access in speech production. *Behavioral and Brain Sciences* 22: 1–75.

Linebarger, M. C.
1990 Neuropsychology of sentence parsing. In: A. Caramazza (ed.), *Cognitive Neuropsychology and Neurolinguistics: Advances in Models of Cognitive Function and Impairment*, 55–122. Hilsdale, NJ: Lawrence Erlbaum.

Linebarger, M. C., M. F. Schwartz, and E. M. Saffran
    1983   Sensitivity to grammatical structure in so-called agrammatic aphasics. *Cognition* 13: 361–392.
Lomas, J., L. Pickard, S. Bester, H. Elbard, A. Finlayson, and C. Zoghaib
    1989   The communicative effectivness index: development and psychometric evaluation of a functional communication measure for adult aphasia. *Journal of Speech and Hearing Disorders* 54: 113–124.
Lutz, L.
    1997   *MODAK – Modalitätenaktivierung in der Aphasietherapie.* Berlin: Springer.
Lyon, J. G.
    1998   *Coping with Aphasia.* San Diego, CA: Singular.
Marshall, J. T.
    1999a   Doing something about a verb impairment: Two therapy approaches. In: S. Byng, K. Swinburn, and C. Pound (eds.), *The Aphasia Therapy File*, 111–130. Hove, UK: Psychology Press.
Marshall, J. T.
    1999b   "Who ends up with the fiver?" – A sentence production therapy. In: S. Byng, K. Swinburn, and C. Pound (eds.), *The Aphasia Therapy File*, 143–149. Hove, UK: Psychology Press.
Marshall, J., T. Pring, and S. Chiat
    1998   Verb retrieval and sentence production in aphasia. *Brain and Language* 63: 159–183.
Martin, N., M. F. Schwartz, and F. P. Kohen
    2006   Assessment of the ability to process semantic and phonological aspects of words in aphasia: A multi-measurement approach. *Aphasiology* 20: 154–166.
Masland, R. L., A. Portera-Sanchez, and G. Toffano (eds.)
    1987   *Neuroplasticity, a New Therapeutic Tool in the CNS Pathology.* Berlin: Sprinter.
Matsui, T. and A. Hirano
    1978   *An Atlas of the Human Brain for Computerized Tomography.* Tokyo: Igako-Shoin.
Mazziotta, J. C., A. W. Toga, and R. S. J. Frackowiak
    2000   *Brain Mapping: The Disorders.* San Diego, USA: Academic Press.
McVicker, S. and L. Winstanley
    2007   A group approach to the long-term rehabilitation of clients with acquired brain injury within the community. In: S. Byng, J. Duchan, and C. Pound (eds.), *The Aphasia Therapy File*, 83–100. Hove, UK: Taylor and Francis Psychology Press.
Meinzer, M., D. Djundja, G. Barthel, T. Elbert, and B. Rockstroh
    2005   Long-term stability of improved language functions in chronic aphasia after constraint-induced aphasia therapy. *Stroke* 36: 1462–1466.
Meinzer, M., T. Elbert, C. Wienbruch, D. Djundja, G. Barthel, and B. Rockstroh
    2004   Intensive language training enhances brain plasticity in chronic aphasia. *BMC Biology* 2: 20.
Menn, L. and L. K. Obler (eds.)
    1990   *Agrammatic Aphasia: A Cross-Language Narrative Sourcebook.* Amsterdam: Benjamins.

Miceli, G., M. C. Silveri, C. Romani, and A. Caramazza
   1989   Variation in the patterns of omissions and substitutions of grammatical morphemes in the spontaneous speech of so-called agrammatic patients. *Brain and Language* 36: 447–492.

Miceli, G., M. C. Silveri, G. Villa, and A. Caramazza
   1984   On the basis for the agrammatics' difficulty in producing main verbs. *Cortex* 20: 207–220.

Mitchum, C. C. and R. S. Berndt
   1991   Diagnosis and treatment of the non-lexical route in acquired dyslexia: an illustration of the cognitive neuropsychological approach. *Journal of Neurolinguistics* 6: 103–137.

Montagu, A. and J. Marshall
   2007   "What's in a name?" Improving proper name retrieval through therapy. In: S. Byng, J. Duchan, and C. Pound (eds.), *The Aphasia Therapy File*, 101–115. Hove, UK: Taylor and Francis Psychology Press.

Morton, J.
   1969   Interaction of information in word recognition. *Psychological Review* 76: 165–178.

Morton, J.
   1979   Facilitation in word recognition: Experiments causing change in the logogen model. In: P. A. Kolers, M. E. Wrolstad, and M. Bouma (eds.), *Proccesing of Visible Language*, 259–268. New York: Plenum Press.

Naeser, M. A., G. Haas, P. Mazurski, and S. Laughlin
   1986   Sentence level auditory comprehension treatment program for aphasic adults. *Archives of Physical Medicine and Rehabilitation* 67: 393–399.

Nickels, L.
   2002   Therapy for naming disorders: Revisiting, revising, and reviewing. *Aphasiology* 16: 935–979.

Nickels, L. and W. Best
   1996a   Therapy for naming disorders (Part I): Principles, puzzles and progress. *Aphasiology* 10: 21–48.

Nickels, L. and W. Best
   1996b   Therapy for naming disorders (Part II): Specifics, surprises and suggestions. *Aphasiology* 10: 109–136.

Ogar, J., S. Willock, J. Baldo, D. Wilkins, C. Ludy, and N. Dronkers
   2006   Clinical and anatomical correlates of apraxia of speech. *Brain and Language* 97: 343–350.

Paivio, A.
   1971   *Imagery and Verbal Processes*. London: Holt, Rinehart and Winston.

Paquier, P. and H. R. van Dongen
   1991   Two contrasting cases of fluent aphasia in children. *Aphasiology* 5: 235–245.

Paquier, P. and H. R. van Dongen
   1996   Review of research on the clinical presentation of acquired childhood aphasia. *Acta Neurologica Scandinavica* 93: 428–436.

Pashek, G. V.
   1997   A case study of gesturally cued naming in aphasia: Dominant versus non-dominant hand training. *Journal of Communication Disorders* 30: 349–366.

Penfield, W. and T. Rasmussen
  1950   *The Cerebral Cortex of Man. A Clinical Study of Localization of Function.* New York, The Macmillan Comp.
Petersen, S. E., P. T. Fox, M. I. Posner, M. I. Mintun, and J. Raichle
  1989   Positron emission tomographic studies of the processing of single words. *Journal of Cognitive Neuroscience* 1: 153–170.
Petersen, R. R. and P. Savoy
  1998   Lexical selection and phonological encoding during language production: Evidence for cascaded processing. *Journal of Experimental Psychology: Learning, Memory, and Cognition* 24: 539–557.
Pound, C.
  2007   Therapy for life: Challenging the boundaries of aphasia therapy. In: S. Byng, J. Duchan, and C. Pound (eds.), *The Aphasia Therapy File*, 129–149. Hove, UK: Taylor and Francis Psychology Press.
Price, C. J.
  2000   Functional imaging studies of aphasia. In: J. C. Mazziotta, A. W. Toga, and R. S. J. Frackowiak (eds.), *Brain Mapping: The Disorders*, 181–200. San Diego: Academic Press.
Prutting, C. A. and D. M. Kirchner
  1987   A clinical appraisal of pragmatic aspects of language. *Journal of Speech and Hearing Disorders* 52: 105–119.
Pujol, J., J. Deus, J. M. Losilla and A. Capdevilla
  1999   Cerebral lateralization of language in normal left-handed people studied by functional MRI. *Neurology* 52: 1038–1043.
Pulvermüller, F., B. Neininger, T. Elbert, B. Mohr, B. Rockstroh, and P. Koebbel
  2001   Constraint-induced therapy of chronic aphasia after stroke. *Stroke* 32: 1621–1626.
Rapp, B. C. and A. Caramazza
  1995   Disorders of lexical processing and the lexicon. In:. M. S. Gazzaniga (ed.), *The Cognitive Neurosciences,* 901–913. Cambridge: The MIT Press.
Raymer, A. M and C. K. Thompson
  1991   Effects of verbal plus gestural treatment in a patient with aphasia and severe apraxia of speech. In: T. E. Prescott (ed.), *Clinical Aphasiology*, 285–297. Austin, TX: Pro-Ed.
Raymer, A. M. and L. J. G. Rothi
  2001   Cognitive approaches to impairments of word comprehension and production. In: R. Chapey (ed.), *Language Intervention Strategies in Aphasia and Related Neurogenic Disorders*, 524–550. Philadelphia, PA: Lippincott Williams and Wilkins.
Riddoch, M. J. and G. W. Humphreys
  1987   Visual object processing in optic aphasia: A case of semantic access agnosia. *Cognitive Neuropsychology* 4: 131–185.
Roach, A., M. F. Schwartz, N. Martin, R. S. Grewal, and A. Brecher
  1996   The Philadelphia naming test: Scoring and rationale. In: M. L. Lemme (ed.), *Clinical Aphasiology,* 121–134. Austin, TX: Pro-Ed.

Robey, R. R.
    1994   The efficacy of treatment for aphasic persons: A meta analysis. *Brain and Language, 47,* 582–608.

Robey, R. R.
    1998   A meta-analysis of clinical outcomes in the treatment of aphasia. *Journal of Speech, Language and Hearing Research* 41: 172–187.

Robey, R. R., M. C. Schultz, A. B. Crawford, and C. A. Sinner
    1999   Review: Single-subject clinical-outcome research: designs, data, effect sizes, and analyses. *Aphasiology* 13: 445–473.

Rodriguez, A. D., A. M. Raymer, and L. J. G. Rothi
    2006   Effects of gesture-verbal and semantic-phonologic treatments for verb retrieval in aphasia. *Aphasiology* 20: 286–297.

Ross, E. D.
    1981   The aprosodias. Functional-anatomic organization of the affective components of language in the right hemisphere. *Archives of Neurology, 38,* 561–569.

Ross, E. D.
    2000   Affective prosody and the aprosodias. In: M. M. Mesulam (ed.), *Principals of Behavioural and Cognitive Neurology,* 316–331. New York: Oxford University Press.

Rothi, L. J. G.
    1995   Behavioral compensation in the case of treatment of acquired language disorders resulting from brain damage. In: R. A. Dixon and L. Mackman (eds.), *Compensating for Psychological Deficits and Declines: Managing Losses and Promoting Gains,* 219–230. Mahwah, NJ: Lawrence Erlbaum.

Saffran, E. M., R. S. Berndt, and M. F. Schwartz
    1989   The quantitative analysis of agrammatic production: Procedure and data. *Brain and Language* 37: 440–479.

Sarno, M. T.
    1969   The functional communication profile manual of directions. *Rehabilitation Monograph* 42; New York University Medical Center.

Schade, U.
    1999   *Konnektionistische Sprachproduktion.* Wiesbaden: Deutscher Universitätsverlag.

Schade, U. and M. Hielscher
    1998   Die Modellierung des Agrammatismus. In: M. Hielscher, P. Clarenbach, S. Elsner, W. Huber, and B. Simons (eds.), *Beeinträchtigungen des Mediums Sprache,* 97–110. Tübingen: Stauffenburg.

Schlenck, C., K.-J. Schlenck, and L. Springer
    1995   *Die Behandlung des schweren Agrammatismus. Reduzierte-Syntax-Therapie REST.* Stuttgart: Thieme.

Schneider, S. L. and C. K. Thompson
    2003   Verb production in agrammatic aphasia: The influence of semantic class and argument structure properties on generalization. *Aphasiology* 17: 213–241.

Schoonen, R.
    1991   The internal validity of efficacy studies: Design and statistical power in studies of language therapy for aphasia. *Brain and Language* 41: 446–464.

Schwartz, M. F.
1987 Patterns of speech production deficit within and across aphasia syndromes: Application of a psycholinguistic model. In: M. Coltheart, G. Sartori, and R. Job (eds.), *The Cognitive Neuropsychology of Language*, 163–199. London: Erlbaum.
Schwartz, M. F., M. Linebarger, E. M. Saffran, and D. Pate
1987 Syntactic transparency and sentence interpretation in aphasia. *Language and Cognitive Processes* 2: 85–113.
Schwartz, M. F., E. M. Saffran, and O. S. Marin
1980 The word problem in agrammatism. I. Comprehension. *Brain and Language* 10: 249–262.
Schwartz, M. F., E. M. Saffran, R. Fink, J. Myers, and N. Martin
1994 Mapping therapy: A treatment programme for agrammatism. *Aphasiology* 8: 19–54.
Scott, C. and S. Byng
1989 Computer assisted remediation of a homophone comprehension disorder in surface dyslexia. *Aphasiology* 3: 301–320.
Shallice, T.
1988 *From Neuropsychology to Mental Structure*. London: Cambridge University Press.
Shallice, T., P. McLeod, and K. Lewis
1985 Isolating cognitive modules with the dual task paradigm: Are speech perception and production separate processes? *Quarterly Journal of Experimental Psychology* 37A: 507–532.
Shallice, T., R. I. Rumiati, and A. Zadini
2000 The selective impairment of the phonological output buffer. *Cognitive Neuropsychology* 17: 517–546.
Shewan, C. M.
1981 *Auditory Comprehension Test for Sentences*. Chicago: Biolinguistics Clinical Institutes.
Simmons-Mackie, N. N.
2001 Social approaches to aphasia intervention. In: R. Chapey (ed.), *Language Intervention Strategies in Adult Aphasia and Related Neurogenic Communication Disorders*, 246–268. Philadelphia: Lippincott Williams and Wilkins.
Simpson, S.
2007 Respecting the rights of a person with aphasia to their own life choices: A longitudinal case study. In: S. Byng, J. Duchan, and C. Pound (eds.), *The Aphasia Therapy File*, 181–208. Hove, UK: Taylor and Francis Psychology Press.
Small, S. L., J. Hart, Jnr., T. Nguyen, and B. Gordon
1995 Distributed representations of semantic knowledge in the brain. *Brain* 118: 441–453.
Stein, D. G., S. Brailowsky, and B. Will
1995 *Brain Repair*. New York: Oxford University Press.
Stemberger, J. P.
1984 Structural errors in normal and agrammatic speech. *Cognitive Neuropsychology* 1: 283–313.

Stirling, A.
  2007   A case study of a client with mild language problems. In: S. Byng, J. Duchan, and C. Pound (eds.), *The Aphasia Therapy File*, 209–218. Hove, UK: Taylor and Francis Psychology Press.
Swinburn, K., G. Porter, and D. Howard
  2004   *Comprehensive Aphasia Test*. London: Psychology Press.
Talairach, J. and P. Tournoux
  1988   *Co-Planar Stereotaxic Atlas of the Human Brain: 3-Dimensional Proportional System: An Approach to Cerebral Imaging*. Stuttgart: Thieme.
Taub E, G. Uswatte, and R. Pidikiti
  1999   Constraint-induced movement therapy: a new family of techniques with broad application to physical rehabilitation: A clinical review. *Journal of Rehabilitation Research Dev.* 36: 237–251.
Thompson, C. K., L. H. Milman, M. W. Dickey, J. E. O'Connor, B. Bonakdarpour, S. C. Fix, J. J. Choy, and D. F. Arcuri
  2006   Functional category production in agrammatism: Treatment and generalization effects. *Brain and Language* 99: 69–71.
Thompson, C. K. and L. P. Shapiro
  1994   A linguistic-specific approach to treatment of sentence production deficits in aphasia. In: M. L. Lemme (ed.), *Clinical Aphasiology*, 307–324. Austin, TX: Pro-Ed.
Thompson, C. K. and L. P. Shapiro
  2005   Treating agrammatic aphasia within a linguistic framework: Treatment of underlying forms. *Aphasiology* 19: 1021–1036.
Toga, A. W. and J. C. Mazziotta
  1998   *Brain Mapping: The Methods*. San Diego, USA: Academic Press. (2nd ed. 2002).
Tompkins, C. A.
  1990   Knowledge and strategies for processing lexical metaphor after right or left hemisphere brain damage. *Journal of Speech and Hearing Research* 33: 307–316.
Tompkins, C. A.
  1994   *Right Hemisphere Communication Disorders. Theory and Management*. Singular Press Publishing Group Inc.: San Diego, CA., USA.
Tompkins, C. A., W. Fassbinder, M. L. Blake, A. Baumgaertner, and N. Jayaram
  2004   Inference generation during text comprehension by adults with right hemisphere brain damage: Activation failure vs. multiple activation. *Journal of Speech, Language, and Hearing Research* 47: 1380–1395.
van Dongen, H. R., P. Paquier, W. L. Creten, J. van Borsel, and C. E. Catsman-Berrevoet
  2001   Clinical evaluation of the conversation speech fluency in the acute phase of acquired childhood aphasia. Does a fluency/nonfluency dichotomy exist? *Journal of Child Neurology* 16: 345–351.
Warrington, E. K. and T. Shallice
  1969   The selective impairment of auditory verbal short-term memory. *Brain* 92: 885–896.
Warrington, E. K. and T. Shallice
  1979   Semantic access dyslexia. *Brain* 102: 43–63.

Warrington, E. K. and T. Shallice
   1984   Category-specific semantic impairments. *Brain* 107, 829–854.
Weiss, S. and H. M. Müller
   2003   The contribution of EEG coherence to the investigation of language. *Brain and Language* 85: 325–343.
Wernicke, C.
   1874   *Der aphasische Symptomenkomplex*. Breslau: Cohn and Weigert (repr. 1974; Berlin: Springer).
Wildgruber, D, I. Hertrich, A. Riecker, M. Erb, S. Anders, W. Grodd, and H. Ackermann
   2004   Distinct frontal regions subserve evaluation of linguistic and emotional aspects of speech intonation. *Cerebral Cortex* 14: 1384–87.
Wildgruber, D., A. Riecker, I. Hertrich, M. Erb, W. Grodd, T. Ethofer, and H. Ackermann
   2005   Identification of emotional intonation evaluated by fMRI. *NeuroImage* 24: 1233–41.
Williamson, J. B., D. W. Harrison, B. V. Shenal, R. Rhodes, and H. A. Demaree
   2003   Quantitative EEG diagnostic confirmation of expressive aprosodia. *Applied Neuropsychology 10: 176–181.*
Wineburgh, L. F. and S. L. Small
   2004   Aphasia treatment at the crossroads: A biological perspective. *The ASHA Leader* 27: 6–7.
Wittler, M.
   2006   Flüssigkeit akut-aphasischer Sprachproduktion: Eine Dichotomie? Dissertation abstracts: Universität Bielefeld.
Wulfeck, B., E. Bates, and R. Capasso
   1991   A crosslinguistic study of grammaticality judgements in Broca's aphasia. *Brain and Language* 41: 311–336.
Ylvisaker M. and T. J. Feeney
   1998   *Collaborative Brain Injury Intervention: Positive Everyday Routines*. San Diego, London: Singular Publishing Group, Inc.
Zaidel, E., A. Kasher, N. Soroker, and G. Batori
   2002   Effects of right and left hemisphere damage on performance of the "Right hemisphere communication battery." *Brain and Language* 80: 510–535.
Zurif, E. B.
   2001   More on sentence comprehension in Broca's aphasia: A response to Caplan. *Brain and Language* 79: 321–328.
Zurif, E. B. and M. M. Pinango
   1999   The existence of comprehension patterns in Broca's aphasia. *Brain and Language* 70: 133–138.

17. The nature and treatment of stuttering

Ashley Craig

Stuttering is a communication disorder involving involuntary disruption to the fluency and flow of speech. It is prevalent across the lifespan with a predominance of males stuttering. It is believed to be a neurological disorder that affects the neural systems of speech. While stuttering is found across all age levels, most begin to stutter before adolescence, between 2 and 5 years of age, with the highest peak at around four years. With increasing age, stuttering can disrupt social and psychological growth and possibly cause distressing experiences that may lead to chronic anxiety and psychological problems. Stuttering also has the potential to limit vocation choices. Best evidence suggests that stuttering can be treated successfully, though the problem becomes more difficult to treat with increasing age. This chapter describes treatment shown to be effective at reducing stuttering within children, adolescents and adults, and will discuss issues related to achieving best outcomes.

1. Introduction

Stuttering is classified in the Diagnostic and Statistical Manual of Mental Disorders (DSM-IV) as a childhood disorder (APA 1994), though it is prevalent across all age levels (Craig, et al. 2002). Most children who stutter (CWS) will begin to stutter before adolescence, most commonly between 2 and 5 years of age, with the highest peak at around four years (APA 1994; Yairi and Ambrose 1992). This is called developmental stuttering. Cases of acquired stuttering do occur where an injury results in damage to the brain (such as in stroke or traumatic brain injury). The risk of ever stuttering is believed to range from 3 to 5% in young children (Bloodstein 1995; Craig et al. 2002). In latest research on the epidemiology of stuttering, the prevalence of stuttering over the entire lifespan (from two years to older age) was found to be 0.72% with at least a 50% higher prevalence rate of stuttering in males (Craig et al. 2002). A 0.72% prevalence rate is expected given that many children naturally recover from stuttering (Bloodstein 1995). A higher prevalence rate of up to 1.4% was found in children and adolescents (2 to 19 years), with males having up to a fourfold higher prevalence (Craig et al. 2002).

Stuttering is believed to be a neurological disorder that affects the motor aspects of speech (Andrews, et al. 1983; Craig 2000; Hulstijn, Peters, and van Lieshout 1997). Therefore, a person who stutters knows what he or she wishes to say, but at the time is unable to communicate it because of an involuntary, motor disruption to their speech (Andrews et al 1983; Bloodstein 1995; Hulstijn et al. 1997). Evidence shows that as a person who stutters (PWS) grows older, many will suffer a lowered quality of life as a consequence of the difficulties experienced when attempting to communicate (Craig et al. 2003). As verbal communication is known to be very important for successful social interaction, stuttering can create barriers to social and psychological development. Coping poorly with stuttering over many years has been associated with problems such as the development of fears of speaking to others, the development of higher than normal levels of chronic trait anxiety, and feelings of helplessness (APA 1994; Baker and Cantwell 1987; Beitchman, et al. 1996; Beitchman, et al. 2001; Cantwell and Baker 1977; Craig 1990; Craig et al. 2003). As can be imagined, stuttering also has the potential to limit the choice of vocation open to the PWS (Craig and Calver 1991). Many people who stutter may not communicate as efficiently as desired when conducting their work duties due to their speech disorder and therefore, stuttering may drive a person to seek employment below their capabilities which possibly results in disappointment and/or lowered self-esteem (Bloodstein 1995; Craig and Calver 1991). Furthermore, PWS also have higher external locus of control scores than people who do not stutter (Andrews and Craig 1988; Craig, Franklin, and Andrews 1984), suggesting they perceive their life (especially their ability to communicate) to be less likely controlled by their own efforts and ability, and more by luck, chance or powerful others. A high external locus of control is known to be associated with feelings of helplessness (Craig et al. 1984).

Given the above dynamics, it is crucial that efficacious treatments be developed for PWS, especially during adolescence where many important lifetime decisions begin to be made. Best evidence does suggest that psychological damage is more a risk for adolescents who stutter in comparison to younger children, thus the urgency for effective treatment by adolescence (Craig and Hancock 1996; Craig et al. 2003). This chapter will describe and discuss treatment rationale and regimens for PWS, including treatment for young children, older children, adolescents and adults. Emphasis will be placed on treatments that have been scientifically trialled and shown to be effective in reducing stuttering to acceptable levels in both the short and long-term, as well as reducing levels of fears about communicating verbally. Before treatment rationale and protocols are described, the definition and nature of stuttering will be discussed.

2. Definition of stuttering

Stuttering has been defined as "interruptions to the fluency and flow of speech, where the person knows what he or she wishes to say, but is unable to because they are experiencing either: (a) involuntary repetitions of syllables, especially when starting words, (b) involuntary prolonging of sounds and (c) unintentional blocking of their speech" (Craig et al. 1996). It may also involve unnatural hesitations, interjections, restarted or incomplete phrases, and unfinished or broken words can also be part of the problem. Associated symptoms can include eye blinks, facial grimacing, jerking of the head, arm waving and so on. As the child grows older there is a risk these behaviours will become more pronounced. Such behaviours are thought to be learned and largely unconsciously acted, and appear to have been adopted by the PWS in an attempt to minimise the severity of the stutter (Bloodstein 1995). Unfortunately, the concomitant behaviour (eg. eye blinks) loses its distraction power to reduce stuttering, and often the PWS can be left with the overt behaviour. Therefore, as the person grows older the stutter develops in complexity and severity. As a consequence, the PWS can become increasingly embarrassed at the moment of the stutter, and eventually they may come to fear a social setting where they have to speak (such as talking to someone using the telephone). Avoidance becomes a more common strategy as a child develops and ages (Bloodstein 1960). Avoidance is the long-term danger for the child who stutters, as it can potentially limit their social and personal growth. Table 1 shows common symptoms experienced in stuttering.

Table 1. Shows possible common symptoms of stuttering

Speech and behavioural symptoms

Involuntary repetitions of syllables, especially when starting words

Involuntary prolonging of sounds

Unintentional blocking on syllables and words

Unnatural hesitations, interjections, restarted or incomplete phrases, and unfinished or broken words.

Concomitant behavioural symptoms can include unusual eye blinks, facial grimacing, jerking of the head, arm waving and so on

Social avoidance behaviour

Psychological and social symptoms

Emotional struggle, frustration and possible embarrassment when stuttering

Shyness due to fear of speaking in specific social contexts

High levels of chronic anxiety, especially social or phobic anxiety

---

3. Who is at risk of stuttering?

As stated above, stuttering is mostly a disorder that begins in early childhood at the time when a child is learning to speak. Therefore, all young children could be said to be at risk of stuttering. However, the population at risk can be narrowed down. We have good evidence that suggests stuttering has a genetic etiology (Yairi, Ambrose, and Cox 1996). We know, for instance, that children who have a parent who stutters have substantially increased risks themselves of stuttering (Andrews et al. 1983). We also know that male children have an increased risk of stuttering compared to female children (Craig et al. 2002). Furthermore, some evidence suggests that children with developmental disabilities have increased risks of stuttering (Andrews et al. 1983; Ardila, et al. 1994; Bloodstein 1995). For example, Ardila et al., (1994) found that university students who stutter had significantly higher risks of having an associated disorder such as dyslexia, minor brain injury, and so on. The population at risk of stuttering (disregarding the population at risk of acquired stuttering) could therefore be defined as "all young children who are developing speech, but especially those who have a history of stuttering in the family, who are male and who have a developmental disability."

4. Rationale for the treatment of stuttering

It is essential that treatments for stuttering attend to the underlying problems associated with the disorder. For instance, if a disorder is known to have a biological cause, then treatment should ideally address the biological factors. It is now accepted that stuttering has a physical/biological basis that is most likely multifactorial in origin (Smith and Kelly 1997). Stuttering likely involves a number of physical dimensions including neurophysiological, perceptual, acoustic, kinematic, electromyographic, respiratory, and linguistic factors (Smith and Kelly 1997). For instance, stuttering involves some disruption to the speech muscles while speaking (eg. rapid repetition of a syllable, or a block on a sound); adults who stutter show greater activity in the non-dominant hemisphere while speaking than non stuttering controls (Fox, et al. 1996); PWS tend to have slower reaction times when speaking (Andrews et al. 1983); they often have irregularities in breathing related to speech (Bloodstein 1995) and they show higher levels of muscle tension (eg. facial and laryngeal) before and during speaking (Craig and Cleary 1982; Bloodstein 1995). Furthermore, stuttering usually begins at an early age of two to six years when the speech-motor cortex is developing (Bloodstein 1995; Craig et al. 1996), and stuttering is unlikely to begin after the maturation of the speech-motor cortex, except in cases of acquired stuttering. PWS have been shown to have delayed speech acquisition and they are more likely to have articulatory problems and reduced capacity to manage motor tasks involved in speech (Andrews et al. 1983; Bloodstein 1995). Research also suggests that stuttering has genetic origins (Andrews et al. 1983; Yairi et al. 1996). That is, males are more likely to stutter and have a family history of stuttering (Bloodstein 1995; Craig et al. 1996). If an identical twin stutters, there is a substantially higher chance that both twins will stutter compared to non-identical twins (about 60% to 20% respectively) (Yairi et al. 1996). Stuttering is possibly inherited by the transmission of a single major gene or a major gene plus multiple genes (Yairi et al. 1996).

The above argues for a treatment protocol that addresses the physical basis of stuttering. However, the best evidence available (Andrews et al. 1991) strongly suggests that inheriting stuttering is an interaction between a genetic predisposition (70%) and the influence of the environment (30%). Therefore, chronic stuttering will be associated with environmental factors. It is suspected that social, psychological and behavioural dimensions influence its development and severity (Craig et al. 2003). It seems understandable that experiencing stuttering will result in psychological consequences. For example, many become embarrassed and frustrated when speaking (and stuttering) in public contexts (eg. talking to a group of people), and some will begin to avoid situations in which the potential for embarrassment and frustration is high. Additionally, the severity of stuttering usually increases when a PWS becomes fatigued or anxious, and particular social contexts and words can be linked to more severe stuttering (Bloodstein 1995; Craig et al. 2003). Because of the societal demands and pressures, stuttering is generally associated with higher levels of trait and state anxiety (Craig et al. 2003). Furthermore, anxiety associated with stuttering often reduces to normal levels following treatment that successfully reduces stuttering severity (Craig 1990).

Ideally then, treatment should be designed to address the biological and psychological aspects of the problem. Of course, treatment should also be tailored to meet the needs and individual circumstances of the client. This becomes clear, for instance, when treating a young child compared to an adolescent or adult. Those PWS who are very socially anxious may require a specialised treatment protocol compared to someone who has little social anxiety linked to their stuttering (Craig and Tran 2006). However, for the majority of PWS, it seems reasonable to begin by employing a treatment regimen that addresses the physical symptoms of stuttering, such as using techniques that directly reduce stuttering severity, resulting in improved fluency and speech rate. It is important to address issues of capacity and demand (Gottwald and Starkweather 1999). For instance, it is desirable that treatment (i) enhance the brain's capacity to process speech, that is, improve coordination of respiratory, supralaryngeal and laryngeal systems (such as delayed auditory feedback or fluency shaping techniques), (ii) reduce the demands associated with speaking (eg. modification of stuttering techniques, speech rate reduction therapy or cognitive behaviour therapies designed to weaken fears associated with speaking), and (iii) reduce motor dysfunction (eg. increased airflow and slowed speech rate techniques, improve control over muscle tension levels before and during speech as taught in EMG feedback therapy). However, given the complexity of stuttering with advancing age and the appearance of secondary psychological factors (eg. social anxiety, shyness and avoidance behaviour and so on), the clinician should also be aware of the potential need for additional therapy components such as social skills training, anxiety management, and behavioural techniques designed to overcome shyness and avoidance behaviour. Additional components designed to enhance neural capacity (and thus improve speech motor resources) could include improving quality of lifestyle, such as improved diet and exercise regimens, and using techniques that increase pleasant activities in daily schedules.

5. Core components of treatment

Regardless of the specialised treatment being delivered, there are core components and principles of treatment that should always be employed by the clinician to ensure that stuttering treatment effectiveness is optimised. In the view of the author, specialised stuttering treatments should be considered core components for the treatment of stuttering. However, specialised treatments will be discussed later on in this chapter. Table 2 presents a list of these essential treatment components.

Table 2. Core components for the treatment of stuttering

Comprehensive assessment and diagnosis of stuttering

Behavioural assessment of the severity of stuttering and communication skills within multiple social contexts

Assessment of the psychological impact of stuttering including social anxiety assessment

Assessment of social skills repertoire specifically related to speech

Assessment of relationship interactions

Treatment

Professional and supportive approach

Provision of specialized speech treatments known to reduce stuttering symptoms

Psychological and social skills therapies for primary and secondary aspects of stuttering

Regular assessment of stuttering throughout treatment to monitor progress

Maintenance and generalisation

Structured maintenance procedures begun in the home, school or work environment

Social support strategies provided by family and friends

Self-help and self control therapies

5.1. A comprehensive diagnosis

A comprehensive diagnosis and assessment should be conducted before treatment is begun. Initial assessment must determine whether the person believed to stutter actually does stutter, and the nature and severity of the stutter should also be determined. For instance, what type of stuttering does the person exhibit (eg. more repetitions rather than blocking), how severe (eg. determine by using behavioural measures of severity such as frequency of syllables stuttered and speech rate), how generalised is the stutter (eg. determine in what contexts the person stutters more frequently) and how anxious the person is about their stuttering (eg. anxiety levels, avoidance behaviour and so on). Usually, severity of stuttering is best measured using a behavioural assessment (Craig et al. 1996) that involves estimating from speech samples the frequency of the stuttering (%SS or percent syllables stuttered) and the speech rate (SPM or syllables per minute). A %SS of greater than 10%SS and a low SPM (less than 100 SPM; most adults will speak at around 200–250 SPM) usually indicates very severe stuttering (frequent stutters and low speech rate). It is important to continue to measure stuttering (at very least %SS and SPM) throughout treatment so that a record of fluency change exists. The diagnosis should also include an assessment of trait anxiety (measured in a comfortable and relaxed setting) as well as state anxiety linked to various speech tasks (for instance, directly before and after a telephone call). Social anxiety should also be measured in addition to scales that measure communication fears and perception of control (e.g. locus of control or self-efficacy expectations). While there is no evidence to suggest that PWS are vulnerable to depression (Craig 2000), a comprehensive mood and personality assessment would be useful for clinical purposes. If possible, an assessment of how the PWS interacts with their family and friends would provide valuable information about the psychosocial and interpersonal dynamics of the stuttering.

In young children, it would be important to distinguish between so called normal disfluency and stuttering. Stuttering is different to normal dysfluency, as it occurs frequently, and signs of struggle or tension often result as the child attempts to speak. Commonly, a PWS will repeat syllables rather than the whole word (unless of course, the word is only one syllable like "me", "to" etc.). It is also important to determine whether the stutter is due to genetic factors or due to other causes such as head injury, as a traumatic injury cause may influence the type and course of treatment. The assessment should elicit information on the onset of stuttering (eg. the age when the person began to stutter), any family history of stuttering, the natural course of the stutter over the person's lifetime, and any prior treatment. Furthermore, complicating factors that are likely to limit treatment efficacy should also be assessed (for instance, coexisting articulation or learning disorder). An evaluation of concomitant behaviours is also useful, and these behaviours may also need to be targeted in therapy, but usually they disappear if the stuttering is eliminated.

5.2. Supportive and professional approach

It is very important that clinicians interact in therapy in a supportive and professional manner. Positive relationships with the client (and their family) are extremely important for producing successful therapeutic outcomes. The clinician should not show favouritism when conducting therapy with a group of children, and it is important to accept that stuttering has a biological basis, not being the fault of the PWS. So often blame can be unnecessarily ascribed to a client if therapy is not going as successful as desired.

5.3. Social support from family and friends

It is very important that family and friends offer social support when a PWS enters into treatment. This is, of course, essential when children are being treated, however, few realise the power of conscripting the support of family and friends in terms of positive therapy outcomes and achieving treatment goals. There are many strategies that the clinician could suggest family and friends use in order to enhance therapy outcomes. Some of these strategies are described below:

5.3.1. *Rewarding fluent speech*

Family members and friends can praise the PWS when they speak fluently. For example, verbal praise ("well spoken" or "that was excellent talking") and nonverbal rewards such as smiling and hugging. Using these will encourage the PWS and help raise their confidence. Praise is a very powerful motivator. The type of praise should be negotiated as frustration or embarrassment can result if they are not comfortable with the type of praise given. Family members must also learn not to punish the PWS by becoming angry or frustrated when they are disfluent. It is not difficult to do this as family are understandably emotionally involved and the PWS is usually very sensitive about their speech. Punishment can also occur if a family member or friend ignores the PWS when they stutter. While punishment may reduce stuttering, usually the effects are minimal and only temporary. In contrast, consistently rewarding fluent speech is likely to result in a sustained increase in fluency.

5.3.2. Highlighting stuttering

Punishment is not always a desirable technique as it can result in aggression and resentment. However, mild forms can be used in conjunction with rewarding statements. For example, "that was a stutter, how about repeating it." It is essential that such statements are said in a non-threatening and positive manner.

5.3.3. Slowed and relaxed speech

It is important for the long-term maintenance of fluency skills that the family become a model for the PWS by regularly using slower speech. It helps to encourage the PWS to slow down their speech and relax their facial, neck and chest muscles.

5.3.4. Structured and regular assistance

A family member can help the PWS by arranging structured and regular periods in which they assist the PWS to practise their fluency skills. Time slots of up to 10–15 minutes each day for say 3–4 days a week can be an effective strategy. The practice session can involve any practice of relevant skills. An example could involve the PWS talking in a controlled conversational session using the treatment skills while monitoring stuttering. Appropriate and achievable goals and targets should be set so that rewards can be used to encourage practice. Appropriate rewards contingent with successful achievements have the potential to make the task of practice easier and more enjoyable. Rewards need to be sophisticated and motivating and both short and long-term rewards need to be used. Rewards will also need to be tailored to the desires of the PWS. It will be necessary to make a list of rewards that each PWS favours. Do not overuse a reward as it may lose its reinforcing power. Use natural rewards more often (such as smiles, hugs, praise and so on).

5.3.5. Relaxed home or work environment

Stuttering will become worse when the PWS is stressed. Family members or friends can help to create a relaxed and accepting environment so the PWS can optimise their ability to control their stuttering. General relaxation prompts such as "calm down", "take it easy", "slowly", "it's ok" can be used to calm the PWS and encourage them to use treatment skills. Use prompts that are encouraging. Prompts are powerful behavioural reinforcers and can be either verbal or non verbal in form. Again, it is imperative that the tone of voice of the family member or friend is not punishing but encouraging. Do not over use these prompts. Encouraging them too frequently could become a punishment!! Allowing the PWS sufficient time to speak will also create a relaxed environment. It is best that the PWS is not unnecessarily interrupted, talked over or have their sentences completed for them when they are having difficulties being fluent.

Practising relaxation at home or in the work environment is also a useful strategy for creating a relaxed atmosphere. There are many ways a PWS can learn to relax such as (a) deep and slow breathing; (b) isometrics, involving tensing up muscles, holding the tension briefly (say five seconds) and then letting the tension go, while saying "relax"; (c) learning imagery or contemplation methods; (d) receiving massage; (e) aerobic exercise and (f) stretch exercises. Details for these techniques are found in Craig (1998a).

5.3.6. Encourage self-responsibility

Family and friends must encourage the PWS to be responsible for their own talking and it is important that they do not to talk for them. Talking on their behalf (when they are present) will only belittle them and reduce their self-esteem. The PWS should be reminded that they can control their stuttering if they put treatment strategies into practise. They should be reminded that they will experience failure now and then, and teaching them to learn from these experiences will help them succeed more often.

6. Specialised treatment programs for young children who stutter

There have been quite a number of treatment programs designed and used to treat early stuttering. It is important to recognise that most programs for young children overlap in many respects in terms of their techniques (Conture 1990; Costello 1983; Gregory 1999; Lincoln et al. 1996; Riley and Riley 1999; Runyan and Runyan 1999; Rustin, Botterill, and Kelman, 1997; Ryan and Ryan 1999; Starkweather, Gottwald and Halfond 1990). Most involve modifying the child's environment so that the potential for a reduction in stuttering is optimised. This may involve parent counselling, encouraging reduced speech rates and the non interruption of children when they speak, and dealing with negative attitudes that may form barriers to fluency. Many also involve measuring and charting the child's stuttering performance throughout therapy. In some cases, treatments involve stuttering modification interventions such as modelling relaxed and slower speech to the child, employing fluency shaping techniques, and changing behaviour through operant techniques such as applying verbal contingencies following stuttered speech. Unfortunately, few of these programs have been shown to be effective using objective and controlled research. There is one exception however, and that is the Lidcombe Program. Details of this program will be presented first, followed by details of two other contrasting examples of stuttering treatment programs for the young child who stutters.

6.1.   Lidcombe Program: Behavioural treatment program for young children

The Lidcombe Program trains the significant carer (here called the parent) in the stuttering child's life to deliver the treatment in the day to day context of the child's environment (Lincoln et al. 1996). Full details of the Program have been described elsewhere (Onslow, Packman, and Harrison 2003). During weekly visits, parents are initially trained to conduct the treatment and measure the progress of the child. Treatment consists of individualised structured sessions in the child's environment, involving the parent delivering verbal contingencies following stutter-free speech and after definite stuttered speech. The power of this program is built upon the laws of operant conditioning, in which the parent delivers positive reinforcement and punishment procedures. The parent encourages fluent behaviour by reinforcing fluent speech. This is achieved by the parent first acknowledging stutter free speech (eg. "that was fluent") and then praising the child (eg. "that was really well spoken" or "well done, excellent talking"). Parents are also encouraged to ask the child to evaluate their performance (eg. "did you have any bumpy words then?"). Stuttering, called bumpy words, is discouraged through parents providing mild punishment following the bumpy word (eg. "that was a bumpy word") and then requesting the child to correct their speech behaviour (eg. "can you repeat the word?"). The Program requires that the parent provide these contingencies as soon as possible following the child's verbal responses and that the ratio of positive reinforcement contingencies to punishment contingencies be around 5:1.

The parents are also trained to measure the child's stuttering each day throughout treatment by rating the severity of their child's stuttering on a 10 point Likert Scale (1=no stuttering and 10=extremely severe stuttering). The Program is divided into two stages. In Stage 1 parents attend the clinic on a weekly basis, and sessions involving parents and child involve structured conversations of around 10–15 minutes at least once a day. Later in Stage 1, parents are encouraged to give verbal contingencies during unstructured more natural conversations at various times during the day. Stage 1 is concluded when the child achieves three consecutive weeks of a stuttering rate of below 1%SS (rated in the clinic by the therapist) and a daily parent severity rating of 1 or 2 (extremely mild stuttering or less). During Stage 2, called the performance-contingent maintenance phase, parents attend the clinic less frequently assuming that the child is maintaining the progress attained during Stage 1. Verbal contingencies are gradually withdrawn as visits to the clinic decline. Any sign of relapse, that is, a return of significant stuttering, results in increased visits and structured sessions till the stuttering declines and maintained at a low level.

Preliminary research suggested the Lidcombe Program is an effective treatment for eliminating stuttering in 12 young stuttering children (Onslow, Andrews, and Lincoln 1994). At 12 months after treatment, the children had achieved a median score of below 1 %SS, with treatment completed in a median time of 11 1 hour sessions. In a randomized clinical trial format, the Lidcombe Program has now been shown to be an efficacious treatment for young stuttering children compared to control children who stutter who did not receive treatment (Harris et al. 2002; Jones et al. 2005).

6.2. Early intervention and stuttering prevention program

Starkweather, Gottwald and Halfond (1990) developed an early intervention program for young children who stutter. The intervention was designed so that demands on the young child's speech were reduced while increasing the child's capacity to speak. Strategies included speech modelling and some fluency shaping, as well as teaching parents to reduce their speech rate, simplifying their language and reducing interruptions to the child's speech, improving any negative attitudes towards the child's speech, and providing daily time devoted to talking. Some evidence is available that demonstrates the efficacy of this treatment. It has been reported that the majority of families entering this treatment successfully complete the therapy (Starkweather et al. 1990), and Gottwald and Starkweather (1999) provided further evidence of its efficacy. They claimed that 14 out of 15 families successfully completed the treatment, meaning that the children significantly improved their fluency. However, there has been no data published providing speech outcomes, nor have there been any comparisons to no treatment controls.

6.3. Parent-child interaction therapy

The Parent-Child Interaction (PCI) program was developed by the Michael Palin Centre for Stammering Children (Rustin, Botterill, and Kelman 1997; Rustin et al. 2001). The main aim of PCI therapy is to identify the interaction styles within the family that may assist the child who stutters to become more fluent. A further goal is to improve the family's confidence and skill in managing their child's problem. It consists of weekly sessions for six weeks followed by a six-week consolidation period with additional appointments as necessary to monitor and review progress. One of the major tasks for the therapist and the parents is to establish what factors might be influencing fluency and stuttering behavior. For example, the way that parents communicate with their child is examined for factors that may deteriorate speech (eg. rapidly paced speaking, with everyone talking at once), with the aim of establishing calmer, more relaxed communication.

Therapy sessions are designed so that they are enjoyed by the child, and during the sessions, the child is videotaped playing with the parent(s). Feedback is given concerning the interactions between parents and child, and discussion is focussed on what aspects of their interaction that might be changed in order to improve fluency prospects. Changes in communication interactions are then practised during regular 5-minute dedicated sessions in the home environment. Parental counseling is also offered during the initial six-week period of therapy, and this may involve individual issues thought to be important for positive outcomes. This may include negative parental and child behaviours that may lead to anxiety and frustration on both sides. Parental concerns about their child's stutter are also dealt with. The program may also work on other speech and language skills if these are behind in development. Again, though the program is well established and successful case studies exist, there has been no data published providing objective speech outcomes, nor have there been any comparisons to no treatment controls.

7. Specialised treatment programs for older children and adolescents who stutter

As for the treatment of the young child, so there has been a number of treatment programs designed and used to treat older children and adolescents who stutter. Furthermore, techniques used in these varied programs also greatly overlap (Azrin, Nunn, and Frantz 1979; Blood et al. 2001; Boberg and Kully 1994; Conture 2001; Craig et al. 1996; Gregory 2003; Hancock et al. 1998; Ladouceur, Boudreau and Theberge 1981; Runyan and Runyan 1986; Ryan and Van Kirk Ryan 1995). Techniques are usually comprised of a mixture of stuttering modification strategies such as fluency shaping, regulated breathing and airflow techniques, and operant technologies are often integrated into treatment (eg. reward for successfully completing stages of treatment, punishment may be imposed such as fines for non completion of treatment stages, and time out procedures may also be implemented such as imposed silence following a stutter). Other techniques include: parents and the PWS may receive counseling; parents may be taught to reduce their rate of speech in the home and to reduce fluency and conversational demands and pressures (eg. non-interruption of the PWS when they speak); dealing with negative attitudes in family members and the PWS that may create barriers to fluency; speech muscle feedback therapy, relaxation techniques and social skills training. Many will also involve assessing and monitoring/charting stuttering performance throughout therapy and into the long-term. The critical issue in treatment for this age group is designing a protocol that maintains their interest.

Operant treatments have been commonly used in school-age children and adolescents who stutter. One example is the graduated increase in length and complexity of utterance (GILCU) method (Ryan 1971). The GILCU program (Ryan 1971) involves the child being told to read fluently, beginning with one-word utterances that are gradually increased to two words, and so on up to five minutes of monologue or conversation. Ryan and Van Kirk Ryan (1995) have recently replicated their earlier study (Ryan and Van Kirk Ryan 1983) with 24 children (seven to 17 years). Twelve children received GILCU and 12 the Delayed Auditory Feedback (DAF) program. DAF involved a slow, prolonged fluent speaking pattern plus DAF (delaying the feedback of speech for short periods), followed by a gradual decrease in the amount of DAF. In each of the programs, operant techniques were also used, where stuttering was negatively reinforced and fluency was rewarded. The results were promising after 14 months, with children significantly reducing their stuttering down to less than one word stuttered per minute in the GILCU program.

Electromyography (EMG) feedback (Bloodstein 1995; Craig and Cleary 1982; Craig et al. 1996) is designed to help the person who stutters to control speech muscle tension associated with stuttering by teaching them to (i) reduce speech muscle tension to low levels before beginning to speak using computer based speech muscle activity feedback. (ii) Lower overall levels of speech muscle tension while speaking. (iii) Learn to control their speech muscle tension, called EMG mastery, in the absence of the computer feedback, and (iv) help the PWS to raise their levels of confidence, increase their feeling of control over their speech and raise their levels of self esteem. Full detail of the EMG Feedback protocol has been published elsewhere (Craig 1998a) and its effectiveness has been demonstrated (Craig et al. 1996; Hancock et al. 1998). Unfortunately, as for early childhood treatments, few of these programs have been shown to be effective using objective and controlled clinical trial research. Craig et al. (1996) and Hancock et al. (1998) have presented objective data from controlled clinical trial research on the effectiveness of a fluency shaping treatment integrated into a behavior therapy regimen. Details of this program will now be presented.

7.1. Fluency shaping techniques for older children and adolescents

Fluency shaping techniques are speech treatments that directly target stuttering (Craig, Feyer, and Andrews 1987). It trains the PWS to control their stuttering by adapting and changing their speech patterns. Smooth speech (a derivative of prolonged speech) is a well known variant of the fluency shaping techniques. It was designed to help the PWS to control their stuttering by teaching them to (i) stabilise their breathing by teaching them to increase levels of airflow before and during speech and taking regular pauses during speech, (ii) stabilise muscle activity by decreasing the amount of muscle tension associated with speech (eg. by using gentle sounds, increased airflow before a phrase and/or speech muscle biofeedback therapy), (iii) improve fluency and social skills by intensive practise of conversations, (iv) monitor speech naturalness, and (v) increase their feelings of control over their speech and reduce anxieties related to speaking. Best available evidence suggests that Smooth Speech should be delivered in a cognitive behavioural therapy context (Craig, Feyer, and Andrews 1987; Craig et al. 1996). This means that it should be delivered in a regimen that sets achievable behavioural goals, assesses behavioural outcomes, rewards outcomes, involves transfer and maintenance procedures and employs behavioural assignments to reinforce skills. An added advantage is that secondary symptoms such as anxiety and psychological upset can also be addressed using cognitive behavioural therapy approaches.

A typical Smooth Speech program could be designed as outlined in Table 3 and an example protocol follows. Details of such a program have been described elsewhere (Craig 1998a; Craig et al. 1996). In the first phase of the program, PWS are trained by the clinician to use a fluency shaping technique like Smooth Speech. This occurs during intensive structured conversation and feedback sessions over a period of at least 3 days, say from 9 am to 4 pm. It is recommended that one parent or family member sit in on therapy and that the group consists of around 4–6 participants. The group is systematically taught to reduce stuttering in structured conversation sessions, beginning at very slow speech rates (about 50 SPM or one quarter of the average adult speech rate). As the participants progress through and they achieve therapy targets, speeds are gradually increased. In addition to slowed speech, they are also required to prolong their syllables and increase the amount of airflow whilst speaking. Essentially, the PWS is taught to speak while breathing out and controlling their rate of speech. This involves receiving instruction on respiratory control, where easy, relaxed breathing during speech is modelled by the therapist. Another fundamental characteristic of Smooth Speech is the use of gentle onsets and offsets. This involves the PWS beginning their phrases with airflow and using soft articulatory contacts. In addition, a phrase/pause speech pattern is taught. Pauses at the end of the phrase serve to reduce difficulties in speaking, that is, pausing helps to restore neural capacity and develop a controlled breathing pattern. To insure that these structured sessions are enjoyable, it is recommended that the clinician use a range of group based games (eg. board or card games) that encourage participants to speak during the sessions. The Program also requires the older child or adolescent to complete a speech assignment with a member of their family in their home environment each night following the daily treatment. This assignment is assessed and discussed the following day with the clinician regarding how successful the participant was in maintaining their fluency at home.

Table 3. Smooth Speech intensive fluency shaping program protocol

Initial assessment

Behavioural assessment of the severity of stuttering and communication skills within multiple social contexts

Psychological assessment

Phase 1 (3 days): Smooth Speech training

Education about stuttering and the role of Smooth Speech treatment

Learning Smooth Speech skills (say 9 am to 4 pm, over a 3 day period) in structured group conversations starting at slow speeds (recommended 50 SPM), increasing gradually up to normal speeds (recommended 180 SPM)

Clinician feedback and modelling of fluency and conversational skills

Practise using fluency and conversational skills at slower speeds in the home setting each night after the daily treatment

Phase 2 (3 days): Transfer and generalisation of fluency skills

Taped speech assignments beginning with easier tasks (eg. typically a conversation with parent), progressing to more difficult communication tasks (eg. shopping)

Self-evaluation of performance and clinician feedback on assignments

Additional skills learned such as thought control and relaxation skills

Phase 3: Maintenance and long-term follow-up (up to 12 months following Phase 2)

Structured maintenance procedures begun in home setting

Social support strategies provided by family and friends

Self-help and self control therapies

As stated above, participants are able to progress to faster speech rates if they complete these sessions stutter free while using acceptable conversational skills. The therapist models appropriate speech throughout these sessions. Video feedback of their performance is provided at regular intervals in the day. The desired target speech outcome consists of normal speech rate levels, emphasising continuous airflow, with unvoiced sounds remaining unvoiced. The emphasis with Smooth Speech is on the end-product being a natural-sounding speech spoken at normal speech rates. It is recommended that progression through the program is rewarded with small cash payments.

When the PWS has completed the required number of structured sessions, and have gained control over their stuttering at normal speech rates, transfer and generalisation sessions are then begun in the second phase of the Program. This involves the participant performing a number of speech assignments based on a hierarchy of difficulty, beginning with easier assignments (eg. speaking at slower speeds with a family member) and ending with challenging tasks (speaking for 5 minutes to a stranger on the telephone or giving a speech in front of an audience). The program requires that participants tape their speech during these assignments and to self-rate the quality of their performance. Self rating sheets should be provided for the self-evaluation. Participants only progress through these assignments if they continue to succeed in producing conversations with minimal stuttering and natural conversational style. Clinicians continue to provide feedback on the participants' performance during the assignments. If the PWS fails an assignment (eg. stutter above the accepted rate during the conversation, use of inappropriate conversation and communication skills, poor intonation used when speaking), then troubleshooting occurs with the clinician in order to correct any faults in their technique or fluency skills. Participants are also trained to cope with failure by talking the problem through and reinforcing fluency strategies.

The Smooth Speech Program should be structured so that the emphasis is shifted away from external control to an expectation of self-control. Specific self-management skills can be employed to achieve this, including training in appropriate self-evaluation and self-monitoring of stuttering. This consists of recording in a speech diary their speech performance following assignments. Completing the speech diary requires the children to record stutters and evaluate correct use of fluency techniques. The children should correct stutters as they occur during therapy in order to increase self-monitoring capability. At home during the evenings of the program, they can be asked to complete a self-monitoring form every two hours. This involves recording on a Likert-type scale how well they spoke in the previous five minutes. They can also be trained to employ self-reward for fluency and for achieving practice goals. In order to reinforce self-responsibility, discussions should be held from day one of Phase 1 on the importance of helping themselves rather than pleasing parents or therapists. In addition, the importance of being motivated to achieve and maintain treatment gains should be reinforced. Specific suggestions can be given on how to improve motivation levels and how to maintain fluent speech despite lifestyle demands. The importance of daily practice and of varying its format in order to remain motivated and maintain treatment gains should be reinforced.

Links between thoughts, feelings and behaviour may also be discussed. Cognitive techniques can be applied to overcome any attitudinal barriers to success. Examples can be given of appropriate self-talk before and during a difficult speaking situation in order to enhance fluency (e.g., "My stuttering is under my control. I am in charge"; "I will think about my fluency skills rather than worrying about stuttering"). Self-talk can also used during treatment to help subjects cope with the experience of stuttering. As stated above, part of the nature of control is the expectation of all possibilities, including failure. The children can be taught skills for dealing with failure when it occurs. For example, they can be trained to recognise high-risk situations such as fatigue, negative mood, threatening environments, and taught methods of coping with these situations (e.g., view stuttering as a sign that they need to focus on fluency skills rather than pushing through stutters and adopting a sense of hopelessness). In addition, the children can be taught simple relaxation techniques such as breath awareness and control, and brief isometric exercises that enable them to enhance control of their muscle tension and anxiety (Craig 1998a). Discussions should be held regarding the need to use physical relaxation so that the participants can think more clearly and use positive thoughts to help cope with difficult speaking situations. They should be encouraged to practise simple relaxation exercises that could be used just before, during or after an anxiety-provoking speaking situation.

In Phase 3 of the Program, maintenance procedures are begun. Family and participants are educated in and trained to use self control strategies that encourage and maintain fluency within their day to day home, school and working schedules. Appointments for the participants and their family to meet the clinician regarding maintenance of fluency skills are made at regular intervals over the 12 month period following Phase 2. Table 3 presents a protocol for an intensive Smooth Speech Program for older children and adolescents.

In a controlled clinical trial format, Smooth Speech has been shown to be an efficacious treatment for older children and adolescents aged 8 to 15 years (Craig et al. 1996; Hancock et al. 1998). Craig et al. (1996) investigated the efficacy of two different Smooth Speech protocols. One consisted of an intensive one-week program in which adolescents were trained to use Smooth Speech over 6–7 days. A group of up to 5 adolescents received instruction in Smooth Speech in formal sessions from 9.30 am to 4 pm involving group conversations in which they practiced their fluency at gradually increasing speeds. They began speaking with Smooth Speech at very slow speeds (around 50 SPM) and they increased this speed in jumps of 5 to 10 SPM as they progressed through the week. By the end of the week they were speaking at speeds of at least 180 SPM and fluency skills were strengthened by performing assignments outside the clinic. Follow-up occurred on a monthly basis for three months, then three monthly up to one year. The other form of Smooth Speech involved a less intensive format in which the participants' family took a more dominant role in conducting the conversation sessions and assignments. Treatment was conducted once a week over 5 weeks, from 9.30 am to 4 pm, with follow-ups monthly for three months, then three monthly up to one year. When the clinician was confident that the parents had successfully learned the Smooth Speech techniques, parents were encouraged to take over the role of therapist, with the clinician supervising. After initially working in structured group conversation sessions, transfer assignments outside the clinic were conducted (eg. talking to shop assistant). The rationale of this therapy was to teach parents to be therapists so that the majority of treatment would take place at home. Standard protocols for the two Smooth Speech treatments were developed and clinicians involved in the treatment were experienced with the protocols.

The purpose of the clinical trial was to evaluate the effectiveness of variations in Smooth Speech stuttering programs that could be applied in the community with older children and adolescents. The results suggest that Smooth Speech could be used in clinics in either an intensive one week program with follow up or a less intensive one day a week program stretched over a five week period with follow-up. The study involved sufficient numbers of subjects to provide convincing evidence for efficacy. That is, 27 participated in the intensive Smooth Speech program and 25 children/adolescents participated in the less intensive home-based Smooth Speech program. Additionally, 20 stuttering children were conscripted into the study as a no treatment control group. The children in the three groups were of a similar age (mean age was around 10 to 11 years) and the ratio of males to females in each group was about 4 to 1. Severity of stuttering was assessed by the percentage of syllables that they stuttered when they were talking in a conversation (%SS) and by their rate of speech in the conversation (SPM).

Children were assessed in three contexts: (a) in a clinic conversation talking to the clinician; (b) on the clinic telephone talking to a family member or friend, and (c) talking to a family member or friend in the home environment. To control for language ability, only those who were progressing normally in their speech for their age were included in the program. Most children began stuttering early (average age 4.7 years, 2 to 11 years range) and they had been stuttering most of their life (average of 6 years). About two-thirds of the children had received therapy prior to the study, though in most cases the intervention had been carried out several years before. No children had received therapy in the three months prior to the Smooth Speech treatment. For ethical reasons, the no-treatment control children were offered therapy after waiting three months.

Both forms of Smooth Speech were found to be very effective techniques for reducing stuttering for older children and adolescents (Craig et al. 1996; Hancock et al. 1998). Typically, up to 95% of stuttering will be removed after a Smooth Speech program and around 80% improvement will be maintained into the long-term. Figure 1 shows the short and long-term fluency outcomes (%SS) of the three groups. Substantial reduction in stuttering frequency occurred in the two Smooth Speech groups compared to the control group. Stuttering severity levels during a conversation at home, in the clinic or during a telephone call were reduced by at least 85% immediately after treatment. Although stuttering severity scores increased slightly at the 3-month, one-year and a mean five-years after treatment, these increases were not substantial. In contrast, the stuttering

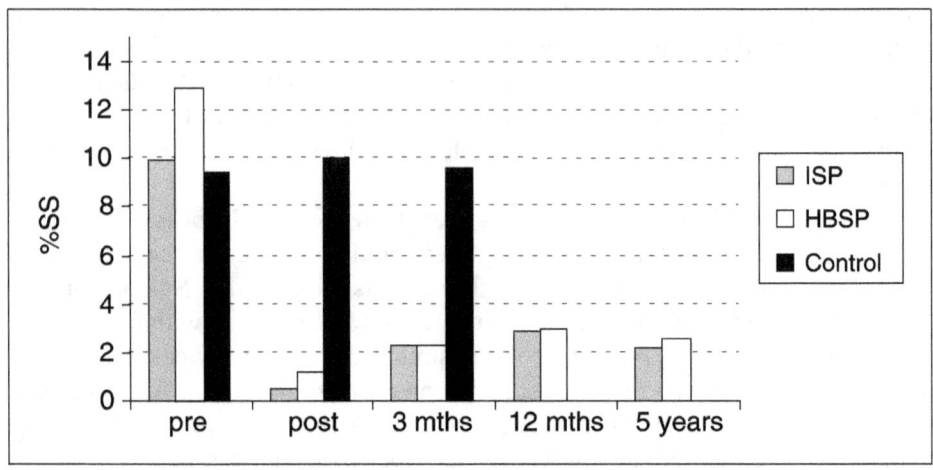

Figure 1. Mean frequency of stuttering (%SS) during a conversation for the two Smooth Speech groups and the control group up to a mean 5 years after treatment began for the treatment groups and up to three months for the control group. After 3 months all control children were withdrawn from the study and offered best treatment. ISP is the Intensive Smooth Speech group and HBSP is the home based Smooth Speech group

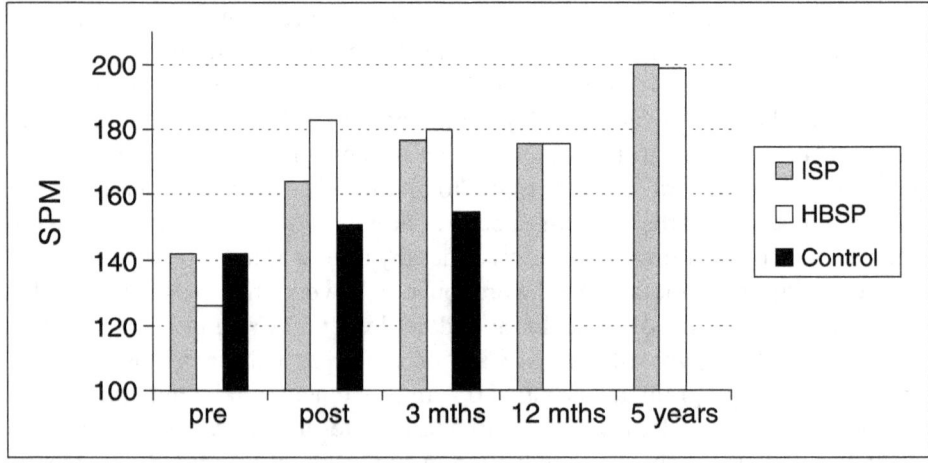

Figure 2. Mean speech rate (SPM) during a conversation for the two Smooth Speech groups and the control group up to a mean 5 years after treatment began for the treatment groups and up to three months for the control group. After 3 months all control children were withdrawn from the study and offered best treatment. ISP is the Intensive Smooth Speech group and HBSP is the home based Smooth Speech group

severity for the stuttering age-matched control children actually remained elevated for the three months in which they participated in the study. Figure 2 shows the mean speech rate outcomes for the treatment and control groups. It is clear that speech rate was increased in the two treatment groups in comparison to the control group. This suggests that the participants in the Smooth Speech programs were speaking faster (with less stuttering) that the untreated controls.

Table 4 shows that Smooth Speech substantially improved the ability to speak fluently in the two treatment groups. Directly after treatment, participants had improved by at least 90% in their capability to talk fluently in different social contexts. While improvements have reduced marginally over time, after 12 months

Table 4. Showing mean % improvement scores for frequency of stuttering (%SS) for the two Smooth Speech treatments

	Intensive Smooth Speech	Home Based Smooth Speech treatment
Pre-treatment to post treatment		
% improvement in stuttering during conversation	95	90
% improvement in stuttering during telephone	94	83
% improvement in stuttering during a conversation at home	–	80
Pre-treatment to 1 year after		
% improvement in stuttering during a conversation	72	76
% improvement during a telephone conversation	72	61
% improvement during a conversation at home	–	72
Pre treatment to a mean 5 years after		
% improvement in stuttering during a conversation	76	80
% improvement during a telephone conversation	76	71
% improvement during a conversation at home	–	79

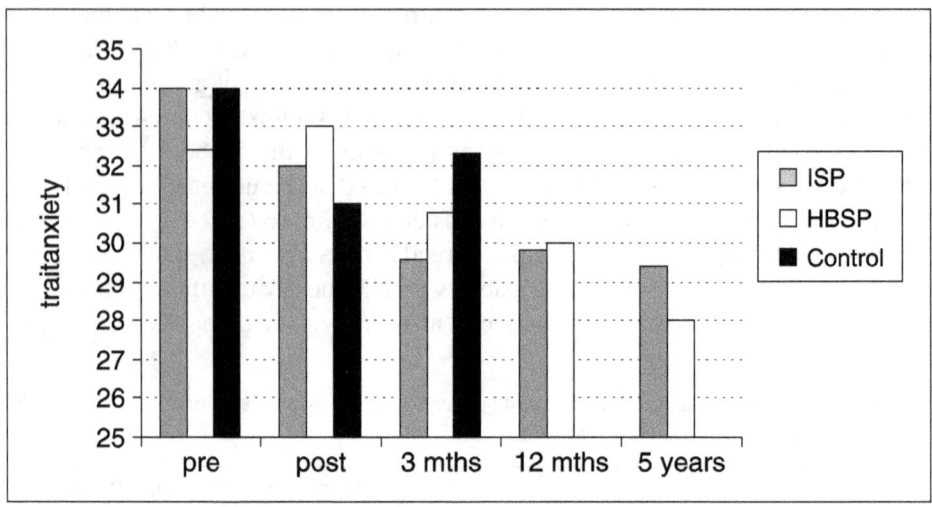

Figure 3. Mean trait anxiety scores for the two Smooth Speech groups and the control group up to a mean 5 years after treatment began for the treatment groups and up to three months for the control group. After 3 months all control children were withdrawn from the study and offered best treatment. ISP is the Intensive Smooth Speech group and HBSP is the home based Smooth Speech group

and five years, the majority of children improved their fluency by at least 70% as a result of treatment. These results are very encouraging as most subjects were able to maintain their speech gains made immediately after treatment. Furthermore, the majority of children were speaking more quickly (ranging from 180 to 200 SPM) and were considered to be speaking acceptably and naturally by themselves, the clinician and the parents of the children (Hancock et al. 1998). Another positive aspect of this study was not only that treatment for older children works, but that the different Smooth Speech formats were found to be efficacious. This allows clinicians to vary confidently the way they may employ a fluency shaping program, and is particularly advantageous when one considers individual differences in client preferences for particular treatment formats. Not receiving one's preferred treatment may negatively influence motivation and thereby limit outcome.

Figure 3 shows that the levels of trait (chronic) anxiety in the two treatment groups decreased in the long-term in comparison to anxiety levels in the control group. This may suggest that treated adolescents worry less about themselves (especially their speech) than PWS who are not treated. These findings are similar to others who have found that stuttering treatments like fluency shaping are psychologically beneficial (Blood 1995; Blood et al. 2001). The results of this clinical trial strongly suggest that the anxiety levels of older children and young adolescents who receive effective treatment will remain lower in anxiety than the norms for their age. Certainly, the participants' communication fears were also found to decrease with Smooth Speech treatment, and this suggests that the treated children were more willing to communicate verbally, providing further evidence of their enhanced psychological well-being. Over all, the results of this controlled trial were very pleasing.

Other independent researchers have also found similar fluency shaping techniques to be effective at reducing stuttering in the short and long term in older children and adolescents (Boberg and Kully 1994). The Fluency Rules Program developed by Runyan and Runyan (1986) employs many of the Smooth Speech fluency shaping components and they (Runyan and Runyan 1993) reported that nine of 12 (75 %) school-age children significantly improved their fluency into the long-term. Kully and Boberg (1991) combined fluency shaping (slow speech) and stuttering modification (pullouts; easy versus hard stuttering) approaches in 10 subjects and found eight of the 10 children who stuttered had near zero stuttering immediately post treatment. A follow-up of eight children suggested these gains were mostly maintained at the 8–18 month follow-up

8. Specialized fluency shaping treatments for adults

A number of adult treatments have been developed over the years, and again, many overlap in terms of the techniques and strategies (Azrin and Nunn 1974; Azrin et al. 1979; Boberg and Kully 1994; Conture 2001; Craig, Feyer, and Andrews 1987; Gregory 2003; Ladouceur et al. 1981; Saint-Laurent and Ladouceur 1987). Gregory (2003) suggests that treatment for adults should consist of a mixture of techniques including attitude therapy (exploring the perceptions of the PWS towards their speech and stuttering), reducing tension, learning new speech styles that are smoother and less tense, increased air flow, resisting time pressure when speaking (learning to delay), voluntary stuttering, cancellations and pull-outs (stopping a stutter when it occurs by pulling out of the block), and time out procedures. He suggests that treatment also include transfer, problem solving techniques and follow-up.

The regulated-breathing technique (Azrin and Nunn 1974) has been investigated a number of times using a randomized clinical trial design. The regulated-breathing therapy employs the airflow techniques utilized in Smooth Speech treatment. That is, it requires the PWS to breathe smoothly and deeply, with regular pauses, while relaxing speech and chest muscles. It is also integrated into a behavioral regimen that includes relaxation techniques, self-correction and self control strategies, social support and encourages long-term maintenance by employing transfer and generalization techniques. Controlled studies with adult PWS have shown immediate reductions in stuttering of around 90 % compared to an active placebo control (Azrin et al. 1979). Ladouceur et al. (1981) and Saint-Laurent and Ladouceur (1987) have also found significant reduction in stuttering in the regulated breathing subjects compared to stuttering controls. Peins, McGough and Lee (1972) compared Van Riper techniques emphasizing anxiety reduction and avoidance reduction strategies with a structured speaking task treatment involving slowed and smooth speech. Both groups were found to be significantly more fluent than a no treatment control.

Evesham and Fransella (1985) studied the efficacy of a fluency shaping technique with two types of maintenance strategies. One group received more of the same, while another received psychological therapy called construct therapy. While both groups were found to have significantly reduced stuttering, the group that received the construct therapy was more likely to maintain treatment gains into the long-term. Smooth Speech has also been found to be very effective for adults (Craig, Feyer, and Andrews 1987; Boberg and Kully 1994). However, the protocol used is more intensive than that presented for adolescents. For example, a longer time may be needed to teach the PWS the fluency skills, and conversation sessions may be run for a whole week rather than say 3 days (Craig et al. 1987). One long-term study that reports the long-term outcome of a fluency shaping technique on 17 adults and 25 adolescents was conducted by Boberg and Kully (1994). Results from surprise phone calls to subjects indicated that 69% maintained a "satisfactory" level of post-treatment fluency after 12 to 24 months.

9. Relapse management following treatment for stuttering

Relapse (i.e. the return of stuttering following successful treatment) and maintaining treatment gains continues to be a significant clinical problem in stuttering (Craig 1998b). From adult research, it is estimated that around a third of treated adults experience difficulties in maintaining fluency in the long-term (Craig 1998b; Craig et al. 1987). Self-report studies suggest that most subjects experience cycles of relapse and fluency (Craig and Calver 1991; Craig and Hancock 1995). In these studies almost all subjects who believed their fluency had decayed also believed they had recovered their fluency through various strategies such as practice of fluency skills, participation in self-help groups, and seeking additional professional help (Craig and Calver 1991; Craig and Hancock 1995). Even less research has been conducted on maintenance and relapse in children and adolescents. However, Craig, Hancock and Cobbin, (2002) and Hancock and Craig (2002) reported data on the benefit of anti-relapse strategies in older children adolescents. These two studies suggest it is essential that structured maintenance strategies be incorporated into the treatment protocol.

Results from the abovementioned clinical trial suggest that relapse or failure to maintain fluency gains occurs in about 25 to 30% of older children and adolescents. For example, parental feedback showed that up to 25% of the treated children were not acceptably fluent in the long-term. Results from the objective behavioral measures such as %SS and SPM also suggests that about 25 to 30% of children had regressed back to unacceptable levels of stuttering after an average five years following treatment (Hancock et al. 1998). While less attention has been given to relapse, a number of factors are believed to contribute to the relapse process. For instance, those with a greater severity of stuttering (eg., higher levels of %SS and low SPM) have a raised chance of relapse (return of stuttering following improvement) in the long-term (Craig 1998b). Relapse management programs or booster programs have now been shown to improve fluency in those who relapse severely or slightly in the long-term following their initial treatment (Craig et al. 2002; Hancock and Craig 2002). We conducted a further study that was designed to investigate the effectiveness of offering an anti-relapse booster treatment for 12 older children/adolescents who had participated in the Smooth Speech controlled trial, and who were experiencing difficulties maintaining their fluency gains following their initial treatment. In addition to strategies such as Smooth Speech, this booster program included strategies known to be effective in reducing risks of relapse (Craig 1998b).

Components included: (a) Smooth Speech skills (b) EMG Feedback skills (c) self-management skills that emphasized the importance of self-responsibility, self-evaluation, self-effort and motivation in the achievement of self-set goals. (d) Cognitive techniques that included positive self-talk aimed at enhancing levels of perceived control over their stuttering (eg., "I am the master of my speech"). Perceived control or self-mastery has been found to be related to long-term outcome in a number of areas as well as stuttering (Craig 1998b). (e) Relaxation exercises which involved simple muscle and thematic relaxation techniques (e.g., breath awareness, isometric exercise, imaging a peaceful scene) designed to enhance their control of muscle tension and anxiety. Discussions were held regarding the need to use the relaxation exercises in order to think clearly and focus on their fluency skills. It was also pointed out that relaxation could be used in combination with their thought control techniques in order to cope with difficult speaking situations.

The results of this study found significant reductions in stuttering (%SS), increases in speech rate (SPM) and speech naturalness after two years. The outcomes for the 12 subjects following the booster treatment were compared with their outcomes from the initial treatment program completed about five years previously. While outcomes were similar up to 12 months after treatment, the booster treatment was associated with significantly reduced %SS and increased SPM two years after the booster program compared with the results following their initial treatment. The efficacy of the booster program is shown in Figure 4 where changes in stuttering resulting from initial treatment are compared to changes in stuttering resulting from the booster treatment.

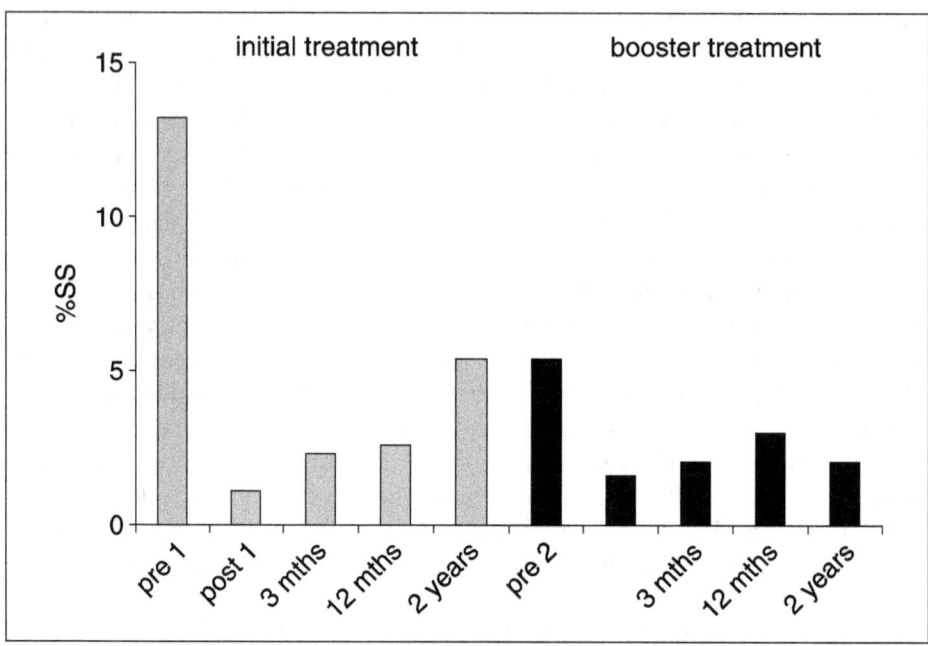

Figure 4. shows the average frequency of stuttering (%SS) for 12 older children in a conversation in the clinic over a period of around seven years as a function of initial treatment for their stuttering and anti-relapse booster treatment. The pre-treatment measure (pre 2) for the booster treatment represents the average 5 year assessment following initial treatment.

10. Conclusions and implications for future treatment

There is now substantial, scientifically reliable information available from clinical trial research with young children, older children, adolescents and adults suggesting that stuttering can be effectively treated using a variety of different treatments. Adult treatments based upon similar treatment strategies to those used for adolescents have also been shown to be effective (Craig et al. 1987). Efficacy was demonstrated by the following changes in the children: (i) reduced stuttering down to acceptable levels, (ii) substantially improved fluency (iii) natural speech at normal speech rate levels, (iv) decreased anxiety and communication related fears, and (v) improved feelings of self-control. Furthermore, this improvement was in evidence in the home, on the telephone and in the clinic. These gains were maintained into the long-term (after at least 2 to 6 years). Given this evidence, there is no doubt that cognitive-behavioural treatment that contains fluency enhancing strategies (eg. Smooth Speech and EMG Feedback therapies) are effective at reducing stuttering for the majority of older children who stutter.

In addition to this, our research suggests that a combination of these treatments has added advantages for older children who stutter (Craig et al. 2002; Hancock and Craig 2002). The evidence strongly suggests that efficacy will be enhanced over either treatment (Smooth Speech or EMG Feedback) offered alone in a behavioural regimen. A combination approach could especially be used for (i) children who experience difficulties in maintaining their fluency following their initial treatment as in the Hancock and Craig (2002) study, or (ii) those children who are expected to be a challenge for standard treatments, for instance, those who have relapsed badly as in the Craig et al. (2002) study. This combination of Smooth Speech and EMG Feedback presented within a cognitive behavioural regimen was shown to be effective in lowering relapse rates in children who had serious difficulties maintaining their fluency skills following their initial treatment. Given the neuronal plasticity of the developing brain in older children, there is a window of opportunity for clinicians to become involved in the management of stuttering using pedigree treatments. Based upon research results, the vast majority of children receiving Smooth Speech and EMG Feedback treatments delivered in a behaviour therapy regimen should improve their stuttering in the long-term by at least 70 to 80%. For these children, stuttering may never be a significant problem ever again.

Acknowledgement. This chapter was written with the support from the National Health and Medical Research Council in Australia, from the Big Brother Movement of Australia, an Australian Rotary Health Research Grant, the Australian Research Council, and from the University of Technology, Sydney. Thanks also to Dr Karen Hancock, other co-researchers and of course, to the many children who we have been able to treat for stuttering over the years.

References

American Psychiatric Association
    1994   *Diagnostic and statistical manual of mental disorders. DSM IV.* Washington, DC: American Psychiatric Association Publication.
Andrews, G. and A. R. Craig
    1988   Prediction of outcome after treatment for stuttering. *British Journal of Psychiatry* 153: 236–240.
Andrews, G., A. Craig, A. M. Feyer, S. Hoddinott, P. Howie, and M. Neilson
    1983   A review of research findings and theories circa 1982. *Journal of Speech and Hearing Disorders* 48: 226–246.
Andrews, G., A. Morris-Yates, P. Howie, and N. Martin
    1991   Genetic factors in stuttering confirmed. *Archives General Psychiatry* 48: 1034–1035.

Azrin, N. and R. Nunn
  1974   A rapid method of eliminating stuttering by a regulated breathing approach. *Behavior Research and Therapy* 12: 279–286.
Azrin, N., R. Nunn, and S. Frantz
  1979   Comparison of regulated-breathing verses abbreviated desensitization on reported stuttering episodes. *Journal of Speech and Hearing Disorders* 44: 331–339.
Baker, L. and D. P. Cantwell
  1987   A prospective psychiatric follow-up of children with speech/language disorders. *Journal of American Academy of Child and Adolescent Psychiatry* 26: 546–553.
Beitchman, J. H., E. R. Brownlie, A. Inglis, J. Wild, B. Ferguson, and D. Schachter
  1996   Seven-year follow-up of speech/language impaired and control children: psychiatric outcome. *Journal of Child Psychology and Psychiatry* 37: 961–970.
Beitchman, J. H., B. Wilson, C. J. Johnson, L. Atkinson, A. Young, E. Adlar, M. Escobar, and L. Douglas
  2001   Fourteen-year follow-up of speech/language impaired and control children: psychiatric outcome. *Journal of American Academy of Child and Adolescent Psychiatry* 40: 75–82.
Blood, G. W.
  1995   A behavioral-cognitive therapy program for adults who stutter: Computers and counseling. *Journal of Communication Disorders* 28: 165–180.
Blood, G. W., I. Blood, M. Bennett, G. Tellis, and R. Gabel
  2001   Communication apprehension and self-perceived communication competence in adolescents who stutter. *Journal of Fluency Disorders* 26: 161–178.
Bloodstein, O.
  1960   The development of stuttering: II. Development phases. *Journal of Speech and Hearing Disorders* 25: 366–376.
Bloodstein, O.
  1995   *A Handbook on Stuttering (5th ed.)*, San Diego: Singular Publishing Group.
Boberg, E. and D. Kully
  1994   Long-term results of an intensive treatment program for adults and adolescents who stutter. *Journal of Speech and Hearing Research* 37: 1050–1059.
Cantwell, D. P. and L. Baker
  1977   Psychiatric disorder in children with speech and language retardation. *Archives of General Psychiatry* 34: 583–591.
Conture, E.
  2001   *Stuttering. Its Nature, Diagnosis and Treatment.* Boston: Allyn and Bacon.
Conture, E.
  1990   *Stuttering (2nd Ed.).* Englewood Cliffs, NJ: Prentice Hall.
Cooper, J. A.
  1990   *Research needs in stuttering: roadblocks and future directions.* ASHA Report, no.18. Rockville, Maryland: ASHA.
Costello, J.
  1983   Current behavioral treatments for children. In: D. Prins and R. Ingham (eds.), *Treatment of Stuttering in Early Childhood: Methods and Issues.* San Diego: College-Hill.

Craig, A. R.
1990   An investigation into the relationship between anxiety and stuttering. *Journal of Speech and Hearing Disorders* 55: 290–294.
Craig, A.
1998a   *Treating Stuttering in Older Children, Adolescents and Adults: A guide for clinicians, parents and those who stutter.* Gosford: Feedback Publications Press.
Craig, A.
1998b   Relapse following treatment for stuttering: A critical review and correlative data. *Journal of Fluency Disorders* 23: 1–30.
Craig, A.
2000   The developmental nature and effective treatment of stuttering in children and adolescents. *Journal of Developmental and Physical Disabilities* 12: 173–186.
Craig, A. R. and P. Calver
1991   Following up on treated stutterers. Studies of perceptions of fluency and job status. *Journal of Speech and Hearing Research* 34: 279–284.
Craig, A., E. Chang, and K. Hancock
1992   Treatment success for children who stutter: A critical review. *Australian Journal of Human Communication Disorders* 20: 81–92.
Craig, A. and P. Cleary
1982   Reduction of stuttering by young male stutterers using EMG feedback. *Biofeedback and Self-Regulation* 7: 241–255.
Craig, A., A. M. Feyer, and G. Andrews
1987   An overview of a behavioural treatment for stuttering. *Australian Psychologist* 22: 53–62.
Craig, A. R., J. Franklin, and G. Andrews
1984   A scale to measure locus of control of behaviour. *British Journal of Medical Psychology* 57: 173–180.
Craig, A. R. and K. M. Hancock
1995   Self reported factors related to relapse following treatment for stuttering. *Australian Journal of Human Communication Disorders* 23: 48–60.
Craig, A. and K. Hancock
1996   Anxiety in children and young adolescents who stutter. *Australian Journal of Human Communication Disorders* 24: 29–38.
Craig. A., K. Hancock, E. Chang, C. McCready, A. Shepley, A. McCaul, D. Costello, S. Harding, R. Kehren, C. Masel, and K. Reilly
1996   A controlled clinical trial for stuttering in persons aged 9 to 14 years. *Journal of Speech and Hearing Research* 39: 808–826.
Craig, A., K. Hancock, and D. Cobbin
2002   Managing adolescents who relapse following treatment for stuttering. *Journal of Speech Language and Hearing: Asia Pacific* 7: 79–91.
Craig, A., K. Hancock, Y. Tran, M. Craig, and K. Peters
2002   Epidemiology of stuttering in the community across the entire lifespan. *Journal of Speech, Language and Hearing Research* 45: 1097–1105.
Craig, A., K. Hancock, Y. Tran, and M. Craig
2003   Anxiety Levels In People Who Stutter: A randomised population study *Journal of Speech, Language, and Hearing Research* 46: 1197–1206.

Craig, A. and Y. Tran
  2006   Chronic and social anxiety in people who stutter. *Advances in Psychiatric Treatment* 12: 63–68.
Evesham, M. and F. Fransella
  1985   Stuttering relapse: the effects of a combined speech and psychological reconstruction programme. *British Journal of Disorders of Communication* 20: 237–248.
Fox, P. T., R. J. Ingham, J. C. Ingham, T. B. Hirsch, J. H. Downs, C. Martin, P. Jerabek, T. Glass, and J. L. Lancaster
  1996   A PET study of the neural systems of stuttering. *Nature* 382: 158–162.
Gottwald, S. and C. Starkweather
  1999   Stuttering prevention and early intervention: A multiprocess approach. In: M. Onslow and A. Packman (eds.), *The Handbook of Early Stuttering Intervention*. San Diego: Singular Publishing Group.
Gregory, H.
  1999   Developmental intervention: Differential strategies. In: M. Onslow and A. Packman (eds.), *The Handbook of Early Stuttering Intervention*. San Diego: Singular Publishing Group.
Gregory, H.
  2003   *Stuttering Therapy. Rationale and Procedures*. Boston: Pearson Education, Inc.
Hancock, K. and A. Craig
  2002   The effectiveness of re-treatment for adolescents who stutter. *Journal of Speech, Language, Hearing. Asia-Pacific* 7: 138–156.
Hancock, K. and A. Craig
  2002   The effectiveness of re-treatment for adolescents who stutter. *Journal of Speech, Language, Hearing. Asia-Pacific* 7: 138–156.
Hancock, K., A. Craig, K. Campbell, D. Costello, G. Gilmore, A. McCaul, and C. McCready
  1998   Two to six year controlled trial stuttering outcomes for children and adolescents *Journal of Speech and Hearing Research* 41: 1242–1252.
Harris, V., M. Onslow, A. Packman, E. Harrison, and R. Menzies
  2002   An experimental investigation of the impact of the Lidcombe Program on early stuttering. *Journal of Fluency Disorders* 27: 203–214.
Harrison, E. and M. Onslow
  1999   Early intervention for stuttering: The Lidcombe Program. In: R. F. Curlee (ed.), *Stuttering and Related Dsorders of Fluency*. New York, Thieme Medical Publishers.
Hulstijn W., H. Peters, and P. van Lieshout
  1997   *Speech Production: Motor Control, Brain Research and Fluency Disorders*. Amsterdam: Elsevier Press.
Ingham, J. and G. Riley
  1998   Guidelines for documentation of treatment efficacy for young children who stutter. *Journal of Speech, Language, and Hearing Research* 41: 753–770.
Jones, M., M. Onslow, A. Packman, S. Williams, T. Ormond, I. Aschwarz, and V. Gebski
  2005   A randomised controlled trial of the Lidcombe Program for early stuttering. *British Medical Journal* 331: 659–664.

Kully, D. and E. Boberg
    1991   Therapy for school-age children. In: E. Perkins (ed.), *Seminars in Speech and Language: Stuttering: Challenges of Therapy.* New York: Thieme Medical Publishers.

Ladouceur, R., L. Boudreau, and S. Theberge
    1981   Awareness training and regulated-breathing method in modification of stuttering. *Perceptual & Motor Skills* 53: 187–194.

Lincoln, M., M. Onslow, L. Wilson, and C. Lewis
    1996   A clinical trial of an operant treatment for school-age stuttering children. *American Journal of Speech-Language Pathology* 5: 73–85.

Menzies, R. G., M. Onslow, and A. Packman
    1999   Anxiety and stuttering: exploring a complex relationship. *American Journal of Speech-Language Pathology* 8: 3–10.

Moscicki, E. K.
    1993   Fundamental methodological considerations in controlled clinical trials. *Journal of Fluency Disorders* 18: 183–196.

Onslow, M., C. Andrews, and M. Lincoln
    1994   A control/experimental trial of an operant treatment for early stuttering. *Journal of Speech and Hearing Research* 37: 1244–1259.

Onslow, M., A. Packman, and E. Harrison
    2003   The Lidcombe Program of Early Stuttering Intervention: A Clinician's Guide. Austin, Texas: Pro-Ed.

Peins, M., W. McGough, and B. Lee
    1972   Evaluation of tape-recorded method of stuttering therapy: improvement in speaking task. *Journal of Speech and Hearing Research* 15: 364–371.

Riley, J. and G. Riley
    1999   Speech motor training. In: M. Onslow and A. Packman (eds.), *The Handbook of Early Stuttering Intervention.* San Diego: Singular Publishing Group.

Runyan, C. and S. Runyan
    1986   A fluency rules program for young children in the public schools. *Language, Speech and Hearing Services in the Schools* 17: 276–285.

Runyan, C. M. and S. E. Runyan
    1993   Therapy for school-age stutterers: An update on the fluency rules program. In: R. F. Curlee (ed.), *Stuttering and Related Disorders of Fluency.* New York: Thieme Medical Publishers.

Runyan, C. and S. Runyan
    1999   The fluency rules program. In: M. Onslow and A. Packman (eds.), *The Handbook of Early Stuttering Intervention.* San Diego: Singular Publishing Group.

Rustin, L., W. Botterill, and E. Kelman
    1997   *Assessment and Therapy for Young Dysfluent Children: Family Interaction.* London: Whurr Publishers.

Rustin, L., F. Cook, W. Botterill, C. Hughes, and E. Kelman
    2001   *Stammering: A Practical Guide for Teachers and Other Professionals.* London: David Fulton.

Ryan, B. P.
    1971   Operant procedures applied to stuttering therapy for children. *Journal of Speech and Hearing Disorders* 36: 264–280.

Ryan, B. and B. Van Kirk Ryan
   1983   Programmed stuttering therapy for children: A comparison of four establishment programmes. *Journal of Fluency Disorders* 8: 291–321.

Ryan, B. and B. Van Kirk Ryan
   1995   Programmed stuttering therapy treatment for children: Comparison of two establishment programmes through transfer, maintenance, and follow-up. *Journal of Speech and Hearing Research* 38: 61–75.

Ryan, B. and B. Ryan
   1999   The Monterey fluency program. In: M. Onslow and A. Packman (eds.), *The Handbook of Early Stuttering Intervention*. San Diego: Singular Publishing Group.

Saint-Laurent, L. and R. Ladouceur
   1987   Massed versus distributed application of the regulated-breathing method for stutterers and its long-term effect. *Behavior Therapy* 18: 38–50.

Smith, A. and E. Kelly
   1997   Stuttering: A dynamic, multifactorial model. In: R. F. Curlee and M. Siegal (eds.), *Nature and Treatment of Stuttering. New Directions,* 204–217. MA: Allyn & Bacon.

Starkweather, C. W., S. R. Gottwald, and M. H. Halfond
   1990   *Stuttering Prevention: A Clinical Method.* Englewood Cliffs, NJ: Prentice-Hall.

Yairi, E. and N. Ambrose
   1992   A longitudinal study of stuttering in children: A preliminary report. *Journal of Speech and Hearing Research* 35: 755–760.

Yairi, E., N. Ambrose, and N. Cox
   1996   Genetics of stuttering: A critical review. *Journal of Speech and Hearing Research* 39: 771–784.

Biographical notes

Mike Allen (PhD, Michigan State University) is Professor and Director of Graduate Studies in the Department of Communication at University of Wisconsin-Milwaukee. His work primarily involves the application of meta-analysis to issues in social influence and he has published more than 100 meta-analyses including those dealing with issues of the treatment and impact of communication anxiety. He is the current editor of *Communication Monographs*.

John Bourhis (PhD, University of Minnesota) is a Professor in the Department of Communication at the Missouri State University where he is also Director of Distance Instruction. His research has focused on the impact of communication anxiety and distance learning. His research has been published in such journals as *Communication Education, American Journal of Distance Education,* and *Communication Quarterly*.

Virginia Berninger (PhD Psychology, Johns Hopkins University) has been a Professor of Educational Psychology at the University of Washington since 1986. She has been Principal Investigator on NICHD-funded research on (a) typical writing and reading development including writing-reading connections and their connections to oral language and (b) a multidisciplinary approach to reading and writing disabilities. She teaches courses on the application of psycholinguistics to assessment, consultation, and intervention for reading and writing problems.

Nancy Burrell (PhD, Michigan State University) is Professor and Chair in the Department of Communication at University of Wisconsin-Milwaukee where she also is Director of the Campus Mediation Center. Her published work focuses on analyzing the discourse of conflict in interpersonal and organizational settings and has been published in such journals as *Human Communication Research, Communication Research,* and *Conflict Resolution Quarterly*. She has been recognized as the Dick Ringler Distinguished Peace Educator for her work with the public schools.

Ashley Craig (PhD) is currently a Professor in the Rehabilitation Studies Unit, Northern Clinical School, Faculty of Medicine, The University of Sydney. He was formerly Professor of Behavioural Sciences in the Department of Medical and Molecular Biosciences, University of Technology, Sydney (1999–2007). He is the Editor-in-Chief of the Journal of Fluency Disorders, the only journal in the world devoted to fluency disorder. Ashley Craig has a long history of research and clinical experience in the field of stuttering. He has completed controlled clinical trials in adolescent stuttering, completed randomized epidemiological studies in stuttering, and is recently investigating the association of stuttering with brain activity, anxiety and quality of life. He has published over 150 refereed papers and book chapters, and has been involved in raising the profile of stuttering in his work with the Australian Stuttering Foundation.

Maureen Ehrensberger-Dow (PhD) is Professor of English in the Institute of Translation and Interpreting IUED of the Zürich University of Applied Sciences (ZHAW). Her main areas of research and teaching are multilingualism, English in Switzerland, technical writing, and translation processes.

Vivian Gramley (PhD, Bielefeld University) was a member of the Graduate Program *Task-oriented Communication* at Bielefeld University. From 2003–2005 she was research assistant at RWTH Aachen in a project on e-learning for the deaf. Since 2005 she has been a tenured lecturer at Bielefeld University for Applied Linguistics and English Language Studies.

Martina Hielscher-Fastabend (PhD, Bielefeld University) (Dipl. Psych, Clinical Linguist) studied Psychology, Mathmatics and Linguistics at Bielefeld University. She worked in projects on reading processes in Cognitive Psychology. After some years of clinical work she took up a position in Clinical Linguistics at Bielefeld University in 1994. She finished her postdoctoral thesis on *Neuropsychological Aspects of Language and Emotion* in 2001. Together with Gert Rickheit she established the curriculum for a consecutive Bachelor and Master programme of Academic Speech and Language Therapy in Bielefeld. She has been an active member in the German Association of Applied Linguistics (GAL) since 1996 for the section Clinical Linguistics. In addition she has been vice-chairwoman of the Bundesverband Klinische Linguistik (BKL) since 2003 and in the German Association of Academic Speech and Language Therapy (Deutscher Bundesverband akademischer Sprachtherapeuten dbs) since 2007.

Thomas Holtgraves (PhD) is professor of Psychological Science at Ball State University. His research focuses on the social and cognitive factors involved in the production and comprehension of language. He is the author of *Language as Social Action: Social Psychology and Language Use*.

Eva-Maria Jakobs (PhD, University of Saarland) is Professor of Text Linguistics of the Institute of Linguistics and Communication Science at RWTH Aachen. Her main areas of research and teaching are text linguistics, professional communication, text production research, technical communication, electronic media, and communicative usability.

Annette Lepschy (PhD, University of Duisburg)) studied German Literature, Catholic Theology, Education and Speech Education (Sprecherziehung) at the Universities of Duisburg and Münster. She is Assistant Professor at the Centrum for Rhetorik, Kommunikation und Theaterpraxis of the University of Münster. She is communication trainer and managing partner of Lepschy & Lepschy GbR Personnel and Organisation Development.

Ralph Axel Müller received his PhD in Neurolinguistics from the University of Frankfurt am Main (Germany) and is now a Professor of Psychology at San Diego State University and Associate Research Scientist at the University of California, San Diego (USA). His research has focused on the brain bases of language development and language impairment, with specific attention to autism, using functional brain imaging techniques.

William Nagy received his PhD in linguistics from the University of California, San Diego. He spent 18 years at the Centre for the Study of Reading at the University of Illinois, Urbana-Champaign, and since 1996 has been a Professor of Education at Seattle Pacific University, where he teaches graduate courses in reading and research methods. His research interests include vocabulary acquisition and instruction, the role of vocabulary knowledge in first- and second-language reading, and the contributions of metalinguistic awareness to learning to read. His published work has examined incidental word learning from context during reading; the acquisition of derivational morphology, bilingual students' recognition of cognate relationships between English and Spanish, and the role of morphological awareness in learning to read in English and in Chinese.

Pekka Niemi (PhD) is currently Professor of Psychology at University of Turku, Finland. He is a founding member of Centre for Learning Research at the same university (1986). From 1988 to 1997 he was professor at Abo Akademi University (the Swedish University of Finland) and in 2000–2006 a part-time professor of special education at University of Stavanger, Norway. Presently he conducts his research within the Finnish Centre of Excellence in Learning and Motivation Research (Academy of Finland, 2006–2011). Research interests include cognitive processes in general and reading acquisition and its difficulties in particular.

Erica Palmer received her PhD in Psychology from Washington University in St. Louis, Missouri. In her graduate work she sought to investigate the neural correlates of single word reading by using functional magnetic resonance imaging to help evaluate cognitive models of lexical processing. Her work has been published in journals such as *NeuroImage* and *Scientific Studies of*

Reading. She continued research using a cognitive neuroscience approach to the study of language during postdoctoral fellowships at Washington University and San Diego State University. She now works as a cognitive scientist for Pacific Science and Engineering Group in San Diego, California, where she applies her background in cognitive psychology and psychophysiology to issues in human performance, training, and education.

Daniel Perrin (PhD) is Professor of Media Linguistics and Director of the Institute of Applied Media Studies IAM of the Zurich University of Applied Sciences (ZHAW). His main areas of research and teaching are media linguistics, text linguistics, methodology of applied linguistics, text production research, and professional communication.

Clair Pond is a postgraduate student in the Department of Psychology, University of Sheffield, UK. Her research is supported by the UK Economic and Social Research Council. It focuses on cognitive processes in the development of conversational understanding. She is particularly concerned with the role of executive functioning in how children interpret meaning in discourse.

Elke Prestin received her PhD in Linguistics from Bielefeld University. Her research focuses both on psycholinguistic processes and pragmatic aspects of language use. Integrating quantitative and qualitative research methods, she currently works on an extensive study on coordination in computer-mediated communication.

Nancy M. Puccinelli (Upton) is Assistant Professor of Marketing at Northeastern University, Boston, Massachusetts, USA. After receiving her PhD in social psychology from Harvard University, she completed a post-doctoral fellowship in marketing at Harvard Business School. Her research focuses on the role of "interpersonal customization" or the tailoring of a communication to a given customer. Building on her research that demonstrates the effect of customer mood on behavior, she identifies ways in which firms can achieve competitive advantage through modifying their behavior to the affective state of their customer. As part of this research Nancy Puccinelli works with companies such as the Four Seasons, Procter & Gamble and Coca-Cola both domestically and internationally.

Wendy Raskind (M.D., PhD Genetics, University of Washington) is Professor of Medicine/ Medical Genetics and Psychiatry and Behavioral Sciences at the University of Washington. Her research is focused on the genetics of reading disability and other neurobehavioral disorders. She has been Principal Investigator for NICHD-funded genetics studies of dyslexia since 1995.

Todd Richards received his academic training at the University of California, Berkeley, where he received his PhD in biophysics. He is currently professor of radiology at the University of Washington and has over 100 scientific publications. He performs neuroimaging research related to learning disabilities, autism, pain, and chemical abnormalities in the brain and has been the Principal Investigator for imaging studies of dyslexia and dysgraphia. He teaches classes in advanced MR imaging techniques such as functional brain imaging, diffusion tensor imaging, perfusion imaging, and MR spectroscopic imaging.

Gert Rickheit studied German Literature and Linguistics in Braunschweig and Linguistics, Psychology and Literature at the University of Bochum, where he obtained his PhD in Linguistics in 1973. Since 1978 he has been Professor of Psycholinguistics at Bielefeld University. He was co-initiator of the specialist course Clinical Linguistics at Bielefeld University in 1985 and initiated the PhD course of study Clinical Linguistics in 1996, which was accredited in summer 2005. He was the initiator and coordinator of the Collaborative Research Centre 360 *Situated Artificial Communicators* at Bielefeld University, which was financed by the German Research Foundation (Deutsche Forschungsgemeinschaft) from 1993 to 2005. He has been a Member of the Board of Reviewers of the German Research Foundation (qualified reviewer for the field of General Language Sciences) since 1996. He was also co-initiator and Member of the Board of the Graduate Programme *Task-Oriented Communication* at Bielefeld University. In 1994 he was co-founder of the Society for Cognitive Science and a Member of the Board of this society until 1996. From 1996 to 2001 he was Rector of Bielefeld University. He is the initiator and coordinator of the Collaborative Research Centre 673 *Alignment in Communication*, which has been financed by the German Research Foundation since 2006. Since 2007 he has been a principal investigator of the Excellence Centre *Cognitive Intelligent Systems* at Bielefeld University.

Katharina J. Rohlfing (PhD) received the Masters degree in Linguistics, Philosophy and Media Science from the University of Paderborn, in 1997. From 1999 to 2002 she was a member of the Graduate Program *Task-Oriented Communication*. She received the PhD degree in Linguistics from Bielefeld University in 2002. Her postdoctoral work at the San Diego State University (Department of Linguistics and Oriental Languages), the University of Chicago (Department of Psychology) and Northwestern University (Department of Communication Sciences and Disorders) was supported by a fellowship within the Postdoc-program of the German Academic Exchange Service (DAAD) from November 2002 to December 2003 and by the German Research Foundation (DFG) from 2004 to 2006. In 2006 she became a Dilthey Fellow (Funding initiative 'Focus on the Humanities') and her research is currently supported by the

Volkswagen Foundation. Katharina Rohlfing is interested in how learning processes are supported by the environment and how they can be modeled. In her research, she is investigating the interface between early stages of language acquisition and conceptual development.

Michael Siegal (PhD) holds the Marie Curie Chair in Psychology at the University of Trieste, Italy, and is a Professor in the Department of Psychology at the University of Sheffield, UK. He has also held appointments at universities in Australia, Canada, and the United States. Michael Siegal has a long history of involvement in research on the development of language and reasoning in typically and atypically developing children, particularly deaf children and children with autism. His work extends to studies of scientific and mathematical understanding in adults following brain damage.

Holly L. Storkel (PhD) is Associate Professor in the Department of Speech-Language-Hearing Sciences and Disorders at the University of Kansas. Her research focuses on sound and word learning by typically developing children and children with phonological or language impairments. Her research has been funded by the National Institute of Deafness and Other Communication Disorders. She received the 2002 Editor's Award for the Article of Highest Merit from *Language, Speech, and Hearing Services in the Schools.*

Hans Strohner (PhD) studied Psychology and Philosophy at the University of Munich as a fellow of the "Studienstiftung des deutschen Volkes". He studied Psychology in a postgraduate programme at Stanford University, USA. He received the PhD degree in Psychology at the University of Tübingen. Afterwards he worked in the Collaborative Research Centre "Linguistics" at the University of Konstanz. In 1979 he was awarded an assistant professorship for Psycholinguistics at Bielefeld University. From 1991 until 2006 he was Professor for Cognitive Linguistics at Bielefeld University. He died on 19th June, 2006.

Constanze Vorwerg (PhD) studied psychology at the Humboldt University of Berlin. She received her PhD degree in Psychology at the University of Mannheim. She is researcher at the Collaborative Research Centre 673 *Alignment in Communication* at Bielefeld University and is a member of the Scientific Board of the Cluster of Excellence *Cognitive Interaction Technlogy* at Bielefeld University. She teaches Psycholinguistics at the Bielefeld University. Her research interests include spatial cognition, perceptual foundations of language, alignment of situation models, robustness of language processing, and intention reading as a basis for communication and imitation.

Keywords

Acquisition 188–189, 192, 193, 200
Adolescence 499–500, 511–513, 517, 520–523
Adults 521–522
Anxiety 500–501, 503–505, 513, 516, 520, 523
Aphasia
- diagnosis 458, 460, 468, 469, 475, 479, 480
- therapy 450, 458, 461–463, 470, 471, 475–477, 478, 480, 481

Aphasic syndroms 442, 450, 451, 452–459, 472
- theoretical models of 463–468, 472–475

Awareness
- phonological 170–178, 180

Behavior
- non-verbal 38
Broca's area 65, 68, 72–73, 88–90

Communication
- apprehension 290–295, 297, 299
- development of 43–46
- sexual 290, 297–298
Communicative competence 15–47, 290–292
Communicator credibility 291–293
Concepts
- language specific 106–108
- universal 104–106
Control
- process 317
- situation 316

Density 135–137, 140
Diagnosis 505
Dyslexia
- brain differences in 401, 403
- developmental 397, 399–400, 402–403, 406, 416
- genetics of 399–400, 412

Event-related potential (ERP) 70–73, 77, 87

Face management 211–214, 216
Fluency shaping 512–515, 521
FOXP2 85–86
functional MRI (fMRI) 66, 70–73, 77–78, 87, 89

Genetic 502–503
Gradual learning 110–113, 117, 118–119

Knowledge
- creation 368–371, 377
- transfer 365–368, 377–378

Language
- comprehension 214–219
- neurophysiology of (language disorders) 443, 444–448, 449, 454, 455–457, 459
Letter knowledge 173, 175–176
Literacy acquisition 171–172, 177, 179

Manual 187–190, 194, 197
Media
- (specific language) competence 277–303
- journalistic 277–278, 283
- language 293, 297–299
- on-line 281
Mirror neuron system 88–89
Motherese 187, 191–192, 200
Motor knowledge and language 110–112, 116–119

Particularized imprimaturs 210–211, 215–216
Perspective taking 219–221
Phonotactic probability 128, 135–136
Plasticity 84–86, 90
Politeness 211–214
Preference organization 217–218
Prevalence 499

Reading 225–248, 359–378
Reading and learning motivation 179–180

Relapse 522–523
Representation 36–38
- lexical 125–126, 135–137, 139–141
- phonological 125–126, 131–132, 138, 141
- semantic 125–126; 133, 135–138, 140–141
Rhythmic 191–192, 198, 200

Speaker status 218–219
Speech acts 208–210
Symptoms 501
Synaptogenesis 81–82

Test (re-)production
Triple word form theory 397, 412

Writing 225–248, 359–378

www.ingramcontent.com/pod-product-compliance
Lightning Source LLC
Chambersburg PA
CBHW050300010526
44108CB00040B/1902